Lecture Notes in Computer Science   3627

Commenced Publication in 1973
Founding and Former Series Editors:
Gerhard Goos, Juris Hartmanis, and Jan van Leeuwen

Christian Jacob   Marcin L. Pilat
Peter J. Bentley   Jonathan Timmis (Eds.)

Artificial
Immune Systems

4th International Conference, ICARIS 2005
Banff, Alberta, Canada, August 14-17, 2005
Proceedings

 Springer

Volume Editors

Christian Jacob
University of Calgary, Dept. of Computer Science and
Dept. of Biochemistry and Molecular Biology
2500 University Drive NW, Calgary, Alberta T2N 1N4, Canada
E-mail: jacob@cpsc.ucalgary.ca

Marcin L. Pilat
University of Calgary, Department of Computer Science
2500 University Drive NW, Calgary, Alberta T2N 1N4, Canada
E-mail: pilat@cpsc.ucalgary.ca

Peter J. Bentley
University College London, Department of Computer Science
Malet Place, London, WC1E 6BT, UK
E-mail: p.bentley@cs.ucl.ac.uk

Jonathan Timmis
University of York, Department of Electronics and Computer Science
Heslington, York YO10 5DD, UK
E-mail: jt517@ohm.york.ac.uk

Library of Congress Control Number: 2005930338

CR Subject Classification (1998): F.1, I.2, F.2, H.2.8, H.3, J.3

ISSN   0302-9743
ISBN-10   3-540-28175-4 Springer Berlin Heidelberg New York
ISBN-13   978-3-540-28175-7 Springer Berlin Heidelberg New York

Springer is a part of Springer Science+Business Media

springeronline.com

© Springer-Verlag Berlin Heidelberg 2005
Printed in Germany

Typesetting: Camera-ready by author, data conversion by Scientific Publishing Services, Chennai, India
Printed on acid-free paper   SPIN: 11536444   06/3142   5 4 3 2 1 0

Preface

Your immune system is unique. It is in many ways as complex as your brain, but it is not centred in one location, like the brain. It is not a single organ—it consists of many different cell types, diverse methods of intercellular communication, and many different organs. Its functionality is blurred throughout you—we can't extract the immune system, or point to where it begins and ends. The immune system is not separable from the system it protects. It has integral links to every organ of our bodies.

This has radical implications for the field of Artificial Immune Systems (AIS), that we are only now beginning to comprehend. One of the first insights is that modelling the immune system, or developing any kind of immune algorithm, is difficult. The immune system is one aspect of biology that we find difficult to apply simple reductionist explanations to. We can very successfully extract sub-processes of the whole and create immune algorithms based on those processes. But we are always aware that we are missing the whole story. This is leading to more holistic views of immune algorithm development: theoretical analyses of how the sub-components contribute to the whole, and identification of missing elements. Artificial immune systems are now beginning to incorporate ideas of innate as well as adaptive immunity, more complex intercellular communication mechanisms, endocrine and neural interfaces, concepts of tissue and broader ideas of organism and environment.

So perhaps the most exciting implication for the future of AIS is that these researchers are on the forefront of unconventional computing—merging the boundaries between biology and traditional computation to achieve new emergent, embodied and distributed processing capabilities.

This year, ICARIS received 68 submissions, and through a peer review process, 37 were selected for publication, giving an acceptance rate of 53%. ICARIS goes from strength to strength, with an increase in numbers of submissions from 2004, but having a lower acceptance rate. This year we continued the theme of streams, hosting technical, conceptual and immunoinformatics papers. However, this year we added a new stream called applications, which was dedicated to the application of AIS techniques in more real world environments. ICARIS is now considered the place to publish leading AIS research, and is becoming more interdisciplinary each year, something we as organisers are very pleased with.

Building on the success of the tutorials introduced in 2004, we again held four tutorials:

- Dr. Emma Hart presented an introductory tutorial on Artificial Immune Systems.
- An exciting Immunoinformatics session was delivered by Dr. Darren Flower.
- Dr. Mark Neal inspired us by a tutorial on bio-inspired approaches to robotics.

– Last but not least, we are very grateful for Dr. Stuart Kauffman's insightful tutorial on the analysis of complex systems.

We were also delighted to have Prof. Stephanie Forrest from the University of New Mexico deliver the plenary lecture. Thank you very much for an exciting keynote!

ICARIS 2005 was hosted in Banff, in the province of Alberta, Canada. It is not without pride that we think we have chosen one of the most spectacular sites Canada has to offer. Banff, located in Banff National Park, is at the heart of the Canadian Rocky Mountains. At the Banff Centre for Conferences ICARIS 2005 participants enjoyed breath-taking scenery, with wildlife in the backyard and majestic mountains all around. What a venue to discuss inspiring and exciting science!

It would not have been possible to organise this conference without the excellent work of the programme committee, our publicity chairs Simon Garrett and Namrata Khemka, our conference secretary Camille Sinanan and the tutorial speakers. Finally, we would like to express our thanks to all authors who submitted and presented their research papers. Without your valued contributions ICARIS would not be as alive as it is today.

We hope you enjoyed ICARIS and find the papers in these proceedings useful and stimulating.

August 2005   Christian Jacob
                                                                             Marcin Pilat
                                                                             Jon Timmis
                                                                        Peter J. Bentley

Organization

Organizing Committee

Conference Chairs	Jonathan Timmis (University of Kent, UK)
	Peter Bentley (University College, London, UK)
Local Chairs	Christian Jacob (University of Calgary, Canada)
	Marcin Pilat (University of Calgary, Canada)
Publicity Chairs	Simon Garret (University of Wales, Aberystwyth, UK)
	Namrata Khemka (University of Calgary, Canada)

Programme Committee

Uwe Aickelin	University of Nottingham, UK
Steve Cayzer	Hewlett-Packard (Bristol), UK
C. Coello Coello	CINVESTAV-IPN, Mexico
Dipankar Dasgupta	University of Memphis, USA
Leandro de Castro	Catholic University of Santos (Unisantos), Brazil
Alex Freitas	University of Kent, UK
Alessio Gaspar	University of South Florida, USA
Fabio Gonzalez	National University of Colombia, Colombia
Emma Hart	Napier University, UK
Colin Johnson	University of Kent, UK
Jungwon Kim	University College, London, UK
Tom Knight	FutureRoute, UK
Henry Lau	University of Hong Kong, P.R. China
Doheon Lee	KAIST, Korea
Wenjian Luo	University of Science and Technology, Anhui, P.R. China
Giuseppe Nicosia	University of Catania, Italy
Susan Stepney	University of York, UK
Alexander Tarakanov	St. Petersburg Institute, Russia
Fernando von Zuben	University of Campinas, Brazil
Andrew Watkins	University of Kent, UK
Slawomir Wierzchon	Polish Academy of Sciences, Poland

Tutorial Speakers

Emma Hart	Napier University, UK
Darren Flower	Edward Jenner Institute for Vaccine Research, UK
Stuart Kauffman	University of Calgary, Canada
Mark Neal	University of Wales, Aberystwyth, UK

Keynote Speaker

Stephanie Forrest   University of New Mexico, USA

Conference Secretary

Camille Sinanan   University of Calgary, Canada

Sponsoring Institutions

University of Calgary, Faculty of Science
Department of Biochemistry & Molecular Biology, University of Calgary
Department of Computer Science, University of Calgary
The academic network ARTIST
iCORE – Informatics Circle of Research Excellence, Alberta, Canada
MITACS – Mathematics of Information Technology and Complex Systems
PIMS – Pacific Institute for the Mathematical Sciences

Table of Contents

Conceptual, Formal, and Theoretical Frameworks

Immunoinformatics

Theoretical and Experimental Studies on Artificial Immune Systems

Applications of Artificial Immune Systems

Fugue: An Interactive Immersive Audiovisualisation and Artwork Using an Artificial Immune System

Peter J. Bentley, Gordana Novakovic, and Anthony Ruto

Department of Computer Science, University College London, London WC1E 6BT, UK
P.Bentley@cs.ucl.ac.uk, gordana.novakovic@btopenworld.com,
a.ruto@cs.ucl.ac.uk

Abstract. Fugue is the result of a collaboration between artist, musician and computer scientists. The result is an on-going project which provides a new way of communicating complex scientific ideas to any audience. Immersive virtual reality and sound provide an interactive audiovisual interface to the dynamics of a complex system – for this work, an artificial immune system. Participants are able to see and interact with immune cells flowing through a lymphatic vessel and understand how the complex dynamics of the whole are produced by local interactions of viruses, B cells, antibodies, dendritic cells and clotting platelets.

1 Introduction

Science often involves abstract formalisms, typically mathematical, of the tangled complexity of the phenomena under study. Communicating these ideas is not easy, whether between colleagues or to the general public. To aid in such endeavors there is a significant need for scientists to employ more direct methods – audio and visual – of representing the systems with which they deal. In scientific education, it has become clear that traditional formal methods of study are increasingly alien to students who have grown up in a world dominated by digital media; at least initially, they require more familiar means of accessing science. Likewise, in communicating science to non-scientists, the constraints of the printed page or the talking head mean that is often necessary to simplify the subject matter to the point where too much is lost or excluded.

Our intention in this work is to examine a new approach. We propose that the best way of enabling both scientists and non-scientists to understand a complex functioning system is not just to present it to him as a spectacle, but to engage him as a participant, and to enable him to interact with the system in a multisensory way, directly appreciating cause and effect, variability, intrinsic dynamics, periodicity, and so on. To achieve this, direct input from an artist and a musician is used to guide the visual and audio experience. In other words: we propose to exploit artists' knowledge of the relation between interactivity and perception, and harness it in the communication of scientific complexity.

Artists and scientists are both concerned with understanding the world and our being in the world, but while the view of the scientist is rooted in consensus and endeavors towards objectivity, the artist emphasises the values of the personal and sub-

C. Jacob et al. (Eds.): ICARIS 2005, LNCS 3627, pp. 1–12, 2005.
© Springer-Verlag Berlin Heidelberg 2005

jective investigation of philosophical questions. Such a dichotomy suggests potential conflict: does the participation of an artist in the communication of science run the risk of introducing some bias antithetical to the very idea of science? And if so, can this potential conflict be managed satisfactorily within the collaborative process? Taken together, these two questions raise a wide range of issues, and as yet there are no definitive answers. The Fugue Project aims to frame and focus the questions in the context of transdisciplinary collaboration in the area of representing the functional dynamics of one of the most complex systems known – the human immune system. This will be achieved by the creation of an immersive virtual reality immune system, which enables participants to interact with and understand various cellular behaviours inside a lymphatic vessel. The hope is that the information uncovered by this research will help to structure future more comprehensive investigations of these fascinating and important issues, for art and science.

2 Background

The human immune system is so complex that it is currently impossible to produce a tractable model of the whole. Nevertheless, computational models are increasingly been seen as important tools to aid our scientific understanding [17]. Separate from immuno-biology, the field of artificial immune systems (AIS) has grown dramatically in the last five years. AIS algorithms are computer programs modeled on different aspects of the human immune system and used to tackle a wide variety of problems, from computer virus detection to data mining, to robot control [14]. Additionally, in recent years issues of public health (from simple allergies to the expansion of AIDS and recent global epidemics of extremely dangerous flu variations) have led to increased and widespread public interest in the immune system [13]. There is a clear need for the lay population to be much better informed about the operation of the one of the most complex and enigmatic biological systems. The confluence of these three factors has both inspired and enabled this research, and forms a strong context for the project.

Audiovisualisation is still a new methodology for presenting scientific findings. Only one virtual reality approach, Planetary Seismology (a Virtual Reality audio/visual representation of seismic phenomena) produced by the German scientist Dombois in 2001 [4], is available for participants at present. Only a handful of immune system visualisations currently exist. They have all been produced exclusively by scientists (Steven Kleinstein, IMMSIM, 1999 [6]; Christian Jacob, 2004 [5]), and the presentational styles are barely accessible to non-experts. (For example, IMMSIM uses a very abstract 2-dimensional lattice representation based on cellular automata.) To date, these visualisations have been presented only within a closed circle of scientists and have not been released for the general public.

Audiovisualisation offers significant advantages for understanding hugely complex systems: it offers a much wider bandwidth than vision alone, and engages both serial and parallel modes of perception. In addition, the intention is to explore the potential of contemporary Virtual Reality technologies for enabling users to actively engage with the production of phenomena, rather than merely observing them passively, within a custom designed virtual reality environment. The user will be able to control certain parameters of the modeled immune system, and will also be able to choose the particular function, particle, or interaction to follow. There are good theoretical reasons pointing in this direction, in particular Merleau-Ponty's analysis of the role of the ear in visual perception [11]. As Dombois, the author of Planetary Seismology, wrote in 2001: 'From philosophical research (…) we can learn that the eye is strong in recognising structure, surface and steadiness. (…..) Now at the same time philosophy finds the ear strong in the recognition of time, dynamics of a continuum and tensions between remembrance and expectation.' [4]

3 Artistic Concept and Method

The development and usage of tools that support visualisation, or audification, usually involves collaborative efforts among scientists, artists, programmers and other expert staff. This is often defined as a Renaissance Team [2]. To achieve the aim of producing interactive, audiovisual representation of a highly complex biological function, that demands full engagement of both artists and scientists, our team is composed of a media artist, Gordana Novakovic (artistic concept); a computer scientist and expert in digital biology, Dr. Peter Bentley; Rainer Linz, a new music composer; Dr. Julie McLeod, and expert in immunology; and computer scientist Anthony Ruto. The aim of creating a scientific tool strongly influences the content and behaviour of the system; however from the point of view of the two artists involved in the creative process, Fugue is an integral interactive art project. Yet, from the scientific point of view, it is essential to ensure the scientific correctness of the underlying model. Will it be art, or will it be science? Our claim is that the first responses to the prototype made it clear that it may be seen as either, depending on the perspective of the user.

The basic concept tests the form of the interaction between the sound and the vision in a way that is inspired by the complexity of one of the greatest musical forms: the art of fugue. The art of fugue is a highly disciplined form of composition of complex structure and exact relationship of parts. The title – Fugue – serves as a metaphor for the transdisciplinary nature of the project, and for the method applied: of interweaving the different perspectives of artists and scientists, different aesthetics, various skills and expertise, and personal philosophies, and uniting them into evolving polyphonic synergy. The emergent, evolving nature of Artificial Immune System algorithm, repetition as a succession of variations of 'events', and the complex structural and functional interrelationship of the particular elements and processes that can be related to the counterpoint, was one of the inspirations for the fugue concept. The Artificial Immune System software creates the dynamics of the virtual immune system drama, and also constructs and implements the architecture of the fugue by providing the functional structure for the communication channels between the visuals and the sound.

On the other hand, this method is well grounded in the already successfully applied artistic method of interweaving, cross-connecting different specialists and specialisms, in an effective cross-disciplinary framework for the emergence of synergy through collaboration; a method resembling the structure of the fugue. In parallel with providing the functional structure for the communication channels between the visuals and the sound, the Artificial Immune System algorithm is a bridge between the scientific and artistic aspect of the project. To establish an appropriate balance between art and science, artists and scientists have been working closely together on both experimentation and evaluation throughout the whole research process, integrating their own assessments with the external feedback. (This method also distinguishes this concept from the mere application of entertainment industry oriented software packages for audiovisualisation.)

Finally, the fugue structure helps to achieve one of the major aims, by not only representing all the processes involved, but also at the same time painting a larger picture of the role of the immune system in the functioning of the human body and mind. This will illustrate the immune system's intimate interconnectedness with the total sum of particulars that constitute each human being. This approach affirms holism as one of the fundamental principles of transdisciplinarity, as seen for example in the neurophenomenology of Varela, Maturana, and Thompson, and the biology of Margulis and Goodwin.

Because we will work towards facilitating a better understanding of the function of the immune system, rather than simply creating 'beautiful imagery', much of our work will be concentrated on processes. The aesthetics of the Fugue are emergent, based upon the essential, fundamental and hidden beauty of the organic processes manifested through the dynamics of the real-time generated, unpredictable Artificial Immune System.

4   The Fugue Architecture

Fugue is designed to be an immersive system, capable of running on platforms ranging from a desktop PC or Macintosh to a full virtual reality CAVE system using SGI IRIX workstations. As such, the hardware may vary from installation to installation, but the software components will remain largely the same. The current prototype is implemented in C++, using OpenGL graphics libraries and TCP/IP communication between processes.

4.1 Hardware

The immediate target for Fugue is to move from the current desktop-based demonstrator to a full-sized system capable of withstanding the rigors of exhibitions. Figure 1 provides an illustration of a possible exhibition installation. An overhead LCD projector and surround-sound speakers will provide the main output, to be experienced by several participants simultaneously. One or more free-standing rotatable LCD "windows" will also be placed in the arena (the exact number depending on the floor area available). These will provide individual views into the same virtual world and permit views from different players in the system (i.e., from a B-cell, or a virus). By rotating the window, the participant rotates their view within the virtual world, enabling interactive control of their immersive experience. The LCD windows will be constructed for the Fugue project and will comprise 17 inch LCD monitors mounted in metal stands, rotatable through at least 300 degrees, with rotation measured by optical sensors and fed back to the server.

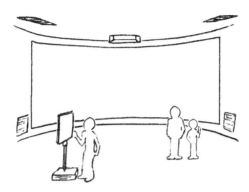

Fig. 1. Illustration of proposed exibition arena, comprising main projection, surround sound speakers and rotatable LCD "windows". (The shape of the projection wall will depend on the space allocated at each venue.).

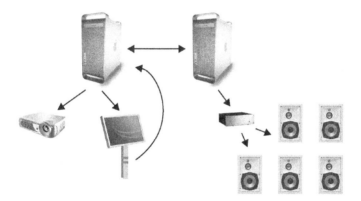

Fig. 2. The Fugue hardware comprises graphics server (top left) driving projector and VGA screens, networked to the audio server (top right) driving amplifier and speakers

Two servers are used to run the Fugue software: a graphics server, which calculates the artificial immune system and corresponding three-dimensional visualisation, and a sound server to calculate corresponding audio. The servers are networked together. Communication between the servers is through TCP/IP. Output from the graphics server feeds to an LCD projector (and the free-standing screens if installed). Output from the sound server feeds to a surround-sound amplifier, which is linked to a minimum of four speakers. Input from sensors such as the window rotation sensors is fed to the graphics server, see figure 2.

4.2 Software

Fugue software comprises five main components, see figure 3. The graphics engine and the audio system demand the most computational power and so these each have their own dedicated servers (the graphics server and audio server). All other components require minimal computational power and so are executed as parallel processes on the graphics server.

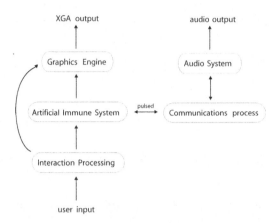

Fig. 3. The Fugue software comprises graphics engine, artificial immune system, interaction processing, a communication process and the audio system

4.2.1 Artificial Immune System

The artificial immune system (AIS) forms the heart of Fugue. The dynamic interplay between the agents in this system feed all outputs, while input from the user alters the dynamics in different ways.

Implemented in C++, the AIS is currently a basic population-based infection model. Several agents are currently implemented: platelets, B-cells, macrophages, antibodies and viruses. All exist in a virtual lymphatic vessel, which is modeled as a large torus (with randomized cross-sectional diameter) to simplify the flow of the agents through the "body" (they simply go round and round inside the torus). Like Jacob's work [5], the spatial modeling is a crucial part of the AIS – all immune activities occur when agents randomly collide and pass or receive information from each other. Movement is computed using force calculations to derive acceleration vectors for each agent, every time step, similar to a swarm algorithm [5]. The major forces are:

- Collision avoidance: agents coming into contact with each other receive a force pushing them apart.
- Wall avoidance: agents too close to the walls of the torus receive a force pushing them away from the wall.
- Pulse: agents are pushed through the vessel in pulses. This is the largest force used in the system. The force (which has a sinusoidal magnitude with frequency equal to the current *pulse* value) is exerted on every agent in a direction determined by the nearest attractor point, where a series of attractor points are precalculated around the inside circumference of the torus. This approach enables future versions to flow within a vessel of arbitrary shape and complexity.

Movement of individual agents can be overridden by the movement of other agents. For example, antibodies stuck to the surface of a cell will have their movement entirely determined by the moment of the cell they are stuck to. A dead cell being consumed by a macrophage has its movement entirely determined by that macrophage and remains in the centre of the macrophage. A virus that has infected a cell will always be in the centre of that cell (with a random oscillation to highlight the infector). In addition, when platelet cells come close enough to an injury, they receive a force pushing them to the source of the injury, with the effect of the pulse and wall avoidance reduced.

The result of these forces produces stochastic and complex three-dimensional dynamics of cell and molecule flow, with completely unpredictable interactions. Nevertheless, although the detail is always different, the general dynamics of the system are determined by preset cellular and molecular behaviours. The current prototype has the following basic behaviours (these are chosen more for demonstration purposes than biological accuracy at this stage; behaviours are designed to be easily extendible or changeable):

- All cells have a cell type: currently either *macrophage*, *B-cell*, or *platelet,* and all live for a randomized lifespan. When their lifespan is reached, the cell type becomes *deadcell* and the resulting inactive cell continues to exist in the environment until either consumed by a macrophage or sufficient time has passed to allow it to decay to nothing. When a cell is lost from the environment, a new cell of random type is introduced back into the system to replace it.

- A single site of injury is introduced into the environment at the start of the run. When a free-floating platelet comes close enough to the site it becomes a clotting platelet and moves to plug the hole where it will stay until it dies.

- Three virus molecules are released into the environment at the site of injury. A virus will decay to nothing after a short period of time unless it comes into contact with either a platelet or B-cell, in which case it infects the cell. If the infected cell is not consumed by a macrophage in time, it will cause its host cell to die after a period of time and release a number of new viruses into the environment.

- If a macrophage (dendritic cell) comes into contact with a dead cell or a cell marked with antibodies, it will consume that cell (the cell it consumes is removed from the system after a short period of digestion). Should the cell it consumes be infected with a virus, the macrophage then becomes an antigen-presenting-cell.

- If a B-cell comes into contact with an antigen-presenting-cell it releases antibodies in response. Currently in this demonstrator it is assumed that the antibodies will always be designed to counter the current viral pathogen.

- If an antibody comes into contact with an infected cell, it sticks to the surface of that infected cell. All antibodies decay to nothing after a fixed period of time.

This basic infection model results in a rapid spread of infection through cells in the initial stages, followed by a response from B-cells and macrophages, which controls the infection. To provide continuous and open-ended"interesting" behaviour, the lifespans, and virus and B-cell production rates are tuned to ensure the infection is controlled but never eradicated from the environment. Maximum population sizes also provide a method of controlling the dynamics (and keep the real-time 3D rendering manageable); currently a 1Ghz PowerBook G4 processor is able to maintain 60 cells, 60 antibodies and 40 viruses and render in real-time at a resolution of 1024 by 768 without difficultly.

4.2.2 Graphics Engine

The 3D graphical visualization of the artificial immune system is created by an OpenGL rendering environment using the Glut interface[1]. It also contains a VRML parser to read in virtual cell surfaces created from clay models (see below). These cells are loaded when the system is started and their different properties are rendered within the OpenGL environment using display lists for efficiency purposes. System dynamics are used to control the movement of both the cells and view of the immune system through the position and manipulation of the cell display lists. This allows for the best overall performance in terms of speed and aesthetics. The display can also support the stereoscopic display of the virtual elements through the Glut interface used. This would enable true 3D effects to be experienced by viewers using appropriate hardware (and also enables the support of multiple monitors).

The shape of each cell is not arbitrary in Fugue. Clay sculptures of cell objects made by Gordana Novakovic were scanned using a Hamamatsu Photonics body scanner[2] to produce 3D point clouds at up to a 1mm resolution. A surface reconstruction process was then used to form canonical representations of the scanned cell point clouds from which a surface was then constructed. This method is commonly used in the 3D scanning of bodies to establish regular sets of points for captured data [12,15] and provides a simple solution for constructing surfaces once the canonical representation has been established. The detail on the reconstructed scan surfaces was reduced in order to speed up the performance of the immune system display by lowering the level of detail. More examples of cells where constructed through the 3D sculpturing of sphere quadrics using an open source 3D editing tool called Blender[3]. The detail on the reshaped quadric surfaces was also reduced through the use of a mesh reduction algorithm provided as part of the Blender software. Both scanned and reshaped cells were stored in a VRML format so that they could be easily imported into the immune system display.

From the point cloud data, a population of randomized cells is created (the different cell images are randomly distorted to create unique shapes). These cell shapes are then translated to the appropriate locations and rendered, each iteration. All cells have a slow random rotation to produce a subtle tumbling effect as they move. Where possible, all movement, scaling and rotations are performed using OpenGL functions on the display lists (rather than recalculating point cloud data), which maximizes rendering speed by exploiting the graphics hardware of the computer.

Viruses and antibodies are rendered as small, glowing OpenGL spheres. Viruses also emit light, designed to light up an infected cell from within (visible because of the partial translucency of cells). When platelets begin to clot, random "tendrils" are rendered from its centre to represent the emission of fibrin.

The "lymphatic vessel" environment is rendered as a torus with walls of partially translucent spheres to represent cells. The radius of the spheres is an inverse function of the sinusoidal pulse used to move the floating cells. This provides the illusion that the internal diameter of the vessel expands and contracts in time with the pulse.

---

[1] Glut Open GL: http://www.opengl.org/resources/libraries/glut.html

[2] Hamamatsu Photonics : http://www.hamamatsu.co.uk

[3] Blender : http://www.blender.org

The graphics engine currently supports two viewing modes: a view from a fixed point, and a "free-floating" view. The former enables a participant to "cut to" an interesting predefined view in the torus, and use basic keyboard controls to rotate and move the view from that point. (Such controls would be replaced by the rotation sensor on the LCD windows or sensors for head mounted displays in a CAVE system.) The free-floating view creates a virtual agent, which is subject to the same forces as all the cells and molecules in the environment, then displays the virtual world from the point of view of that agent. To avoid a disconcerting somersaulting view, the viewing angle is kept at right angles to a vertical axis at the torus centre, ensuring the view is always towards the centre of the torus. There are also options to look backwards or simplify the view by showing wireframe only or the torus without the cells on its walls.

Future work on Fugue will extend the viewing modes and interactivity of the system, enabling more control over the perception and allowing participants to take the role of any cell or molecule and both see and interact with the virtual world from their chosen perspective.

4.2.3 Communications

On execution, the Graphics Engine spawns a communication process to send and receive signals to and from the Audio System without incurring visible computation overheads on its graphical output. The comms process uses TCP with a streaming UNIX domain socket to communicate with the Graphics Engine (the comms process acts as server and both processes run on the same processor). It uses TCP with an Internet socket to communicate with the Audio System (the audio system acts as server; the use of Internet sockets enables the two computers to communicate over any network, including the Internet).

Data is squirted from the artificial immune system, to the comms process and onwards to the audio system on every pulse. A 25-byte packet of data representing the main population sizes, views and other global dynamics indicators updates the audio system with details of the main behaviours, enabling it to alter the audio in synchronization with the changes occurring in the artificial immune system.

4.2.4 Audio System

Composer and Sound Artist, Rainer Linz, will be creating the audio system for Fugue. Written in Java, the system will interpret the data sent from the communications process and provide an audio accompaniment designed to complement the current system dynamics and view chosen by the participant. Because the system data is received in pulses, the audio will inevitably mirror the pulses in its own dynamics. This provides the rhythm for the piece, a rhythm that will speed up or slow down depending on the pulse of the "virtual organism". It is not proposed that an explicit heartbeat or other biological noises be duplicated in Fugue. The audio is intended as a second method of communicating information to the participant. 'Sound is emphatically not just for sound tracks': as Brown and Hershberger observed in 1994: 'Sound does not merely enhance the beauty of a presentation; it can be used to give fundamental information.'[1]

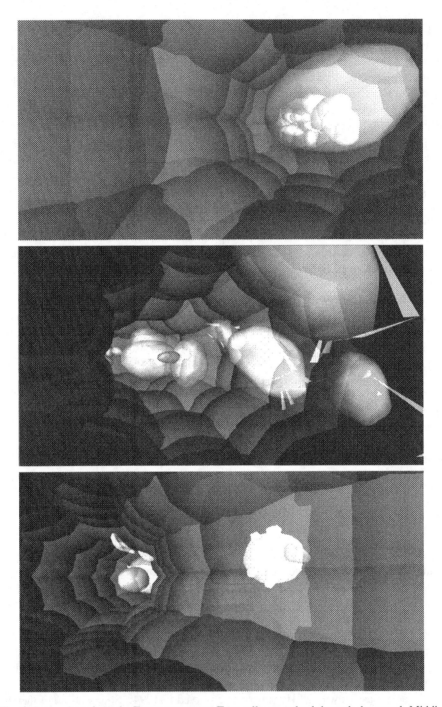

Fig. 4. Screenshots from the Fugue prototype. Top: cells are pulsed through the vessel; Middle: platelets begin to clot at the site of the injury; Bottom: an infected cell attracts antibodies on its surface.

The sound, envisaged as a 'mental soundsacpe'; a resonance of the function of immune system in the body, will provide a major channel for interaction. By overlaying and modulating the sonic pulsation, cycles - such as circadian, or other inputs such as stress level, will be introduced. The dynamics of the sound system may be fed back to the artificial immune system (changing the pulse, increasing stress levels) causing another level of fascinating dynamics for the participant.

This aspect of Fugue is still under development.

5 Performances

A prototype of Fugue has been implemented and DVD movie of the project been created (under the name of Algorithmica). Running on a desktop computer, the prototype did not have the audio system or communications described above. It was also producing output in shades of red instead of black and white, and did not have the "pulsing" feature of Fugue. The work was presented at several venues in early 2005:

- the GAGE Festival, Hull Time Based Arts, Hull
- the Creative Evolution Conference, Goldsmith's College
- Smartlab Seminar, Central St Martins College of Art and Design
- EVA Conferences (Electronic Imaging & the Visual Arts), UCL
- Hypermedia Research Centre, University of Westminster.

The response has been overwhelmingly positive from both the artistic community and the science community. The validity of the approach, both artistically and scientifically has clearly been demonstrated, and work is now underway to improve both, through: (1) enhancements to existing visuals and audio (2) enhancements to hardware, through large-scale projection and audio broadcasting (3) additions to the methods of interaction with the components of the immune system by participants (4) collaboration with immunobiologist Dr Julie McLeod to improve cell imagery through digital microscopy photographs and (5) improvements to cellular behaviours by using more scientifically plausible artificial immune systems.

Figure 4 show some example screen shots from the current version of Fugue (as described in this paper).

6 Conclusions

Fugue is an on-going project which aims to explore a new way of communicating complex scientific ideas to any audience. Immersive virtual reality and sound provide an interactive audiovisual interface to an artificial immune system. Participants are able to see and interact with immune cells flowing through a lymphatic vessel and understand how the complex dynamics of the whole are produced. Fugue is a demonstration of the benefits to be gained from art/science collaborations. The response so far has been overwhelming positive from both the artistic community and the scientific community. Further work and plans for several new exhibitions are underway. Through this work we aim to explore the dichotomy between artist and scientist: how personal and subjective views compare and influence consensus and objectivity, and also how a complex, algorithmic, immersive environment affects perception, mood and emotion.

References

1. Brown, M. H. and Hershberger, J. (1991). Color and Sound in Algorithm Animation (Technical Report No. 76a). DEC Systems Research Center.
2. D. Cox, 1988 : Renaissance Teams and Scientific Visualization: A Convergence of Art and Science, Collaboration in Computer Graphics Education, SIGGRAPH '88 Educator's Workshop Proceedings
3. D. Cox, 1989: The Tao of Postmodernism: Computer Art, Scientific Visualization, and Other Paradoxes, ACM SIGGRAPH '89 Leonardo: International Journal of Art, Technology and Science Supplemental Issue
4. F. Dombois, 2001: Using Audification in Planetary Seismology, Proceedings of the 2001 International Conference on Auditory Display, Espoo
5. Christian Jacob, Julius Litorco and Leo Lee 2004. Immunity through swarms: agent-based simulations of the human immune system. In Proc. of the Third International Conference on Artificial immune Systems (ICARIS 2004), Catania, Sicily. pp. 400-412.
6. S. Kleinstein, J. Pal Singh, Philip E. Seiden: Putting limits on selection and mutation in a simulation of the humoral immune response, Pacific Symposium on BioComputing. 1999
7. Brian Goodwin, 2001: How the Leopard Changed Its Spots : The Evolution of Complexity; Princeton University Press
8. O. Grau, 2000: Ancestors of the virtual, historical aspects of virtual reality and its contemporary impact,Thirtieth International Congress of the History of Art, London
9. L. Margulis, D. Sagan, 1986: Microcosmos: Four Billion Years of Evolution from Our Microbial Ancestors, University of California Press
10. H. Maturana and F. Varela, 1992: The Tree of Knowledge: The Biological Roots of human understanding,The MIT Press
11. M. Merleau-Ponty, 2002: Phenomenology of Perception, Routledge Classics
12. Ruiz M., Buxton, B.F., Douros I., Treleaven, P.C., "Web-based Software Tools for 3D Body Database Access and Shape Analysis", Scanning 2002 Proceedings, Paris, May 2002.
13. New Scientist Editorial 2005. Bring back bugs to finish off allergies. We have eliminated so many childhood diseases and risky micro-organisms that our immune systems are undereducated - how do we redress the balance? New Scientist 2495. 16 April 2005
14. Nicosia, G., Cutello, V., Bentley, P. J. and Timmis J. (Eds) (2004) Artificial Immune Systems. Proceedings of the Third International Conference (ICARIS 2004). Lecture Notes in Computer Science 3239. Springer-Verlag. ISBN 3-540-23097-1.
15. A Tahan, B Buxton and M.C Ruiz. "Point Distribution Models of Human Body Shape from a Canonical Representation of 3D Scan Data". Proceedings of 3D Modelling 2003, Paris, April 2003.
16. F. Varela, E. Thompson, and E. Rosch,1992: The Embodied Mind
17. A. Yates, C.C.W. Chan, R. E. Callard, A.J.T. George and J. Stark, An Approach to Modelling in Immunology, In Briefings in Bioinformatics, 2, 2001, 245-257

Clonal Selection Algorithms: A Comparative Case Study Using Effective Mutation Potentials

Vincenzo Cutello, Giuseppe Narzisi, Giuseppe Nicosia, and Mario Pavone

Department of Mathematics and Computer Science,
University of Catania,
V.le A. Doria 6, 95125 Catania, Italy
{vctl, narzisi, nicosia, mpavone}@dmi.unict.it

Abstract. This paper presents a comparative study of two important Clonal Selection Algorithms (CSAs): CLONALG and opt-IA. To deeply understand the performance of both algorithms, we deal with four different classes of problems: toy problems (one-counting and trap functions), pattern recognition, numerical optimization problems and NP-complete problem (the 2D HP model for protein structure prediction problem). Two possible versions of CLONALG have been implemented and tested. The experimental results show a global better performance of opt-IA with respect to CLONALG. Considering the results obtained, we can claim that CSAs represent a new class of Evolutionary Algorithms for effectively performing searching, learning and optimization tasks.

Keywords: Clonal Selection Algorithms, CLONALG, opt-IA, one-counting, trap functions, pattern recognition, numerical optimization, NP-complete problems, 2D HP Protein Structure Prediction.

1 Introduction

Clonal Selection Algorithms (CSAs) are a special class of Immune algorithms (IA) which are inspired by the Clonal Selection Principle [1,2,3] of the human immune system to produce effective methods for search and optimization. In this research paper two well known CSAs are analyzed: CLONal selection ALGorithm (CLONALG) [4] and optimization Immune Algorithm (opt-IA)[5], which both use a simplified model of the Clonal Selection Principle . To analyze experimentally the overall performance of those two algorithms, we will test them on a robust set of problems belonging to four different classes: toy problems, pattern recognition, numerical optimization problems and NP-complete problems. Both algorithms are population based. Each individual of the population is a candidate solution belonging to the fitness landscape of a given computational problem. Using the cloning operator, an immune algorithm produces individuals with higher affinities (higher fitness function values), by introducing blind perturbation (by means of a hypermutation operator) and selecting their improved mature progenies.

C. Jacob et al. (Eds.): ICARIS 2005, LNCS 3627, pp. 13–28, 2005.

1.1 CLONALG

CLONALG is characterized by two populations: a population of antigens, Ag, and a population of antibodies, Ab (denoted with $P^{(t)}$). The individual antibody and antigen are represented by string attributes $m = m_L, \ldots, m_1$, that is, a point in a L−dimensional shape space $S, m \in S^L$. The Ab population is the set of current candidate solutions, and the Ag is the environment to be recognized. After a random initialization of the first population $P^{(0)}$, the algorithm loops for a predefined maximum number of generations (N_{gen}). In the first step, it determines the fitness function values of all Abs with respect to the Ag (the given objective function). Next, cloning operator selects n Abs that will be cloned independently and proportionally to their antigenic affinities, generating the clone population P^{clo}. Hence, the higher the fitness, the higher the number of clones generated for each of the n Abs. The hypermutation operator performs an affinity maturation process inversely proportional to the fitness values generating the matured clone population P^{hyp}. After computing the antigenic affinity of the population P^{hyp}, CLONALG creates randomly d new antibodies that will replace the d lowest fit Abs in the current population.

In this paper we use the CLONALG version for optimization tasks (except for pattern recognition where we will use the other version proposed in [4]), varying the same parameters (N, n, β, d) plus ρ (not studied in [4]) that controls the shape of the mutation rate with respect to the following two equations:

$$\alpha = e^{(-\rho * f)}, \qquad \alpha = \left(\frac{1}{\rho}\right) e^{(-f)} \qquad (1)$$

where α represents the mutation rate , and f is the fitness function value normalized in $[0.1]$. The number of mutations of a clone with fitness function value f is equal to $\lfloor L * \alpha \rfloor$ where L is the length of the clone receptor. The first potential mutation has been proposed in [4], the original mutation law used by CLONALG; while the second potential mutation has been introduced in [6]. We will show how setting the mutation rates and the parameter ρ is crucial for the algorithm performance. In the optimization version of CLONALG the affinity proportionate cloning is not useful; we use the same law defined in [4]: $N_c = \sum_{i=1}^{n} round\,(\beta * N)$; where N_c represents the total number of clones created at each generation, in this way, each antibody (or B cell) produces the same number of clones. Moreover, we assign $N = n$, so all Abs from the population will be selected for cloning in step 4 of the algorithm. For the pseudo-code of CLONALG see [4].

The experimental study was conducted using two versions of CLONALG, CLONALG$_1$ and CLONALG$_2$, with different selection scheme in step 8 of the algorithm and using the two potential mutations above defined (equations 1):

CLONALG$_1$: at generation (t), each Ab will be substituted by the best individual of its set of $\beta * N$ mutated clones.

CLONALG$_2$: the population at the next generation $(t + 1)$ will be formed by the n best Ab's of the mutated clones at time step t.

1.2   opt-IA

The opt-IA algorithm uses only two entities: antigens (Ag) and B cells (or Ab) like CLONALG. At each time step t, we have a population $P^{(t)}$ of size d. The initial population of candidate solutions, time $t = 0$, is generated randomly. The function *Evaluate(P)* computes the fitness function value of each B cell $\boldsymbol{x} \in P$. The implemented IA uses three immune operators, cloning, hypermutation and aging. The cloning operator, simply, clones each B cell *dup* times producing an intermediate population P^{clo} of size $d \times dup$, where each cloned B cell has the same age of its parent.

The hypermutation operator acts on the B cell receptor of P^{clo}. The number of mutations M is determined by *mutation potential*. We tested our IA using inversely proportional hypermutation operators, hypermacromutation operator, and combination of hypermutation operators and hypermacromutation. The two hypermutation operators and the Hypermacromutation perturb the receptors using different mutation potentials, depending upon a parameter c. In particular, the two implemented operators try to mutate each B cell receptor M times without using probability mutation p_m, typically used in Genetic Algorithms.

In the *Inversely Proportional Hypermutation* the number of mutations is inversely proportional to the fitness value, that is it decrease as the fitness function of the current B cell increases. So at each time step t, the operator will perform at most $M_i(f(\boldsymbol{x})) = ((1 - \frac{E^*}{f(\boldsymbol{x})}) \times (c \times \ell)) + (c \times \ell))$ mutations, where E^* is the optimum of the problem and l is the string length. In this case, $M_i(f(\boldsymbol{x}))$ has the shape of an hyperbola branch. In the *Hypermacromutation* the number of mutations is independent from the fitness function f and the parameter c. In this case, we choose at random two sites in the string, i and j such that $(i + 1) \leq j \leq \ell$ the operator mutates at most $M_m(\boldsymbol{x}) = j - i + 1$ directions, in the range $[i, j]$.

The aging operator eliminates old B cells in the populations $P^{(t)}$, $P^{(hyp)}$ and/or $P^{(macro)}$, to avoid premature convergence. The value τ_B is the maximum number of generations B cells are allowed to remain in the population. When a B cell is $\tau_B + 1$ old it is erased from the current population, no matter what its fitness value is. We call this strategy, *static pure aging*. We can also define a *stochastic aging* where the elimination process is based on a stochastic law. The probability to remove a B cell is governed by exponential negative law with parameter τ_B, using the function $P_{die}(\tau_B) = (1 - e^{-ln(2)/\tau_B})$ [2]. During the cloning expansion, a cloned B cell takes the age of its parent. After the hypermutation phase, a cloned B cell which successfully mutates, will be considered to have age equal to 0. Such a scheme intends to give an equal opportunity to each new B cell to effectively explore the landscape. The best B cells which "survived" the aging operator, are selected from the populations $P^{(t)}$, $P^{(hyp)}$ and/or $P^{(macro)}$, in such a way each B cell receptor is *unique*, i.e. each B cell receptor is different from all other receptors. In this way, we obtain the new population $P^{(t+1)}$, of d B cells, for the next generation $t + 1$. If only $d' < d$ B cells survived, the $(\mu + \lambda)$-*Selection operator* creates $d - d'$ new B cells (*Birth phase*). The boolean function *Termination_Condition()* returns true if a solu-

```
opt-IA(ℓ, d, dup, τ_B, c, h, hm)
1. t := 0
2. P^(t) := Initial_Pop()
3. Evaluate(P^(0))
4. while (¬ Termination_Condition()) do
5.     P^(clo) := Cloning (P^(t), dup)
6.     if (H is TRUE) then
7.         P^(hyp) := Hypermutation(P^(clo), c, ℓ)
8.         Evaluate(P^(hyp))
9.     if (M is TRUE) then
10.        P^(macro) := Hypermacro(P^clo)
11.        Evaluate (P^(macro))
12.     Aging(P^(t), P^(hyp), P^(macro), τ_B)
13.     P^(t+1) := (μ + λ)-Selection(P^(t), P^(hyp), P^(macro))
14.     t := t + 1
15.end_while
```

Fig. 1. Pseudo-code of opt-IA

tion is found, or a maximum number of fitness function evaluations (T_{max}) is reached. Figure 1 shows the pseudo-code of the proposed Immune Algorithm. The boolean variables H, M control, respectively, the hypermutation and the hypermacromutation operator.

2 Toy Problems

Toy problems play a central role in understanding the dynamics of algorithms [7]. In fact, they can be used to show the main differences between different algorithms. In this section we test and study the dynamic of CLONALG and opt-IA for two classical toy problems: *one-counting* and *trap functions*.

2.1 One-Counting Problem

The one-counting problem (or one-max problem), is simply defined as the problem of maximizing the number of 1 in a bit-string x of length ℓ: $f(x) = \sum_{i=1}^{\ell} x_i$, with $x_i \in \{0, 1\}$. In this work we set $\ell = 100$. The one-max problem is a classical test to assess if an evolutionary algorithm is able to reach an optimal solution starting from a randomly initialized population.

Experimental results. All the experimental results reported in this sections were averaged over 100 independent runs, and we fixed the max number of fitness function evaluations (T_{max}) to 10^4. Figure 2 shows the Success Rate (SR) parameters surface for CLONALG$_1$ and CLONALG$_2$ varying $\beta \in \{0.1, 0.2, \ldots, 1.0\}$ and $\rho \in \{10.0, 20.0, \ldots, 100.0\}$ for the second type of mutation rate previously

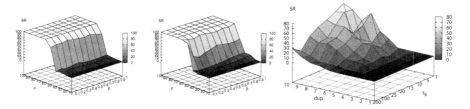

Fig. 2. SR as a function of the values β and ρ using mutation rate $\alpha = \left(\frac{1}{\rho}\right) e^{(-f)}$ for CLONALG$_1$ (left plot) and CLONALG$_2$ (center plot). SR as a function of the values dup and τ_B for opt-IA (right plot).

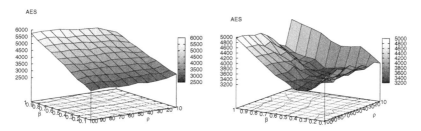

Fig. 3. AES as a function of the values β and ρ using mutation rate $\alpha = e^{(-\rho*f)}$ for CLONALG$_1$ (left plot) and CLONALG$_2$ (right plot)

defined: $\alpha = \left(\frac{1}{\rho}\right) e^{(-f)}$. From the plots it is clear that the parameter ρ plays an important role in reaching the optimum solution. For $\rho < 40.0$, CLONALG (both versions) is unable to find the optimum ($SR = 0$). Instead, using the first type of mutation rate $\alpha = e^{(-\rho*f)}$, CLONALG$_1$ and CLONALG$_2$ solve the one-counting problem for $\ell = 100$ for each setting of the parameters ρ and β (the parameter surface are not shown), but the performance is different, as shown by the Average number Evaluation to Solution (AES) in figure 3. For CLONALG$_1$ the only parameter that influences the behavior of the algorithms is β: if β increases, AES increases also. For CLONALG$_2$ instead both parameter are crucial. Figure 2 shows also the SR parameter surface for opt-IA varying $dup \in \{1, 2, \ldots, 10\}$ and $\tau_B \in \{1, 5, \ldots, 25, 100, 200\}$. The behavior of the algorithm depends on both parameters dup and τ_B, but it is not able to reach $SR = 100$. Figure 4 shows the population average fitness versus generation for CLONALG and opt-IA on the first 100 generations. For CLONALG we show both versions (CLONALG$_1$ and CLONALG$_2$) using the two possible mutation rates defined in section 1.1. The convergence speed of CLONALG is inferior respect to opt-IA but its SR is superior. In about 40 generations, opt-IA reaches a fitness value of $\simeq 95$ but from now on the aging process is more intensive refraining the convergence speed. For opt-IA we show versions with the usage of the static or stochastic aging coupled with an elitist or no-elitist strategy (i.e., the best candidate solution is always maintained from a generation to another). The better results are obtained using static aging.

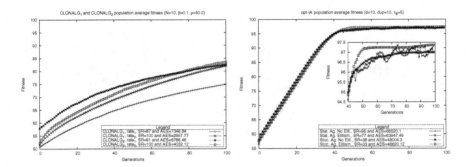

Fig. 4. Population average fitness for CLONALG (left plot) and opt-IA (right plot) (rate$_1$: $\alpha = e^{(-\rho * f)}$, rate$_2$: $\alpha = \left(\frac{1}{\rho}\right) e^{(-f)}$)

2.2   Trap Functions

Trap functions [8] [9], simply, take as input the number of 1's in a bit strings of length ℓ:

$$f(x) = \widehat{f}(u(x)) = \widehat{f}\left(\sum_{k=1}^{\ell} x_k\right) \tag{2}$$

We can define two different types of trap functions: *simple trap function* and *complex trap function*. Their definitions follow:

$$\widehat{f}(u) = \begin{cases} \frac{a}{z}(z-u), & \text{if } u \leq z \\ \frac{b}{\ell-z}(u-z), & \text{otherwise.} \end{cases} , \qquad \widehat{f}(u) = \begin{cases} \frac{a}{z_1}(z_1-u), & \text{if } u \leq z_1 \\ \frac{b}{\ell-z_1}(u-z_1), & \text{if } z_1 < u \leq z_2 \\ \frac{b(z_2-z_1)}{\ell-z_1}\left(1-\frac{1}{\ell-z_2}(u-z_2)\right) & \text{otherwise.} \end{cases} \tag{3}$$

The parameters a, b and z, will take on the values used in [8]: $z \approx (1/4)\ell$; $b = \ell - z - 1$; $1.5b \leq a \leq 2b$; a a multiple of z. The simple trap function is characterize by a global optimum (for a bit string of all 0's) and a local optimum (for a bit string of all 1's) that are the complement *bit-wise* of each other. The complex trap function is more difficult to investigate, in fact there are two directions to get trapped. We note that for $z_2 = \ell$ the complex trap function becomes the simple trap function. In this case the values of parameter z_2 are determined by the following equation $z_2 = \ell - z_1$. Next section tables show the experimental results. Trap functions are labeled either $S(type)$ or $C(type)$, where S and C mean respectively Simple and Complex trap function. *type* varies according to the used parameter values: type I ($\ell = 10, z = 3, a = 12, b = 6$), type II ($\ell = 20, z = 5, a = 20, b = 14$), type III ($\ell = 50, z = 10, a = 80, b = 39$), type IV ($\ell = 75, z = 20, a = 80, b = 54$), type V ($\ell = 100, z = 25, a = 100, b = 74$). For the complex trap function $z_1 = z$ and $z_2 = \ell - z_1$.

Experimental results. All the experimental results reported in this sections have been averaged over 100 independent runs. Table 1 shows the best results obtained

Table 1. Best results obtained by CLONALG (both versions) with population size $N = 10$, varying $\beta \in \{0.1, 0.2, ..., 1.0\}, \rho \in \{1.0, 2.0, ..., 10.0\}$ and $d \in \{1, 2, 3, 4, 5\}$

| | CLONALG$_1$ | | | | | | CLONALG$_2$ | | | | | |
| | $\left(\frac{1}{\rho}\right) e^{(-f)}$ | | | $e^{(-\rho * f)}$ | | | $\left(\frac{1}{\rho}\right) e^{(-f)}$ | | | $e^{(-\rho * f)}$ | | T_{max} |
Trap	SR	AES	(β, ρ)	SR	AES	(β, ρ)	SR	AES	(β, ρ)	SR	AES	(β, ρ)	
S(I)	100	1100.4	(.5,3)	**100**	**479.7**	(.8,2)	100	725.3	(.9,4)	100	539.2	(.7,2)	10^5
S(II)	**100**	**27939.2**	(.8,8)	100	174563.4	(.1,4)	30	173679.8	(.1,6)	31	172191.2	(.1,4)	2×10^5
S(III)	0	-		0	-		0	-		0	-		3×10^5
S(IV)	0	-		0	-		0	-		0	-		4×10^5
S(V)	0	-		0	-		0	-		0	-		5×10^5
C(I)	100	272.5	(.7,3)	100	251.3	(.9,4)	100	254.0	(.3,3)	**100**	**218.4**	(.5,4)	10^5
C(II)	**100**	**17526.3**	(1,8)	10	191852.7	(.2,1)	29	173992.6	(.1,6)	24	172434.2	(.1,4)	2×10^5
C(II)	0	-		0	-		0	-		0	-		3×10^5
C(IV)	0	-		0	-		0	-		0	-		4×10^5
C(V)	0	-		0	-		0	-		0	-		5×10^5

Table 2. Best results obtained by opt-IA with population size $d = 10$, duplication parameter $dup = 1$, varying $c \in \{0.1, ..., 1.0\}$ and $tau_B \in \{1, ..., 15, 20, 25, 50, 100, 200, \infty\}$

| | Inv | | | Macro | | | Inv+Macro | | | |
Trap	SR	AES	(τ_B, c)	SR	AES	(dup, τ_B)	SR	AES	(τ_B, c)	T_{max}
S(I)	100	504.76	(5, 0.3)	100	1495.9	(1, 1)	100	477.04	(15, 0.2)	10^5
S(II)	97	58092.7	(20, 0.2)	28	64760.25	(1, 1)	100	35312.29	(100, 0.2)	2×10^5
S(III)	0	-	-	23	19346.09	(4, 13)	100	20045.81	$(2 \times 10^5, 0.1)$	3×10^5
S(IV)	0	-	-	28	69987	(10, 12)	100	42089	(25, 0.2)	4×10^5
S(V)	0	-	-	27	139824.41	(7, 1)	100	80789.94	(50, 0.2)	5×10^5
C(I)	100	371.15	(10, 0.2)	100	737.78	(5, 3)	100	388.42	(10, 0.2)	10^5
C(II)	100	44079.57	(10, 0.2)	**100**	**27392.18**	(5, 3)	100	29271.68	(5, 0.2)	2×10^5
C(III)	0	-	-	54	115908.61	(4, 7)	24	149006.5	(20, 0.1)	3×10^5
C(IV)	0	-	-	7	179593.29	(2, 9)	2	154925	(15, 0.4)	4×10^5
C(V)	0	-	-	2	353579	(1, 15)	0	-	-	5×10^5

by CLONALG (both versions) in terms of Success Rate (SR) and Average number of Evaluations to Solutions (AES), the population size has been set to the minimal value $N = 10$. The third column in table 1 reports the best parameter values that allowed the hypermutation operators to reach the best results. The last column of the tables reports the maximum number of evaluations allowed, T_{max}, for each kind of trap function.

The results show clearly that, in terms of problem solving ability, facing toy problems is not an easy game. The cases III, IV and V for simple and complex trap functions remain no solved. Moreover, the better result are obtained using mutation rate $(1/\rho) e^{(-f)}$, respect to the ones-counting problem, where the better performance is obtained using $e^{(-\rho * f)}$.

Table 2 shows results obtained with opt-IA using a population size $d = 10$, a minimal duplication parameter $dup = 1$, and varying the parameter $c \in \{0.1, ..., 1.0\}$ and $\tau_B \in \{1, ..., 15, 20, 25, 50, 100, 200, \infty\}$. If we compare the results of opt-IA using only the inversely proportional hypermutation operator with the results obtained by CLONALG for population size of 10 Ab's we note how CLONALG outperforms opt-IA. Using the hypermacromutation operator, opt-IA obtains $SR > 0$ for all cases of the simple and complex trap function. Finally, the usage of coupled operators (Inv+Macro) is the key feature to effectively face the trap functions as shown in the third column of table 2. The results obtained with this setting are comparable with the results in [8], where the authors, in their theoretical and experimental research work, use only cases C(I), C(II) and C(III) for the complex trap function.

3 Pattern Recognition

In this section we consider the simple pattern recognition task to learn ten binary characters. Each character is represented as a bitstring of length $L = 120$ corresponding to a resolution of 12×10 bits for each picture. The original characters are depicted on figure 6, those characters are the same used in [4]. The fitness measure is the standard Hamming distance for bit strings.

Experimental results. Figure 5 shows the opt-IA dynamic for each input pattern to be learned. The algorithm is able to recognize all the characters in only 90 generations. This is not true for CLONALG, the overall convergence happens after 250 generations. This is visible in figure 6, where the representations of the antibodies after 200 generations of the algorithms contain a bit of noise.

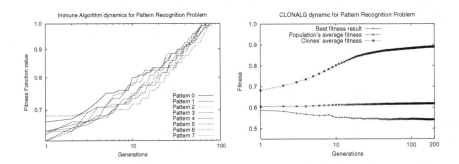

Fig. 5. opt-IA dynamics for each pattern using $d = 10$, $dup = 2$ and $\tau_B = 5$ (left plot). CLONALG population, clones and best Ab average fitness using mutation rate $\alpha = (1/\rho)\,e^{(-f)}$ on 100 independent runs using the same setting of the parameters in [4]: $N = 10, n = 5, m = 8, \beta = 10, d = 0$ (right plot). For both plots, fitness values in axis y are normalized in $[0, 1]$ and axis x is in log scale.

Fig. 6. CLONALG results on pattern recognition. From left to right: patterns to be learned; initial Abs set; Abs set after 200 generations.

4   Numerical Optimization

Numerical optimization problems are fundamental for every field of engineering, science, and business. The task is that of global optimization of a generic objective function. However, often, the objective function is difficult to optimize because the function possesses numerous local optima which could trap the algorithm. Moreover this difficulty increases with the increase of the problem dimension. In this paper we consider the following numerical minimization problem:

$$\min(f(\boldsymbol{x})), \qquad L \leq \boldsymbol{x} \leq U \tag{4}$$

where $\boldsymbol{x} = (x_1, x_2, \ldots, x_n)$ is the variable vector in $\mathcal{R}^n$, $f(\boldsymbol{x})$ denotes the objective function to minimize and $L = (l_1, l_2, \ldots, l_n)$, $U = (u_1, u_2, \ldots, u_n)$ represent, respectively, the lower and the upper bound of the variables, such that $x_i \in [l_i, u_i]$.

Test Functions. Twentythree functions from three categories are selected [10], covering a broader range. Table 3 lists the 23 functions and their key properties (for a complete description of all the functions and the parameters involved see [10]). These function can be divided into three categories of different complexities:

- unimodal functions $(f_1 - f_7)$, which are relatively easy to optimize, but the difficulty increases as the problem dimension increases;
- multimodal functions $(f_8 - f_{13})$, with many local minima, they represent the most difficult class of problems for many optimization algorithms;
- multimodal functions which contain only a few local optima $(f_{14} - f_{23})$.

Some functions possess unique features: f_6 is a discontinuous step function having a single optimum; f_7 is a noisy quartic function involving a uniformly distributed random variable within $[0, 1]$. Optimizing unimodal functions is not a major issue, so in this case the convergence rate is of main interest. However, for multimodal functions the quality of the final results is more important since it reflects the algorithm's ability in *escaping* from local optima.

We used binary string representation: each real value x_i is coded using bitstrings of length $L = 22$ corresponding to a precision of six decimal places.

Experimental results. In table 4 we report results obtained with CLONALG and opt-IA with respect to one of the best evolutionary algorithms for numerical optimization in literature: Fast Evolutionary Programming (FEP) [10]. FEP is based on Conventional Evolutionary Programming (CEP) but uses a new mutation operator based on Cauchy random numbers that helps the algorithm to escape from local optima. In the experiments of this section, opt-IA uses the same mutation potentials above defined for CLONALG (equation 1) for the inversely proportional hypermutation operator. Parameters for CLONALG and opt-IA are setted respectively as follow: $N = n = 50, d = 0, \beta = 0.1$ and $d = 20, dup = 2, \tau_B = 20$. If we compare the two versions of CLONALG, we can see that for unimodal functions $(f_1 - f_7)$ CLONALG$_2$ is in general more effective

Table 3. The 23 benchmark functions used in our experimental study; n is the dimension of the function; f_{min} is the minimum value of the function; $S \subseteq \mathcal{R}^n$ are the variable bounds (for a complete description of all the functions and the parameters involved see [10])

Test function	n	S	f_{min}
$f_1(\boldsymbol{x}) = \sum_{i=1}^{n} x_i^2$	30	$[-100, 100]^n$	0
$f_2(\boldsymbol{x}) = \sum_{i=1}^{n} \lvert x_i \rvert + \prod_{i=1}^{n} \lvert x_i \rvert$	30	$[-10, 10]^n$	0
$f_3(\boldsymbol{x}) = \sum_{i=1}^{n} \left(\sum_{j=1}^{i} x_j \right)^2$	30	$[-100, 100]^n$	0
$f_4(\boldsymbol{x}) = \max_i \{ \lvert x_i \rvert, 1 \leq i \leq n \}$	30	$[-100, 100]^n$	0
$f_5(\boldsymbol{x}) = \sum_{i=1}^{n-1} [100(x_{i+1} - x_i^2)^2 + (x_i - 1)^2]$	30	$[-30, 30]^n$	0
$f_6(\boldsymbol{x}) = \sum_{i=1}^{n} (\lfloor x_i + 0.5 \rfloor)^2$	30	$[-100, 100]^n$	0
$f_7(\boldsymbol{x}) = \sum_{i=1}^{n} i x_i^4 + random[0, 1)$	30	$[-1.28, 1.28]^n$	0
$f_8(\boldsymbol{x}) = \sum_{i=1}^{n} -x_i \sin(\sqrt{\lvert x_i \rvert})$	30	$[-500, 500]^n$	-12569.5
$f_9(\boldsymbol{x}) = \sum_{i=1}^{n} [x_i^2 - 10\cos(2\pi x_i) + 10]$	30	$[-5.12, 5.12]^n$	0
$f_{10}(\boldsymbol{x}) = -20\exp\left(-0.2\sqrt{\frac{1}{n}\sum_{i=1}^{n} x_i^2}\right)$ $- \exp\left(\frac{1}{n}\sum_{i=1}^{n} \cos 2\pi x_i\right) + 20 + e$	30	$[-32, 32]^n$	0
$f_{11}(\boldsymbol{x}) = \frac{1}{4000}\sum_{i=1}^{n} x_i^2 - \prod_{i=1}^{n} \cos\left(\frac{x_i}{\sqrt{i}}\right) + 1$	30	$[-600, 600]^n$	0
$f_{12}(\boldsymbol{x}) = \frac{\pi}{n}\{10\sin^2(\pi y_1)$ $+ \sum_{i=1}^{n-1} (y_i - 1)^2 [1 + 10\sin^2(\pi y_{i+1})] + (y_n - 1)^2\}$ $+ \sum_{i=1}^{n} u(x_i, 10, 100, 4),$ $y_i = 1 + \frac{1}{4}(x_i + 1)$ $u(x_i, a, k, m) = \begin{cases} k(x_i - a)^m, & \text{if } x_i > a, \\ 0, & \text{if } -a \leq x_i \leq a, \\ k(-x_i - a)^m, & \text{if } x_i < -a. \end{cases}$	30	$[-50, 50]^n$	0
$f_{13}(\boldsymbol{x}) = 0.1\{\sin^2(3\pi x_1)$ $+ \sum_{i=1}^{n-1} (x_i - 1)^2 [1 + \sin^2(3\pi x_{i+1})]$ $+ (x_n - 1)[1 + \sin^2(2\pi x_n)]\} + \sum_{i=1}^{n} u(x_i, 5, 100, 4)$	30	$[-50, 50]^n$	0
$f_{14}(\boldsymbol{x}) = \left[\frac{1}{500} + \sum_{j=1}^{25} \frac{1}{j + \sum_{i=1}^{2}(x_i - a_{ij})^6}\right]^{-1}$	2	$[-65.536, 65.536]^n$	1
$f_{15}(\boldsymbol{x}) = \sum_{i=1}^{11} \left[a_i - \frac{x_i(b_i^2 + b_i x_2)}{b_i^2 + b_i x_3 + x_4}\right]^2$	4	$[-5, 5]^n$	0.0003075
$f_{16}(\boldsymbol{x}) = 4x_1^2 - 2.1x_1^4 + \frac{1}{3}x_1^6 + x_1 x_2 - 4x_2^2 + 4x_2^4$	2	$[-5, 5]^n$	-1.0316285
$f_{17}(\boldsymbol{x}) = \left(x_2 - \frac{5.1}{4\pi^2}x_1^2 + \frac{5}{\pi}x_1 - 6\right)^2$ $+ 10\left(1 - \frac{1}{8\pi}\right)\cos x_1 + 10$	2	$[-5, 10] \times [0, 15]$	0.398
$f_{18}(\boldsymbol{x}) = [1 + (x_1 + x_2 + 1)^2(19 - 14x_1 + 3x_1^2 - 14x_2$ $+ 6x_1 x_2 + 3x_2^2)] \times [30 + (2x_1 - 3x_2)^2(18 - 32x_1$ $+ 12x_1^2 + 48x_2 - 36x_1 x_2 + 27x_2^2)]$	2	$[-2, 2]^n$	3
$f_{19}(\boldsymbol{x}) = -\sum_{i=1}^{4} c_i \exp\left[-\sum_{j=1}^{4} a_{ij}(x_j - p_{ij})^2\right]$	4	$[0, 1]^n$	-3.86
$f_{20}(\boldsymbol{x}) = -\sum_{i=1}^{4} c_i \exp\left[-\sum_{j=1}^{6} a_{ij}(x_j - p_{ij})^2\right]$	6	$[0, 1]^n$	-3.32
$f_{21}(\boldsymbol{x}) = -\sum_{i=1}^{5} \left[(\boldsymbol{x} - a_i)(\boldsymbol{x} - a_i)^T + c_i\right]^{-1}$	4	$[0, 10]^n$	-10.1422
$f_{22}(\boldsymbol{x}) = -\sum_{i=1}^{7} \left[(\boldsymbol{x} - a_i)(\boldsymbol{x} - a_i)^T + c_i\right]^{-1}$	4	$[0, 10]^n$	-10.3909
$f_{23}(\boldsymbol{x}) = -\sum_{i=1}^{10} \left[(\boldsymbol{x} - a_i)(\boldsymbol{x} - a_i)^T + c_i\right]^{-1}$	4	$[0, 10]^n$	-10.53

than CLONALG$_1$. Otherwise, for multimodal functions ($f_8 - f_{23}$), CLONALG$_1$ has a better performance. This is in agreement with the type of selection scheme used by the two versions. Since CLONALG$_1$ at each generation replaces each Ab by the best individual of its set of $\beta * N$ mutated clones, it is able to maintain more diversity in the population. On the other hand, CLONALG$_2$ focuses the search on the global optimum, with the consequence of a higher probability to be trapped in a local optimum.

Considering the two versions of opt-IA, the four versions of CLONALG, and the results obtained by FEP, opt-IA outperforms CLONALG and FEP on 11

Table 4. Comparison between FEP[10], CLONALG$_1$, CLONALG$_2$ and opt-IA on the 23 test functions. Results have been averaged over 50 independent runs, "mean best" indicates the mean best function values found in the last generation, "std dev" stands for standard deviation and T_{max} is the maximum number of fitness function evaluation allowed. In **boldface** overall better results for each function, in *italics* the best results among CLONALG and opt-IA.

Fun. T_{max}	FEP[10] mean best (std dev)	CLONALG$_1$ $e(-\rho*f)$, $\rho=10$ mean best (std dev)	CLONALG$_1$ $(\frac{1}{\rho})e(-f)$, $\rho=150$ mean best (std dev)	CLONALG$_2$ $e(-\rho*f)$, $\rho=10$ mean best (std dev)	CLONALG$_2$ $(\frac{1}{\rho})e(-f)$, $\rho=150$ mean best (std dev)	opt-IA $e(-\rho*f)$, $\rho=10$ mean best (std dev)	opt-IA $(\frac{1}{\rho})e(-f)$, $\rho=150$ mean best (std dev)
f_1 150.000	5.7×10^{-4} (1.3×10^{-4})	9.6×10^{-4} (1.6×10^{-3})	3.7×10^{-3} (2.6×10^{-3})	3.2×10^{-6} (1.5×10^{-6})	5.5×10^{-4} (2.4×10^{-4})	6.4×10^{-8} (2.6×10^{-8})	*3.4×10^{-8}* *(1.3×10^{-8})*
f_2 200.000	8.1×10^{-3} (7.7×10^{-4})	7.7×10^{-5} (2.5×10^{-5})	2.9×10^{-3} (6.6×10^{-4})	1.2×10^{-4} (2.1×10^{-5})	2.7×10^{-3} (7.1×10^{-4})	7.4×10^{-5} (4.5×10^{-6})	*7.2×10^{-5}* *(3.4×10^{-6})*
f_3 500.000	**1.6×10^{-2}** **(1.4×10^{-2})**	2.2×10^4 (1.3×10^{-4})	1.5×10^4 (1.8×10^3)	2.4×10^4 (5.7×10^3)	5.9×10^3 (1.8×10^3)	3.6×10^3 (1.1×10^3)	*2.6×10^2* *(6.8×10^2)*
f_4 500.000	0.30 (0.50)	9.44 (1.98)	4.91 (1.11)	*5.9×10^{-4}* *(3.5×10^{-4})*	8.7×10^{-3} (2.1×10^{-3})	1.0×10^{-2} (5.3×10^{-3})	4.9×10^{-3} (3.8×10^{-3})
f_5 2×10^6	**5.06** **(5.87)**	31.07 (13.48)	*27.6* *(1.034)*	4.67×10^2 (6.3×10^2)	2.35×10^2 (4.4×10^{02})	28.6 (0.12)	28.4 (0.42)
f_6 150.000	**0.0** **(0.0)**	0.52 (0.49)	2.0×10^{-2} (1.4×10^{-1})	*0.0* *(0.0)*	*0.0* *(0.0)*	0.2 (0.44)	*0.0* *(0.0)*
f_7 300.000	7.6×10^{-3} (2.6×10^{-3})	1.3×10^{-1} (3.5×10^{-2})	7.8×10^{-2} (1.9×10^{-2})	4.6×10^{-3} (1.6×10^{-3})	5.3×10^{-3} (1.4×10^{-3})	**3.4×10^{-3}** **(1.6×10^{-3})**	3.9×10^{-3} (1.3×10^{-3})
f_8 900.000	-12554.5 (52.6)	-11099.56 (112.05)	-11044.69 (186.73)	-12228.39 (41.08)	-12533.86 (43.08)	-12508.38 (155.54)	*-12568.27* *(0.23)*
f_9 500.000	**4.6×10^{-2}** **(1.2×10^{-2})**	42.93 (3.05)	37.56 (4.88)	21.75 (5.03)	22.41 (6.70)	19.98 (7.66)	*5.68* *(1.55)*
f_{10} 150.000	1.8×10^{-2} (2.1×10^{-3})	18.96 (2.2×10^{-1})	1.57 (3.9×10^{-1})	19.30 (1.9×10^{-1})	1.2×10^{-1} (4.1×10^{-1})	0.94 (3.56×10^{-1})	**4.0×10^{-4}** **(1.8×10^{-4})**
f_{11} 200.000	1.6×10^{-2} (2.2×10^{-2})	3.6×10^{-2} (3.5×10^{-2})	*1.7×10^{-2}* *(1.9×10^{-2})*	9.4×10^{-2} (1.4×10^{-1})	4.6×10^{-2} (7.0×10^{-2})	9.1×10^{-2} (1.36×10^{-1})	3.8×10^{-2} (5.5×10^{-2})
f_{12} 150.000	**9.2×10^{-6}** **(3.6×10^{-6})**	0.632 (2.2×10^{-1})	*0.396* *(9.4×10^{-2})*	0.738 (5.3×10^{-1})	0.573 (2.6×10^{-1})	0.433 (1.41×10^{-1})	0.364 (5.6×10^{-2})
f_{13} 150.000	**1.6×10^{-4}** **(7.3×10^{-5})**	1.83 (2.7×10^{-1})	*1.39* *(1.8×10^{-1})*	1.84 (2.7×10^{-1})	1.69 (2.4×10^{-1})	1.51 (1.01×10^{-1})	1.75 (7.7×10^{-2})
f_{14} 10.000	1.22 (0.56)	1.0062 (4.0×10^{-2})	*1.0021* *(2.8×10^{-2})*	1.45 (0.95)	2.42 (2.60)	1.042 (0.11)	1.21 (0.54)
f_{15} 400.000	**5.0×10^{-4}** **(3.2×10^{-4})**	1.4×10^{-3} (5.4×10^{-4})	1.5×10^{-3} (7.8×10^{-4})	8.3×10^{-3} (8.5×10^{-3})	7.2×10^{-3} (8.1×10^{-3})	*7.1×10^{-4}* *(1.3×10^{-4})*	7.7×10^{-3} (1.4×10^{-2})
f_{16} 10.000	-1.03 (4.9×10^{-7})	*-1.0315* *(1.8×10^{-4})*	-1.0314 (5.7×10^{-4})	-1.0202 (1.8×10^{-2})	-1.0210 (1.9×10^{-2})	-1.0314 (8.7×10^{-4})	-1.027 (1.0×10^{-2})
f_{17} 10.000	**0.398** **(1.5×10^{-7})**	0.40061 (8.8×10^{-3})	0.399 (2.0×10^{-3})	0.462 (2.0×10^{-1})	0.422 (2.7×10^{-2})	*0.398* *(2.0×10^{-4})*	0.58 (0.44)
f_{18} 10.000	3.02 (0.11)	3.00 (1.3×10^{-7})	3.00 (1.3×10^{-5})	3.54 (3.78)	3.46 (3.28)	*3.0* *(3.3×10^{-8})*	*3.0* *(0.0)*
f_{19} 10.000	**-3.86** **(1.4×10^{-5})**	-3.71 (1.1×10^{-2})	-3.71 (1.5×10^{-2})	-3.67 (6.6×10^{-2})	-3.68 (6.9×10^{-2})	-3.72 (1.5×10^{-4})	*-3.72* *(1.4×10^{-6})*
f_{20} 20.000	-3.27 (5.9×10^{-2})	-3.30 (1.0×10^{-2})	-3.23 (5.9×10^{-2})	-3.21 (8.6×10^{-2})	-3.18 (1.2×10^{-1})	-3.31 (7.5×10^{-3})	**-3.31** **(5.9×10^{-3})**
f_{21} 10.000	-5.52 (1.59)	-7.59 (1.89)	-5.92 (1.77)	-5.21 (1.78)	-3.98 (2.73)	**-8.29** **(2.25)**	-3.73 (0.26)
f_{22} 10.000	-5.52 (2.12)	-8.41 (1.40)	-5.90 (2.09)	-7.31 (2.67)	-4.66 (2.55)	**-9.59** **(1.72)**	-3.79 (0.25)
f_{23} 10.000	-6.57 (3.14)	-8.48 (1.51)	-5.98 (1.98)	-7.12 (2.48)	-4.38 (2.66)	**-9.96** **(1.46)**	-3.86 (0.19)

functions over 23, analogously to FEP, while CLONALG performs better only in 3 functions (see boldface results in table 4).

By inspecting the entries on the table 4 in terms of results obtained by CSAs only, we note that, opt-IA outperforms CLONALG on 15 functions over 23 benchmark functions (execept for function 6 where both algorithms obtain the same statistical results), while CLONALG obtains the best results on 7 functions only (results reported in italic in table 4).

5   Protein Structure Prediction: HP Model

The Protein Structure Prediction problem (PSP) is simply defined as the problem of finding the 3D conformation of a protein starting from the amino-acids composition. A simplified version of this problem was introduced by Dill in [11] which is called the HP model. It models proteins as two-dimensional *self-avoiding walk chains* of ℓ monomers on the square lattice: two residues cannot occupy the same node of the lattice. Residues are classified into two major classes: H (hydrophobic) and the P (polar). In this model, each H–H topological contact, that is, each lattice nearest-neighbor H–H contact interaction, has energy value $\epsilon \leq 0$, while all other contact interaction types (H–P, P–P) have zero energy. In general, in the HP model the residues interactions can be defined as follows: $e_{HH} = - \mid \epsilon \mid$ and $e_{HP} = e_{PH} = e_{PP} = \delta$. When $\epsilon = 1$ and $\delta = 0$ we have the typical interaction energy matrix for the standard HP model [11]. The native conformation is the one that maximizes the number of contacts H–H, i.e. the one that minimizes the free energy function. Finding the global minimum of the free energy function for the protein folding problem in the 2D HP model is NP-hard [12]. The input for the algorithms is a protein sequence of $s \in \{H, P\}^{\ell}$ where ℓ represents the number of amino-acids. The candidate solution is a sequence of *relative directions* [13] $r \in \{F, R, L\}^{\ell-1}$, where each r_i is a relative direction with respect to the previous direction (r_{i-1}), with $i = 2, \ldots, \ell - 1$ (i.e., there are $\ell - 2$ relative directions) and r_1 the non relative direction. We obtain an overall sequence r of length $\ell - 1$.

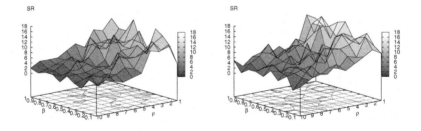

Fig. 7. CLONALG$_1$: SR as a function of the values β and ρ for mutation rate $\alpha = e^{(-\rho * f)}$ (left plot) and mutation rate $\alpha = \left(\frac{1}{\rho}\right) e^{(-f)}$ (right plot) on seq2 instance

Experimental results. In this section we report the results obtained for both versions of CLONALG and opt-IA on 12 instances from the *Tortilla 2D HP benchmarks*[1]. Since opt-IA was well studied for the HP model [5,14,15], first of all we made a parameter tuning process for CLONALG in order to choose between CLONALG$_1$ and CLONALG$_2$ the version with the best performance for PSP, and also in order to set the best values for parameters β and ρ. In particular, parameter surfaces were determined in order to predict the best delimited region

---

[1] http://www.cs.sandia.gov/tech report/compbio/tortilla-hpbenchmarks.html

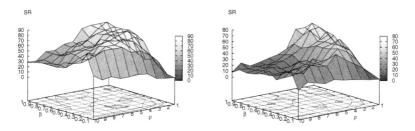

Fig. 8. CLONALG$_2$: SR as a function of the values β and ρ for mutation rate $\alpha = e^{(-\rho * f)}$ (left plot) and mutation rate $\alpha = \left(\frac{1}{\rho}\right) e^{(-f)}$ (right plot) on seq2 instance

Table 5. opt-IA algorithm ($d = 10, dup = 2$). Results have been averaged on 30 independent runs, where $b.\,f$ indicates the best values found, symbol μ stands for mean and symbol σ stands for standard deviation.

	Protein			$\tau_B = 1$				$\tau_B = 5$			
No.	ℓ	E^*	SR	AES	b. f.	μ	σ	SR	AES	b. f.	μ	σ
1	20	-9	100	23710	-9	-9	0	100	**20352.4**	-9	-9	0
2	24	-9	100	69816.7	-9	-9	0	100	**39959.9**	-9	-9	0
3	25	-8	100	**269513.9**	-8	-8	0	100	282855.7	-8	-8	0
4	36	-14	**100**	2032504	-14	-13.93	0.25	73.33	4569496.3	-14	-13.73	0.44
5	48	-23	**56.67**	6403985.3	-23	-22.47	0.67	6.67	4343279	-23	-21.47	0.62
6	50	-21	100	**778906.4**	-21	-21	0	100	1135818.9	-21	-21	0
7	60	-36	0	//	-35	-33.73	0.68	0	//	-35	**-34.5**	**0.5**
8	64	-42	0	//	**-39**	**-36.13**	**1.28**	0	//	-38	-35.1	1.25
9	20	-10	100	**18085.8**	-10	-10	0	100	18473.6	-10	-10	0
10	18	-9	100	**69210**	-9	-9	0	100	130342	-9	-9	0
11	18	-8	100	**41724.2**	-8	-8	0	100	50151.2	-8	-8	0
12	18	-4	100	87494.5	-4	-4	0	100	**74426.5**	-4	-4	0

that maximizes SR values and minimize AES value. The maximum number of fitness function evaluation (T_{max}) allowed for this first set of experiments is 10^5. The results are averaged on 100 independent runs.

From figures 7 and 8 it is obvious that CLONALG$_2$ has a better behavior with respect to CLONALG$_1$, the best SR found by CLONALG$_2$ is 85 using mutation rate $\alpha = e^{(-\rho * f)}$, while the best SR found by CLONALG$_1$ is 18. The worse performance of CLOANLG$_1$ is consequence of the structure of the selection scheme for the creation of the new population of antibody, as explained in section 1.1. In fact, this version is more useful for multimodal optimization problems where is necessary to find the greatest number of peaks of a specific function (maximization), as shown in [4] and as demonstrated from results on numerical optimization in section 4. Again, we want to put in evidence the crucial importance of selecting the better mutation rate for each problem, and the tuning of the parameter to which is correlated (ρ).

Tables 5 and 6 show the best results for CLONALG (both versions) and opt-IA on the 12 PSP instances setting $T_{max} = 10^7$. All the results have been averaged over 30 independent runs. For CLONALG the values of β and ρ have been chosen according to figures 7 and 8 when the best SR is found. The mutation rate $\alpha = e^{(-\rho * f)}$ was used, according to its better performance as shown

Table 6. CLONALG$_1$ and CLOANLG$_2$ using mutation rate $\alpha = e^{(-\rho * f)}$ ($N = n = 10, d = 0$). Results have been averaged on 30 independent runs, where $b.\ f$ indicates the best values found, symbol μ stands for mean and symbol σ stands for standard deviation.

Protein			CLOANLG$_1$ ($\beta = 0.4, \rho = 1.0$)					CLOANLG$_2$ ($\beta = 0.3, \rho = 5.0$)				
No.	ℓ	E^*	SR	AES	b. f.	μ	σ	SR	AES	b. f.	μ	σ
1	20	-9	100	322563.50	-9	-9	0	100	**22379.60**	-9	-9	0
2	24	-9	90	2225404.75	-9	-8.9	0.3	100	**69283.34**	-9	-9	0
3	25	-8	96.67	1686092.38	-8	-7.96	0.17	**100**	907112.56	-8	-8	0
4	36	-14	0	//	-13	-12.23	0.46	**23.33**	5189238.50	-14	-13.2	0.47
5	48	-23	0	//	-21	-18.93	0.92	**3.33**	8101204.50	-23	-20.76	1.02
6	50	-21	0	//	-20	-17.43	0.95	**46.67**	6019418.50	-21	-20.2	0.87
7	60	-36	0	//	-34	-30.43	1.33	0	//	**-35**	-32.43	0.98
8	64	-42	0	//	-35	-29.26	1.74	0	//	**-39**	-33.43	2.21
9	20	-10	100	649403.00	-10	-10	0	100	**27391.67**	-10	-10	0
10	18	-9	**96.67**	2143456.50	-9	-8.96	0.18	90	1486671.25	-9	-8.9	0.3
11	18	-8	96.67	742352.56	-8	-7.96	0.18	**100**	52349.10	-8	-8	0
12	18	-4	100	740468.31	-4	-4	0	100	**70247.73**	-4	-4	0

previously. Best results for opt-IA are obtained using coupled operators, inversely proportional hypermutation and Hypermacromutation. As for the traps, this is again the key feature to effectively face the problem. Both algorithms use the same minimal population dimension ($N = d = 10$). For the simple sequences 1,2,3,9,11 and 12 the algorithms have a similar behavior, but when we consider more difficult instances, like sequences 4,5 and 6, the overall performance of opt-IA is evident. Both algorithms are unable to solve the hard sequences 7 and 8, but although they reach the same minimum values, opt-IA has lower mean and standard deviation, showing a more robust behavior.

6   Conclusions

In this experimental work we made a comparative study of two famous Clonal Selection Algorithms, CLONALG and opt-IA, on significant test bed: ones-counting and trap functions (toy problems), pattern recognition, numerical optimization (23 functions) and 2D HP Protein Structure Prediction problem (NP-Complete problem). A robust test bed is important in order to analyze theoretically and experimentally the overall robustness of evolutionary algorithms, as reported in [16]. Two possible versions of CLONALG have been implemented and tested, coupled with two possible mutation potential for the hypermutation operator. The experimental results show a deep influence of the mutation potential for each problem and the setting of the respective parameter. Parameter tuning was made for both algorithms, and an overall better performance of opt-IA was found on all problems tackled. In particular, simulation results on numerical optimization problems show how CSAs (in particular opt-IA) are effective methods also for numerical optimization problems, obtaining comparable results respect to one of the most effective method in literature, Fast Evolutionary Programming. Obviously, the presented clonal selection algorithms can be applied to any other combinatorial and numerical optimization problem using suitable representations and variable operators [17,18,2].

In last years there have been many applications of CSAs to search, learning and optimization problems [19,20,21]. In particular, this new class of evolutionary algorithms seem to be effective to face protein structure prediction problem [14,15,22]. This article and all the above cited research works demonstrate that the clonal selection algorithms are mature and effective computational tools [21,23].

The evolutionary computation scientific community has a new class, *immune algorithms* [4,17], that along with *genetic algorithms* [24,25], *evolution strategies* [26], *evolutionary programming* [27] and the *genetic programming* [28] constitutes the overall set of evolutionary algorithms.

References

1. Burnet F.M.: "The Clonal Selection Theory of Acquired Immunity". Cambridge, UK: *Cambridge University Press*, (1959).
2. Cutello V., Nicosia G.: "The Clonal Selection Principle for in silico and in vitro Computing", *in Recent Developments in Biologically Inspired Computing*, L. N. de Castro and F. J. Von Zuben, Eds., (2004).
3. De Castro L. N., Timmis J.: "Artificial Immune Systems: A New Computational Intelligence Paradigm" London, UK: *Springer-Verlag*, (2002).
4. De Castro L.N., Von Zuben F.J.: "Learning and optimization using the clonal selection principle". *IEEE Trans. on Evolutionary Computation*, vol 6, no 3, pp. 239-251, (2002).
5. Cutello V., Nicosia G., Pavone M.: "Exploring the capability of immune algorithms: A characterization of hypermutation operators" in *Proc. of the Third Int. Conf. on Artificial Immune Systems (ICARIS'04)*, pp. 263-276, (2004).
6. De Castro L. N., Timmis J.: "An Artificial Immune Network for Multimodal Function Optimization", *CEC'02, Proceeding of IEEE Congress on Evolutionary Computation*, IEEE Press, (2002).
7. Prugel-Bennett A., Rogers A.: "Modelling GA Dynamics", *Proc. Theoretical Aspects of Evolutionary Computing*, pp. 59–86, (2001).
8. Nijssen S., Back T.: "An analysis of the Behavior of Simplified Evolutionary Algorithms on Trap Functions", *IEEE Trans. on Evolutionary Computation*, vol 7(1), pp. 11-22, (2003).
9. Nicosia G., Cutello V., Pavone M., Narzisi G., Sorace G.: "How to Escape Traps using Clonal Selection Algorithms", *The First International Conference on Informatics in Control, Automation and Robotics* (ICINCO) INSTICC Press, Vol. 1, pp. 322-326, (2004).
10. Yao X., Liu Y., Lin G.M.: "Evolutionary programming made faster", *IEEE Trans. on Evolutionary Computation*, vol 3, pp. 82-102, (1999).
11. Dill K.A.: "Theory for the folding and stability of globular proteins", in *Biochemistry*, vol. 24, pp. 1501-1509, (1985).
12. Crescenzi P., Goldman D., Papadimitriou C., Piccolboni A., Yannakakis M.: "On the complexity of protein folding" in *J. of Comp. Bio.*, vol. 5, pp. 423-466, (1998).
13. Krasnogor N., Hart W.E., Smith J., Pelta D.A.: "Protein Structure Prediction with Evolutionary Algorithms", *GECCO '99*, vol 2, pp. 1596-1601, (1999).

14. Cutello V., Morelli G., Nicosia G., Pavone M.; "Immune Algorithms with Aging operators for the String Folding Problem and the Protein Folding Problem" in *Proc. of the Fifth Europ. Conf. on Comp. in Combinatorial Optimization (EVOCOP'05)*, LNCS, vol. 3448, pp. 80-90, (2005).
15. Nicosia G., Cutello V., Pavone M.: "An Immune Algorithm with Hyper-Macromutations for the Dill's 2D Hydrophobic-Hydrophilic Model", *Congress on Evolutionary Computation, CEC 2004, IEEE Press*, vol. 1, pp. 1074-1080, (2004).
16. Goldberg D.E.: "The Design of Innovation: Lessons from and for Competent Genetic Algorithms", *Kluwer Academic Publisher*, vol 7, pp. Boston, (2002).
17. Cutello V. , Nicosia G.: "An Immunological Approach to Combinatorial Optimization Problems". *Proc. of 8th Ibero-American Conf. on Artificial Intelligence* (IBERAMIA'02), (2002).
18. Nicosia G., Cutello V., Pavone M.: "A Hybrid Immune Algorithm with Information Gain for the Graph Coloring Problem", *Genetic and Evolutionary Computation Conference*, GECCO 2003, vol. 2723, pp. 171-182.
19. Garrett S. M.: "Parameter-free, Adaptive Clonal Selection" *Congress on Evolutionary Computing*, Portland Oregon, June (2004).
20. Nicosia G., Cutello V., Bentley P. J., Timmis J.: "Artificial Immune Systems", *Third International Conference*, ICARIS 2004, Catania, Italy, September 13-16, Springer (2004).
21. Nicosia G.: "Immune Algorithms for Optimization and Protein Structure Prediction", PHD Thesis, *University of Catania"*, Italy, December 2004.
22. Cutello V., Narzisi G., Nicosia G.: "A Class of Pareto Archived Evolution Strategy Algorithms Using Immune Inspired Operators for Ab-Initio Protein Structure Prediction." *EvoWorkshops 2005*, LNCS, vol. 3449, pp. 54-63, (2005).
23. Garrett S. M.: "A Survey of Artificial Immune Systems: Are They Useful?" *Evolutionary Computation*, vol. 13(2), (2005) (to appear).
24. Holland J.: "Genetic algorithms and the optimal allocation of trials", *SIAM J. Computing*, vol. 2, pp. 88-105, (1973).
25. Holland, J. H.: "Adaptation in Natural and Artificial Systems". Ann Arbor, Michigan: *The University of Michigan Press*, (1975).
26. Rechenberg, I.: "Evolutions strategie: Optimierung Technischer Systeme nach Prinzipien der Biologischen Evolution". *Frommann-Holzboog*, Stuttgart, (1973).
27. Fogel, L. J., Owens, A. J., Walsh, M. J. "Artificial Intelligence Through Simulated Evolution". *New York: Wiley Publishing*, (1966).
28. Koza, J. R.: "Evolving a computer program to generate random numbers using the genetic programming paradigm". *Proc. of the Fourth Int. Conf. on GA*, (1991).

Not All Balls Are Round: An Investigation of Alternative Recognition-Region Shapes

Emma Hart

Napier University, Scotland, UK
e.hart@napier.ac.uk

Abstract. The purpose of this paper is three-fold. Firstly, it aims to demonstrate empirically that networks evolved using different shaped recognition regions in a real-valued shape-space exhibit different dynamics during their formation, and vary in both their capabilities to tolerate antigens and in their memory capacity. Secondly, the paper serves as a useful comparison to previous published work which investigated the properties of a network evolving in a simple, small Hamming shape-space. This work represents the first steps in a proper analysis of a real-valued shape-space with differing recognition shapes. Finally, and perhaps most importantly, the experiments presented illustrate the importance of paying careful attention to the choice of recognition region and algorithm parameters when applying an AIS based on a network-model to practical problems.

1 Introduction

Since Jerne first suggested the notion of an idiotypic network [6] in which antibody cells are able to interact with other antibody cells as well as with antigenic material, there has been a great deal of interest in understanding and applying such networks, ranging from experimental and theoretical studies in the immunological communities [11,2] to practical applications such as data-clustering [7] in the AIS (Artificial Immune Systems) domain.

The computational implementation and study of Jerne's ideas was to a large extent made possible by the introduction of the notion of shape-space by Perelson and Oster [8], which provides a formal model that can quantitatively describe the interactions between cells. The model assumes that the generalised shape of any cell can be represented by a vector of L attributes, where the attributes represent for example the width, height and charge of a combining site, and can be real-valued, integers, binary, symbols, or a combination, depending on the application. A degree of affinity can then be calculated for any cell pair by defining a measure of distance between the two vectors, thus a shape-space is simply a metric space with an associated distance function, where small distances correspond to high affinity and vice-versa. Shape-space can take any form; typically, Hamming shape-spaces and real-valued shape-spaces are often chosen in practical AIS applications.

C. Jacob et al. (Eds.): ICARIS 2005, LNCS 3627, pp. 29–42, 2005.

According to the shape-space model, cells recognise other cells lying within a *ball of stimulation*. In Perelson and Oster's original work, the *shape* of the ball of stimulation is exactly as the term suggests, namely a hyper-spherical region centered on the cell itself. This idea is propagated through much future work; for example, Smith [10] uses it explain the associative properties of immunological memory. Bersini [2] adopts the model in building a simulation of an idiotypic work that is used to lend weight to the argument of Varela and Coutinho [11] that the immune system is self-assertive rather than a self-recognition system, and elaborates on the engineering implications of this in [1,3]. In the AIS domain, the network inspired algorithms of Timmis and Neal [7] apply the idea in an practical context through the use of a parameter called the *network affinity threshold* which effectively creates a hyper-spherical region around a point outside of which recognition is not deemed to take place.

As engineers however, we are at liberty to abstract ideas from the biological models we use as our inspiration and adapt them according to our needs. Hart and Ross in [5] present some observational results from graphical simulations of an idiotypic network based on earlier work by Bersini in [1] in which the shape of the recognition region of any cell *can be varied*. Their work represents a shift in perspective from earlier studies which have simulated idiotypic networks — instead of focusing attention on understanding the biological immune system, their purpose was to gain a clearer understanding of the behaviour of idiotpyic networks so that they could be better used in engineering AIS solutions to practical applications. In this paper, we extend the qualitative work of [5] by providing empirical evidence that the shape of the recognition region of a cell in a real-valued shape-space can be usefully altered in order to manipulate the properties of the resulting emergent networks. In particular, the ability of a network to tolerate antigen and the memory capacity of the networks can be affected by judicious choice of recognition region shape.

2   Related Work

Hart *et al* in [5] present a study of the effects of altering the shape of the recognition region of cells in an idiotypic network simulation in a real-valued shape-space, from an engineering perspective. However, their work mainly addresses the emergence of such networks in the absence of any antigenic stimulation, and whilst very interesting from a theoretical point of view, it has less relevance for an AIS engineer, where a problem to be solved usually has data represented by antigens, and the aim of evolving a network is (for example) to represent the data in some manner. Furthermore, their work only presented some qualitative observations, without any proper empirical analysis, and therefore it is difficult to predict more general behaviour from their study, particularly if the parameters of the algorithm are varied from those used in the experiments described.

More relevant related work is that of Bersini [2], who presents empirical results from experiments with an idiotypic network which evolves in a binary shape-space. In this work, cells are represented by binary string of N bits, and affinity is calculated using Hamming distance between two strings. This work presents many interesting conclusions, in relation to the behaviour of the networks in the presence of antigen, and in relation to their ability to tolerate antigen and maintain an antigenic memory as a function of the matching probability between cells. However, as previously mentioned, the focus of the work is in studying the network to address conflicting immunological questions, rather than to understand how the models may be best adapted to help solve engineering problems. Also, the use of a binary shape-space renders the outcomes less relevant for the majority of practical applications which lend themselves naturally to a real-valued representation. Nevertheless, this work serves as a very useful benchmark against which the work in this paper can be contrasted, and we adopt much of the methodology stated in this paper so that a useful comparison can be made.

3   Modelling of Recognition Regions

The models used in the experiments are described below and shown in figure 1. Theses shapes are identical to those described in [5].

Circle. A simple, symmetrical recognition region is investigated, which consists of a circular region centered on the complement of any given point (x,y) and is shown in figure 1(a). This shape of region is also used by Bersini in [2].

Cross. The second shape is shown in figure 1(b). In this model, one co-ordinate of a cell must match the complement of a cell to which it binds closely and the other co-ordinate matches within the specified recognition radius. This is an attempt to model multiple, distinct, binding sites on a single cell. The length of the long side of the cross shape is determined by the experimentally variable parameter R, and the short side is fixed at length $2N$, where N is the radius of the short arm.

Box. In figure 1(c,d), the complementary regions are engineered such that there is not necessarily mutual recognition between a pair of cells; thus, if cell B lies in the complementary region of cell A, then cell A does *not necessarily* also lie in the complementary region of cell B. The complementary regions in this case essentially consist of a square of side R positioned at a point in the space dependent on the coordinates of the cell.

Note that for any given value of R, the corresponding *area* of the recognition region for the three models just described will differ. For example, the area of the circular shape of radius R will be π times greater than that of the corresponding box shape of side R. Thus, when directly comparing experimental results at any given value of R, one should be aware that there will be a different probability of a randomly generated antigen being matched by a cell in each of the three models described. Whilst this has implications if one is merely studying and comparing the evolution of networks from a theoretical standpoint, from an engineering perspective, the value of R chosen is often of greater importance than the *size* of the recognition region. For example, consider figure 2 which shows an artificially

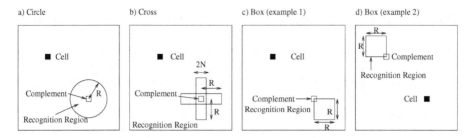

Fig. 1. The shapes of recognition region used in the experimental work — in each case, R represents the recognition radius of each shape

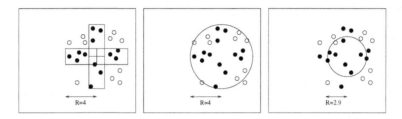

Fig. 2. The figure illustrates the importance of choosing the correct radius and shape for a recognition region. In a), the cross has radius $R = 4$. In b), the circle has identical radius $R = 4$. In c), the circular region has identical area to the cross in a), which is obtained when $R = 2.9$.

constructed problem in which a cell is required to match the antigens shown by the solid circles only. The first diagram shows that the required cells are easily matched by a cross-shaped region with $R = 4$. The second figure shows the effect of using a circular region of *identical* radius — in this case, some extra antigens of a different type are also matched. Finally, the third diagram shows a circular region of identical area to the cross region in the first figure, and therefore will identical probability of matching some randomly generated cell. In this case, some of the black antigens are not matched. In general, practical problems have a non-random distribution of data, and hence the recognition radii becomes of great importance.

4   The Algorithm

The algorithm governing the network simulation is described below. All cells (both antibodies and antigens) are represented as a 2-dimensional points (x, y) on a grid on size (X, Y).

Cell Dynamics. One new antibody P is created at each iteration, and placed randomly on a grid of pre-specified size with an initial concentration of P_c. Then, at each cycle, the total affinity P_a of each cell is calculated as follows. If the cell P is at (x, y), then the contents of a region S of radius R centered at the complementary point $Q = (X - x, Y - y)$ are deemed to be an adequately close complement to the cell and influence the value of P_a as follows:

$$P_a = \sum_{\text{antigens } A \in S} A_c(r - ||A - Q||) \qquad \text{or} \qquad (1)$$

$$P_a = \sum_{\text{antigens } A \in S} A_c(r - ||A - Q||) + \sum_{\text{cells } E \in S} E_c(r - ||E - Q||) \quad (2)$$

depending on whether the user chooses to let cells 'see' just antigens or both cells and antigens in the complementary region (and where A_c is antigen concentration and E_c is cell concentration). Thus, antigens (and maybe cells) closest to the centre of the complementary region have potentially much more effect on the affinity than those close to the edge of the region. In the above equations, the term r represents the maximal distance of any point from the complement Q that lies within the recognition region of radius R. Thus for the circle shape, $R = r$, however, for the box shape, $r = R\sqrt{2}$, and for the cross, $r = \sqrt{(R^2 + N^2)}$.

If a cell P's total affinity P_a satisfies $L \le P_a \le U$ then its concentration is increased by 1, otherwise it is decreased by 1. A cell dies, and is removed, if its concentration falls to 0. This, the model is not strictly *idiotypic* in the sense that there is idiotypic suppression between molecules, rather, the upper boundary U acts as a mechanism for preventing over-stimulation.

Antigen Dynamics. Antigens can be added at any iteration of the algorithm, either as a "batch" in which a number of antigens are added simultaneously at some iteration x, or individually. Each newly-created antigen has a experimentally pre-specified concentration. At each cycle, the total affinity A_a of an antigen A at (x, y) is computed in a somewhat similar way by looking at the cells in the complementary region S centered at the complementary point $B = (X - x, Y - y)$:

$$A_a = \sum_{\text{cells } E \in S} E_c(r - ||E - B||)$$

If $A_a \le L$ the concentration of A is unaffected, but if $A_c > L$ then the concentration decreases by an amount $A_c/(100L)$. If the concentration falls to 0 the antigen dies and is removed. Thus, antigens never *increase* in concentration, their concentration either stays the same, or decreases.

5   Experimental Parameters

All experiments in the following sections were performed using a modified version of the idiotypic network simulator code downloadable from [9]. The code was modified to be able to run offline without graphics for the purpose of experimentation, and so that antigen data could stored in files and added to the simulation at any point during an experiment. All experiments were performed on a grid of size 100x100. Antibodies were always added with a fixed concentration of 10, and one antibody is randomly recruited at each iteration of the algorithm. The lower limit of the threshold value, L was held constant at 100, and the upper limit U at 10000. In all experiments, the network emergence is investigated over the complete range of possible values of R, i.e for 1-100. Clearly, at large values of R, so much of the space is covered by any single cell a network cannot serve any practical function. However, the results are presented for completeness.

6   Investigation of Network Emergence

In the initial simulations, we investigate the dynamics of the emergence of three idiotypic networks, using the shape-spaces described in section 3. In all experiments, a network is evolved over 10000 iterations, entirely in the absence of antigens, with parameters as given in section 5. Experiments with each network are repeated 10 times, using recognition radii varying over the full width of the 2d grid, i.e from 1 (representing very specific matching) to 100 (representing completely unspecific matching). Figure 3 shows the average number of cells present in the system after 10000 iterations as a function of the recognition radius of each shape and the average number of other antibodies each antibody present is stimulated by (i.e that lie within its recognition region).

For each of the three shape-spaces, there is some minimum probability of matching, p_{min}, below which a network is unable to spring into existence. The exact value of R, the recognition radius, at which this is reached varies between the shape-spaces (see figure 3(b) which clearly illustrates this). The same effect is observed by Bersini in [2] in his discussion of Hamming shape-spaces, which he labels *network percolation*. For each shape-space, the precise value of p_{min} is determined by the interplay between the values of the radius R, the initial concentration of each cell, and the affinity thresholds L and U (see section 4). Altering these values changes the value of p_{min} in each case, however the same general pattern is observed.

Each of the shape-spaces exhibits different behaviour immediately following the percolation however; in the case of the circle and box shape-spaces, *self-regulation* of the network occurs, i.e overall, there is a decrease in cell numbers

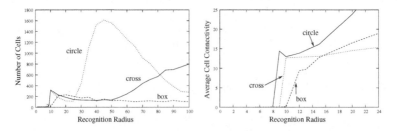

Fig. 3. The dynamics of Network formation in the absence of antigen

as the radius is increased — the higher the probability of a match between cells, the fewer the number of cells that are required overall to sufficiently stimulate any given cell. This effect is also noted by Bersini in [2]. For the circle and cross shape-spaces, the self-regulation effect initially occurs immediately following percolation, however, interestingly, there appears to be a second percolation in each case (at approximately $R = 25$ for the circle and $R = 50$ for the cross) — this is not observed in the similar experiments using Hamming shape-space described in [2]. In the circle case, the system the begins to again self-regulate as the radii increases beyond $R = 50$, although the second self-regulation point is not reached in the case of the cross. Simulating the algorithm visually clearly illustrates the reason (although these screen shots are not shown through lack of space). For $R = 25$, a self-sustaining line of cells is observed, in which each cell in the lines is supported by others also in the line, which requires very few cells to separate the space into tolerant and reactive zones. At $R \geq 50$ however, the network formation is inhibited — some cells are sustained by interaction with transient cells in the intolerant region, but by $R = 100$, most cells are inhibited due to over-stimulation occurring very rapidly. This secondary percolation effect does not occur in the simulations using binary shape-spaces reported in [2], presumably due to the small number of cell possibilities in a small, binary shape-space.

The box-shape space exhibits slightly different behaviour, although there is clearly a percolation followed by a self-regulatory effect. Following this percolation, the number of cells in the system remains almost constant despite the increase in R. This is explained by three factors; firstly, the unsymmetrical nature of the match function results in a network with quite different dynamics (for further evidence of this, see [5]). Secondly, for any given R, the area of the match region is smallest for the box shape, and hence there is a smaller probability of interaction between one cell and another. Finally, as the box shape-space is unsymmetrical with respect to the complementary point, at large R, a large part of the recognition region of most cells will actually lie off the edge of the 2D grid, resulting in an even smaller *effective* area of recognition. This effect also occurs of course with the other two models but is to a large extent lessened by the symmetrical nature of the region in the other cases.

7   Formation of Networks in the Presence of Exogenous Antigens

Although the previous experiments provide us with some interesting theoretical insight into the emergence of idiotypic networks in the absence of antigen, from a practical view-point, networks are almost always evolved in the presence of antigen in order to serve some useful purpose; for example, to cluster data, [7], or to segment a data-space into tolerant and non-tolerant regions for the purpose of recognising anomalous behaviour. Therefore in this section, we investigate the emergence of networks in the presence of exogenous antigen. In particular, we are interested in how the emergence of a network is affected by antigen present in the system, and in determining whether or not there is added value in maintaining a network with idiotpyic interactions as opposed to a classical Burnetian system with only antigen-antibody interactions. This is interesting from an engineering and computational perspective due to the high computational overhead in maintaining an idiotypic network.

In the following experiments, 50 antigens are introduced into the simulation over 10000 iterations. One antigen is recruited every 200 iterations with an initial concentration c. Values of c investigated are 100 and 1000. The number of antigens remaining in the system at the end of the 10000 iterations is recorded over a series of experiments in which R varied from 1-100. All experiments are repeated 10 times and the results averaged. Each simulation is performed twice — once using a classical Burnetian system in which there are only antigen-antibody interactions, and secondly using an idiotypic network where there are antibody-antibody and antibody-antigen interactions.

7.1   Exogenous Antigens with High Concentration

Figures 4 and 5 show the number of tolerated antigens when antigens are added with concentration $c = 1000$, and the repertoire size, as a function of increasing recognition radius. We observe that without the network, for the circle and cross regions, the system is only able to tolerate antigen when the recognition radius is very low, and therefore, there is an extremely low probability of any cell matching an antigen. The recruitment rate of antibodies simply does not outweigh the very small likelihood of a newly recruited cell matching an antigen. By approximately $R = 10$ however, both circle and cross shape-spaces are able to almost completely remove all antigens from the system. At high R however, these two models are once again unable to remove all antigens from the system — this effect is not observed in Bersini's Hamming experiments in [2]. Note however that Bersini's experiments are only performed with antigen concentration equal to 100. Clearly, there is a fine balance between cells becoming stimulated by being able to match antigens with very high probability, but then being removed from the system due to over-stimulation *before* they are able to completely eliminate the antigens

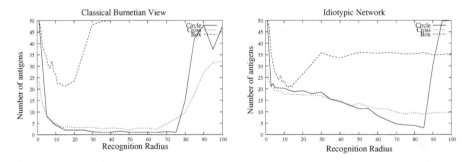

Fig. 4. Number of antigens vs recognition radius R for systems evolved in the presence of 50 exogenous antigen added with concentration 1000

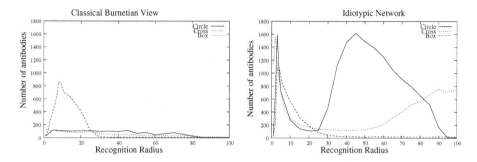

Fig. 5. Number of cells vs recognition radius for systems evolved in the presence of 50 exogenous antigen added with concentration 1000

which are added with very high concentration, relative to the cells themselves (1000 vs 10) — see figure 5. In the box case, the same overall pattern is observed, except that the balance point between enough cells being able to match antigens to remove them and over-stimulation occurring occurs at much lower R. The precise value at which this balance occurs could theoretically be calculated in a simple Burnetian model such as this — we hope to present these results in forthcoming work. Qualitatively, the observed differences can be explained by comparing the area of the recognition regions for equivalent radii in the two systems. For example, a value of $R = 1$ for the circle space gives an area of π. In the cross-space, the area of the region is 20, therefore, there is much higher probability of being able to match antigen. For the box region, for the reasons outlined in section 6, the system is able to tolerate antigens over a wide variation in R, because a high-value of R effectively results in a very low match-probability.

The results obtained from the idiotypic network are more interesting results. Firstly, for all 3 models, as observed in section 6, there is a minimum probability of match before a network is able to spring into existence. However, this percolation value is now lower than when then networks are evolved in the absence of antigen — this effect is also observed in [2]. The presence of the network divides the space into tolerant and intolerant regions, and thus antigens which happen to occur in the tolerant regions are sustained throughout the experiments.

The network effectively inhibits some of the antibodies that could remove antigen, so we see a higher tolerance of antigen for all values of R — this is most apparent with the circular region. As in Bersini's Hamming spaces experiments, at high R, i.e. very unspecific matching, almost all cells are inhibited and the size of the network is maintained at a very low value. In the case of idiotypic matching, the precise value of R at which this effect is observed is affected by both the area and nature of the matching region (recall the unsymmetric nature of the box-region matching). Thus, the cross-region can maintain sufficient self-sustaining cells to tolerate some antigens even at high R, and the box-region is able to eliminate more antigens due to the network presence than the Burnetian system. Hence, although figure 5 clearly shows the computational overhead in maintaining a network compared to a Burnetian system over certain ranges of

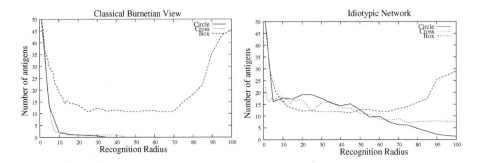

Fig. 6. Number of antigens vs recognition radius R for systems evolved in the presence of 50 exogenous antigen added with concentration 100

R, a change in behaviour is observed in the system with regard to its ability to tolerate antigens. Note also however, there appears to be no obvious advantage to using a network over some specific range of R in each case.

7.2   Exogenous Antigens with Low Concentration

Figure 6 shows the results of identical experiments to those above but when the concentration of added antigen is reduced to 100. Comparing the figures to those just presented shows that the concentration of antigens clearly plays a large part in the behaviour of the system. Firstly, without a network, the behaviour obtained by the circular and cross regions is exactly comparable to Bersini's results obtained in Hamming space across all values of R. When compared to those results obtained when $A_c = 1000$, comparable behaviour is observed until approximately $R = 75$ (circle) and $R = 65$ (cross). However, when the concentration of added antigen is low, even over-stimulated cells occurring when R is large are able to remain in the system just long enough to be able to completely remove all antigens. The box-region model fares somewhat better at removing antigens when their concentration is low, a factor which compensates somewhat for the low match probability.

Although the results obtained at $A_c = 100$ are qualitatively similar to those obtained at $A_c = 1000$, the network is never able to completely inhibit all cells. Hence even at high R, all three models are able to remove more antigens from the system than the corresponding experiments with $A_c = 1000$ — this is particularly noticeable in the circular case, and contrast directly with the results obtained by Bersini at this value of antigen concentration. These experiments therefore illustrate the critical importance of the choice of the algorithm parameters R, antigen concentration and antigen concentration when applying this algorithm to a practical problem. Their complex interplay determines the possible outcome of any simulation, and hence they must be chosen with care, depending on the desired effects.

8   Investigating the Network Memory Capacity

Memory is often cited as one of the key distinguishing features of immune algorithms, and therefore we investigate whether an idiotypic network in a real-valued shape-space is able to show any capacity to remember previous encounters with antigen, and if so, whether the shape of the recognition region can play an important role in determining the memory capacity — in the following experiments, we consider that a memory effect has occurred if the network behaves differently when presented with antigens similar to those it has previously encountered than to those which are completely random.

In each experiment, a network is first allowed to develop and stabilize in the presence of 50 external antigens for 10000 iterations (set A, S_a). As in previous experiments, one antigen is submitted to the network every 200 iterations, with concentration 1000. Following this, a further set of 50 antigens, S_b, is submitted to the network and the experiment continued for a further 2000 iterations, at which the total number of antigens remaining in the system is measured. In the first experiment S_b consists of antigens which are produced by applying a random mutation to each antigen in S_a — the mutation adds a random number between -2 and 2 to each coordinate of the original antigen. In the second experiment, S_b consists of a new set of antigens generated at random, each coordinate lying in the range (0,100). The antigens in S_b each have concentration 1000 and are added simultaneously at iteration 10000. Figure 7 shows the total number of antigens remaining in the system at iteration 12000 as a function of recognition radius for each shape. Each point on the graph is an average of 100 simulations, and the same S_b is used in each experiment.

The graph shows that for the circular recognition region over the range $R = 35 - 85$, slightly more of the *similar* antigens are rejected from the system than those that are generated totally at random. In the cross and box case, no discernible difference is observed, and in fact in the box case, the random antigens are removed more efficiently over the range $R = 10 - 17$. This result is at odds with the results reported by Bersini in Hamming shape-space, where he fined that at two values (out of a possible 20) of recognition radius, lying close to the percolation value of the system, the idiotpyic network is more likely to reject antigens similar to those observed during network development than those that are random. (Around 10 extra antigens are rejected in this case). In Bersini's experiments, the antigens in the "similar" set were at Hamming distance 1 from the originals. In the above experiments, the maximum distance of a mutated antigen from the original is $\sqrt{8}$ - further experiments, currently in progress, will examine results over a narrower range, and will also average the results over a number of *different* sets of mutated antigens, to determine whether Bersini's results can be replicated with the real-valued shape-space.

A modified version of the above experiment is now reported in which sets of antigens are added in *batches* to the evolving network, rather than individually over a number of iterations. Furthermore, two sets of antigens are added to the evolving network during the stabilisation period — one early in its development, and the second much later. After the network has stabilised, it is then presented

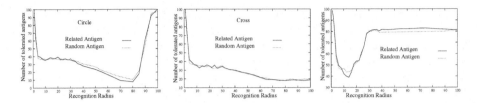

Fig. 7. The graph shows the total number of tolerated antigens after 12000 iterations for various recognition radii R following addition of 3 sets of antigens

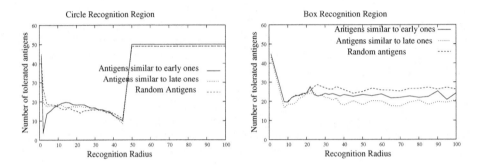

Fig. 8. Total number of tolerated antigens among 3 different sets of antigens. The first set is random, the second similar to antigens added early in the network evolutuion, and the third similar to antigens added late in the evolution.

with a further set of antigens in order to try and determine whether a memory capacity can be observed at all, and if so, whether the network retains better memory of those antigens it has encountered relatively recently compared to those it encountered early in its development. The experiments are performed as follows: at iteration 0, S_1 consisting of 50 random antigens with concentration 1000 is added. At iteration 6000, S_2, consisting of a further 50 random antigens is added. At iteration 10000, a new set S_3 of antigens is added — this set can either be similar to S_1, similar to S_2, or random. The results (averaged over 10 experiments for each point) are show in in figure 8 which show the number of antigens tolerated from S_3 after 12000 iterations. For the circle, no significant differences in network behaviour are noticed between the 3 possible sets S_3, however, the results are noticeably different from those obtained when the network is developed in the presence of gradually appearing antigens. For $R \geq 50$, none of the antigens in S_3 are removed. In the box case however, for $R \geq 20$, we observe that the system best rejects those antigens which are similar to those in S_2 (added late in the development), shows slightly more tolerance to those similar to S_1, and best tolerates the randomly added antigens. This result is in agreement with that observed by Bersini in Hamming shape-space, and in accordance with the classical vision of immunology that a network can show tolerance to very early antigenic encounters. This result also implies that the frequency of antigen encounters seems to be important in network memory — stimulating the network with large number of antigens in a short period of time appears to affect its emergence more clearly than when antigens are encountered infrequently. However, further experiments need to be performed with all recognition region shapes before conclusive evidence can be drawn.

9   Conclusions and Further Work

This paper has presented some early empirical evidence into the emergence of idiotypic networks in a real-valued shape-space, using a variety of different shaped recognition regions. The results clearly show that the dynamics and size of the emergent networks are heavily influenced by the recognition region shape, and that the networks show varying ability to tolerate antigens over different ranges of recognition radius. This is crucial information for the AIS engineer; on the one hand it emphasises the need for careful parameter setting; on the other however, it provides some flexibility and control over network evolution which can be used to our advantage, depending on the problem being tackled. In respect to the network evolution in the presence of antigens, the overall picture is somewhat similar to that painted by Bersini in his investigation of Hamming shape-spaces, although there are clearly some differences. The major differences tend to occur at high values of R, i.e when matching is very unspecific — as noted earlier, over these ranges, the network is unlikely to produce any useful behaviours from a practical perspective anyway.

The results from the investigation into memory capacity are less clear; more experimentation needs to be performed before conclusive results regarding the memory capacity of the models investigated can be drawn, although it does appear that the frequency which antigen is encountered may play a critical part in the network development. Further analysis is also required to explain the differences between the circle and box models observed in figure 8. If immunological memory is really to be exploited in artificial immune algorithms, particularly when applied to problems in dynamic environments, then it is crucial to gain an understanding of the mechanisms and limitations of any such memory features.

This work represent the tip of the iceberg concerning our understanding of the behaviour of idiotypic networks from a practical perspective. We are currently continuing the investigations described above over a wider parameter range, to better understand the interplay between cell concentrations, recognition radius, and recognition region shape, and to determine more clearly how the rate of exposure to antigen can affect ultimate performance. In future work, an important strand of investigation will be to investigate the behaviour of the system when exposed to sets of exogenous antigens which are not uniformly distributed throughout the data-space in order to better reflect real-world data. In relation to this, we also wish to explore the effects of cells utilising variably-sized recognition regions (an effect which has been explored in anomaly detection by [4]. Finally, there has been a considerable amount of interest in recent years in the concept of scale-free network connectivity, which endows a network with a

near-optimal method of communication between nodes, and improved robustness. This has been tentatively explored by Bersini in [2] in relation to networks
in binary shape-space and hence we also wish to pursue this line of research
using in real-valued shape-space.

References

1. H. Bersini. Self-assertion vs self-recogntion: A tribute to francisco vare la. In
   Proceedings of ICARIS 2002, 2002.
2. H. Bersini. Revisiting idiotypic immune networks. In W. Banzhaf and *et al*, editors,
   Advances in Artificial Life, 7th European Conference, Proceedings of ECAL 2003,
   Lecture Notes in Computer Science, pages 164–174. Springer, 2003.
3. H. Bersini. The endogenous double plasticity of the immune network and the
   inspiration to be drawn for engineering artifacts. In D. Dasgupta, editor, *Artificial
   Immune Systems and Their Applications*, pages 22–41. Springer, 99.
4. D. Dasgupta, K. KrishnaKumar, D. Wong, and M. Berry. Negative selection algorithm for aircraft fault detection. In *Proceedings of the 3nd International Conference on Artificial Immun e Systems, ICARIS02*, volume 3239 of *Lecture Notes in
   Computer Science*. Springer, 2004.
5. E. Hart and P. Ross. Studies on the implications of shape-space. In *Artificial Immune Systems, Proceedings of ICARIS 2004*, Lecture Notes in Computer Science,
   pages 413–426. Springer, 2004.
6. N.K. Jerne. Towards a network theory of the immune system. *Annals of Immunology (Institute Pasteur)*, 1974.
7. M. Neal. Meta-stable memory in an immune network. In J. Timmis, P. Bentley,
   and E. Hart, editors, *Artificial Immune Systems: Proceedings of ICARIS 2003*,
   volume 2787 of *Lecture Notes in Computer Science*, pages 168–180. Springer, 2003.
8. A. Perelson and G.F. Oster. Theoretical studies of clonal selection: Minimal antibody repe rtoire size and reliability of self-nonself discrimination in the immune
   system. *J. Theoretical Biology*, 158, 1979.
9. Peter Ross. http://www.dcs.napier.ac.uk/~peter/.
10. D.J Smith, S Forrest, and A.S Perelson. Immunological memory is associative.
    In *Artificial Immune Systems and Their Applications*, pages 105–112. Springer-
    Verlag, 1999.
11. F. Varela and A. Coutinho. Second generation immune network. *Immunology
    Today*, 12(5):159–166, 1991.

A Generic Framework for Population-Based Algorithms, Implemented on Multiple FPGAs

John Newborough and Susan Stepney

Department of Computer Science, University of York, Heslington, York, YO10 5DD, UK

Abstract. Many bio-inspired algorithms (evolutionary algorithms, artificial immune systems, particle swarm optimisation, ant colony optimisation, ...) are based on populations of agents. Stepney *et al* [2005] argue for the use of conceptual frameworks and meta-frameworks to capture the principles and commonalities underlying these, and other bio-inspired algorithms. Here we outline a generic framework that captures a collection of population-based algorithms, allowing commonalities to be factored out, and properties previously thought particular to one class of algorithms to be applied uniformly across all the algorithms. We then describe a prototype proof-of-concept implementation of this framework on a small grid of FPGA (field programmable gate array) chips, thus demonstrating a generic architecture for both parallelism (on a single chip) and distribution (across the grid of chips) of the algorithms.

1 Introduction

Many bio-inspired algorithms are based on populations of agents trained to solve some problem such as optimising functions or recognising categories. For example, Evolutionary Algorithms (EA) are based on analogy to populations of organisms mutating, breeding and selecting to become "fitter" [Mitchell 1996]. The negative and clonal selection algorithms of Artificial Immune Systems (AIS) use populations of agents trained to recognise certain aspects of interest (see de Castro & Timmis [2002] for an overview): negative selection involves essentially random generation of candidate recognisers, whilst clonal selection uses reinforcement based on selection and mutation of the best recognisers. Particle swarm optimisation (PSO) [Kennedy & Eberhart 2001] and social insect algorithms [Bonabeau 1999] use populations of agents whose co-operations (direct, or stigmergic) result in problem solving.

Stepney *et al* [2005] argue for the use of conceptual frameworks and meta-frameworks to capture the principles and commonalities underlying various bio-inspired algorithms. We take up this challenge, and, in section 2, outline a generic framework abstracted from the individual population-based models of the following classes: genetic algorithms (GA), AIS negative selection, AIS clonal selection, PSO, and ant colony optimisation (ACO). The framework provides a basis for factoring out the commonalities, and applying various properties uniformly across all the classes of algorithms, even where they were previously thought particular to one class (section 3).

In section 4 we describe our proof-of-concept prototype implementation of the generic framework on a platform of multiple field programmable gate array (FPGA)

C. Jacob et al. (Eds.): ICARIS 2005, LNCS 3627, pp. 43–55, 2005
© Springer-Verlag Berlin Heidelberg 2005

chips. Thus the generic architecture naturally permits both parallelism (multiple individuals executing on a single chip) and distribution (multiple individuals executing across the array of chips) of the algorithms. In section 5 we outline what needs to be done next to take these concepts into a fully rigorous framework architecture and implementation.

2   The Generic Framework for Population Algorithms

There are many specific algorithms and implementation variants of the different classes. To take one case, AIS clonal selection, see, for example [Cutello *et al* 2004] [Garrett 2004] [Kim & Bentley 2002]. It is not our intention to capture every detail of all the variants in the literature. Rather, we take a step back from the specifics, and abstract the *basic underlying concepts*, particularly the more bio-inspired ones, of each class of algorithm. So when we refer to "GA" or "AIS clonal selection", for example, we are not referring to any one specific algorithm or implementation, but rather of the general properties of this class. We unify the similarities between these basics in order to develop a generic framework. The intention is that such a framework provides a useful starting point for the subsequent development of more sophisticated variants of the algorithms.

Basic Underlying Concepts

The generic algorithm is concerned with a population of *individuals*, each of which captures a possible solution, or part of a solution. Each individual contains a set of *characteristics*, which represent the solution. The characteristics define the (phase or state) space that the population of individuals inhabit. The goal of the algorithm is to find "good" regions of this space, based on some *affinity* (a measure that relates position in the space to goodness of solution, so defining a *landscape*). The individuals and characteristics of the specific classes of algorithm are as follows:

GA: The individuals are *chromosomes*; each characteristic is a *gene*.

AIS negative selection: The individuals are *antibodies*; each characteristic is a *shape receptor*.

AIS clonal selection: There are two populations. In the *main population* the individuals are *antibodies*; each characteristic is a *shape receptor*. There is also a population of *memory cells* drawn from this main population.

Swarms: The individuals are *boids*; the characteristics are *position*, *velocity* and *neighbourhood group* (the other visible individuals).

Ants: The individuals are the *complete paths* (not the ants, which are merely mechanisms to construct the complete paths from *path steps*); the characteristics are the *sequence of path steps*, where each step has an associated characteristic of *length* and *pheromone level*.

Algorithm Stages

The different specific algorithms each exhibit six clearly distinct stages, comprising a *generation*. These are generalised as:

1. **Create** : make novel members of the population
2. **Evaluate** : evaluate each individual for its affinity to the solution
3. **Test** : test if some termination condition has been met
4. **Select** : select certain individuals from the current generation, based on their affinity, to be used in the creation of the next generation
5. **Spawn** : create new individuals for the next generation
6. **Mutate** : change selected individuals

We describe each of these stages, covering the generic properties, and how they are instantiated for each specific class of algorithm. Using this framework results in descriptions that sometimes differ from, but are equivalent to, the traditional descriptions of the algorithms. For example, rather than saying that some individuals survive from generation to generation, for uniformity we consistently consider each generation to be a completely fresh set of individuals, with some possibly being *copies* of previous generation individuals. As another example, the pheromone changes in the Ant algorithm is mapped to the generic mutate step.

Create

Creation makes novel members of the populations. In the first generation, the whole population is set up, and the members have their characteristics initialised. On subsequent generations, creation "tops up" the population with fresh individuals, as necessary.

GA: An individual chromosome is created usually with *random* characteristics, giving a broad coverage of the search space.

AIS negative selection: An individual antibody is created usually with *random* shape receptors.

AIS clonal selection: An individual antibody in the main population is created usually with *random* shape receptors; memory cells are not created, rather they are *spawned* from the main population.

Swarms: An individual boid is created usually with *random* position and velocity characteristics, giving a broad coverage of the search space; the neighbourhood characteristic is usually set to implement a ring, grid or star connection topology.

Ants: Each path step is initially set up usually with a *fixed* pheromone level, and with the relevant (fixed) path length; the population of paths is *created* by the ants from these steps each generation.

Evaluate

The *affinity* measures how well each individual solves (part of) the problem. It is a user-defined function of (some of) an individual's characteristics. This function should ideally (but does not always) have the structure of a *metric* over the space defined by the characteristics.

GA: The affinity is the *fitness* function, a function of the values of the genes.

AIS: The affinity is a measure of how closely the shape receptors *complement* the target of recognition, inspired by the "lock and key" metaphor.

Swarms: The affinity, or *fitness* function, is a function of the current *position*.

Ants: The affinity is the (inverse of the) *path length*.

Test

The test for termination is either (a) a sufficiently good solution is found, or (b) enough generations have been run without finding a sufficiently good solution. On termination, the solution is:

GA, Swarms, Ants: The highest affinity (fittest) individual.

AIS negative selection: The set of individuals with above-threshold affinities.

AIS clonal selection: The population of memory cells.

Select

High affinity individuals are *selected* to contribute somehow to the next generation's population. There are several selection algorithms commonly used. *n best* selects the *n* highest affinity individuals from the current population. *Threshold* selects all the individuals with an affinity greater than some given threshold value. *Roulette wheel* selection randomly chooses a given number of individuals, with probability of selection proportional to their affinity, or to their ranking. *Tournament* randomly selects teams of individuals, and then *selects* a subset of individuals from each team.

GA: Different variants use any of the above methods of selection, to find the *parents* that will produce the next generation.

AIS negative selection: *Threshold* selection is used to find the next generation.

AIS clonal selection: A combination of *n best* and *threshold* selection is used to find the next generation of the main population; *all* individuals of the memory cell population are selected to become the basis of its next generation.

Swarms: *All* individuals are selected to become the basis of the next generation.

Ants: *No* individuals are specifically selected to become the next generation: each generation is *created* afresh from the path steps (whose characteristics are changed by the *mutate* step).

Spawn

Production of new individuals for the next generation usually involves *combining* the characteristics of *parent* individuals from the *selected* population (ants are a special case).

GA: The characteristics of *pairs* of selected parents are combined by using a *crossover* mask (predefined or randomly generated) to generate two new individuals. If the crossover mask is set to the identity, then the two new individuals are clones of the two parents.

AIS negative selection: The selected parents become the basis of the new generation (which is topped up to the population size by *creating* sufficient new individuals). If the threshold is a constant value throughout the run, this has the effect that an individual, once selected, continues from generation to generation, and only the newly created individuals need be evaluated.

AIS clonal selection: In the main population new individuals are spawned as *clones* of each parent, with the number of clones being produced proportional to the parent's affinity; in the memory cell population, the selected parents become the basis of the new generation, and a new individual is spawned, as (a copy of) the best individual of the main population.

Swarms: A new individual is spawned from the sole parent and the highest affinity individual in that parent's neighbourhood group, with the intention of making the new individual "move towards" the best neighbour. The new position is derived from the parent's position and velocity, the velocity is modified to point towards the best neighbour, and the neighbourhood group is copied from the parent.

Ants: *No* individuals are specifically spawned for the next generation: each generation is *created* afresh from the path steps (whose characteristics are changed by the *mutate* step).

Mutate
Mutation involves altering the characteristics of single individuals in the population. It would be possible to unify spawning and mutation into a single *generate* stage, but since most algorithms consider these to be separate processes, we have followed that view, rather than strive for total generality at this stage. The mutation rate might be globally random, or based on the value of a characteristic or the affinity of each individual. How a characteristic is mutated depends on its type: a boolean might be flipped, a numerical value might be increased or decreased by an additive or multiplicative factor, etc.

GA, Swarms: Individuals are mutated, usually randomly, in order to reintroduce lost values of characteristics; *evolutionary strategy* algorithms encode mutation rates as characteristics.

AIS negative selection: No mutation occurs. (That is, the next generation consists of copies of the selected above threshold individuals, topped up with newly created individuals. An alternative, but equivalent, formulation in terms of this framework would be to consider that *all* the individuals are *selected*, and that only the below-threshold individuals are *mutated*, into completely random individuals. However, this is at odds with the traditional description of the algorithm, and also with the view that mutation makes relatively small alterations.)

AIS clonal selection: The new *clone* individuals are mutated, by an amount inversely proportional to their affinity.

Ants: New pheromone is *laid* on each path step by an amount proportional to the affinity of the complete paths in which it occurs, and decreased by a constant *decay* factor.

3   Generalising Across Algorithms and Implementations

Once we have all the algorithms in a common framework, we can see ways of generalising each in a natural manner (that is bio-inspired, but by a different aspect of biology). We discuss two such cases here – niching and elitism – and outline other possibilities.

Niching

Some population-based algorithms include "niching": developing sub-populations separately, with occasional migration of individuals [Brits *et al* 2002] [Mahfoud 1995] [Watkins & Timmis 2004]. Niching is motivated by the biological evolution of populations on separate islands. It is useful for solving multi-objective problems, with sub-populations focussing on separate objectives, but we do not here consider that aspect. Here we are interested in its use for efficiently distributing the algorithm across multiple processors, by minimising the amount of communication (of details of the high affinity individuals) needed between processors. We use these ideas to add a *migrate* step to the generic framework.

In niching, we have *N islands* of separately developing sub-populations, with each island following the simple algorithm, and each having a neighbourhood that is of a subset of the other islands (capturing locality of islands). Every *g* generations, modify the current population by replacing *n* individuals (suitably *selected* to be of low affinity, or chosen randomly) with *n* migrants from the neighbourhood (suitably *selected* to be of high affinity, or chosen randomly). This results in the following specifics:

GA: Migration is simple population replacement; the solution is the fittest individual across all islands.

AIS negative selection: Migration is simple population replacement; the solution is the union of all above-threshold individuals across all islands.

AIS clonal selection: Migration can occur for both the main population and the memory cell population; the solution is the union of all memory cell populations across all islands.

Swarms: Migration is simple population replacement, where the replaced individuals copy in the position and velocity characteristics of the migrants, but retain their original neighbourhood characteristic; the solution is the fittest individual across all islands. (Swarms admit another distribution strategy that can be efficiently implemented if the nearest individual neighbourhood relation is that of a simple ring topology. A single swarm can be distributed across a ring of processors, with the only communication between processors being the very local neighbourhood properties.)

Ants: Migration is simple population replacement; the solution is the fittest individual (shortest path) across all islands. The (affinity of the) migrated paths will affect only the pheromone update stage; the migrated paths need not be recreated in the next generation.

Elitism

Some GAs include *ad hoc* elitism: copying the best individual(s) into the next generation, in order to preserve the currently best solution (and hence make the best solution monotonic with generations). This is not a particularly bio-inspired process. AIS algorithms with their (constant) threshold selection, on the other hand, are naturally elitist: if an antibody exceeds the threshold, (a copy of) it survives in future generations. We use these ideas to modify the *spawn* step, and add generic elitism to the framework.

When spawning the next generation, copy the n best of the previous population, as well as spawning any new individuals from the selected parents. Also, these particular n individuals should be exempt from mutation in this stage. This results in the following specific modifications:

GA: n fewer individuals need to be spawned by crossover.

AIS: No change, provided n individuals are above the threshold.

Swarms: The solution is a property of the position characteristic only, and the position is modified by the velocity. So the previous best solution is copied, with its velocity set to zero, so that it "hovers" over the current best solution.

Ants: An "elite ant" recreates the current shortest path, ensuring that the solution remains in the population, and that its steps get their pheromone levels updated.

Other Generalisations

The generic framework allows further features of one specific algorithm to be generalised to the others.

- Evolutionary Strategies encode the mutation rates as characteristics: a similar approach can be used in the other algorithms. For example, the ant algorithm could allow the pheromone decay rate to be a characteristic.
- Genetic Algorithms use crossover to combine characteristics of parents: a similar spawn operator can be used in the other algorithms. For example, AIS clonal selection could spawn new antibodies by crossover.
- Traditionally unchanging characteristics could be mutated, for example, swarm neighbourhood.
- AIS use affinity-based mutation, to preferentially shake up poorer solutions: all mutation schemes could take this approach.
- AIS clonal selection increases the number of good solutions by affinity based cloning (thereby increasing their probability of being selected, so allowing more exploration of the nearby space). The other algorithms could be adapted to variable population size with cloning.

- The range of selection strategies can be employed across all the algorithms that have a non-trivial selection stage. In particular, AIS clonal selection has two populations: selection strategies could be used on the memory cell population too.

4 The Prototype Implementation

There is much opportunity for *parallelism* in these algorithms: individuals can (to some degree) be evaluated, selected, and created in parallel. This suggests efficiency gains by executing these algorithms on parallel hardware.

FPGAs and Handel-C

We chose as our prototype implementation platform a small grid of FPGAs, executing the framework implemented in Handel-C.

An FPGA is *programmable hardware*: its array of logic gates can be configured and connected for each specific program. This removes the need to fetch and decode instructions, fetch data, and store results; it is programmed to be a direct hardware representation of the code. It can be configured to provide genuine parallel execution (see for example [Brown & Rose 1996]). So each individual FPGA can host multiple individuals executing in parallel, and multiple FPGAs allow distributed implementations.

The framework described above has been prototyped as a proof of concept. It demonstrates that a suitably flexible generic framework can indeed be developed to support multiple classes of population-based algorithms, and that it can be distributed on a grid of FPGAs. It has been tested on an array of four FPGA algorithm engines, each connected to a fifth monitoring FPGA, in turn connected to a PC.

The prototype framework is implemented in Handel-C [Celoxica 2004], a (relatively) high level language designed specifically for writing applications for FPGAs. Handel-C code is compiled down into the relevant FPGA net-list, which specifies how the FPGA is to be configured.

Handel-C is based on the process calculus of CSP (Communicating Sequential Processes) [Hoare 1985]. Handel-C is essentially an executable subset of CSP [Stepney 2003], with some extensions to support FPGA hardware. In particular, it has explicit support for parallel execution of processes:

```
for (i=0; i < imax; i++) {
  // the imax iterations execute in sequence
  // and occupy space independent of imax
}

par (i=0; i < imax; i++) {
  // the imax iterations execute in parallel
  // and occupy space proportional to imax
}
```

Being based on CSP, Handel-C uses *synchronous* communication between its parallel processes. There is currently no Handel-C language support for programs distributed across multiple FPGAs, and such configurations do not support synchronous communication between chips as a primitive. It would have been possible to design a protocol to implement this, allowing the distributed program to be (very close to) a pure Handel-C program. However, the communication between chips is deliberately restricted, to just the occasional migration data. So for this prototype, a simple handshaking protocol has been used, and the inter-chip communication hidden in a wrapper.

The Implemented Framework

The prototype implementation of the framework provides much of the functionality described above. The genericity means that there are many parameters and options: the prototype includes support for specific options, and hooks for a range of user-definable functions. The framework is structured so that the basic algorithm needs no alteration: the user merely selects certain features (such as population sizes, characteristics, mutation rates, style of creation and selection, crossover masks, number of FPGAs, and number of islands per chip), and provides the code for certain functions (the evaluation function and stopping condition, and, as required, creation, selection, spawning, and mutation functions).

The framework code and user-defined functions, both written in Handel-C, are compiled on the PC, then downloaded on to the FPGA array to run. The Handel-C compiler optimises away dead code, so options that are not selected by the user (such as various choices of creation or selection functions) do not appear in the compiled code.

When the algorithm terminates, the relevant results are communicated back to the PC. It is also possible to return intermediate results every generation, to allow investigation of the performance, or for debugging, but this introduces a communication bottleneck.

Each individual is represented as a bit string, with each bit or combination of bits in the string representing a characteristic. A user-specified flag selects whether these bits are initialised to 0s, to 1s, to random bit values, or to a user-defined alternative. Each FPGA chip holds a certain number of islands, each of which holds its individuals. Migration information is passed between the islands, and hence between the chips, as required.

Ideally, all individuals should be able to evaluate their own affinity in parallel, by a call to the user-defined evaluation function. For completely parallel implementation on an FPGA, this would require one copy of the function per individual. This can result in much of the FPGA's resource being used by evaluation functions, limiting the number of individuals per chip. The framework instead allows a trade-off between number of individuals and amount of parallelism. During certain of the algorithm steps, the individuals in an island are considered to be grouped into f *families*, each with m *members*, giving at total of $f \times m$ individuals. Families are processed in parallel, but the members of a family are processed in sequence. Thus each family requires only one copy of each function, and space is proportional to f and execution time is proportional to m:

```
par (family=0; family < f; family++) {
  for (member=0; member < m; member++) {
    // ... code for  individual[family*m + member]
  }
}
```

The prototype implementation provides a timer function, to help the user chose a suitable trade-off for each step, and for each application.

The probabilistic nature of (parts of) the algorithm require the use of random numbers. The implementation provides one 32-bit linear feedback shift register per family for this purpose.

Tournament selection is used to divide the population into *teams*. If no tournament is required, the entire population forms one large team. Then the appropriate selection method is used on each team in parallel.

Restrictions Due to the Platform Choice

Some of the design decisions for the framework prototype are due to specific features and limitations of FPGAs and Handel-C, and different platform choices could result in different decisions. For example, the use of *families* is to cope with the limited size of the FPGAs.

Another example of this choice is the selection implementation. Although each team performs selection in parallel, the selection within each team is sequential. One might think that roulette wheel, or even a random, selection from a collection of individuals could be performed in parallel. However, this would result in the need for many parallel accesses to random number generators, and the FPGA's silicon would quickly become dedicated to these. Certain parts of the selection can be performed in parallel, for example, to find the n best, where each individual can read the affinity of all its team-mates in parallel. Even so, care needs to be taken, because the highly interconnected read accesses can result in quite complex (and therefore slow to compile) routing.

Handel-C supports variable bit-width values, requiring explicit casting between values with different widths. This can lead to arcane code, particularly when trying to write generic routines. For example, consider the case where some particular size n (such as population size) is a power of 2. Then the variable that stores the size is one bit larger than the variable used for indexing into an array of this size, running from 0 to $n-1$, so comparing the index and the size requires some fancy casting.

5 Preliminary Results

Sizes: The number of (families of) individuals possible per chip varies depending on the settings. For example, if no survival, generation, or niching is done, it is possible to have 30–40 individuals per chip, each with 8 bit-characteristics. With all the capabilities turned on, this number drops to about 18 individuals run sequentially, or four if run in parallel, the reduction being due to the increased routing and copies of code. The limiting constraint is routing tables rather than logic gates: every individual is accessed by each of the six algorithm stage functions, and the implementation uses all the routing tables, but only about 10-15% of the logic gates. Similar size results apply when hosting two islands on a single chip: this halves the *total* population possible, because of code replication and routing constraints.

The FPGAs being used (300K gate Xilinx SpartanIIE chips) are relatively small: it was thought more important for this proof of concept work to get the maximum *number* of FPGAs for the budget, rather than the maximum size of each one. Clearly, more individuals would be possible with larger FPGAs. However, the architectural design needs to be done carefully to optimise use of the resources: design experience of these style of algorithms for FPGAs is still in its infancy.

Parallelism: How much speedup does *parallelism* give?

The experiment compares running four individuals in parallel (the most supportable in this experiment) against running four in sequence, solving a simple optimisation problem. Linear speedup would result in a 400% improvement, but the parallel form has a speed-up of only about 30% over the sequential form. This low value indicates that there is still a great deal of sequential execution in this prototype implementation. This sequential bottleneck occurs mainly in the *select* stage of the framework: the speedup in the *evaluate* stage (calculation of the affinity function) is essentially linear. More complicated evaluation functions would therefore result in an increase in the parallel efficiency, but would also increase the demand on silicon resource if the complicated functions physically took up more space.

Parallelism versus population size: More parallelism takes up more silicon, resulting in few individuals being supportable. Parallelism lets the algorithm run faster, in that each generation takes less time to execute, but larger populations allow greater diversity and exploration of the search space per generation, so the algorithm could require fewer generations to find a solution. What is better: more parallelism or a larger population?

The experiment compares running four individuals in parallel (the most supportable in this experiment) against running 12 in sequence (the most supportable sequential individuals in this experiment). The parallel form gives no speed-up overall compared to the sequential form. However, looking at only the *evaluate* stage shows the sequential form taking about twice as long as the parallel form. Given the linear speedup noted above, the sequential case takes 12 times as long per generation, and so is executing only about one sixth the number of generations before finding a solution. Even so, the parallel form is taking less time overall (in the *evaluate* state), suggesting that parallelism outweighs population size in this case.

However, these experiments need to be tried on larger populations, and a wider range of affinity function complexity (which affects the parallel to sequential population size ratio), before any more definitive statements can be made.

Niching: What is the effect of using multiple chips? How much speedup does *distribution* give?

The experiment compares running four individuals in parallel on one chip versus four individuals in parallel on each of the five chips (20 individuals in total), migrating the two best individuals every 100 generations. There is a speedup of about a factor of two (over the whole algorithm run, not just the *evaluate* stage). These experiments need to be repeated for different migration rates to see if there is an optimum rate.

6 Discussion and Future Work

The unified framework allows the generalisation of concepts from across a range of algorithms types, for example, elitism and niching. Thus we have a chimerical computational framework that is inspired by biology, but not restricted to any one particular biological domain. Implementation of the framework on parallel and distributed architectures is (relatively) straightforward, and provides performance benefits (although currently significantly less than linear improvement). So this proof of concept has shown that the approach to generalising and parallelising population-based algorithms is feasible and useful. Thus it is worth pursuing the approach with more rigour and detail.

The relatively small speedups indicate the need for removing the remaining sequential bottlenecks, and the constraints on parallel individuals caused by routing limitations indicate the need for a more sophisticated parallelisation architecture targeted at the opportunities and limitations of FPGAs. Allowing six islands per chip to use the hardware for the six algorithm steps in a pipeline might provided further speedup.

An alternative distributed architecture would be to dedicate certain chips to algorithm steps, and move the individuals around. Different numbers of chips could be dedicated to each step, depending on the complexity of that step, to balance the processing load.

The prototype framework needs to be extended with more built-in options, and made more usable, by providing a configuration language for selecting parameter values, etc. It also needs to be made more flexible to accommodate other arrangements of FPGA arrays.

Future work also includes formalising the generic framework, to make it clearer which features of each algorithm are being represented and captured, and to generalise and include more details and capabilities from the range of variant algorithms in the literature. A more rigorous framework will allow *analysis* at the generic and specific levels, *comparison* of instantiations, and further generalisations of various properties.

Acknowledgments

We would like to thank Wilson Ifill and AWE, who provided funding for the FPGAs used in this work. Also thanks to Neil Audsley and Michael Ward for turning a large box of components into a usable FPGA grid, and to Fiona Polack and Jon Timmis for detailed comments on earlier versions.

References

[1] E.W. Bonabeau, M. Dorigo, G. Theraulaz. *Swarm Intelligence: from natural to artificial systems.* Addison Wesley, 1999

[2] R. Brits, A.P. Engelbrecht, F. van den Bergh. A niching Particle Swarm Optimizer. *4th Asia-Pacific Conference on Simulated Evolution and Learning*, 2002.

[3] S. Brown, J. Rose. Architecture of FPGAs and CPLDs: a tutorial. *IEEE Design and Test of Computers*, **13**(2):42-57, 1996.

[4] Celoxica. *Handel-C Reference Manual, development kit v3.0.* 2004. http://www.celoxica.com/techlib/files/CEL-W0410251JJ4-60.pdf

[5] V. Cutello, G. Nicosia, M. Pavone. Exploring the capability of immune algorithms: a characterization of hypermutation operators. *ICARIS 2004*, LNCS **3239**:263-276

[6] L.N. de Castro, J. Timmis. *Artificial Immune Systems: A New Computational Intelligence Approach.* Springer, 2002

[7] S.M. Garrett. Parameter-free, adaptive clonal selection. *CEC 2004*, pp 1052-1058. IEEE Press, 2004

[8] C.A.R. Hoare. *Communicating Sequential Processes.* Prentice Hall, 1985

[9] J. Kennedy, R.C. Eberhart. *Swarm Intelligence.* Morgan Kaufmann, 2001

[10] J. Kim, P.J. Bentley. Immune memory in the dynamic clonal selection algorithm. *ICARIS 2002*, pp 59-67, Kent, 2002

[11] S.W. Mahfoud. A comparison of parallel and sequential niching methods. In L.J. Eshelman, ed, *Proc. 6th International Conference on Genetic Algorithms*, pp 136-143. Morgan Kaufmann, 1995.

[12] M. Mitchell. *An Introduction to Genetic Algorithms.* MIT Press, 1996

[13] S. Stepney. *CSP/FDR2 to Handel-C translation.* Technical Report YCS-2003-357, University of York. June 2003.

[14] S. Stepney, R.E. Smith, J. Timmis, A.M. Tyrrell, M.J. Neal, A.N.W. Hone. Conceptual Frameworks for Artificial Immune Systems. *Int. J. Unconventional Computing.* **1**(3) 2005

[15] A. Watkins, J. Timmis. Exploiting Parallelism Inherent in AIRS, an Artificial Immune Classifier. *ICARIS 2004*, LNCS **3239**:427-438. Springer, 2004.

An AIS-Based Dynamic Routing (AISDR) Framework

Henry Y.K. Lau[1] and Eugene Y.C. Wong[2]

[1] Department of Industrial and Manufacturing Systems Engineering,
The University of Hong Kong, Pokfulam Road, Hong Kong, PRC
hyklau@hku.hk
[2] Orient Overseas Container Line (OOCL) Limited,
Harbour Centre, 25 Harbour Road, Wanchai, Hong Kong
eugene.wong@oocl.com

Abstract. An Artificial Immune System-based Dynamic Routing (AISDR) framework is engineered through the adoption of the characteristics that are analogous to human immune system for solving dynamic routing problems. The framework covers the profound features on recognition, selection, learning, memory, and adaptation capabilities. An AISDR algorithm is developed that incorporates the features of clonal selection, affinity maturation, and immunological memory features. Simulation study is carried out to evaluate the performance of the algorithm in the global shipment operation.

1 Introduction

The human immune system exhibits the capability of recognition, selection, learning, memory, and adaptation that can be adopted to solve dynamic routing problems. This paper presents a framework with associated algorithms for route planning with characteristics of the immune system. It adopts relevant theories and methodologies found in the immune systems and develops corresponding algorithms for solving dynamic routing problems such as those commonly encountered in the global shipment and transshipment.

Algorithms for solving routing problems, in particular, the Vehicle Routing Problem (VRP) including classical linear programming to more recent meta-heuristic and Artificial Intelligence (AI) algorithms were developed by various researchers. Brandao (1999; 2002; 2003) used meta-heuristic algorithms, whereas Braysy (2001), Jung and Haghani (1998), and Filipec (2000) adopts Genetic Algorithms (GA) to solving VRP. Jean-Yves (1996), Thangiah et al. (1994), and Lalinka & Fernando (2002) adopted a hybrid AI approach.

Traditionally, dynamic routing algorithms are developed based on business logics. New business rules are often continuously added into the algorithm without the consideration of complementary effects. Based on such an approach, the risk of the existence of system loopholes and software defects is often high (Landwehr et al., 1993). Building algorithms analogous to the immune system inspires new insights and approaches to the problem with the development of novel algorithms. This paper presents a conceptual framework that applies the clonal selection theory, affinity

C. Jacob et al. (Eds.): ICARIS 2005, LNCS 3627, pp. 56–71, 2005.

maturation, cross reactive response theory, and immune network theory of human immune system known as the AIS-based Dynamic Routing (AISDR) framework, which aims at solving dynamic routing problems in an automated manner.

2 Biological Immune Systems

The human immune system is a rapid and effective defense mechanism against infections. The response falls into two categories, namely, innate immune response and adaptive or acquired immune response. In the innate immune system, cells are immediately available to combat against foreign invasions, without requiring previous exposure to them. For the adaptive immune system, antibodies are produced only in response to specific infections. The response improves with each successive encounter with the same pathogen; in effect the adaptive immune system memorizes the infective agents and prevents it from causing disease.

The immune system is made up of a number of components with lymphocytes mainly mediating the adaptive immune response. Lymphocytes are categorized into two main types: B lymphocytes and T lymphocytes. The former recognizes antigen by releasing antibodies that bind to antigens. The latter consists of two types of T-cells, namely the Helper T cells (T_H) that control B lymphocyte development, produce antibodies, and interact with phagocytic cells to help destroy pathogens; and the Cytotoxic T-cells (T_{CR}) that recognize cells infected by virus with a view to destroy them.

In the human immune system, the B-lymphocyte, T-lymphocyte, antigen presenting cells (APC), Natural killer cells, and Plasma cells work in a corporative environment to fight against antigen invasion. There are specific mechanisms in the process of recognition, categorization, and defense. APC obtains information from an antigen and presents information (for example, cell wall, defense mechanism of bacteria in order to let white blood cells or other defensive cells to kill the antigen) of the antigen to the immune system memory. B cells then recognizes and categorizes the antigen, and the memory B cells will distinguish whether existing antibodies can kill the antigen. If the antigen is recognized by specific antibodies, B cells will be activated to be Plasma cells and produce antibodies to destroy the antigen. When a pathogen invades a body cell, which then becomes an infected cell. Major Histocompatibility Complex (MHC) will present peptide of the pathogen of these infected cells to cytotoxic T precursors. Cytotoxic T cells will then destroy the infected cell.

3 Artificial Immune System

An artificial immune system is a computational system based upon the metaphors of the natural immune system (Timmis, 2000). There a number of potential benefits of adopting the theories and mechanisms of natural immune systems to solving complex engineering problems. Recently, increasing interest has been found in formalizing and adapting the theories and underlying mechanisms of the immune system to solving engineering problems (Luh et al., 2004).

Immunological theories had been applied to produced solutions for complex problems, including pattern recognition (White and Garrett, 2003; Nicosia et. al., 2001), fault detection (Taylor and Corne, 2003), scheduling (Coello et al., 2003), and optimization (Coello & Cortes, 2002; Nicosia & Cutello, 2002).

In route planning, Keko et al. (2003) adopted the immunizing features of the immune system to a classical genetic algorithm using vaccine inserting method to solving the traveling salesman problem (TSP). Genetic Algorithm (GA) used by Keko was vaccinated to become less susceptible to changing parameters and improve the speed of generating the smallest total distance in a TSP problem. A heuristic operator, the Lin-Kerninghan operator, was implemented to improve the population with the applied action is considered as vaccination. In this research, the full potential application of the immunity theory to solving the routing problem had not been fully explored. de Castro and Von Zuben (2000) applied the clonal selection algorithm in immune system to solve a 30 cities instance of the TSP. An AIS-based routing algorithm developed in this research adopted the characteristics of the immune system, namely, its dynamic property, immunological memory, self-regulation, cross-reactive response, adaptability, and diversity of the immune system.

As solving complex dynamic routing problems requires the processes of selection, prioritization, regulation, memory, and self-recognition, in which AIS is able to offer corresponding mechanisms for undertaking these processes, this paper aims to introduce an integrated framework known as the artificial immune system-based dynamic routing (AISDR) framework for tackling this complex problem.

4 Artificial Immune System-Based Dynamic Routing (AISDR) Framework

The emergence of global logistics networks imposes the pressing need of a dynamic routing system for global shipment and transshipment of commodities that covers various industrial and country specific booking requirements in a global perspective. Due to its high complexity, such systems that are commonly built and operated on business and human logic will not be able to provide the necessary quality and performance; and often ends up in disaster situations when the underlying logic is being manipulated by a fully manual process. An AISDR framework is therefore developed to provide first-line assistance for dynamic-planning and evaluating of routes so as to alleviate the shortcomings of the traditional manual operation. The proposed AISDR capitalizes some of the features of AIS in shipment route computation.

The proposed immune system-based routing framework has a number of properties that is adopted from the nature of biological immune system, having some advantages over other dynamic routing solutions. These include the clonal selection, immunological memory, immune regulation, cross-reactive response, and immune network capabilities. One of the major advantages of an AIS-based system is that its memory will not be continuously built up on a centralized system in an uncontrolled manner. A centralized approach often incurs a significant investment in the upgrading of new servers and database for the ever expanding memory usages. The localized immune memory feature is much desirable for generating a set of optimal dynamic routes where prompt localized response and action generation that is similar to the immunological responses is essential for efficient and effective operation of such a routing system. In addition, the characteristics immune cells cooperation and distribution of work are also key features that are being incorporated to the proposed AISDR algorithm.

4.1 The Organization of the AISDR Framework

The proposed dynamic routing framework is highlighted by the following characteristics:

- *Dynamic*. The system assists system users to select the best route in respond to changes in the operating environment by adopting the clonal selection theory using binding affinity as the key measurement. The ability to recognize and classify different route patterns and to generate selective response in a dynamic manner is similar to the behavior of the human immune system.
- *Distributed Memory*. The system facilitates the efficient storage and retrieval of active and inactive routes and their respective costs and selection priorities in a distributive manner, which is parallel to the organization and operation of the immune memory.
- *Self-regulation*. It assists users to regulate the number of routes and nodes that is analogous to the regulation of hyper-mutation mechanism of the immune system.
- *Cross-reactive Response*. It assists users to handle bookings (the requests of new routes) that are structurally fit to the existing routes in the system. This is analogous to the cross–reactive response theory.
- *Adaptability*. It assists users and the routing system to constantly renew the routing structure of the system through the continuous recruitment of newly formed elements and the destruction of non-simulated or self-reactive elements. This feature is adopted from the immune network theory or the immune recruitment mechanism of the immune system.
- *Diversity*. The system contains a diverse set of elements of various types to fulfill various roles to identify the booking characters and to select the best route.

The corresponding analogies of the AISDR to the immune system are shown in Table 1 and the organization of the framework is illustrated in Figure 1.

Route Selection by Clonal Selection
Burnet (1957) has modified Jerne's natural selection theory (1955) for antibody formation as the theory of clonal selection. It focuses on the distinctive feature of immune system that can respond to millions of different foreign antigens in a highly specific way. Burnet's theory shows that each human first randomly generates a vast diversity of lymphocytes, and then those cells that react with the foreign antigens which the human actually encounters are specifically selected for the action. This theory is based on the proposition that during development each lymphocyte becomes

Table 1. Behavioral states of AIS agent

Immune System	AISDR
Humoral immune System	Dynamic routing system that has nodes and routes/component routes
Self	- Existing nodes, routes, solutions - New routes - Test routes (for tolerance behaviour)
Non-self	Requirements, i.e. a booking with origin, destination, cargo information, and other important information that contributes to route selection. (Bookings required existing optimized standard routes; bookings require new routes)
Antigen / Receptors of Antigen	Incoming bookings (Bookings required existing optimized standard routes or bookings require new routes. Latter booking type is considered as non-self)
Antibody / Receptors of antibodies	Routes
Antigen Presenting Cell (APC)	A major functional unit within the system that handles bookings and job assignments
B lymphocytes (B cell)	A functional unit within the system that handles job order bookings, and derive routes
T lymphocytes (Helper T cell)	A functional unit within the system that handles job order bookings, and derive routes
Amino acid sequence on antibody that binds to antigen	Route components and sequences that combine to form standard routes as possible solutions to incoming bookings
Binding Affinity – a measurement of the strength of the bond between an antibody's combining site and a single epitope	Fitting Priority – measurement for evaluating the best fit route
Clonal-Selection Theory	First generate a vast diversity of feasible routes, those routes that fit the problem best will be used
Immune memory – stored antibodies which has not been binded to an antigen before	Stored existing routes that are not in service but may be changed to active when in use (inactive)
Immune memory – stored antibodies which has bind to an antigen before	Stored existing route that is in service (active)
Primary Response	Response to new bookings that has not been handled previously
Secondary Response	Repeat bookings with faster selection with a better fitting process
Hypermutation	Manuel editing of routes or other information/special request handling
Cross-reactive response theory	To allow standard routes fit to structurally related new routes
Immune Network Theory – Immune Recruitment Mechanism and Metadynamics	Continuously improved route structures and new booking selection criteria that are subject to new internal or external factors
Innate Immune Response	Inborn routes provided by the system
Adaptive Immune Response	Newly created standard routes provided by the system

committed to react with a particular antigen before ever being exposed to it. Each lymphocyte is committed to specifically fitting to the antigen with its cell-surface receptor proteins. This binding of antigens to the receptors activates the cell, causing immune cell to both proliferate and mature. A foreign antigen thus selectively stimulates those cells that express complementary antigen-specific receptors and are thus already committed to respond to it.

Similarly, AISDR first generates a vast amount of routes that connects through nodes with various modes of transportation. They are in an inactive status but may be changed into active status when they are being used. To serve an incoming booking, a standard route should be used. This could be a set of connected routes or a route connecting with two nodes all with active status. A functional unit within the system will handle bookings and derive routes. It is done by recognizing the requirements, including origin, destination, cargo types, container types, cargo volume, etc. Then it selects a list of standard routes that serves the bookings. Based on the rating that is associated to the binding affinity, the functional unit further selects the best route with the highest priority and lowest cost that best fits to the requirement. The operation of the system, which is analogous to the immune system, functions on the ready-made rather than the made-to-measure principle.

Specificity through Affinity Maturation
The AISDR inherits the affinity maturation characteristics of the immune system. During the cell division process that is stimulated by antigen binding to a specific clone, the repertoire of antigen-activated B-cells is diversified basically by two mechanisms: hypermutation and receptor editing. High-affinity variants are selected and put into the pool of memory cells. This phenomenon in which antibodies present in a secondary response is generally having a higher affinity than those of the early primary response is referred to the maturation of the immune response. This maturation requires the antigen-binding sites of the antibody molecules in the matured response be structurally different from those present in the primary response through mutation events. Such events may lead to an increase in the affinity of these antibodies. Those with higher affinity variants are then selected to the pool of memory cells. The immune system will keep these best fit cells as well as those routes created in the infant stage with a sort of resting states that will act more efficiently on incoming antigens.

Through the adoption of the affinity maturation and immunological memory characteristics, AISDR behaves dynamically to increase its ability to cater for the incoming bookings requirement and stored its package (routes and services) for future bookings with the same requirement. The division of B-cells to cater vast amount of antigens is analogous to a booking or a large number of bookings which may require a lot of planned transportation capacity to handle the cargos that navigate in the selected route. Short- or mid-term capacity planning facilitates the resource reservation for the bookings. The selected standard route could be edited to further fitting into the requirement to ship particular cargos from an origin to a destination.

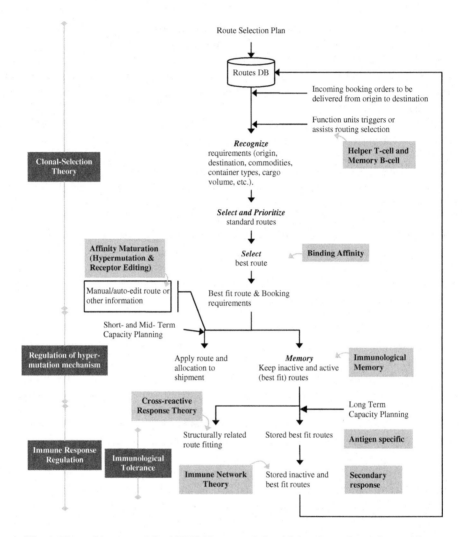

Fig. 1. The architecture of the AISDR Framework for solving dynamic routing problems

Regulation with the use of Hypermutation Mechanism

The hypermutation mechanism in the immune system serves to regulate the amount of stored routes based on the receptor affinity. As the continuing deleterious changes by mutation may cause the loss of advantageous mutation, a short burst of somatic hypermutation, followed by a pause for antibodies selection and clonal expansion, also forms the basis of maturation process. The selection mechanism then regulates the hypermutation process based on the receptor affinity in order to allow storing the best fit antibodies. Low affinity cells will further undergo the mutation process to improve their affinities; otherwise they will die through apoptosis. Hypermutation will also be deactivated when there are cells that contain high-affinity antibody receptors (Kepler and Perelson, 1993).

A regulation mechanism is built in the AISDR to cope with the sudden request on the increase or deletion of nodes and routes. The requested actions affect the standard routes and call sequences. Some affected routes that are best fitted to a particular booking can undergo further binding affinity evaluation, route selection, and then stored in memory. Suboptimal fitted routes will be stored in resting state. The route selection provides a means to categorize good and suboptimal fitted routes for future reference. This provides a mechanism for regulating the storage of routes.

Despite the hypermutation regulation mechanism, the immune response is subject to a variety of regulation and control mechanisms which serve to restore the immune system to a resting state when response to a given antigen is no longer required. Antibody, APC, lymphocytes, and the antigen itself contribute to the regulatory mechanism of the immune system. Antibody exerts feedback control on an immune response. IgM antibody together with an antigen specifically could stimulate an immune response to the antigen, where as IgG antibody could suppress the response. The effectiveness of APC in presenting the antigen is also a determining factor as it decides whether a responsive or tolerance action should take place. The nature of antigen also influences the type of immune response that occurs. Lymphocytes, with $CD4^+$ T cells that prevent the induction of autoimmunity, T_H cell subsets involving in the regulation of immunoglobulin production, and $CD8^+$ T cells transferring resistance and tolerance play an important role on the immune system regulation mechanism. Cross-reactive response and the immune network theory also provide a regulatory effect on the immune system. Regulation in a dynamic routing system is also needed to control booking responses, the availability of active routes, resource, and capacity.

Diversity and Efficiency of Second and Cross Reactive Responses
Primary, secondary, and cross-reactive responses characteristics demonstrate a learning and memory capability acquired for antibody production and antigen defense. Primary response occurs when specific antibodies is defending against antigens with an increase in the concentration and affinity up to a level in their first exposure to an antigen. When infection is eliminated, the concentration will decline. Secondary response occurs when antibodies react on the same antigen after the primary response. It shows a faster and more efficient response against the antigen. When another antigen with structurally related to the antigen in the primary response is introduced, B-lymphocytes can adapt to the antigen and present a faster and more efficient secondary response to the structurally related antigen. This demonstrates an associative memory and the cross-reactive response. Smith (1997) developed a discrete object model of immune system on analyzing the cross-reactive response and immunological associative memory.

To cope with a more rapid response, booking specificity fulfillment, and flexibility to handle new bookings with routes that are structurally related to the standard routes are required. In addition, a dynamic routing system requires the processing of secondary, cross-reactive response, and associative memory characteristics.   This would allow a more rapid routing selection process and improved flexibility in fitting new booking requirements.

Route Repository against Immunological Memory

The routing repository that is similar to the immunological memory, not only keeps the best fit routes and routes that are in the resting state for handling efficient future bookings; it also allows capacity planning for the stored routes and its equipments. This planning mechanism is based on the first response, customer information and their background. Thus, faster selection, resource arrangement, and order completion process could be achieved with the incorporation of secondary response using the concept of immune memory and capacity planning features.

Functional Unit Interaction and Routes Renewal

Jerne (1974) proposed the immune network theory suggesting that the immune system is composed of a regulated network of molecules and cells that recognizes one another even in the absence of antigens.

   The theory also suggests that the immune system has the ability to continuously produce and recruit novel cells and molecules. The constant renewal of network structure via recruitment into activity of these newly formed elements and the death of non-simulated or self-reactive elements enable the system to survive and adapt to the changing environment. This immune network metadynamics, also regarded as immune recruitment mechanism, allows for the selection of new elements into the network according to the global state of the system. The selection showing the networking sensitivity that is measured by the affinity of this element has with the actual elements already present in the immune network. In a routing system, this could also be considered as an application of network sensitivity: functional unit interaction of the routing systems, and the self-renewal process of the AISDR.

System Security and Tolerance

For the immune system to function properly, it is required that molecules of its own cells (self) to be distinguished from foreign molecules (non-self). Otherwise, an immune response will be triggered against the self-antigens, causing autoimmune disease. Immunological tolerance mechanisms are essential as the immune system randomly generates a vast diversity of antigen-specific receptors and some of these will be self reactive; tolerance prevents reactivity against the body's own tissues. Artificial tolerance can be induced artificially by various regimes that may eventually be exploited to prevent rejection of foreign transplants and to deal with autoimmune diseases. Functional testing and distributive complementary cooperative activities are essential in complex artificial immune systems. It is necessary for a system to be able to differentiate self and non-self in order to function efficiently.

4.2 The AISDR Algorithm

Key Cost Factors

Vessel/Voyage and equipment are considered as fixed cost items whereas the followings key cost factors are regarded as variable cost factors:

1. *Transit Time*
2. *Distance*
3. *Transportation Cost*

Transportation cost is the total transportation cost of door transportation cost, inter-modal transportation cost, and public feeder transportation cost.

4. *Terminal Cost*

The terminal cost is the average unit cost for loading or unloading of cargo at a port, for example, the lift on/off, shifting and other handling charges. It is a variable cost and is associated with all water legs of a labeled route. The terminal cost mainly involves the transshipment commission.

Transshipment commission is the cost of handling transshipments. This cost is presented either as a flat rate per TEU or a percentage of revenue.

5. *Equipment Cost*

Equipment cost includes depot cost, maintenance and repair cost, and equipment rental cost. Depot cost is the average unit cost of container storage for rental and leasing a box.

6. *Vessel Voyage Cost*

Vessel cost includes cost on vessels, public feeders, and public barge service.

7. *Cargo Assessment Cost.*

Cargo assessment is a local charge given to government or other entity other than the carrier.

8. *Agency Commission Cost.*

Agency commission is the third party commission. It is paid to an agent who handles business activities for the carrier.

9. *Cost on Cargo Nature*

The cost on cargo nature includes cost on pre-trip inspection, reefer monitoring, and hanger container

10. *Freight Tax*

Freight taxes and dues is the local tax demanded by a local government. The cost is associated to the place of receipt or the final destination.

11. *Empty Reposition Cost*

Empty repositioning cost represents the slot and other transportation cost related to empty reposition. The cost is associated to the empty pick up and empty return facilities.

Empirical Mathematical Model
Definitions:
For a selected route, R_s

R_{si}	- Component route i of R_s;	V_{si}	- Vessel voyage cost of R_{si}
T_S	- Total transit time of T_{si};	C_s	- Total cargo assessment cost of R_s

T_{Si} - Transit time of R_{si};

D_S - Total distance of R_s;

D_{Si} - Distance of R_{si};

P_{si} - Cost of transportation of R_{si};

P_s - Total cost of transportation of R_s;

M_s - Total terminal cost of R_s;

M_{si} - Terminal cost of R_{si};

E_s - Total equipment cost of R_s;

E_{si} - Equipment cost of R_{si};

V_s - Total vessel voyage cost of R_s;

C_{si} - Cargo assessment cost of R_{si}

A_s - Total agency commission cost of R_{si}

A_{si} - Agency commission cost of R_{si}

N_s - Total cargo nature cost, including reefer pre-trip inspection, reefer monitoring, hanger container

F_s - Freight tax

ER_s - Empty reposition cost

α - Weighting factor for the transit time

β - Weighting factor for the total cost

VC - Variable Costs

FC - Fixed Costs

Objective Function:

To select the best route for delivering a consignment of cargo from an origin to a destination:

Select best route R_s such that: $f\left[(-1)(\alpha)(\min \text{ transit time}) \times (-1)(\beta)(\min \text{ total costs})\right]$

where transit time: $f\{\alpha[c(T_S)]\}$

and total cost function:

$$f\{\beta[C(E_s) \pm C(V_s) \pm C(P_s) \pm C(M_s) \pm C(C_s) \pm C(A_s) \pm C(N_s) \pm C(F_s) \pm C(ER_s)]\}$$

Hence, to find the best route, minimize

$$f\{\alpha[C(T_s)] \cdot \beta[C(E_s) \pm C(V_s) \pm C(T_s) \pm C(M_s) \pm C(C_s) \pm C(A_s) \pm C(N_s) \pm C(F_s) \pm C(ER_s)]\}$$

Cost of total transit time:

$$c(T_S) \alpha (T_{S1} + T_{S2} + \ldots + T_{SN}) \Rightarrow c(T_S) \alpha \sum_{i=1}^{N} T_{Si}$$

Cost of transportation:

$$c(P_S) \alpha (P_{S1} + P_{S2} + \ldots + P_{SN}) \Rightarrow c(P_S) \alpha \sum_{i=1}^{N} P_{Si}$$

Cost of terminal handling:

$$c(M_S) \alpha (M_{S1} + M_{S2} + \ldots + M_{SN}) \Rightarrow c(M_S) \alpha \sum_{i=1}^{N} M_{Si}$$

Constraints:

The selection of a specific route is subjected to the following constraints:

1. Functional relationship of total transit time to total cost (total cost is a function of equipment rental cost)
2. Functional relationship of total transit time to total distance
3. Total transit time also depends on the waiting/idle time between transshipment
4. Vehicle capacity (vessel/feeder/barge)
5. Time window
6. Cost has a seasonal fluctuation
7. Customs clearance
8. Ports and inter-modal transportation performance

4.3 Simulation Studies

A number of tools are available for development and simulation on immune-based systems, including C-ImmSim (Castiglione, 2004), IMMSIM (Kleinstein, 2000), MATLAB, and LISYS (Steven & Stephanie, 2000). In this study, MATLAB is selected for its flexibility, dynamic functionality and efficient simulation time. A MATLAB model named AISDR is developed for studying the dynamic route selection problem.

In particular, AISDR implements the mechanism of clonal selection for dynamic routing selection following the procedures defined in Figure 1, namely, (a) by storing a diversity of routes in the system; (b) receiving incoming bookings from an origin to a destination; (c) recognizing requirements; (d) selecting a list of possible standard routes; and (e) selecting the best fit route based on the requirements.

For a typical shipment scenario, a set up with 71 nodes and 28 routes was adopted. Each route passes through a number of nodes that ranges from 4 to 28 nodes. In addition, AISDR adopts binding affinity to fit the incoming requirement for the start and end node by selecting the best route among the set of possible routes. In particular, the 71 nodes represent international ports that are located in the seven continents while the routes are the vessel routes that provide Trans-pacific, Asia-Europe, Trans-Atlantic and Australia with New Zealand services. Based on the design, the model can be applied to problem involving generic cases of global cargo transshipments for a logistics business.

The start nodes and end nodes are referred to the origin and the destination respectively. For example, there are eight calls in Route 9 and they are 23>17>16>13>36>35>13>23. If an incoming request is initiated from 17 to 35, Route 9 will be one of the possible choices of route to be selected as the best fit route based on a score that is computed with the function of shipment cost and transit time.

Simulation Case 1

The requirements received by the AISDR are:

Origin: Node 13 (Pusan)

Destination: Node 25 (Hong Kong)

Route 2 is selected as the best route by the AISDR as shown in Table 1 and Figure 2.

Table 2. AISDR Simulation 1 Results

Route	Route Details	AISDR
R2	*13>23>25*	*-3.722*
R6	13>50>21>23>17>25	-9.566
R10	13>23>27>25	-6.75
R11	13>16>23>27>25	-12.612
R16	13>42>35>18>25	-7.696
R27	13>16>23>17>24>25	-14.792

Table 3. AISDR Simulation 2 Results

Route	Route Details	AISDR	
R15	36>18>25	-4.684	-
R18	36>40>50>22>18>26>25	-13.366	-

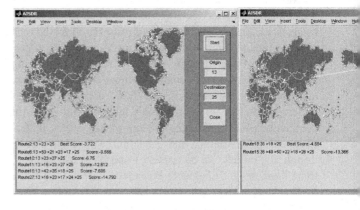

Fig. 2. Output from Simulation Case 1   **Fig. 3.** Output from S

With AISDR, Simulation Case 1 shows an input of node 13 as
25 as the destination. The system recognized the requirement and
fit such requirement. Based on the value of the correspondi
computed in the AISDR, Route 2 is found to be best fitte
requirement based on the total cost and transit time.

Simulation Case 2
The requirements received are:
Origin: Node 36 (Long Beach)
Destination: Node 25 (Hong Kong)

is shown that AISDR successfully adopted the distinctive behaviour of immune system, especially clonal selection and distributive immunological memory. Figure 4 compares the computation time for route planning using the prototyped AISDR simulation system and manual operation with increasing number of nodes involved. From the observation, being a computer-aided approach, AISDR provides remarkable saving of processing time compared with using manual operation alone.

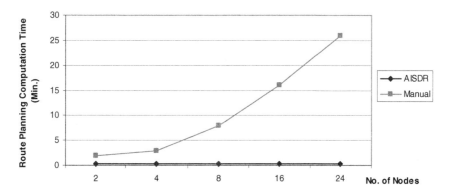

Fig. 4. Route planning time between AISDR and manual processes against number of nodes

5   Conclusion

An AISDR framework is developed through the adoption of the main features of human immune system for solving dynamic routing problems. These features include recognition, selection, learning, memory, and adaptation capabilities. With the proposed framework, associated algorithms are developed based on the clonal selection and immunological memory mechanisms. In this research, a prototyped of the MATLAB-based AISDR simulator was developed and simulation studies were performed on a number of typical shipment bookings. The results of two representative simulations show a high specificity and accuracy on route selection. From this study, the adoption of the immune system features has benefited the process of selecting best fit route in an accurate and highly efficient way.

- Build on the current development of the route selection functionality given by the AISDR framework, future developments include:
- To incorporate the notion of maximum route priority in the objective function where route priority is referred to the priority due to special reasons, for example, customer request, government regulations, etc.
- To consider the case of transshipment with a variety of routes that is to be set up.
- To determine contingency plans dynamically such as a substitute routes when a section of a route is unable to provide the necessary service or a port that cannot be berthed.

70 H.Y.K. Lau and E.Y.C. Wong

- To incorporate added functionality including system regulation with the use of hypermutation mechanism, routing memory adopting immunological memory, and inter-route recognition with the use of immunological tolerance.

Based on the prototyped system, future research and development will also focus on producing a practical and stable version for shipment route planning and re-planning for the global logistics industry.

References

[1] Brandao J. C. S, Metaheuristics for the Vehicle Routing Problem with Time Windows, Meta-heuristics Advances and Trends in Local Search Paradigms for Optimization, Inria, (1999).

[2] Brandao J. C. S., A lower bound based meta-heuristic for the vehicle routing problem, Ribeiro, C.: Hansen, P., Essays and surveys in metaheuristics, Kluwer Academic Publishers, Boston, pp. 151-168, (2002).

[3] Brandao, J. C. S., A tabu Search Algorithm for the Vehicle Routing, European Journal of Operational Research, (2003).

[4] Burnet, F. M., "A Modification of Jerne's Theory of Antibody Production Using the Concept of Clonal Selection", *The Australian Journal of Science 20*: 67-69.(1957).

[5] Coello Coello C. A. and Cortes N. C., An Approach to Solve Multiobjective Optimization Problems Based on an Artificial Immune System, Artificial Immune Systems: First International Conference, ICARIS 2002, (2002).

[6] Coello Coello C. A., Rivera D. C., and Cortes N. C., Use of an Artificial Immune System for Job Shop Scheduling, Artificial Immune Systems: Second International Conference, ICARIS 2003, Edinburgh, UK, September 1-3, 2003, Proceedings, Springer-Verlag GmbH, pp. 1-10, (2003).

[7] Darden L. and Cain J. A., Selection Type Theories, *Philosophy of Science 56* (1989):106-129, (1989).

[8] de Castro L. N. and Von Zuben F. J., The Clonal Selection Algorithm with Engineering Applications, In Workshop Proceedings of GECCO'00, pp. 36-37, Workshop on Aritificial Immune Systems and Their Applications, Las Vegas, USA, (2000).

[9] Filipec M. D. and Krajcar S. S., Genetic Algorithm Approach for Multiple Depot Capacitated Vehicle Routing Problem, Solving with Heuristic Improvements Build-in, Int. Jour. Of Modeling and Simulation, Vol 20, No. 4, (2000).

[10] Gomes, L.C.T., Von Zuben, F.J., A Neuro-fuzzy Approach to the Capacitated Vehicle Routing Problem, Proceedings of the IEEE International Joint Conference on Neural Networks (IJCNN'2002), Vol. 2, pp. 1930-1935, in the 2002 IEEE World Congress on Computational Intelligence (WCCT'2002), Honolulu, Hawaii, May 12-17, (2002).

[11] Hofmeyr S. A. and Forrest S., Architecture for an Artificial Immune System, Massachusetts Institute of Technology, Evolutionary Computation 8(4): 443-473, (2000).

[12] Jerne. N. K., "The Natural-Selection Theory of Antibody Formation", Proceedings of The National Academy of Sciences 41: 849-857, (1995).

[13] Jerne, N. K., Towards a Network Theory of the Immune System", Ann. Immunol. (Inst. Pasteur), 125C, pp. 373-389, (1974).

[14] Jung, S., A. Haghani, Genetic Algorithm for the Time-Dependent Vehicle Routing Problem, Proceedings of the 5th World Congress on Intelligent Transport Systems, Seoul, Korea, October 12-16, (1998).

[15] Kepler, T. B., and Perelson, A. S., Somatic Hypermutation in B Cells: An Optimal Control Treatment, J. theor. Biol., 164, pp. 37-64, (1993).

[16] Kleinstein S. H., and Seiden P. E., Simulating the Immune System, Computing in Science and Engineering, pp. 69-77, (2000)

[17] Landwehr, C. E., Bull, A. R., McDermott, J. P. and Choi, W. S. A Taxonomy of Computer Program Security Flaws, with Examples, Naval Research Laboratory, NRL/FR/5542-93-9591, (1993).

[18] Luh G. C., Wu C. Y., and Cheng W. C., Artificial Immune Regulation (AIR) for Model-Based Fault Diagnosis, Artificial Immune Systems: Third International Conference, ICARIS 2004, (2004).

[19] Nicosia G., Cutello V., An Immunological Approach to Combinatorial Optimization Problems, Advances in Artificial Intelligence, IBERAMIA 2002, Proceedings of 8th Ibero-American Conference, November 12-15, 2002. Lecture Notes in Computer Science, vol. 2527, pp. 361-370, (2002).

[20] Nicosia G., F. Castiglione. F., Motta S., Pattern Recognition by primary and secondary response of an Artificial Immune System, Theory in Biosciences, Vol. 120, No. 2, 93-106, (2001).

[21] Potvin J. Y., Dubé D., Robillard C., A Hybrid Approach to Vehicle Routing using Neural Networks and Genetic Algorithms, Applied Intelligence, Volume 6., (1996).

[22] Smith D. J., The Cross-Reactive Immune Response: Analysis, Modeling and Application to Vaccine Design, PhD Thesis, University of New Mexico, (1997).

[23] Taylor D. W. and Corne D. W., An Investigation of the Negative Selection Algorithm for Fault Detection in Refrigeration Systems, Second International Conference, ICARIS 2003, Edinburgh, UK, September 1-3, 2003, Proceedings, Springer-Verlag GmbH, pp. 34-45, (2003).

[24] Thangiah S. R., Osman I. H., Sun T., Hybrid Genetic Algorithm Simulated Annealing and Tabu Search Methods for Vehicle Routing Problem with Time Windows, Technical Report 27, Computer Science Department, Slippery Rock University, (1994).

[25] Timmis, J. & Neal, M., "Investigating the Evolution and Stability of a Resource Limited Artificial Immune System", Proc. of the Genetic and Evolutionary Computation Conference, Workshop on Artificial Immune Systems and Their Applications, pp. 40-41, (2000).

[26] White J. A. and Garrett S. M., Improved Pattern Recognition with Artificial Clonal Selection?, Artificial Immune Systems: Second International Conference, ICARIS 2003, Edinburgh, UK, September 1-3, 2003, Proceedings, Springer-Verlag GmbH, pp. 181-193, (2003).

Biomolecular Immune-Computer: Theoretical Basis and Experimental Simulator

Larisa B. Goncharova[1], Yannick Jacques[2], Carlos Martin-Vide[3],
Alexander O. Tarakanov[4], and Jonathan I. Timmis[5]

[1] Institute Pasteur of St. Petersburg,
Mira 14, St. Petersburg, 197101, Russia
goncharova_lara@mail.ru
[2] Institut National de la Sante et de la Recherche Medicale,
Institut de Biologie, 9 quai Mocousu, Nantes, 44093, France
yjacques@nantes.inserm.fr
[3] Research Group on Mathematical Linguistics, Universitat Rovira i Virgili,
Plaza Imperial Tarraco, 1, Tarragona, E-43003, Spain
carlos.martin@urv.net
[4] St. Petersburg Institute for Informatics and Automation, Russian Academy of Sciences,
14th line 39, St. Petersburg, 199178, Russia
tar@iias.spb.su
[5] Departments of Electronics and Computer Science, University of York,
Heslington, York, YO10 5DD, United Kingdom
jt517@ohm.york.ac.uk

Abstract. We propose to develop a theoretical basis and experimental simulator of the first Immune-Computer (IC) as a new kind of biomolecular computer. This IC will be able to control a fragment of the natural immune system in an autonomous and intelligent manner. Such control has proved unobtainable with other methods.

1 Introduction

Biological organisms show amazing computational capabilities at many levels from individual molecules of DNA and protein, to complete organisms and populations. The immune system is called "the second brain of vertebrates" and plays a major role in the ability of higher organisms to survive in rapidly varying and hostile environments. This system displays many characteristics required for autonomy and cognition: the ability to learn, the ability to reason (in a distributed manner) and the ability to deal with threats.

1.1 State of the Art

How do we construct truly autonomous systems that are capable of controlling human immune system? How do we construct biomolecular systems that can implement intelligent control mechanisms that are beyond the capabilities of current approaches? How do we create truly representative models of biomolecular processes that help us gain an insight into their operation? These are crucial questions that have faced the

C. Jacob et al. (Eds.): ICARIS 2005, LNCS 3627, pp. 72–85, 2005.

research community for many years. Clearly, progress has been made to some degree towards tackling these issues, with more traditional software engineering techniques and computer system construction. However, with the progress in miniaturization and complexity come new and ill-understood demands on computational systems intended for control. This has resulted in many systems being inflexible, ad hoc, difficult to configure and impenetrably arcane to maintain. To try and address this, attempts have been made to utilize techniques such as differential equations, artificial neural networks, genetic algorithms, cellular automata and the myriad of novel computational systems that are present in the literature [27]. However, these approaches are proving to be insufficient at addressing these issues and providing realistic computational models of key biomolecular mechanisms: in particular when concerned with the immune system. For example, none of these approaches is able to explain the sense of natural dualism in the network-field which has been supposed for cytokines. These represent a key biomolecular mechanism of the immune (as well as neuro-immune) modulation.

Modern biocomputing approaches have also shown themselves to be insufficient to solve these problems. This is due to the fact that the principles of information processing by proteins and immune networks have been out of its scope. Today, the notion of biocomputing refers to the use of biological elements such as DNA molecules, light-sensitive protein rhodopsin, biopolymers etc, for solving various computational problems, e.g. travelling salesman, simulation of artificial neural networks, control of mobile robots, etc. For example, tools of molecular biology are used to solve an instance of the directed Hamiltonian path problem by so called DNA-computer [3]. In this work, a small graph is encoded by DNA molecules, and computational "operations" are performed with standard protocols and enzymes. Another relevant work has been devoted to the development of computer memory based on bacterial protein rhodopsin. Chemical-based reaction-diffusion media for image processing, control of autonomous robots, and graph optimization are also under development [1].

Besides, a large number of works have been published in audio-video information fusion and representation (see e.g. [8], [17]). However, the efficiency of existing techniques is very far from the effectiveness of natural systems, which are able to represent, to manipulate and to fuse complex information. This feature is especially important, e.g., for public security metaphor of the immune system which provides the ability to survive in rapidly varying and hostile environment.

Current approaches of both conventional and biomolecular computing are obviously insufficient for an autonomous and intelligent control of ex vivo immune system. We propose it is necessary to develop and exploit a strict mathematical basis and experimental simulator of the IC to overcome the existing gap.

1.2   The Why

Given the above state of the art, there is a clear need for the use of *biomolecular immune-computer*, i.e. the IC. This need also emerges from a closing of silicon and biomolecular components in modern *biochips* (DNA and protein chips for genomics, medical diagnostics, drug design, etc.), as well as from recent findings in molecular immunology (immune network theory, cytokine networks-fields, immune synapse, psycho-neuro-immune modulation). We envisage that biochips in areas such as medicine and ecology will soon be miniature (up to *nanochips*) and soft (i.e. implemented and/or implanted in wetware or tissue). In addition, we also propose that the current principles of their autonomous control will not work.

For example, it would be very problematic to control a biochip-based autonomous *artificial immune cell* with a conventional computer. Moreover, an immune network-field of such cells would require a distributed and "intelligent" (adaptive, self-control, "self-conscious") mechanism permissive also to be implanted into the natural immune system.

Therefore, we propose it is necessary to meet this challenge with the construction of an IC that exploits the strategy of natural cytokine "computations" (modulations) of immune networks.

1.3 The What

We propose to develop a theoretical basis and experimental simulator of the IC as a new kind of biomolecular computer. This IC will be able to control a fragment of the natural immune system in an autonomous and intelligent manner. Such control has proved unobtainable with other methods.

We believe there are a number of objectives that will allow us to obtain a *computer controlled immune system*. Specifically we need to:

1. Create a mathematical basis of the IC which allows for the augmentation of biocomputing by utilizing a cytokine control of immune networks;
2. Build a software simulator of the IC, which will be accessible (in terms of usability and flexibility) to a wide variety of users, thus increasing the potential take up of this technology;
3. Build faithful and powerful simulator of an ex vivo fragment of the immune system and ultimately simulate the IC control of this fragment;
4. Develop a concept of special cytokine biochip as an interface between computer hardware and ex vivo immune system;
5. Work up a demonstrator application of the IC to cytokine-modulated apoptosis in immune-cancerology.

Therefore, we view the IC as a computer controlled fragment of the natural immune system (i.e. *ex vivo*) where cytokines (messenger proteins) collaborate in performing computation with conventional computer. This IC will be specialized in the "soft" control of immune networks and its programmability will consist of manipulating cytokine combinations to modulate immune response. Loosely speaking, cytokines form a kind of alphabet of a language of intercommunications between immune cells. Thus, the IC will be able to understand this language and to talk to the immune system in health and disease.

1.4 Approach

Our approach is based on artificial immune systems [11], [12], as well as on recent development within an EU project IST-2000-26016 IMCOMP of a new kind of computing which implements the principles of information processing by proteins and immune networks. The feasibility of this approach has been proved recently through the successful application of the developed computational paradigm *immunocomputing* for such computational intensive problems as: a) virtual clothing by 3 times faster than conventional approaches; b) learning by at least 40 times faster and recognition capabilities twice as effective than artificial neural networks and genetic algorithms on the tasks of environmental monitoring and laser physics; c) recognition of results in immunoassay-based diagnostic arrays 10 times faster than direct recognition by comparing them with a mask sample; d) powerful, robust and flexible on-line detection of dangerous ballistic situations in near-Earth space; e) predicting the danger of the plague infection outburst, which is beyond the capabilities of traditional statistics [29],[30].

Also, the feasibility of our approach can indirectly be confirmed by the approach of a new integrated project FET6-IST PACE (Programmable Artificial Cell Evolution). However, the "nanoscale robot ecology" of PACE project based on general cell prototype is also insufficient to provide autonomous intelligent control of ex vivo immune system, "where mathematics, computer science, linguistics and biology meet" [6], [20], [21], [22].

Therefore, within our approach, we propose to develop a methodology that will identify pertinent characteristics of functional regulatory networks in the cytokine field for an autonomous intelligent control. These characteristics will be used as the basis for the creation of new mathematical and computational models, and the augmenting of existing models. This will allow a greater understanding of the operation of such control systems to be developed in a biomolecular context. The work will then be extended to develop a computer simulator of an ex vivo fragment of the immune system and a concept of cytokine biochip as an *internal interface* of the IC with ex vivo immune system.

Concurrently with this development, we propose to develop a simulator of the IC. The simulator will capture the salient features of the IC and be constructed in such a way as to allow easy access, in terms of usability and flexibility, to the technology. Once this has been completed, an experimental phase will be undertaken with the simulator. Such experiments will use the simulator of ex vivo immune system to switch its immune response from Th1 to Th2 type, and vice versa.

In addition, we propose to build a demonstration application of the IC to a real-life task related to cytokine-modulated apoptosis in immune-cancerology. However, in order to make this a more rigorous test scenario, the notion of dual-acting cytokine will be introduced in which its normal physiological functions may be related to specific aspects of the immune system and over-expression culminates in cancer-specific apoptosis. This will check the ability of the IC to adapt and assess the benefits over and above more traditional methods: in essence assess the value added nature of the IC approach.

2   Immune-Computer

2.1   Main Components

Main components of the IC are shown in Fig. 1. This IC is expected to perceive the current status of the immune cell system (ICS) fragment and to correct it, if necessary.

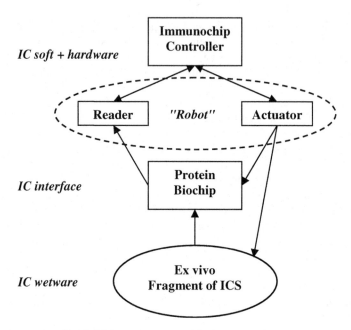

Fig. 1. Main components of the immune-computer

The protein biochip serves as a sensor (input) of the IC. The biochip reader acts as a scanning detector system and measures the concentration of several proteins (cytokines) in the fragment.

Processing these data, the immunochip recognizes general (cytokine) status of the fragment and computes the necessary control actions. This immunochip will implement in silicon the mathematical and computational models of immunocomputing approach as well as the soft/hardware simulator of ex vivo fragment of ICS that we propose to develop.

The IC actuator, as a liquid delivery system, performs the output control over the ICS fragment by means of cytokines.

2.2 Biochip

A biochip is a biological equivalent for computer microchip, but instead of performing of millions of mathematical operations, it is intended for carrying out thousands of biological interactions per minute, thousands of times faster than existing technologies. Biochips appeared as a result of application of the ideas of miniaturization, integration and parallel processing of information from microelectronics, where they were born, to biological processes. The chip principle, together with miniaturization, has now become the dominating theme for a number of new genomics and proteomics technologies, some of them are already used for comprehensive analysis of clinical samples in an attempt to describe disease and disease risk at the molecular level. However, all of these technologies are far from routine in clinical use.

The main advantage of biological microchips over conventional analytical devices is the possibility of massive parallel analysis. Biological microchips are smaller than conventional testing systems and highly economical in the use of specimen and reagents. Major progress has been achieved in the manufacturing and application of DNA microchips, but DNA is not the only biological entity that can be arrayed or spotted onto the surface of biochips. Proteins, lipids or carbohydrates can serve as receptors in the biochip-type analysis and their applications in genomic and proteomic research are being developed. The possibility to configure arrays of proteins is a real fact now, but their construction is vastly more complicated than creating DNA chips, popular research tools for analyzing suits of genes involved in everything from cancer to normal cell development.

In our previous work [28] we had developed a macro prototype of a protein biochip for immunoassay based diagnostics, where bioarray was a macro-prototype of the biochip microarray, while the software was a core of the biochip reader and controller. The method detected bound complexes of human immunoglobulin G (IgG) with recombinant protein G (pG).

2.3 Ex Vivo Immune System

The ICS fragment will include ex vivo complex of human T cells during their differentiation into the subsets of CD4+ T helper cells Th1 and Th2, thus producing regulatory cytokines. At the same time, the process may be influenced and partly directed by exogenous cytokines that originate from outside of the fragment.

The ICS fragment is expected to involve the expression and regulation activity of such cytokines as interferon family IFN-γ, IFN-α, IFN-β, tumor necrosis factor TNF-α, interleukins IL-1, IL-2, IL-4, IL12, IL-5, IL-6, IL-10, IL-13, etc. The naive T cells are expected to undergo a series of precise proliferation and differentiation events that will result in the generation of immune T cells with appropriate functional capabilities.

The differentiation of CD4+ T-helper cells into Th1 or Th2 subsets has profound effects on the outcome of autoimmune diseases, infectious diseases and graft rejection. Thus, understanding of the mechanism underlying Th cell differentiation and molecular events controlling T cell development is essential for therapeutic manipulation of the cytokine system phenotype in disease conditions and may allow the selective manipulation of Th subsets in vivo.

As a result, the developing IC may also be used in medical diagnostics to detect cytokine status of the immune system and, possibly, to measure C-reactive protein, which functions are rather close to those of cytokines. Besides, the increased level of this protein serves as a marker of the increased risk of severe cardiovascular diseases [34].

3 Theoretical Challenges

3.1 Cytokines

Cytokines (messenger proteins) are a group of biologically active mediator molecules that provide the intercellular interactions within the immune system. They are the central regulators of leukocyte growth and differentiation, being produced by a wide variety of cell types, targeting various cell subsets and exhibiting numerous biological activities.

Up to now more than 100 different human cytokines are identified. An increasing volume of experimental data suggests that cytokines play one of the central roles in the immune regulation as well as in the neuro-immune-endocrine modulation [2]. Such concept of cytokines as a network modulating and switching several cascades of immune reactions [23] adjoins with the concept considering such molecules as a field or a milieu, which local properties mediate immune response [16].

There is a relationship between cytokine levels in human body fluids and disease pathogenesis, including the inflammation and even depression [7]. Many types of cancers have taken advantage of the regulatory role of cytokines to down-regulate appropriate immune responses targeted at destroying cancer cells. They do this by secreting immunosuppressive cytokines that induce generalized and specific inhibition of immune responses [18]. Therefore, the use of immunostimulatory cytokines to boost protective anti-tumor immunity and to enhance the efficacy of tumor vaccines has become a promising strategy in cancer immunotherapy [15]. Conversely, several antagonists of cytokine action are now used in the treatment of inflammatory disorders [32].

Recent developments show that several cytokines induce apoptosis (programmed cell death) in cancer cells [33]. The induction of apoptosis is associated with a dose-dependent inhibition of cancer cell division, and this activity has been demonstrated for a wide range of cancer types including bladder, breast, leukemia, melanoma, ovarian and prostate.

Apoptosis is a natural mechanism by which cells "commit suicide" when they have outlived their purpose, become defective, or have aged. Apoptosis prevents cells from accumulating and forming tumors. Understanding of the control of apoptosis in normal and malignant cells will help to improve the diagnosis and treatment of malignancies. The goal of many treatments, including chemotherapies is to induce malignant cells to undergo apoptosis. Current data also suggests that a cytokine may function as a dual-acting cytokine in which its normal physiological functions may be related to specific aspects of the immune system and over-expression culminates in cancer-specific apoptosis [13].

3.2 From Natural Languages to Languages of Nature

In recent years, several research lines and speculations have suggested that some common principles of information processing cover both natural languages and languages of Nature (see e.g. [29]). The matter concerns construction and behavior of words and bio-molecules. For example, a weak but suggestive analogy is the observation that natural proteins represent chains (words of an alphabet) of 20 amino-acids. This number of amino-acids in Nature is approximately equal to the number of letters in the alphabets of the so called "classical" Indo-European languages: the Italian alphabet has 21 letters, the Greek alphabet has 24 letters, and the English alphabet has 26 letters. A somewhat sounder analogy between protein structures and languages is the observation that although the universe of distinct amino acid sequences is essentially unlimited the number of different folding patterns for the domains is not. The existing databases of protein sequence and structure indicates that most of the natural domain sequences assume one of a few thousand folds [24]. It should be noted that this number is of the same order of magnitude of a natural language dictionary.

Finally, an interesting and provoking proposal assumes that common principles govern both the evolution of genes and of languages [10].

Another example gives the theory of linguistic valence by L. Tesniere [31]. Tesniere claimed that a verb can be imagined as an original "atom with hooks", which can attract to itself a greater or smaller numbers of actants depending on the greater or smaller number of hooks which it has to hold these actants to itself. This theory has been acknowledged and developed, especially by the French and Russian linguistic schools. Nevertheless, this theory occupies a somewhat isolated position in linguistics, since it strongly differs from the widely spread generative grammars of N. Chomsky [9].

On the other hand, we can clearly distinguish strong and weak bindings as two kinds of connections both at the level of biomolecules and words.

First - strong (or valence) bindings - construct DNA's chain of nucleic acids or protein's chain of amino-acids. In linguistics it corresponds to the morphology, or construction of word's chain from letters.

Second - weak (or non-valence) bindings - form working complexes of biomolecules, like the double helix of DNA or Y-form of immunoglobulins. In linguistics it corresponds to the syntax, or forming sentences from words.

However, the most widespread mathematical constructions (see e.g. [19], [25]) usually make no distinction between morphology and syntax. From the viewpoint of finite automata and formal grammars, the so called "correctly constructed word" or "correctly constructed sentence" are just the same. In our opinion, such state of the art contradicts both molecular biology and modern linguistics.

Our project will make an attempt to overcome the above contradiction by introducing a new kind of formal system. We also consider our attempt as a first step towards a common formalism that describes realistic "working complexes" of words and biomolecules. The need for such an approach proceeds also from the new findings in brain research regarding the receptor mosaics of proteins and basic principles of molecular network organization [4], [5].

4   Mathematical Basis

4.1   Cytokine Formal Immune Network

Definition 1. Cell is a pair $V = (c, P)$, where "cytokine" c is natural number $c \in N$, whereas $P = (p_1, p_2, p_3)$ is a point of three-dimensional (3D) Euclidian space: $P \in R^3$, and P lies within unit cube: $\max\{| p_1 |, | p_2 |, | p_3 |\} \leq 1$.

Let distance ("affinity") $d_{ij} = d(V_i, V_j)$ between cells V_i and V_j be as follows:

$$d_{ij} = \max\left\{ \left|(p_1)_i - (p_1)_j\right|, \left|(p_2)_i - (p_2)_j\right|, \left|(p_3)_i - (p_3)_j\right| \right\}. \tag{1}$$

Fix some finite non-empty set of cells ("innate immunity") $W_0 = (V_1,...,V_m)$ with non-zero distance between cells: $d_{ij} \neq 0$, $\forall i, j : i \neq j$.

Definition 2. Cytokine formal immune network (cFIN) is a set of cells: $W \subseteq W_0$.

Definition 3. Cell V_i recognizes cell V_k if the following conditions are satisfied: $c_i = c_k$, $d_{ik} < h$, $d_{ik} < d_{ij}$, $\forall V_j \in W$, $j \neq i$, $k \neq j$, where $h \geq 0$ is given "threshold of affinity".

Let us define the behavior ("maturation") of cFIN by the following two rules.

Rule 1 (Apoptosis). If cell $V_i \in W$ recognizes cell $V_k \in W$ then remove V_i from cFIN.

Rule 2 (Auto-Immunization). If cell $V_k \in W$ is nearest to cell $V_i \in W_0 \setminus W$ among all cells of cFIN: $d_{ik} < d_{ij}$, $\forall V_j \in W$, whereas $c_i \neq c_k$, then add V_i to cFIN.

Let W_A be cFIN as a consequent of application of apoptosis to all cells of W_0. Let W_I be cFIN as a consequence of auto-immunization of all cells of W_A by all cells of W_0. Note that the resulting sets W_A and W_I depend on the ordering of cells in W_0. Further it will be assumed that the ordering is given.

It is obvious that neither the result of apoptosis W_A nor the result of auto-immunization W_I can overcome W_0 for any innate immunity: $W_A \subseteq W_0$, $W_I \subseteq W_0$, $\forall W_0$. Consider more important and less evident properties of cFIN.

Proposition 1. For any innate immunity W_0 there exists threshold of affinity h_0 such that apoptosis does not change W_0 for any h less than h_0: $W_A = W_0$, $\forall h < h_0$.

Let h_0 be minimal distance (1) for any pair of cells of cFIN with the same cytokines:

$$h_0 = \min_{i,j}\{d_{ij}\}: c_i = c_j, i \neq j.$$

Then, according to Definition 3, none of the cells of cFIN can recognize other cells, because $d_{ij} > h_0$ for any pair of cells V_i and V_j. According to Rule 1, none of the cells can be removed from cFIN for any h less than h_0, because $d_{ij} > h$, $\forall h < h_0$, $\forall V_i, V_j \in W_0$. Thus, $W_A = W_0$, $\forall h < h_0$.

Proposition 2. For any innate immunity W_0 there exists such threshold of affinity h_1 that consequence of apoptosis and auto-immunization $W_1 = W_I(h_1)$ provides the minimal number of cells $|W_1|$ for given W_0 and any h: $|W_1| \leq |W_I(h)|$, $\forall h$, $\forall W_I \subseteq W_0$.

Let h_1 be maximal distance (1) for any pair of cells of cFIN with the same cytokines:

$$h_1 = \max_{i,j}\{d_{ij}\}: c_i = c_j, \ i \neq j.$$

Then, according to Definition 3, any cell V_i can recognize the nearest cell V_j if the last one has the same cytokine: $c_i = c_j$. Let W_- be the set of all such cells V_i. Then, according to Rule 1, $|W_A(h_1)| = |W_0| - |W_-|$, and such number of cells after apoptosis is minimal among any h: $|W_A(h_1)| \leq |W_A(h)|, \forall h$. Let W_+ be set of cells, which is added to $W_A(h_1)$ as a consequence of auto-immunization: $W_1 = W_A(h_1) \cup W_+$. It is also evident that W_+ is a subset of W_-: $W_+ \subseteq W_-$, and $|W_+|$ represents a number of "mistakes" of apoptosis when cFIN "kills" some cells, which lead to further recognition errors. Such cells are then "restored" by auto-immunization (Rule 2). Let $W_* = W_- \setminus W_+$ be cells which yield apoptosis without further recognition errors. Then $|W_*| = |W_-| - |W_+|$. On the other hand: $|W_1| = |W_A(h_1)| + |W_+|$. Substitutions of $|W_A(h_1)|$ and $|W_+|$ lead to the following result: $|W_1| = |W_0| - |W_*|$. Thus, $|W_1| \leq |W_I(h)|$, proves Proposition 2.

4.2 Binding System

As usual, for a finite set X we denote by X^* the free monoid generated by X and ε denotes the empty string.

Definition 4. A binding system (BS) is a system

$$M = (X, s_0, s_1, r_1, r_2),$$

where

- X is a finite alphabet;
- $s_0, s_1 \notin X$ are the initial and the final symbols;
- $r_1 : s_0 \cup X - X \cup s_1$ is the linking map associating to s_0 and each letter $x \in X$ a set of letters or s_1;
- $r_2 : X - X \cup \varepsilon$ is the binding map associating to each letter $x \in X$ a set of letters or empty string.

Consider a *primary structure* as a chain $a \in X^*$, generated by BS according to the linking map $r_1(s_0) = x$, $r_1(x) = y$, ..., $r_1(z) = s_1$ as follows:

$$s_0 - s_0x - s_0xy - \ldots - s_0xy...z - s_0as_1.$$

Consider x_y as a *binding site* of the letter x to the letter y, if $r_2(x) = \{y,...,z\}$, or no binding sites, if $r_2(x) = \varepsilon$.

Consider a pair of the sites x_y and y_x as *bound* $(x_y :: y_x)$ in the primary structure $a_1 x a_2 y a_3$ if $r_2(x) = y$, $r_2(y) = x$, and either $x \notin a_1$, $y \notin a_2$, or all previous pairs of such sites are bound.

Consider a secondary structure of BS as the primary structure with all sites bound.

The behavior of BS is the language of the secondary structures:

$$L(M) = \{\omega \in X^* \mid x_y :: y_x, \forall x, y \in \omega\} .$$

Definition 5. A language $L \subseteq X^*$ is called *binding language*, if there exists a BS such that $L = L(M)$.

We denote by $BL(X)$ the family of all languages over X generated by BSs. *BL* denotes the family of binding languages over each alphabet.

A BS is called deterministic (DM) if $card(r_1(x)) : 1$, $card(r_2(x)) : 1$, for each $x \in X$.

$DBL(X) \subseteq BL(X)$ is the class of languages generated by BS.

Example 1. Consider the alphabet $X = \{a, b, c\}$. We are going to display a BS generating $L = \{a^n b^n c^n \mid n > 0\}^*$. Let M be the BS with $r_1(s_0) = a$, $r_1(a) = \{a, b\}$, $r_1(b) = \{b, c\}$, $r_1(c) = \{c, s_1\}$, $r_2(a) = \{b, c\}$, $r_2(b) = \{a\}$, $r_2(c) = \{a\}$.

It is an easy task to see that the behavior of M is exactly the language L.

Example 2. With a slight modification in the construction of the previous example we can prove that the language

$$\{(a^n)^k (b^n)^k (c^n)^k \mid k \geq 0\} \in BL .$$

To this end we just extend the binding map as follows: $r_2(a) = \{b,...,b,c,...,c\}$, $r_2(b) = \{a,...,a\}$, $r_2(c) = \{a,...,a\}$, where each letter repeats n times. Thus, the letter a has $2n$ binding sites and the letters b, c have n binding sites. It is obvious that

$$L(M) = \{(a^n)^k (b^n)^k (c^n)^k \mid k \geq 0\} .$$

4.3 Remarks

As mentioned in Section 1.3, cytokines form a kind of alphabet of a language of intercommunications between immune cells. Thus, for the IC will be able to understand this language and to talk to the immune system in health and disease, it is necessary to develop both mathematical models of cFIN and BS as well as a united "mathematical linguistics" of the IC.

5 Conclusion

The aim of our approach is to create a basis for the first biomolecular IC. This is a new opportunity for science and technology within emerging multidisciplinary area of ex vivo human immune system (see e.g. [26]). The IC represents a novel and extremely innovative approach, which involves high (technical) risk and establishes a truly interdisciplinary collaboration between computer scientists, mathematicians, engineers and immunologists. As a new computer paradigm, the IC could have a very high potential payoff in the long term, in particular for testing new vaccine constructs and immunomodulators that provide superior protection against threat agents as well as for public and information security assurance.

Potential benefits of this technology will be wide-ranging and diverse. An immediate benefit of our approach will be new possibilities of computer-aided testing and design of new vaccines and immunomodulators to minimize both testing on animals and preclinical and clinical trials. For this purpose, the primary and most laborious stages could be substituted by "virtual testing" within the IC controlled fragment of the immune system ex vivo. Such IC-aided analysis and predicting of final output of immunomodulators and vaccine testing at the outset of testing stage could lead to a significant reducing of the number of testing experiments, which are extremely time-consuming, laborious, and very expensive. It is also worth noting that further specification of how the proposed IC could be implemented for such virtual testing needs the involving of actual test protocols. Although we have started such technical work based on the prototype of our biochip (see e.g. [28]), its description in detail seems not so appropriate for a conceptual paper.

Expected users of this technology are companies producing soft and hardware tools for biotech sector, as well as pharmacology and biotech companies, medical tool producing companies and biological research laboratories. New mathematical and computational paradigm of the IC and its software implementation could also be used by producers of soft- and hardware tools for conventional (silicon) computing, information security and government agencies (or private companies) involved in public security (or production and industrial security).

Apart from medicine, the principles of such IC can also be applied successfully in such traditional fields of computation as computer networks security, public security design (conceive, optimization and management), environmental monitoring, space engineering, etc. In addition, to the best of our knowledge, there is no current computing method that could provide an intelligent adaptive control of public security related real-life applications.

References

1. Adamatzky, A. Computing in Nonlinear Media and Automata Collectives. Institute of Physics Publishing, Bristol (2001)
2. Ader, R., Felten, D.L., Cohen, N. (eds.): Psychoneuroimmunology. Academic Press, New York (2001)
3. Adleman, L.M. Computing with DNA. Scientific American 279/2 (1998) 54-61
4. Agnati, L.F., Tarakanov, A.O., Ferre, S., Fuxe, K. Receptor-receptor interactions, receptor mosaics, and basic principles of molecular network organization: possible implications for drug development. J. Mol. Neurosci. 26/2-3 (2005) (in press)
5. Agnati, L.F., Tarakanov, A.O., Guidolin, D. A simple mathematical model of cooperativity in receptor mosaics based on the "symmetry rule". BioSystems 80/2 (2005) 165-173

6. Bernard, J., Harb, C., Mortier, E., Quemener, A., Meloen, R.H., Vermont-Desroches, C., Wijdeness, J., Van Dijken, P., Grotzinger, J., Slootstra, J.W., Plet, A., Jacques, Y. Identification of an interlukin-15 {alpha} receptor-binding site on human interlukin-15. J. Biol. Chem. 279 (2004) 24313-24322

7. Bunk, S. Signal blues: stress and cytokine levels underpin a provocative theory of depression. The Scientists, August 25 (2003) 24-28

8. Caumont, A. On the right track of Triverity: data device finds a niche in racing, extreme sports. The Washingtonpost, January 24 (2005) E05

9. Chomsky, N. Reflections of Language. Pantheon Books, New York (1975)

10. Dawkins, R. The Selfish Gene. Oxford University Press (1989)

11. Dasgupta, D. (ed.): Artificial Immune Systems and Their Applications. Springer-Verlag, Berlin (1999)

12. De Castro, L.N., Timmis, J. Artificial Immune Systems: A New Computational Intelligence Approach. Springer-Verlag, London (2002)

13. Fisher, P.B., Gopalkrishnan, R.V., Chada, S., Ramesh, R., Grimm, A., Rosenfeld, M.R., Curiel, D.T., Dent, P. mda-7/IL-24, a novel cancer selective apoptosis inducing cytokine gene: from the laboratory into the clinic. Cancer Biology and Therapy 2 (2003) S023-S037

14. Goncharova, L.B., Melnikov, Y.B., Tarakanov, A.O. Biomolecular immunocomputing. Lecture Notes in Computer Science, Vol. 2787. Springer-Verlag, Berlin (2003) 102-110

15. Hisada M., Kamiya, S., Fujita, K., Belladonna, M.L., Aoki, T., Koyanagi, Y., Mizuguchi, J., Yoshimoto, T. Potent antitumor activity of interleukin-27. Cancer Research 64 (2004) 1152-1156

16. Kourilsky, P., Truffa-Bachi, P. Cytokine fields and the polarization of the immune response. Trends in Immunology 22 (2001) 502-509

17. Kung, S.Y., Mak M.W., Lin, S.H. Biometric Authentication: A Machine Learning Approach. Prentice Hall (2005)

18. Kurzrock, R. Cytokine deregulation in cancer. Biomedecine & Pharmacotherapy 55/9/10 (2001) 543-547

19. Lallement, G. Semirings and Combinatorial Applications. John Wiley & Sons, New York (1979)

20. Magrangeas, F., Boisteau, O., Denis, S., Jacques, Y., Minvielle, S. Negative cross-talk between interleukin-3 and interleukin-11 is mediated by suppressor of cytokine signalling-3 (SOCS-3). Biochem. J. 353 (2001) 223-230

21. Martin-Vide, C., Mitrana, V. (eds.): Where Mathematics, Computer Science, Linguistics and Biology Meet. Kluwer, Dordrecht (2001)

22. Martin-Vide, C., Mitrana, V. (eds.): Grammars and Automata for String Processing: From Mathematics and Computer Science to Biology, and Back. Taylor and Francis, London (2003)

23. O'Garra, A. Cytokines induce the development of functionally heterogeneous T helper cell subsets. Immunity 8 (1998) 275-283

24. Sali, A., Glaeser, R., Earnest, T., Baumeister, W. From words to literature in structural proteomics. Nature 422 (2003) 216-225

25. Salomaa, A., Jewels of Formal Language Theory. Computer Science Press, Rockville (1981)

26. Special Focus Area: Engineering Tissue Constructs. DARPA BAA 01-42 Addendum 8 (2002)

27. Stepney, S., Clark, J., Tyrell, A., Johnson, C., Timmis, J., Partridge, D., Adamatzky, A., Smith, R. Journeys in Non-Classical Computation: A Grand Challenge for Computing Research [http://www.nesc.ac.uk/esi/events/Grand_Challenges/] (2003)

28. Tarakanov, A., Goncharova, L., Gupalova, T., Kvachev, S., Sukhorukov, A. Immunocomputing for bioarrays. The 1st Int. Conf. on Artificial Immune Systems (ICARIS'02). Univ. of Kent at Canterbury, UK (2002) 32-40

29. Tarakanov, A.O., Skormin, V.A., Sokolova, S.P. Immunocomputing: Principles and Applications. Springer-Verlag, New York (2003)
30. Tarakanov, A.O., Tarakanov, Y.A. A comparison of immune and neural computing for two real-life tasks of pattern recognition. Lecture Notes in Computer Science, Vol. 3239. Springer-Verlag, Berlin (2004) 236-249
31. Tesniere, L. Elements de Syntaxe Structurale. Klincksieck, Paris (1979)
32. Vilcek, J, Feldmann, M. Historical review: Cytokines as therapeutics and targets of therapeutics. Trends Pharmacol. Sci. 25 (2004) 201-209
33. Wall, L., Burke, F., Caroline, B., Smyth, J., Balkwill, F. IFN-gamma induces apoptosis in ovarian cancer cells in vivo and in vitro. Clinical Cancer Research 9 (2003) 2487-2496
34. Yu, H., Rifai, N. High-sensitivity C-reactive protein and atherosclerosis: from theory to therapy. Clinical Biochemistry 33/8 (2000) 601-610

What Have Gene Libraries Done for AIS?

Steve Cayzer[1], Jim Smith[2], James A.R. Marshall[3], and Tim Kovacs[3]

[1] HP Laboratories, Bristol, BS34 8QZ, UK (SC)
[2] Faculty of Computing Engineering and Mathematical Sciences,
University of the West of England, Bristol, BS16 1QY, UK (JS)
[3] Department of Computer Science, University of Bristol,
Bristol BS8 1UB, UK (JM, TK)

Abstract. Artificial Immune Systems (AIS) have been shown to be useful, practical and realisable approaches to real-world problems. Most AIS implementations are based around a canonical algorithm such as clonotypic learning, which we may think of as individual, lifetime learning. Yet a species also learns. *Gene libraries* are often thought of as a biological mechanism for generating combinatorial diversity of antibodies. However, they also bias the antibody creation process, so that they can be viewed as a way of guiding the lifetime learning mechanisms. Over time, the gene libraries in a species will evolve to an appropriate bias for the expected environment (based on species memory). Thus gene libraries are a form of *meta-learning* which could be useful for AIS. Yet they are hardly ever used. In this paper we consider some of the possible benefits and implications of incorporating the evolution of gene libraries into AIS practice. We examine some of the issues that must be considered if the implementation is to be successful and beneficial.

1 Introduction

In any biologically inspired algorithm, one is obliged to make a number of concessions to simplicity. Indeed, one might argue that excessive biological realism is undesirable, since it will lead to building a system rather too specifically tailored to the biological environment. Nevertheless, the danger of oversimplification is that one may make a generic system, full of sweeping assumptions, that is not well suited for real world tasks [9]. In this paper we focus on two such broken assumptions. Firstly, *random creation of antibodies*. As any machine learning student knows, the naïve *generate and test* metaphor is the canonical algorithm, cheap yet unsystematic and often hopelessly inefficient. In the AIS world the approach may bring scalability problems [19]. The second broken assumption states that *antigens are uniformly distributed in non-self space*. We think this is unlikely to be representative of real world problems, and is certainly not true of the well-known UCI datasets [3].

In the biological system, of course, neither assumption holds. Firstly, antibodies are created from genes spliced from the so-called *gene libraries*; this ensures that antibody creation is far from random. Secondly, uniform coverage of non-self space is not only unnecessary, it is impractical; non-self space is too big! Thus, from a computational point of view, libraries introduce *initialisation bias* and provide a 'species memory' to tackle the antigen mapping task.

C. Jacob et al. (Eds.): ICARIS 2005, LNCS 3627, pp. 86–99, 2005.

What could this mean for AIS? Could gene libraries be used to intelligently seed our algorithm? In the paper we consider whether gene libraries might:

1. improve non-self space coverage – through better placement of detectors (antibodies), over and above random creation;
2. reduce the cost of detector generation by more effectively avoiding self;
3. map the antigen population more accurately; and
4. help deal with co-evolving antigens

At a trivial level, the answer to all these questions is affirmative. Yet, of course, the computational cost of maintaining and evolving gene libraries may make the approach infeasible. In this paper, we outline a method for a principled evaluation of each feature. We include some preliminary results suggesting that option 2 is somewhat easier to achieve than option 1. Our work is intended to shed light on the sort of real world problems for which gene libraries should be considered.

We start by reviewing the relevant biology. We then consider the criteria outlined above in more detail before presenting our preliminary results. The considerable body of related work is reviewed before we make our concluding remarks.

2   Biological Metaphor

In this section, we give sufficient biological background for the purposes of this paper. This is not intended to be an exhaustive review; the interested reader is directed to sources such as Kuby [11] or Travers [16].

In the human immune system (HIS), gene libraries are used to generate both T cell (T cell receptor; TCR) and B cell (antibody) diversity. Antibody molecules are composed of four *immunoglobulin* chains; two identical pairs of heavy and light chains. Each chain contains a variable region which determines its antigen specificity; the DNA encoding this region is constructed by sampling from so-called V, D and J *gene libraries* (see Table 1); usually one from each, although sometimes multiple D segments can be sampled [16]. This DNA mixing occurs during B cell maturation, during which further diversity is encouraged by *junctional flexibility*, *P-additions* and *N-additions* (insertion or deletion of base pairs between gene library segments). Of course, such variability inevitably means many such generated gene sections are unviable. There are two interesting mechanisms to counter this. Firstly, there are two 'flavours' of light chain, κ and λ. If a viable κ gene segment cannot be built, then an attempt is made to build λ (thus typically κ is more prevalent than λ). Secondly, being diploid, B cells have 2 chromosomes for each immunoglobulin chain type. This allows two attempts to generate valid chain DNA (although a successful combination suppresses further attempts; this is *allelic exclusion*). Nevertheless, only about 10% of the pre-B cells in the bone marrow progress to maturity. Once a B cell is mature, however, it is immunologically committed[1].

The gene library mechanism appears at first to be wasteful: to make an immunoglobulin variable region of 223 amino acids we supply enough DNA to

---

[1] In fact there is a further choice to be made, at *transcription* (DNA to mRNA) time, about which C region to choose. However this *isotype switching* mechanism does not affect the antigen specificity, so it is not considered here.

encode 11,975 amino acids. However this redundancy enables 2M combinations (which if stored linearly would require 2M × 223 = 446M). Combinatorial diversity is further enhanced by the join errors described above, and by *somatic hypermutation,* in which B cells activated by antigens are stimulated to divide with a mutation rate of about 0.001 per base pair per generation (this compares to a spontaneous mutation rate of about 10^{-8}). To encode 223 amino acids needs 669 base pairs, so this mutation rate is expected to change one base pair almost every division. Estimates of total antibody diversity vary from 10^{10} [11] to 10^{14} [16], with somatic hypermutation pushing the number even higher to maybe 10^{16} [7]. The expressed diversity is, of course, likely to be somewhat lower because not all combinations are equally likely (in the mouse, some are actually disallowed). One assumes also that some variants are never expressed because they are autoreactive. Finally, it should be noted that only a subset (estimated 10^6-10^7) of these types are actually represented at any one time.

TCR diversity is similar, although a larger number of J segments (61) leads to a much higher gene library diversity, 10^{18} [16]. TCRs also do not undergo somatic hypermutation (perhaps a protection against generating autoreactive T cells). So for TCRs the diversity is more heavily germline encoded; conversely, some non-human species rely much more on somatic mechanisms.

Table 1. Human antibody diversity generation These numbers are taken from a single individual and are not the same for all individuals. The first three rows show the size of each V, D and J gene, and the number of genes in each library. It is a simple matter to sum the gene lengths to arrive at the total number of amino acids in an immunoglobulin chain variable region (4th row, first 2 columns). Multiplying the library size and gene length shows the number of amino acids encoded in each gene library (e.g. 4971 = 51×94 + 27×3 + 6×16). Combining the gene library sizes (final row) shows the diversity generated from each library (e.g. 8262=51×27×6). Finally, using both light chain alternatives in combination gives the expected total diversity (1982880 = (8262×200) + (8262×120)). Note that since 3 base pairs encode one amino acid, you should multiply by 3 to get the number of base pairs. Adapted from Kuby [11].

Library	Gene length (amino acids encoded)		Gene library size (number of gene segments)			Total
	Heavy	Light	Heavy	Light κ	Light λ	
V	94	97	51	40	31	
D	3	N/a	27	0	0	
J	16	13	6	5	4	
(amino acids)	113	110	4971	3945	3059	**11,975**
(combinations)			8262	200	120	**2,643,840**

However, even this extraordinary diversity may not be sufficient for all possible antigen encounters. In principle, since there are 20 amino acids, there are 20223 = 10390 ways of expressing the variable regions of an antibody. This renders almost negligible the antibody diversity expressible by an individual, even if we multiply this by every human on the planet. Bakács et al [28] concur, and point out that antigenic variation is a hallmark of several RNA viruses, thus providing a fast moving target. Yet we seem able to mount an immune response to pretty much any foreign molecule, "even those…never having appeared before in evolutionary time" [7]. One simplification is that vast swathes of this antibody shape space will be identical, or topologically infeasible, or simply non-functional. So it would seem reasonable that gene libraries bias the antibody creation process towards creating viable immunoglobulin chains. But we suspect that some antigen shapes are simply more likely than others, due to the energetics of protein folding. Perhaps gene libraries may help to focus the antibody creation process into the most promising areas of shape space, a possibility suggested by the fact that multiple antibody types bind a single antigen [7], and the finding that V region genes are clustered into related families and clans [16].

Taking inspiration from this account, we can see that gene libraries, shaped by evolution, are used to guide the B cell creation process to create antibodies with a good chance of success, while preserving the ability to respond to novel threats. This has obvious parallels in AIS, in instances where random creation does not scale, or where memory enabled by lifetime learning mechanisms is not sufficiently persistent.

3 What Are Gene Libraries for?

3.1 Enhanced Coverage

The most naïve way of looking at antibody creation is a way of covering a multidimensional area (antigen space). If one uses gene libraries to bias the creation process, then it is easy to see that evolution should encourage the emergence of diverse gene libraries, which perform some coarse grain mapping on antigen space. Indeed, Oprea and Forrest [21] found precisely this mechanism at work. Yet in the real world, such a mechanism is highly expensive. If all one wants to do is to cover a well understood antigen space (say, binary strings with Hamming distance matching), then an enforced distribution would be the simplest mechanism. There are well understood algorithms for dealing with other types of spaces, for example Wierzchon's schema match [26] for r-contiguous matching.

Of course, generally the task is to map antigen space *while avoiding self*. This is a more involved task, yet even here there are simple algorithms that might do a superior job to gene libraries, particularly when computational cost is taken into account. For example, de Haeseleer's greedy algorithm [6] generates a number of non-self 'templates' and uses these to create an antibody which binds to the most unmatched antigens. Singh [23] extended this algorithm to deal with non-binary alphabets. A somewhat simpler approach is Ayara's NSMutation [2] which generates detectors randomly, mutating those that match self. Gonzalez [12] uses idiotypic suppression to maximise antibody diversity. Finally, Wierzchon's schema matching algorithm [26] can be used to effectively generate self-avoiding, non-self-matching antibodies [25].

This, then, provides a convenient place to start our investigation into gene library function. We propose a comparative study on these algorithms in order to find what characteristics of a real world problem (if any) would suggest the use of gene libraries might be advantageous. It should be noted that complete coverage will almost certainly be impossible in presence of self [6]. An advantage of using a binary string representation with r-contiguous bits is that one can work out the theoretical optimum [26] and compare the coverage obtained by any one individual against it.

3.2 Avoiding Self

As mentioned in the last section, simple coverage is probably not a sophisticated enough aim for gene libraries. The avoidance of self is a different slant on the same problem. In the HIS, this is essential to protect against autoimmune reactions. Whilst it is true that there is a negative selection mechanism operating in the HIS, it would clearly be beneficial for the creation process to have a bias *against* creating self reactive antibodies. In the context of AIS, this amounts to making the creation process cheaper. In other words, the number of attempts to create a valid (i.e. not self-reactive) antibody should be considerably *less* using gene libraries than a naïve random approach, which is exponential in the size of self [8]. Of course the benefit may still not justify the computational expense of using gene libraries. Also, alternative algorithms (see the last section) may be a rather cheaper way of attaining the same benefit. Thus, the cost of avoiding self is a plausible evaluation function which we can use as an additional comparison point.

3.3 Mapping Antigens

Antigens correlate to things we want to detect, or classify. In a sense, they are 'points of interest' in the non-self space. If we accept that it is impossible (given the computational resources, i.e. number of antibodies available) to map all of non-self space, even in principle, then it clearly behoves the system to bias antibody creation towards these areas of interest.

This, now, starts to move towards more realistic scenarios. Imagine, for example, a document classifier that identifies 'interesting' documents. Given a training set of interesting and uninteresting documents it will generate a set of detectors to identify, and generalise from, interesting documents. Such documents tend to form clusters in non-self space. A gene library would bias the creation process so that rather than fumbling blindly in non-self space, antibody creation would be guided towards the clusters of interest.

A more subtle point is that gene libraries provide a long term memory. Say, for example, that a set of randomly created antibodies are subject to clonotypic learning, such that they cover the clusters in one particular training set but not all clusters ever seen. Gene libraries provide a way of remembering past encounters so that antibody creation is more likely to match novel clusters which are nevertheless similar to those seen some time ago. This motivation has guided several previous implementations of the gene library metaphor [14,20]. In a variant of this approach, gene libraries have been used as metaphor in an email filtering system [31]. Here words found in "interesting" emails were archived, then during the mutation stage of clonal selection, a word (gene) chosen to be mutated was replaced by one chosen from the archive, rather than subjected to random perturbation.

Of course, evolving these gene libraries will take time, during which a great deal of random searching (or searching guided by a cheap heuristic) might have taken place. Whether the trade-off is worth it is a moot point, and will depend greatly on the problem characteristics. For example, there is a choice about whether to use self; if so, the task is transformed into a 3-class problem (self, non-self, don't care). Another consideration is the evaluation function, for example: number of antigens successfully detected after X generations; number of antibodies created before all antigens detected; average cost before 1st antigen detected. Our work should provide some principled guidance for AIS practitioners.

3.4 Winning the Evolutionary Arms Race

A further consideration is that in the real world, antigens (i.e. whatever you want to map) are unlikely to stay still. Mapping dynamic antigens is a more complex problem, akin to non-stationary landscapes, for which problem generators [24] are available. The species-level memory afforded by gene libraries could prove to be a boon here, since they may evolve to track a moving target. This assumes that gene libraries can 'keep up' with the rate of antigen change, of course; a point illustrated by Oprea and Forrest's work [21].

A further complication is that antigens may be moving purposefully, to avoid detection by the immune system. For example, a sensible strategy for an antigen is to get close to self, ideally within a 'cove' or 'hole' [6]. Such possibilities can be explored using coevolutionary models, and this is a major focus of our ongoing research. Interestingly, Gathercole and Ross [10] use a predator-prey model for effective coverage, which links in nicely with our original scenario.

What practical implications could such work have? In almost all real world problems the target is constantly moving (for example, the definition of: an 'interesting' or 'relevant' document; an anomalous network event; a suspected fraudulent mortgage application, a spam email). Could gene libraries provide the basis for a more robust, adaptive and responsive system?

4   Implementing Gene Libraries

The preceding discussion describes the areas where we intend to focus our investigation. As a validation scenario, we repeated Forrest's canonical experiments on self/non-self discrimination [8]. In this paper, the authors use a random generate and test algorithm to create a set of detectors covering non-self with some desired (low) probability of failure. They used a simple binary string universe with self, non-self and an r-contiguous matching measure. For example, using a 32 bit string with 16 self strings and r set to 8, 105 attempts were needed to create 46 detectors which between them covered about 90% of non-self space.

It is worth commenting a little on this experimental setup. The r-contiguous matching function is often argued to be more biologically plausible than Hamming distance, although this view is strongly criticised by Timmis & Freitas [9]. In fact, Forrest et al., who pioneered the metric, call it "[an] arbitrary decision [made] in order to simplify the mathematical analysis". As an example, they calculate the chance of 2 random strings matching as roughly 0.05 using the parameters above.

In an elegant paper, Wierzchon [26] extended this mathematical analysis to sets of detectors. In general, non-self space is likely to contain 'holes' that cannot be detected [6]; these are regions where matching detectors would also match self. Wierzchon showed how to calculate the number of holes for any given self set, giving a upper bound to the amount of non-self coverage possible. In a similar vein Esponda, Forrest and Helman have analysed the trade-offs between postivie and negative selection for the r-chunks matching function [29], arguing that this is a prefrable matching function, and Stibor, Bayarou and Eckert have investigated the propoerties of this matching function as the underlying alphabet is extended beyond the binary case [30].

The evaluation measure is also important. In fact, we would say it is key to understanding the system. The evaluation function in some sense <u>defines the task</u>. One measure is the <u>ease of avoiding self</u>, or equivalently the cost of generating a system. The <u>detection rate</u>, in contrast, measures the performance of the generated system. It can be calculated either for a fixed number of detectors (number of antigens matched divided by number of antibodies in system), or for a fixed number of attempts to generate a detector.

Following Forrest then, we used a set of antigens (sampled from a fixed population). The antibodies are subject to negative selection, but in our case rather than employing random creation we create the antibodies from gene libraries. The overall algorithm is as follows, where TERMINATION_CRITERION occurs when NR non-self antibodies have been generated, or the full set of combinations has been tested, whichever is sooner.

```
Create self
Create non-self
LOOP foreach generation
   LOOP foreach individual (= gene library)
      While (TERMINATION_CRITERION not met)
      DO
         Choose genes from gene libraries
         Create antibody
         IF match self THEN destroy
      END WHILE
      Evaluate fitness of individual
   END LOOP
   Do selection/recombination/mutation of individuals
   Do replacement of individuals
END LOOP
```

4.1 Some Preliminary Results

We conducted a series of experiments looking at the effort required (number of antibodies generated) to produce a set of NR (= 46) detectors, and the coverage they provide of the non-self region, as defined by its complementarity to a randomly created set of 128 "self" strings. The parameters are shown in table 2.

Initially we considered random generation to verify that our system was equivalent to Forrest's. For 1000 repetitions we generated strings at random until we had created a set of 1024 non-self strings (i.e., not matching the self region), noting the total number of strings created (NS_Attempts). We then generated antibodies at random, discarding those which matched self until we had NR detectors, again noting the effort required (number of antibodies created, NR0). Finally we measured the coverage provided by the set of detectors, calculated as the percentage of the non-self set which were matched by at least one of the detectors. These results are shown in Table 3. The coverage values obtained are higher than those Forrest noted, but their measure was slightly different – they changed one eight-bit block of one string from self and saw whether any of the detectors matched the mutated string.

Table 2. Parameters and choices for our experiments

Parameter	Choice	Comments
Antigen representation	Binary string	32 bits
Antibody representation	Binary string	32 bits
Matching function	r-contiguous	8 bits
Antibody creation	Try a maximum of LC times from gene library or until NR antibodies created	LC =8000; NR =46 No mutation at this stage.
Fitness evaluation	% antigens matched from f antigens sampled randomly from non-self space.	f = 1024. Static; not changed between individuals or generations
Self	S randomly created strings.	s = 128. Static; not changed between individuals or generations
Genotype	20V11, 20D10, 20J11 LC = 20×20×20 = 8000	20V11: V library has 20 genes each with 11 bits.
GA parameters	Mutation: 0.01 per bit Crossover: 0.1 one point Selection: Binary Tournament Replacement: generational, no elitism Population size: 128 Learning: 500 generations	Tournament selection Avoids many problems with fitness-proportionate selection
Fitness of an individual	See below	

Table 3. Results of Random Antibody Generation

Measure	Min	Max	Mean	Std.Dev	Skewness
NS_Attempts	433,846	1,543,945	777,525.3	147027	0.718
NR0	16,863	80,105	35135.37	8386.91	0.803
Coverage	96.68	99.8	98.67	0.46	-0.61

The values for NR0 are similar – they reported a mean of 34,915 with a standard deviation of 8513.

Next, we considered the effects of evolving gene libraries. During the evolution, each population member was evaluated as follows. First, a random permutation of the LC possible antibodies was generated. The antibodies were then created and tested for matches against self in this order, until either the number of detectors created (ND) equalled NR, or all possibilities had been exhausted (NR0 = LC). In addition to ND and NR0, the efficiency and coverage were calculated and the mean per generation noted, defined as:

$$Efficiency = \frac{ND}{NR} * \frac{(LC - NR0)}{(LC - NR)} , \ Coverage = \frac{match(NonSelf)}{all(NonSelf)} *100\%$$

We considered three different fitness functions to be maximised: efficiency, coverage, and a equal linear combination of the two. Preliminary experiments used a simpler version of efficiency, which discarded individuals which could not produce the full set of NR detectors. This proved to be highly ineffective since in the early generations many population members had ND < NR and so were assigned fitness

0.0, removing any fitness gradients and preventing evolution. For each fitness function we conducted 25 runs, each using a different set of self and non-self, but the same set of seeds were used across the fitness functions to avoid the possibility of one seeing "easy" or "hard" sets of self/ non-self strings.

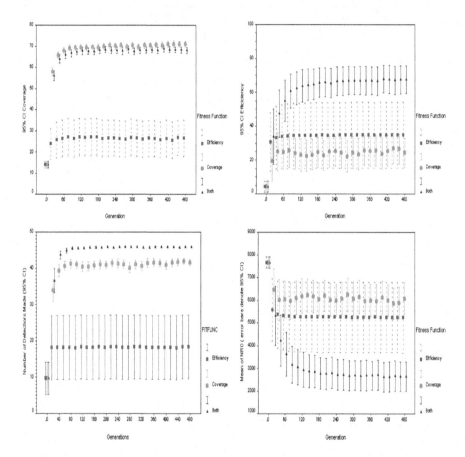

Fig. 1. Evolution of metrics under different fitness functions: Coverage (top left), Efficiency (top right), Number of detectors made: ND (Bottom left), Effort: NR0 (bottom right). Markers are for mean over 25 runs, with error bars showing 95% confidence interval for mean.

Figure 1 shows the evolution of the metrics considered under the three different fitness functions. From this figure we can make the following observations:

- Evolution solely under the influence of avoiding self (efficiency) produces results which are highly variable and are, on average poor. Closer examination shows that this is because around half of the runs cannot produce solutions providing many, let alone the full complement of, detectors.

- Evolution under the influence solely of coverage of non-self, reaches around 70% coverage, but produces less detectors (ND ~40) and uses considerable effort to produce them (NR0 ~6000).
- Evolution under the combined influence of efficiency and coverage quickly learns to produce NR detectors at low cost (NR0 < 3000), while reaching similar levels of coverage (maximum recorded 77.2%, mean over last 400 generations 68.03% with std. deviation 3.06). Clearly in this case the GA is managing to evolve gene libraries which efficiently avoid self and cover the non-self regions.

In each case evolution has nearly stopped by the 100th generation. Taking the results for the combined fitness function, and sampling every tenth of the last four hundred generations gives us 25 runs × 40 samples = 1000 samples to compare with the random results. Statistical analysis using a variety of non-parametric tests confirms that the coverage is worse than the random case (68% vs 98%), but that the effort required to avoid self is considerably (tenfold) lower.

4.2 Evaluation and Extensions

It would appear that the use of evolved gene libraries can produce significant improvements in terms of the efficient generation of antibodies which do not match self, but that the resultant coverage of the non-self regions is clearly not uniform. One possibility is that the gene libraries are in fact modelling self, or more accurately its inverse (in the r-contiguous matching sense). Another is that during the initial phase of evolution fitness gains are made by improving efficiency, but that diversity is lost, so that coverage does not improve as much. These will be tested in future work by incorporating explicit diversity preservation measures into the genetic algorithm.

To investigate whether gene libraries could produce reasonable coverage, we simplified the gene libraries so that there was only one library (46V32). We were now able to obtain the 90% coverage reported by Forrest et al. In addition, if we allow the AIS a fixed number of attempts (NR0 =105) to generate as many detectors as it can, then the performance goes to about 95% with about 60 detectors. This, of course, amounts to using a GA to search for a set of optimal antibodies, which is rather less ambitious than a search for a set of optimal gene libraries. What is rather interesting is that similar results were obtained even without using any self. This adds weight to our supposition that the block for gene libraries is the capability of covering a large space with a small number of detectors, rather than the problem of avoiding self.

It is worth emphasising that improved results could probably be obtained by using a more sophisticated GA, or one with a larger population. We could also combine the fitness measures together using a Pareto-based approach [1]. Our parameter choices were domain led - we chose to use one-point crossover because of its positional bias: it is more likely to keep together adjacent genes than, for example, uniform crossover. The gene library fragments are coded as contiguous segments.

One problem of fitness evaluation is that there are a large number of potential antibodies to be evaluated before we get a good idea of the 'worth' of a gene library. Other authors have faced the same problem, and either limited evolutionary learning to a partial fitness measure [15] or resorted to less computationally expensive algorithms, such as hill climbing [21]. Also, the 'meaning' of a gene in a library depends on which genes it is combined with (a form of *epistasis*).

An important consideration here is the use of gene libraries for coding efficiency. As discussed above, the HIS encodes 2M combinations of 223 amino acids using 12000 amino acid coding units[2], a compression rate of 223×2M:12K = 37K:1. Our naïve gene libraries managed to encode 8000 combinations of 32 bits using 640 bits, a compression ratio of only 400:1. Clearly, there is trade-off between encoding efficiency (the most efficient being a random generator) and preservation of species memory (the extreme being 1 gene per antibody, as per our 46V32 encoding).

We made several simplifications to the biology, some of which are straightforward to explain. For example, no lifetime learning mechanism is included here; we are simply testing for the initial coverage. Further work is likely to involve a mechanism for clonotypic learning; this would be a good way to introduce a Baldwin effect which may well be essential to leverage gene library diversity and hence achieve better coverage [21]. Another example is the encoding, which was binary, rather than, say, 20 letters (for amino acids) or 4 letters (for DNA bases). The motivation here is to evaluate gene libraries in established, analytically tractable, scenarios.

Other possibilities suggest interesting areas to explore. For example, we used a static definition of self, using random selection of 128 binary strings. Different sizes of self may influence the results, as might the distribution of self (should it be clustered?). Self might also be dynamic, though in a principled way. Perhaps inter-individual variation could be captured using Gaussian perturbation, while species drift could be modelled by including self in an individual's genotype. The antigens used here consisted of 1024 randomly created strings (screened against self): an enforced uniform selection might be a more principled way to check coverage. Another possibility is to use a static, perhaps clustered definition of antigen, which could be generated from its own set of gene libraries or antigen schema. Such possibilities of course take us into the more complex scenarios introduced earlier.

5   Related Work

We make no claim to be the first researchers to look at gene libraries. That claim, at least for AIS, perhaps belongs to Stephanie Forrest's group at the University of New Mexico. Perelson et al [22] showed that gene libraries can enhance coverage. They constructed antibodies by taking segments from 4 gene libraries. Fitness was evaluated by calculating the coverage of a varying size antigen universe. Unsurprisingly, the fitness asymptotically approached random levels as the antigen universe size increased, but approached perfection as the number of antigens decreased. Their work differs from that presented here in that the matching function used was Hamming, and (more significantly) there was no 'self' to avoid. Interestingly, they experimented with both straight Hamming scores (fitness of an antibody is its closeness of match with an antigen) and thresholds (fitness of an individual is the number of antigens to which at least one antibody binds sufficiently).

---

[2] Recall an amino acid coding unit is 3 base pairs of DNA.

They also show that a modest degree of somatic (clonotypic) learning may provide a Baldwinian acceleration.

Extending this work, Hightower et al [15] investigated the evolution of effective coverage. They showed that the 'best' coverage was achieved by a high Hamming distance (spread out antibodies) – but not too high. A maximal separation actually allows gaps in coverage (analogous to gaps between disjoint spheres). Oprea & Forrest [21] showed that as the pathogen set size decreases, the structure of the gene library changes, moving from a 'coarse mapping' of antigen space towards a more focused targeting of pathogenic clusters. They also show that since gene library size increases coverage only logarithmically, it must be augmented with somatic learning.

Forrest et al [7] do not use explicit gene libraries, but they do consider bias in the antibody creation process, which they evolve to map an antigen population. Interestingly, this process requires a minimal number of antibody types to bind to a particular antigen.

Other groups have also studied gene libraries. Hart & Ross [13] used a genetic algorithm (GA) to evolve libraries for a scheduling immune system. Essentially, the gene libraries preserved useful fragments of antibody (building blocks) that could successfully be reused. The same authors [14] develop this notion by suggesting that the germline (gene library) could be 'seeded' with antibodies during learning. Coello Coello et al employ a similar approach [27]. We would suggest that such an approach is akin to having species level memory cells. Kim & Bentley [17] mention the notion of gene libraries as a way of encoding 'some knowledge of antigens'. In their companion paper [18] they model gene libraries as a single population of successful genes which are combined to form detectors. Thus the gene library evolves in parallel with AIS itself. More recently, these authors [20] have used deleted memory detectors as 'gene library' – i.e. long term memory. Kim and Bentley point out that "the fact they managed to become memory detectors at all implies that they hold valid information about non-self antigens in previous clusters".

In much of this work [13,14,17,18,20] the gene library metaphor is used as an engineering artefact rather than in the more biologically faithful way that we investigate here. Conversely, the theoretical work [7,15,21,22] is distanced from existing AIS applications (e.g. by absence of self). The current work attempts to build a bridge between the established theoretical foundations and current AIS engineering practice.

6 Conclusion and Future Directions

In this paper, we have shown that gene libraries are an interesting, and perhaps useful, tool in the AIS practitioner's repertoire. We have outlined some areas where gene libraries might help and shown how to evaluate gene libraries in each area. Our preliminary results suggest that gene libraries may not be well suited to simply enhancing coverage, and may be better employed for improving the average quality of created antibodies (here exemplified by the task of avoiding self). These results need to be extended and analysed, and we have proposed a plan for testing the gene library metaphor in progressively more complex scenarios.

References

1. Anchor, K.P., Zydallis, J.B., Gunsch G.H.,Lamont, G.B.: Extending the Computer Defense Immune System: Network Intrusion Detection with a Multiobjective Evolutionary Programming Approach. In: J. Timmis and P. J. Bentley, (eds.) Proceedings of the 1st International Conference on Artificial Immune Systems (ICARIS) Canterbury, UK. (2002) 12-21

2. Ayara, M., Timmis, J., de Lemos, R., de Castro, L.N., Duncan, R.: Negative Selection: How to Generate Detectors. In: J. Timmis and P.J. Bentley (Eds.) 1st International Conference on Artificial Immune Systems, University of Kent at Canterbury, September 2002. (2002) 89-98

3. Blake, C.L., Merz, C.J.: UCI Repository of machine learning databases [http://www.ics.uci.edu/~mlearn/MLRepository.html]. Irvine, CA: University of California, Department of Information and Computer Science. (1998) Accessed 25 April 2005.

4. Burnet, F.M. (1959) The clonal selection theory of immunity. Nashville, TN: Vanderbilt University Press

5. de Castro, L.N., Timmis, J.: Artificial Immune Systems: A New Computational Approach. Springer-Verlag, London UK (2002)

6. D'haeseleer P., Forrest, S., Helman, P.: An Immunological Approach to Change Detection: Algorithms, Analysis and Implications. In: Proceedings of the 1996 IEEE Symposium on Computer Security and Privacy (1996)

7. Forrest, S., Javornik, B., Smith, R.E., Perelson, A. S.: Using genetic algorithms to explore pattern recognition in the immune system. Evolutionary Computation, Vol. 1, No. 3 (1993), 191-211.

8. Forrest, S., Perelson, A.S., Allen, L., Cherukuri, R.: Self-nonself discrimination in a computer. In: Proceedings of the 1994 IEEE Symposium on Research in Security and Privacy, Los Alamitos, CA: IEEE Computer Society Press. (1994) 202-212

9. Freitas, A., Timmis, J.: Revisiting the Foundations of Artificial Immune Systems: A Problem Oriented Perspective. In: Timmis, J., Bentley, P., Hart, E. (Eds.) Proceedings of the 2nd International Conference on Artificial Immune Systems. Lecture Notes in Computer Science Vol 2787 Springer-Verlag, Berlin Heidelberg New York (2003) 229-241

10. Gathercole, C. Ross, P.: Dynamic Training Subset Selection for Supervised Learning in Genetic Programming. In: Davidor, Schwefel and Manner (eds.): PPSN III: Proceedings of the 3rd Conference on Parallel Problem Solving from Nature. Lecture Notes in Computer Science, Vol. 866. Springer-Verlag, Berlin Heidelberg New York (1994) 312—321

11. Goldsby, R.A., Kindt, T.J., Osborne, B.A., Kuby, J.: "Immunology" W H Freeman, New York 5th edition (2003)

12. González, F., Dasgupta, D.: Combining Negative Selection and Classification Techniques for Anomaly Detection. In: Proceedings of the Congress on Evolutionary Computation, Honolulu, Hawaii May (2002) 705-710

13. Hart, E., Ross, P.: An Immune System Approach to Scheduling in Changing Environments. In: W.Banzhaf, J.Daida, A.E.Eiben, M.H.Garzon, V.Honavar, M.Jakiela, R.E.Smith (Eds.) Proceedings of Genetic and Evolutionary Computation Conference (GECCO) July 13-17 Morgan Kaufmann (1999) 1559-1566

14. Hart, E., Ross, P.: The Evolution and Analysis of a Potential Antibody Library for Job-Shop Scheduling. In: New Ideas in Optimisation. D. Corne, M.Dorigo & F. Glover (eds), K. McGraw-Hill, London. (1999) 185-202

15. Hightower, R., Forrest, S., Perelson, A.S.: The evolution of emergent organization in immune system gene libraries. In: Proceedings of the Sixth International Conference on Genetic Algorithms, Los Altos, CA. Eshelman L.J. (Ed.) Morgan-Kauffman, San Francisco, CA (1995) 344-350
16. Janeway, C.A., Travers, P., Walport, M., Shlomchik, M.: "Immunobiology: The immune systems in health and disease" Garland Publishing, New York. 5th edition (2001)
17. Kim, J., Bentley, P., The Human Immune System and Network Intrusion Detection. In: 7th European Congress on Intelligent Techniques and Soft Computing (EUFIT '99), Aachen, Germany, September 13- 19. (1999)
18. Kim, J., Bentley, P.: The Artificial Immune Model for Network Intrusion Detection. In: 7th European Congress on Intelligent Techniques and Soft Computing (EUFIT'99), Aachen, Germany, September 13- 19. (1999)
19. Kim, J. and Bentley, P. J.: Evaluating Negative Selection in an Artificial Immune System for Network Intrusion Detection. In: Genetic and Evolutionary Computation Conference 2001 (GECCO-2001), San Francisco, July 7-11, 2001. (2001) 1330 - 1337
20. Kim, J., Bentley, P. J.: A Model of Gene Library Evolution in the Dynamic Clonal Selection Algorithm. In: Proceedings of the First International Conference on Artificial Immune Systems (ICARIS) Canterbury, pp., September 9-11, 2002. (2002) 175-182
21. Oprea, M., Forrest, S.: Simulated evolution of antibody libraries under pathogen selection. In: Proceedings of the 1998 IEEE International Conference on Systems, Man and Cybernetics, San Diego, CA (1998)
22. Perelson, A.S., Hightower, R., Forrest, S. "Evolution and somatic learning in V-region genes. Research in Immunology 147 (1996) 202-208
23. Singh S.: Anomaly detection using negative selection based on the r-contiguous matching rule. In: J. Timmis and P. J. Bentley, (eds.) Proceedings of the 1st International Conference on Artificial Immune Systems (ICARIS) Canterbury, UK. (2002) 99-106
24. Spears.W. (contact) Repository of Test Problem Generators. Available at: http://evonet.lri.fr/evoweb/resources/software/record.php?id=393 Accessed 22 April 2005
25. Wierzchoń, S.T.: Generating Optimal Repertoire of Antibody Strings in an Artificial Immune System. In M. Klopotek, M. Michalewicz and S. T. Wierzchon (eds.) Intelligent Information Systems. Advances in Soft Computing Series of Physica-Verlag/Springer Verlag, Heidelberg/New York, Physica-Verlag. (2000) 119-133
26. Wierzchoń, S. Deriving a concise description of non-self patterns in an artificial immune system. In: New Learning Paradigms in Soft Computing Physica-Verlag (2002) 438-458
27. Coello Coello, C. A., Rivera, D. C., Cortés, N. C.: Use of an Artificial Immune System for Job Shop Scheduling. In: J. Timmis, P. J. Bentley, E. Hart (eds.) Proceedings of the 2nd International Conference on Artificial Immune Systems (ICARIS) Edinburgh, UK. (2003) 1 – 10
28. Bakács, T., Szabados, T., Varga, L., Tusnády, G.: Axioms of mathematical immunology. Studia Scientiarum Mathematicarum Hungarica 38 (2001) 13-43
29. Esponda, F., Forrest, S., Helman, P.: A formal framework for positive and negative detection schemes. IEEE Transactions on Systems, Man and Cybernetics Part B 34 (2004) 357–373
30. Stibor, T., Bayarou, K., Eckert, C.: An investigation of R-chunk detector generation on higher alphabets. In: LNCS 3102. (2004) 26–30
31. Secker A and Freitas A and Timmis J (2003). AISEC: An Artificial Immune System for E-mail Classification. Proc. Congress on Evolutionary Computation pp 131-139. IEEE

Why the First Glass of Wine Is Better Than the Seventh

Hugues Bersini

IRIDIA – ULB, CP 194/6, 50, av. Franklin Roosevelt, 1050 Bruxelles, Belgium
bersini@ulb.ac.be

Abstract. The response to the title would simply be that the state of the organism has changed between the first and the seventh glass and that, before the seventh, this state was much closer to some kind of "homeostatic limit". Although the external impact i.e. the glass of wine is identical in both cases, the reaction of the receptive organism might be different, depending on its current state: accept the first glass then reject the seventh. It is the couple "wine and current state of the organism" which is important here and not just the wine. Introducing this paper, I will attempt to clarify the famous self-nonself controversy by referring attentively to the debate which took place in 1997 between more traditional immunologists (Langman) and less ones (Dembic, Coutinho), and by proposing a very simple and illustrative computer simulation allowing a beginning of "formalization" of the self-assertion perspective. I will conclude by discussing the practical impact that such a perspective should have on the conception of "intrusion detectors" for vulnerable systems such as computers, and why a growing number of immunologists, like Varela twenty years ago, plead for going beyond this too narrow vision of immune system as "intrusions detector" to rather privilege its "homeostatic character".

1 Introduction: The Self-nonself Debate

The response to the title would simply be that the state of the organism has changed between the first and the seventh glass and that, before the seventh, this state was much closer to some kind of "homeostatic limit". Obviously, among other things, the swallowing of all precedent glasses i.e. the history of the drinking organism must be taken into account in order to assess the effect of this last glass. Although the external impact i.e. the glass of wine is identical in both cases, the reaction of the receptive organism might be different, depending on its current state: accept then reject. It is the couple "wine and current state of the organism" which is important here and not just the wine. The wine is neither self nor non-self, dangerous or inoffensive as such, but rather pleases or disturbs the drinker as a function of his stomach. An important question logically follows: "would you prevent yourself from drinking a first glass of wine, aware that the seventh could be much more harmful". What a pity and what an enormous "false positive" this would be. Such a rejection would be useless in the first place. But even worse, this rejected impact (rejected because it can be hurtful in some particular context), could in other circumstances play a positive curing effect (wine is famous for that). Not taking the state into account can lead to too conservative protection policy, up until missing some curing opportunities.

C. Jacob et al. (Eds.): ICARIS 2005, LNCS 3627, pp. 100–111, 2005.

In 1997, a very interesting, long and vivid debate took place among immunologists, some more classical and others proposing alternative views such as the "danger" model (Matzinger [14]), the "integrity" one (Dembic [10]), together with models around the idiotypic networks (Varela, Coutinho, Stewart [21][24]) (this debate is available on the Web at http://www.cig.salk.edu/BICD_140_W99/debate/). Among other issues, one very warmly discussed was the classical self-nonself distinction and the importance given by immunologists to "detection and recognition" processes. To quote this debate moderator Kenneth Schaffner: "All postings thus far accept a major role for the immune system in detecting and eliminating pathogens, while not attacking the body or the immune system. In recognizing some things as "to be eliminated" and others as not, is this tantamount to an implicit definition of the self-nonself distinction?". Even stronger, the following claim of Rod Langman (an immunologist more on the classical side): "I see no escape from the conclusion that all biodestructive protective mechanisms will have to do something that can be described as a self-nonself or dangerous-nondangerous or integrate-nonintegrate, etc. discrimination based on specific recognition and exercise of the biodestructive consequence of recognition". According to him, all the debate boils down to a simple wordy issue, a semantic game, that provides no better way to construe the immune functions. Since many years, I have tried to encourage researchers in AIS, above all if interested in "intrusions detection", to watch more attentively for these alternative views yet having a marginal impact [4] [6]. It is time now to attempt a more pedagogical effort to help to better understand the differences between these positions and above all the impact these differences could have further on their practical developments. Exactly as it is for the immune system, the state of our research community might be today more mature to better receive and echo these once marginal voices.

I believe with many others (Varela, Coutinho, Stewart, Tauber, Cohen, Dembic) that the self-nonself debate largely goes beyond a simple labeling issue and that the real focus is not so much on defining what is "self", which clearly, as Langman rightly pointed, can be substituted by "non-dangerous" or any synonymous for a homeostatic viable entity. The problem resides much more in the nature and the characterization of the "yes/no" dichotomy. How does it arise? Is this dichotomy just dependent on some proper features of the external impact, like accepted by the whole AIS community (who majoritarily engeneerizes his immune knowledge in a classification system separating data distributed in a space bounded by axis corresponding to external features) or, like I rather defend, is it dependent also on the state of the impacted system at the moment of the impact (making this classification much more problematic)? Is an impact dangerous per se or dangerous because the system at the moment of the impact is much more vulnerable than it usually is? I believe the second interpretation to be a more correct way to see things, both for living organisms but equally so for computers. To quote Tauber [22,23] (a very convincing advocate of the alternative views): "The meaning of a given antigen is governed by the complex interplay of the endogenous and exogenous factors in which it appears" and Cohen [8]: "Rejection of infectious agents depends more on the site and circumstances of the infected tissue than it does on the identity of the infectious agent"

Polly Matzinger, today one of the best known critics of the self-nonself dichotomy of immunology, and exerting a recent influence on some AIS developments [1] [7], remains quite ambiguous on this specific issue. It is clear that the problem with self and nonself lies in the determination, namely the nature and the location, of the frontier. What she proposes is to maintain the duality, i.e. the immune system keeps two ways of being in response to external impact: defensive and tolerant, but no more depending on a physical evasive frontier to cross. She insists in getting rid of the self-nonself discrimination as such but to substitute it with an alternative dichotomy: dangerous/inoffensive. The fact that this move at first simply consists of a semantic substitution makes a lot of immunologist very skeptic against Matzinger's position. According to Janeway (another famous classical immunologist): "The problem with this model is its inherent tautology ... The immune response is induced by a danger signal but the danger signal is defined as just about anything that can induce an immune response" [15]

To clarify the issue, there is no better way than taking advantage of the metaphor exploited by Matzinger herself in an interview she gave to advocate her position (in http://www.info-implants.com/Walt/01.html): "Let me use an analogy to explain it. Imagine a community in which the police accept anyone they met during elementary school and kill any new migrant. That's the self-nonself model. In the danger model, tourists and immigrants are accepted, until they start breaking windows. Only then do the police move to eliminate them. In fact, it doesn't matter if the window breaker is a foreigner or a member of the community.... In the danger model, the police wander around, waiting for an alarm signaling that something is doing damage. If an immigrant enters without doing damage, the white cells simply continue to wander, and after a while, the harmless immigrant becomes part of the community". Taking that metaphor literally, it is obvious that what she presents as an alternative view is not really so since the familiar/foreign dichotomy just gives place to the gentle/nasty one, the invader's feature "country of origin" being simply replaced by the feature "basic personal psychology". A real departure from the classical dichotomy would be for the migrant to make the choice between adopting a gentle or a nasty attitude depending also and perhaps essentially on the internal state of the community at the time he comes in. Such a state will obviously depend on the presence of the previous migrants and thus on the whole flux of them since the origin of this community. However, it will also depend on other internal aspects of this community: the lodging capacity, the social welfare, economical inequalities and the usual police attitude, comprised the one adopted when encountering the migrants. A migrant, usually nice in many circumstances, might turn out to be angry and destructive in very specific contexts.

Presented as she presents it, this Matzinger's vision of what is dangerous or not is not such an exciting one, because it still demands from the system the ability to discriminate and to defend. The self-nonself frontier is simply re-designed but is maintained outside the system to protect. With such a view, the recognition ability of the immune system still plays the leading role in separating the dangerous impact from the non-dangerous one. A more interesting perspective, which would make Matzinger to integrate the circle of the radical immunologists, instigated by Varela, Coutinho and Cohen, sees the danger as a consequence of the interaction between the external impact and the current state of the immune system. In such a case, a stimulus is no more dangerous per se, but is dangerous in the current context of the immune system. An outside separation in two classes, making the immune system behaves in two ways, simply collapses. No discriminative recognition is at play any more. We remain with an immune system behaving in one only way but, depending on its current state and the nature of the impact, proposing different responses to it. For instance, a same external impact could drive the system to react differently at different times. The internal perturbation caused by the external impact, i.e. the way the internal dynamics "digests" it, is what really counts in order to locate this impact on one side or the other of the immune system. The set of the antigenic attributes is one part of the problem, the state and the history of the system since its appearance is the other key part and definitely not something easy to discriminate upon. At the end of the debate, Langman still remains skeptic and claims "My challenge is to ask whether you would consider the possibility of a set of mechanistic details and boundary conditions that offer a way of establishing a set of criteria that amount to a workable self-nonself discrimination that does not require nonself markers such as "danger", "disintegration", "inflammation", "toxicity"", whereas Dembic rightly answers that we all need to move from a discriminatory process taking place in some feature spaces whatever it is, to a new space, yet to define, that would simultaneously incorporate time and the regulatory dynamics of the system.

In the following section, a more formal reading will be proposed to support and clarify this alternative vision. I'll show that the main difference between the classical view and the new one (designated as "the self-assertion perspective" in previous works [24] [6]) asks to replace a "linear causality", where the whole immune reaction just starts from and is only conditioned by the antigenic impact, with a "circular causality", maintaining some autonomy in the immune behavior, now simply perturbed but no longer initiated from and only conditioned by the antigenic impacts. The third section will briefly recall why the well-known idiotypic network, popularized by Jerne some thirty years ago [12], was an essential but still very preliminary step on the way to this alternative vision. Since "intrusion detection" remains the main engineering use and perhaps abuse of the immune metaphor, the fourth section will describe a little computer simulation in which a complex system is being impacted from outside. A defensive mechanism built around it and aiming at preserving it inside a viability domain will be gradually learned. The simulation will show the need for the adaptive defensive mechanism to take into account not only the nature of the impact but also the state of the system at the moment of the impact. Many false positives are avoided and a finer curing attitude becomes possible. The final section will emphasize again the same shift in perspective as the one advocated many years ago. The internal homeostasis of a system to be protected goes beyond the severity of its frontiers. One needs to re-concentrate the attention on the inside of the system to the detriment of the outside, and to understand better its internal regulatory mechanisms both while isolated and in response to an impact.

2   Linear Causality vs Circular Causality

In figure 1, a very intuitive mathematical formulation will help to differentiate the two perspectives. We suppose on the left an antigenic intrusion $Ik(t)$ occurring at time t and impacting a first stage of immune cells $Xk(t+1)$. We suppose that the interaction occurs by means of some kind of structural binding between the antigen and these cells, inducing a stimulatory effect on the cells. In the right part of the figure, these latter cells Xk, in their turn, stimulate by structural binding a second stage of immune

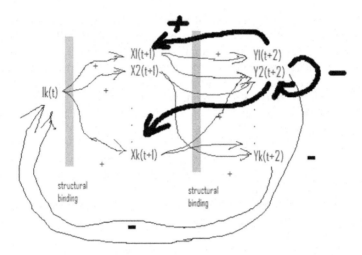

Fig. 1. Linear vs Circular causality

cells Yk(t+2). Finally these latter have the possibility to inhibit the antigen by decreasing its concentration. Without accounting for the thicker feedback arrows, this
figure depicts a linear causation in which the antigen is the initiator of the whole sequence of interaction. Everything happens in reaction to the antigen intrusion and the
precise effect will depend on the nature of the antigen, from that the classical self-
nonself distinction. Now by adding the feedback thicker arrows, a circular causality is
induced, driving the system to manifest a dynamical behavior on its own, perturbed
but now longer impelled and impressed by the antigens.

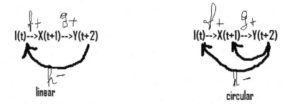

Simplifying this scheme even further, we can see how the two figures above lead
to two different mathematical dependencies. In the first linear case: $X(t+1)=f_+(I(t))$,
$Y(t+2)=g_+(X(t+1))$ and $I(t+3)=h_-(Y(t+2))$ which, by concatenating all dependencies,
gives $I(t+3)=f_+ (g_+ (h_- (I(t))))$, reducing so the becoming of the antigen to its sole intrinsic nature. In contract, in the second case: $X(t+1)=f_+(I(t),Y(t))$, $Y(t+2)=g_+(X(t+1))$
and $I(t+3)=h_-(Y(t+2))$ which, by concatenating all dependencies, gives $I(t+3)=$
$h_-(g_+(f_+(I(t),Y(t))))$ and making the future of the antigen still dependent on the state
of the impacted system at the moment of the impact, here the variable Y. The value of
this variable, depending on the previous impacts, the reaction to any antigen depends
on the whole evolution of the system, comprised all previous impacts. So the nature
of the antigen alone i.e. the structural category it fits in is far from enough to predict
what will happen to it. Only a complete knowledge of the couple (antigen, system
state) can allow predicting the antigen destiny.

3   Idiotypic Networks Show This Circular Causality

In the middle of a Nobel lecture given the 8th December 1984 in France [13], Niels Jerne discoursed on a topic he considered to be a major breakthrough in immunology: *"I shall now turn to some remarkable discoveries, made during the past years, showing that the variable regions of antibody molecules are themselves antigenic and invoke the production of anti-antibodies.... Jacques Oudin and his colleagues in Paris [18, 19], showed that ordinary antibody molecules that arise in an immunized animals are antigenic and invoke the formation of specific anti-antibodies. In other words, the variable region of an antibody molecule constitutes not only its "combining site", but also presents an antigenic profile (named its idiotype) against which anti-idiotypic can be induced in other animals."* Since Oudin's experimental finding and Jerne's enthusiastic emphasis on the existence of idiotypic network, that antibodies can mutually stimulate themselves in a way very similar to the stimulation antigen exerts on antibody has been convincingly revealed by a large set of experiments [15,16,24]. The Burnetian clonal selection theory, which describes how an antibody is selected to proliferate in response to antigen recognition, extends now to antibodies themselves that turn out to be as much selector as selected. Jerne had many reasons to be so enthusiastic, since this discovery was the first rupture with the classical linear causality, still so vivid among its immunological colleagues.

The circular causality is obvious by watching the simplest scheme below:

An antigen stimulates a first antibody Ab1 which in its turn stimulates and is stimulated (creating the circularity) by a second antibody Ab2. In the self-assertion simulation presented in [6], the program instructions changing the concentration of any antibody are:

if (low $< \alpha\Sigma_i$ affinityOfAntibodies$_i$ $+ \beta \Sigma_i$ affinityOfAntigen$_i$ $<$ high)
$$Cj(t) = Cj(t) + 1$$
else
$$Cj(t) = Cj(t) - 1$$

indicating that the concentration of any antibody $Cj(t)$ changes, not only as a function of the antigens stimulating it, but also of the other antibodies present in the network. We show in the simulation how indeed the evolution of an antigen concentration depends in part on its own characteristics but also on the evolution of the antibodies concentration and the network interactions. Despite the lack of attention and interest for this network in today immunology, many other immunological ways exist to induce this circular causality. It is enough that any cell, lymphocyte or macrophage of any sort, stimulated by the antigen, mutually stimulates themselves, to have feedback loops and memory effects in the system, relaxing the importance of the external stimuli.

4 Defending Complex Systems

The small computer simulation to be presented in the following aims at illustrating how the self-assertion perspective can lead to some practical advantages (as compared with the self-recognition one) in the construction of effective defenses for complex systems such as computer ones. The complex system to be protected here is a fully connected Hopfield network composed of 8 units:

$$x_i(t+1) = \tanh(\sum_{j=1}^{8} w_{ij} xj(t)) \text{ with } w_{ii} = 1 \text{ and } w_{ij} \text{ taken randomly in } [-0.5, 0.5]$$

This structure should be construed as a generic metaphor for complex systems since it displays a strong circular causality, each variable influencing all the others. The weights being not symmetric and the diagonal unitary, the network does not stabilize into fixed points but into cyclic attractors instead. After a long transient, we define a viability interval Vi for each variable as the interval in between the boundaries of its range of variation $[x_{imin}, x_{imax}]$. The viability domain of the whole system becomes the union of all these intervals. A viable and "healthy" system has all its variables comprised in their viable intervals. It is no longer the case as soon as one of its units leaves its interval. The mission of the whole defensive process to be described consists in maintaining viable this system.

A deleterious impact here amounts to a perturbation I_j taken randomly in [-2,2] and exerted at time t on one variable $x_j(t)$ randomly chosen:

$$x_i(t+1) = \tanh(\sum_{j=1}^{8} w_{ij}(x_j(t) + Ij))$$

As figure 2 illustrates the whole defensive strategy is organized around three types of agent: monitoring, filtering and curing agents.

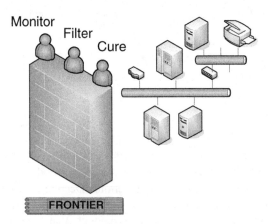

Fig. 2. The defense of complex systems organized around three types of agent: monitoring, filtering and curing

The system is experimented in two phases. During the first phase, the defensive strategy is gradually built in the presence of the monitoring agent whereas this strategy is evaluated in the second phase.

The learning phase and the role of the monitoring agent: During this phase, at each time step, an impact is exerted on the system at time t and, if the system exits its viability domain at time t+1, the couple $(I_j, x_j(t))$ is memorized in a data base as a bad impact. In the following, any impact will consist in this couple of data. The impacts are memorized with a certain granularity threshold g. Whenever a new impact arrives and makes the system unviable at t+1, this new impact will be memorized only if not similar to an existing impact. The similarity is defined by computing the Euclidean distance with the existing impacts and by checking if the result is inferior to the granularity threshold. Once the system unviable and the impact memorized, the system is reset into its original position and a new impact is tested. The learning terminates as soon as no more deleterious impacts can be memorized.

The evaluation phase and the role of the filtering agent: During this successive phase, every three time steps, an impact is exerted on the system. However, the data base learned previously, composed of the bad impacts, will be the basis of a filtering mechanism. Only if the impact is authorized, it will be allowed to perturb the system. To be authorized, the impact needs to be dissimilar (taking into account the same granularity g) from all impacts included in the learned data base.

In order to compare the self-recognition perspective with the self-assertion one, in a second set of experiments, an impact will now consist in the couple $(I_j, X(t))$. By $X(t)$, it is intended all the variables and not only the impacted one. It is now the whole state of the system (the eight variables) that is being memorized for each impact. As referred in the previous sections, the alternative vision of the immune system takes the state at the moment of the impact to be as important as the nature of the impact itself. In both cases, following the learning phase, the system is fully safe; none of the authorized impacts can throw the system away from its viability zone. During the evaluation phase, the filtering is playing a perfect role, no false negative occurs. The results are shown in figure 3. In the graph, the number of authorized impacts is shown as a function of the number of impacts memorized in the data base, both for the self-recognition and the self-assertion cases. This data base grows as a function of the granularity. The smaller the granularity, the bigger the number of impacts to be memorized is in order to cover the whole set of possibilities. It resorts clearly that the more precise the learning is (i.e. the smaller the granularity) the more impacts are being authorized.

However, the most interesting result lies in the comparison of the two curves. The self-assertion curve remains always above the self-recognition one, meaning that the first strategy avoids many false positive. The explanation is obvious. By ignoring the state, it is enough for one impact to make the system unviable, independently on its current state, to prevent any similar impact. Whereas by adding the state information, only for specific value of the state will a same I_j be prevented from entering the system again. It is the simulation replica of the story of the glass of wine. Taking the state into account allows the defensive strategy to be much less conservative, some glasses are allowed others not.

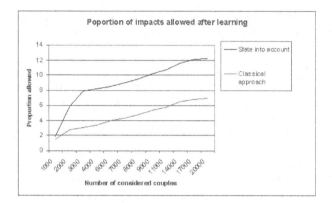

Fig. 3. The proportion of authorized impacts as a function of the number of memorized impacts during the learning phase. This figure compares the self-recognition approach (with no account for the state) and the self-assertion one (where the state is taken into account).

Beyond the avoidance of many false positives, taking the state into account allows some impacts to play an extra curing role. This curing part, once again, takes place in two successive phases: the learning and the evaluation phases.

<u>The learning phase and the role of the monitoring agent:</u> At each time step, the system is set in a random but non-viable state. Thus an impact is exerted on it. If that impact makes the system viable in the next time step, this impact is memorized as a curing impact and the couple $(I_j, X(t))$ is added in the data base. The learning terminates when no more curing impact can be added in the data base.

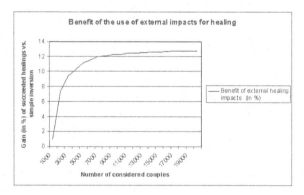

Fig. 4. This graph shows the percentage of time that the application of a curing impact, retrieved from the learned date base, can compensate for the failure of the "inversion strategy".

<u>The evaluation phase and the role of the curing agent:</u> We have supposed a first very intuitive default curing strategy in the case the system exits out of its viability zone. It just consists in inverting the previous impact and impacting the same variable again but now in this "inverse" way. The intuition behind is that in systems not knowing

anything about the potential cure coming from the precedent learning phase, there must always exist a "safety procedure" that can take very urgent but not accurate recovery action. However, as the figure 4 shows, this rough recovery strategy works for only 70% of the cases. An additional cure can be tried that consists in searching in the data base an impact which, for such state condition of the system, was able during the learning phase to bring the system back to a viable situation. In the best case, 19000 memorized impacts, the figure shows that an improvement of 13% is possible with respect to the sole "inversion strategy".

The cure can consist in fact in regulating some internal variables of the system, included the ones not directly impacted. An impact exerted on one connected unit can re-equilibrate the system after the perturbation exerted on another specific unit. The graph also shows that the bigger the data base the more successful is the curing strategy since more and more information is obtained on the curing potentialities.

5 Conclusions and Still Open Perspectives

At one point of the debate referred previously, Ephraim Fuchs, a close colleague of Matzinger, pertinently says: "It is easy to see how the self-nonself distinction was important during an era in which the major challenges to human health were viral and bacterial infections. Now, however, we have to deal with problems like autoimmune disease, cancer, and transplants … It is difficult to see how a self-nonself paradigm would be of much assistance in understanding these phenomena". And Rod Langman, although the most attached at this distinction, surprisingly concludes by: "The organism is a complicated thing with lots of different activities going on inside. We assume that a normal organism is in a state of homeostasis, under the control of many regulators. These regulators have to know when the system is becoming disordered, and these regulators then attempt to restore the old order"

For many years, Varela, Coutinho and Cohen have plead for a radically different understanding of autoimmunity that could give rational to other forms of successful treatment such as the injection of antibody serum (coming from healthy subject [16]) or the T-cell vaccination [9], where the vaccine is composed of a key member of the immune system itself. They expect immunologists to be less obsessed by characterizing what comes from outside the system and how it gets in but instead to have them more concentrated on what happens inside, autonomously. They encourage them to pay more attention on the very sophisticated self-regulation mechanisms which allow such a complicated system, characterized by so many different dynamical actors, to still maintain a viable organization. It appears that while an increasing number of biological disciplines are becoming more and more influenced by the "network or systemic thinking", immunologists are still very reluctant in sympathizing with these views. Nevertheless, this thinking seems inescapable if one wants to tackle with diseases more logically imputable to network deregulation than to the presence of an undesirable foreigner. Beyond the prevention of impacts, how these impacts influence the whole system might be more precious as knowledge to have and to gain that just their intrinsic characteristics.

15 years ago, together with Francisco Varela, we tried in a succession of papers to propose new principles for distributed control of complex processes based on our

understanding of the immune functions [2-5]. Nothing has changed from that time expect the sad premature disappearance of the instigator. Among these principles, we proposed to control the process by a set of small operators distributed in time and space and organized into a network structure represented by an affinity matrix. The aim of the controller was to maintain the viability of the process to control. The controller learned to maintain this viability despite perturbations affecting this process. The learning was based on mechanisms of reinforcement type, by modifying some parameters associated with the controller but also by adding some fresh new ones. The homeostatic maintain was the main mission of these controllers and the whole methodology was tested and illustrated in part for robotic and non-linear control toy applications. For process control application, such as the cart-pole, the aim of the control was to keep the pole balancing the longest period of time. In a robot control, the aim of the control was to find viable path preventing the robot to bump obstacles. In the control of chaotic systems, the aim was to control the chaotic trajectory about fixed points that are embedded in the attractor but are unstable.

Very similar principles could have interesting roles to play in the conception of protective systems for computer while it is again the recognition ability of the immune system which is set to work in order to distinguish bad invading programs from inoffensive ones. Interestingly enough, it seems that computer engineers are encountering exactly the same kind of conceptual difficulties immunologist encounter when trying to separate a priori the good files from the bad files. Roughly said, what is self and nonself for computer systems? It would not be surprising that the computer engineers had to step back a pace and envisage this problem under the new lights presented in this paper. What is safe and non-safe for a computer has to be seen by the computer itself in its current state and in the context of its current operations. It might be possible to first identify a set of characteristic variables of the computer operations which should remain in between decent values, let's say to define what could be the viable operational zone or data for a computer, and thus to teach the computer how to organize its own defense (i.e. which program to tolerate and which to reject) in order to maintain this viability.

More recently, Somayaji and Forrest [11][20] proposed a very exciting work, totally in line with the view we defended for all these years. They design defensive mechanisms in which the computer autonomously monitors its own activities, routinely making small corrections to remain in a viable state. They pertinently write that what they work on supposes a move to recognize that immune systems should be more properly thought of as homeostatic mechanisms than pure defense mechanisms. This time, I can't agree more with them.

References

1. Aicklen, U., P. Bentley, S. Cayzer, J. Kim and J. Mc Leod. 2003. Danger Theory: The Link Between AIS and IDS? In J. Timmis, P. Bentley, E. Hart(Eds) LNCS 2787, pp. 156-167, Springer.
2. Bersini, H. and F. Varela. 1990: Hints for Adaptive Problem Solving Gleaned from Immune Network. In *Parallel Problem Solving from Nature*, H.P. Schwefel and H. Muhlenbein (Eds.) – Springer Verlag, pp. 343-354.

3. Bersini, H. 1991: "Immune Network and Adaptive Control" in the Proceedings of the first European Conference on Artificial Life - Paul Bourgine and Francisco Varela (Eds.) - Bradford Books - MIT Press - pp. 217-226.
4. Bersini H. and F. Varela. 1993: The Immune Learning Mechanisms: Recruitment Reinforcement and their applications in *Computing with Biological Metaphors* - Chapman and Hall - R. Patton (Ed.).
5. Bersini, H. 1993. Immune Network and Adaptive Control. In *Toward a Practice of Autonomous Systems – the first European Conference on Artificial Life* – Varela and Bourgine (Eds.), pp. 217-225 – MIT Press.
6. Bersini, H. 2002. Self-Assertion vs Self-Recognition: A Tribute to Francisco Varela. Proc. of the first ICARIS Conference – pp. 107-112.
7. Burgess, M. 1998 Computer Immunology. Proceedings of LISA XII, pp. 283-297.
8. Cohen, IR. 2000: Tending Adam's Garden: Evolving the Cognitive Immune Self, Academic Press, San Diego
9. Cohen, IR. 2002: T-cell vaccination for autoimmune disease: a panorama. In Vaccine 20, pp. 706-710.
10. Dembic, Z. 2000. About theories and the integrative function of the immune system. The Immunologist 8/6, 141-146.
11. Forrest, S., Balthrop, J. , Glickman, M. and D. Ackley. 2002. Computation in the Wild. In The Internet as a Large-Scale Complex System – Park and Willinger (Eds.) – Oxford University Press.
12. Jerne, N. 1974: Towards a network theory of the immune system – *Annals of Institute Pasteur/Immunology (Paris)* – 125C: 373-389.
13. Jerne, N. 1984: The Generative Grammar of the Immune System – Nobel Lecture, 8 December – Chateau de Bellevue – France. – also in *EMBO Journal*, Vol. 4, No 4.
14. Matzinger, P. 2002: The Danger Model: A Renewed Sense of Self – In *Science* – Vol. 296. pp. 301 – 305
15. Medzhitov, R. and C. Janeway. 2002: Decoding the pattern of self and nonself by the innate immune system. *Science* 296 – pp. 298-300.
16. Mouthon,L., Lacroix-Desmazes, S., Nobrega, A., Barreau, C. , Coutinho, A. and Kazatchkine, MD. - 1996. The self-reactive antibody repertoire of normal human serum IgM is acquired in early childhood and remains conserved throughout life. *Scand. J. Immunol.* 44(3): pp. 243-251
17. Mouthon, L., Nobrega, A., Nicolas, N., Kaveri, SV., Barreau, C., Coutinho, A., Kazatchkine, MD. – 1995. Invariance and restriction toward a limited set of self-antigens characterize neonatal IgM antibody repertoires and prevail in autoreactive repertoires of healthy adults – In *Proc. Natl. Acad. Sci. USA* – 92(9) – pp. 3839-3843.
18. Oudin, J., and M. Michel – 1963 *C.R. Acad. Sci.* Paris, 257, 805.
19. Oudin, J. and M. Michel – 1969. *Journal of Exp. Med.* 130, 595, 619.
20. Somayaji, A. and S. Forrest. 2000 Automated response using system-call delays. In Proceedings of te ninth USENIX Security Sumposium, pp. 185-197.
21. Stewart, J. 1994: *The Primordial VRM System and the Evolution of Vertebrate Immunity.* Austin, TX: R.G. Landes.
22. Tauber, A.I. 1994: *The Immune Self: Theory or Metaphor* ? New York and Cambridge: Cambridge University Press.
23. Tauber, A.I. 2002: The Biological Notion of Self and Non-Self – *Stanford Encyclopedia of Philosophy* – http://plato.stanford.edu/entries/biology-self.
24. Varela, F. and A. Coutinho. 1991: Second Generation Immune Network – in *Immunology Today*, Vol. 12 No5 – pp. 159-166.

Towards a Conceptual Framework
for Innate Immunity

Jamie Twycross and Uwe Aickelin

School of Computer Science, University of Nottingham, UK
jpt@cs.nott.ac.uk

Abstract. Innate immunity now occupies a central role in immunology. However, artificial immune system models have largely been inspired by adaptive not innate immunity. This paper reviews the biological principles and properties of innate immunity and, adopting a conceptual framework, asks how these can be incorporated into artificial models. The aim is to outline a meta-framework for models of innate immunity.

1   Introduction

Immunology has traditionally divided the immune system into innate and adaptive components with distinct functional roles. For many years, research was focused on the adaptive component. However, the prevailing view in immunology now shows the innate system to be of central importance [1]. The first part of this paper focuses on the innate immune system and on ways in which it interacts with and controls the adaptive immune system and discusses research over the last decade which has uncovered the molecular basis for many of these mechanisms, reviewed in [2]. It first contrasts the innate and adaptive immune systems and briefly reviews essential biology. It then discusses specific mechanisms of interaction between cells of the innate and adaptive immune systems, and concludes by showing how these mechanisms are examples of more general systemic properties.

While the integral role of the innate immune system has been established in immunology, artificial immune system models, surveyed in [3,4], have largely taken their inspiration from adaptive immunity. The second part of this paper adopts the conceptual framework of Stepney et al. [5] and addresses how ideas from innate immunity might be modelled in artificial immune systems. The conceptual framework is first briefly summarised and then a general meta-framework for models incorporating innate immunity is presented and refined through the discussion of specific models properties.

2   Innate Immunity

This section begins with an overview of well-established conceptions of innate immunity. Research which over the last decade has served to highlight the central

C. Jacob et al. (Eds.): ICARIS 2005, LNCS 3627, pp. 112–125, 2005.

role of the innate immune system is then discussed. Lastly, general properties of the innate immune system which have been drawn out by this research are presented. Review papers as well as the original articles are cited, and original figures are reproduced to enhance the necessarily brief summaries of the mechanisms.

2.1   Contrasting Innate and Adaptive Immunity

Differences between the innate and adaptive immune systems can be seen on a number of levels (Table 1). The adaptive immune system is organised around two classes of cells: *T cells* and *B cells*, while the cells of the innate immune system are much more numerous, including natural killer (*NK*) cells, dendritic cells (*DCs*), and *macrophages*. The receptors of innate system cells are entirely *germline-encoded*, in other words their structure is determined by the genome of the cell and has a fixed, genetically-determined specificity. Adaptive immune system cells possess *somatically generated* variable-region receptors such as the TCR and BCR (T and B cell receptors) with varying specificities, created by a complex process of gene segment rearrangement within the cell. On a population level, this leads to a *non-clonal distribution* of receptors on innate immune system cells, meaning that all cells of the same type have receptors with identical specificities. Receptors on adaptive immune system cells however, are distributed *clonally* in that there are subpopulations of a specific cell type (clones) which all possess receptors with identical specificities, but that generally, cells of the same type have receptors with different specificties [1,6,7].

Table 1. Differences between innate and adaptive immunity

property	innate immune system	adaptive immune system
cells	DC, NK, macrophage.	T cell, B cell.
receptors	germline-encoded.	encoded in gene segments.
	rearrangement not necessary.	somatic rearrangement necessary.
	non-clonal distribution.	clonal distribution.
recognition	conserved molecular patterns.	details of molecular structure.
	selected over evolutionary time.	selected over lifetime of individual.
response	cytokines, chemokines.	clonal expansion, cytokines.
action time	immediate effector activation.	delayed effector activation.
evolution	vertebrates and invertebrates.	only vertebrates.

The molecules which a receptor is able to bind with and recognise are known as ligands. While all receptors at the most basic level recognise molecules, ligands are often discussed in terms of higher-level structures. The variable-region receptors of adaptive immunity recognise features of pathogen structure, with BCRs directly recognising peptide sequences on pathogens, such as components of bacterial cell membranes, and TCRs recognising peptide sequences which have first been processed by DCs. These receptors are selected for over the lifetime of the organism by processes such as clonal expansion, deletion or anergy and are under *adaptive* not evolutionary pressure. Conversely, innate immune system receptors recognise a genetically-determined set of ligands under *evolutionary* pressure. One key group of innate receptors is the pattern recognition receptor (PRR) superfamily which recognises evolutionary-conserved pathogen-associate molecular patterns (PAMPs). PRRs do not recognise a specific feature of a specific pathogen as variable-region receptors do, but instead recognise common features or products of an entire class of pathogens. The immune system utilises adaptation of variable-region receptors to keep pace with evolutionary more rapid pathogens [1,6].

The environment of a cell *in vivo* is the tissue in which it is located. Tissue is formed by specialised groups of differentiated cells, and itself forms major components of organs. A substantial part of tissue volume is extracellular space and filled by a structured network of macromolecules called the extracellular matrix. Many of the molecules found in the extracellular matrix are actively produced by cells and involved in intercellular signalling [8,9]. Cytokines are secreted molecules which mediate and regulate cell behaviour, two important subsets of which are tissue factors, inflammation-associated molecules expressed by tissue cells in response to pathogen invasion, and chemokines, cytokines which stimulate cell movement and activation. Cytokines bind to germline-encoded cytokine receptors present on all cells and are widely produced and consumed by both innate and adaptive immune system cells during an immune response. Recognition by the innate immune system leads to the immediate initiation of complex networks of cytokine signalling which orchestrate the ensuing immune response. Adaptive responses additionally involve processes of cell selection such as clonal expansion, deletion and anergy, which take several days [1,6].

2.2 Recent Developments

This section reviews key developments over the last decade in our understanding of the innate immune system. Over this period, intense research has highlighted the central role of the innate system in host defense through its interaction with the adaptive immune system and with tissue, and uncovered the molecular basis for these interactions. These developments have lead immunologists to reevaluate the roles of both the innate and adaptive immune systems in the generation of immunity, installing innate immunity as a vital component in the initiation and modulation of the adaptive immune response [2].

NK cells of the innate immune system respond to the disruption of normal cell physiology in what has been termed the *"missing self"* model of NK cell activation [10]. Most normal tissue cells constitutively express MHC class I molecules, which present intracellular host-derived peptides on the cell surface. Presentation of virus-derived peptides leads to activation of CTL (cytotoxic T lymphocyte) cells and apoptosis in the infected cell through ligation with the TCR of the CTL [11]. However, viruses and other infectious agents have evolved to interfer with MHC class I antigen presentation [12] and so evade a CTL response. In the *"missing self"* model (Figure 1), NK cells are activated either by reduced signalling through receptors of the KIR family, inhibitory receptors

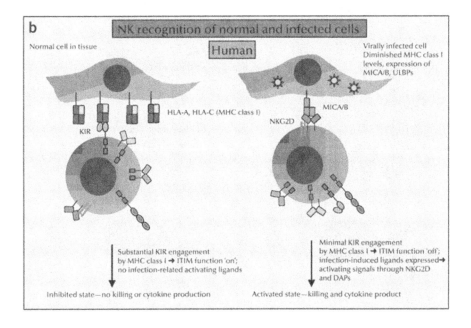

Fig. 1. NK receptors and NK recognition, from [2]

specific for host MHC class I, leading to apoptosis of the cognate cell [13]. This creates a no-win situation for the virus: if MHC class I expression is unaffected, it will be open to detection and removal through a CTL-based adaptive immune response, but if it affects MHC class I expression, it will be open to detection and removal through an NK-based innate immune response.

Some of the most exciting recent advances have been made in uncovering the role of TLRs in determining DC differentiation and so a mechanism by which the innate immune system mediates the quality of an adaptive immune system response [2,15] (Figure 2). Initial ligation by different PAMPs and tissue factors of different TLRs on DCs *"primes"* DCs to differentiate along different pathways, resulting in mature and immature DCs which produce different Th (T helper) cell polarisation factors. Release of these polarisation factors upon interaction with naive T cells causes the naive cell to differentiate into Th1, Th2 or Treg cells, all distinct types of T cell [14]. DCs, through TLRs, couple the quality of the adaptive immune effector response to the nature of the pathogen. Other PRR receptor families have also been implicated in Th polarisation [16]. Interestingly, recent research [17] suggests a renewed role for variable-region receptors not just in the determination of the antigen specificity of an immune response, but also in the regulation of this response. In place of the purely *"instructive"* DC to T cell paradigm, the responding Th1 or Th2 cells reinforce signals to B cell or CTL effectors in a *"success-driven"* consensual model of T cell polarisation.

As well as polarising Th cells, DCs play a key role in maintenance of populations of T cells. Tolerance is the ability of the immune system to react in a

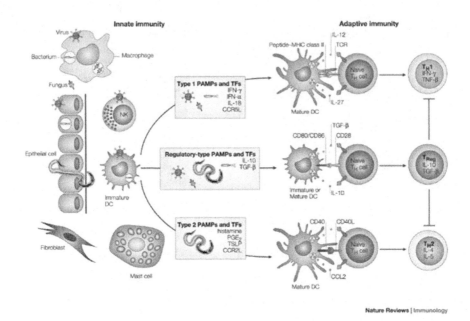

Fig. 2. DC polarisation of Th cells, from [14]

non-biodestructive manner to stimuli and has long been associated with adaptive immunity. Tolerance is usually discussed in terms of apoptosis or anergy of self-reactive T and B cells, and was initially proposed to occur centrally in a relatively short perinatal period, as epitomised in the clonal selection theory of Burnet [19,20]. While recent research shows the continuing importance of central tolerance mechanism [21], it is now accepted that peripheral tolerance mechansims which operate to censor cells throughout the lifetime of the host are of equal importance. DCs of the innate immune system lie at the heart of the generation of peripheral tolerance. Models propose that DCs continually uptake apoptotic and other material from peripheral tissues under normal steady-state, nonpathogenic conditions. Periodically, DCs migrate to draining lymph nodes where they delete lymphocytes by presenting the processed material which, as representative of tissue in the absence of pathogen, needs to be tolerated by the host [22]. Signals received by DCs *'license"* [18] (Figure 3) them to promote either T cell clonal expansion, or T cell clonal anergy or deletion. Research has established the molecular basis for such models. The absence of TLR signalling on DCs [22,23] or the presence of signalling through receptors involved in the uptake of apoptotic material [24,25] leads to distinct semimature and mature DC populations which interact with T cells to promote tolerance or immunogenicity respectively.

Cosignalling receptors and their ligands provide another mechanism by which DCs determine the qualitative and quantitative nature of adaptive immune responses. CD80 and CD86 are costimulatory molecules expressed on DCs and

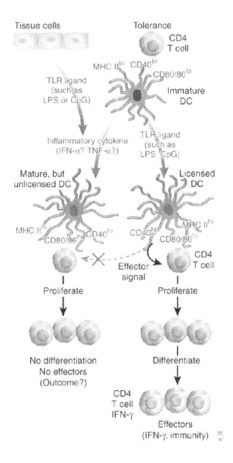

Fig. 3. DC Th tolerance, from [18]

bind with the CD28 and CTLA-4 cosignalling receptors on Th cells. Binding to CD28 leads to upregulation of Th activity and an immunogenic response, whereas CTLA-4 binding to downregulation of activity and tolerance. CD28 is constitutively expressed by Th cells, whereas the latter in proportion to the strength of TCR stimulation. CD80 and CD86 do not bind equivalently to CD28 and CTLA-4, and through selective expression by DCs of these molecules, innate immune system cells initiate and regulate Th cell activity. A key concept which has emerged from this research is the importance of sequential and properly timed interactions in the development of an immune response [2,26,27].

2.3   Summary

As the biology described in this section shows, the protection afforded to the host by the immune system *as a whole* arises from mechanisms of the innate *and* adaptive immune systems, which help form an *integrated system* of host protection. While there can be no doubt that specific recognition by the adaptive immune system plays an important role in functions such as pathogen recognition and removal, it is now clear that innate immune system mechanisms play an *equally* important role. The mechanisms discussed above are specific examples of more general properties of innate and adaptive immune system function and interaction, which are summarised in Table 2.

Table 2. General properties of the innate immune system

property 1	pathogens are recognised in different ways by the innate and adaptive immune systems.
property 2	innate immune system receptors are determined by evolutionary pressure.
property 3	response to pathogens is performed by both the innate and adaptive systems.
property 4	the innate immune system initiates and directs the response of the adaptive immune system.
property 5	the innate immune system maintains populations of adaptive immune system cells.
property 6	information from tissue is processed by the innate immune system and passed on to the adaptive immune system.

Considering the innate as well as adaptive immune system highlights how immune system cells interact with pathogens on multiple levels (Property 1). While the variable-region receptors of adaptive immunity are often specific for *one* feature of *one* particular pathogen, germline-encoded receptors such as PRRs of innate immunity are specific for features belonging to an entire *class* of pathogens. Innate immune system cells also respond not only to pathogen structure, but also to pathogen behaviour, either directly through PAMPs and TLRs, or indirectly through changes in tissue cell behaviour (NK cells). Innate receptor specificity is determined by evolutionary pressures, whereas adaptive processes such as peripheral tolerance determine the range of specificities of adaptive receptors (Property 2).

Innate immune system cells, as well as recognising pathogen, respond to them directly (Property 3), as with NK cell monitoring of MHC class I expression. Such recognition and response mechanisms when taken together show how the innate and adaptive immune systems work together to provide a broad coverage of protection to the host. Recognition by the innate immune system does not usually lead to a solely innate response, but instead also initiates and modulates an adaptive response through DC polarisation of Th cells and modulation of costimulatory signals (Property 4). Mechanisms such as DC tolerisation of Th cells, as well as relying on antigen processed by DCs, also shows how innate immune system cells maintain populations of cells (Property 5). The adaptive response is driven by information not only directly sensed by adaptive immune system cells, but equally by information gathered and processed by innate immune system cells, as with DC collection, processing and presentation of antigen to T cells (Property 6).

3   Modelling Innate Immunity

As artificial immune systems develop in their sophistication and so are more able to realise the functions of biological immune systems, they will need to incorporate properties of innate immunity into their models. This section first reviews the conceptual framework for artificial immune systems of Stepney et al. [5]. Adopting this framework and drawing on the biology of the previous section, it then proposes a number of general properties of models incorporating innate immunity. Looking first at the mechanisms of the previous section as a whole, and then individually, these general properties are discussed and refined. The aim is to suggest a meta-framework which highlights the key properties of models in general and how they might be realised in various individual models.

3.1   Conceptual Frameworks

In [5], Stepney et al. present a conceptual framework within which biologically-inspired models and algorithms can be developed and analysed. Figure 4 summarises their framework, in which probes provide the experimenter with an incomplete and biased view of a complex biological system which then allows the construction and validation first of simplifying abstract representations, and consequently of analytical computational frameworks, which themselves provide principles for the design and analysis of biologically-inspired algorithms.

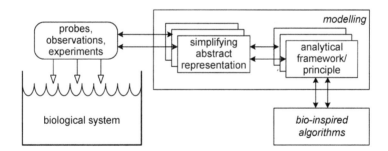

Fig. 4. A conceptual framework for biologically-inspired algorithms [5]

Stepney et al. (ibid.) also apply similar ideas to develop a meta-framework, Figure 5, which allows common underlying properties of classes of models to be analysed by asking questions, called meta-probes, of each of the models under consideration. They suggest a number of questions based around properties which are thought to affect complex behaviour in general. These areas relate to openness, diversity, interaction, structure and scale (ODISS). Using this meta-framework, the authors analyse the commonalities of population and network models.

While Stepney et al. use the meta-framework to analyse *artificial* models for essential features and commonalities, this paper uses it to analyse *biological*

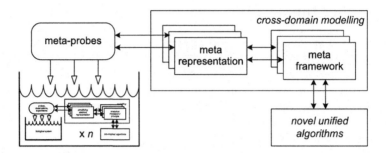

Fig. 5. A conceptual framework for integrating biologically-inspired computational domains [5]

models. The latter approach, apart from being pragmatic as very few artificial models currently exist, also allows biology to have much more of an influence on the meta-framework. Whichever approach is taken, meta-frameworks and the development of computational and mathematical models present a route through which artificial immune system research can help biologists answer research questions in their field.

3.2   A Meta-framework for Innate Models

This section takes the general properties of the innate immune system presented in Section 2 and abstracts them by adopting the conceptual framework. The abstracted properties form the basis of a meta-framework for innate models and are presented in terms of each of the ODISS areas of the conceptual framework:

openness: the interaction between the immune system and the host is one of a poised system in dynamic equilibrium coupled to an ever-changing environment. The relatively constant populations of innate immune system cells contrasts with the fluctuating populations of the adaptive system. The innate immune system provides examples of mechanisms for controlling the dynamic allocation of resources of populations of agents.

diversity: the different classes of cells of the innate and adaptive immune systems leads to the idea of distinct groups of functionally similar agents. At a different level, clonal distribution of receptors is an good example of different ways in which diversity manifests itself in biological systems. The underlying processes which drive diversity of innate receptors are evolutionary, while adaptive receptor diversity is established through adaptation.

interaction: in the wider sense considering the innate immune system shows how computation is largely communication, with immunity arising from the cytokine networks of signalling interactions between intercommunicating tissue cells and the innate and adaptive immune systems. Adaptive and innate immune cells are also specialised to access different informational levels. Innate cells focus on class features, while adaptive cells on individual features. Crosstalk between signalling networks is also a prevalent property in the immune system. Spatiality and temporally are key features of interactions across all levels.

structure: considering the innate immune system necessitates a view of the immune system composed of distinct subsystems. Functional similarities as well as differences can be seen between the innate and adaptive subsystems. The innate and adaptive are themselves composed of interacting populations of agents. Cell differentiation pathways provide an even more fine-grained division of cells into types.

scale: diverse populations of large numbers of cells is a hallmark of the immune system. A challenge for artificial immune systems is the need to simulate large populations of agents. Exploiting the emergent properties of distinct populations of large numbers of *simple* agents rather than a smaller number of more complex agents, along with distributed and parallel architectures for artificial immune systems [28] may provide a way forward.

3.3   Refining the Framework

As seen in the previous section, the innate immune system provides examples of general properties for artificial systems. Systems of agents form a convenient meta-representation of artificial systems, and many artificial systems are based on populations of interacting agents. This section adopts this meta-representation and refines the general properties of the previous section by discussing how they might be instantiated in models.

Cells seen as autonomous agents forms the basis of the meta-representation discussed here. The intercellular communication involved in all the mechanisms of Section 2 suggests the need for similar means of intercommunication between agents. Signals which allow groups of agents to control the functions and state of other groups of agents are necessary. A finer-grain representation of intercellular signals into distinct classes, as seen in the biological immune system, such as costimulatory, primer or chemokine signals, would allow artificial systems to more closely approximate the control mechanisms and systemic properties of biological systems. A key role of the environment which these agents exist in, termed *artificial tissue* here, is the provision of a milieu in which agents can interact via signalling. As well as passing signals between agents, mechanisms such as antigen processing and presentation to Th cells by DCs suggest the need for agents with the ability to "*consume*", process and pass on information to other agents. Some groups of agents, akin to Th or CTL cells, would not have direct access to information, but instead see it through the filter provided by these information processing agents. Artificial tissue would provide the mechanisms for these kinds of interaction with the environment and other agents.

The representation of pathogens at multiple levels suggests another "*service*" which artificial tissue has to provide. A problem must be represented at multiple levels. The artificial tissue allows agents of the artificial immune system to access different levels of information about events. At the very least, information concerning the structure of events and signals relating to the way elements behave or interact with the tissue as a whole needs to be accessible. Classical static classification problems could perhaps be translated into such a multilevel representation by clustering algorithms or statistical methods which give indications of how individual feature vectors relate to a whole set of other vectors. However, the innate immune system clearly relies on sensing the behaviour as well as structure of pathogens, and tissue models built entirely from information derived from structural considerations, such as similarity or differences between feature vectors, fail to capture this reliance. Dynamic, realtime problems such as intrusion detection offer a much more amenable domain as they naturally include notions of behaviour. For example, a computer virus not only has a particular structure, its program code, but also behaves in a certain way through its interactions with other programs and operating systems, searching for other machines, subverting the function of existing programs, installing backdoors on systems, and so on.

Over its lifetime a cell differentiates along a particular pathway, with each differentiation stage along this pathway representing a specific cell type. All cells at the same stage of differentiation are of the same type and have the same phenotypic configuration and functional characteristics. Which pathway a cell follows is the result of the environmental pressures the cell experiences. Little of the dynamics of the immune system can be captured if agents in artificial immune system models do not possess similar developmental characteristics. This could be modelled by endowing agents with a set of functions, subsets of which the agent performs at any one time and which represent the current type of the agent. Transitions from one type to another are a result of interactions of the agent with its environment and could be pictured as a branching tree structure.

While cells act as individuals, differentiating along their own individual pathways, they also act as part of a group. At this population level, considering the innate immune system highlights the need for groups of agents which respond to different types of information. Certain agents might identify fixed patterns in this information, embodying some type of notional TLR, while others would identify variable patterns, akin to TCRs. The processes which drive the specificity of receptors may be adaptive or evolutionary, with different pressures biasing the type of information surveyed by agents.

Cells control other cells on an individual contact-dependant level. They also control cells in a local neighbourhood through the production of cytokines. This localised control leads to dynamical patterns at the population level. DC control of Th proliferation through costimulatory molecules is a good example of how local interactions control the population of Th cells and determine population-level phenomena such as clonal distribution. Effects of the artificial tissue on one group of agents should have resulting effects on populations of other agents. The generation of peripheral tolerance by DCs suggests a mechanism by which signals presented by the artificial tissue are received by one group of agents and have a direct effect on other groups of agents. This control might not be as clearcut as live or die, but more a direction of differentiation pathways, of which polarisation of Th cells by TLRs on DCs is a good example.

Lastly, mechanisms of trust or obligation are established. The NK *"missing self"* model is a good example of this. The provision of sufficient quantities of MHC can be seen as a monitoring requirement, imposed by NK cells, of the system. If tissue cells fail to provide MHC they are destroyed. In realtime monitoring situations, models of such a suppression-based mechanism might be used to establish if groups of data providing agents are functioning.

3.4 Summary

Using the biology of the previous section as a basis, this section has sketched out a meta-framework for models of innate immunity, discussing general properties of such models and also how they might be realised more concretely. While the properties presented have tried to capture the core features of innate immunity, due to space and intellectual constraints they are not exhaustive and need to be combined with existing frameworks of adaptive models [5] if integrated models are to be built.

4   Conclusion

This paper has presented a summary of current biological understanding of the innate immune system, contrasting it with the adaptive immune system. Adopting a conceptual framework it then proposed and refined a meta-framework for artificial systems incorporating ideas from innate immunity. While emphasising the role of innate immunity, in reality, the innate and adaptive systems are intimately coupled and work together to protect the host. As already suggested, combining the properties suggested here with those of traditional population and network models would enable artificial systems to more closely reflect their biological counterparts.

Other possibilities for future work include a review within the proposed framework of artificial immune system models such as [29,30] which already include innate immunity. This would help evaluate and compare these models, discerning commonalities and providing direction for future research. Developing more detailed mathematical and computational models would be an important next step in a more detailed understanding of the properties of innate immunity. These models could then be used to instantiate a range of systems in different application domains. More realistic and principled models could also extend understanding on the dynamics of competing immunological models such as those of instructive or consensual regulation of Th1/2 responses, or modulation of costimulatory signals.

Couching ideas of innate immunity within an accepted conceptual framework provides a step in developing more integrated artificial immune system models which take into account the key role the innate immune system plays in host protection. As always, the beauty and subtlety of the immune system will continue to provide a rich source of inspiration for designers of artificial systems.

Acknowledgements

Many thanks to Adrian Robins for discussions on the immunology, and to my coworkers Uwe Aickelin, Julie Greensmith, Jungwon Kim, Julie McLeod, Steve Cayzer, Rachel Harry, Charlotte Williams, Gianni Tedesco and Peter Bentley, without whom this work would not have been possible. This research is supported by the EPSRC (GR/S47809/01).

References

1. Medzhitov, R., Janeway, C.A.: Innate immunity. The New England Journal of Medicine **343** (2000) 338–344
2. Germain, R.N.: An innately interesting decade of research in immunology. Nature Medicine **10** (2004) 1307–1320
3. Aickelin, U., Greensmith, J., Twycross, J.: Immune system approaches to intrusion detection - a review. In G Nicosia et al., ed.: Proc. of the Third International Conference on Artificial Immune Systems. Number 3239 in Lecture Notes in Computer Science, Springer (2004) 316–329
4. de Castro, L.N., Timmis, J.: Artificial Immune Systems: A New Computation Intelligence Approach. Springer (2002)
5. Stepney, S., Smith, R., Timmis, J., Tyrrell, A., Neal, M., Hone, A.: Conceptual frameworks for artificial immune systems. International Journal of Unconventional Computing **1** (2005)
6. Janeway, C.A., Medzhitov, R.: Innate immune recognition. Annual Review of Immunology **20** (2002) 197–216
7. Janeway, C.A., Travers, P., Walport, M., Shlomchik, M.: Immunobiology. 5th edition edn. Garland Science, available online at http://www.ncbi.nlm.nih.gov/books/ (2001)
8. Alberts, B., Johnson, A., Lewis, J., Raff, M., Roberts, K., Walter, P.: Molecular Biology of the Cell. 4th edn. Garland Science, available online at http://www.ncbi.nlm.nih.gov/books/ (2002)
9. Lodish, H., Berk, A., Matsudaira, P., Kaiser, C.A., Krieger, M., Scott, M.P., Zipursky, L., Darnell, J.: Molecular Cell Biology. 4nd edn. W. H. Freeman and Co., available online at http://www.ncbi.nlm.nih.gov/books/ (1999)
10. Ljunggren, H.G., Karre, K.: In search of the 'missing self': MHC molecules and NK cell recognition. Immunology Today **11** (1990) 237–244
11. Germain, R.N.: MHC-dependent antigen processing and peptide presentation: Providing ligands for T lymphocyte activation. Cell **76** (1994) 287–299
12. Lorenzo, M.E., Ploegh, H.L., Tirrabassi, R.S.: Viral immune evasion strategies and the underlying cell biology. Seminars in Immunology **13** (2001) 1–9
13. Lanier, L.L.: Natural killer cell receptor signaling. Current Opinion in Immunology **15** (2003) 308–314
14. Kapsenberg, M.L.: Dendritic-cell control of pathogen-driven T-cell polarization. Nature Reviews in Immunology **3** (2003) 984–993
15. Reis e Sousa, C.: Toll-like receptors and dendritic cells: from whom the bug tolls. Seminars in Immunology **16** (2004) 27–34
16. Pulendran, B., Kumar, P., Cutler, C.W., Mohamadzadeh, M., Van Dyke, T., Banchereau, J.: Lipopolysaccharides from distinct pathogens induce different classes of immune responses in vivo. The Journal of Immunology **167** (2001) 5067–5076

17. Kalinski, P., Moser, M.: Consensual immunity: success-driven development of T-helper-1 and T-helper-2 responses. Nature Reviews in Immunology **5** (2005) 251–260

18. Heath, W.R., Villadangos, J.A.: No driving without a license. Nature Immunology **6** (2005) 125–126

19. Baxter, A.G., Hodgkin, P.G.: Activation rules: the two-signal theories of immune activation. Nature Reviews in Immunology **2** (2002) 439–446

20. Mondino, A., Khoruts, A., Jenkins, M.K.: The anatomy of T-cell activation and tolerance. Proc. of the National Academy of Science USA **93** (1996) 2245–2252

21. Kyewski, B., Derbinski, J.: Self-representation in the thymus: an extended view. Nature Reviews in Immunology **4** (2004) 688–698

22. Scheinecker, C., McHugh, R., Shevach, E.M., Germain, R.N.: Constitutive presentation of a natural tissue autoantigen exclusively by dendritic cells in the draining lymph node. The Journal of Experimental Medicine **196** (2002) 1079–1090

23. Spörri, R., Reis e Sousa, C.: Inflammatory mediators are insufficient for full dendritic cell activation and promote expansion of CD4+ T cell populations lacking helper functions. Nature Immunology **6** (2005) 163–170

24. Lutz, M.B., Schuler, G.: Immature, semi-mature and fully mature dendritic cells: which signals induce tolerance or immunity? Trends in Immunology **23** (2002) 445–449

25. Mahnke, K., Knop, J., Enk, A.H.: Induction of tolerogenic DCs: 'you are what you eat'. Trends in Immunology **24** (2003) 646–651

26. Sharpe, A.H., Freeman, G.J.: The B7-CD28 superfamily. Nature Reviews in Immunology **2** (2002) 116–126

27. Carreno, B.M., Collins, M.: The B7 family of ligands and its receptors: new pathways for costimulation and inhibition of immune responses. Annual Review of Immunology **20** (2002) 29–53

28. Watkins, A., Timmis, J.: Exploiting parallelism inherent in AIRS, an artificial immune classifier. In G Nicosia et al., ed.: Proc. of the Third International Conference on Artificial Immune Systems. Number 3239 in Lecture Notes in Computer Science, Springer (2004) 427–438

29. Zhang, X., Dragffy, G., Pipe, A.G., Zhu, Q.M.: Artificial innate immune system: An instant defence layer of embryonics. In G Nicosia et al., ed.: Proc. of the Third International Conference on Artificial Immune Systems. Number 3239 in Lecture Notes in Computer Science, Springer (2004) 302–315

30. Na, D., Park, I., Lee, K., Lee, D.: Integration of immune models using petri nets. In G Nicosia et al., ed.: Proc. of the Third International Conference on Artificial Immune Systems. Number 3239 in Lecture Notes in Computer Science, Springer (2004) 205–216

Inspiration for the Next Generation of Artificial Immune Systems

Paul S. Andrews[1] and Jon Timmis[2]

[1] Department of Computer Science, University of York, UK
psa@cs.york.ac.uk
[2] Departments of Electronics and Computer Science, University of York, UK
jtimmis@cs.york.ac.uk

Abstract. In this conceptual paper, we consider the state of artificial immune system (AIS) design today, and the nature of the immune theories on which they are based. We highlight the disagreement amongst many immunologists regarding the concept of self–non-self discriminations in the immune system, and go on describe on such model that removes altogether the requirement for self–non-self discrimination. We then identify the possible inspiration ideas for AIS that can be gained from such new, and often radical, models of the immune system. Next, we outline a possible approach to designing AIS that are inspired by new immune theories, following a suitable methodology and selecting appropriate modelling tools. Lastly, we follow our approach and present an example of how the AIS designer might take inspiration from a specific property of a new immune theory. This example highlights our proposed method for inspiring the design of the next generation of AIS.

1 Introduction

Through the collaborative effort of many interdisciplinary researchers, the field of Artificial Immune Systems (AIS) is beginning to mature. The AIS researcher now has at their disposal an extensive body of literature, including an AIS textbook [1], and a wide ranging collection of successful application papers [2,3,4]. Invaluable to the maturation process of any research area, is the ability to reflect and comment on the way work in that field is conducted. This kind of activity is starting to be seen in AIS [1,5,6]. As a continuation of these ideas, we have focused on how and where the AIS practitioner gains inspiration from the immunology on which AIS are based. By looking at the state of AIS today, and the nature of the immunological theories on which these AIS are based, we highlight the importance of actively seeking out new and often controversial immune theories. From these theories it is possible to gather new ideas and processes for AIS inspiration. As an example, we summarise the details of such a theory of the immune system that has been presented by Cohen [7]. Using this example, we then show the type of ideas that could be used for AIS inspiration, and highlight a possible approach to exploiting this inspiration for AIS development by following a conceptual framework approach [6] and selecting appropriate modelling

C. Jacob et al. (Eds.): ICARIS 2005, LNCS 3627, pp. 126–138, 2005.

tools. Finally, following our outlined approach, we present a simple example in which we select receptor degeneracy as a property present in Cohen's immune model that has not previously been used in AIS design. Within this example, we highlight how inspiration can be taken from it to design an AIS, and what can be gained from doing this.

2   Current AIS

The current state of AIS research can be gauged from the proceedings of the previous three international conferences on AIS [2,3,4]. Year on year, we see an increase in both the number of papers published, and the number of successful applications to which AIS have been applied. The immunological inspiration on which the majority of these AIS are built, comes from either the processes based on Burnet's clonal selection theory [8], or Jerne's immune network theory [9]. Although these are competing and contradictory theories for the functioning of the immune system, they have both been able to inspire examples of AIS that satisfactorily perform their desired tasks. Thus, from an AIS perspective, both the clonal selection and immune network theories are equally useful for the purpose of providing the AIS designer with inspiration. It is important, however, that the theory chosen from which to take inspiration is appropriate, based on the behaviours required from the AIS. As Freitas and Timmis [5] have pointed out, the AIS practitioner needs to consider the application area of the AIS when designing it.

It is clear from many recent examples of AIS, that the way in which they are designed has changed from the early days of AIS research. The original AIS, such as those by Bersini [10], Forrest et al. [11], and Hightower et al. [12], were developed using an interdisciplinary approach, with clear attention paid to the biology from which inspiration was being taken. More recently, however, the design focus of many AIS has become more engineering oriented, with less emphasis placed on trying to understand and extract key biological properties. Consequently, these AIS have been built directly from naïve biological models, thus suffering from a case of 'reasoning by metaphor' [6]. It is noted, however, that not all recent AIS are designed in this way. For example the works of Hart and Ross [13], Wilson and Garrett [14] and Jacob et al. [15], have all used modelling techniques to build AIS in order to understand underlying immune properties.

3   Immunological Arguments

The success of an AIS practitioner owes much to the theories presented by the immunologist. Many immune processes, however, are not well understood, and there is little agreement amongst many immunologists regarding many of the key immune principles, such as self–non-self discrimination. This is clearly evident from a number of articles published in volume 12 of *Seminars in Immunology*

[16,17,18,19,20,21,22] from 2000. In this journal volume, many leading immunologists discuss their views on the nature and importance of self–non-self discrimination in the immune system. Tauber [22] points out that the concept of self and the idea of discriminating between self and non-self in the immune system, was first explicitly suggested by Burnet in his formulation of the clonal selection theory [8]. By the 1970s, this theory had been widely accepted amongst immunologists, and it still forms the basis for many of the processes described in textbooks on immunology today. Jerne's immune network theory [9] presented in the early 1970s, however, presented a challenge to the idea of an immune self. The immune network theory is characterised by a self-organising model in which there is no concept of self and non-self, only the elements of the network. It is to perturbations of the self-organised network itself that a reaction occurs. Tauber believes that the alternative models of the immune system presented in the aforementioned journal volume, fall to various degrees between the ideas of Burnet and Jerne, and are thus a continuation of the arguments between these two points of view.

On closer examination of the articles presented in volume 12 of *Seminars in Immunology*, one appreciates more the level to which many immunologists differ in their views. This is summed up by Langman and Cohn, who state in their editorial summary:

> "There is an obvious and dangerous potential for the immune system to kill its host; but it is equally obvious that the best minds in immunology are far from agreement on how the immune system manages to avoid this problem." [23]

Of the immune models presented in the journal, Langman and Cohn's own minimal model of self–non-self discrimination [20] is the one closest to the original ideas of Burnet, whereas Cohen's [18] is the closest to Jerne's. Between these, and to various degrees, fall the models of Bretscher [17], Medzhitov and Janeway [21], Anderson and Matzinger [16] and Grossman and Paul [19]. This raises the question that if the immunologists are themselves unclear as to the functioning of many immune processes, where does this leave the AIS practitioner when deciding which aspects of immunological theory to take inspiration from? As mentioned above in section 2, both the clonal selection and immune network theories have provided inspiration for successful AIS, so, we would like to suggest that alternative theories of immune processes can be equally useful for inspiring AIS. Indeed, we believe that the AIS practitioner should actively investigate these theories as they are likely to highlight new and different models of immune processes, and thus alternative ideas from which to take inspiration.

4   Cohen's Immune Model

Having established our belief that alternative immune theories can be beneficial to AIS, we describe ideas from Cohen's model of the immune system that are presented in [18,7,24]. We will then highlight the scope for inspiration for AIS that could be taken from Cohen's ideas.

4.1   The Immune System

Cohen's model of the immune system is a holistic one, being presented as a complex, reactive and adaptive system, whose role is body maintenance. This departs from the classical view that defence against pathogen and self–non-self discrimination is the main purpose of the immune system. Removal of pathogen, however, is beneficial to the health of the body, and thus defence against pathogen is considered to be just a special case of body maintenance. In order to carry out body maintenance, the immune system must be able to detect the current state of the body's tissues and elicit an appropriate response. To explain how this is achieved in Cohen's model, we first need to examine the elements of the immune system.

The immune system comprises a set of immune agents consisting of specialised cells and molecules, which are distributed around the body. The immune cells include the lymphocytes (e.g. T and B cells), monocytes (e.g. macrophages) and granulocytes. The immune molecules consist of those molecules that stimulate, or are utilised by, immune cells for the purposes of the immune system, and include the cytokines, antigen receptors and plasma proteins. The input to the immune system constitutes the molecular shapes that are sensed by immune cell receptors when binding to a ligand occurs. There exists two types of immune cell receptor: the innate receptors that have evolved to recognising germ-line molecules such as cytokines, and the somatically generated antigen receptors of the T and B cells. The observed response of the immune system to receptor input is a complex reaction between the immune agents that causes a change in the states and activities of immune cells. This change then causes the immune agents to produce a number of different effects on the body, including cell growth and replication, cell death, cell movements, cell differentiation and the modification of tissue support and supply systems. The range of processes that the immune system can have on the body is termed inflammation, and this is seen to be the output of the immune system. The task of the immune system, therefore, is to produce the correct inflammatory response to the receptor input in order to keep the body functioning.

4.2   Specificity, Co-respondence and Patterns

According to the clonal selection theory, immune specificity is a property of the somatically generated immune receptors of the T and B cells, which both initiates and regulates the immune response. Initiation is achieved via the binding between an antigen and a receptor that is specific to it. The response will then stop only when there is no antigen or receptor left for binding. Cohen, however, points out that immune receptors are intrinsically degenerate, i.e. they can bind more than one ligand. Immune specificity, therefore, cannot be purely dependent on molecular binding as no one receptor can be specific to a single antigen. Instead, affinity, the strength of binding between a receptor and its ligand, is a matter of degree. In Cohen's model, immune specificity requires diagnosing varied conditions in the body and producing a specific inflammatory response. This specificity emerges from the co-operation between immune agents, and does so despite receptor degeneracy and the fact that immune agents are pleiotropic and functionally redundant. Pleiotropism refers to the fact that a single immune agent is able to produce more than one effect, for example the same cytokine is able to kill some cells whilst stimulate others. Functional redundancy concerns the ability of one class of immune agents to perform the same function as another, for example cell apoptosis can be induced by different immune cells. There are two processes provided by Cohen to explain the generation of immune specificity in his model: co-respondence, and patterns of elements.

Co-respondence is a process whereby the agents of the immune system respond simultaneously to different aspects of its target, and to its own response. This results in a specific picture of an antigen emerging from immune agent co-operation, and is explained by the following process. As previously noted, immune receptors provide the input to the immune system by recognising molecular shapes. There are three different types of immune receptor that recognise different aspects of antigen. These are the somatically generated receptors of the T and B cells and the innate receptors of macrophages. The T cell receptors are restricted to recognising processed fragments of antigen peptides bound to a MHC molecule, whereas the B cell receptors (antibodies) recognise the conformation of a segment of antigen. The innate receptors of macrophages don't recognise antigen, but germ-line molecules. These molecules form a set of ancillary signals that describe the context in which lymphocytes are recognising antigen. These ancillary signals can be classified into three classes: the state of body tissues (some receptors detect molecules only expressed on damaged cells), the presence and effects of pathogen (some receptors are unique to infectious agents such as bacterial cell wall) and the states of activation of nearby lymphocytes (some receptors detect immune molecules produced by lymphocytes). In addition to interacting with their target object, the T cells, B cells and macrophages use immune molecules to communicate their response to each other, and other tissues of the body. This forms an immune dialogue comprised of an on-going exchange of chemical signals between the immune cells. Subject to this exchange of information, they update their own responses accordingly, be it to increase or decrease the vigour of their response. The exchange of information between immune cells is also affected by the existence of networks of immune agents, such as cytokine and idiotypic networks, and by the processes of positive and negative feedback in these networks. The process of co-respondence can be summed up by figure 1.

Patterns of elements help generate immune specificity as the specificity of a pattern can extend beyond that of the individual elements that make up the pattern. Immune patterns are a complex arrangement of populations of immune agents, which, through their individual activity, produce a specific pattern of activity. For example, a pattern can emerge toward a particular antigen from the overlapping reactions of a population of degenerate immune receptors. Even though each immune receptor is non-specific to its target, the result of all the receptor reactions together will be unique, and thus specific to that antigen. Patterns can also be built with the help of immune agent pleiotropism and

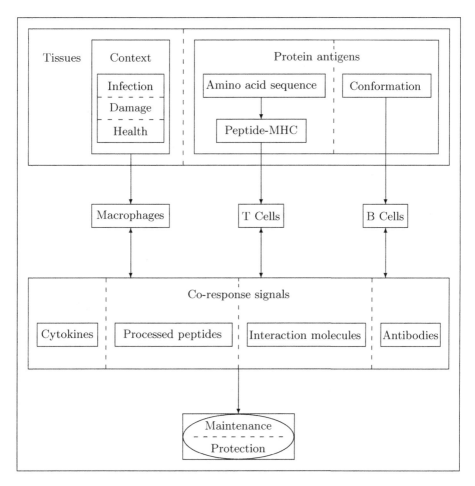

Fig. 1. Co-respondence, as taken from [7], where rectangles represent objects, ellipses within rectangles represent states of objects, arrows designate directions of relationships and items separated by broken lines can be combined to generate joint products

functional redundancy. Here, the ability of different immune agents each being capable of responding to a situation with a number of different immune effects, allows more response options to be available than just having a single mapping between immune agent and its effect. Thus, specificity emerges through a cooperative pattern of degenerate, redundant and pleiotropic immune agents.

4.3   Maintenance

In order to achieve body maintenance, the immune system selects and regulates an inflammatory response according to the current condition of the body, utilising the mechanisms of co-respondence and patterns of activity. Thus, immune recognition and response is not just a function of the adaptive arm of the immune system, but a collaborative effort between both the adaptive and innate arms. Also central to the idea of immune maintenance, is the ability to recognise the state of the body's own tissues. This is called autoimmunity, and refers to the existence of antigen receptors that recognise the body's own molecules. According to the clonal selection theory, this is undesirable as the receptor will initiate an attack on the molecule it recognises, causing an autoimmune disease such as rheumatoid arthritis. In Cohen's model, healthy autoimmunity is a requirement of the immune system, and an explanation is provided for how healthy autoimmunity and autoimmune diseases co-exist in [7]. Cohen also goes on to present the immune system as a cognitive system that, like the brain, forms an internal history, self-organises (learning and memory) and makes deterministic decisions. The details of this are too many to include in this paper, but the interested reader is referred to [7] for more details.

4.4   Ideas for Inspiration

From Cohen's immune model, we can identify a number of properties not present in the clonal selection theory that could provide inspiration for AIS. Some of these ideas are present in Jerne's immune theory and have already been used as inspiration for AIS, but we still discuss them here as they form key parts of Cohen's model, and the way in which they are integrated into it may highlight alternative inspiration. There are two levels of scale of inspiration from Cohen's model, the high level ideas and paradigms that describe the functioning and behaviour of the immune system, and the lower level processes that are proposed to achieve the described functions. The high level ideas include:

- *Maintenance*: The role that Cohen sees the immune system as fulfilling, rather than the discrimination of self from non-self.
- *Co-operation*: The immune response is a collaborative effort between the innate and adaptive immune agents.
- *Emergent Behaviours*: The observed immune responses and properties, such as immune specificity, emerge from the functioning of immune agents rather than a one-to-one mapping between a receptor and antigen.
- *Autoimmunity*: Receptors that are able to recognise the state of the body's own tissue are beneficial rather than undesirable.

Examples of the low level processes include:

- *Multiple Immune Agents*: Co-respondence involves the interactions of different agents such as macrophages, T and B cells.
- *Signalling Networks*: Immune agents communicate using an immune dialogue of signalling molecules.
- *Feedback*: Positive and negative feedback help to co-ordinate the immune response.
- *Degeneracy*: The degeneracy of antigen receptors provides a many-to-one relationship between the receptors and specificity of recognition.

– *Pleiotropia and Redundancy*: The pleiotropic and redundant nature of immune agents are also important in providing specificity of response.

By highlighting these properties, it is then possible to identify application areas to which they might be applied. For example, the notion of the immune system as a concurrent and reactive maintenance system, lends itself well to application domains that operate in dynamic environments, such as embedded systems and robotics.

5   Exploiting the Inspiration

Once the AIS designer has investigated the immune theories and identified the relevant immune properties, the AIS must then be built in way that utilises these properties effectively. To do this, we suggest that the designer adopts a suitable design methodology and a set of appropriate modelling techniques suited to the nature of the immune processes chosen for inspiration.

5.1   A Conceptual Framework

One of the main problems involved in designing bio-inspired algorithms, is deciding which aspects of the biology are necessary to generate the required behaviour, and which aspects are surplus to requirements. To help tackle this and enable the development of bio-inspired algorithms in a more principled way, Stepney et al. [6] have suggested a conceptual framework for designing these algorithms. This framework promotes the use of an interdisciplinary approach to developing and analysing these algorithms. It encompasses a number of modelling stages, the first of which utilises biological observations and experiments to provide a partial view of the biological system from which inspiration is being taken. This view is used to build abstract models of the biology, which are then open to validation. Frameworks can then be built and validated from these models to provide the principles for designing and analysing the required bio-inspired algorithms. Using such a framework aims to stop the designer from making naïve assumptions about the biological processes that are providing the inspiration, and thus preventing the development of algorithms that are just a weak analogy of the process on which they are based.

We suggest that when taking inspiration for AIS from immune theories not previously exploited, the adoption of the conceptual framework approach is especially important. For instance, the theory may not be fully formed or well understood, so it is possible that unexpected or unexplained behaviours will arise from the properties being modelled. Following the conceptual framework ideas should help capture such occurrences. Additionally, the immune models built by the AIS practitioner to investigate the properties of immune theories may be of help to immunologists. By following a principled design methodology, these models should be able to provide experimental evidence for, or against, the assertions made by immunologists in their theories. This should provide useful insights and help to develop these theories further.

5.2   Modelling Tools

Following the conceptual framework approach requires the building of models of the biological processes. Building models of immune processes is an aid to understanding how these processes work, and has been carried out by theoretical immunologists and AIS practitioners for many years. These immune models naturally fall into two main classes: mathematical models and computational models. The majority of the mathematical models consist of differential equations that model the population dynamics of interacting immune agents, Perelson [25] provides an overview of many of these techniques. Successful computational models that have been used for immune process modelling include cellular automata [26], Boolean networks [27] and UML statecharts [28].

To model a particular immune process effectively, the modeller needs to select appropriate techniques. For example, if the immune process being modelled is an emergent behaviour, then the designer needs to choose a modelling technique that allows emergence to occur. By considering the description in section 4, we are able to highlight suitable techniques that can be used to model the immune processes within Cohen's model. In [7], Cohen states that most experimental immunological research has been concerned with a reductionist approach, taking apart the system to identify the basic building block in order to understand the system as a whole. The immune system, however, has been presented as an adaptive, reactive and concurrent system in which many immune functions are emergent properties of the interactions amongst the immune agents. Thus, to build models based on Cohen's description requires modelling tools that take the reductionist experimental data as its building blocks and allow behaviours to emerge. Such modelling tools are used extensively by the Artificial Life (ALife) community. ALife, as described by Langton [29], takes a synthetic, bottom-up approach to biology, putting together the interacting elements of a system in order to understand it. The interactions between these elements produce emergent dynamic behaviours such as those in Cohen's immune model. We suggest, therefore, that the models used by the ALife community are suitable in the design process of AIS inspired by immune models such as Cohen's. Examples of these ALife modelling techniques include recursive developmental systems, such as cellular automata and L-systems, evolutionary systems, such as genetic algorithms, (multi-)agent based systems, such as swarms, and networks of automata, such as Boolean networks.

In addition to the tools that have already been used to model the immune system and the proposed ALife tools described above, techniques that have been utilised in other biological modelling areas may be appropriate to immune modelling, and should thus be investigated. For example the work by Johnson et al. [30] utilises object-oriented methods to model intra-cellular processes, and a similar approach could be used successfully in immune modelling. An effective example of a modelling technique taken from a different modelling area is given by Chao et al. [31], where a stochastic age-structured model that is often used in ecology has been applied to modelling immune cell populations and transitions.

5.3   Example: Receptor Degeneracy

In section 4.2 we discussed Cohen's rejection of the classically held clonal selection theory view of immune specificity, where specificity arises from the molecular binding between a target antigen and a single receptor specific to that antigen. Instead of this one-to-one mapping between receptor and antigen, immune receptors were described as being degenerate, each interacting with a target antigen to various degrees. This meant that the differentiation between target antigens by a population of degenerate receptors, is a function of the interactions between each receptor in the population and an antigen. This was presented in terms of patterns of response, where recognition occurs as a many-to-one relationship between receptors and antigen. The majority of AIS designed to date that utilise the antigen-receptor matching paradigm, have taken the one-to-one mapping route to recognition. Additionally, the dimensionality of the receptor and antigen representations in the AIS algorithms is typically the same, which is biologically implausible as immune receptors (antibodies and T cell receptors) only recognise parts of a target antigen. Thus, we have chosen the idea of receptor degeneracy as our case study of a possible new area for AIS inspiration. To describe how this might be done, we need to address three questions: what are the details of the observed immune mechanism, how can we exploit this mechanism for AIS design, and why might this be useful? These questions can be analysed within the conceptual framework approach to AIS design described in section 5.1.

The first stage in the conceptual framework approach will determine the details of the observed biological mechanism from which inspiration is being taken, by using biological observations to provide a partial view of the biology. For the example of receptor degeneracy, this could fall into two parts. Firstly, the analysis of Cohen's ideas from the literature [18,7,24] is needed to help understand the general details of what receptor degeneracy means. Secondly, via the use of experimental research articles, ideas can be gleaned from the specific biological detail of how the receptor degeneracy process works as part of the immune system. For example, we might focus on the cell-mediated biology of T cells, where different processed fragments of target antigen are presented via MHC to a randomly generated population of T cell receptors. This detail will help inform the abstract biological models that need to be built in the next step of the framework.

The second stage in the conceptual framework approach involves building abstract models of the biology and will provide the detail on how to exploit the receptor degeneracy mechanism for AIS design. At this point, as described in section 5.2, we need to make an informed choice of which modelling tools to use. We have seen that the previous stage of the framework approach will provide the reductionist biological data with which to build our models, and so the choice of a first modelling tool will rest on this data as well as our intended goal. A suitable choice might be a cellular automaton, as this is able to provide dynamic and emergent behaviours whilst still providing a spatial element to the modelling, thus being close to the original biology. This should help maintain the required properties of the observed biology. The choice of subsequent models of the biology will be informed by the previous ones, dependent on what these models were able to show. The type of models used will naturally become more abstract and general in order to get closer to the algorithm design stage. The modelling stage of the conceptual framework approach will proceed until we can produce a suitable framework for algorithm design.

The last stage in the conceptual framework approach before designing the specific AIS, is to produce the concrete framework using insight gained during the modelling phase, which should provide the suitable general principles for the algorithm design. In the case of receptor degeneracy, we would hope to uncover insight into the size of processed antigen fragment needed, the number of T cell receptors needed to recognise antigen, suitable affinity metrics, and so on. It is also at this stage that we can make an informed decision on what receptor degeneracy might be a useful property for, leading to the choice and production of specific AIS algorithms. It is anticipated, for example, that receptor degeneracy may be a useful generalisation property for rationalising about unseen antigen, and also a technique for reducing the dimensionality of a problem. It may be that an analogy with neural network models will become apparent [32].

Throughout the whole process of following the conceptual framework method, there are five general system properties to be considered. These, as stated by Stepney et al. [6], are openness, diversity, interactions, structure and scale, and are all linked to and influence each other. As a last point, we note that the conceptual framework method does not always end with the production of the designed AIS. The process of producing a framework from which to design an AIS is cyclical, with the knowledge gained by following it fed-back into producing still better models, frameworks and algorithms. Additionally, the investigation of mechanisms like receptor degeneracy can be used as a building block to producing AIS inspired by more complex processes such as Cohen's process of co-respondence.

6   Conclusion

In this paper, we have first considered how the majority of AIS are designed today by examining them from a historical perspective. It was seen that these AIS are almost exclusively inspired by immune processes based on either the theories of Burnet or Jerne. By investigating the state of current thinking amongst immunologists today, it is clear, however, that certain immune concepts, such as self–non-self discrimination, are far from agreed upon. This lead us to examine the perceived benefits to AIS design of exploring an alternative immune theory, such as Cohen's. Cohen's immune theory was able to highlight a number of ideas for inspiration that are not present in either the clonal selection or immune network theories. We have then highlighted a possible approach to designing an AIS based on an alternative immune theory, advocating the use of a suitable design methodology, and the choice of appropriate modelling techniques. As a final exercise, we presented an example of how we could following our outlined approach to take inspiration from the idea of receptor degeneracy that is described in Cohen model. Future work will involve performing practical steps similar to those described in section 5.3 to follow the conceptual framework approach to designing an AIS inspired by Cohen's work.

References

1. de Castro, L.N., Timmis, J.: Artificial Immune Systems: A New Computational Intelligence Approach. Springer (2002)
2. Timmis, J., Bentley, P.J., eds.: Proceedings of the 1st International Conference on Artificial Immune Systems (ICARIS 2002), University of Kent Printing Unit (2002)
3. Timmis, J., Bentley, P., Hart, E., eds.: Proceedings of the 2nd International Conference on Artificial Immune Systems (ICARIS 2003), Springer (2003)
4. Nicosia, G., Cutello, V., Bentley, P.J., Timmis, J., eds.: Proceedings of the 3rd international Conference on Artificial Immune Systems (ICARIS 2004), Springer (2004)
5. Freitas, A., Timmis, J.: Revisiting the foundations of artificial immune systems: A problem oriented perspective. In: Proceeding of the 2rd International Conference on Artificial Immune Systems (ICARIS), Springer (2003) 229–241
6. Stepney, S., Smith, R.E., Timmis, J., Tyrell, A.M.: Towards a conceptual framework for artificial immune systems. In: Proceeding of the 3rd International Conference on Artificial Immune Systems (ICARIS 2004), Springer (2004) 53–64
7. Cohen, I.R.: Tending Adam's Garden: Evolving the Cognitive Immune Self. Elsevier Academic Press (2000)
8. Burnet, F.M.: The Clonal Selection Theory of Acquired Immunity. Cambridge University Press (1959)
9. Jerne, N.K.: Towards a network theory of the immune system. Ann. Immunol. (Inst. Pasteur) **125C** (1974) 373–389
10. Bersini, H.: Immune network and adaptive control. In: Proceedings of the 1st European Conference on Artificial Life (ECAL), MIT Press (1991) 217–226
11. Forrest, S., Perelson, A., Allen, L., Cherukuri, R.: Self–nonself discrimination in a computer. In: Proceedings of the IEEE Symposium on Research Security and Privacy. (1994) 202–212
12. Hightower, R.R., Forrest, S.A., Perelson, A.S.: The evolution of emergent organization in immune system gene libraries. In: Proceedings of the 6th International Conference on Genetic Algorithms, Morgan Kaufmann (1995) 344–350
13. Hart, E., Ross, P.: Studies on the implications of shape-space models for idiotypic networks. In: Proceedings of the 3rd international Conference on Artificial Immune Systems (ICARIS 2004), Springer (2004) 413–426
14. Wilson, W.O., Garrett, S.M.: Modelling immune memory for prediction and computation. In: Proceedings of the 3rd international Conference on Artificial Immune Systems (ICARIS 2004), Springer (2004) 386–399
15. Jacob, C., Litorco, J., Lee, L.: Immunity through swarms: Agent-based simulations of the human immune system. In: Proceedings of the 3rd international Conference on Artificial Immune Systems (ICARIS 2004), Springer (2004) 400–412
16. Anderson, C.C., Matzinger, P.: Danger: the view from the bottom of the cliff. Seminars in Immunology **12** (2000) 231–238

17. Bretscher, P.: Contemporary models for peripheral tolerance and the classical 'historical postulate'. Seminars in Immunology **12** (2000) 221–229
18. Cohen, I.R.: Discrimination and dialogue in the immune system. Seminars in Immunology **12** (2000) 215–219
19. Grossman, Z., Paul, W.E.: Self-tolerance: context dependent tuning of t cell antigen recognition. Seminars in Immunology **12** (2000) 197–203
20. Langman, R.E., Cohn, M.: A minimal model for the self–nonself discrimination: a return to basics. Seminars in Immunology **12** (2000) 189–195
21. Medzhitov, R., Janeway, C.A.: How does the immune system distinguish self from nonself? Seminars in Immunology **12** (2000) 185–188
22. Tauber, A.I.: Moving beyond the immune self? Seminars in Immunology **12** (2000) 241–248
23. Langman, R.E., Cohn, M.: Editorial summary. Seminars in Immunology **12** (2000) 343–344
24. Cohen, I.R.: The creation of immune specificity. In Segal, L.A., Cohen, I.R., eds.: Design Principles for Immune Systems and Other Distributed Autonomous Systems. Oxford University Press (2001) 151–159
25. Perelson, A.S., Weisbuch, G.: Immunology for physicists. Reviews of Modern Physics **69** (1997) 1219–1267
26. Kleinstein, S.H., Seiden, P.E.: Simulating the immune system. Computing in Science and Engineering **2** (2000) 69–77
27. Weisbuch, G., Atlan, H.: Control of the immune response. Journal of Physics A: Mathematical and General **21** (1988) 189–192
28. Efroni, S., Harel, D., Cohen, I.R.: Towards rigorous comprehension of biological complexity: Modeling, execution, and visualization of thymic t-cell maturation. Genome Research **13** (2003) 2485–2497
29. Langton, C.G.: Artificial life. In Nadel, L., Stein, D., eds.: 1991 Lectures in Complex Systems. Addison-Wesley (1992) 189–241
30. Johnson, C.G., Goldman, J.P., Gullick, W.J.: Simulating complex intracellular processes using object-oriented computational modelling. Progress in Biophysics and Molecular Biology **86** (2004)
31. Chao, D.L., Davenport, M.P., Forrest, S., Perelson, A.S.: A stochastic model of cytotoxic t cell responses. Journal of Theoretical Biology **228** (2004) 227–240
32. Gurney, K.: An Introduction To Neural Networks. Taylor and Francis (1997)

Two Ways to Grow Tissue for Artificial Immune Systems

Peter J. Bentley[1], Julie Greensmith[2], and Supiya Ujjin[3]

[1] Department of Computer Science, University College London, London WC1E 6BT, UK
P.Bentley@cs.ucl.ac.uk
[2] School of Computer Science (ASAP), University of Nottingham, NG8 1BB, UK
jqg@cs.nott.ac.uk
[3] Computing Research and Development Division,
National Electronics and Computer Technology Center, Thailand
supiya.ujjin@nectec.or.th

Abstract. An immune system without tissue is like evolution without genes. Something very important is missing. Here we present the novel concept of tissue for artificial immune systems. Much like the genetic representation of genetic algorithms, tissue provides an interface between problem and immune algorithm. Two tissue-growing algorithms are presented with experimental results illustrating their abilities to dynamically cluster data and provide useful signals. The use of tissue to provide an innate immune response driving the adaptive response of conventional immune algorithms is then discussed.

1 Introduction

Multicellular organisms are very attractive places for viruses, bacteria, fungi and parasites. They provide protection against the uncertainties of the world: stable temperatures, food, machinery to help reproduction, and sometimes even help remove their waste products. But unfortunately, the cellular structure of multicellular organisms (which for simplicity, we will call *tissue* in this paper) is not always designed to cope with such uninvited guests. When infected, tissue may degrade or deteriorate, leading to, at worst, the death of the entire organism. To overcome such problems, some of the cells of organisms fight back. They actively search out and destroy pathogens, in order to maintain the tissue of the organism. (In immunobiology, it is known that tissue also provides an innate immune response, with cells such as B and T cells providing the adaptive response .)

So the immune system exists to protect tissue from harm. In one sense, an immune system without tissue is meaningless. Yet in the field of artificial immune systems there is no real concept of tissue. Data is typically mapped directly to antigens. In many cases there is not even the concept of immune cells, let alone tissue cells. Both conceptually and technically, this can cause difficulties − for if every new artificial immune system (AIS) is directly "wired" to a specific problem, then it becomes difficult to compare, analyse and even to apply the AIS to new problems.

Here we propose an alternative treatment for artificial immune systems. Instead of joining the AIS to its application directly, it is proposed that an intermediary represen-

C. Jacob et al. (Eds.): ICARIS 2005, LNCS 3627, pp. 139–152, 2005

tation is employed, much like the genetic representation of the genetic algorithm. This intermediary will be a dynamic encoding of the current problem providing the equivalent of an innate immune response to support the adaptive response of an AIS. The encoding will be modified according to the problem like the genetic encoding of a GA [1]. But regardless of the underlying data, it will present a consistent interface to an artificial immune system. That interface will be *tissue*, fig 1.

Fig. 1. Tissue should act as the interface between problem and AIS

2 Background

The concept of artificial tissue is used extensively in cell modelling and simulation, with additional applications in electronics and biotechnology. One well-known example was the POEtic project, which used the concept of cellular tissue and immune cell modelling within hardware devices [11]. In this architecture each cell is treated as an individual processing device, with the tissue performing the role of providing an interface between a biologically inspired processing mechanism and data provided by the environment. Similarly, in [3], fault tolerant electronic circuits were constructed and used a combination of embryonically grown cells coupled with immune-inspired negative selection. This model provides an immune inspired component and entity to protect, though the protected cells did not provide feedback signals to the AIS. The protected cells in this system were embryonically grown, sending out signals to support each other. The system partitioned the AIS and the cells into separate layers, providing communication between the two components. This architecture was implemented and applied to various hardware devices. Examples of developmental models that include aspects of tissue growth are becoming more popular; interested readers should consult [7].

In biology, tissue has long been known to be a crucial component of the immune system, and this role was highlighted further by Matzinger. The Danger Model, proposed by Polly Matzinger in 1994 [9], attempted to alter the perspective from which the immune system was viewed. This involved abandoning the belief that the immune system is conditioned at an early age to distinguish self from non-self proteins. Instead, this model proposes that the immune system contains cells sensitive to cellular damage. In her words: "The Danger model … suggests that neither the innate nor adaptive immune systems are in ultimate control. This function belongs to the ancient innate responses of the normal bodily tissues themselves" [8].

The theory suggests that signals are innately released from cells under stress, due to damage, often derived from pathogens, physical disruption, radiation, extreme pHs or temperature. These signals may cause tolerance to proteins through regulatory cell activation or lead to the activation of effector cells [10]. This discrimination is based on the information gathered from proteins collected within the body, in combination with various signals derived from host tissue cells. The combination of antigens-plus-signals can give information regarding damage to a specific area of tissue. In order to understand what the signals are and under what conditions they arise, two important types of cell death have to be examined.

1. Apoptosis. Tissue cells can die in a number of different ways, forming part of the life cycle of a cell. It is essential for cells to die under controlled conditions to provide regulation of tissue growth and to remove defective and virally infected cells. This type of pre-programmed cell death is known as apoptosis. On receipt of an apoptotic signal the cell releases a number of degrading enzymes which have dramatic effects on the internal structure of the cell. The cell's DNA is fragmented into orderly portions, nuclear condensation is initiated and organelles are broken down. During this period of degradation, the integrity of the outer cell membrane remains intact, while expressing greater quantities of signalling molecules on the membrane surface. These molecules are detected by innate immune cells, such as macrophages, which are triggered to ingest the cell, ultimately resulting in removal of the apoptotic cell from the tissue[5].

2. Necrosis. In contrast, unexpected, chaotic cell death does not involve an intricate removal system. Unlike apoptotic cells, the necrotic cell swells up, the internal material is chaotically fragmented and the membrane integrity is lost. Ultimately, the cell explodes, releasing its contents into the fluid surrounding the cell. Cellular products released as a result of necrotic cell death are known as danger signals - endogenous activators of the innate immune system. This includes molecules derived due to cell degradation, inclusive of uric acid, adenosine-tri-phosphate, and heat shock proteins[12], in addition to an array of pro-inflammatory cytokines.

Without tissue there would be no endogenous danger signals, no innate immune activation and nothing to protect. Additionally it is thought that the absence of tissue derived danger signals is as equally important as their presence, through the generation of proteins that do not belong to the host, yet cause no damage, e.g. bacterial gut flora. The detection of an apoptotic signal is translated into the activation of the adaptive immune system's regulatory cells [10].

It is clear that tissue has been highlighted as an integral part of immune function. Danger signals released from cells dying under stressful conditions activate cells belonging to the innate immune systems. These cells ultimately control the effector cells, and giving direction to the immune response. Yet, the concept of tissue has not been widely used within AIS. The question remains: is it possible to construct artificial tissue to provide an interface between an application and an artificial immune system?

3 Defining Tissue

Focussing for now on the task of anomaly detection, it is proposed that tissue designed for artificial immune algorithms should comprise a series of linked cells, each cell "grown" in response to specific data, in a data stream being input to the system.

Cells should grow and be supported by homogeneous data. Where data does not exist to support a cell, the cell dies. Where too much/too diverse data exists for a cell, the cell divides. Cells should exist in a dynamic network structure, with similar cells linked or placed near to each other. The use of a cellular representation is also intended to enable distributed processing and the support of multiple datastreams simultaneously.

In the 'tissue paradigm' all communication between a problem and AIS is mediated via the tissue. Tissue thus provides some functionality of the innate immune system, with the AIS performing the common role of adaptive immune system.

3.1 Uplinks

Given a data stream of temporally homogeneous data items, the tissue will quickly grow to form a specific shape, structure and size, which will be maintained indefinitely. The artificial immune system should consult all cells in the tissue, examining them and any corresponding danger signals. If the data changes, the tissue will change in response. Those aspects of the data that remain the same will continue to support the corresponding parts of tissue. Those aspects that differ will result in a restructuring or even cell death. An artificial immune system should thus be able to ignore static tissue and quickly cause an immune response on and near to the cells where the changes (and corresponding signals) are occurring. In this way the tissue provides more than an interface to the underlying data – it provides a spatial and temporal structure, enabling the AIS to specialise and focus to different extents, spatially and temporally.

It is recognised (and experiments confirm later) that the tissue will not perform perfectly as a clusterer and anomaly detector – if it did there would be no reason to have the AIS. Instead, the tissue provides useful data preprocessing, gathering similar data items together, and presenting gross, short-term anomalies to the AIS. (Specific, problem dependent knowledge can also be incorporated and exploited in the cells in order to present other innate signals to the AIS.) It is expected that critical anomalies will still occur within "normal" tissue. Thus the role of the AIS in the 'tissue paradigm' is now to consult cells within the tissue and identify fragments of data (antigens) presented by the cells that together may indicate a critical anomaly. Note that there is no real concept of a self/non-self division; here the concept is more one of stability/entropy. A stable tissue is considered 'healthy'; unstable or entropic tissue is 'unhealthy' and will attract attention from the AIS.

3.2 Downlinks

The natural immune system is designed to both detect harmful anomalies and remove the causal agents. However, an artificial immune system using the 'tissue paradigm' cannot simply remove 'infected' cells from the tissue – this would only prevent the tissue from presenting information about the anomaly to the AIS, it would not prevent the underlying anomaly in the application from reoccurring. Instead, the AIS should use the tissue as an interface to the application. If a critical anomaly is discovered, cells should be informed which antigens are responsible. The cells then pass this information down to the underlying application, where the information should be used to remove the cause of the anomaly. For example, in a computer network intrusion detection application, if the AIS identifies a specific antigen in one cell, the cell will then communicate this information to the network management software. This software might terminate a corresponding process and thus remove the 'infection' from the input data stream, or just inform the system administrator. If there is a one-to-one correspondence between cell and anomaly, then by identifying the anomalous antigen within the cell, and causing the subsequent prevention of the anomalous data in the input stream, the corresponding cell will no longer be supported by the data stream and will die. In other words, it is possible for the AIS to cause tissue cell death by interacting with the application via the tissue.

```
create zygote (initial cell) with first data point (antigen)

    get next antigen from data steam
    find nearest cell (cell with mean antigen closest to current antigen)

    if current antigen is sufficiently similar* to nearest cell mean
      add antigen to nearest cell
      if nearest cell has number of antigens == maxantigenspercell
        split current cell into two linked cells s.t. antigens are shared
equally**
        update cell means, danger signals and linked neighbours
    else
      create new cell at current antigen; nearest cell is linked parent

    for every cell
      for every antigen in the cell
        age antigen
        if antigen age > maxantigenage
          remove antigen
      if antigens in cell == 0
        cell dies (can no longer respond to input)
        create new dangersignal, origin = final antigen,
                range = cell stddev,
                strength = max (or inversely proportional to cell age)
        pass all danger signals of dying cell to linked neighbouring cells

    for every dangersignal
      reduce stength
      if stength == 0
        delete dangersignal
```

```
    *similarity measures depend on the matching function used and underlying appli-
cation; in the experiments reported here, data values are normalised and the
Euclidian distance between cell mean and antigen compared against a similarity
threshold of 0.2 (default).
    **the cell split function should use the same distance function to divide anti-
gens into two groups; in the experiments reported here, all antigens greater than
the mean are placed in one cell, all antigens less than the mean are placed in the
other.
```

```
    In addition to the similarity measures, there are 2 important constants:
    maxantigenage - determines number of antigens held by tissue cells at any point
in time.
    maxantigenspercell - affects how many cells there will be in the tissue
```

Fig. 2. The network tissue algorithm

4 Tissue Algorithms

There are many ways in which tissue can be developed. Here we present two different approaches: a network tissue growing algorithm, and a swarm tissue growing algorithm. Both effectively act as dynamic clusterers, using danger signals as approximate alerts of anomalies in the input stream. Both are independent of the size of any data set – computational time depends on the size of the window on the data and the bitrate of the data stream (which will determine the size of the tissue being maintained).

4.1 Network Tissue Algorithm

The network-based algorithm explicitly maintains cells in a dynamic network, with parent cells pointing to daughter cells, and link restructuring on cell death to maintain network coherence (e.g., the death of a parent cell results in the oldest daughter cell taking the parent's position in the network). In this algorithm, each cell may hold up to `maxantigenspercell` antigens before dividing into two. Figure 2 outlines the network tissue algorithm.

4.1.1 Biological Analogies

Figure 3 summarises the model with respect to natural biology. In this model a single cell may represent a particular cell type of a living organism. While there is data to support a cell (i.e., while the impact of the environment and genes results in a particular type of tissue structure), the cell will survive indefinitely (the tissue will have a certain cell type and structure indefinitely). If the input stream changes permanently (or for a sufficiently long duration), even if the change is dramatic, the new data will cause corresponding new tissue to develop and be supported (i.e. a long-term change in the environment causes long-term useful changes in tissue structure). But if an anomalous datum creates a cell, and there is insufficient subsequent similar data to support that cell, then the cell will die. (In an organism, cells can be created in response to the environment, affected by the existing tissue; but the environment might include some form of pathogen, which infects and destroys cells of that type). It is not necessary for apoptosis to be modelled explicitly – it is assumed that a single cell represents many cells of that type growing and dying to be replaced by new cells naturally. So should a cell die in the model, this can only be necrosis – and thus it causes the release of a danger signal, to be passed to the neighbouring cells in the tissue.

In an attempt to match biological characteristics of danger signals, in the model, danger signals emitted as a result of necrosis are general indicators of an anomaly, but are spatially and temporally specific. The danger signals from a dead cell are held by its neighbouring cells (which, through automatic network restructuring or swarming after necrosis, "fill the gap" left by the dead cell). It is possible for cells to hold many danger signals at once. Danger signals decay over time; they are removed once their strength falls to zero.

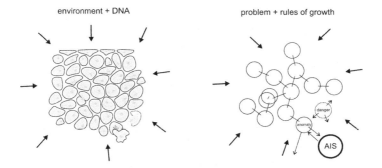

environment + DNA   problem + rules of growth

Fig. 3. Left: Organic tissue grows according to its DNA, and interactions with its environment. To create a new cell, an existing cell divides into two. Necrosis results in "danger signals". Immune cells consult antigens presented by tissue cells and respond by destroying infection. Right: AIS tissue grows according to its rules of growth and interactions with a problem. To create a new cell, an existing cell may split into two. Unnatural cell death results in danger signals. The AIS consults antigens presented by tissue cells and responds by signalling the underlying application via the cells, potentially resulting in the destruction of cells that are presenting anomalous antigens.

4.1.2 Experiments

A series of experiments were performed using the standard "breast cancer" UCI machine learning data set, comprising 240 'malignant' items in class 1 and 460 'benign' items in class 2. (Each data item, or antigen, comprised a vector of 9 real-valued numbers, which describe various cancer cell measurements.) For each system setting, the same experiment was repeated 30 times. Implemented in 'C' and running on a Mac Powerbook G4, each run of 10,000 iterations (with one randomly picked data item presented to the tissue each iteration) lasted less than 5 seconds. Class 2 (benign) is treated as the "normal" class of data, with items from class 1 (malignant) being introduced into the datastream every 25 iterations (this value is investigated in the first 3 experiments). Table 1 lists the different parameter settings used in the experiments.

Table 1. System setups for the nine experiments

Experiment	Max antigen age	Max antigens/cell	Similarity threshold	Class 1 item freq.
1	40	10	0.2	25
2	40	10	0.2	10
3	40	10	0.2	5
4	40	10	0.1	25
5	40	10	0.3	25
6	40	5	0.2	25
7	40	15	0.2	25
8	20	10	0.2	25
9	60	10	0.2	25

Table 2. Results for experiments 1-9, showing mean number of danger signals per run, standard deviation, and percentage of danger signals that correspond to data items in class 1 and class 2.

experiment	Class 1			Class 2		
	mean	stddev	percent	mean	stddev	Percent
1	382.8	2.6	98.1%	1008.5	25.1	10.5%
2	933.4	5.8	95.6%	946.7	20.2	10.5%
3	1801.7	20.2	92.3%	842.6	22.0	10.5%
4	390.1	1.4	99.9%	1378	27.2	14.4%
5	373.5	3.5	95.7%	849.7	20.0	8.9%
6	383.7	2.4	98.3%	2165.8	27.3	22.6%
7	384.0	2.2	98.4%	796.7	24.8	8.3%
8	389.6	1.6	99.6%	1046.1	19.5	10.9%
9	378.7	3.0	97.2%	946.0	24.0	9.9%

4.1.3 Analysis

Table 2 shows the results for the nine experiments (t-tests were used to corroborate the following comments). As is to be expected from a deterministic algorithm (where the only stochastic element is the data item order in the data stream), the results for all experiments were very consistent across runs, as shown by the low standard deviation values. Experiments 1 to 3 indicate how the frequency of anomalous data items influences the accuracy of danger signals, i.e., more frequent items from class 1 reduces the tendency of the tissue to treat class 1 items as anomalous (true positive), while the percentage of items in class 2 treated as anomalous remains unchanged (false positive). Experiments 4 and 5 (also compare with experiment 1) show how changing the similarity threshold affects danger signal accuracy. A smaller threshold produces near perfect detection of anomalies from class 1, but also increases the tendency for items in class 2 to be detected as anomalies. The opposite effect occurs when the threshold is increased. Experiments 6 and 7 (also compare with experiment 1) show how the number of antigens per cell affects danger signals. No real change occurs to the accuracy of detection of anomalous items from class 1, but a smaller number of antigens produces far less tolerance for different items in class 2 (the cells are more specialised, increasing the chances for even slightly different antigens to be treated as anomalous). Increasing the number of antigens has the opposite effect – causing a significant reduction in the number of items in class 2 that are treated as anomalous. Finally, experiments 8 and 9 (also compare with experiment 1) show the effect of varying the maximum antigen age. In the experiments, this has only a minor effect on danger signal accuracy, although the results suggest that the age should be set in relation to the expected frequency of anomalies in the datastream, i.e., a long age for frequent anomalies increases the tolerance of the tissue for the anomalies, while a short age causes infrequent but normal data items to be treated as anomalies.

4.2 Swarm Tissue Algorithm

The swarm-based algorithm is a second, alternative approach to tissue development. It is designed to follow much the same "tissue growing" principles as outlined previously, but now clusters in the tissue are formed by cell movement in a two-dimensional space (of size 1000 by 1000 units) which is unrelated to the data values, with similar cells moving together and dissimilar cells moving apart. In this algorithm, each cell holds just one data item; cells are created by new data and die constantly – thus apoptosis is modelled in this algorithm. If cells have not grouped themselves into a cluster by the time they die, they produce a danger signal, i.e. necrosis is modelled by the death of "abnormal"cells that do not participate in normal tissue development. Figure 4 outlines the algorithm, which uses the following swarming rules to drive the motion of cells:

```
get next antigen from data steam
create cell using antigen and place in swarm-tissue

for every cell, (current cell = C₁)
    for every cell in neighbourhood* of C₁ (neighbour cell = C₂)

        if C₁ is sufficiently similar** to C₂/cell-cluster***
            C₁ joins/makes cluster with C₂/cell-cluster
            if C₁ and C₂ were in clusters
                with mean antigen differences < current similarity
                they form a new cluster together
        else
            C₂/cell-cluster*** is added to cell avoidance list

        if C₁ is in a cluster, C₁ best position is mean pos. of cells in C₁ cluster
        else C₁ best position is mean tissue position

        update velocity of C₁ using best pos, mean avoidance values (Rules 1 to 3)

        update C₁ position based on velocity (Rule 4)

        increase age of C₁
        if C₁ age is greater than celllifespan
            remove C₁ from swarm-tissue
            if C₁ was not in a cluster
            create dangersignal, origin = C₁,
                    range = cell stddev,
                    strength = max
        (pass all danger signals of dying cell to neighbouring cells)


    for every dangersignal
        reduce strength
        if stength == 0
            delete dangersignal
```

* defined by radius around C₁ where radius = 300
** similarity measures depend on the matching function used and underlying application; in the experiments reported here, data values are normalised and the Euclidian distance between the two cell values are compared against a similarity threshold of 0.2 (default). In addition, the similarity measure between C₁ and C₂ where C₂ is in a cluster is scaled by the inverse of the number of cells in the cluster, making larger clusters more attractive.
*** if C₂ is in a cluster, the mean value of cells in the cluster is used, otherwise the value of C₂ is used.

Fig. 4. The swarm tissue algorithm

$$v_i^{attr} = wv_i + c_1 r_1 (x_{pbest,i} - x_i) \qquad \text{Rule 1}$$

$$v_i = v_i^{attr} - f_2 c_2 r_2 (x_{avoid,i} - x_i) \qquad \text{Rule 2}$$

$$if\ (|v_i| > v_{max})\ v_i = (v_{max}/|v_i|)v_i \qquad \text{Rule 3}$$

$$x_i = x_i + v_i \qquad \text{Rule 4}$$

where:

x_i is the current position of data item i
$x_{pbest,i}$ is the current best position of data item i
$x_{avoid,i}$ represents the current avoidance position of data item i.
v_i is the velocity of data item i
w is a random inertia weight between 0.5 and 1 [4]
c_1 and c_2 are spring constants set to 1.494 [4]
r_1 and r_2 are random numbers between 0 and 1 [2]
f_2 is the repulsive factor (default value 2). Defines the effect of the repulsive force on velocity; the higher the value the more that dissimilar items repel each other.
v_{max} is the maximum velocity (default value of 300)

Note: $x_{pbest,i}$ is either the central position of all items in the same cluster as i or the central position of all items in the swarming space (if i does not belong to a cluster)

$x_{avoid,i}$ represents the central position of all data items in i's neighbourhood whose similarity value falls below the similarity threshold.

4.2.1 Biological Analogies

Figure 5 summarises the model with respect to natural biology. In this model cells are modelled more directly. New data generates new cells which all live for a fixed lifespan before dying. While they live they move with respect to each other, with similar cells clustering and dissimilar cells moving apart (i.e., the impact of the environment and genes results in a particular type of tissue structure, with similar cells adhering to each other and forming organs). As with the previous algorithm, if the input stream changes permanently (or for a sufficiently long duration), even

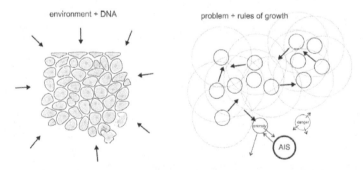

environment + DNA   problem + rules of growth

Fig. 5. Left: Organic tissue grows according to its DNA, and interactions with its environment. Right: AIS tissue grows by moving cells relative to each other according to their rules of growth and interactions with a problem. A cell that has not formed part of the tissue before it dies is necrotic and produces a danger signal. The AIS consults antigens presented by tissue cells and responds by signalling the underlying application via the cells.

if the change is dramatic, the new data will cause corresponding new tissue to develop and be supported (i.e. a long-term change in the environment causes long-term useful changes in tissue structure). But if an anomalous datum creates a cell, and there is insufficient subsequent similar data to produce similar cells, then the cell will be unable to form a cluster before it dies. (In an organism, cells can be created in response to the environment, affected by the existing tissue; but the environment might include some form of pathogen, which infects and alters cells of that type). In this algorithm, apoptosis is modelled explicitly – cells grow and die to be replaced by new cells naturally. So in this model, necrosis is modelled by a dying cell that has not formed part of a group of other cells – and thus it causes the release of a danger signal, to be passed to the neighbouring cells in the tissue.

4.2.2 Experiments
Again, a series of experiments were performed using the standard "breast cancer" UCI machine learning data set. As before, for each system setting, the same experiment was repeated 30 times. This time implemented in Java J2SE and running on a 2.4 Ghz Pentium 4 PC, each run of 10,000 iterations lasted between 30 and 145 seconds. The same parameter settings as listed in table 1 were used for the experiments, although experiments 6 and 7 could not be performed as each cell only holds one antigen in this model.

4.2.3 Analysis
Table 3 shows the results for the nine experiments. Accuracy of danger signals for class 1 is consistently high for all experiments, but the changes in parameter settings do appear to affect the percentage of items in class 2 treated as anomalous. Presenting items from class 1 more frequently (see results for experiments 1,2,3) produces a subtle increase in class 2 anomalies; this may be caused by a disturbance effect of more cells in class 1 disrupting the path of class 2 cells as they try to cluster. A lower similarity threshold allows fewer cells to cluster and so produces a considerably worsened percentage for class 2 anomalies, while a higher threshold has the reverse effect (see results for experiments 1,4,5). The same effect occurs when cell age is modified (see results for

Table 3. Results for experiments 1-9, showing mean number of danger signals per run, standard deviation, and percentage of danger signals that correspond to data items in class 1 and class 2.

experiment	Class 1			Class 2		
	mean	sstdev	Percent	mean	stdev	Percent
1	398.0	0.18	99.99%	1973.6	39.2	20.6%
2	996.0	0.18	100.0%	1903.1	38.4	21.2%
3	1991.9	0.37	100.0%	1783.4	46.0	22.4%
4	398	0	100.0%	4045.0	61.7	42.3%
5	397.3	0.92	99.82%	1434.4	44.8	15.0%
8	399	0.0	100.0%	6425.9	75.4	67.1%
9	396.9	0.25	99.98%	1422.4	44.5	14.9%

experiments 1,8,9) – a lower age produces fewer chances for clusters to form in time; a higher age increases the chance and thus reduces the class 2 signals. Further experiments showed that increasing the lifespan to 100 and using a threshold of 0.3 produced accuracy in class 1 of 99.8% and in class 2 of 8.9%, although execution times increased to 145 seconds for 10,000 items.

5   Discussion

Like immunobiology, the field of artificial immune systems has been obsessed with the workings of the adaptive immune system and its capabilities of specificity, diversity and memory, with little work spent on the innate immune system. This work attempts to lay the foundations of a more complete view of the immune system for AIS. We propose that the concept of tissue is important for several reasons:

- Tissue provides a generic data representation which interfaces between problem and conventional AIS, simplifying future AIS development.
- Tissue stores the current state of the application, providing a clearer concept of "organism" and enabling the AIS to learn to detect changes in the organism, correct harmful changes and prevent future damage by similar agencies.
- For applications such as anomaly detection, tissue provides a dynamic window of the input data stream; the data is dynamically organized and spatially structured, encapsulating the important concepts of temporal and spatial variability. An AIS exploiting tissue would be able to specialize and focus on different areas of the problem, at different times, enabling a more precise response.
- Tissue encapsulates ideas of homeostasis – if the problem becomes heterogenous or chaotic, the tissue will reorganize its structure in response. An AIS collaborating with the tissue would be able to correct harmful changes and work to maintain homeostasis.
- Tissue is essential for the innate immune system, and tissue algorithms can be used to provide desirable "automatic" processing and signals from data.

It is proposed that an AIS will employ tissue by traversing its spatial representation and allocating resources according to the spatial and temporal requirements. A network-based AIS might form distinct and functionally diverse subnetworks to focus on tissue cells of different types. A population-based AIS would be able to allocate subpopulations of agents (e.g., antibodies, B-cells or T-cells) for specific regions of tissue. In all cases, all aspects of the problem should be presented to the AIS through tissue, and all AIS responses should be presented to the underlying application by the tissue.

In this work we have focused on the task of anomaly detection, and both tissue-growing algorithms were developed with this in mind. However, we propose that the concept of tissue should be employed for all AIS applications. This may inevitably involve different forms of tissue growth. For example, in a robot control application [6], sensor input might be used as an input data stream and the algorithms presented above could be used. Alternatively, the state of sensors and actuators might be represented by a fixed and predefined tissue structure (e.g. a cell for each sensor, and a cell for each motor). Such a structure would change if sensors or motors were lost through damage – obviously requiring a significant response from the controlling AIS. But normal control would occur through the robot presenting its changing state via antigens and signals from the cells, interpreted by the AIS, with responses made to the cells being mapped back to robot motor control.

Like the genetic representations of genetic algorithms, the exact tissue representation necessary is likely to be application-specific, but the AIS used to consult with the tissue and respond to it should be generic. It is conceivable that evolutionary computation could be employed to evolve useful innate tissue responses for a given application and AIS. Indeed if each tissue cell contained an evolving GP function [1], cells would be able to present one or more evolved interpretations (i.e., signals) derived from the raw data, in addition to the raw data.

6 Conclusions

In this work we have presented the novel concept of tissue for artificial immune systems. Much like the genetic representation of genetic algorithms, tissue provides an interface between problem and immune algorithm. From the perspective of immunobiology, tissue provides an innate immune response, with the AIS providing an adaptive response. Two tissue-growing algorithms were presented with experimental results illustrating their abilities to dynamically cluster data and provide useful signals. Both algorithms are able to detect anomalous data items with accuracies up to 100% depending on the parameter settings. Future work will investigate the integration of these algorithms with artificial immune systems for intrusion detection.

Acknowledgements

Thanks to all the members of the "Danger Project" http://www.dangertheory.com/ for their helpful comments, feedback and discussions which helped shape the ideas in this paper. This project is supported by the EPSRC (GR/S47809/01), Hewlet Packard Labs, Bristol, and the Firestorm intrusion detection system team. This work is ODISSIAC-friendly.

References

[1] Bentley, P. J. 1999. An Introduction to Evolutionary Design by Computers. Chapter 1 in Bentley, P. J. (Ed.). *Evolutionary Design by Computers*. Morgan Kaufman Publishers Inc., San Francisco, CA, 1-73.

[2] Blackwell, T.M. and Bentley, P.J. 2002. Dynamic Search with Charged Swarms. In Proceedings of the Genetic and Evolutionary Computation Conference 2002. New York.

[3] Canham, R. and Tyrell, A.M. 2003. A Hardware Artificial Immune System and Embryonic Array for Fault Tolerant Systems. Genetic Programming and Evolvable Machines. vol 4, issue 4, pp.359-382.

[4] Eberhart, R.C. and Shi, Y. 2001. Particle Swarm Optimization: Developments, Applications and Resources. In Proceedings of the 2001 Congress on Evolutionary Computation. vol.1, pp.81-86.

[5] Edinger, A.L. and Craig B Thompson. 2004. Death by Design: apoptosis, necrosis and autophagy. Current Opinion in Cell Biology. vol.16, pp663-669.

[6] Ko, A., Lau, H. Y. K., and Lau, T. L.. 2004. An Immuno Control Framework for Decentralised Mechatronic Control. In Proc. of the Third International Conference on Artificial Immune Systems (ICARIS 2004). Catania, Sicily. pp. 91-105.

[7] Kumar, S. and Bentley, P. J. (contributing editors). 2003. On Growth, Form and Computers. Academic Press Ltd, London.

[8] Matzinger, P. 1998. An Innate Sense of Danger. Seminars in Immunology.vol.10, pp.399-415.

[9] Matzinger, P. 1994. Tolerance, Danger and the Extended Family. Annual Reviews In Immunology 12:991-1045.

[10] Matzinger, P. 2002. The Danger Model: A Renewed Sense of Self. Science. 296, pp301-305.

[11] Thoma,Y., Tempesti, G,. Sanchez, E. and Arostegui, J.M.M. 2004. POEtic: an electronic tissue for bioinspired cellular applications. Biosystems. 76, pp.191-200.

[12] Wallin, R.P.A., Lundquist, A., More, S.H., Von Bonin, A., Keissling, R. and Ljunggren, H.G. 2002. Heat Shock Proteins as Activators of the Innate Immune System. Trends in Immunology. 23, no. 3, pp.130-135.

Introducing Dendritic Cells as a Novel Immune-Inspired Algorithm for Anomaly Detection

Julie Greensmith[1], Uwe Aickelin[1], and Steve Cayzer[2]

[1] ASAP, School of Computer Science and IT, University of Nottingham,
Jubilee Campus, Wollaton Road, Nottingham, UK, NG8 1BB
{jqg, uxa}@cs.nott.ac.uk
[2] Hewlett-Packard Labs plc, Filton Road, Stoke Gifford,
Bristol, UK. BS32 0QZ
steve.cayzer@hp.com

Abstract. Dendritic cells are antigen presenting cells that provide a vital link between the innate and adaptive immune system. Research into this family of cells has revealed that they perform the role of co-ordinating T-cell based immune responses, both reactive and for generating tolerance. We have derived an algorithm based on the functionality of these cells, and have used the signals and differentiation pathways to build a control mechanism for an artificial immune system. We present our algorithmic details in addition to some preliminary results, where the algorithm was applied for the purpose of anomaly detection. We hope that this algorithm will eventually become the key component within a large, distributed immune system, based on sound immunological concepts.

Keywords: artificial immune systems, dendritic cells, anomaly detection, Danger Theory.

1 Introduction

In 2003, Aickelin et al outlined a project describing the application of a novel immunological theory, the Danger Theory to intrusion detection systems[1]. The authors of this work suggested that the Danger Theory encompassed pathogenic detection, where the basis for discrimination was not centred around 'self' or 'non-self', but to the presence or absence of danger signals. The paper described how danger signals are released from the body's own tissue cells as a result of necrotic cell death, triggered by an invading pathogen. The immune system was thought to be sensitive to changes in concentration of danger signals and hence an appropriate response is generated. Aickelin et al propose that by differentiating between the chaotic process of necrotic cell death and the safe signals derived from regulated apoptotic cell death, pathogenic agents can be detected within an artificial immune system context.

Currently, the majority of artificial immune systems (AIS) encompass two different types of immune inspired algorithms, namely negative selection (T-cell

C. Jacob et al. (Eds.): ICARIS 2005, LNCS 3627, pp. 153–167, 2005.
© Springer-Verlag Berlin Heidelberg 2005

based), and clonal selection with somatic hypermutation(B-cell based). Exceptions to this include [16], where defined patterns of misbehaviour was used to create danger signals within mobile ad-hoc networks. Danger signals are used in [2] to define the context for collaborative filtering. Implementations including Danger Theory so far, have monitored danger signals directly and have not taken into account any of the cells responsible for signal detection. It is thought that danger signals are detected and processed through 'professional' antigen presenting cells known as **dendritic cells**. Dendritic cells are viewed as one of the major control mechanisms of the immune system, influencing and orchestrating T-cell responses, in addition to acting as a vital interface between the innate (initial detection) and adaptive (effector response) immune systems.

Dendritic cells (DCs) are responsible for some of the initial pathogenic recognition process, sampling the environment and differentiating depending on the concentration of signals, or perceived misbehaviour, in the host tissue cells. Strong parallels can be drawn from this process to the goal of successful anomaly detection. Current anomaly detection systems frequently rely on profiling 'normal' user behaviour during a training period. Any subsequent observed behaviour that does not match the normal profile (often based on a simple distance metric) is classed as anomalous. At this point an 'alert' is generated. However, these systems can have problems with high levels of false positive errors, as behaviour of users on a system changes over a period of time. Anomaly detection systems remain a high research priority as their inherent properties allow for the detection of novel instances, which could not be detected using a signature based approach. AIS featuring negative selection algorithms have been tried and tested for the purpose of anomaly detection [6]. They produced promising results, but were tarnished by issues surrounding false positives and scalability[8]. Some moderately successful non-AIS systems have been implemented, often involving adaptive sampling[4] and adaptive alert threshold modification.

The aim of this research is to understand the Danger Theory and its implications and to be able to derive an anomaly detection system. More specifically, section 2 of this paper explores the process of cell death and the debate surrounding immune activating signals. Section 3 focuses on dendritic cells with respect to changing morphologies, functions, control of the immune system and in terms of the infectious non-self and danger theories. Section 4 outlines an abstraction from DC functioning and the derivation of a bio-inspired anomaly detection unit. Section 5 shows a worked example of how a DC algorithm can be used as a signal processor, complete with pseudo-code and preliminary results. Section 6 includes a brief analysis of the results and details of future work followed by conclusions.

2   Death, Danger and Pathogenic Products

2.1   Cell Death and Tissues

Our organs are made up of a collection of specialised cells - generically named tissues. Tissue cells communicate with each other through the use of secreted messenger chemicals known as **cytokines**. These cytokines can have different effects on the tissue cells in the vicinity and can be either pro or anti-inflammatory in nature. The tissue coupled with the surrounding fluid containing cytokines forms the environment for the DC. The cytokine profile of the tissue changes according to differences in the type of cell death occurring in the tissue at the time, and can be used to assess the state of the tissue.

Pre-programmed cell death, **apoptosis** is a vital part of the life cycle of a cell. Without it, we would not be able to control the growth of our bodies, and we would be subject to out of control tumours. On the initiation of apoptosis all nuclear material is fragmented in an orderly manner, digestive enzymes are secreted internally and new molecules are expressed on the surface of the cell. The cell is ingested by macrophages, with the membrane still intact. It is thought that the resulting cytokines released from apoptotic cells have an **anti**-inflammatory effect. However, apoptosis is not the only means by which cells can die. If a cell is subject to stress (by means of irradiation, shock, hypoxia or pathogenic infection), it undergoes the process of **necrosis**. Due to its unplanned nature, there is no careful repackaging of internal cell contents, or preservation of the membrane. The cell swells up, loses membrane integrity and explodes, releasing its contents into the interstitial fluid surrounding neighbouring tissue cells inclusive of uric acid crystals and heat shock proteins. This type of cytokine environment is said to be **pro**-inflammatory. This also includes host derived antigens and all other polypeptides which can be phagocytosed by a DC.

The differences in the cytokine profile as a result of cell death are integral for understanding the way in which pathogens and other harmful activities are sensed by the immune system. There have been a number of theories over the last century which have attempted to explain the phenomena of pathogenic recognition. Two of the most hotly debated theories - the Infectious Non-self Model and the Danger Theory are relevant to understanding DCs and imperative to the abstraction of a useful algorithm.

2.2   Infectious Non-self - The World According to Janeway

Since 1959 the central tenet of immunology revolved around the specificity of lymphocytes to antigen. According to this theory, proteins belonging to the body (self) are not recognised by the immune system due to the deletion of self reactive T-cells in the thymus. However, this theory did not fit with an amassing volume of evidence. A new perspective emerged in 1989 with Janeway's insightful article [7], which provided an explanation as to why adjuvants added to vaccines were necessary in order to stimulate an immune response. These ideas formed the basis for the infectious non-self model. This model, also known as the detection of microbial non-self, is an augmentation of the long established self non-self principles, though the focus is on innate immune function[5]. This theory proposes that the detection of pathogens is done through the recognition of conserved molecules known as PAMPs (pathogen associated molecular patterns), essentially **exogenous signals**. PAMPs are produced by all microorganisms irrespective of their pathogenicity, and can be recognised by human immune system cells through the use of pattern recognition receptor e.g. toll-like receptors[13]. The effects of PAMPs on DCs will be explored in more detail in the coming section.

2.3 The Danger Theory - The World According to Matzinger

The Danger Theory, proposed by Polly Matzinger in 1994[10], also emphasises the crucial role of the innate immune system for guiding the adaptive immune responses. However, unlike detecting exogenous signals, the Danger Theory rests on the detection of **endogenous signals**. Endogenous danger signals arise as a result of damage or stress to the tissue cells themselves. The crucial point of the Danger Theory is that the only pathogens detected are the ones that induce necrosis and cause actual damage to the host tissue. The damage can be caused by invading micro-organisms or through defects in the host tissue or innate immune cells. Irrespective of the cause, the danger signals released are always the same. These signals are thought to be derived from the internal contents of the cell[11] inclusive of heat shock proteins, fragmented DNA and uric acid. It is proposed that the exposure of antigen presenting cells to danger signals modulates the cells' behaviour, ultimately leading to the activation of naive T-cells in the lymph nodes. Alternatively, the absence of danger signals and the presence of cytokines released as a result of apoptosis can lead to antigen presentation in a different context, deleting or anergising a matching T-cell[12]. The Danger Theory suggests that the tissue is in control of the immune response.

In [14] it is suggested that DCs have the capability to combine signals from both endogenous and exogenous sources, and respond appropriately. Different combinations of input signals can ultimately lead to the differentiation and activation of T-cells. Both theories have implications for the function of DCs.

3   Introducing Dendritic Cells

Dendritic cells (DCs) are white blood cells, which have the capability to act in two different roles - as macrophages in peripheral tissues and organs and as a vehicle for antigen presentation within the secondary lymphoid organs. DCs can be sub-categorised dependent on their location within the body. For the purpose of this investigation and the subsequent algorithm, dermal or tissue resident DCs have been examined. Essentially, the DCs' function is to collect antigen from pathogens and host cells in tissues, and to present multiple antigen samples to naive T-cells in the lymph node. DCs exist in a number of different states of maturity, dependent on the type of environmental signals present in the surrounding fluid. They can exist in either **immature, semi-mature** or **mature** forms. The various different phenotypes of DC are shown in Figure 1.

3.1 Immature DCs

Immature DCs (iDCs) are cells found in their initial maturation state. They reside in the tissue where their primary function is to collect and remove debris

Immature DC   **'Semi-mature' DC**   **Mature DC**

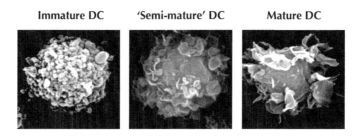

Fig. 1. Three differentiation states of DCs as shown from the ESEM photographs shown (see acknowledgements)

from the interstitial fluid. The ingested material is then processed by the cell. It is either metabolised for use by the cell, returned to the environment, or is re-packaged for presentation to another immune cell. At this point the matter can be termed antigen, and could be a 'self' molecule or something foreign. The re-presentation of antigenic material is performed by complexing the antigen with another molecule namely the MHC molecule family, necessary for binding to T-cell receptors. In order to present antigen to T-cells, DC needs sufficient antigen presented with MHC. However, the expression of inflammatory cytokines are needed in order to activate T-cells. Therefore a T-cell encounter with an iDC results in the deactivation of the the the T-cell. Differentiation of iDCs occurs in response to the receipt of various signals. This leads to full or partial maturation depending on the combination of signals received.

3.2   Mature DCs

Due to the low levels of inflammatory cytokines expressed by iDCs, they are not able to activate T-cells on contact. In order to present antigen **and** activate T-cells, the increased expression (or **up-regulation**) of a number of proteins and cytokines is necessary. DCs which have the ability to activate naive T-cells are termed mature DCs (mDCs). For an iDC to differentiate and become a mDC, the iDC has to be exposed to a certain number of signals. This includes activation of toll-like receptors through exposure to both the exogenous and endogenous signals (previously described). On exposure to various combinations of these signals, the DC up-regulates a number of molecules vital for stimulating a T-cell response. Perhaps most importantly, it up-regulates a number of costimulatory molecules, pro-inflammatory cytokines (namely IL-12), and migrates from the tissue to the local draining lymph node. During this migration period, the iDC changes morphologically too. Instead of being compact (optimal for antigen collection), the DC develops whispy, finger-like projections - characterising it as a mDC, as seen in Figure 1. The projections not only make it distinguishable from iDCs, but also increase the surface area of the cell, allowing it to present a greater quantity of antigen.

3.3   Semi-mature DCs

During the antigen collection process, iDCs can experience other environmental conditions. This can affect the end-stage differentiation of a DC. These different conditions can give rise to semi-matureDCs (smDCs). The signals responsible for producing smDCs are also generated by the tissue - endogenous signals. During the process of apoptosis, a number of proteins are actively up-regulated and secreted by the dying cell. The release of TNF-α (tumor necrosis factor) from apoptosing cells is thought to be one candidate responsible for creating semi-mature DCs [9]. As a result of exposure to apoptotic cytokines (TNF-α included), an iDC also undergoes migration to the lymph node, and some maturation as shown in Figure 1. Costimulatory molecules are up-regulated by a small yet significant amount and, after migration to the lymph node, the cell can present antigen to any matching T-cell. However, smDCs do not produce any great amount of pro-inflammatory cytokines, necessary for promoting activation of T-cells. Instead, smDCs can produce small quantities of IL-10 (anti-inflammatory cytokine), which acts to suppress matching T-cells.

3.4   Summary

In brief, DCs can perform a number of functions, related to their state of maturation. Modulation between these states is facilitated by the release of endogenous and exogenous signals, produced by pathogens and the tissue itself. The state of maturity of a DC influences the response by T-cells, either immunogenic or tolerogenic, to specific presented antigen. Immature DCs reside in the tissue where they collect antigenic material and are exposed to exogenous and endogenous signals. Based on the combinations of signals, mature or semi-mature DCs are generated. Mature DCs have an activating effect while semi-mature DCs have a suppressive effect. The different cytokine output by the respective cells differ sufficiently to provide the context for antigen presentation. In the following section this information is utilised to derive a signal processor based on the explored functionality of the DCs.

4   DC's Meet AIS

There are a number of desirable characteristics exhibited by DCs that we want to incorporate into an algorithm. In order to achieve this, the essential properties, i.e. those that heavily influence immune functions, have to be abstracted from the biological information presented. From this we produce an abstract model of DC interactions and functions, with which we build our algorithm.

4.1   Abstraction

As shown, the orchestration of an adaptive immune response via DCs has many subtleties. Only the essential features of this process are mapped in the first

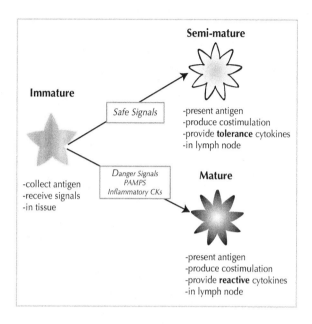

Fig. 2. The iDC, smDC and mDC behaviours and signals required for differentiation. CKs denote cytokines.

instance as we are interested in building an anomaly detector, not an accurate simulation. DCs are examined from a cellular perspective, encompassing behaviour and differentiation of the cells and ignore the interactions on a molecular level and direct interactions with other immune system cells.

DCs have a number of different functional properties that we want to incorporate into an algorithm. Bearing this in mind, we can abstract a number of useful core properties, listed below and represented graphically in Figure 2:

- iDCs have the ability to differentiate in two ways, resulting in mature or semi-mature cells.
- Each iDC can sample multiple antigens within the cell, leading to generalisation of the antigen context.
- The collection of antigen by iDCs is not enough to cause maturity. Exposure to certain signals causes the up-regulation of various molecules that initiate antigen presentation.
- Both smDCs and mDCs show expression of costimulatory molecules, inferring that both types have antigen presenting capabilities.
- The cytokines output by mature and semi-mature cells are different, providing contextual information. The concentration of the output cytokines is dependent on the input signals and can be viewed as an interpretation of the original signal strength.

The effects of individual cytokines and antigen binding affinities have not yet been incorporated into this model, as the initial implementation does not feature T-cells. As stated in [14], we are treating DCs as processors of both exogenous and endogenous signal processors. Input signals are categorised either as PAMPs (P), Safe Signals (S), Danger Signals (D) or Inflammatory Cytokines (IC) and represent a concentration of signal. They are transformed to output concentrations of costimulatory molecules (csm), smDC cytokines (semi) and mDC (mat) cytokines. The signal processing function described in Equation 1 is used with the empirically derived weightings presented in Table 1. These weightings are based on unpublished biological information (see acknowledgements) and represent the ratio of activated DCs in the presence and absence of the various stimuli e.g. approximately double the number of DCs mature on contact with PAMPs as opposed to Danger Signals. Additionally, Safe Signals may reduce the action of PAMPS by the same order of magnitude. Inflammatory cytokines are not sufficient to initiate maturation or presentation but can have an amplifying effect on the other signals present. This function is used to combine each of the input signals to derive values for each of the three output concentrations, where C_x is the input concentration and W_x is the weight.

$$C_{[csm, semi, mat]} = \frac{(W_P * C_P) + (W_S * C_S) + (W_D * C_D) * (1 + IC)}{W_P + W_S + W_D} * 2 \qquad (1)$$

Table 1. Suggested weighting values for the signal processing function based on DC maturation ratios

W	csm	semi	mat
PAMPs(P)	2	0	2
Danger Signals(D)	1	0	1
Safe Signals (S)	2	3	-3

In order to use this model, input signals have to be pre-classified (either manually or from a signature based intrusion detection system, another anomaly detector, or 'artificial' tissue) based on the following schema:

PAMPs - signals that are known to be pathogenic
Safe Signals - signals that are known to be normal
Danger Signals - signals that may indicate changes in behaviour
Inflammatory Cytokines - signals that amplify the effects of the other signals

In nature, DCs sample multiple antigens within the same section of tissue. To mirror this, we create a population of DCs to collectively form a pool from which a number of DCs are selected for the sampling process, in a similar manner to [17]. An aggregate sampling method should reduce the amount of false positives generated, providing an element of robustness. For such a system to work, a DC can only collect a finite amount of antigen. Hence, an antigen collection threshold must be incorporated so a DC stops collecting antigen and migrates from the sampling pool to a virtual lymph node. In order to achieve this we will use a fuzzy threshold, derived in proportion to the concentration of costimulatory molecules expressed. In order to add a stochastic element, this threshold is within a range of values, so the exact number of antigens sampled per DC varies in line with the biological system.

On migration to the virtual lymph node, the antigens contained within an individual DC are presented with the DC's maturation status. If the concentration of mature cytokines is greater than the semi-mature cytokines, the antigen is presented in a 'mature' context. It is possible to count how many times an antigen had been presented in either context to determine if the antigen is classified as anomalous. In order to crystallise these concepts, a worked example and details of a basic implementation are given in the next section.

5   Implementing a DC Based Algorithm

To illustrate the signal processing capabilities of a DC we have designed and implemented a simple prototype system. The purpose of this implementation is to demonstrate the signal processing capability of a population of DCs and their ability to choose between the mature and semi-mature pathways. We expect to see differentiation pathway switching when the data items change from one class to another. In essence a DC algorithm should transform a representation of input data items and signals into the form of antigen-plus-context. From this we can then derive information based on the analysis of the output cytokines.

For such an algorithm to work, some data attributes have to be classed as signals. We use the standard UCI Wisconsin Breast Cancer data-set[15], containing 700 items, each with nine normalised attributes representing the various characteristics of a potentially cancerous cell. Each data item also has a tenth attribute, which is a classification label of class 1 or class 2. Although this is a static dataset, it is suitable for use with our algorithm as data is used in an event driven manner. In order to reduce the difficulty of interpreting the inital experiments only a subset of the data was used. Data items with the largest standard deviation form the danger signals, namely cell size, cell shape, bare nuclei and normal nucleoli. For each of these attributes the mean was calculated over all data items in class 1. Subsequently, the absolute difference from the mean was calculated for each data item, within each attribute, v. The average of the four attribute mean differences comprises the derived danger signal concentration.

To generate concentrations for safe signals and PAMPs, the clump size attribute was chosen as it had the next greatest standard deviation. The median clump size value for all the data items was calculated and each item is compared to the median. If the attribute value is greater than the median, safe signals are derived, equalling the absolute difference between the median and the clump size, and the PAMP concentration is set to zero. If the value is less than the median, then the reverse is true, i.e. safe signals are set to zero and PAMPs are equal to the absolute distance. A worked example is presented in Tables 2 and 3, using one data item and the weightings from Table 1. An example of how to transform the input signals into csms is presented in Equation 2, using a modified version of Equation 1. This example data item was taken from class 1 and, as expected, produces a higher concentration of smDC than mDC cytokines.

Table 2. Sample data item with calculated threshold and signal values (in bold)

Sample Data Attribute	Data Value	Mean/Threshold	Derived Signal
Clump Size	10	4	**6**
Cell Size	8	6.59	1.41
Cell Shape	8	6.56	1.44
Bare Nuclei	4	7.62	3.62
Normal Nucleoli	7	5.88	1.12
Mean Danger Signal	-	-	**1.8975**

$$C_{csm} = \frac{(2*0) + (2*6) + (1*1.8975)}{2+2+1} \qquad (2)$$

Table 3. The output of the signal processing calculations

Output Signal	Output Conc.
csm	2.7795
semi	6
mat	-16.1025

Although we incorporate inflammatory cytokines into the model, they are not used in this example, as no obvious mapping is available. Antigen is represented in its simplest form, as the identification number of a data item within the dataset. The antigen label facilitates the tracking of data items through the system. Once the signals have been derived and associated with an antigen label, they are processed by the population of DCs. All featured parameters are derived from empirical immunological data. In our experiments, 100 DCs are created for the pool and ten are selected at random to sample each antigen. The signals relating to the antigen are processed by each selected DC and the total amount of output cytokines expressed are measured. The fuzzy migration threshold is set to ten. Once this has been exceeded, a particular DC is removed from the pool and replaced by a new one. After all antigen has been sampled, the context of each antigen is determined based on the number of times it was sampled as either mature or semi-mature. The threshold for classification is derived from the distribution of the data.

```
create DC pool of 100 cells

for each data item
    pick 10 DCs from pool
        for each DC
            add antigen(DataLabel) to antigenCollected list
            update input signal concentrations
            calculate concentrations for output cytokines
            update running total of each output cytokine
            if total csms > fuzzy threshold
                    removeDC from pool and migrate
                    create new DC

for each DC that migrates
    if concentration of semi  > mature
        antigenContext = semi
    else
        antigenContext = mature

for each antigen that entered the system
    calculate number of times presented as mature or semi
        if semi > mature
            antigen = benign
        else
            antigen = malignant
```

Fig. 3. Pseudocode for our simple example of a DC algorithm

The algorithmic details are presented in the pseudo-code as shown in Figure 3:

5.1   Experiments and Preliminary Results

Two experiments are performed using the standard Breast Cancer machine learning data-set. This data is divided into class 1 (240 items) and class 2 (460 items). The order of the data items is varied for the two experiments. Experiment 1 uses data on a class by class basis i.e. all of class 1 followed by all of class 2. Experiment 2 uses 120 data items from class 1, all 460 items of class 2 followed by the remaining 120 items from class 1. Each experiment is run 20 times on a Mac iBook G4 1.2MHz, with code implemented in C++(using g++ 3.3). Each run samples each data item 10 times, giving 7000 antigen presentations per run, with 20 runs performed per experiment. The time taken to perform 100 runs is under 60 seconds, giving approximately 10,000 data items sampled per second. The threshold for classification is set to 0.65 to reflect the weighting - items exceeding the threshold are classed as class 2, with lower valued antigen labelled as class 1. These classifications are compared with the labels presented in the original data-set so false positive rates can be measured, in addition to observations of the algorithm's behaviour. Preliminary results are presented in Table 4, and graphically in Figure 4.

6   Discussion and Future Work

It is important to note that we are not primarily trying to build a new classification algorithm. However, the classification accuracy in these simple experiments

Table 4. Table of results to compare two different data orders

Experiment	Actual Class	Predicted Class 1	Predicted Class 2
Experiment 1	Class 1	236	4
	Class 2	0	460
Experiment 2	Class 1	234	6
	Class 2	1	459

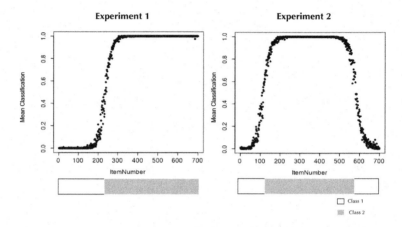

Fig. 4. This figure shows the classification of the 700 items. The bar underneath represents the ordering of the data. The results for the two different data distributions are presented. The y-axis represents the degree of maturity, from 0 (semi-mature, class1) to 1 (mature, class 2) . Data points above the threshold of 0.65 were classified as class 2 and vice-versa.

exceeds 99%. Rather, we are using this benchmark data-set to show how our dendritic cell model exhibits timely and accurate behavioural switches to changes in context. This is illustrated by our experiments, in which the system rapidly switches to 'danger' mode (Figure 4, Experiment 1) and back again (Figure 4, Experiment 2). Closer examination shows that the misclassifications occur exclusively at the transition boundaries. This is because each DC gathers multiple antigens over a period of time. If an iDC differentiates to an mDC, then every antigen contained in that DC is perceived as dangerous (class 2). Similarly, antigens within an smDC are all perceived as safe (class 1). It is not surprising that during a transition phase there is a small degree of confusion regarding temporally and spatially clustered antigens. A corollary to this is that the DC model is expected to make more mistakes if the context changes multiple times in quick succession; preliminary experiments (results not shown) confirm this. It is important to stress that the data set used was not the ideal application for this algorithm, but it provides data which we can interpret easily to observe the behaviour of the prototype itself.

The implementation of a DC algorithm that we present utilises a relatively simple, well understood data-set. This was useful as it demonstrated the signal processing and change detection potential of a DC based algorithm. However, as stated in the introduction, the ultimate use for this system is as an anomaly detection system with potential applications in computer security. This could be the detection of e-mail worms from an 'outbox'. The presence and type of attachment, rate of sending and content of the mail message could comprise the various signals, with a representation for the content of an attachment and the structure of the message could be an 'antigen'. Alternatively, the algorithm could be used to monitor network behaviour. Various attributes e.g. bandwidth consumption, could be mapped as danger signals, with safe signals and PAMPs derived from the output of various signature matching components e.g. an antivirus scanner. Antigen could be represented by data flowing through the system in terms of specific patterns of process execution, or perhaps the network packets themselves.

In addition to a more suitable data-set, a number of modifications can be made to the algorithm itself. For instance, we did not include any inflammatory cytokines in our worked example due to data constraints. It would be interesting to explore their proposed amplifying effects on the other signals and on the behaviour across a population of DCs. The current weighting function is simplistic and the weights are empirically derived. Perhaps replacing it with a more sophisticated signal processor based on multi-sensor data fusion techniques would be worth exploring. It will be interesting to see if making the algorithm more biologically plausible results in improved, finer grained detection. Potential improvements could include using a network of cytokines, specifically the cytokines responsible for T-cell activation and proliferation (e.g. IL-12, IL-10, IL-2), and dynamics taken from the accumulating body of immunological experimental results. DCs are only one component of the immune system - the incorporation of other 'cells' such as tissue (for endogenous signals) or T-cells (for an effector response) may give an improved performance.

7   Conclusions

In this paper we have presented a detailed description of dendritic cells and the antigen presentation process, from which an algorithm was abstracted. We have also presented a worked example and prototype implementation based on this abstraction The preliminary results are encouraging as both data orders produced low rates of false positive errors.

It is worth making two points about these results. Firstly, it is very encouraging that our simple model illustrates a prediction from the Danger Theory [10]: "...self-reactive killers should be found during the early phases of most responses to foreign antigens, and they should disappear with time". Secondly, it must be remembered that DCs are only part of a system, and that auto-reactive T cells will be tolerised if they subsequently encounter the same antigen in a safe context. A DC model is expected to work in partnership with a T cell system within the larger framework of a distributed immune inspired security system[3].

Acknowledgements

This project is supported by the EPSRC (GR/S47809/01), Hewlet Packard Labs, Bristol, and the Firestorm intrusion detection system team. ESEM photographs provided courtesy of Dr Julie McLeod, UWE, UK. The authors would like to thank Dr Rachel Harry and Charlotte Williams for the additional biological information. Thanks to Jamie Twycross for assistance throughout. Also, many thanks to Dr Jungwon Kim, William Wilson, Markus Hammonds, Dr Christian Lambert, Gillan Cash, Jim Greensmith and the rest of the Danger Team for their help, support and useful comments.

References

1. U Aickelin, P Bentley, S Cayzer, J Kim, and J McLeod. Danger theory: The link between ais and ids. In *Proc. of the Second Internation Conference on Artificial Immune Systems (ICARIS-03)*, pages 147–155, 2003.
2. Uwe Aickelin and Steve Cayzer. Danger theory and its applications to ais. In *Proc. of the Second Internation Conference on Artificial Immune Systems (ICARIS-02)*, pages 141–148, 2002.
3. Uwe Aickelin, Julie Greensmith, and Jamie Twycross. Immune system approaches to intrusion detection - a review. In *Proc. of the Second Internation Conference on Artificial Immune Systems (ICARIS-03)*, pages 316–329, 2004.
4. E. Eskin, M. Miller, Z. Zhong, G. Yi, W. Lee, and S. Stolfo. Adaptive model generation for intrusion detection. In *Proceedings of the ACMCCS Workshop on Intrusion Detection and Prevention, Athens, Greece, 2000.*, 2000.
5. Ronald N Germain. An innately interesting decade of research in immunology. *Nature Medicine*, 10(12):1307–1320, 2004.
6. Steven Hofmeyr. *An immunological model of distributed detection and its application to computer security*. PhD thesis, University Of New Mexico, 1999.
7. Charles A Janeway. Approaching the asymptote? evolution and revolution in immunology. *Cold Spring Harb Symp Quant Biol*, 1:1–13, 1989.
8. J Kim and P J Bentley. Towards an artificial immune system for network intrusion detection: An investigation of clonal selection with a negative selection operator. In *Proceeding of the Congress on Evolutionary Computation (CEC-2001), Seoul, Korea*, pages 1244–1252, 2001.
9. Manfred B. Lutz and Gerold Schuler. Immature, semi-mature and fully mature dendritic cells: which signals induce tolerance or immunity? *Trends in Immunology*, 23(9):991–1045, 2002.
10. P Matzinger. Tolerance, danger and the extended family. *Annual Reviews in Immunology*, 12:991–1045, 1994.
11. P Matzinger. An innate sense of danger. *Seminars in Immunology*, 10:399–415, 1998.
12. Polly Matzinger. The danger model: A renewed sense of self. *Science*, 296:301–304, 2002.
13. Ruslan Medzhitov and Charles A Janeway. Decoding the patterns of self and nonself by the innate immune system. *Science*, 296:298–300, 2002.
14. Tim R Mosmann and Alexandra M Livingstone. Dendritic cells: the immune information management experts. *Nature Immunology*, 5(6):564–566, 2004.

15. C.L. Blake S. Hettich and C.J. Merz. UCI repository of machine learning databases, 1998.
16. Slavisa Sarafijanovic and Jean-Yves Le Boudec. An artificial immune system for misbehavior detection in mobile ad-hoc networks with virtual thymus, clustering, danger signal, and memory detectors. In *Proc. of the Second Internation Conference on Artificial Immune Systems (ICARIS-04)*, pages 342–356, 2004.
17. Robert E. Smith, Stephanie Forrest, and Alan S. Perelson. Searching for diverse, cooperative populations with genetic algorithms. *Evolutionary Computation*, 1(2):127–149, 1993.

Cooperative Automated Worm Response and Detection ImmuNe ALgorithm(CARDINAL) Inspired by T-Cell Immunity and Tolerance

Jungwon Kim[1], William O. Wilson[2], Uwe Aickelin[2], and Julie McLeod[3]

[1] Department of Computer Science, University College London, UK
j.kim@cs.ucl.ac.uk
[2] School of Computer Science, University of Nottingham, UK
wow,uxa@cs.nott.ac.uk
[3] Faculty of Applied Science, University of the West England, UK
julie.mcleod@uwe.ac.uk

Abstract. The role of T-cells within the immune system is to confirm and assess anomalous situations and then either respond to or tolerate the source of the effect. To illustrate how these mechanisms can be harnessed to solve real-world problems, we present the blueprint of a T-cell inspired algorithm for computer security worm detection. We show how the three central T-cell processes, namely T-cell maturation, differentiation and proliferation, naturally map into this domain and further illustrate how such an algorithm fits into a complete immune inspired computer security system and framework.

1 Introduction

Self-propogating malicious code represents a significant threat in recent times as the ability of these programs to spread and infect systems has increased dramatically. The recent SQL Slammer worm infected more than 90% of vulnerable hosts on the Internet within 10 minutes [10], and at its peak the Code-Red worm infected over 2,000 hosts every minute [11]. Under such a constantly hostile environment, the traditional manual patching approach to protecting systems is clearly not effective.

An alternative solution to this problem is to have an automated detection and response system which could identify malicious self propogation and stop the spread of the worm as early as possible. Current automated detection and response systems involve such actions as blocking unsecure ports, dropping potentially threatening packets, and eliminating emails carrying malicious codes, breaking communication between infected and non-infected hosts to slow down worm propagation and minimise potential damage [12]. This appears to be a simple and obvious solution, however there are a number of significant hurdles to overcome in order to employ such automated responders. The most noteworthy obstacle is the high false positive error problem [16]. If an automated responder disconnects communication between two hosts based on a false positive result,

C. Jacob et al. (Eds.): ICARIS 2005, LNCS 3627, pp. 168–181, 2005.
© Springer-Verlag Berlin Heidelberg 2005

the effect of this inappropriate disconnection could be as bad, if not worse than, the damage caused by the worm itself.

The objective of this paper is to propose a solution to this problem by taking inspiration from the Human Immune System (HIS). Previous research into computer security in the context of Artificial Immune Systems (AIS) has been focused on detecting unknown intrusions [2] [8]; detecting anomalous events such as abnormal network traffic patterns or abnormal sequences of system calls. However the reliability of these systems to handle non trivial problems is still in question as they have not yet passed tests to indicate that low false positives are achievable in a real environment [2] [8].

Instead of developing these existing AIS, we propose a novel AIS model that adopts numerous mechanisms inspired from the differentiation states of T cells. These differentiation states can be grouped into particular status subsets which can be used to classify the types of T cell. From these classifications, the various roles of the diverse T cell types can be seen in terms of their contribution to the unique aspects of overall immunity and tolerance within the HIS. In this paper we carefully study the significant properties and physiological mechanisms of each T cell subset, with regard to the way they influence the interaction of immunity and tolerance. This study allows us to design a new AIS model, CARDINAL(Cooperative Automated worm Response and Detection ImmuNe ALgorithm) which has the potential to operate as a cooperative automated worm detection and response system. The paper starts by addressing the research issues associated with such a system. Section 3 introduces the different differentiation states of T cells within the HIS. Section 4 presents a novel cooperative automated worm detection and response system which adopts CARDINAL and finally the paper concludes with details of future work planned.

2   Cooperative Automated Worm Detection and Responses

In order to detect the presense of a novel worm virus various automated anomaly detection and response based systems have been developed [12]. These systems trigger automated responses when they observe such things as abnormal rates of outbound connections, emails sent, or port scanning, etc. In order to improve the false positive error rate made by local anomaly detectors, an alternative cooperative strategy has also been suggested [3] [13] [14]. The motivation behind this approach is that additional information on the infectious status of the worm, and the responding states of other peer hosts, would help local responders make better decisions by taking into account the collective evidence on an attack's severity and certainty, and an infection growth rate. Indeed, some work has already reported that such a suggestion reduces false positive errors [16].

However, there are some significant issues to be tackled in order to make a cooperative strategy truly effective. Firstly, information shared between peer hosts should be lightweight, as the transfer of unnecessary and excessive information can create the potential for self denial-of-service attacks [3] [13]. Secondly response mechanisms should be robust against inaccurate information passed amoung hosts [3]. If the reaction to a false positive error is isolated to a single host, the impact is minimal. However because of the cooperative nature of the system, this inappropriate response could be disseminated to the rest of the network, causing other hosts to react in a similar fashion and exascerbate the problem. Thus, a cooperative system needs to localise the negative impact of such errors, and this could be done by constantly redefining the range of information to be shared in terms of an estimated certainty of detection results. In order to address these issues, we identify the following to be studied:

- **Optimise the number of peer hosts polled**: the CARDINAL system needs to determine which peer hosts are able to share information, and how many peer hosts should be selected to share that information. These decisions are directly aimed at preventing a possible break of self denial-of-service attack. Determining the set of peer hosts is done by identifying all the possible peer hosts that can be directly contacted and thus infected by a given host. However, the number of all possible peer hosts may be unnecessarily large as information shared by a smaller number of peer hosts might be sufficient to mitigate and stop worm propagation. An optimal number of peer hosts is desirable to mitigate the propogation of a worm to a sufficient degree whilst minimising the number of resources that are required to achieve that objective. The determination of the size of this optimal set of peer hosts would be influenced by factors such as the severity of the worm's threat, the certainty of attack detection, and the growth rate of the infection. The more severe an attack, the more certain we are of it being detected, or the faster is its propagation, then the larger the peer set needs to be so information can be shared by more peer hosts to counterattack the worm successfully.
- **Types of system responses should be determined by attack severity and certainty**: in order to reduce the negative effects of false detection results, CARDINAL selects its response to the threat depending on the certainty of an attack being detected and the severity of that attack. CARDINAL would respond to severe and certain attacks with strong actions, such as blocking ports showing anomalous outbound connection patterns, eliminating emails appearing to carry worms, or dropping hostile network packets containing attack signatures. Alternatively, when presented with relatively uncertain or less severe attacks, CARDINAL would take less severe action, such as logging the potential situation for an administrator or limiting the network connection rates.
- **For performing adequate magnitudes of responses, both local and peer information needs to be taken into account**: the severity and certainty of attacks should not be staticly measured. A worm detected at a local host, at a given time, might appear to be relatively less severe, however if CARDINAL later observes that the number of peer hosts infected by the worm greatly increases within a short time frame, responses to this worm should be upregulated in terms of detection certainty and attack severity. The total number of infected peer hosts could be estimated based on the

collective information passed between the peer set. Alternatively, when a severe attack is detected by a particular host, which disseminates this information to the remaining designated peer hosts, those hosts do not necessarily have to take the same corrective action as the original host. If the infectious symptoms are not shown at the peer hosts receiving this information, and the total number of infected peer hosts does not increase quickly, the peer host can change its response from a very strong reaction to a weaker one. In turn this host would decrease the number of other peer hosts to which it sends its detection and response information, curtailing the response to the worm and returing the system to a stable state. Considering these factors together, we see CARDINAL will determine the apppropriate number of hosts to be polled and the degree of response to a worm according to the severity and certainty of attacks, which are dynamically measured based on both local and peer information.

Table 1. Mapping between CARDINAL and HIS

CARDINAL	HIS
Optimise the number of peer hosts polled	Dynamically adjust the proliferation rate for each effector T cell
Types of system responses should be determined by attack severity and certainty	Differentiate appropriate types of effector T cells depending on interaction with cytokines and other molecules during the maturation proccess
For performing adequate magnitudes of responses, both local and peer information needs to be taken into account	T cell effector function is amplified and suppressed via interaction among different types of effector T cells

We believe that several mechanisms constituting T cell immunity and tolerance of the HIS could provide insight into intelligent approaches to implementing the previous three properties. Table 1 shows these three specific properties of T cells in the HIS, which were used to design CARDINAL. Section 4 discusses the details of these properties together with the proposed model of CARDINAL. Before this discussion, section 3 briefly reviews the various differentiation states of T cells and how they contribute to the HIS in balancing immunity and tolerance.

3   T-Cell Immunity and Tolerance of HIS

The immune response is an incredibly complex process that one can argue begins with the dendritic cell (DC). DC's are a class of antigen presenting cell that migrate to tissue in order to ingest antigen or protein fragments. Whilst ingesting the antigen, DC's are also receptive to molecules in the environment that may be associated with the circumstances of that antigen's existence. These molecules are identified as a form of danger signal [9]. Once the antigen has been ingested in the tissue, the DC's travel back to the lymph nodes where they present the antigen peptides to naive or memory T cells via their MHC molecules, this allows a T cell to be able to identify that antigen. In addition, the DC will interpret the molecules it experienced during the ingestion process, and release particular cytokines[1] to influence the differentiation of the T cell it is presenting antigen to. In this way, the DC drives the T cell to react to the antigen in an appropriate manner and as such the DC can be seen as the interpretative brain behind the immune response. Given we now know what drives the T cell differentiation process, we turn to look at the different T cell differentiation stages. Much of this information has been taken from [5] [7] and reference to that work should be made if further detail is required.

3.1   Naive T Cells

Naive T cells are T cells that have survived the negative and positive selection processes within the thymus, and have migrated to continuously circulate between the blood and lymphoid organs as they await antigen presentation by DC's. The important fact is that naive T cells have not experienced antigen and they do not as yet exhibit effector function.

3.2   Activated T Cells

Naive T cells reach an activated state when the T cell receptor (TCR) on the surface of the naive T cell successfully binds to the antigen peptide-MHC molecules on the surface of the DC, and co-stimulatory molecules are sufficiently upregulated on the surface of the DC to reflect the potential danger signal. The degree of signaling from the DC influences the degree of activation of the T cells. T cells that receive high signal strengths adopt the potential for effector function and gain the ability to migrate from their current location in the lymph node to the periphery. These activated T cells gain the ability to proliferate and their clones will begin to differentiate into either helper T cells or cytotoxic T cells. These cells will finally reach effector status when they interact with a second antigen source. T cells that receive excessive levels of signalling die through a process of activation induced cell death (AICD) to prevent an excessive immune response taking place.

3.3   Helper T Cells (Th)

Naive T cells express either CD4 or CD8 co-receptor molecules on their surface, so called as they are clustered with the TCR and bind to the MHC molecules presented on the DC. Naive T cells expressing CD4 differentiate into Th cells

---

[1] Cytokines are chemical messengers within the HIS [5]. They are proteins produced by virtually all cells in the HIS and they play an important role in regulating the development of effector immune cells.

after activation. When they achieve effector status, through further antigenic stimulation, Th cells can develop into either Th1 or Th2 cells. The divergence between Th1 and Th2 is driven by the cytokines released from the DC when the T cell is first activated. Th1 and Th2 cells have different functionality as Th1 cells release cytokines that activate cytotoxic T cells whilst Th2 cells release cytokines that activate B cells.

In addition, a cross regulation mechanism exists between Th1 and Th2 cells. Cytokines released by Th1 cells directly impede the proliferation of Th2 cells, whilst Th1 cytokines downregulate the production of the cytokine IL-12 in DC's which in turn downregulates the proliferation of Th2 cells. This feedback mechanism leads to an immune response dominated by the particular Th cell subtype that is primarily stimulated, ensuring the more suitable immune response is initiated to resolve the current threat.

3.4   Cytotoxic T Cells (CTL)

Naive cells that express the CD8 molecule on their surface are predestined to become CTL cells after activation. If the DC's themselves do not express sufficient co-stimulatory molecules to cause activation, then DC's can be induced to upregulate those signals by Th1 cells who also bind to the DC. Activated CTL's will undergo proliferation and migrate to inflamed peripheral tissues. When they receive stimulation from subsequent antigen, they will reach an effector status and develop the ability to produce antiviral cytokines and cytotoxic molecules, which when released will kill infected host cells that exhibit the antigen trace identified by the CTL. A CTL can bind to, and therefore kill, more than one infected cell at a time.

Current theories disagree as to whether, after reaching an effector state and carrying out their helper or killer function, CTL and Th cells either die as they have reached a terminally differentiated state or whether some proportion of the CTL / Th effector cell population differentiate into longer lived memory cells to facilitate a suitable secondary response.

3.5   Summary of T Cell States

From the above sections, we can see that given the presentation of antigen by an APC and the existence of sufficient signals that indicate the presence of danger, a naive cell will become activated, will proliferate and differentiate into effector cells which can take on numerous alternative states. Depending on the co-receptors expressed on the effector T cell surface, these cells will either differentiate into Th or CTL cells. CTL cells lead the immune response by eliminating antigenic threats. Th cells provide assistance to this protective process but also provide regulation via a comprehensive feedback mechanism to ensure stabilisation. Naive cells that do not receive sufficient danger signals do not become activated and so the system becomes tolerant to such antigen strains. All these cells interact in a competitive environment that results in tolerance and immunity within the system.

4   Cooperative Automated Worm Response and Detection ImmuNe ALgorithm(CARDINAL)

As described in the previous section, different differentiation statuses of T-cells play varying roles in evoking overall immunity and tolerance in the HIS. This section introduces the overall architecture and components of the AIS that adopts CARDINAL, which employs various the T-cell immunity and tolerance mechanims reviewed in the previous section.

4.1   Overall Architecture

The overall architecture of CARDINAL is presented in Fig. 1. It consists of *periphery* and *lymph node* processes [15]. Both processes reside on a monitoring host and any host running these two processes becomes a part of an artificial body which CARDINAL monitors. The periphery is comprised of DCs and various types of artificial T cells and they directly interact with input data such as network packets, email outbox or TCP connection requests etc. The input data also exists as a part of the periphery. DCs gather and analyse the input data and carry their analysis results to the lymph node. At the lymph node, *naive T cells* are created which subsequently differentiate into various types of *effector T cells* based on the input data analysis results continuously passed from DCs. Within CARDINAL, effector T cells are automated responders that react to worm related processes in the periphery. Effector T cells are assigned to a response target, a response type, and the number of peer hosts polled. Before the effector T cells migrate from the lymph node to the periphery, they interact with other effector T cells passed from peer hosts. This interaction allows locally generated effector T cells to determine whether they should perform assigned types of responses or not, and the numbers of peer hosts to be polled if they decide a response is appropriate. The local effector T cells assigned to particular responses, and the number of peer hosts to be polled are passed to

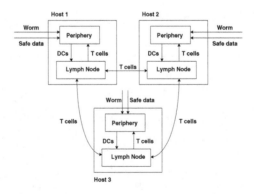

Fig. 1. Overview Architecture of CARDINAL

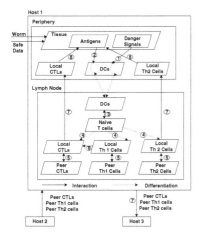

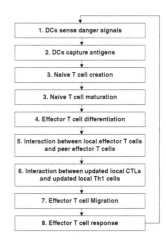

Fig. 2. Periphery and Lymph Node Processes in CARDINAL

Fig. 3. A flow chart of CARDI-NAL

the periphery processes at the local host and the peer hosts. These effector T cells now respond to the response targets, which are also defined as a part of the periphery process. In the next section, we provide more detailed descriptions of artificial cell interactions occuring at the periphery and lymph node processes within CARDINAL.

4.2 Periphery and Lymph Node Processes

DCs sense danger signals and capture antigens. The artificial tissue layer provides the location for two primary activities, the monitoring of danger signals (see ① in Fig. 2) and the collection of antigen in the form of input data (see ② in Fig. 2). Here danger signals are seen in the context of the symptoms arising from a worms infection. Well known worm infection symptoms include excessive cpu load at the host level, bandwidth saturation at the network level, and abnormal rates of email communication etc. Mechanisms of converting infection symptoms into danger signals that can be acted upon can be seen in [6] and are not discussed here. The DC's within CARDINAL then assess these danger signals and ascertain the severity of the attack and the certainty of its detection. The second purpose of the tissue layer is to provide a mechanism for the DC's to gain access to the input data reflecting the antigens, so that the threat level derived from the danger signal can be associated with its respective source and remembered. The extraction of antigen from the tissues by DC's is discussed in [4] [6].

Naive T cell creation. Once collected in the periphery, DCs carry the danger signal assessment results and captured antigens to the lymph node. At the lymph node, *naive T cells* are created and these are subsequently differentiated based on the danger signal assessment results into their various states (see ③ in Fig. 2). In nature, the receptors on naive T cells (TCR's) allow the cell to identify a particular type of antigen. For the sake of simplicity, our model assumes that the system will target the worm which always has a consistent attack signature and so can be detected by our naive T cells via these receptors. This assumption will be changed in future work to allow for the detection of polymorphic worms, which constantly change their form or functionality. In this way, the receptors of the naive T cells are simply copies of the antigens presented by DCs.

Naive T cell maturation. Naive T cells continuously encounter DCs passed from the periphery (see ③ in Fig. 2). During this process, DCs present danger signal assessment results to the naive T cells in three forms, as a form of a *costimulatory signal* and as two types of *cytokines* that reflect the potential danger signal, and each is affected differently based on the scale of the attack. The costimulatory signal is increased if a DC detects a severe attack, needing a strong response, and the certainty of that attack is assessed to be high. The cytokine IL-12 increases when a DC detects a severe attack requiring a strong response but with a relatively lower certainty, whereas the value of the cytokine IL-4 is incremented when a DC detects a less severe attack which only needs a weak response[2].

Naive T cells have three numerical values associated with them, these represent the "accumulated" certainties and severities of attacks recognised for each cell type: *CTL activation values*, *Th1 activation values*, and *Th2 activation values*. Whenever naive T cells interact with DCs, they evaluate whether the antigen presented by DCs are identical to their TCRs. If they are identical, naive T cells adjust these three activation values by taking account into the values of the costimulatory signals and the cytokines IL-12 and IL-4 produced by the DC's (see ③ in Fig. 2). The costimulatory signal will influence the CTL activation value whilst IL-12 and IL-4 will influence the Th1 and Th2 activation values respectively. After a suitable period of time, these naive T cells are considered as ready to respond and differentiate.

Effector T Cell differentiation. There are three different types of local effector T cells : *local CTL*, *local Th1*, and *local Th2 cells* (see ④ in Fig. 2). The CTL activation , Th1 activation and Th2 activation values associated with the naive T cells will determine the types of local effector T cells that naive T cells will differentiate into. When one of these activation values exceeds a given threshold, via stimulation from the costimulatory molecules or cytokines from DCs, naive T cells will differentiate into the respective type of cell for which the threshold was exceeded. The newly differentiated local effector T cell will have an identical TCR pattern to the orginal naive T cell. In addition, they are cloned, and the *number of clones* reflects the numbers of polled peer hosts. This clonal rate is determined by the CTL, the Th1, and the Th2 activation values respectively. The

---

[2] For a less severe attack, CARDINAL does not take into account the certainty of this kind of attack since a negative effect of a response triggered by a false positive error would be minor.

larger the CTL activation value, the larger is the number of clones allocated to that CTL. Similarly, the larger the Th1 or Th2 cell activation values, the larger is the numbers of clones assigned to the Th1 cell or Th2 cell.

Interaction between local effector cells and peer effector cells. Each type of local effector T cell only interacts with the same corresponding type of peer effector T cell transferred from the peer hosts (see ⑤ in Fig. 2). This interaction takes place over four distinct stages. During the initial stage, at each host, CARDINAL selects local effector T cells whose numbers of clones are large enough to indicate that the antigens recognised by those effectors are severe in terms of their attack, and that the evidence of this attack is certain. During the second stage, CARDINAL reviews the local effector T cells that were not selected during the first stage and compares them to the peer effector T cells. Local effector T cells are then chosen if they match the required number of peer effector T cells, which detect the same antigens recognisied by local effector T cells. During the third stage, CARDINAL recalculates the number of clones assigned to the local effector T cells that were selected during stages one and two. The numbers of clones produced is determined by comparing the historical growth rate of the worm infection against the historical effector cell clone growth rate[3]. If the worm infection growth rate exceeds, or is equal to, the clone growth rate, CARDINAL increases the numbers of clones currently assigned to local effector T cells, otherwise CARDINAL decreases the numbers of clones of local effector T cells.

During the fourth and final stage, CARDINAL reviews the peer effector T cells received by the local host and identifies those cells that do not have a local effector T cell that are capable of detecting the same antigen. The numbers of clones assigned to these peer effector T cells is then decreased because those antigen have not been detected at this local host, and so are not considered a threat. Therefore, CARDINAL starts to suppress the response to that antigen. After this suppression, CARDINAL examines the the number of clones assigned to the peer effector T cells sent to the local host. If the number of clones exceeds zero, then this reflects a potential threat that the local host has yet to experience. In order to prepare the local host for this potential threat the local host will create a local naive T cell that is an exact copy of a peer effector T cell. This naive cell will have lower activation thresholds for its CTL, Th1 and Th2 activation values to ensure a rapid response is initiated to any subsequent antigen exposure. In this way, we create a form of memory within the CARDINAL system.

Interaction between updated local CTLs and updated local Th1 cells. Up to this point, effector T cells have only interacted with other effector T cells of the same type. However, CARDINAL also incorporates interactions amongst

---

[3] The worm infection growth rate is estimated from the total number of responses which the peer hosts made during the previous two time steps. The clone growth rate is also measured as the change in the number of clones over the previous two time steps.

different types of effector cells. Before local effector T cells migrate to the periphery, another interaction between local CTLs and local Th1 cells occurs at the lymph node. During this interaction, the local Th1 cells can further increase the number of clones assigned to local CTL's if the two cells recognise the same antigen (see ⑥ in Fig. 2). As the certainty of an attack detected by a local Th1 cell is lower compared to that detected by a CTL, some fraction of the number of clones which a local Th1 cell has could be added to the number of clones of the local CTL. This variation in attack certainty between CTL's and Th1's depends on the type and timing of the danger signals' occurrence (infection symptoms). The interaction between a local Th1 and a local CTL would result in the fusion of various information related to an antigen, which is collected from diverse input sources over different time steps. This additional support from a Th1 cell reinforces the response of a CTL by increasing the number of CTL clones specific to that antigen. This is because they provide additional evidence as to the existence of an antigen threat.

Effector T Cell migration and response. After the cell interaction phase is complete, local and peer effector T cells with positive clone values begin a migration process either to respond to a threat in the periphery at a local level (see ⑦ ⑧ in Fig. 2) or communicate the existence of such a threat to other peer hosts (see ⑦ in Fig. 2). Local CTLs and local Th2 cells migrate to the periphery of the local host and commence their assigned response roles to counter the antigen attack. Th1 cells influence the number of CTL clones whilst in the lymph node, so their impact on the periphery is indirect. If the numbers of clones assigned to local effectors are positive, and there are no matching peer effector cells detecting identical antigens, CARDINAL creates new peer effectors which are copies of the local effectors. These new peer effector T cells, along with the existing peer effector T cells, migrate to other peer hosts if the number of clones associated with these cells is positive. This ensures that the knowledge of the antigen attack is communicated to the selected peer hosts. As described previously, the number of peer hosts selected for migration is determined by the severity and certainty of an attack. The actual hosts chosen for this migration subset are selected randomly from "all the possible peer hosts".

4.3   T Cell Immunity and Tolerance Within CARDINAL

As illustrated in previous sections, CARDINAL adopts various immune inspired components in order to implement an effective cooperative strategy for worm detection and response. Table 2 summarises these components and their roles within CARDINAL. In section 2, we highlighted three properties desirable for an effective worm detection and response system. We believe that CARDINAL would provide these properties through implementing T cell immunity and tolerance as follows:

– **Types of system responses should be determined by attack severity and certainty**: CARDINAL determines appropriate types of responses

Table 2. CARDINAL components and their roles

CARDINAL Components	Roles	CARDINAL Components	Roles
Periphery	Input data access and responding targets	Lymph Node	T cell creation, differentiation and interaction
Tissue	Local anomaly detectors	DC Costimulatory Signals	Frequencies of severe and certain attacks
DC Cytokine IL12	Frequencies of severe and less certain attacks	DC Cytokine IL4	Frequencies of less severe attacks
Danger Signals	Infection symptoms	Antigens	Attack Signatures
TCRs	Attack signatures	CTLs	Strong Automated Responders
Th1 Cells	CTL controller	Th2 Cells	Weak Automated Responders
Activation Values of a Naive T cell	Accumulated severities and certainties of attacks	Number of clones of an Effector T cell	Number of polling peer hosts

based on the attack severity and certainty assessed by DCs. DCs exposed to various types of danger signals produce different levels of costimulatory signals and cytokines, which in turn stimulate naive T cells recognising the antigen presented by DCs. The different degrees of accumulated costimulatory signals and cytokines reflect the severity and certainty of an attack measured collectively over multiple time steps and data sources. This kind of collective measurement would provide more accurate grounds to determine appropriate types of responses.

- **For performing adequate magnitudes of reponses, both local and peer information needs to be taken into account**: a local effector T cell assigned to a specific type of response can be further stimulated or suppressed by the interaction with peer effector T cells. This stimulation and suppression is realised through updating the number of clones assigned to each effector T cell, which performs a specific type of response.
- **Optimise the number of peer hosts polled**: CARDINAL optimises the number of clones(=the number of peer hosts polled) assigned to each effector T cell by dynamically estimating the severity of the worm's threat, the certainty of attack detection, and the growth rate of the infection. This estimation is implemented via several stages of different types of cell interactions. These interactions include tissue and DC, DC and naive T cell, local effector T cell and peer effector T cell, and local CTL and local Th1 cell interactions. As a result of these interactions, if CARDINAL considers the identified attacks to be more severe, certain, and to propagate faster, CARDINAL triggers a larger number of hosts to evoke an automated reponse. In addition, CARDINAL immediately suppresses the number of peer hosts polled when it observes that the severity and certainty of an attack becomes less, and the propagation speed of an observed attack becomes slower.

The current mechanisms within CARDINAL, inspired by T cell immunity and tolerance, would provide these three desirable properties, which will help an automated worm detection and response system to reduce a false positive error.

5   Conclusion

In this paper, we have shown how the link between the the innate immune system(DCs) and the adaptive immune systems(T-cells), can be computationally modelled to form the basis of a novel worm detection algorithm. In particular, we identified three key properties of T- cell and mapped these into the CARDINAL system: *T-cell proliferation - to optimise the number of peer hosts polled. *T-cell differentiation - to assess attack severity and certainty and *T-cell modulation and interaction - to balance local and peer information.

Further extensions of the presented T-cell algorithm are possible. In particular, performance could be enhanced by including the notion of antigen generalisation leading to T-cell memory. Additionally, immunologists have recently discovered a potentially third T-cell line in the shape of regulatory T-cells. It is currently thought that these cells form an important part in inducing tolerance by regulating other T-cell behaviour. However, more details have yet to emerge before this class of cell can be efficiently incorporated into our computational model.

It is also worth noting here that the proposed T-cell algorithm does not operate in isolation, but in unison as a part of the novel danger theory inspired system [1]. Thus, it is essential for the algorithm to work with artificial tissue [4] and dendritic cell algorithms [6]. Once integrated, these systems should mirror the robustness and effectiveness of their human counterparts.

Current work is focusing on implementing a simulated model of AIS adopting CARDINAL. To reflect worm propagation in the real world, the simulated model needs to accommodate a number of settings and parameters such as the type of worm (random-scan worm or topology-based worm), a network topology, a rate of worm infection depending on selected worm types and the network topology etc. In order to provide such a realistic environment in the CARDINAL simulated model, the epidemic models defining the state transitions and conditions of infections are being currently studied [3] [13] [14].

Acknowledgements

This project is supported by the EPSRC (GR/S47809/01), Hewlett-Packard Labs, Bristol, and the Firestorm intrusion detection system team. Special thanks to Jamie Twycross for initiating the study of worm detection problems. Great thanks to all the members of the "Danger Project" (www.dangertheory.com) for their helpful feedback and inspiring discussion.

References

1. U. Aickelin, P. Bentley, S. Cayzer, J. Kim, and J. McLeod. Danger theory: The link between ais and ids. In *Proceedings of the International Conference on Artificial Immune Systems (ICARIS'03)*, pages 156–167, Edinburgh, UK, 2003.
2. U. Aickelin, J. Greensmith, and J. Twycross. Immune system approaches to intrusion detection - a review. In *Proceedings of ICARIS'04*, pages 316–329, Catania, Italy, September 2004.
3. K. G. Anagnostakis, M. B. Greenwald, S. Ioannidis, A. D. Keromytis, and D. Li. A cooperative immunization system for an untrusting internet. In *Proceedings of the 11th International Conference on Networks (ICON), 2003*, Sydney, October 2003.
4. P. J. Bentley, J. Greensmith, and S. Ujjin. Two ways to grow tissue for artificial immune systems. In *Proceedings of ICARIS'05*, 2005.
5. R. Coico, Sunshine G., and E. Benjamini. *Immunology : A Short Course*. John Wiley & Son, fifth edition, 2003.
6. J. Greensmith, U. Aickelin, and S. Cayzer. Introducing dendritic cells: A novel immune-inspired algorithm for anomaly detection. In *Proceedings of ICARIS'05*, 2005.
7. C. A. Janeway, P. Travers, M. Walport, and M. J. Shlomchik. *Immunobiology : the immune system in health and disease*. Garland Science Publishing, sixth edition, 2005.
8. J. Kim. *Integrating Artificial Immune Algorithms for Intrusion Detection*. PhD thesis, Department of Computer Science, University College London, 2002.
9. P. Matzinger. An innate sense of danger. *Seminars in Immunology*, 10:399–415, 1998.
10. D. Moore, V. Paxson, S. Savage, C. Shannon, S. Staniford, and N. Weaver. Inside the slammer worm. *IEEE Security and Privacy*, 1(4):33–39, August 2003.
11. D. Moore and C. Shannon. Code-red: a case study on the spread and victims of an internet worm. In *Proceedings of the 2002 ACM SIGCOMM Internet Measurement Workshop*, pages 273–284, Marseille, France, November 2002.
12. J. Nazario. www.wormblog.com, 2005.
13. D. Nojiri, J. Rowe, and K. Levitt. Cooperative response strategies for large scale attack mitigation. In *DARPA Information Survivability Conference and Exposition*, pages 293–302, 2003.
14. P. Porras, L. Briesemeister, K. Skinner, K.Levitt, J. Rowe, and Y. A. Ting. A hybrid quarantine defense. In *Proceedings of the 2004 ACM workshop on Rapid malcode (WORM'04)*, pages 73 – 82, Washington DC, USA, October 2004.
15. J. Twycross. Soma - a self-orgnasing mobile agent immune system for computer networks. Unpublished working report, September 2004.
16. N. Weaver, S. Staniford, and V. Paxson. Very fast containment of scanning worms. In *Proceedings of the 13th Usenix Security Conference*, 2004.

Mathematical Modeling of Immune Suppression*

Dokyun Na and Doheon Lee**

Dept. of BioSystems, KAIST, 373-1 Guseong-dong, Yuseong-gu,
Daejeon 305-307, Republic of Korea
{dkna, dhlee}@biosoft.kaist.ac.kr

Abstract. Administered antibodies can suppress humoral immune response. Though there are two hypotheses explaining the suppression, such as the epitope-masking and Fc-receptor mediated suppression, the epitope-masking hypothesis has garnered more supports. To better understand how the immune suppression works and to gain a quantitative and qualitative insight, we developed the first mathematical immune suppression model based on the epitope-masking hypothesis. However, because the hypothesis does not account for the actual B suppression mechanism, the fact that antigen-depletion induces the arrest of proliferating B cells was incorporated to the model. The model can reproduce immune suppression phenomena and complement the epitope-masking hypothesis by suggesting that the key mechanism for the suppression is the arrest of proliferating B cells and it was shown to be feasible. It is expected that our model gives a new insight to researchers in designing experiments for discovering the underlying mechanism of immune suppression.

1 Introduction

Humoral immune response can be suppressed by administered antibodies [1] and this phenomenon has been used to treat Rhesus prophylaxis [2, 3]. Briefly, a Rh- mother who lacks Rh+ erythrocytes can develop antibodies against the Rh+ erythrocytes acquired from her Rh+ baby at her childbirth. From the following pregnancy, the developed antibodies are delivered through placenta and damage Rh+ erythrocytes of her fetus. To treat Rhesus prophylaxis extrinsic anti-Rh+ antibodies are administered to the Rh- mother at her childbirth and which prevents the development of anti-Rh+ immune response and enables her to give a next birth without any complication. Though the immune suppression by administered antibodies has been used for medical treatments [2], the underlying mechanism is not fully understood yet.

In order to explain the suppression, two prominent hypotheses have been developed The first model, called epitope-masking, claims that passively administered antibodies bind to epitopes on antigens and prevent B cell receptors (BCR) from

* This work was supported by National Research Laboratory Grant (2005-01450) from the Ministry of Science and Technology. We would like to thank CHUNG Moon Soul Center for BioInformation and BioElectronics and the IBM-SUR program for providing research and computing facilities.
** Corresponding author.

C. Jacob et al. (Eds.): ICARIS 2005, LNCS 3627, pp. 182–192, 2005.
© Springer-Verlag Berlin Heidelberg 2005

recognizing the epitopes [1, 4, 5, 6, 7]. Therefore, B cells cannot be stimulated by antigens any more. The other model, Fc-receptor-mediated suppression, claims that administered antibodies form antigen-antibody complexes that induce co-crosslinking of BCR and FcγRIIB receptors, recognizing the Fc part of the antibody, on the B cell membrane [8, 9, 10]. The co-crosslinked FcγRIIB inhibits B cell activation signaling via immunoreceptor tyrosine-based inhibitory motif residing in intracellular domain of FcγRIIB [8].

Though each model has a strong point over the other, the epitope masking hypothesis has garnered more supports. For example, the FcR-mediated suppression model can explain the fact that antibodies against one epitope could suppress not only the epitope-specific immune response but also the immune responses against the other epitopes on the same antigen [10]. However, it has been also reported that $F(ab')_2$ fragments, lacking the Fc part recognized by the Fc-receptors, and intact antibodies showed similar suppression [1, 6]. In addition, Mikael C. I. explained the non-epitope specific suppression and supported the epitope masking by suggesting that microgram antibody completely covers antigens by binding to the epitopes and blocks other epitopes from being recognized by the corresponding BCR [11]. A decisive experimental result is that immune responses were effectively suppressed even in Fcγ receptor-deficient mice and there was no significant difference of suppression between normal mice and the knockout mice [12].

Until now many mathematical models on immunity have been developed, for example, for the prediction of immune response against Mycobacterium tuberculosis [13], vesicular stomatitis virus (VSV) [14], Hamophilus influenzae [15], Epstein-Barr Virus [16], Lymphocytic Choriomeningitis Virus [17], HIV [18, 19, 20] and so on. In spite of many attempts to develop immune models, to our knowledge, models on immune suppression have not been reported yet. Moreover, because previously developed humoral immune models focused on the way of B cell proliferation, not the way of B cell suppression, they could not be applied to predict immune suppression phenomenon.

In order to describe suppression by administered antibodies and to gain new insights on the suppression mechanism, we present the first immune suppression model. Specifically, the development of such a model would allow us to address how the suppression mechanism works and to predict the suppression quantitatively. Because the epitope-masking hypothesis is plausible [1, 6, 11, 12], the model is developed based on the hypothesis. However, the hypothesis though simply claims that due to the masking of epitopes by administered antibodies B cells are suppressed [21], it does not explain how B cells are actually suppressed. Thus, in order to explain the suppression mechanism and rapid reduction of B cell population, we complement the hypothesis by incorporating the 'B cell survival signal' to our model, that proliferating B cells require signals from antigen-BCR complexes for their survival [22, 23, 24]. In other words, our model not only supports the epitope masking hypothesis but also complements it by suggesting that the actual mechanism of immune suppression is the arrest of proliferating B cells resulted from the depletion of antigens. To test the model, it is simulated and model results are compared with experimental data in literatures.

2 Mathematical Model

We developed a mathematical immune suppression model based on the epitope masking hypothesis [21], but the difference from the original epitope-masking hypothesis is that in order to describe the suppression mechanism, which is not

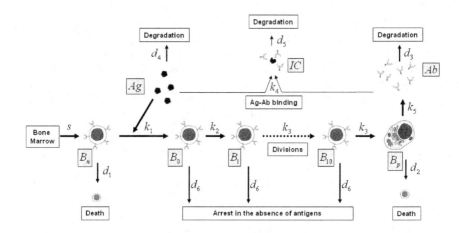

Fig. 1. Our immune suppression model is based on the epitope masking hypothesis which claims that the suppression of humoral immune response is resulted from the blockage of epitopes on antigens from B cell receptors by administered antibodies. Furthermore, our model incorporated the fact that B cells require antigens in order to keep dividing through their B cell receptors. Otherwise, they arrest in their cell cycles.

Table 1. Variables and function used in the model

Variables/Function	Description
Bn	Naïve B cell
B_0	Stimulated B cell by antigens before starting division
B_i	Dividing B cell. i denotes a division stage
Bp	Antibody producing plasma cell
Ab	Anti-SRBC antibody
Ag	SRBC
IC	Antigen-antibody complex
$D(x)$	The decreasing rate of the number of proliferating B cells in the absence of available antigens. $$D(x) = \begin{cases} 0 & \text{for } [Ag] \geq a[Ba] \\ d_6 x & \text{for } [Ag] < a[Ba] \end{cases} \quad \text{where } Ba = \sum_{i=0}^{10} B_i$$

explained in the hypothesis, the 'B cell survival signal' was incorporated in our model [22, 23, 24]. The model overview is shown in figure 1. Injected antigens are recognized by corresponding BCR-expressing B cells. The antigen-recognizing B cells delay one day before starting their divisions [25]. If sufficient antigens are available, the B cells proliferate and then differentiate into plasma cells to secret antibodies. Otherwise, they arrest in their cell cycles [23].

Table 2. Parameters used in the model

Para-meter	Value	Unit	Description	Ref
s	10	B-cell/day	Rate of naïve B cell production from bone marrow	Estimated
k_1	1.78×10^{-7}	1/(Ag day)	B cell stimulation rate	Fitted
k_2	1	1/day	Delay of stimulated B cells for division	[24]
k_3	3	1/day	B cell division rate	[24]
k_4	1.4×10^{-10}	IC/(Ab Ag day)	Rate of antigen-antibody complex formation	Estimated
k_5	10^8	Ab/(B-cell day)	Antibody production rate from plasma cells	[26, 27]
d_1	0.1	1/day	Death rate of naïve B cell	[28]
d_2	0.4	1/day	Death rate of plasma cell	[28]
d_3	0.18	1/day	IgG decay rate	[29]
d_4	0.05	1/day	Ag decay rate	[30]
d_5	2.4	1/day	Decay rate of antigen-antibody complex	Estimated
d_6	1.6	1/day	Death rate of proliferating B cell in the absence of antigen	Estimated
a	10		Minimum number of antigens required to sustain survival signal in proliferating B cells	Estimated
b	2		B cells produced per division	
e	10		Minimum number of antigens required to sustain survival signal in proliferating B cells	[31]

We used parameters from sheep red blood cell (SRBC) experiments in mice, a widely studied subject in the context of the immune suppression. The mathematical equations are listed below and the variables and parameters are described in Table I and II.

$$\frac{d[Bn]}{dt} = s - k_1[Ag][Bn] - d_1[Bn] \tag{1}$$

$$\frac{d[B_0]}{dt} = k_1[Ag][Bn] - k_2[B_0] - D([B_0]) \tag{2}$$

$$\frac{d[B_1]}{dt} = k_2[B_0] - k_3[B_1] - D([B_1]) \tag{3}$$

$$\frac{d[B_i]}{dt} = bk_3[B_{i-1}] - k_3[B_i] - D([B_i]) \quad (i = 2..10) \tag{4}$$

$$\frac{d[Bp]}{dt} = bk_3[B_{10}] - d_2[Bp] \tag{5}$$

$$\frac{d[Ab]}{dt} = k_5[Bp] - k_4[Ag][Ab] - d_3[Ab] \tag{6}$$

$$\frac{d[Ag]}{dt} = -\frac{k_4[Ag][Ab]}{e} - d_4[Ag] \tag{7}$$

$$\frac{d[IC]}{dt} = \frac{k_4[Ag][Ab]}{e} - d_5[IC] \tag{8}$$

3 Results

3.1 Immune Response Against SRBC

The stimulation rate of the naïve B cell was estimated to fit the experimental data where 4×10^6 SRBC were administered [11, 12, 32]. The number of B cell at day 3, 4 and 5 were from [11, 12]. The estimated B cell stimulation rate was 1.78×10^{-7} Ag^{-1}day^{-1}. The immunological profiles against SRBC are shown in Figure 2. It has been known that the stimulated B cells start to increase in their numbers from about one day after immunization to subsequent 3~6 days [33] as shown in figure 2A. In figure 2B, the number of antibody begins to increase 3 days after the immunization. It is because that stimulated B cells take 3~4 days to become antibody-secreting plasma cells [25]. The number of the antigens decreases by the produced antibodies (Fig. 2C). Specifically, according to our model results, around day 6 the number of the antigen-antibody complexes reaches its peak (Fig. 2D) because the antigens are most rapidly removed over the period (Fig. 2C).

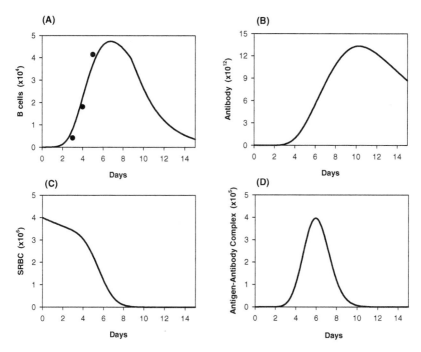

Fig. 2. For the simulation, 4×10^6 SRBC were injected and the humoral immune responses are shown. The B cell response to SRBC is shown in (A). The experimental data (closed circles) are from experimental data [11, 12]. The number of the B cell is the sum of the proliferating B cells and the plasma cells. The profiles of the secreted antibodies (B), antigens (C), and the formed antigen-antibody complexes (D) are also shown.

3.2 Immune Suppression

In order to simulate immune suppression, 4×10^6 SRBC were administered alone (Fig. 3A) and then 10µg anti-SRBC antibody approximately containing 4×10^{13} molecules [11] was administered at 0, 1, 2 and 5 days after the antigen injection (Fig. 3B~F). As shown in figure 3B~3F, the B cell peaks appeared 1~2 days after the antibody injection [12, 33], because the administered antibodies eliminated most antigens within a day (Fig. 3G), which resulted in the arrest of the dividing B cells. Even though antibodies were administered 5 days after the immunization, they also suppressed the immune response (Fig. 3F) as demonstrated previously in [12].

The earlier the antibodies were administered, the more the immune responses were suppressed (Fig. 3) [12]. The suppression results are in agreement with the experimental results [12]. For example, the administration of antibodies 3 days after the immunization could suppress immune response by 43% at day 5 while simultaneous administration could result in 1% suppression percentage at day 5 [4, 11, 12, 33, 34]. The suppression percentages were calculated by [34]:

$$\text{suppression percentage} = 100\times\frac{\text{No. of B cell in case of antibody injection}}{\text{No. of B cell in control}}$$

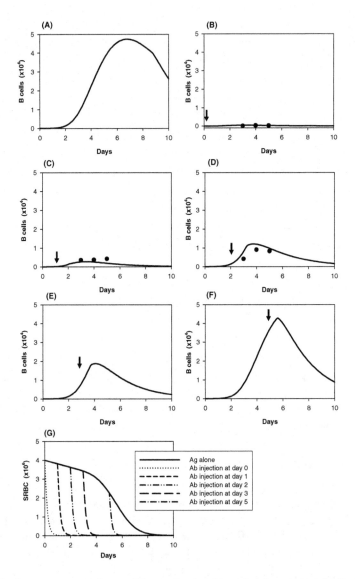

Fig. 3. The immune suppression model was simulated by administrating antibodies at various days, 0, 1, 2, 3 and 5 days after the immunization. The number of B cells and SRBC are shown. As a control, 4×10^6 SRBC were injected alone (A). B cell responses, when antibodies were administered at day 0 (B), 1 (C), 2 (D), 3 (E) and 5 (F), are shown. Arrows in (B)~(F) indicate the time of antibody administration. The closed circles in (B), (C) and (D) were calculated from the experimental results (12, 13). The SRBC profiles when antibodies were administered at various points are also shown in (G).

It has been known that not only the timing of antibody administration but also the amount of administered antibody affects the suppression. We simulated it by administering various amounts of antibody at day zero; 0.1, 2, and 10μg antibody approximately contained 4×10^{11}, 8×10^{12}, and 4×10^{13} molecules, respectively. In figure 4, the fewer antibodies were administered, the fewer antigens were cleared and the response was less suppressed. While 0.1μg of antibody did not make any significant suppression, more than 2μg of antibody suppressed the response significantly (Fig. 4A). It is because that 0.1μg antibody cannot eliminate the antigens, but more than 2μg antibody is enough to clear the antigens within a couple of days (Fig. 4B). This model results are also in accord with previous experimental results [11].

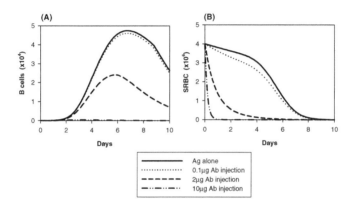

Fig. 4. 4×10^{6} SRBC with 0.1, 2 and 10μg antibody is administered together at day 0. The B cell profiles and SRBC profiles are shown in (A) and (B), respectively. As more antibodies were administered, they eliminated the antigens more rapidly and thus immune response was more suppressed. Administering antibodies less than 0.1μg did not make a significant suppression while more than 2μg antibody made a significant suppression.

4 Discussion

We have presented the first immune suppression model in order to understand the suppression phenomena. Though the model was based on the epitope-masking hypothesis, because the hypothesis does not explain the actual suppression mechanism but claims that the suppression would be initiated by the elimination of antigens, to account for the suppression mechanism and dramatic decrease of B cell population, the hypothesis was complemented by incorporating the concept of B cell survival signal [22, 23, 24].

According to reported experimental results, the number of B cell decreases 1~2 days after antibody administration [33, 35]. Without the arrest, the B cell population starts to decrease 3~4 days after antibody injection because the programmed divisions of stimulated B cells are not interrupted. This reflects that without suppressing proliferating B cells the population cannot be rapidly reduced. Thus, the arrest of B cell is the key process for immune suppression. In our simulation results, when antibodies were administered, it took one day before the number of B cells started to decrease because the antibodies took one day to remove the available antigens. Then, due to the depletion of the antigens, dividing B cells started to arrest and the number of the B cell population decreased consequently. Antibodies administered up to as many as 5 days after the antigen injection can suppress the B cell response [12]. Moreover, calculated suppression percentages were also in good agreement with previous experimental results.

We also simulated the effect caused by various amounts of administered antibodies and found that less than 0.1µg antibody against 4×10^6 SRBC cannot make any suppression while more than 2µg antibody makes significant suppression. It is possible to apply our model to clinical treatments such as the Rhesus prophylaxis [2, 4]. Using the model, an optimum antibody concentration inducing maximal suppression can be predicted for the treatment.

Conclusively, the model successfully reproduced the suppression phenomena and which supports the hypothesis and we suggest that the key process for the dramatic decrease of B cell population is due to their arrests in the absence of available antigens. We expect that our model results give researchers a new insight as to how the immune suppression works and it would help them to design experiments for discovering the underlying mechanism of immune suppression.

References

1. Tao, T., and Uhr, J. W. Capacity of pepsin-digested antibody to inhibit antibody formation. Nature 212 (1966) 208-209
2. Chilcott, J., Jones , M.L., Wight , J., Forman, K., Wray, J., Beverley, C., Tappenden, P. A review of the clinical effectiveness and cost-effectiveness of routine anti-D prophylaxis for pregnant women who are rhesus-negative. Health Technol. Assess. 7 (2003) iii-62
3. Gottvall, T., and Selbing, A. Alloimmunization during pregnancy treated with high dose intravenous immunoglobulin. Effects on fetal hemoglobin concentration and anti-D concentrations in the mother and fetus. Acta Obstet. Gynecol. Scand. 74 (1995) 777-783
4. Karlsson, M.C.I., de Ståhl, T.D., Heyman, B. IgE-mediated suppression of primary antibody response in vivo. Scand. J. Immunol. 53 (2001) 381-385
5. Heyman, B., Dahlström, J., de Ståhl, T.D., Getahun, A., Wernersson, S., Karlsson, M.C.I. No evidence for a role of FcγRIIB in suppression of *in vivo* antibody response to erythrocytes by passively administered IgG. Scand. J. Immunol. 53 (2001) 331-334
6. Cerottini, JC., McConahey, P.J., Dixon, F.J. The immunosuppressive effect of passively administered antibody IgG fragments. J. Immunol. 102 (1969) 1008-1015
7. Quintana, I.Z., Silveira, A.V., Möller, G. Regulation of the antibody response to sheep erythrocytes by monoclonal Ig antibodies. Eur. J. Immunol. 17 (1987) 1343-1349
8. Ravetch, J.V., and Lanier, L.L. Immune inhibitory receptors. Science 290 (2000) 84-89
9. Coggeshall, K.M. Inhibitory signaling by B cell FcγRIIb. Curr. Opin. Immunol. 10 (1998) 306-312
10. Heyman, B. Fc-dependent IgG-mediated suppression of the antibody response: fact or artifact? Scand. J. Immunol. 31 (1990) 601-607

11. Karlsson, M.C.I., Wernersson, S., de Ståhl, T.D., Gustavsson, S., Heyman, B. Efficient IgG-mediated suppression of primary antibody responses in Fcγ receptor-deficient mice. Proc. Natl. Acad. Sci. 96 (1999) 2244-2249

12. Karlsson, M.C.I., Getahun, A., Heyman, B. FcγRIIB in IgG-mediated suppression of antibody responses: different impact *in vivo* and *in vitro*. J. Immunol. 167 (2001) 5558-5564

13. Marino, S., Kirschner, D.E. The human immune response to *Mycobacterium tuberculosis* in lung and lymph node. J. Theor. Biol. 227 (2004) 463-486

14. Funk, G.A., Barbour, A.D., Hengartner, H., Kalinke, U. Mathematical model of a virus-neutralizing immunoglobulin response. J.Ttheor. Biol. 195 (1998) 41-52

15. Rundell, A., DeCarlo, R., Hogenesch, H., Doerschuk, P. The humoral immune response to Haemophilus influenzae type b: a mathematical model based on T-zone and germinal center B-cell dynamics. J. Theor. Biol. 194 (1998) 341-381

16. Davenport, M.P., Fazou, C., McMichael, A.J., Callan, M.F.C. Clonal selection, clonal senescence, and clonal succession: the evolution of the T cell response to infection with a persistent virus. J. Immunol. 168 (2002) 3309-3317

17. De Boer, R.J., Oprea, M., Antia, R., Murali-Krishna, K., Ahmed, R., Perelson, A.S. Recruitment times, proliferation, and apoptosis rates during the CD8+ T-cell response to lymphocytic choriomeningitis virus. J. Virol. 75 (2001) 10663-10669

18. Wodarz, D., Lloyd, A.L., Jansen, V.A.A., Nowak, M.A. Dynamics of macrophage and T cell infection by HIV. *J. Theor. Biol.* 196 (1999) 101-113

19. Stafford, M.A., Corey, L., Cao, Y., Daar, E.S., Ho, D.D., Perelson, A.S. Modeling plasma virus concentration during primary HIV infection. J. Theor. Biol. 203 (2000) 285.

20. Perelson, A.S. Modelling viral and immune system dynamics. Nat. Rev. Immunol. 2 (2002) 28-36

21. Heyman, B. Feedback regulation by IgG antibodies. Immunol. Lett. 88 (2003) 157-161

22. Rosado, M.M., and Freitas, A.A. The role of the B cell receptor V region in peripheral B cell survival. Eur. J. Immunol. 28 (1998) 2685-2693

23. Pittner, B.T. and Snow, E.C. Strength of signal through BCR determines the fate of cycling B cells by regulating the expression of the Bcl-2 family of survival proteins. Cell. Immunol. 186 (1998) 55-62

24. Smith, S.H., and Reth, M. Perspectives on the nature of BCR-mediated survival signals. Mol. Cell 14 (2004) 696-697

25. Hodgkin, P.D., Lee, J., Lyons, A.B. B cell differentiation and isotype switching is related to division cycle number. J. Exp. Med. 184 (1996) 277-281

26. Hager, A.-C.M., Ellmark, P., Borrebaeck, C.A.K., Furebring, C. Affinity and epitope profiling of mouse anti-CD40 monoclonal antibodies. Scand. J. Immunol. 57 (2003) 517-524

27. Kierzek, A.M., Zaim, J., Zielenkiewicz, P. The effect of transcription and translation initiation frequencies on the stochastic fluctuations in prokaryotic gene expression. J. Biol. Chem. 276 (2001) 8165-8172

28. Perelson, A.S. Immunology for physicists. Rev. Modern Phys. 69 (1997) 1219-1268

29. Maynard, J. and Georgiou, G. Antibody engineering. Annu. Rev. Biomed. Eng. 2 (2000) 339-376

30. Giles, R.C.Jr., Berman, A., Hildebrandt, P.K., McCaffrey, R.P. The use of ^{51}Cr for sheep red blood cell survival studies. Proc. Soc. Exp. Biol. Med. 148 (1975) 795-798

31. Leanderson, T., Källberg, E., Gray, D. Expansion, selection and mutation of antigen-specific B-cells in germinal centers. Immunol. Rev. 126 (1992) 47-61

32. Bocharov, G.A., and Romanyukha, A.A. Mathematical model of antiviral immune response III. Influenza A virus infection. J. Theor. Biol. 167 (1994) 323-360
33. Göran Möller, M.D. and Wigzell, H. Antibody synthesis at the cellular level. J. Exp. Med. 121 (1965) 969-989
34. Heyman, B. and Wigzell, H. Immunoregulation by monoclonal sheep erythrocyte-specific IgG antibodies: suppression is correlated to level of antigen binding and not to isotype. J. Immunol. 132 (1984) 1136-1143
35. Kettman, J. and Dutton, R.W. An *in vitro* primary immune response to 2,4,6-trinitrophenyl substituted erythrocytes: response against carrier and hapten. J. Immunol. 104 (1970) 1558-1561

Evaluating Theories of Immunological Memory Using Large-Scale Simulations

M.J. Robbins and S.M. Garrett

Computational Biology Group,
Dept. Computer Science,
University of Wales, Aberystwyth
Wales, UK
SY23 3DB
{mjr00, smg}@aber.ac.uk

Abstract. Immunological simulations offer the possibility of performing high-throughput experiments *in silico* that can predict, or at least suggest, *in vivo* phenomena. In this paper, we first validate an experimental immunological simulator, developed by the authors, by simulating several theories of immunological memory with known results. We then use the same system to evaluate the predicted effects of a theory of immunological memory. The resulting model has not been explored before in artificial immune systems research, and we compare the simulated *in silico* output with *in vivo* measurements. We conclude that the theory appears valid, but that there are a common set of reasons why simulations are a useful support tool, not conclusive in themselves.

1 Introduction

The field of Artificial Immune Systems (AIS) has successfully established itself as a discipline that investigates the computational properties of immune system abstractions. As a result, AIS researchers are in the unique position of being able to offer to immunologists simultaneous expertise in computational methods, and in the ability to apply these methods to immunological problems.

One such useful computational application is the *immune system simulation*. Immune system simulators will be required if there is to be a significant increase in the generation of new immunological ideas, because computational simulation is considerably faster than lab experiments. So far, however, this has not been practical because the granularity of the simulations has been far too large, and a single system can either generate high-level, global immune simulations, or detailed but partial simulations.

In this paper we outline a system, still under development, that can provide fast, detailed immune simulations, and which is beginning to suggest *in vivo* effects with enough accuracy to be useful as an immunology support tool. We choose immunological memory as our application area. This paper:

1. Provides a survey of immunological memory, particularly with regard to a new immunological memory theory that may be of interest in AIS.

C. Jacob et al. (Eds.): ICARIS 2005, LNCS 3627, pp. 193–206, 2005.

2. Provides a survey of existing immune simulation systems. Due to space constraints we have restricted this to global simulators, rather than more specialised simulations such as (6).
3. Describes how we validated our immune system simulator on existing data.
4. Describes how we tested the validity of a new theory of immunological memory (3), by using our immune simulator to generate *in silico* results from a model of it, and evaluating the reliability of that theory by comparing our *in silico* results with the *in vivo* results.

Our simulator is fast, even when simulating tens of millions of immune cells, and it has the ability to simulate cytokine concentrations, which proved vital in simulating the work of (3). The simulator's speed and flexibility allows it to be applied to tasks that were previously impossible. Furthermore, our new simulator is designed from the ground up as a reusable, flexible tool for complex adaptive systems research, not just a one-off immune simulation.

2   Background

2.1   Immune Memory

Immune (or serological) memory is one of the hallmarks of the immune system but, as Zinkernagel et al say, in their seminal paper on viral immunological memory, *"Browsing through textbooks and authoritative texts quickly reveals that the definition of immunological memory is not straightforward."* (35), and many of the questions they raise are still relevant almost ten years later.

Once the immune system has mounted a primary response to an antigen, a memory of that antigen is retained for several years or even decades (23; 21). One way to measure the strength of a memory to an antigen is by counting the population of specific memory cells. This figure tends to fall rapidly immediately after an infection, reaching a stable level which is maintained over many years or decades, even in the absence of re-exposure to the antigen. The challenge facing immunologists is to discover how these cells are maintained.

Long-Lived Memory Cell Theory: The majority of our cells have a lifespan much shorter than that of the body as a whole, and so cells are continually dying, and being renewed. It has been speculated that some lymphocytes (both B- and T-cells) that have a close match to an antigenic source differentiate into 'memory cells', and that these memory cells are then highly responsive to the original antigenic trigger. This theory assumes that there is no cell-division, and the cells live a very long time, preserving immunity for many years (19).

Emergent Memory Theory: A similar theory proposed says that there are no special memory cells, rather the effector cells naturally evolve towards highly specific cells, and are preserved from apoptotic death via some sort of 'preservase' such as telomerase (30). Although it is unlikely that emergent memory is stable in itself (31), the process would explain how the quality of the memory evolves.

It is now widely accepted that these hyper-sensitive memory cells do exist, and exhaustive research has been conducted in order to describe their attributes and behaviours, e.g. (19). However recent experimental evidence has contradicted the theory that memory cells they are extremely long-lived. A series of experiments (29; 28) on mice showed that memory T-cells can continue to divide long after any primary response. Since a stable population is maintained, this means that memory cells must also be dying at a similar rate, and are therefore not as long-lived as originally believed.

Residual Antigen Theory: It is possible that the immune system does not completely remove all antigenic material from the host, either because small concentrations of antigenic cells may remain long-enough to reproduce, or because the immune system itself has retained some of the antigenic material in follicular dendritic cells (FDCs) – these FDCs then slowly release the antigenic material into the host, to stimulate a low-level immune response. In either case, this would keep the immune system active enough to sustain memory cell populations. This idea has been supported by research suggesting that B-cell memory is particularly sensitive to residual antigen (27).

In recent years however, compelling evidence has been presented suggesting that the cycling of memory T-cells continues to occur without any of the specific antigen being present (15), which would mean that these cells must be responding to some other stimulus. This view is widely accepted by immunologists (2), but it should be noted that some debate remains (17; 34)

Immune Network Theory: Network theory is based around the idea that the immune system retains memory by internal, not external stimulation. It suggests that immune cells, particularly lymphocytes, present regions of themselves that are antigenic to other immune cells. This causes chains of stimulation and suppression, which while begun by an external antigenic source, are continued and maintained even in their absence, and thus are a form of memory (9; 8). Nevertheless, general opinion in immunology says that the amount of interaction between antibodies is not sufficient to explain immunological memory.

Heterologous Memory Theories: It has been observed that during an immune response, populations of memory T- cells unrelated to the antigen may also expand (3; 28), suggesting that perhaps serological memory could be maintained by a degree of *polyclonal stimulation* during all immune responses.

According to (2), two possible mechanisms have been suggested to explain these results - Bystander Stimulation and Cross-Reactive Stimulation. The Bystander Stimulation theory suggests that the antigen-specific T-cell produces a cytokine that somehow stimulates all nearby memory T-cells to divide. The Cross-Reactive Stimulation theory is based on speculation that memory cells could be more sensitive to stimulation than naïve cells, and might therefore be stimulated by different antigens, perhaps even a self-antigen. It has been shown experimentally that memory T-cells specific to a particular antigen can be directly stimulated by a different, unrelated antigen (24).

Both of these theories are examples of *heterologous memory*. In other words, they suggest that once memory T-cells have been created, they can be stimulated during immune responses to unrelated antigen. The difference is that in one case the cells are directly stimulated by antigen, and in the other they are stimulated by cytokines released by other, antigen-specific cells.

Memory Maintenance in General: It seems likely that one, some, or all of the above theories have some basis in fact, but there are further general issues of memory maintenance. There are a number of problems with current theories of B-cell memory maintenance. These stem from an apparent paradox that can be seen in measurements of antibody concentrations in serum in the months following an infection. It has been known for decades (23; 21) that antibody produced in response to an antigen can persist at significant levels in serum for years after the initial infection has occurred. Antibodies cannot survive in the body for any length of time, so we can conclude that plasma cells are sustaining these concentrations. The problem is that plasma cells in mice have been shown to live for just a few months (25), and that they are only produced by differentiating memory cells. This evidence contradicts theories of long-lived memory B-cells, and draws us to the conclusion that memory B-cells – like their T-cell equivalents – are being continually cycled long after any infection has been removed.

2.2   A Brief Survey of Immune Modelling

Mathematical Models: Mathematical immunological models are often developed for a highly focussed area of interest (e.g. (22; 26)). Generally, they use ordinary differential equations (ODEs) or partial differential equations (PDEs) to encapsulate their chose immune dynamics.

Perelson's HIV equations (22), and Smith's influenza dynamics (26), are illustrations of models of small parts of the immune system dynamics that have had significant benefits to human health, but which do not set out to model the immune system as a whole. Slightly larger scale models have been used to explain gross-scale features of the immune system (33), but they are rare.

Immunological memory has been modelled in this way; the classic example is Farmer, Packard and Perelson's work (8), but there are more recent attempts to model immunological memory too (1). Although these models say a lot about certain details, they are not intended to be global models of immunological memory. For example, the important work of Antia, Ganusov and Ahmed on understanding $CD8^+$ T-cell memory (2) is based on a few, relatively simple equations. This is not to say that it is easy to generate such equations (it is not); rather, we are saying that the applicability of these equations is limited. Indeed, the difficulty in building and managing these equations is precisely the reason that a computational simulation approach is sometimes more appropriate.

Computational Models: Computational models are not as well established as mathematical models, but are usually either population-based (entities that are tracked as they freely interact with each other), or cellular automata (entities that are tracked in a discrete grid-like structure) (32). There are surprisingly few immunological simulators, and those that do exist have often not been peer-reviewed by the academic community.

ImmSim: The work of Seiden, Kleinstein and Celada on on ImmSim was the first real attempt to model the immune system as a whole. (14; 13), and it is still the only simulator to have been fairly widely peer reviewed. It is similar in style to the work of Farmer et al (8), but is a true simulation, not a set of ODEs.

Simmune: There are at least two "SIMMUNE" immunology simulators: Meier-Schellersheim's version (20), which was developed in the late-1990s, and a Derek Smith and Alan Perelson's version. Of the two, Meier-Schellersheim is the more advanced, implemented as a full cellular automata with the ability to define almost any rules that the user desired, whereas Smith and Perelson's was a relatively simple, unpublished Lisp simulation.

Synthetic Immune System (SIS): Although SIS appears to be significantly faster and more powerful, it does much less. SIMMUNE can simulate large numbers of complex interactions, whereas SIS is designed only to investigate self-nonself relationships. SIS is a cellular automata. SIS can only be found on the web, at: http://www.cig.salk.edu/papers/SIS_manual_wp_M.pdf

ImmunoSim: Ubaydli and Rashbass's Immunosim set out to provide researchers with an "Immunological sandbox" - it was a customizable modelling environment that simulated cell types, receptors, ligands, cascades, effects, and cell cycle, with experiments run in silico. A key requirement was that it should have a purely visual interface, with no programming necessary. It received the Fulton Roberts Immunology prize (twice) from Cambridge University but does not appear to available as a publication, or on the web.

Other systems: These simulations (5; 11) are smaller scale than that proposed here, but have still had benefits to medicine and immunology, and/or highlight problems that need to be overcome. Others have emphasised the importance of the binding mechanism, the type of cell-cell and cell-antigen interaction chosen, and the multitude of other possibilities that should be considered (10).

We have been using immunological memory as an area to help develop an generic immune simulator (31) – i.e. one that can simulate far more than just immunological memory.

3   Methods and Materials

3.1   About the Simulation System

The simulations that form the basis of this paper were modelled using our software, 'Sentinel'. Sentinel is a complex system simulation platform for immunology and AIS research that currently exists as a prototype. Its design is based largely around the principals of cellular automata, with the environment divided into a discrete grid of locations. Entities within the simulation are free to move around in this environment, but are only able to respond to events that occur within closely neighbouring cells. 'Engines', such as those used in computer games for managing graphics, physics, etc., manage the physical and chemical interactions that occur within this environment.

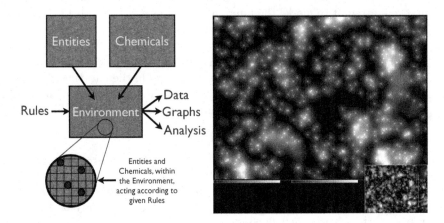

Fig. 1. (left) The structure of the Sentinel system. (right) Sentinel models the diffusion of chemicals to implement realistic chemotaxis and, crucially, to model the effects of cytokines (see text). The main figure shows the different concentrations of chemicals over a detailed view of the simulator's simulation environment. The inset shows the location of the detailed view in the whole space being modelled.

The physics engine allows accurate simulation of the physical properties of agents, restricting their movements according to attributes such as mass or energy output. Whereas many simulations or differential equation models are exclusively based on cells that exhibit some form of Brownian motion, agents (cells) in Sentinel move according to the chemical stimuli they receive, their motor capabilities, and external forces acting upon them. This ensures that movement is as realistic as possible, and is a novel feature of Sentinel.

A chemistry engine is responsible for managing chemical and biochemical reactions, and also the distribution of extra-cellular molecules throughout the environment. For example, if a cell releases a particular kind of cytokine at its location, the chemistry engine will cause that cytokine to gradually disperse across the environment (see Fig. 1) by diffusion, spreading a proportion of the molecules in one cell equally across its neighbours. This feature is essential for the accurate simulation of cell movement by chemotaxis – the process by which immune cells move towards higher concentrations of chemotactic factors, i.e. chemicals that attract them. Clearly, this also enables a cell to influence a larger expanse of its environment than would typically be allowed in a cellular automata, spreading their influence beyond merely their immediate neighbours. The implementation of chemotaxis is another novel feature of Sentinel.

Given a set of entities and chemicals (B-cells, memory cells, cytokines, etc.), the influence of the physics and chemistry engines is defined by a number of *rules* (see Fig. 1). These rules define when an entity can interact with another cell, and the nature of that interaction; how one cell releases chemicals, or other entities, into its near environment, and any global features, such as currents that affect all entities and chemicals.

Sentinel is in fact two applications - a simulator and an integrated development environment that simplifies the process of building complex models. Having defined the simulation model in the IDE, by coding the entities, chemicals and rules, the simulator is run and information is output according to user-defined data-feeds. These data can then be viewed in the form of various graphs and samples, or streamed to log files for analysis, all within the Sentinel system. It seems likely that this simulator architecture will be useful in other areas too, such as Biochemistry and abstract work in Genetic and Evolutionary Computing. Further details of the structure of Sentinel can be found in (9).

Sentinel can simulate several million cells, and their interactions, on a typical high-end desktop. Although this figure varies depending upon the complexity of the model, it appears to be one of the most powerful simulators currently available, especially in view of the complex interactions that it is able to simulate without resorting to lazy evaluation techniques or mathematical short-cuts. We believe Sentinel's ability to simulate realistically the movement of cells and chemical agents within the environment is very important, removing some of the assumptions about motion and distribution that are often made in simpler models, and providing a platform for more ambitious experiments.

3.2   Experiments and Tests

Before using Sentinel to evaluate Bernasconi et al's theory, we validated its performance. Both the validation and the evaluation models ran with of the order of 10^8 antibodies.

Simulator Validation Tests: Three theories of immune memory, outlined earlier, will be simulated in order to validate our Sentinel system: (i) Long-Lived Memory B-cells; (ii) Emergent Memory, and (iii) Residual Antigen. These theories have been simulated before, by us (31). If the results are qualitatively the same then we will have demonstrated that Sentinel can reproduce previous results. Each simulation was run 7 times, in order to ensure that the results were consistently reproduced and not merely one-offs. A more comprehensive validation is presented in (9); this is the only validation provided here.

Theory Evaluation Experiment: This experiment is designed to explore the veracity of Polyclonal Activation Memory, via simulation – something which has not been done before. We could not use our simpler simulator (31) because the experiment required implementation of cytokine gradients (of IL-15), and needed to be performed on a much larger scale to obtain meaningful results. Sentinel was the only simulation platform available that provided both realistic cell dynamics and a comprehensive data output.

The construction of Bernasconi et al's model is based on the theory described in (3). They suggested their theories as a result of *in vivo* experiments, and claim that the experimental results provide compelling evidence for bystander stimulation of memory B-cell populations. The comprehensive set of results published in (3) will be tested against the data from our simulation, so our aim is to simulate the implications of Bernasconi et al's theory, and assess whether it could indeed be responsible for the *in vivo* results that they observe.

It is likely that the results produced by Sentinel can only be legitimately used for their qualitative properties. Since the validation process described above is fairly limited, and the process of parameterising any simulation is complex, we can only safely look for qualitative similarities in the results.

3.3   Assumptions

In constructing these models, a number of assumptions were made. These have been kept consistent through all the simulations conducted.

Longer-lived memory cells: Memory B-cells live longer than their naïve equivalents. In nature a naïve B-cell tends to live for about 24 hours unless it receives stimulus, at which point it is rescued, and may go on to live for a few months (3) This is reflected in our models.

Antigen: Antigen does not reproduce or mutate during the simulation.

Clonal selection: In response to antigen, B-cells undergo clonal selection and hypermutation, as described by Burnet's 1959 theory. (4).

Simplified binding: In order to provide the best possible performance, a very simple binding mechanism was used. A strain of antigen is given a number between 0 and 20000, which remains constant across the population. Every new B-cell is assigned a random number within that range, and the binding success is measured as the distance between the two numbers.

Simplified Immune Repertoire: The simulation consists of only three entities: B-cells, antibodies and antigen, and one cytokine. B-cell T-cell interaction is not simulated in these tests, but are planned (see Further Work). We needed to keep the model as similar to our previous system as possible (no plasma cells) to make the validation process as meaningful as possible.

4   Results

4.1   Simulator Validation Results

As in (31), the results in Fig. 2 show that Sentinel produces a secondary response to a repeat infection of the same antigen, for all these memory theories. Furthermore, Sentinel's results also agree with (31) (Fig. 3) in that only the Residual Antigen model could maintain a stable population of memory cells, and produced a much less drastic drop in antibodies – down to about 10^6 antibodies before second infection, compared to near zero for the other memory models.

In both simulators, the models of the Memory Cell and 'Preserveron' theories sustained good short-term memory, and in both we observed the memories stored in this manner failing when the cells carried them died. Unless we accept that the primary immune response produces memory cells that live for years, such models will always result in an immune memory that fades over time.

The model of the Residual Antigen theory sustained a stable level of memory cells in both simulators, and was able to produce a substantial secondary

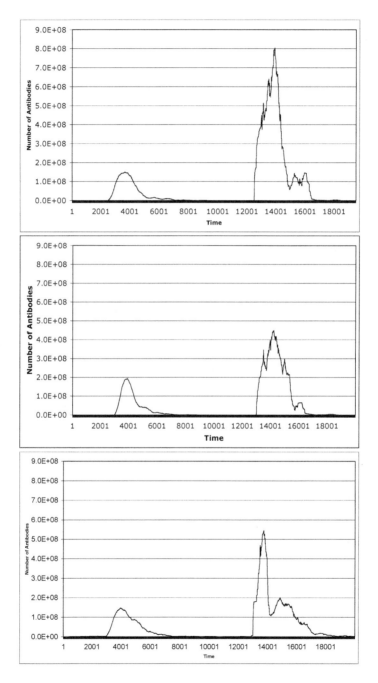

Fig. 2. Validation graphs produced by Sentinel for the number of cells over arbitrary time for: (i) the Memory Cell model; (ii) the 'Preserveron' model, and (iii) the Residual Antigen model. Antigen A is injected at t=3000, and t=13,000.

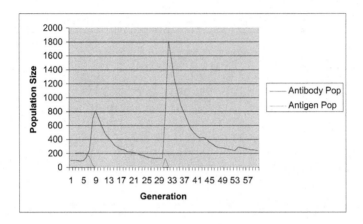

Fig. 3. A reproduction of the secondary response graph from (31). This graph was used to summarise the nature of the secondary response of all theories in (31), although that paper also described differences in the amount of memory loss between various theories.

response regardless of the length of time between the first infection and subsequent re-infection. It appears to be a viable model of immune memory; however, the requirements to sustain such a system seem unlikely to be met in nature because the immune system would have to produce such material over a highly extended period. Indeed this point was debated several years ago (18).

There are some differences in details, such as the more pronounced secondary peak in the secondary response, but the two simulators are close enough to proceed with the qualitative comparison of the *in vivo* and *in silico* results.

4.2   Theory Evaluation Results

Since we stated in the 'Experiments and Tests' subsection that we have not validated the finer-grained elements of Sentinel's results, we have compared the results, in a qualitative way. Fig. 4 shows two plots from Sentinel (top and middle) – each for different model parameters – and a presentation of the graph from (3) (bottom).

Note that the Anti-A plot, caused by re-injected Antigen A, in (top) and (middle) has a shallower peak than the plot of Anti-TT in the bottom plot. The parameter values for the (top) graph are bad, but in (middle) are better, and this need to find good parameters is discussed in the Further Work section below. Still, allowing for this, the *relative* increases seem to indicate that here is some degree of match between the simulated and *in vivo* results. Both parameter choices result in some features of the Bernasconi et al plot.

Although not perfectly confirmed, Bernasconi et al's theory has been shown to be qualitatively reasonable, relative to the *in vivo* measurements. But what causes the quantitative differences? The disparities may be due to: (i) *incorrect modelling* of the Bernasconi et al theory; (ii) *lack of detail* in the model; (iii)

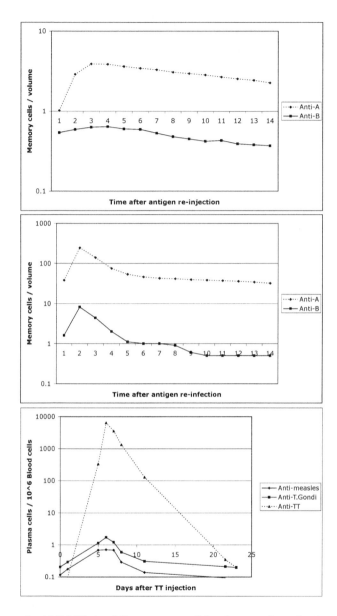

Fig. 4. (top and middle) Plots of the memory cell-levels per volume for two antigens, A and B, which are too dissimilar to directly cause a response in each other's memory cells. The immune system has already been exposed to both Antigen A and B; Antigen A is re-introduced at t=0. (top) and (middle) are for two different model parameterisations (see text). Both cases show an unexpected increase in the memory cells that are specific to the non-injected antigen. Since plasma cells levels are roughly linear, relative to memory cell levels, the *in silico* results are qualitatively consistent with the *in vivo* results in (3) (bottom).

incorrect parameterisation of that model, and/or (iv) a fundamentally *faulty theory* underlying the model. The next step is to isolate the cause of disparity. The first and last of these points can be addressed by opening a dialogue with Bernasconi's group, but points (ii) and (iii) will require significant further work.

In conclusion, the simulated theory of polyclonal activation produced interesting results, similar to those obtained by residual antigen theory, but without requiring a long-lived supply of antigen. The signalling provided by IL-15 seems to be essential for this phenomenon. It appears consistent with Nature's efficient ways that the body would use the constant attack by antigen to strengthen itself, and we have demonstrated a polyclonal memory effect that is qualitatively similar to the experimental observations of (3).

5   Further Work

The logical extension of our somewhat basic model of polyclonal memory is to create a more detailed B-cell model, and to use that as the basis for a combined model attempting to simulate both B- and T-cell memory. Once this has been implemented, we can begin to explore questions surrounding the relationship between B- and T-lymphocyte memory, and look at new rules for plasma cell and memory cell creation, death and homeostasis.

The level of detail of a simulation should be as simple as possible (invoking Occam's razor), but a simulation that is too simple will not be effective. This is a standard dilemma of machine learning, and we intend to address this issue by means of automatic feedback. In other words, we will generate a population of simulations, and evolve them to find the simplest, most effective candidate.

The choice of parameters for any model is known to be a hard problem (16), but creation of the model is much harder (12). We are examining several methods of assisted parameterisation of the models, so that a 'best-fit' can be found by Sentinel. This will allow the research to focus on the scientifically interesting model-building task, rather than the more mechanical parameterisation task, and will help to remove of the of four possibilities for the differences in between the *in silico* and *in vivo* results in the previous section.

One of our long-term goals is to produce an integrated model of immunological memory that explains the experimental evidence used to support many of, if not all, the theories explored here. Such a model could used to explore more detailed issues in immunological memory, such as the unusual effects of the SAP gene (which controls long-term memory, but has no effect on short-term memory) (7). Furthermore, a general theory of immunological memory would have implications for machine learning.

As Sentinel continues to develop, and becomes ever more sophisticated, we will be able to develop larger, more complex models than at present. It will be interesting to see if the increase in complexity is important, or whether there is a level of complexity that is sufficient for the majority of immunological research.

References

[1] E. Ahmed and A. H. Hashish, *On modelling of immune memory mechanisms (sic)*, Theory Biosci. **122** (2003), 339–342.

[2] R. Antia, V. V. Ganusov, and R. Ahmed, *The role of models in understanding cd8⁺ T-cell memory*, Nature Review of Immunology **5** (2005), 101–111.

[3] N. L. Bernasconi, E. Traggiai, and A. Lanzavecchia, *Maintenance of serological memory by polyclonal activation of human memory B-cells*, Science **298** (2002), 2199–2202.

[4] F. M. Burnet, *The clonal selection theory of acquired immunity*, Cambridge University Press, 1959.

[5] F. Castiglione, V Selitser, and Z. Agur, *The effect of drug schedule on hypersensitive reactions: a study with a cellular automata model of the immune system*, Cancer Modelling and Simulation (Luigi Preziosi, ed.), CRC Press, LLC, (UK), 2003.

[6] D. L. Chao, M. P. Davenport, S. Forrest, and A. S. Perelson, *Stochastic stage-structure modelling of the adaptive immune system*, Proceedings of the IEEE Computer Society Bioinformatics Conferences (CSB 2003), 2003.

[7] S. Crotty, P. Felgner, H. Davies, J. Glidewell, L. Villarreal, and R. Ahmed, *SAP is required for generating long-term humoral immunity*, Nature **421** (2003), 282–287.

[8] J.D. Farmer, N. Packard, and A. Perelson, *The immune system, adaptation and machine learning*, Physica D **22** (1986), 187–204.

[9] S. Garrett and M. J. Robbins, *Simulating immunological memory*, In Silico Immunology (D. Flower and J. Timmis, eds.), Springer Verlag, 2006, p. to be published.

[10] S. M. Garrett, *A paratope is not an epitope: Implications for immune networks and clonal selection*, 2nd International Conference in Artificial Immune Systems (Edinburgh), Springer-Verlag, September 1–3 2003, pp. 217–228.

[11] C. Jacob, J. Litorco, and L. Lee, *Immunity through swarms: Agent-based simulations of the human immune system*, 3rd International Conference in Artificial Immune Systems (ICARIS-2004) (Catania, Italy), September 1–3 2004, pp. 477–489.

[12] R.D King, S.M. Garrett, and G.M. Coghill, *On the use of qualitative reasoning to simulate and identify metabolic pathways*, Bioinformatics **To Appear** (2005), (in print).

[13] S. H. Kleinstein, Y. Louzoun, and M. J. Shlomchik, *Estimating hypermutation rates from clonal tree data*, The Journal of Immunology **171** (2003), no. 9, 4639–4649.

[14] S. H. Kleinstein and P. E. Seiden, *Simulating the immune system*, Computing in Science and Engineering (2000), 69–77.

[15] L. Lau, B. Jamieson, T. Somasundraram, and R. Ahmed, *Cytotoxic T-cell memory without antigen*, Nature **369** (1994), 648–652.

[16] L. Ljung, *System identification: Theory for the user, 2nd ed.*, PRT Prentice Hall, Upper Saddle River, N.J., 1999.

[17] R. A. Manz, S. Arce, G. Cassese, A. E. Hauser, F. Hiepe, and A. Radbruch, *Humoral immunity and long-lived plasma cells*, Curr. Opin. Immunol. **14** (2002), 517.

[18] P. Matzinger, *Tolerance, danger ad the extended family*, Annual Review of Immunology **12** (1994), 991 – 1045.

[19] L. J. McHeyzer-Williams and M. G. McHeyzer-Williams, *Antigen-specific memory B cell development*, Annual Review of Immunology **23** (2005), 487–513.

[20] M. Meier-Schellersheim and G. Mack, *Simmune, a tool for simulating and analyzing immune system behavior.*, 1999, http://www-library.desy.de/.

[21] J. R. Paul, J. T. Riordan, and J. L. Melnick, *Antibodies to three different antigenic types of poliomyelitis in sera from north alaskan eskimos*, Am. J. Hyg. **54** (1951), 275–285.

[22] A. Perelson, *Modelling viral and immune system dynamics*, Nature **2** (2002), 28–36.

[23] W. Sawyer, *The persistance of yellow fever immunity*, J. Prev. Med. **5** (1931), 413–428.

[24] L. Selin, S. Nahill, and R. Welsh, *Cross-reactivities in memory cytotoxic t-lymphocyte recognition of heterlogous viruses*, J. Exp. Med. **179** (1994), 1933–1943.

[25] M. K. Slifka, R. Antia, and J. K. Whitmire an R. Ahmed, *Humoral immunity due to long-lived plasma cells*, Immunity **8** (1998), 363–372.

[26] D. J. Smith, S. Forrest, D. H. Ackley, and A. S. Perelson, *Variable efficacy of repeated annual influenza vaccination*, PNAS **96** (1999), 14001–14006.

[27] J. G. Tew, M. H. Kosco, G. F. Burton, and A. K. Szakal, *Follicular dendritic cells as accessory cells*, Immunological Reviews (1990), 185–212.

[28] D. Tough, P. Borrow, and J. Sprent, *Induction of bystander T-cell proliferation by viruses and type i interferon in vivo.*, Science **272** (1996), 1947–1950.

[29] D. Tough and J. Sprent, *Turnover of naive- and memory- phenotype cells*, J. Exp. Med. **179** (1994), 1127–1135.

[30] N-P. Weng, L. Granger, and R. J. Hodes, *Telomere lengthening and telomerase activation during human B cell differentiation*, Proc. Natl. Acad. Sci. **94** (1997), 10827–10832.

[31] W. Wilson and S. Garrett, *Modelling immune memory for prediction and computation*, 3rd International Conference on Artificial Immune Systems (ICARIS-04), Springer-Verlag, 2004, pp. 343–352.

[32] S. Wolfram, *A new kind of science*, Wolfram Media Incorporated, 2002.

[33] A. Yates, C.C.W Chan, R.E. Callard, A.J.T. George, and J. Stark, *An approach to modelling in immunology*, Briefings in Bioinformatics **2** (2001), 245–257.

[34] R. M. Zinkernagel, *On differences between immunity and immunological memory*, Curr. Opin. Immunol. (2002), no. 14, 523–536.

[35] R. M. Zinkernagel, M. F. Bachmann, T. M. Kündig, S. Oehen, H. Pirchet, and H. Hengartner, *On immunological memory*, Annual Review of Immunology **14** (1996), 333–367.

The Quaternion Model of Artificial Immune Response

Maoguo Gong[1], Licheng Jiao[1], Fang Liu[2], and Haifeng Du[1,3]

[1] Institute of Intelligent Information Processing, P.O. Box 224, Xidian University,
Xi'an, 710071, P.R. China
maoguo_gong@hotmail.com
[2] School of Computer Science and Engineering, Xidian University,
Xi'an, 710071, P.R. China
[3] School of Mechanical Engineering, Xi'an Jiaotong University,
Xi'an, 710049, P.R. China

Abstract. A quaternion model of artificial immune response (AIR) is proposed in this paper. The model abstracts four elements to simulate the process of immune response, namely, antigen, antibody, rules of interaction among antibodies, and the drive algorithm describing how the rules are applied to antibodies. Inspired by the biologic immune system, we design the set of rules as three subsets, namely, the set of clonal selection rules, the set of immunological memory rules, and the set of immunoregulation rules. An example of the drive algorithm is given and a sufficient condition of its convergence is deduced.

1 Introduction

In 1980s, Farmer et al[1] put forward a dynamic model of immune system based on immune network theory, and discussed the relationship between immune system and artificial intelligence methods. Until 1996, the international workshop on immune system was hold, putting forward the concept of Artificial Immune Systems (AIS) for the first time. In 1997, the IEEE International Conference on Systems, Man, and Cybernetics organized the 'Special Session on Artificial Immune Systems and Their Applications' for the first time. Subsequently, the artificial immune systems came into 'Silver Age'. D. Dasgupta et al[2] considered that AIS has been a research hotspot of theories and applications in artificial intelligence. After analyzing the similarities and differences between AIS and artificial neural network, D. Dasgupta [3] indicates that natural immune system is the important origin of artificial intelligence methods. Gasper et al[4] considers that diversity is the basic character of self-adaptive dynamics, while AIS is a better optimization method than GA in preserving the population diversity. Applications of AIS include machine learning, fault diagnosis, computer security, scheduling, virus detection, and optimization. As L.N. de Castro et al said, the field of AIS is showing great promise of being a powerful computing paradigm[5].

The immune response is the way the body recognizes and defends itself against microorganisms, viruses, and substances recognized as foreign and potentially harmful to the body. When bodies are exposed to antigens, immune system actually learns from the experience. The next time bodies are exposed to the same antigens, immune system often recognizes the culprit and sets out to destroy it, namely,

C. Jacob et al. (Eds.): ICARIS 2005, LNCS 3627, pp. 207–219, 2005.

secondary immune response. Embodying the mechanism of secondary immune response in artificial immune systems may be one of the superiority of AIS to evolutionary computation and neural networks. But first of all, we have to design a mathematical model to describe immune response from an information-processing perspective.

In this paper, we introduce a systematic description for a quaternion model of artificial immune response. After introducing the immunology background, the new artificial immune systems model, the quaternion model of artificial immune response is defined. Some general descriptions of heuristic rules are introduced. Then we take a simple drive algorithm for example to analyze its characters and a sufficient condition of its convergence is deduced.

2 Immunology Background

The ability of the immune system to respond to an antigen exists before it ever encounters that antigen[7]. The immune system relies on the prior formation of an incredibly diverse population of B cells and T cells. The specificity of both the B-cell receptors (BCRs) and T-cell receptors (TCRs); that is, the epitope to which a given receptor can bind, is created by a remarkable genetic mechanism. Each receptor is created even though the epitope it recognizes may never have been present in the body. If an antigen with that epitope should enter the body, those few lymphocytes able to bind to it will do so. If they also receive a second co-stimulatory signal, they may begin repeated rounds of mitosis. In this way, clones of antigen-specific lymphocytes (B and T) develop providing the basis of the immune response. This phenomenon is called clonal selection. Clonal selection leads to the eventual production of a pool of plasma cells and a pool of 'memory' cells.

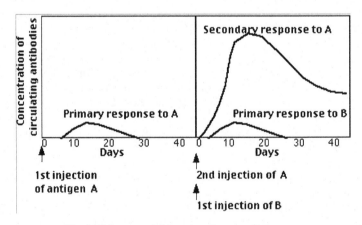

Fig. 1. Primary and Secondary Immune Responses

After recovering from an infection, the concentration of antibodies against the infectious agent gradually declines over the ensuing weeks, months, or even years. A time may come when antibodies against that agent can no longer be detected.

Nevertheless, the individual often is still protected against a second case of the disease; that is, the person is still immune. In fact, a second exposure to the agent usually calls forth a more rapid and larger response to the antigen. This is called the secondary response. The secondary response reflects a larger number of antigen-specific cells, called memory cells, than existed before the primary response. During the initial expansion of clones, some of the progeny cells neither went on dividing nor developed into plasma cells. Instead, they reverted to small lymphocytes bearing the same BCR on their surface that their ancestors had. This lays the foundation for a more rapid and massive response the next time the antigen enters the body.

3   The Quaternion Model of Artificial Immune Response

The immune system incorporates mechanisms that enable antibodies (lymphocytes) to learn the structures of specific foreign proteins, essentially, the immune system evolves and reproduces antibodies that have high affinities for specific antigens. It is difficulty or unnecessary to apply the definitions of immunology and copy the process of biology mechanically. In this paper, we put forward a novel mathematic model of artificial immune systems, the quaternion model of artificial immune response (AIR).

Immune response can be modeled as a quaternion (G, I, R, A), where G is exterior stimulus or antigen, I is the set of antibodies available, R is the rules of interaction among antibodies, A is an algorithm describing how the rules are applied to antibodies.

3.1   Antigen G

In immunology, an antigen is any substance that causes immune system to produce antibodies against it. In artificial immune response, antigens usually refer to problems and its constraints. Taking optimization problem (P) for example

$$(P) \begin{cases} \text{minimize} \quad f(x) = f(x_1, x_2, ...x_n) \\ \text{subject to} \quad g_i(x) < 0 \quad i = 1, 2, \cdots, p \\ \qquad\qquad h_j(x) = 0 \quad j = p+1, p+2, \cdots, q \end{cases} \tag{1}$$

where $x = (x_1, x_2, ...x_n)$, antigen is the function of objective function $f(x)$, namely, $G(x) = g(f(x))$, similar to the effect of antigen in immunology, it is the initial factor of artificial immune response.

3.2   Antibody Space I

Let $I = \{b_1, b_2, b_3, \cdots, b_n\}$, which is called antibody space, is the set of antibodies available during artificial immune response, n can be random integer. The representation of antibody b varies with antigen G, can be binary string, real number sequence, symbolic sequence, and characteristic sequence. Antibodies are the foundation of artificial immune response, whose representation is crucial for designing R.

Taking antibody $b = b_1 b_2 \cdots b_l$ for example, depending on biological term, b_i is regarded as genetic gene, called allele, whose value is correlative to the coding method. In practice, binary coding and decimal coding are used frequently. i.e., an antibody is represented as 8 bits binary digits, '0-1-1-1-0-1-0-0'. The antibody population $B = \{b_1, b_2, b_3, \cdots, b_m\}$, is an m-dimensional group of antibody b, and it is a subset in the antibody space I, positive integer m is called the size of antibody population.

3.3 The Set of Rules R

The set $R = \{r_1, r_2, r_3, \cdots, r_l\}$, which describes all the possible actions among antibodies in antibody space I. A rule, $r_i \in R$, can be designed inspired by the interactions between antigens and antibodies, or between antibodies and antibodies in biologic immune system. For antibody population $B = \{b_1, b_2, b_3, \cdots, b_n\}$, a rule $r_i \in R$ can be expressed as

$$r_i(b_1 + b_2 + \cdots + b_n) = b_1' + b_2' + \cdots + b_m' \tag{2}$$

Where n, m are positive integers, the size of m depends on rule r_i, and the representation '+' is not the arithmetical operator, but only separates the antibodies on either side in Equation (2).

Equation (2) shows that n antibodies on the left evolve into m antibodies on the right by the effect of rule r_i. For simulating biologic immune response in detail, it is necessary to design enough rules inspired by biologic immune system.

3.4 Drive Algorithm A

A is the algorithm simulating the process of antibody evolution and dominating interactions among antibodies during artificial immune response, including the format of the set R acting on antibody space I, the judgment of halt conditions in artificial immune response, and so on. In artificial immune response, the judgment of halt conditions is usually set as maximal generations or solving precision or both of them. Although A can be any iterative algorithms, its designing also should depend on special problems.

4 Rule Design Inspired by Immune Response

Among the four elements of AIR model (G, I, R, A), antibody space I and drive algorithm A depend on the antigen G, and the designing and selection of rules in the set R depend on the antigen G and the representation of antibodies. In this paper, we design the set R composed of three subsets, namely, the set of clonal selection rules R_{CS}, the set of immunological memory rules R_M, and the set of immunoregulation rules R_A. Then $R = R_{CS} \cup R_M \cup R_A$, described as follows.

4.1 The Set of Clonal Selection Rules R_{CS}

The clonal selection theory is used in immunology to describe the basic features of an immune response. Its main idea lies in that the antibodies can selectively react to the antigens, which are the native production and spread on the cell surface in the form of peptides. The reaction leads to cell clonal proliferation and the colony has the same antibodies. Some clonal cells divide into the eventual production of a pool of plasma cells, and others become immune memory cells to boost the secondary immune response.

4.1.1 Clonal Proliferation
In immunology, Clone means asexual propagation so that a group of identical cells can be descended from a single common ancestor, such as a bacterial colony whose members arise from a single original cell as the result of mitosis. In artificial immune systems, the clonal proliferation $R\_proliferation$ on antibody population $B = \{b_1, b_2, b_3, \cdots, b_n\}$ is defined as:

$$R\_proliferation(b_1 + b_2 + \cdots + b_n) \tag{3}$$
$$= \{b_1^1 + b_1^2 + \cdots + b_1^{q_1}\} + \{b_2^1 + b_2^2 + \cdots + b_2^{q_2}\} + \cdots + \{b_n^1 + b_n^2 + \cdots + b_n^{q_n}\}$$

where $b_i^j = b_i$, $i = 1, 2, \cdots n$; $j = 1, 2, \cdots q_i$, $q_i \in [1, n_c]$ is an self-adaptive parameter, or set as an constant, n_c is a given value related to the upper limit of clone scale, $q_i = 1$ represents that there is no clonal proliferation on antibody b_i. It is obvious that clonal proliferation above is similar to that of immunology, which is a simple process of asexual propagation. All the antibodies in sub-population $B_i = (b_i^1, b_i^2, \cdots, b_i^{q_i})$ result from the clonal proliferation on the same antibody b_i, and have the same property as antibody b_i.

4.1.2 Genic Mutation
Genic mutation $R\_mutation$ is a simulation of immune system recognizing external pattern in the form of antibody gene mutation and compilation. Genic mutation $R\_mutation$ on antibody population $B = \{b_1, b_2, b_3, \cdots, b_n\}$ is defined as:

$$R\_mutation(b_1 + b_2 + \cdots + b_n) = b_1' + b_2' + \cdots + b_n' \tag{4}$$

The essential content of genic mutation is changing genic values in some genic positions of antibodoes. As far as the binary representation is concerned, mutation means make some genic positions inverse with a certain probability (i.e. $1 \rightarrow 0$ or $0 \rightarrow 1$). For decimal representation, uniform mutation, Gaussian mutation, Cauchy mutation and some stochastic mutations can be used.

4.1.3 Genic Inversion
Inversion is the main mode of recomposition of light chain immunoglobulin antibody gene. Genic inverstion $R\_inversion$ is the operation that distorting a section of

genes in antibodies with a certain probability. Genic mutation R_inversion on antibody population $B = \{b_1, b_2, b_3, \cdots, b_n\}$ is defined as:

$$R\_inversion(b_1 + b_2 + \cdots + b_n) = b_1' + b_2' + \cdots + b_n' \qquad (5)$$

Selecting antibodies with probability p_i from antibody population, and choosing two points p and q, where $p<q$, then the R_inversion operation on antibody $b_i = \{b_{i1}, b_{i2}, \cdots, b_{ip}, \cdots, b_{iq}, \cdots, b_{il}\}$ is as follows.

$$b_i' = R\_inversion(b_i) = \{b_{i1}, b_{i2}, \cdots, b_{iq}, b_{iq-1}, \cdots, b_{ip+1}, b_{ip}, \cdots, b_{il}\} \qquad (6)$$

For example, after the R_inversion operation on antibody $b_i = 00110011$ between the 3rd and 6th section, the antibody becomes $b_i' = 00001111$. R_inversion can change the antibody acutely, if the length of antibody encoding is very large, it may be extraordinary useful.

4.1.4 Clonal Selection

Clonal selection R_selection is an operation contrary to clonal proliferation, which selects an excellent individual from the sub-population generated by clonal proliferation. For antibody population $B(b_1^1, b_1^2, \cdots, b_1^{q_1}, b_2^1, b_2^2, \cdots, b_2^{q_2}, \cdots, b_n^1, b_n^2, \cdots, b_n^{q_n})$, clonal selection R_selection is defined as:

$$R\_selection(\{b_1^1 + b_1^2 + \cdots + b_1^{q_1}\} + \{b_2^1 + b_2^2 + \cdots + b_2^{q_2}\} + \cdots + \{b_n^1 + b_n^2 + \cdots + b_n^{q_n}\}) \qquad (7)$$
$$= b_1' + b_2' + \cdots + b_n'$$

Where $R\_selection(b_i^1 + b_i^2 + \cdots + b_i^{q_i}) = b_i'$, namely, the sub-population $\{b_i^1, b_i^2, \cdots, b_i^{q_i}\}$ generated by the clonal proliferation on antibody b_i improves local affinity through clonal selection after the compilation of antibodies. Concretely, $\forall i = 1, 2, \cdots n$, $\exists j \in \{1, 2, \cdots, q_i\}$, making the antibody b_i^j with the highest affinity in sub-population $(b_i^1, b_i^2, \cdots, b_i^{q_i})$ has the largest selection stress, namely, the probability of $b_i' = b_i^j$ is largest.

4.2 The Set of Immunological Memory Rules R_M

Clonal selection not only produces plasma cells but also leads to a pool of memory cells. These memory cells are B lymphocytes with receptors of the same specificity as those on the original activated B cell. During the initial expansion of clones, some of the progeny cells neither went on dividing nor developed into plasma cells. Instead, they reverted to small lymphocytes bearing the same BCR on their surface that their ancestors had. This lays the foundation for a more rapid and massive response the next time the antigen enters the body. In this paper, we simulate the immunological memory by setting up a memory antibody population. The set of immunological memory rules include the nonself learning operation $R\_m\_L_{nonself}$ and the self learning operation $R\_m\_L_{self}$.

4.2.1 Nonself Learning of Memory Antibody Population

If the memory antibody population is $\boldsymbol{B}^M = \{\boldsymbol{b}_1^M, \boldsymbol{b}_2^M, \boldsymbol{b}_3^M, \cdots, \boldsymbol{b}_n^M\}$, antibody $\boldsymbol{b}_0$ is an excellent antibody outside $\boldsymbol{B}^M$, then the nonself learning operation $R\_m\_L_{nonself}$ is defined as

$$R\_m\_L_{nonself}(\boldsymbol{B}^M + \boldsymbol{b}_0 = \{\boldsymbol{b}_1^M + \boldsymbol{b}_2^M + \boldsymbol{b}_3^M + \cdots + \boldsymbol{b}_n^M + \boldsymbol{b}_0\}) \tag{8}$$

$$= \{\boldsymbol{b}_1^{M'} + \boldsymbol{b}_2^{M'} + \boldsymbol{b}_3^{M'} + \cdots + \boldsymbol{b}_m^{M'}\} = \boldsymbol{B}^{M'}$$

where $R\_m\_L_{nonself}$ designed as follows: calculating the antibody-antibody affinities (Ab-Ab affinity, can be thought as a function of the distance between two antibodies) between $\boldsymbol{b}_0$ and all the antibodies in $\boldsymbol{B}^M$. Ab-Ab affinities embody the relative distribution of antibodies in antibody space $\boldsymbol{I}$, the larger the value, the bigger difference of genes the two antibodies have, contrariwise, it is still right. If the Ab-Ab affinity between $\boldsymbol{b}_s^M \in \boldsymbol{B}^M$ and $\boldsymbol{b}_0$ is the minimum one, and its value is δ_{s0} , then there are two cases to be considered: if $\delta_{s0} \le \delta_0$, where δ_0 is the minimum distance between every two individuals of $\boldsymbol{B}^M$, then compared the antibody-antigen affinities (Ab-Ag affinity, can be thought as a measurement of the value of objective functions) $G(\boldsymbol{b}_0)$ and $G(\boldsymbol{b}_s^M)$, and let

$$\boldsymbol{b}_s^M = \begin{cases} \boldsymbol{b}_0 & if \quad G(\boldsymbol{b}_0) > G(\boldsymbol{b}_s^M) \\ \boldsymbol{b}_s^M & else \end{cases} \tag{9}$$

Then the number of antibodies in memory antibody population is $N_m = n$; otherwise, namely, $\delta_{s0} > \delta_0$, let $\boldsymbol{b}_{n+1}^M = \boldsymbol{b}_0$, the number of antibodies in memory antibody population is $N_m = n+1$, if $n+1$ is larger than the upper limit of the memory antibody population size N_{max} , then delete the worst antibody in memory antibody population.

4.2.2 Self Learning of Memory Antibody Population

Memory antibody population not only learning external information pattern by $R\_m\_L_{nonself}$, but also learning new pattern in the form of antibody gene mutation and compilation for affinity maturation, which we named self learning operation $R\_m\_L_{self}$. The self learning of memory antibody population $R\_m\_L_{self}$ on $\boldsymbol{B}^M = \{\boldsymbol{b}_1^M, \boldsymbol{b}_2^M, \boldsymbol{b}_3^M, \cdots, \boldsymbol{b}_n^M\}$ is defined as

$$R\_m\_L_{self}(\boldsymbol{b}_1^M + \boldsymbol{b}_2^M + \boldsymbol{b}_3^M + \cdots + \boldsymbol{b}_n^M) = \boldsymbol{b}_1^{M'} + \boldsymbol{b}_2^{M'} + \boldsymbol{b}_3^{M'} + \cdots + \boldsymbol{b}_m^{M'} \tag{10}$$

Each antibody in memory antibody population has its own clonal space size S_m around itself. Applied the set of clonal selection rules $\textbf{\textit{R}}_{CS}$ to each memory antibody in its own clonal space, the way depends on the drive algorithm A.

4.3 The Set of Immunoregulation Rules R_A

The immune system consists of a network of cells that have developed to recognize and eradicate a wide variety of pathogens. Pathogen-derived products (inartificial or artificial) can trigger immune cells to produce cytokines, soluble molecules that promote the immune response. However, the immune system is a double-edged sword since cytokines can also result in damage to the host tissue (for example, in inflammatory diseases). Cytokine production is therefore subject to intricate regulation, in order to control the immune response and prevent such damage.

4.3.1 Vaccination
In immunological, vaccination is also called active immunization because the immune system is stimulated to develop its own immunity against the pathogen. The principle of vaccination is inserting strong promoter plasmid carriers in antigen encoding genes, and then inserting this recombined plasmid in cells, the antigen encoding synthesizes plasma cells to cause protective immune response.

In this paper, given an antibody, vaccination means modifying the genes on some bits in accordance with vaccines so as to gain higher affinity with greater probability. A vaccine is abstracted from the prior knowledge of the pending problem. A vaccine can be regarded as estimation on some genes of the optimal individual, and the accuracy of this estimation depends on the further test. Thus it can be seen that the correctness of selecting a vaccine plays an important role in the operational efficiency. All the vaccines form the initial storage of vaccines $vaccine\_storage_0$.

The vaccines in $vaccine\_storage_0$ may be as three kinds: an entire antibody, a section of genes, and a bit gene. It is necessary to note that there is usually not only one vaccine in a certain problem, therefore, during the course of vaccination, the injection can be carried out by either selecting any vaccine randomly or getting them together according to a certain logic relationship. A vaccine can also be obtained during the evolution process of antibody population, such as be abstracted from the memory antibody population.

If the antibody population is $\textbf{\textit{B}} = \{b_1, b_2, b_3, \cdots, b_n\}$, then the vaccination of $vaccine\_storage$ on populations $\textbf{\textit{B}}$ means modifying the genes on some bits of all the antibodies in $\textbf{\textit{B}}$ with a certain probability. It can be described as follows

$$R\_vaccine(\textbf{\textit{B}} + vaccine\_storage) = \textbf{\textit{B}}' + vaccine\_storage \tag{11}$$

We can find out the influence of correct selection of a vaccine on the functions of the vaccination with a straightforward example. Given that the encoding of a pending problem is binary with n bits, it can form a space with 2^n pending solutions. If we could define the gene of a certain bit by analyzing the problem, then the population with this gene will centralize in the half space in which the optimal individual is forecast, and therefore the searching efficiency will be improved greatly. On the contrary, if our estimation is wrong, then the vaccination will hold back the searching actions, and even exert a negative influence.

4.3.2 Immunological Death

Immunological death R_death is a simple simulation of immunological tolerance. In immunology, the negative adjustment during the antibody creating of B cells may be clonal deletion or clonal anergy. This paper intitules those as clonal death without any difference. Immunological death R_death on the antibody population $B = \{b_1, b_2, b_3, \cdots, b_n\}$ is defined as:

$$R\_death(b_1 + b_2 + \cdots + b_n) = \alpha_1 b_1 + \alpha_2 b_2 + \cdots + \alpha_n b_n \qquad (12)$$

where $\alpha_i b_i$ represents that the number of b_i is α_i after clonal death, in which α_i is a integer with $\alpha_i \geq 0$, $\alpha_i = 0$ means antibody b_i presents immune tolerance, or clonal deletion, the reason of which may be the low Ab-Ag affinity of b_i, or may be the decline of the diversity of antibody population result from the common genotype between antibody b_i and other antibodies. $\alpha_i > 1$ means the antibodies with high affinity (i.e. target cells) have a local proliferation with the positive feedback immunoregulation of target cells. In artificial immune response model, for holding the durative of algorithms, there is $\alpha_1 + \alpha_2 + \cdots + \alpha_n = n$ in common.

Different from biologic evaluation system varying with different sex, immune system is an asexual system. From the description above, it can be concluded that the rules in the set $R = R_{CS} \cup R_M \cup R_A$ are asexual process, which can be comprehended as a simple depiction on the characteristic of immune system by artificial immune response.

5   An Example of the Drive Algorithm A

The following algorithm is an example of the drive algorithm in AIR.

```
While (the antibody population B(k) doesn't satisfy the
conditions of affinity maturity) do
```

> {

>> Implement immunological death R_death on $B(k)$, get new antibody population $B^{(1)}(k)$;

>> Implement Clonal proliferation $R\_proliferation$ on $B^{(1)}(k)$, get new antibody population $B^{(2)}(k)$;

>> Implement Genic mutation $R\_mutation$ on $B^{(2)}(k)$, get new antibody population $B^{(3)}(k)$;

```
        Implement Clonal selection R_selection  on
        B⁽³⁾(k), get new antibody population B⁽⁴⁾(k);

        Set  B(k+1)=B⁽⁴⁾(k),  k=k+1;

    } End
```

In this drive algorithm, every generation can be comprehend as a four-step transferred process of antibody population $B(k)$. For any antibody space and the rules $R = \{R\_death, R\_proliferation, R\_mutation, R\_selection\}$, there is:

$$B(k+1) = \vartheta[B(k)] = \vartheta\left[\bigcup_{i=1}^{n} g^{-1}\left(Max\left(\bigcup_{j=1}^{\alpha_i \times q_i} g\left(b_i(k) + \Delta b_{ij}(k)\right)\right)\right)\right] \tag{13}$$

where $g(\bullet)$ denotes the method of calculating Ab-Ag affinity, the means of α_i and q_i are the same as those described in section 4, $\Delta b_{ij}(k)$ is the mutation scale. Specially, $\bigcup_{j=1}^{0} g(b_i(k) + \Delta b_{ij}(k))$ means empty operation while $\alpha_i = 0$. In this algorithm, three parameters need to be adjusted: α_i, q_i and $\Delta b_{ij}(k)$.

Let deviation $e(k) = |g(b_0) - g(b^*(k))|$, where b_0 is the antibody coding of optimal solution, $b^*(k)$ is the best antibody in generation k, get discrete Lyapunov function

$$V(k) = \frac{e^2(k)}{2} = \frac{(g(b_0) - g(b^*(k)))^2}{2} \tag{14}$$

Then

$$\Delta V(k) = V(k+1) - V(k) = \frac{1}{2}(e^2(k+1) - e^2(k)) \tag{15}$$

$$= (e(k+1) - e(k))(e(k) + \frac{1}{2}(e(k+1) - e(k)))$$

$$= \Delta e(k)(e(k) + \frac{1}{2}\Delta e(k))$$

where $\Delta e(k) = e(k+1) - e(k)$, use one order Taloyer Series to approximate:

$$e(k+1) - e(k) = \left[\frac{\partial e(k)}{\partial b^*}\right]^T \times \left[b^*(k+1) - b^*(k)\right] + o\left[b^*(k+1) - b^*(k)\right] \tag{16}$$

as well as

$$g(b^*(k+1)) = g(b^*(k)) + \left[\frac{\partial g(b^*(k))}{\partial b^*}\right]^T \times \left[b^*(k+1) - b^*(k)\right] + o\left[b^*(k+1) - b^*(k)\right] \tag{17}$$

so $\dfrac{\partial e(k)}{\partial \boldsymbol{b}^*} = -\dfrac{\partial g(\boldsymbol{b}(k))}{\partial \boldsymbol{b}^*}$, and then

$$g(\boldsymbol{b}^*(k+1)) - g(\boldsymbol{b}^*(k)) = -\Delta e(k) = \left[\dfrac{\partial g(\boldsymbol{b}^*(k))}{\partial \boldsymbol{b}^*}\right]^T \times \left[\boldsymbol{b}^*(k+1) - \boldsymbol{b}^*(k)\right] + o\left[\boldsymbol{b}^*(k+1) - \boldsymbol{b}^*(k)\right] \tag{18}$$

let $\boldsymbol{b}^*(k+1) - \boldsymbol{b}^*(k) = \Delta \boldsymbol{b}^*(k)$, then

$$\Delta V(k) \approx \left[\dfrac{\partial e(k)}{\partial \boldsymbol{b}^*}\right]^T \times \Delta \boldsymbol{b}^*(k) \left\{ e(k) + \left[\dfrac{\partial e(k)}{\partial \boldsymbol{b}^*}\right]^T \times \Delta \boldsymbol{b}^*(k) \right\} \tag{19}$$

Let $\Delta \boldsymbol{b}^*(k) = \eta \nabla \varphi = \eta \dfrac{\partial g(\boldsymbol{b}^*(k))}{\partial \boldsymbol{b}^*}$, η is the length of search step, then

$$\Delta V(k) \approx -\left\Vert \dfrac{\partial g(\boldsymbol{b}^*(k))}{\partial \boldsymbol{b}^*} \right\Vert^2 \left(\eta e(k) - \eta^2 \left\Vert \dfrac{\partial g(\boldsymbol{b}^*(k))}{\partial \boldsymbol{b}^*} \right\Vert^2 \right) \tag{20}$$

For assuring the convergence of algorithm, need to satisfy:

$$\eta e(k) - \eta^2 \left\Vert \dfrac{\partial g(\boldsymbol{b}^*(k))}{\partial \boldsymbol{b}^*} \right\Vert^2 > 0 \tag{21}$$

namely,

$$0 < \eta < \dfrac{e(k)}{\left\Vert \dfrac{\partial g(\boldsymbol{b}^*(k))}{\partial \boldsymbol{b}^*} \right\Vert^2} \tag{22}$$

So we can have the theory as follow:

The drive algorithm A employed the rules

$R = \{R\_death, R\_proliferation, R\_mutation, R\_selection\}$

is convergent and the dynamic process decided by the algorithm is gradually reaching the stability when the best antibody evolves along the direction of grads of objective function and the step length satisfies Equation (22).

The complex biologic inspirations of bionic algorithms determine that the algorithms should pay more attention to the operations on gene and simulating the biologic process as vividly as possible. As a result, in practice, the conditions of convergence above are difficult to satisfy strictly in bionic algorithms.

6 Concluding Remarks

The goal of this paper was to introduce a systematic description for a quaternion model of artificial immune response. After introducing the immunology background such as antibody clonal selection and immunological memory, a new artificial immune systems model, the quaternion model of artificial immune response was defined. The four elements were antigen, antibody, the set of rules, and the drive algorithm, where antibody space and the drive algorithm depend on the antigen, and the rule designing depend on antigen and the representation of antibodies. Without aiming at any specific problems, some general descriptions of heuristic rules were introduced, namely, the set of clonal selection rules, the set of immunological memory rules, and the set of immunoregulation rules. Then we took a simple drive algorithm for example to analyze its characters and a sufficient condition of its convergence was deduced.

Applications of AIR are broad, such as learning, optimization, and information processing. The application in learning ranges from pattern recognition to machine learning. The application of AIR in optimization can replace or make up other algorithms to find solutions of difficult problems. The application in information processing includes real immunological computing and a design paradigm for new hardware or software architectures and so on. All of these are interesting and meaningful.

References

1. Farmer, J. D., Packard, N. H., Perelson, A. S.: The immune system, adaptation, and machine learning. Physica D, Elsevier Science Publishers. Vol. 2, No. 1–3. (1986) 187–204
2. Dasgupta, D., Forrest, S.: Artificial immune systems in industrial applications. In: Proceedings of the Second International Conference on Intelligent Processing and Manufacturing of Materials, Hawaii, USA, July 10–15 (1999) 257–267
3. Dasgupta, D.: Artificial Neural Networks and Artificial Immune Systems: Similarities and Differences. In: Proceedings of the IEEE International Conference on Systems, Man and Cybernetics, Vol. 1, Orlando, USA, October 12–15 (1997)
4. Gasper, A., Collard, P.: From GAs to artificial immune systems: improving adaptation in time dependent optimization. In: Proceedings of the Congress on Evolutionary Computation (CEC 99). IEEE press (1999) 1859–1866
5. de Castro, L. N., Timmis, J.: Artificial Immune Systems: A New Computational Intelligence Approach. Springer-Verlag, Berlin Heidelberg New York (2002)
6. Dasgupta, D.: Artificial Immune Systems and Their Applications. Springer-Verlag, Berlin Heidelberg New York (1999)
7. Abbas, A.K., Lichtman, A.H., Pober, J.S.: Cellular and Molecular Immunology. 4th edn. W B Saunders Co., New York (2000)
8. Dittrich, P., Ziegler, J., Banzhaf, W.: Artificial Chemistries–A Review. Artificial Life, 7, (2001) 225–275
9. Tarakanov, A.O., Skormin, V.A., Sokolova, S.P.: Immunocomputing: Principles and Applications. Springer-Verlag, Berlin Heidelberg New York (2003)
10. de Castro, L. N., Von Zuben, F. J.: Learning and Optimization Using the Clonal Selection Principle. IEEE Transactions on Evolutionary Computation, Special Issue on Artificial Immune Systems, Vol.6, No.3 (2002) 239–251
11. Kim, J., Bentley, P.J.: Towards an Artificial Immune System for Network Intrusion Detection: an Investigation of Clonal Selection with a Negative Selection Operator. In: IEEE Neural Networks Council. Proceedings of the 2001 Congress on Evolutionary Computation. Vol. 2. Seoul Korea, IEEE (2001) 1244–1252

12. Jiao, L., Wang, L.: A novel genetic algorithm based on immunity. IEEE Transactions on Systems, Man and Cybernetics, Part A. Vol.30, No.5 (2000) 552–561
13. Gong, M., Du, H., Jiao, L., Wang, L.: Immune Clonal Selection Algorithm for Multiuser Detection in DS-CDMA Systems. In: Webb, G.I, Yu, X. (eds.): Advances in Artificial Intelligence: Proceedings of the 17th Australian Joint Conference on Artificial Intelligence, Cairns, Australia, December 4–6 (2004) 1219–1225
14. Bäck, T.: Evolutionary Algorithms in Theory and Practice. Oxford University Press, New York (1996)
15. Wolpert, D. H., Macready, W. G.: No Free Lunch Theorems for Search. Santa Fe Institute Techinical Report SFI-TR-05-010, Santa Fe Institute, Santa Fe, NM. (1995)
16. Forrest, S., Hofmeyr, S.A.: Immunology as information processing. In: Segel, L.A., Cohen, I. (eds.): Design Principles for the Immune System and Other Distributed Autonomous Systems. Santa Fe Institute Studies in the Sciences of Complexity. New York: Oxford University Press (2001)
17. Warrender, C., Forrest, S., Legal, L.: Effective Feedback in the Immune System. In: Genetic and Evolutionary Computation Conference Workshop Program, Morgan Kaufman (2001) 329–332
18. Hofmeyr, S., Forrest, S.: Immunity by Design: An Artificial Immune System. In: Proceedings of the Genetic and Evolutionary Computation Conference (GECCO), Morgan-Kaufmann, San Francisco, CA (1999) 1289–1296
19. Jiao, L.C., Gong, M.G., Shang, R.H., DU, H.F., Lu, B.: Clonal Selection with Immune Dominance and Anergy Based Multiobjective Optimization. In: Coello Coello, C.A., Aguirre, A.H., Zitzler, E. (Eds.): Proceedings of the Third International Conference on Evolutionary Multi-Criterion Optimization, EMO 2005, Guanajuato, Mexico, March 9-11, 2005. Springer-Verlag, LNCS 3410, 2005. 474–489
20. Du, H.F., Gong, M.G., Jiao, L.C., Liu, R.C.: A novel artificial immune system algorithm for high-dimensional function numerical optimization. PROGRESS IN NATURAL SCIENCE. Taylor & Francis Ltd press. Vol.15, No.5, May 2005: 463–471

A Comparative Study on Modeling Strategies for Immune System Dynamics Under HIV-1 Infection

Zaiyi Guo and Joc Cing Tay

Evolutionary and Complex Systems Lab,
Nanyang Technological University
asjctay@ntu.edu.sg

Abstract. Considerable research effort has provided mathematical and computational models of the human immune response under viral infection. However, the quality of simulated results are highly dependent on the choice of modeling strategy. We examine two modeling approaches of HIV pathogenesis: Mathematical and Multi-Agent (or MA) Models. The latter has relatively wider Model Scope due to the agent-rule specification method. Mathematical Models employ Parameter and Population/Subpopulation Level entity granularities with equation-based interaction, while MA Models specify entities at Individual Level, implemented with agents to describe interactions via IF-THEN rules. Compared to the former, MA Models naturally handles entity heterogeneity and spatial non-uniformity, and suffers less from the issue of directly designed dynamics. Both approaches are however, not directly accessible to immunologists due to the need for programming knowledge; hence, closer collaboration between computer scientists and immunologists is necessary.

Keywords: Multi-Agent Simulation, Mathematical Models, Immune System, HIV, Systems and Models.

1 Introduction

The amalgamation between computing and biology can be classified into three categories [10]: biologically motivated computing, computationally motivated biology and computing with biological mechanisms. There has been considerable research in the first category, where biological functions inspire solutions for generic real-world problems (see [10] for a survey of immunology motivated computational methods and various applications). The modeling of immune system dynamics described in this paper falls into the second category, where the primary role of computing is to provide tools that benefit the interpretation of biological data and to advance our understanding beyond mere intuition-driven rationalizations. Research between the two categories can be synergistic as modeling itself provides a summarization that forms a framework for deriving new computational methods.

The human immune system is highly complex, dynamic and adaptive; it has attracted considerable research effort to develop mathematical and computational models in order to verify its inner workings. Some popular modeling subjects include

C. Jacob et al. (Eds.): ICARIS 2005, LNCS 3627, pp. 220–233, 2005.

emergence of immune memory [19,23], idiotypic networks [23,29], completeness issue of immune repertoire [9,34], helper T cell differentiation [4-6], and system dynamics under HIV-1 infection [11,14,27,30,39]. We observe that the models for these diverse phenomena differ greatly in terms of modeling strategies. Employing a particular strategy implies a certain way of thinking which may impose its own preconceptions and inherited shortcomings [24].

In this paper we compare two popular modeling approaches: ODE Models and Multi-Agent (or MA) Models. Given the diversity in modeling areas, attempting a complete coverage of all modeling areas could make our study superficial. We therefore focus on the computational models for immune dynamics under HIV-1 infection. This is a heavily researched area, where many models have been developed to explain why the immune system ultimately collapses despite the apparently controlled viral replication during the asymptomatic phase [7]. Studying these models can provide better insights in immunological modeling techniques and the target domain features that are considered important. We propose three model characteristics as our basis for comparison: Model Scope, Entity Granularity, and Interaction Descriptions. The examination of differences in terms of these model characteristics will enable in-depth discussions on each modeling strategy with an aim towards more effective verification of HIV-1 pathogenesis through model-based simulations.

This paper is organized as follows. Section 2 briefly introduces the human immune system and HIV-1 pathogenesis. Section 3 compares the model characteristics of ODE and MA Models, and discusses the potential model shortcomings due to these inherited characteristics. Section 4 discusses the practical considerations for immunological models based on the issues we observe. Section 5 concludes the paper.

2 Immune System and HIV-1 Pathogenesis

The immune defense mechanism involves many kinds of cells and molecules [2,21]. A brief overview of the major players and functions following a viral infection is as follows. One possible scenario involves Macrophages (MPH) and dendritic cells ingesting the pathogen and presenting the antigen fragments on the cell surface in the form of a MHC-peptide complex. The MPH then secretes interleukin-1 (IL-1) that activates helper T cells (TH). TH cells have receptors on their surface, which bind to the antigen presented on the antigen-presenting-cell (APC) by shape matching. Activated TH cells upon antigen recognition secrete a variety of stimulatory molecules, such as IL-2, to trigger proliferation of cytotoxic T cells (TK) and/or B cells (B). TK cells can mount an immediate attack on infecting and infected cells that present unusual surface antigens, a process known as cellular immune response. On another front, B cells produce antibodies which bind to matched free antigens, neutralizing the antigen's virulence and serve as a marker for MPHs (which then perform phagocytosis). This latter form of immune defense is known as a humoral response.

Acquired Immune Deficiency Syndrome (or AIDS) is characterized by a combination of opportunistic infections and a markedly reduced circulating TH cell count [36]. Due to their central role in stimulating and regulating an immune response, the abnormal loss of TH cells is considered a convincing explanation of the immune system failure at the AIDS stage [25]. Hence, a widely accepted hypothesis is that the Human Immunodeficiency Virus (or HIV) directly infects cells bearing CD4+ molecules (especially the TH cells). The progression of HIV infection towards AIDS typically follows three phases [26,32], as shown in Figure 1. The patient exhibits acute symptoms during the early phase of infection. With the onset of HIV-specific antibodies and TK cells, the amount of virus sharply declines by a factor of 100 or more. Viral load then remains at a relatively low but constant level, while TH cell count slowly decreases for a period up to 12 years. TH cell count falls below 200/μl and is characterized as onset of AIDS [30].

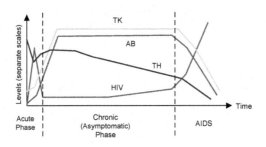

Fig. 1. Typical 3-Stage Disease Progression of HIV-Infected Patient [26]

Besides the direct infection of TH cells, other hypothesized explanations have been proposed. These include: rapid viral mutations [26], syncytium formation [16,37], filling of CD4 receptor sites [41], HIV-induced cell apoptosis [13], impaired production of new TH cells [25] and the existence of viral reservoirs [12]. In addition to clinical verifications, these mechanisms have been modeled mathematically for quantitative analysis. We now examine the characteristics of these models.

3 A Comparison of Immunological Models

We define the following concepts for the specification of immunological models.

Entity: An object of interest in the system. Entities are *nouns* that describe the system.
Interaction: An event taking place among one or more entities. Interactions are *verbs* that describe the system.

In the context of modeling HIV pathogenesis, examples of entities include T cells, HIV variants and MPHs. Examples of interactions include proliferation, infection, activation and killing. We now compare ODE and MA models from three model characteristics whose definitions are based on the concept of Entity and Interaction.

3.1 Model Scope

Models are abstractions of reality, often simplified to allow a computationally tractable means of predicting and simulating the phenomena by identifying the *key* variables. This raises the issue of choosing the Model Scope:

Model Scope: The entities and interactions that are present in the model.

For HIV pathogenesis, a wide range of entities and interactions are possible but only a subset is typically modeled. The extent of the Model Scope is usually dependent on goals that the model developers want to achieve, as illustrated below.

We start with several models with minimum Model Scope. In the work by Phillips [35], Wei et al. [43], and Perelson et al. [33], the only entities present are TH cells and HIV virions. The main interactions include HIV infection of TH cells, virion production by infected TH cells, and metabolic activities for TH cells (cell production, death) and HIV (virion decay). The Phillips [35] model attempts to demonstrate that the sharp decline in viral load after the initial peak that is observed during the acute phase is due to insufficient amount of TH cells available for infection rather than an adaptive immune response. This is referred to as the Target-Cell-Limited theory [8]. This model removes factors that are relevant to immune response, such as TK cells, B cells and antibodies, so as to achieve the goal of proving the Target-Cell-Limited Theory. Wei et al. [43] and Perelson et al. [33] were mainly concerned with measuring the loss rates of TH cells and HIV virions from patient data. They assume that the population size of healthy TH cells remains constant and the drug is 100% effective. Their Model Scope is kept minimal for the ease of parameter measurement, while the Phillips model restricts the Model Scope to exclude an immune response. In both cases, the Model Scope though restricted, serves the modeling objectives well.

The HIV infection of TH cells appears to be fundamental to most HIV pathogenesis models [8,18,32,33,35,39,43]. The extension to a larger Model Scope is specific for certain modeling objectives. Stafford et al [39] quantitatively verified the Target-Cell-Limited theory using patient data; parameter values that were determined through regression analysis consistently predicted a viral load that was higher than the actual measurement after about 100 days of infection. The authors attributed this difference between prediction and reality to the existence of an immune response, leading to an extension of their Model Scope to include 1) TK cells which increased the death rate of infected TH cells and 2) soluble factors secreted by TK cells that inhibited the production of virion particles from infected TH cells. In this case, the Model Scope was extended to account for the difference between prediction and reality.

Model Scope extension can also be seen in a series of *therapy models* which explicitly considers drug effects. As described above, the therapy models used by Wei et al. [43] and Perelson et al. [33] possessed minimum Model Scope and imposed several assumptions for the ease of parameter measurement. Perelson [30] performed a more formal study on drug effects by relaxing the assumptions of constant population of healthy TH cells and of perfect drug effects. The extension of Model Scope to include drug effects (in the form of efficacy coefficient) allows theoretical studies of imperfect drugs. In another model of Perelson et al. [31], the Model Scope was further extended to cover long-lived victim cells of HIV infection, which are known as virus reservoirs. This was motivated by the observation that after drug treatment, the viral load declines exponentially but the decline rate slows down over time [20]. Perelson et al. [31] postulated the existence of viral reservoir. By including long-lived cells and their interactions with HIV, the new model produced a viral decay pattern similar to the clinical observation after the drug treatment. The ODE models we have seen have scopes that are as minimum *as required* (this may be subjective due to what model developers understand as 'required' for their purposes), and are extended only when necessary. This gives rise to an ordering of models where there is incremental extensions of previous ones. As seen above, Stafford et al [39] verified and extended Phillips [35], Perelson [30] generalizes Wei et al. [43] and those by Perelson et al. [33], and Wein at al. [44] are extensions of Perelson et al. [31].

However, we observe that MA Models possess much wider Model Scopes in general. The MA Models by Guo et al.[15] were constructed for verifying four well-known HIV pathogenesis hypotheses. Their models include HIV virions, TH cell, TK cells, B cells, antibodies and Syncytia. Grilo et al. [14] {#240}implemented an Agent-Rule-Based simulation model based on a Cellular Automata (or CA) structure. Their model includes HIV virions, TH cells, TK cells, Macrophages, B cells, antibodies and a series of molecules such as IL-1, IL-2, IL-5 and γ-IFN. A similar coverage of cells and chemical molecules by Sieburg et al. [38] is based on a strict CA structure. In ODE models, TK cells, B cells and antibodies are usually omitted and chemical molecules are not explicitly identified.

3.2 Entity Granularity

The task of modeling TH cell population dynamics under viral infection considers questions like: should their receptors be modeled? What are their activation states? should we distinguish every TH cell, or treat them as a homogenous population? This raises the issue of entity granularity, which we define as follows:

Entity Granularity: The level of detail at which entities are specified. We refer to an ordered and discrete categorization rather than a continuous measurement.

From our survey of immunological models, we define three levels of entity granularity:

1. *Parameter Level:* Entities here do not appear as population variables; only their functions and effects are present in the form of parameters of other dynamical descriptions.
2. *Population Level or Subpopulation Level:* Entities here are treated as a group. They are typically described by population variables.
3. *Individual Level:* Entities here are distinct and stateful.

Many ODE models [8,18,27,28,30-33,35,39,43] specify the main entities of interest, particularly TH cell and HIV virions at the Population Level. The Target Cell Limited Model by Phillips [35] contains one population of HIV and three subpopulations of TH cell types; namely, healthy, productively infected (which produce HIV virions upon death), and latently infected (which do not produce HIV virions) cells. The verification model by Stafford et al. [39] reduced TH cells into two subpopulations: healthy and infected cells as Phillips [35] noted that latently infected TH cell populations do not impact population dynamics significantly. The therapy models, such as the one proposed by Perelson et al. [30,31] divides HIV into two subpopulations: infectious and noninfectious as the drug Protease Inhibitor was designed to produce noninfectious virions from infected cells.

We observe that the number of subpopulations increases with the number of heterogeneous entities modeled within a single population. Essunger and Perelson [11] investigated the virulence of HIV towards memory TH cells by modeling naïve, activated, and memory TH cells; each of which had a corresponding infected subpopulation, and the infected memory TH cells were further divided into transiently (revertible to a healthy state) and permanently infected, resulting in a total of 7 TH cell subpopulations and one HIV population. In another example, Wein at al. [44] extended the post-treatment model by Perelson et al. [31] (which tries to explain the slowing down of viral decay after drug treatment by introducing long-lived victim cells) with two types of virions: those that are easily eradicated by drugs (type 1) and those that are not (type 2), resulting in 4 subpopulations of HIV (infectious type 1 and 2, noninfectious type 1 and 2), 2 subpopulations for both infected TH cells and long-lived infected cells (type 1 and 2). Together with healthy TH cells and long-lived cells, a total of 10 subpopulations were required. The increased number of subpopulations gives rise to more complex equations and interactions among subpopulations.

For entities modeled at the Parameter Level, their existence is reflected as parameters of other dynamical descriptions. A parameter can either be a constant or be dependent on other factors in the model. For example, in many models [30,35,39,44], there is a constant input rate of births to the healthy TH subpopulation, which denotes the function of a thymus, and its constant value indicates that the thymus is assumed to be functioning well over time. In the model by Essunger and Perelson [11], this birth inflow is a decreasing function of HIV population size, implying that the new TH cell production is impaired by the increase in viral load. Drug modeling [30] is another example; it's use is described by a parameter called *efficacy*, which specifies the proportion of infections that are blocked (efficacy of Reverse Transcriptase Inhibitor) or the proportion of virions produced from infected cells that are noninfectious (efficacy of Protease Inhibitor).

Entities modeled at the Individual Level are typically found in MA Models. Referred to as *agents*, each is autonomous and stateful. Each agent interacts with others according to its own set of rules. Instead of having to partition a population into many subpopulations, the implementation of different states is more intuitive here; an agent, based on its type, can transition among a set of possible states over time. For example, in the model by Sieburg et al. [38], there are 8 states for a TH cell (naïve, secretory, proliferating, memory and their correspondent infected states), 4 states for a TK cell (similar to TH cell), 5 states for a B cell (naïve, antigen-presenting, activated, antibody-producing, and memory), 3 states for a macrophage (non-binding, antigen-presenting, and stimulated). On top of this, 3 types of interleukins (IL-1, IL-2, IL-5) and γ-Interferon are also modeled. This is more complicated and detailed than the models at (Sub)Population Level as described above. The model developers have to properly identify the states, state transitions and the associated conditions, but with domain knowledge, this is straightforward as the cognitive mapping is direct from one rule to another, unlike mapping from a rule to a mathematical relationship.

Immune Specificity is another type of entity granularity that quantifies the specific matching between immune cell receptors and antigen shapes. Nowak et al. [27] modeled the TH cells at Subpopulation Level based on an integer-valued specificity. In their model, the TH cell subpopulation of strain *s* only recognizes the HIV of strain *s*, while HIV does not face such shape-matching restrictions when infecting TH cells. New HIV strains (with different integer values) are created over time, simulating rapid mutation. There is a special subpopulation of TH cells that can recognize all HIV strains with the assumption that they can only recognize the conserved parts of the HIV antigen [27]. The results from Nowak et al [27] show a successful reproduction of the 3-stage dynamics of HIV pathogenesis when the total number of strains was set to 8. That is, there are 8 HIV subpopulations, 8 TH cell subpopulations and one special TH cell subpopulation that can recognize any HIV virions.

The work by Hershberg et al. [17] was similar to Nowak et al. [27] except that they modeled different strains (essentially different shapes) with letter strings. With this model, they introduced the concept of *shape space*. Each letter string is a point in this space, differing from its neighbours in one letter through mutation. This model also attained the 3-stage disease progression dynamics.

It is surprising that there are relatively few models that actually consider immune specificity; those that do, target models for rapid viral mutation theory where immune specificity is a crucial factor. Similar to choosing the Model Scope, the choice of Entity Granularity is also greatly influenced by the model developers' perception of what is "required" for their purpose. This subjectivity may hinder the discoveries of important causes of the diseases progression dynamics.

3.3   Interaction Description

The entities in the system are interdependent due to interactions. For example, a viral infection can trigger a chain of activations of immune cells; the different cytokines secreted by TH cells can activate or suppress other cells. What interactions are included and excluded from the model concerns its scope as described in Section 3.1. Here we concentrate on the issue of the method of interaction description.

Interaction Description: Form of representation used for describing entity interactions.

There exist two different methods of interaction descriptions. An *Equation-based* approach uses a set of coupled ordinary or partial differential equations to describe entity interactions by expressing relationships among observables quantitatively. Observables are measurable variables of interest - for instance, population size, concentrations, growth rate, and infection efficiency. They are usually an averaged measurement over the population. ODE models [8,18,27,28,30-33,35,39,43] typically adopt a Population/Subpopulation Level of entity granularity and the Equation-based interaction description. An *Agent-rule-based* approach describes interactions by specifying interacting rules at the cellular and molecular level. The rules are usually described with IF-THEN clauses. MA models [14,15,19] the Individual Level of entity granularity with a corresponding Agent-rule-based interaction description.

Table 1. Comparison of Equation- and Agent-rule-based Interaction Descriptions

	Equation-based	**Agent-rule-based**
Defined by	Linear combination of products of population sizes weighted by interaction rates	Agent rules: If some conditions are met, then act
Concerned with	System Level Observables	Individual Behaviors
Level of view	Macroscopic	Microscopic
Representation	*Implicit* representation: embedded in equations	*Explicit* representation: actually happen in simulation

Table 1 compares the Equation- and Agent-rule-based interaction description approaches. An Equation-based approach is only concerned with system level observables such as population sizes and interaction rates; hence it takes a *macroscopic* view of the real system to be modeled. Conversely, the Agent-rule-based approach explores the cellular and molecular levels by predicting behaviors of each cell and molecule through agent rule specifications; hence it models the real system from a *microscopic* view. With respect to what actually happens in the real immune system, we believe that the agent-rule-based interaction description is more *explicit* as each distinguishable cellular or molecular interaction is modeled and designed to occur individually and possibly distinctively in the simulation, while the Equation-based approach is *implicit* since cellular and molecular interactions are not distinctively computed but rather, homogeneously combined and embedded within a mathematical model of population change. We exemplify the point made above about Equation-based approaches through a simple ODE Model by Perelson [30], given in Eq. 1 to Eq. 3. This model involves three entity population sizes: healthy TH cells (T), infected TH cells (I) and HIV virions (V).

Table 2. Equations and Schematic Diagram of the Model by Perelson [30]

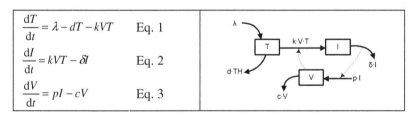

$$\frac{dT}{dt} = \lambda - dT - kVT \qquad \text{Eq. 1}$$

$$\frac{dI}{dt} = kVT - \delta I \qquad \text{Eq. 2}$$

$$\frac{dV}{dt} = pI - cV \qquad \text{Eq. 3}$$

In the Equation-based approach, the amount of cellular interaction (right-hand side of equations) is quantified by the sizes of involved populations and weighted by a rate parameter. For example, the amount of infection is equal to the product of virion population size (V) and healthy TH cell population size (T) multiplied by the infection rate k . The relationship between interactions and populations is illustrated in Table 2. Rectangular boxes represent entity populations. Solid arrows represent the *flows*, which are factors causing the change in population sizes. The flows depicted by perforated arrows are quantitatively dependent on the factors or population sizes that originate it. Such a graphical form of ODE Models is also employed by simulation tools such as STELLA® [40] and VenSim® [42].

Table 3. TH Cell Agent Rules with Schematic Diagrams by Guo et al. [15]

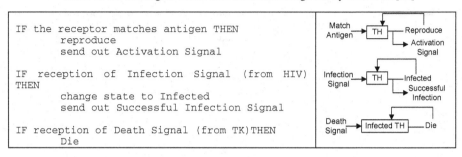

IF the receptor matches antigen THEN
    reproduce
    send out Activation Signal
 	
IF reception of Infection Signal (from HIV)
THEN
    change state to Infected
    send out Successful Infection Signal
 	
IF reception of Death Signal (from TK)THEN
    Die

We next exemplify the Agent-rule-based Interaction Description using the model by Guo et al. [15]. Each type of agent has a set of agent rules which governs their inter-action with other agents. Table 3 gives three agent rules that governs antigen match-ing, infection and death due to cytotoxic effect for TH cells. From the corresponding graph, incoming arrows denote conditions of the rule. If the condition is met, then the rule is fired and the decision part of the rule is carried out (shown as outgoing ar-rows). Feedback causes agent state changes as a result of rule firing. Agent rules can be specified from a description of a single cell's (or a molecule's) biological function and MA Model developers do not need to explicitly enforce any Population Level relationships, such as the flows among populations common seen in ODE Models. While rule specification is done at a microscopic level, macroscopic level properties such as changes in population sizes and the amount of interactions are emergent prop-erties as a result of a large collection of local interactions.

The reason why MA Models [14,15,19,38,38] tend to have wider scopes than ODE Models can be explained by the cognitive process of agent rule specification. The specification of agent rules only requires a description of the biological func-tion of a single cell (or a molecule); constructing mathematical equations requires a further translation of these rules (and the abstraction of many of these) into Popula-tion Level relationships such as birth-death flows. The direct mapping from bio-logical functions to agent rules naturally results in models with greater details and wider scope.

Table 4 summarizes the model comparisons we have discussed so far. ODE Mod-els usually have restricted Model Scope where a minimum number of entity types and interactions are included based on the model developers' understanding. MA Models have wider Model Scope, which appears to be a direct implication of the intuitively straightforward agent-rule specification method. ODE Models specify entities at Parameter, Population and Subpopulation Level, while MA Models specify entities at Individual Level through the implementation of agents. Many models do not imple-ment immune specificity. Among those that do, different strain-labeling methods include integer-valued [27,28] (which are essentially disjoint symbols) and letter strings [17] (which implies a shape space). ODE Models rely on a set of ordinary differential equations to describe interactions among entities, while MA Models spec-ify interactions by defining a set of rules for each type of agent.

Table 4. Comparison of ODE and MA Model Characteristics

	ODE Models	MA Models
Model Scope	Limited types of entities	Many types of entities
Entity Granularity: w.r.t Entity	Parameter / (Sub)population level	Individual level
Entity Granularity: w.r.t Specificity	Modeled or not modeled	Modeled or not modeled
Interaction Description	Equation-based	Agent-rule-based

4 Practical Considerations for Immunological Modeling

In this section we discuss issues beyond the apparent differences in model characteristics. In particular, we investigate the limitation of ODE Models in terms of entity heterogeneity and spatial non-uniformity, the amount of effort necessary for developing the computational models, and the issue of emergent and designed dynamics.

4.1 Entity Heterogeneity and Spatial Non-uniformity

The entities we have seen in immunological models have many states. For example, a TH cell can be in a quiescent, activated, productively infected, latently infected, or memory state. For ODE Models this would mean dividing the cell population into more subpopulations, each of which is dedicated to one cell state, modeled by a single differential equation. Solving a system of coupled differential equations for as many cell types as there are in the human immune system easily surpasses the capabilities of any modeling tool. As a result, ODE Models generally assume homogeneity of entity types so as to limit the number of computable states while compromising on the 'realism' of their predictions. MA Models, on the other hand, can afford many entity types and entity states without significantly affecting computational tractability.

To model agent interactions realistically, MA Models specify rules that are dependent on spatial proximity; that is, agents should only interact when they are close to each other. Cellular Automata is a possible choice [14,15,38] for implementing such an environment, where agents and interactions are located on a spatial dimension. This dependence on spatial proximity is typically absent with ODE Models as only Population Level factors are considered, spatial (questions of positional effects) and topological (questions of positional responses) dependencies on individual interactions are ignored. The resulting equations imply that entity interactions are uniformly occurring at the same frequency at all places. We believe that this assumption is unjustifiable. As demonstrated in [24], models that explicitly take spatial non-uniformity into consideration can lead to drastically different simulation results. To consider the spatial non-uniformity using equation-based description, PDE models are used; they specify the dynamics with respect to x, y and z-axes in space in addition to the time dimension. This results in an increased number of coupled equations, making the model computationally more expensive.

4.2 Implementation Effort

Software simulation tools such as STELLA® [40] and VenSim® [42] provide a graphical user interface which allows the dragging-and-dropping of ODE model components and automatic generation of the equations. However, such tools face practical difficulties when the number of populations increase; a result of increased entity granularities with respect to either entity or immune specificity. With more subpopulations identified, the number of equations increases accordingly, and the number of interconnections to be drawn on the diagram increases quickly. When immune specificity is modeled, duplicate diagrams have to be drawn, each diagram for one strain.

For MA models, once domain knowledge is acquired, specifying agent rules is intuitively straightforward. However, an *executable* Multi-Agent Model is not as easy to construct as compared to ODE Models due to the extra effort needed to create the basic framework (such as virtual environment, agent communication channels, agent life span modeling) in addition to the agent rules. Although programming toolkits (such as RePast [1] and BREVE [22]) exist for generic MA Model construction, the need for programming knowledge may make them less accessible.

4.3 Emergent vs. Designed Dynamics

We clarify the differences between *emergent dynamics* (from model and simulation) and *designed dynamics* (by model developer) in this section. In the Stafford et al. [39] model, TK cells are not explicitly modeled; only its cytotoxic effect (i.e., to kill infected cells) is present as a parameter which represents an increase in death rate of infected TH cells. This parameter is a function of viral load and time, which peaks at about 200 days after infection, as shown in Figure 3. Its dynamics are directly *designed* through a mathematical formula also shown in Figure 3. The peak position can be directly controlled by the model developer by specifying the relevant parameters (t_1, t_2). In the model by De Boer and Perelson [8], TK cells are modeled as a population. The interactions between TK cell population and infected TH cell subpopulations follows the famous Lotka-Volterra equations [3]. In their model, TK cells are the predators whose population reproduction rate is proportional to the infected TH cell population size, and infected TH cells are preys whose death rate is proportional to the TK cell population size. The interactions are directly specified, but the patterns in population dynamics and rate dynamics are *emergent*. Model developers can only *indirectly influence* the pattern by changing the parameters in interactions (equations).

The difficulty with *designed* dynamics is that the result may only be valid for that particular design, and may not hold when the designed factors are altered. Model developers are hence responsible for justifying each parameter in the formula, in particular, their correspondence to the biological phenomena. Often however, there is no uniquely correct way for such formulation (as is often qualified by researchers themselves) nor are justifications always provided. A directly designed expression of macroscopic observables may approximate observed dynamics well but its results are only as good as the assumptions and mathematical relationships chosen *for* the model. They lack the provision to allow serendipitous discoveries through the collective causality of microscopic interactions.

ODE Models rely on equation-based interaction description, which in turn relies on certain rate parameters that quantify the outcome of the interactions. These rate parameters often arise with only intuitive justifications. MA Models however, suffer less from this issue of designed dynamics because the macroscopic dynamics are not formulated but emerge from the microscopic interactions among agents.

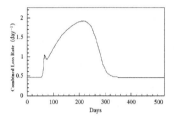

TH Cell Loss Rate δ as a function of viral load V and time t :

$$\delta(V,t) = \begin{cases} \delta_0 & t < t_1 \\ \delta_0 + V\left(\dfrac{\beta}{1 + \kappa e^{\frac{-(t-t_1)}{\Delta T_1}}} - \dfrac{\beta}{1 + \kappa e^{\frac{-(t-t_2)}{\Delta T_2}}} \right) & t \geq t_1 \end{cases}$$

Fig. 2 TH Cell Loss Rate Dynamics with Cytotoxic Effect (Adopted from [39])

5 Conclusions

We have presented HIV pathogenesis models based on the model characteristics of Scope, Entity Granularity and Interaction Description. ODE Models have relatively restricted Model Scope, selected based on the model developers' understanding of the relevance of each entity type and interaction. A restricted Model Scope risks omitting potentially important factors. MA Models have relatively wider Model Scope, which we believe to be a direct implication of the intuitively straightforward agent-rule specification method. ODE Models employ Parameter Level and Population/Subpopulation Level entity granularity with equation-based interaction, while MA Models specify entities at Individual Level, implemented as agents, and interactions are described via agent-rules. ODE Models are relatively easy to construct but its complexity grows with increased number of subpopulations as a result of striving for a higher entity granularity level. ODE Models are not suitable for modeling spatial non-uniformity unless PDEs are used. MA Models can naturally handle entity heterogeneity and spatial non-uniformity, and suffer less from the issue of directly designed dynamics. Even though specifying agent rules is intuitively straightforward, a complete Multi-Agent Model requires effort to build the basic framework that implements a virtual environment and agent communication channels, which are nontrivial. Close collaboration between computer scientists and immunologists is necessary for developing useful modeling tools.

References

1. RePast: http://repast.sourceforge.net.
2. Banchereau, J.: The long arm of the immune system. Scientific American 287 (2002) 52-59
3. Bar-Yam, Y.: Dynamics of Complex Systems. Westview Press (1997)

4. Bergmann, C., Van Hemmen, J. L., Segel, L. A.: Th1 or Th2: how an appropriate T helper response can be made. Bull Math Biol. 63 (2001) 405-430
5. Caetano, A., Grilo, A.: Modeling thymic selection and concomitant immune responses on CD4+T lymphocyte sub-populations. In: Proc. 2nd workshop on BEMC (1996)
6. Callard, R., George, A. J., Stark, J.: Cytokines, chaos, and complexity. Immunity. 11 (1999) 507-513
7. Coffin, J. M.: HIV population dynamics in vivo: implications for genetic variation, pathogensis, and therapy. Science 267 (1995) 483-489
8. De Boer, R. Perelson, A. S.: Target cell limited and immune control models of HIV infection: a comparison. J. theor. Biol. 190 (1998) 201-214
9. De Boer, R. J. Perelson, A. S.: T cell repertoires and competitive exclusion. J. theor. Biol. 169 (1994) 375-390
10. De Castro, L.N. and Timmis, J.: Artificial Immune Systems: A New Computational Intelligence Approach. Springer (2002)
11. Essunger, P. Perelson, A. S.: Modeling HIV infection of CD4+ T-cell subpopulations. J. theor. Biol. 179 (1994) 367-391
12. Fauci, A. S. Chun, T.-W.: Latent reservoirs of HIV: obstacles to the eradication of virus. Proc. Natl. Acad. Sci. USA 96 (1999) 10958-10961
13. Gougeon, M.-L.: Apoptosis as an HIV strategy to escape immune attack. Nature Reviews Immunology 3 (2003) 392-404
14. Grilo, A., Caetano, A., Rosa, A.: Immune System Simulation through a Complex Adaptive System Model. In: Proceeding of the 3rd Workshop on Genetic Algorithms and Artificial Life (1999)
15. Guo, Z., Han, H. K., Tay, J. C.: Sufficiency Verification of HIV-1 Pathogenesis based on Multi-Agent Simulation. In: GECCO 2005, Washington D.C. (2005)
16. Heinkelein, M., Sopper, S., Jassoy, C.: Contact of human immunodeficiency virus type 1-infected and uninfected CD4+ T lymphocytes is highly cytolytic for both cells. Journal of Virology 69 (1995) 6925-6931
17. Hershberg, U., Louzoun, Y., Atlan, H., Solomon, S.: HIV time hierarchy: winning the war while, loosing all the battles. Physica A 289 (2001) 178-190
18. Ho, D. D., Neumann, A. U., Perelson, A. S., Chen, W., Leonard, J. M., Markowitz, M.: Rapid turnover of plasma virions and CD4 lymphocytes in HIV-1 infection. Nature 373 (1995) 123-126
19. Jacob, C., Litorco, J., Lee, L.: Immunity Through Swarms: Agent-Based Simulations of the Human Immmune System. In: 3rd International Conference on Artificial Immune Systems (2004)
20. Janeway, C.A., Travers, P., Walport, M., and Shlomchik, M.: Immunobiology: the immune system in health & disease. Garland Science Publishing (2001)
21. Johnson, G.B.: The Living World 2nd Edition. Mc Graw Hill (2000)
22. Klein, J.: BREVE: a 3D simulation enviornment for the simulation of decentralized systems and artificial life. In: Proceedings of ARtificial Life VIII, the 8th International Conference on the Simulation and Synthesis of Living Systems. (2002)
23. Lagreca, M. C., de Almeida, R. M. C., Zorzenon dos Santos, R. M.: A dynamical model for the immune repertoire. Physica A 289 (2001) 191-207
24. Louzoun, Y., Solomon, S., Atlan, H., Cohen, I. R.: Modeling complexity in biology. Physica A 297 (2001) 242-252
25. McCune, J. M.: The dynamics of CD4$^+$ T-cell depletion in HIV disease. Nature 410 (2001) 974-979

26. Nowak, M. A. McMichael, A. J.: How HIV defeats the immune system. Scientific American 273 (1995) 58-65

27. Nowak, M. A., Anderson, R. M., McLean, A. R., Wolfs, T. F. W., Goudsmit, J., May, R. M.: Antigenic diversity thresholds and the development of AIDS. Science 254 (1991) 963-969

28. Nowak, M. A., May, R. M., Anderson, R. M.: The evolutionary dynamics of HIV-1 quasispecies and the development of immunodeficiency disease. AIDS 4 (1990) 1095-1103

29. Perelson, A. S.: Immunology for physicists. Reviews of Modern Physics 69 (1997) 1219-1267

30. Perelson, A. S.: Modelling viral and immune system dynamics. Nature Reviews Immunology 2 (2002) 28-36

31. Perelson, A. S., Essunger, P., Cao, Y., Vesanen, M., Hurly, A., Saksela, K., Markowitz, M., Ho, D. D.: Decay characteristics of HIV-1-infected compartments during combination therapy. Nature 387 (1997) 188-191

32. Perelson, A. S. Nelson, P. W.: Mathematical Analysis of HIV-1 Dynamics in Vivo. SIAM Review 41 (1999) 3-44

33. Perelson, A. S., Neumann, A. U., Markowitz, M., Leonard, J. M., Ho, D. D.: HIV-1 Dynamics in vivo: virion clearance rate, infected cell life-span, and viral generation time. Science 271 (1996) 1582-1586

34. Perelson, A. S. Oster, G. F.: Theoretical studies of clonal selection: minimal antibody repertoire size and reliability of self-non-self discrimination. J. Theor. Biol. 81 (1979) 645-670

35. Phillips, A. N.: Reduction of HIV concentration during acute infection: independence from a specific immune response. Science 271 (1996) 497-499

36. Rowland-Jones, S. L.: AIDS pathogenesis: what have two decades of HIV research taught us? Nature Reviews Immunology 3 (2003) 343-348

37. Selliah, N. finkel, T. H.: Biochemical mechanisms of HIV induced T cell apoptosis. Cell Death and Differentiation 8 (2001) 127-136

38. Sieburg, H. B., McCutchan, J. A., Clay, O. K., Cabalerro, L., Ostlund, J. J.: Simulation of HIV infection in artificial immune systems. Physica D 45 (1990) 208-227

39. Stafford, M. A., Corey, L., Cao, Y., Daar, E. S., Ho, D. D., Perelson, A. S.: Modeling plasma virus concentration during primary HIV infection. J. theor. Biol. 203 (2000) 285-301

40. STELLA software. High Performance Systems, Inc. Home Page: www.hps-inc.com.

41. Stine, G. J.: AIDS Update. Prentice Hall (1999)

42. Vensim. Ventana Systems. Ventana Systems Home Page. http://www.vensim.com.

43. Wei, X., Ghosh, S. K., Taylor, M. E., Johnson, V. A., Emini, E. A., Deutsch, P., Lifson, J. D., Bonhoeffer, S., Nowak, M. A., Hahn, B. H., Saag, M. S., Shaw, G. M.: Viral dynamics in human immunodeficiency virus type 1 infection. Nature 373 (1995) 117-122

44. Wein, L. M., D'Amato, R. M., Perelson, A. S.: Mathematical analysis of antiretroviral therapy aimed at HIV-1 eradication or maintenance of low viral loads. J. theor. Biol. 192 (1998) 81-98

Handling Constraints in Global Optimization Using an Artificial Immune System

Nareli Cruz-Cortés, Daniel Trejo-Pérez, and Carlos A. Coello Coello

CINVESTAV-IPN, Evolutionary Computation Group,
Depto. de Ingeniería Eléctrica, Sección de Computación,
Av. Instituto Politécnico Nacional No. 2508 Col. San Pedro Zacatenco,
México, D. F. 07360, Mexico
{nareli, dtrejo}@computacion.cs.cinvestav.mx,
ccoello@cs.cinvestav.mx

Abstract. In this paper, we present a study of the use of an artificial immune system (CLONALG) for solving constrained global optimization problems. As part of this study, we evaluate the performance of the algorithm both with binary encoding and with real-numbers encoding. Additionally, we also evaluate the impact of the mutation operator in the performance of the approach by comparing Cauchy and Gaussian mutations. Finally, we propose a new mutation operator which significantly improves the performance of CLONALG in constrained optimization.

1 Introduction

Many bio-inspired algorithms (particularly evolutionary algorithms) have been very successful in the solution of a wide variety of optimization problems [3]. However, all of these approaches (including evolutionary algorithms and artificial immune systems), when used for numerical optimization, can be seen as unconstrained search techniques. This means that they require a suitable mechanism to incorporate constraints, such that they can deal with the general nonlinear optimization problem.

Within evolutionary algorithms (EAs), external penalty functions have been the most popular mechanism adopted to incorporate constraints into the fitness function [17]. The idea of an external penalty function is to "punish" (or penalize) a solution for being infeasible by increasing its fitness value (when solving a minimization problem). Despite their popularity, penalty functions have several problems, from which the main one relates to the difficulties to define accurate penalty factors. A large penalty value discourages the exploration of the infeasible region since the very beginning of the search process (this may cause difficulties when dealing, for example, with a disjoint feasible region). On the other hand, if the penalty value is too low, a lot of the search time will be spent exploring the infeasible region because the penalty will be negligible with respect to the objective function.

Recently, several researchers have proposed constraint-handling techniques for EAs which avoid the use of a penalty function or do not require any fine-tuning of the penalty factors [11,16,7,9]. Such approaches have been found to outperform traditional penalty functions and can handle all types of constraints (linear, nonlinear, equality, inequality).

C. Jacob et al. (Eds.): ICARIS 2005, LNCS 3627, pp. 234–247, 2005.

The main motivation of the work presented in this paper was to explore the capabilities of an artificial immune system in the context of constrained global optimization. For that sake, we decided to adopt the algorithm based on the clonal selection principle (called CLONALG) which is described in [4,6]. CLONALG was proposed as a learning algorithm particularly well-suited for solving pattern recognition and multimodal optimization problems. However, as far as we know, it hasn't been properly validated in the context of constrained global optimization.

CLONALG is a population-based algorithm and its only variation operator is mutation. Evidently, the main search power of CLONALG relies on this mutation operator and therefore, such operator became the main focus of our study.

There is well-documented evidence (in the specialized literature) of the superiority of evolution strategies (over genetic algorithms) in constrained optimization [16]. Also, we were aware of the proposal by Yao and Liu [18] of adopting Cauchy-distributed random numbers for an evolution strategy, instead of the traditional Gaussian distribution. Yao and Liu [18] found that this probability distribution allowed the mutation operator of an evolution strategy to behave as a sort of crossover operator, thus improving the performance of the algorithm in (unconstrained) numerical optimization problems (including multimodal functions). Apparently, this behavior was due to the fact that Cauchy-distributed random numbers allow relatively coarse-grained steps, which contrast with the fine-grained steps of the traditional Gaussian-distributed random numbers.

Thus, being aware of this work, we decided to incorporate Cauchy-distributed random numbers into CLONALG. We hypothesized that this would considerably improve the performance of CLONALG in constrained optimization (with respect to the use of Gaussian mutations). However, the results (as we will see later on) were rather disappointing and led us to propose our own mutation operator which turned out to be better than any of the two other operators initially adopted. Finally, we also evaluated CLONALG with binary encoding, in order to assess the impact of the representation in the performance of the approach (in the context of constrained optimization).

The remainder of the paper is organized as follows. In Section 2, we define the problem we want to solve. Section 3 describes some previous related work. In Section 4, we describe the modifications done to CLONALG so that it can handle constraints. In Section 5, we present our experiments adopting a binary representation (both with and without Gray coding). In Section 6, we report our experiments adopting real-numbers representation (adopting different mutation operators). In Section 7, some changes to CLONALG's mutation operator are proposed, our results are presented and they are discussed. Finally, in Section 8, our conclusions and some possible paths for future research are provided.

2   Statement of the Problem

The problem that we want to solve is the general nonlinear programming problem which is defined as follows:

$$\text{Find } x \text{ which optimizes } f(x) \tag{1}$$

subject to:

$$g_i(\boldsymbol{x}) \leq 0, \quad i = 1, \ldots, n \tag{2}$$

$$h_j(\boldsymbol{x}) = 0, \quad j = 1, \ldots, p \tag{3}$$

where $\boldsymbol{x}$ is the vector of solutions (or decision variables) $\boldsymbol{x} = [x_1, x_2, \ldots, x_r]^T$, n is the number of inequality constraints and p is the number of equality constraints (in both cases, constraints could be linear or nonlinear).

3   Previous Related Work

We were able to find very few papers in which the main focus was the solution of constrained global optimization problems using an artificial immune systems. Such work is briefly described next.

Hajela and Yoo [19,8] proposed a hybrid between a Genetic Algorithm (GA) and an artificial immune system, aiming to solve constrained optimization problems. In this approach, the authors adopted two populations. The first is composed by the antigens (which are the best solutions), and the other by the antibodies (which are the worst solutions). The idea is to have a GA embedded into another GA. The outer GA performs the optimization of the original (constrained) problem. The second GA is run for a few generations, and uses as its fitness function a Hamming distance (binary encoding was adopted for the GA) so that the antibodies are evolved to become "very similar" (at the genotypic level) to the antigens, without becoming identical. The interesting effect of this evolution was that the infeasible individuals would normally become feasible. This approach was tested with some structural optimization problems.

Kelsey and Timmis [10] proposed an immune inspired algorithm based on the clonal selection theory to solve multimodal optimisation problems. Its highlight is the mutation operator called "Somatic Contiguous Hypermutation" where mutation is applied on a subset of contiguous bits. The length and beginning of this subset is determined randomly.

Coello Coello and Cruz-Cortés [2] proposed an extension of Hajela and Yoo's algorithm. In this proposal, no penalty function is required (as in the original approach), and some extra mechanisms are defined to allow the approach to work in cases in which there are no feasible solutions in the initial generation. Additionally, the authors proposed a parallel version of the algorithm and validated it using some standard test functions reported in the specialized literature.

Balicki's proposal [1] is very similar to the two previous approaches. Its main difference is the way in which the antibodies' fitness is computed. In this case, Balicki introduces a ranking procedure. This approach was validated using a constrained three-objective optimization problem.

Luh and Chueh [13,12] proposed an algorithm (called CMOIA, or Constrained Multi Objective Immune Algorithm) for solving constrained multi-objective optimization problems. In this case, the antibody's population is composed by the potential solutions to the problem, whereas antigens are the objective functions. CMOIA transforms the constrained problem into an unconstrained one by associating an interleukin (IL) value with all the constraints violated. IL is a function of both the number of constraints violated and the total magnitude of this constraint violation (note that this IL function is actually a penalty function). Then, feasible individuals are rewarded and infeasible individuals are penalized. Other features of the approach were based on the clonal selection theory and other immunological mechanisms. CMOIA was evaluated through six test functions and two structural optimization problems.

4   Clonal Selection Algorithm for Constrained Optimization

Nunes and Von Zuben [4,6] proposed the CLONALG algorithm, which is inspired in the clonal selection theory of the immune system. CLONALG was used by its authors to solve pattern recognition and multimodal optimization problems.

Next, we will describe the main elements that comprise the general framework of any biological-inspired system as described in [5] and considering the context of constrained optimization:

- **Representation of the components**: *Antigens* are represented by the objective function $f(x)$ that we want to optimize (minimize or maximize) and *antibodies* are represented by the variables of the problem (x) which are potential solutions.
- **Mechanisms to evaluate the interaction among individuals and their environment**: antibody's affinity corresponds to the evaluation of the objective function given by the antigen.
- **Adaptation Procedures**: The clonal selection theory of the immune system.

Now, we will briefly describe the CLONALG algorithm [6]:

1. Generate j antibodies randomly.
2. Repeat a predetermined number of times:
   (a) Determine the affinity of each antibody (Ab). This affinity corresponds to the evaluation of the objective function.
   (b) Select the n highest affinity antibodies.
   (c) The n selected antibodies will be cloned proportionally to their affinities, generating a repertory C of clones: the higher the affinity is, the higher becomes the number of clones generated for each of the n selected antibodies.
   (d) The clones from C are subject to a hyper-mutation process inversely proportional to their antigenic affinity: the higher the affinity, the smaller the mutation rate.
   (e) Determine the affinity of the mutated clones C.
   (f) From this set C of clones and antibodies (Ab), select the j highest affinity clones to compose the new antibodies' population.
   (g) Replace the d lowest affinity antibodies by new individuals generated at random.
3. End repeat

The number of clones generated from the n selected antibodies is given by:

$$Nc = \sum_{i=0}^{n} round\left(\frac{\beta * j}{i}\right) \qquad (4)$$

where Nc is the total number of clones, and β is a multiplier factor (generally equal to 1).

In order to apply CLONALG to constrained optimization problems, we introduced the following changes:

- In step 2.(a), it is necessary that each antibody evaluates the objective function, and the constraints of the problem in order to know if it is a feasible solution or not.
- In step 2.(b), the antibodies' affinity is defined not only by the objective function value, but also based on feasibility or infeasibility, considering that feasible individuals must have a higher affinity value. Within this group, the best individuals are those whose objective function value is best (i.e., the larger value if we are maximizing). Within the group of infeasible individuals, those having the lowest constraint violation quantity will obtain the highest affinity values (since they are closest to the feasible region).
- In step 2.(f), when the individuals that will make it for the next generation are determined, it is necessary to ensure that at least q infeasible individuals will survive (q is a user-defined parameter). This is because we want to promote a reasonable diversity right in the boundary between the feasible and the infeasible region (this is done because it is known that the most difficult constrained optimization problems for EAs are those in which the global optimum is located precisely in the boundary between the feasible and the infeasible regions).
- In step 2.(g), the criterion that determines the individuals who will be replaced is driven by feasibility criteria as well. That means that if infeasible individuals become a majority, more of them will be replaced and vice versa.

In order to assess the performance of CLONALG in constrained optimization, we conducted a set of experiments using different representations and mutation operators. For these experiments, we adopted the benchmark originally proposed in [15] and extended in [16]. The test functions chosen contain characteristics that are representative of what can be considered "difficult" global optimization problems for an evolutionary algorithm (or any other bio-inspired algorithm used for global optimization). The mathematical description of these test functions can be found in [16].

To get an estimate of how difficult is to generate feasible points through a purely random process, we computed the ρ metric for the 13 test functions of the benchmark (as suggested by Michalewicz and Schoenauer [15]) using the expression:
$\rho = |F|/|S|$, where $|S|$ is the number of random solutions generated ($S = 1,000,000$ in our case), and $|F|$ is the number of feasible solutions found (out of the total $|S|$ solutions randomly generated). The values of ρ for each of the functions chosen are shown in Table 1.

CLONALG was compared with respect to two approaches that are representative of the state-of-the-art in constrained optimization: Stochastic Ranking [16] and the Adaptive Segregational Constraint Handling Evolution Strategy (ASCHEA) [9].

Table 1. Values of ρ for the 13 test problems. n=number of decision variables, LI=number of linear inequalities, NI=number of nonlinear inequalities, LE=number of linear equalities and NE=number of nonlinear equalities

Problem	n	Type of function	ρ	LI	NI	LE	NE
g01	13	quadratic	0.0003%	9	0	0	0
g02	20	nonlinear	99.9973%	1	1	0	0
g03	10	nonlinear	0.0026%	0	0	0	1
g04	5	quadratic	27.0079%	0	6	0	0
g05	4	nonlinear	0.0000%	2	0	0	3
g06	2	nonlinear	0.0057%	0	2	0	0
g07	10	quadratic	0.0000%	3	5	0	0
g08	2	nonlinear	0.8581%	0	2	0	0
g09	7	nonlinear	0.5199%	0	4	0	0
g10	8	linear	0.0020%	3	3	0	0
g11	2	quadratic	0.0973%	0	0	0	1
g12	3	quadratic	4.7697%	0	9^3	0	0
g13	5	nonlinear	0.0000%	0	0	1	2

The versions that were evaluated are the following:

– Binary representation
  • Standard
  • Gray coding
– Real-numbers representation
  • Self-adaptive mutation using Gaussian distribution
  • Self-adaptive mutation using Cauchy distribution
  • Uniform mutation without self-adaptation

5   Binary Representation

The CLONALG algorithm with the extensions for handling constrained optimization problems, was first implemented using a binary representation. Since other researchers have reported advantages of using Gray codes when dealing with numerical optimization problems (and adopting genetic algorithms) [14], we decided to try both versions: normal binary encoding and binary encoding with Gray codes.

For these experiments, we adopted the following parameters:

– Number of antibodies $j = 50$.
– Minimum number of infeasible solutions that must survive q=2.
– Type of mutation: uniform (same as in the simple genetic algorithm).
– Mutation rate: Clones are sorted by their affinity values in a descendent manner. The mutation operator was implemented using a small value at the beginning and then we increased it until a certain predetermined value was reached. The initial mutation rate was= $(1/len)$, where len is the length of the binary string. The final mutation rate was set to 0.3.

– Percentage d of replaced antibodies: 0.20.
– Total number of objective function evaluations: 238,750.

The parameters used to compute the number of clones (Eq. (4)) were the following:
$\beta = 1$ and $n = j$.

Tables 2 and 3 summarize the statistical results obtained by our binary versions of CLONALG (with and without Gray coding, respectively) over 30 independent runs.

Table 2. Results obtained by CLONALG using standard binary representation. INF means that the algorithm converged to an infeasible solution. In the functions marked with *, the approach converged to a feasible solution only in 75% of the runs.

Test Function	Optimal	Best	Mean	Worst	Std. Dev
g01*	-15.0	-14.8686	-14.660287	-12.789464	0.501459
g02	0.803619	0.775589	0.749575	0.683894	0.025699
g03*	1.0	0.99891	0.97078	0.92849	0.024912
g04	-30665.539	-30650.00697	-30460.85416	-30366.98548	96.1407
g05	5126.498	INF	INF	INF	INF
g06	-6961.814	-6921.48749	-6248.9307	-6182.9937	181.4024
g07	24.306	24.80870	30.8661	35.4455	2.4353
g08	0.095825	0.095825	0.093398	0.09313	0.00080
g09	680.630	684.12886	704.87263	753.22103	17.58436
g10	7049.25	INF	INF	INF	INF
g11	0.75	0.750295	0.865079	1.567670	0.22056
g12	1.0	0.999996	0.907750	0.725285	0.077762
g13	0.053950	INF	INF	INF	INF

Table 3. Results obtained by CLONALG using binary representation with Gray coding. INF means that the algorithm converged to an infeasible solution. In the functions marked with *, the approach converged to a feasible solution only in 50% of the runs. The use of ** indicates cases in which the algorithm converged to a feasible solution only in 15% of the runs.

Test Function	Optimal	Best	Mean	Worst	Std. Dev.
g01	-15.0	-15.0	-15.0	-15.0	0.0
g02	0.803619	0.760753	0.700945	0.562943	0.049646
g03	1.0	1.0	0.999688	0.997992	0.000579
g04	-30665.539	-30665.504	-30662.678	-30658.778	1.946
g05*	5126.498	INF	INF	INF	INF
g06	-6961.814	-6961.813	-6961.813	6961.810	0.000552
g07	24.306	24.945	27.017	30.007	1.709
g08	0.095825	0.095825	0.095825	0.095825	0.0
g09	680.630	680.727	681.649	682.853	0.599
g10*	7049.25	7451.54	8344.18	10509.34	962.58
g11	0.75	0.75	0.76	0.79	0.011
g12	1.0	1.0	1.0	1.0	0.0
g13**	0.053950	0.059553	0.059215	0.062709	0.003000

Table 4. Results obtained by ASCHEA [9] performing 1,500,000 objective function evaluations. N.A.=Not available.

Test Function	Optimal	Best	Mean	Worst
g01	-15.0	-15.0	-14.84	N.A.
g02	0.803619	0.785	0.59	N.A.
g03	1.0	1.0	0.99989	N.A.
g04	-30665.5	-30665.5	-30665.5	N.A.
g05	5126.4981	5126.5	5141.65	N.A.
g06	-6961.814	-6961.81	-6961.81	N.A.
g07	24.306	24.3323	24.6636	N.A.
g08	0.095825	0.095825	0.095825	N.A.
g09	680.63	680.630	680.641	N.A.
g10	7049.33	7061.13	7497.434	N.A.
g11	0.75	0.75	0.75	N.A.
g12	-1.0	N.A.	N.A.	N.A.
g13	0.05395	N.A.	N.A.	N.A.

Table 5. Results obtained by the Stochastic Ranking algorithm [16] performing 350,000 objective function evaluations

Test Function	Optimal	Best	Mean	Worst	Std. Dev.
g01	-15.0	-15.0	-15.0	-15.0	0.0E+00
g02	0.803619	0.803515	0.7858	0.726288	2.0E-02
g03	1.0	1.0	1.0	1.0	1.9E-04
g04	-30665.539	-30665.539	-30665.539	-30665.539	2.0E-05
g05	5126.498	5126.497	5128.881	5142.472	3.5E+00
g06	-6961.814	-6961.814	-6875.940	-6350.262	1.6E+02
g07	24.306	24.307	24.374	24.642	6.6E-02
g08	0.095825	0.095825	0.095825	0.095825	2.6E-17
g09	680.63	680.630	680.656	680.763	3.4E-02
g10	7049.33	7054.316	7559.192	8835.655	5.3E+02
g11	0.75	0.75	0.75	0.75	8.0E-05
g12	-1.0	-1.0	-1.0	-1.0	0.0E+00
g13	0.05395	0.053957	0.067543	0.216915	3.1E-02

Clearly, the version that uses Gray coding outperforms its traditional binary counterpart. When standard binary representation is used, the algorithm is not capable of finding feasible solutions in functions g5, g10 and g13. For all the other functions, a reasonable approximation to the optimal value is attained.

When Gray coding is adopted, in 10 of the 13 functions, the algorithm is capable of reaching the optimal value. However, in functions g5, g10, and g13, the algorithm has problems even for reaching the feasible region, as indicated before.

To have an idea of how competitive are the results produced by our two binary versions of CLONALG, we present in Table 4 the results produced by ASCHEA [9]. These results were obtained with 1,500,000 objective function evaluations (let's keep in mind that CLONALG performed only 238,750 evaluations). It can be clearly seen that CLONALG (in its two versions) is outperformed by ASCHEA in most cases. Note however that ASCHEA does not report results for g12 and g13.

Table 5 the results produced by Stochastic Ranking [16]. These results were obtained with 350,000 objective function evaluations. As can be seen in Table 5, Stochastic Ranking obtained better results for six functions, and CLONALG outperformed Stochastic Ranking only in one test function.

6   Real-Numbers Representation

In this Section we present our experiments using a version of CLONALG with real-numbers representation. In [6], the authors proposed to use self-adapting mutation parameters in CLONALG as in Evolution Strategies (ES). In such case, the mutation rate is proportional to the antibodies' affinities using the following equation:

$$\alpha = exp(-\rho f) \tag{5}$$

where α is the step size, ρ controls its decay, and $f(x)$ is the antigenic affinity. The sizes of $f(x)$ and α are normalized over the interval [0,1].

Based on what we discussed in Section 1, we decided to experiment with both, Gaussian-distributed and Cauchy-distributed random numbers for our mutation operator. The parameter values adopted for our experiments were the following:

- Number of antibodies j: 20
- Percentage d of replaced antibodies: 0.20
- Objective function evaluations: 350,000

The parameters to compute the number of clones using Eq.(4) were the following: $\beta = 1$ and $n = j$.

The parameter to compute α (Eq.(5)) was: $\rho = 20$

6.1   Gaussian-Distributed Mutations

In the first set of experiments, the mutation applied to a variable x_k (step 2.d) was computed using: $x_k^{new} = x_k + G(0, \alpha)$, where $G(0, \alpha)$ is a random number between 0 and α with Gaussian distribution.

In order to assess the algorithm's performance after this small modification, we utilized the benchmark described in [16], as before. The results obtained from 30 independent runs using Gaussian-distributed numbers are shown in Table 6. In this case, CLONALG was able to converge to a feasible solution in 11 of the 13 test functions. The quality of the results obtained with Gaussian mutations is similar to that of the algorithm with traditional binary representation. However, the results are outperformed by CLONALG with Gray coding.

Table 6. Results obtained by CLONALG with real-numbers representation, using Gaussian mutations. INF mean that the algorithm converged to an infeasible solution.

Test Function	Optimal	Best	Mean	Worst	Std. Dev.
g01	-15.0	-14.9665	-14.835	-14.559	0.0887
g02	0.803619	-0.7920	-0.710	-0.5	0.0583
g03	1.0	-0.99674	-0.551	-0.0852	0.2943
g04	-30665.5	-30665.2360	-30663.09370	-30661.36	1.0620
g05	5126.4981	INF	INF	INF	INF
g06	-6961.814	-6961.1488	-6949.6321	-6928.9176	8.7312
g07	24.306	31.32150	36.041	40.3094	2.1601
g08	0.095825	-0.095825	-0.095825	-0.095825	0.0000
g09	680.63	682.94	686.4131	689.61	1.7149
g10	7049.33	7099.6346	8953.5650	12146.8123	1698.2081
g11	0.75	1.0	1.0	1.0	0.0000
g12	-1.0	-1.0	-1.0	-1.0	0.0000
g13	0.05395	INF	INF	INF	INF

6.2 Cauchy-Distributed Mutations

In our second set of experiments, we tested Cauchy-distributed mutations, aiming to improve the performance of our real-numbers version of CLONALG. In this case, we adopted: $x_k^{new} = x_k + C(0, \alpha)$, where $C(0, \alpha)$ is a random number between 0 and α with Cauchy distribution.

Table 7 shows the results obtained from 30 independent runs using Cauchy-distributed random numbers for our mutation operator. It was quite surprising for us to see that Cauchy-distributed mutations produced the worst overall results for our real-numbers version of CLONALG. These results seem to indicate that the behavior produced by

Table 7. Results obtained by CLONALG with real-numbers representation, using Cauchy mutations. INF means that the algorithm converged to an infeasible solution.

Test Function	Optimal	Best	Mean	Worst	Std. Dev.
g01	-15.0	-14.4501	-13.7009	-12.7895	0.3616
g02	0.803619	-0.35507	-0.3055	-0.256481	0.0264
g03	1.0	0.0	0.0	0.0	0.0
g04	-30665.5	-30664.5824	-30662.4466	-30659.6513	1.3475
g05	5126.4981	INF	INF	INF	INF
g06	-6961.814	-6957.24841	-6917.8961	-6854.0776	26.6042
g07	24.306	40.56171	46.04928	52.1685	3.333
g08	0.095825	-0.095825	-0.09579	-0.0957	0.0
g09	680.63	685.05423	690.51003	696.7897	2.8512
g10	7049.33	7110.1621	8138.4531	11043.2050	986.6993
g11	0.75	1.0	1.0	1.0	0.0
g12	-1.0	-1.0	-1.0	-1.0	0.0
g13	0.05395	INF	INF	INF	INF

Cauchy-distributed mutations (emulating a crossover operator) is not the most appropriate when dealing with constrained optimization problems.

7   CLONALG with Controlled and Uniform Mutations

Given the disappointing results that we obtained when using CLONALG in constrained optimization problems, we decided to introduce a modification in its mutation operator aiming to improve the algorithm's performance. Considering that the binary representation version with Gray coding had produced the best results so far, we decided to analyze only the possible changes to the mutation operator for real-numbers representation. Our first modification was to remove the self-adaptation mechanism suggested in [6]. The motivation for this decision was the fact that this self-adaptation mechanism was apparently designed for unconstrained problems and it wasn't obvious to us how to extend it for constrained problems. Thus, it would be easier to analyze the impact of any changes to the mutation operator if this self-adaptation mechanism was removed.

The second change was the introduction of a control mechanism that allowed to increase the algorithm's capability of exploring neighboring regions. This corresponds to step 2.(d) of the algorithm shown in Section 4. All the other steps remained without changes. In this modified mutation operator, the step size is a function of the mutated variable search space size, the antibody's affinity value and the population size.

So, our proposal was to apply mutation in the following way:

1. For each decision variable x_k, compute $R_k = UB - LB$, where UB and LB are the upper and lower bounds of that variable, respectively, and R_k is the search space size of the k-th variable.
2. Compute $\Delta_k = R_k/j$ where j is the number of antibodies in the population.
3. The clones population is sorted by affinity values in descending order.
4. The mutation operator is applied to each size-g clone group coming from the same parent.
   (a) For each variable k, compute $\delta_k = \Delta_k/g$.
   (b) Apply mutation to each variable x_k by using $x_k^{new} = x_k + U(0, \delta_k)$, where U is a random number in the range from 0 to δ_k with a uniform distribution.

As the search progresses, the value Δ_k is gradually decreased. The purpose of that is that at the beginning of the search process large mutations are applied to the individuals. Then, as the search progresses (and the algorithm starts converging to a solution), the mutations will become smaller and smaller.

The sorting process mentioned in step 3 is accomplished by placing at the top of the list the antibodies that are feasible and have the best objective function values. After that, we place the infeasible solutions that have the lowest amount of constraint violation and so on. Note how the step sizes of this mutation operator depend on the range of each decision variable, on the size of the antibodies' population and on their affinity.

As mentioned earlier, higher affinity antibodies are allowed to generate more clones g (see step 2.(c) from the algorithm in Section 4). Based on this fact, in step 4.(a) we obtain smaller step sizes when g is large. We argue that this mutation operator increases the exploratory capabilities of the algorithm.

Table 8. Results obtained by CLONALG with real-numbers representation and controlled uniform mutation. The asterisk (*) indicates a case in which only 90% of the runs converged to a feasible solution.

Test Function	Optimal	Best	Mean	Worst	Std. Dev.
g01	-15.0	-14.9874	-14.7264	-12.9171	0.6070
g02	0.803619	-0.8017	-0.7434	-0.6268	0.0414
g03	1.0	-1.000	-1.000	-1.000	0.0000
g04	-30665.539	-30665.5387	-30665.5386	-30665.5386	0.0000
g05*	5126.498	5126.9990	5436.1278	6111.1714	300.8854
g06	-6961.814	-6961.8105	-6961.8065	-6961.7981	0.0027
g07	24.306	24.5059	25.4167	26.4223	0.4637
g08	0.095825	-0.095825	-0.095825	-0.095825	0.0000
g09	680.63	680.6309	680.6521	680.6965	0.0176
g10	7049.33	7127.9502	8453.7902	12155.1358	1231.3762
g11	0.75	0.75	0.75	0.75	0.0000
g12	-1.0	-1.0	-1.0	-1.0	0.0000
g13	0.05395	0.05466	0.45782	1.49449	0.37900

Our third set of experiments was performed on the same set of test functions as before. However, in this case, our CLONALG implementation performed 350,000 objective function evaluations. The summary of results (from 30 independent runs) is presented in Table 8. It is clear that the new mutation mechanism produced a remarkable improvement in the results. In this case, the algorithm was able to reach the optimal (or best known) solution in 8 of the 13 test functions adopted. These results are competitive with respect to both ASCHEA and Stochastic Ranking.[1]

Our results seem to suggest that the use of local search (i.e., small step sizes in the mutation operator) has a more significant impact on performance when dealing with constrained search spaces. This contrasts with the case of unconstrained multimodal optimization, in which large step sizes are preferred, to avoid converging to a local optimum [18]. However, other issues such as the most proper balance between feasible and infeasible solutions (i.e., to avoid having only feasible solutions at any time during the search process) remain to be explored (we have adopted a user-defined parameter in our approach, but evidently other alternatives need to be explored). This issue in particular, has been found to have a very significant impact on performance when using evolutionary algorithms for solving constrained optimization problems [9,16] and therefore its importance.

8   Conclusions and Future Work

We have presented a study of the use of the CLONALG approach for solving constrained optimization problems. As part of our study, we have experimented with both

---

[1] It is worth remembering that ASCHEA performs a much higher number of objective function evaluations than our approach.

binary and real-numbers representation. In the case of binary representation, we also studied the impact of Gray coding, which we found to be positive in terms of the performance of CLONALG.

Regarding real-numbers encoding, we analyzed the use of both Gaussian and Cauchy random numbers. Surprisingly, the use of Cauchy-distributed mutations (which have been found useful in unconstrained numerical optimization) resulted in the worst overall performance of CLONALG.

The poor results obtained in our experiments led us to propose an alternative mutation operator for real-numbers representation. In our proposed mutation operator, the step size depends not only of the antibodies' affinity, but also of the allowable range of each decision variable and of the size of the antibodies' population. This mutation operator was implemented using random numbers with a uniform distribution. As seen in our results, the use of this operator significantly improved the performance of CLON-ALG with real-numbers representation.

Although there is evidently more room for improvement (we still cannot outperform Stochastic Ranking), the main aim of this paper was to point out the need to do more research on the potential use of CLONALG (and other artificial immune systems) for constrained optimization. As we have seen in this paper, the mechanisms that have been proposed for unconstrained optimization (even if dealing with multimodal functions) are not necessarily the most appropriate for dealing with constrained optimization problems. However, we have also seen that the search capabilities of algorithms such as CLONALG can be regulated through a more carefully designed mutation operator as to provide a competitive performance in constrained optimization. However, other issues such as robustness, balance between feasible and infeasible solutions and how sensitive the algorithm is to the parameters given remain as part of our future work.

Acknowledgements

We thank the comments of the anonymous reviewers which greatly helped us to improve the contents of this paper. The first and third authors gratefully acknowledge support from NSF-CONACyT through project 42435-Y. The second author acknowledges support from CONACyT through a scholarship to pursue graduate studies at CINVESTAV-IPN.

References

1. Jerzy Balicki. Multi-criterion evolutionary algorithm with model of the immune system to handle constraints for task assignments. In L. Rutkowski, J. Siekmann, R. Tadeusiewicz, and L.A. Zadeh, editors, *Artificial Intelligence and Soft Computing – ICAISC 2004 7th International Conference, Proceedings*, volume 3070, pages 394–399. Springer, Lecture Notes in Computer Science, 2004.
2. Carlos A. Coello Coello and Nareli Cruz-Cortés. Hybridizing a genetic algorithm with an artificial immune system for global optimization. *Engineering Optimization*, 36(5):607–634, October 2004.
3. David Corne, Marco Dorigo, and Fred Glover, editors. *New Ideas in Optimization*. McGraw-Hill, London, UK, 1999.

4. Leandro Nunes de Castro and Jon Timmis. An artificial immune network for multimodal function optimization. In *Proceedings of the special sessions on artificial immune systems in the 2002 Congress on Evolutionary Computation, 2002 IEEE World Congress on Computational Intelligence*, volume I, pages 669–674, Honolulu, Hawaii, May 2002.
5. Leandro Nunes de Castro and Jonathan Timmis. *An Introduction to Artificial Immune Systems: A New Computational Intelligence Paradigm*. Springer-Verlag, 2002.
6. Leandro Nunes de Castro and F. J. Von Zuben. Learning and Optimization Using the Clonal Selection Principle. *IEEE Transactions on Evolutionary Computation*, 6(3):239–251, 2002.
7. Raziyeh Farmani and Jonathan A. Wright. Self-Adaptive Fitness Formulation for Constrained Optimization. *IEEE Transactions on Evolutionary Computation*, 7(5):445–455, October 2003.
8. Prabhat Hajela and Jun Sun Yoo. Immune network modelling in design optimization. In D. Corne, M. Dorigo, and F. Glover, editors, *New Ideas in Optimization*, pages 167–183. Mc Graw-Hill, 1999.
9. S. B. Hamida and M. Schoenauer. ASCHEA: New results using adaptive segregationsl constraint handling. In *Proceedings of the Congress on Evolutionary Computation 2002 (CEC'02)*, volume 1, pages 884–889, Piscataway, New Jersey, 2002. IEEE Service Center.
10. J. Kelsey and J. Timmis. Immune Inspired Somatic Contiguous Hypermutation for Function Optimisation. In E. Cantú-Paz et al, editor, *Genetic and Evolutionary Computation Conference - GECCO 2003 of Lecture Notes in Computer Science*, volume 2723, pages 207–218, Chicago, USA., 2003. Springer-Verlag.
11. Slawomir Koziel and Zbigniew Michalewicz. Evolutionary Algorithms, Homomorphous Mappings, and Constrained Parameter Optimization. *Evolutionary Computation*, 7(1):19–44, 1999.
12. G. C. Luh and C. H. Chueh. Multi-objective optimal designof truss structure with immune algorithm. *Computers and Structures*, 82:829–844, 2004.
13. G. C. Luh, C. H. Chueh, and W. W. Liu. MOIA: Multi-Objective Immune Algorithm. *Engeneering Optimization*, 35(2):143–164, 2003.
14. Keith E. Mathias and L. Darrel Whitley. Transforming the search space with Gray coding. In J. D. Schaffer, editor, *Proceedings of the IEEE International Conference on Evolutionary Computation*, pages 513–518. IEEE Service Center, Piscataway, New Jersey, 1994.
15. Zbigniew Michalewicz and Marc Schoenauer. Evolutionary Algorithms for Constrained Parameter Optimization Problems. *Evolutionary Computation*, 4(1):1–32, 1996.
16. Thomas P. Runarsson and Xin Yao. Stochastic ranking for constrained evolutionary optimization. *IEEE Transactions on Evolutionay Computation*, 4(3):284–294, 2000.
17. Alice E. Smith and David W. Coit. Constraint Handling Techniques—Penalty Functions. In Thomas Bäck, David B. Fogel, and Zbigniew Michalewicz, editors, *Handbook of Evolutionary Computation*, chapter C 5.2. Oxford University Press and Institute of Physics Publishing, 1997.
18. X. Yao and Y. Liu. Fast evolution strategies. *Control and Cybernetics*, 26(3):467–496, 1997.
19. J. Yoo and P. Hajela. Enhanced GA Based Search Through Immune System Modeling. In *3rd. World Congress on Structural and Multidisciplinary Optimization*. IEEE Press, 1999.

Multiobjective Optimization by a Modified Artificial Immune System Algorithm

Fabio Freschi and Maurizio Repetto

Dept. of Electrical Engineering, Politecnico di Torino,
corso Duca degli Abruzzi,
24, 10129 Torino, Italy
{fabio.freschi, maurizio.repetto}@polito.it
http://www.polito.it/cadema

Abstract. The aim of this work is to propose and validate a new multi-objective optimization algorithm based on the emulation of the immune system behavior. The *rationale* of this work is that the artificial immune system has, in its elementary structure, the main features required by other multiobjective evolutionary algorithms described in literature. The proposed approach is compared with the NSGA2 algorithm, that is representative of the state-of-the-art in multiobjective optimization. Algorithms are tested versus three standard problems (unconstrained and constrained), and comparisons are carried out using three different metrics. Results show that the proposed approach have performances similar or better than those produced by NSGA2, and it can become a valid alternative to standard algorithms.

1 Introduction

Many real world applications involve the simultaneous optimization of various and often conflicting objectives. Traditional approaches for solving the Multi-objective Optimization Problem (MOP) aggregate all objectives into one function, then a single objective problem is solved by using standard optimization techniques. Several optimization runs with different parameter settings are performed, in order to achieve a set of solutions.

In the middle of the '80s Schaffer published the first attempt to solve the MOP by using evolutionary algorithms [1,2]. The use of population-based techniques is preferable with respect to aggregating approaches, because multiple solutions can be found in one single run. From this work, several Multi Objective Evolutionary Algorithms (MOEAs) have been proposed in the last two decades. Coello Coello maintains an updated Evolutionary Multiobjective Optimization repository (http://delta.cs.cinestav.mx/~ccoello/EMOO/) in which the references of almost all the proposed algorithms can be found.

Despite the considerable efforts to extend Evolutionary Algorithms for solving MOPs, very few direct approaches to the MOP using the emulation of the Immune System behavior have been proposed. Most of the work concerns the use of Artificial Immune System (AIS) as a tool for maintaining diversity in the

C. Jacob et al. (Eds.): ICARIS 2005, LNCS 3627, pp. 248–261, 2005.

population of a Genetic Algorithm (see for example [3]) or for handling constraints in Evolutionary Algorithms [4]. In literature, one of the first reported approaches which uses AIS for solving MOPs is proposed in [5], but also in this case AIS is coupled with GA. Recently Coello Coello and Cruz Cortes develop a MOEA directly based on the emulation of the immune system [6]. The resulting algorithm, called Multiobjective Immune System Algorithm (MISA), can be considered the really first attempt to solve the general MOP directly with AIS. The performances of MISA have been improved in a further work of the same authors [6].

In this paper we propose a new approach for solving MOPs, based on the multimodal AIS optimization algorithm proposed by De Castro and Timmis [7]. The aim is to show that AIS intrinsically include some common features required by classical MOEAs, and that the extension to multiobjective optimization can be done by introducing only few modifications into the standard algorithm. The resulting algorithm is then tested on standard problems and results are compared with the ones obtained by NSGA2 algorithm [8], universally considered as representative of the state-of-the-art in multiobjective optimization.

2   Multi Objective Optimization Problem

Generally the MOP requires to optimize the vector function

$$f(x) = [f_1(x), f_2(x), \ldots, f_m(x)]^T \tag{1}$$

subject to inequality and equality constraints

$$\begin{aligned} g_i(x) &\geq 0 \ i = 1, 2, \ldots, k \\ h_i(x) &= 0 \ i = 1, 2, \ldots, p \end{aligned} \tag{2}$$

where $x = [x_1, x_2, \cdots, x_n]^T \in \Omega$ is the vector of decision variables and Ω is the feasible region. Because of the presence of several objective functions, the aim of a MOEA is to find compromise solutions rather than a single optimal point as in scalar optimization problems. In this case the trade-off solutions are usually called Pareto optimal solutions.

Considering, without loss of generality, a minimization problem for each objective, it is said that a decision vector x_P *dominates* another vector x_Q (denoted by $x_P \prec x_Q$) if

1. x_P is no worse than x_Q in all objectives, AND
2. x_P is strictly better than x_Q in at least one objective.

Mathematically:

$$\forall i = 1, \ldots, m \quad f_i(x_P) \leq f_i(x_Q) \quad \wedge \quad \exists i = 1, \ldots, m \quad f_i(x_P) < f_i(x_Q) \tag{3}$$

If there is no solution x_Q that dominates x_P, then x_P is a *Pareto optimal solution*. The set P

$$P \triangleq \{x \in \Omega : \neg \exists x^* \in \Omega, f(x^*) \prec f(x)\} \tag{4}$$

of all feasible Pareto optimal decision vectors is referred to as *Pareto optimal set*, while the corresponding image PF

$$PF \triangleq \left\{ \boldsymbol{f}(\boldsymbol{x}) = [f_1(\boldsymbol{x}), \dots f_m(\boldsymbol{x})]^{\mathrm{T}} : \boldsymbol{x} \in P \right\} \tag{5}$$

of objective vectors is called *Pareto optimal front*. Pareto optimal solutions are also called *noninferior* or *nondominated* solutions.

In this work we distinguish between the actual Pareto front, termed PF_{true}, and the final set of nondominated solutions returned by a MOEA, termed PF_{known} as defined in [9].

3 Algorithm

3.1 Artificial Immune System: Brief Overview

The main characteristic of the Immune System (IS) is that it must fight against external intruders (nonself) but must be tolerant with body cells (self). The main characters of IS are

- antigen (Ag): any substance capable of triggering an immune response;
- antibody (Ab): molecule (lymphocytes) that can match and counteract Ag.

Once a lymphocyte shows a high *affinity* toward an Ag, it is activated that is it undergoes an affinity maturation, a process that is aimed at improving the binding with Ag. New cells are *clones* of the older ones, diversity of new cells is ensured by a somatic *hypermutation* where genes of new cells are pieced together from widely scattered bits of DNA. This process is called *clonal selection* principle. The higher the affinity of the new cells with Ag, the higher their possibility to generate new clones. Despite its efficiency to increase affinity with Ag, somatic hypermutation has the risk of generating autoimmune cells. IS must inhibit new cells which are not self-tolerant (*suppression* of similar cells). Ag recognition does not start every time from scratch; after being stimulated some of the lymphocytes become *memory cells* of the system.

The behavior of the Immune System can be artificially emulated for optimization or, more generally, for machine learning [10]. An algorithm based on emulation of the IS behavior is referred to as Artificial Immune System (AIS). A deep investigation of the AIS can be found in [11,12].

In the optimization field, AIS has shown to have a great ability for searching multiple optimal solutions [7]. In this case Ags are represented by the optimal points of a function, while Abs are the test configurations. Basically, the optimization algorithm is structured into two nested levels (Fig. 1). The inner one takes into account the Ab-Ag affinity relations, stimulating most promising cells, while the outer level manages the network of cells of the system, eliminating the similar ones. Cardinality of the population can be fixed or dynamic, but new cells are generated throughout the process in order to explore as much as possible the space of configurations. Deep details of the multimodal single objective optimization algorithm are provided in [7].

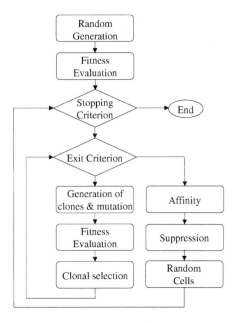

Fig. 1. AIS optimization algorithm flowchart

3.2   Multi Objective Algorithm

Following the structure of the AIS optimization algorithm, we propose a new multiobjective optimization algorithm. The algorithm, called Vector Artificial Immune System (VAIS) has the same structure as the one for the single objective shown in Fig. 1.

1. Initially a random uniformly distributed population is created and the fitness is assigned to each solutions, as it will be described in the next section. The memory is initialized to be empty.
2. Each cell is reproduced in N_{clones} copies of the original one and each clone is locally mutated by a random perturbation. The amplitude of mutation decreases when the fitness of the original parent cell increases, according to Eqs. (6)

$$\begin{aligned}
\boldsymbol{x}_{\text{new}} &= \boldsymbol{x}_{\text{old}} + \alpha \ \boldsymbol{x}_{\text{random}} \\
\alpha &= \beta \exp(-f^*)
\end{aligned} \tag{6}$$

where $\boldsymbol{x}_{\text{random}}$ is a vector of Gaussian random numbers of mean 0 and standard deviation 1, f^* is the normalized value of fitness from the values $[f_{\min}, f_{\max}]$ into the range $[0, 1]$. The value of the parameter β is chosen to set the maximum amplitude of mutation. $\boldsymbol{x}_{\text{new}}$, $\boldsymbol{x}_{\text{old}}$ and $\boldsymbol{x}_{\text{random}}$ are real valued vectors defined in a normalized parameter space.
3. For each clone the values of the objective functions and Pareto dominance relations are evaluated. Because the fitness depends on the actual population,

its value is assigned to the clones and recalculated for the parent cells. The nondominated individuals are copied into the memory.

4. The best (with respect to the fitness value) mutated clone for each cell replaces the original parent (clonal selection).
5. Steps 2-4 (which represent the inner loop) are repeated for N_{in} times.
6. The affinity operator is applied to the memory: the Euclidean distance between memory cells is measured; despite of the traditional AIS algorithm, the distance is evaluated in the objective space, in order to obtain an uniformly distributed Pareto front.
7. All but the highest fitness cells whose distances are less than a threshold are suppressed. The threshold value must be related to the number of solutions desired on the PF_{known} (N_{memory}); if the objectives are normalized into the range $[0, 1]$, the value of $\frac{\sqrt{m}}{N_{memory}}$ (m: number of objectives) represents the distance among solutions uniformly distributed on a straight continuous Pareto front. We choose this value as threshold for suppression.
8. The memory is copied into the original population. New randomly generated cells fill the remaining population, in order to maintain the diversity of solutions. A minimum percentage of newcomers is guaranteed at each iteration to obtain a good exploration of the solution space.
9. The process is repeated N_{out} times from step 2.

The *rationale* of this work is that AIS has, in its elementary structure, the main characteristics required by MOEAs described in literature. One of the main characteristic of classical MOEAs is that they present selection pressure (genetic drift) phenomenon [13] and some tricks must be adopted for enhancing diversity in solutions and space exploration. Instead, AIS makes parallel searches of optimal solutions, leaving the management of the network of cells to the *suppression* operator in the upper level of the algorithm. This operator gives another advantage: when defining the fitness assignment, several MOEAs require information about crowding (density) of solutions [14], while AIS does not need them because similar solutions are suppressed. There are at least two other characteristics intrinsically defined in AIS which are usually needed by other multiobjective algorithms. AIS do not need an additional memory for storing nondominated solutions (like, for example, the MultiObjective Particle Swarm Optimization, MOPSO, algorithm [15]), because this feature is already defined. Finally the clonal selection is always elitist, so AIS does not present *backward* effects during the iteration [16].

Fitness Assignment. In literature there are several Pareto-based fitness assignment strategies for MOPs. All non-aggregating techniques require the evaluation of the Pareto dominance among the individuals of the population [17]. This approach has the advantage that it is insensitive to the nonconvexity of the Pareto Optimal Set [18]. In their famous algorithm NSGA2 [19,8], Deb *et al.* apply a pure Pareto ranking for assigning the fitness value to the population. At each iteration all the nondominated solutions are assigned rank 1 and they are temporary removed from the assignment. Then rank 2 is assigned to the new set of nondminated solutions and so on. In SPEA [17] algorithm and in its evolution SPEA2 [14], instead of calculating the standard Pareto ranking, Zitzler *et al.* assign to the population a fitness value which incorporates both dominance and density information. In particular all nondominated solutions have a fitness, called *strength*, proportional to the number of individuals dominated by each of them: let N_i denote the number of individuals dominated by the nondominated i-th cell and N_{dom} the total number of dominated solutions, then the strength of i is

$$s_i = \frac{N_i}{1 + N_{\text{dom}}} \tag{7}$$

The fitness of a dominated solution j is calculated from the strength of the solutions i which dominate it

$$f_j = \sum_{i:i \prec j} s_i \tag{8}$$

The NSGA2 fitness assignment approach does not distinguish among nondominated solutions and the hierarchical classification of solution can become computationally intensive if the population is large. On the other side, the SPEA2 approach includes density information that are not required by the VAIS algorithm described in the previous section, because AIS has in itself operators which preserve diversity (such as affinity and suppression) and prevent the crowding of solutions. For these reasons we have adopted a simpler fitness assignment, which overcome these problems called Simple Strength Approach, SiSA. For each nondominated individual the fitness is equal to the strength, as defined in SPEA2, while for a dominated cell, the fitness is the number of individuals which dominate it. The resulting fitness guarantees a partial ranking, because all nondominated solutions have fitness values lower than 1, while the dominated ones always greater than 1.

Constraint Handling. Constraints can be classified into two different types:

- constraints on objectives;
- constraints on variables.

This classification comes from the consideration that in real world problems the evaluation of objectives is the most time consuming operation in the optimization process (think, for example, to objective functions evaluated by Finite Element Analisys software) so constraints on objectives must be carefully treated in order to avoid wasting time and resources. Constraints on decision variables can be treated more easily because they can be managed before evaluating the objective functions.

In literature constraints are usually handled by using penalty functions techniques. Reference [20] gives a good survey of these strategies. Another approach, based on the definition of *constrained dominance* is developed by Deb *et al.* [8]. This technique does not require the definition of penalty functions, but simply modify the definition of dominance given in Eq. (3) including infeasible solutions.

In this work we propose a technique for handling inequality constraints on variables preserving the feasibility of solution [21]. For what concerns equality

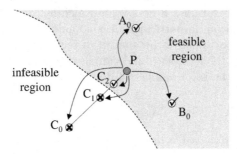

Fig. 2. Constraint handling: from a parent cell P, three clones are generated and mutated. Clones A_0 and B_0 are in the feasible region. Given that clone C_0 falls in the infeasible region, the amplitude of mutation is progressively reduced with a bisection rule, until a feasible clone, C_2, is obtained.

constraints on variables, these can be often rearranged decreasing the dimension of the search space. Sometimes equality constraints can be transformed into inequality one [22]. The VAIS algorithm can generate infeasible solutions in two cases. The first one is when a new random individual is generated. In this case any infeasible solution is simply discarded. An infeasible solution can also occur after applying the mutation operator to a cell close to the constraint. In this case the feasibility of the solution is maintained by progressively reducing the mutation amplitude with the bisection rule. This process stops when the mutated clone becomes feasible (Fig. 2). This technique can be applied without any hypothesis on the type of constraints (linearity, convexity, ...).

4   Experiments

The proposed algorithm, called Vector Artificial Immune System (VAIS) is compared versus NSGA2. This algorithm has achieved the largest attention in the multiobjective optimization literature and has been used as reference algorithm in various studies. For all tests NSGA2 has been run using a population size of 100; other parameters are set according to the values suggested by the developers in [8]. The results of VAIS are obtained using the following parameters: population size $= 100$, number of clones for each cell $= 4$, number of inner iteration $= 5$, percentage of random cells at each outer iteration $= 20\%$, $\beta = 0.05$. These values have been determined after an intensive preliminary test phase of the algorithm on different test functions. The number of generations for both algorithms is set depending on the maximum number of function evaluations allowed in the test.

Three different measures have been used for numerical comparisons of the trade-off fronts produced by the algorithms, each of them takes into account a particular desired characteristic of the PF_{known}.

1. **Spacing** (S): first introduced by Schott [23], this metric measures how well the solutions throughout the PF_{known} are distributed. This metric is mathematically defined as

$$S \triangleq \sqrt{\frac{1}{N_{\text{known}} - 1} \sum_{i=1}^{N_{\text{known}}} \left(\bar{d} - d_i\right)^2} \tag{9}$$

where, for each i in the set of N_{known} solutions of the PF_{known},

$$d_i \triangleq \min_j \sum_{k=1}^{m} \left| f_k^i(\boldsymbol{x}) - f_k^j(\boldsymbol{x}) \right| \tag{10}$$

and $\bar{d}$ is the mean value of all d_i. A value of 0 for this metric states that the solutions on the PF_{known} are equally spaced and the representation of the front is as smooth and uniform as possible.

2. **Reverse Generational Distance** (RGD): one of the main issue for measuring the performance of a MOEA is the ability to produce solutions on the PF_{known} as near as possible to the PF_{true}. In order to evaluate this characteristic, Van Veldhuizen and Lamont [24] have introduced a particular metric called *Generational Distance* (GD). It is defined as

$$GD \triangleq \frac{1}{N_{\text{known}}} \sqrt{\sum_{i=1}^{N_{\text{known}}} d_i^2} \tag{11}$$

where N_{known} is the number of nondominated vectors in the PF_{known} and d_i is the Euclidean distance measured in the objective space between each of them and the nearest member of the PF_{true}. Obviously $GD = 0$ means $PF_{\text{known}} \equiv PF_{\text{true}}$. As noted by Bosman and Thierens [25] a PF_{known} consisting on only a single solution can have a low value for this indicator. In order to include the goal of diversity, they propose to compute for each j solution in the PF_{true} the distance $\tilde{d}_j$ to the closest solution in the PF_{known} set

$$RGD \triangleq \frac{1}{N_{\text{true}}} \sqrt{\sum_{j=1}^{N_{\text{true}}} \tilde{d}_j^2} \tag{12}$$

where N_{true} is the cardinality of the PF_{true} set. We refer to this metric as *Reverse Generational Distance*.

3. **Error Ratio** (ER): presented by Van Veldhuizen in [26] this metric measures the number of nondominated vectors of the PF_{known} that are not member of the PF_{true}

$$ER \triangleq \frac{\sum_{i=1}^{N_{\text{known}}} e_i}{N_{\text{known}}} \tag{13}$$

where $e_i = 1$ if solution i is not on the PF_{true}, $e_i = 0$ otherwise.

In their analysis, Knowles and Corne [27] have noted that the use of these metrics can not draw final conclusions on outperformances among MOEAs. However these indicators are commonly used in standard evolutionary multiobjective optimization literature [22].

The MOEA community has developed several test functions, that have become a standard reference for testing new algorithms. We choose three representative problems which point out some difficulties for the optimization algorithms. The following results are evaluated after having performed 20 independent runs of both algorithms.

4.1   Test Function 1

The first test is performed using the problem proposed by Tanaka [28]:
Minimize

$$
\begin{aligned}
f_1(\boldsymbol{x}) &= x_1 \\
f_2(\boldsymbol{x}) &= x_2
\end{aligned}
\tag{14}
$$

subject to

$$
g_1(\boldsymbol{x}) = x_1^2 + x_2^2 - 1 - 0.1 \cos\left(16 \arctan \frac{x_1}{x_2}\right) \geq 0
$$

$$
g_2(\boldsymbol{x}) = \left(x_1 - \frac{1}{2}\right)^2 + \left(x_2 - \frac{1}{2}\right)^2 \leq \frac{1}{2}
\tag{15}
$$

and $x_1, x_2 \in [0, \pi]$. The final number of fitness function evaluations in this case has been set to 12000. The function presents a discontinuous and concave Pareto front which entirely lies on the first constraint. It has been proved that some MOEAs can have difficulties in finding Pareto optimal solutions with discontinuous and concave segments [29]. Fig. 3 shows the PF_{true} (continuous line) and the PF_{known} (circles) found by VAIS and NSGA2. The solutions shown correspond to the median result with respect to the RGD metric. It can be seen that the the average performances of VAIS are better than NSGA2 with respect to the spacing and the reverse generational distance (Table 1); the opposite happens with respect to the error ratio. It must be noticed that in this case differences are very small and not statistically significant.

Table 1. Results of the metrics for the Tanaka test function

	S		RGD		ER	
	VAIS	NSGA2	VAIS	NSGA2	VAIS	NSGA2
Best	0.00144	0.00479	1.82779E-4	4.56689E-4	0.00552	0.00000
Worst	0.00260	0.00857	3.82790E-4	7.29166E-4	0.03191	0.05000
Average	0.00201	0.00640	2.56854E-4	5.65629E-4	0.02009	0.01700
Median	0.00204	0.00642	2.54257E-4	5.30819E-4	0.02139	5.30819E-4
Std. Dev.	2.77208E-4	8.40962E-4	8.28494E-5	4.25030E-5	0.00640	8.28494E-5

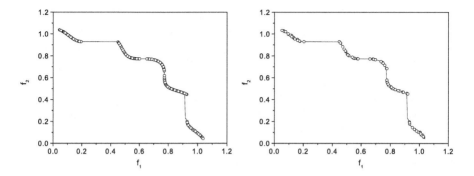

Fig. 3. Pareto Front produced by VAIS (left) and NSGA2 (right) for the Tanaka test function

4.2   Test Function 2

The second function has been proposed by Viennet [30]:
Minimize

$$f_1(\boldsymbol{x}) = \frac{1}{2}\left(x_1^2 + x_2^2\right) + \sin\left(x_1^2 + x_2^2\right)$$
$$f_2(\boldsymbol{x}) = \frac{(3x_1 - 2x_2 + 4)^2}{8} + \frac{(x_1 - x_2 + 1)^2}{27} + 15 \tag{16}$$
$$f_3(\boldsymbol{x}) = \frac{1}{(x_1^2 + x_2^2 + 1)} - 1.1\exp\left(-x^2 - y^2\right)$$

with $x_1, x_2 \in [-3, 3]$. The final number of fitness function evaluations in this case has been set to 6000. This function presents several challenging characteristics, such as a high dimensional objective space, discontinuous Pareto optimal set and several local minima in objective functions. Because of the PF_{true} has not an analytical expression, in this case it is obtained by enumeration of all possible solutions. By looking at the Pareto fronts produced in this case (Fig. 4), it can be seen that VAIS has a better representation of the PF_{true}. This fact is confirmed by the analisys of the numerical results presented in Table 2 which shows a better behavior of VAIS for all metrics.

Table 2. Results of the metrics for the Viennet test function

	S		RGD		ER	
	VAIS	NSGA2	VAIS	NSGA2	VAIS	NSGA2
Best	0.01150	0.03009	5.06375E-4	0.00172	0.00000	0.00000
Worst	0.03868	0.04599	0.00388	0.01022	0.01765	0.04000
Average	0.01526	0.04028	8.67047E-4	0.00308	0.00345	0.01650
Median	0.01284	0.04098	5.84390E-4	0.00190	0.00217	0.01000
Std. Dev.	0.00640	0.00408	7.76958E-4	0.00287	0.00406	0.01226

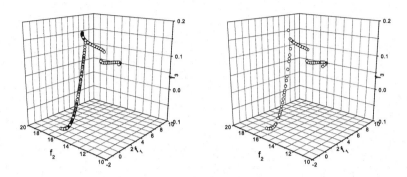

Fig. 4. Pareto Front produced by VAIS (left) and NSGA2 (right) for the Viennet test function

4.3   Test Function 3

The last test is performed on a function proposed by Zitzler [31] and character-ized by a high dimensional decision space and local Pareto fronts in the objective space. The problem is defined as:
Minimize

$$f_1(\boldsymbol{x}) = 1 - \exp(-4x_1)\sin^6(6\pi x_1)$$
$$f_2(\boldsymbol{x}) = w(\boldsymbol{x})\left(1 - \frac{f_1(\boldsymbol{x})}{w(\boldsymbol{x})}\right)^2 \tag{17}$$

where

$$w(\boldsymbol{x}) = 1 + 9\left(\frac{\sum_{i=2}^{5} x_i}{4}\right)^{0.25} \tag{18}$$

with $x_i \in [0,1]$ and $i = 1,\ldots,5$. The true Pareto front is obtained when $w(\boldsymbol{x}) = 0$, that is with $x_1 \in [0,1]$ and $x_2 = \cdots = x_5 = 0$. Another challenging characteristic of this function is that the Pareto optimal front is not uniformly represented because the function f_1 is non linear (for more details in problem difficulties for MOP see [32]). For this test function both algorithms stop after 40000 fitness function evaluations. The comparison between the algorithms with respect to the spacing measure shows that NSGA2 has a more uniform spread of solutions than VAIS. But VAIS has better performance with respect to the other two metrics (Table 3). This result can be explained looking at Fig. 5: NSGA2 has difficulties in finding the global Pareto front, getting stuck at a local one.

5   Conclusion and Further Work

In this paper it has been shown that AIS has in its elementary structure the main characteristics of MOEA described in literature. Following this idea, a new MOEA based on the clonal selection principle, has been developed. First comparisons with another state-of-the-art algorithm show that performances

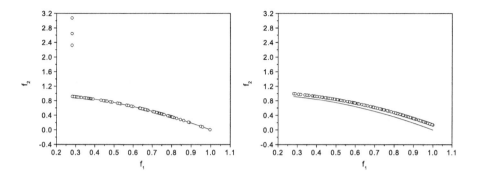

Fig. 5. Pareto Front produced by VAIS (left) and NSGA2 (right) for the Zitzler test function

Table 3. Results of the metrics for the Zitzler test function

	S		RGD		ER	
	VAIS	NSGA2	VAIS	NSGA2	VAIS	NSGA2
Best	0.03140	0.00570	8.58313E-5	1.48321E-4	0.06818	0.10000
Worst	0.55028	0.00712	0.00935	0.00613	0.41463	1.00000
Average	0.21017	0.00651	0.00186	0.00473	0.14747	0.95500
Median	0.16552	0.00669	8.11857E-4	0.00493	0.12162	1.00000
Std. Dev.	0.16224	4.24203E-4	0.00227	0.00137	0.07991	0.20125

of VAIS are similar or better than those produced by NSGA2. These results encourage the authors to continue the research and tests on the algorithm.

Some improvements will be done in order to produce a competitive, general purpose algorithm for MOPs, that can become a valid alternative to standard MOEAs:

- some other strategies for constraint handling will be tested, especially for managing constraints on objectives;
- the possibility of including problems with integer and mixed-integer decision variables will be added;
- other tests will be performed with other multiobjective optimization algorithms which represent the state-of-the-art in evolutionary multiobjective optimization; in this study other performance measures will be implemented;
- finally the algorithm will be tested on some high dimensional real world problems, especially in the field of electromagnetism.

Acknowledgements

The authors would like to thank Ms Eloisa Salina Borello for her preliminary studies about Multiobjective Optimization and Artificial Immune Systems.

References

1. Schaffer, J.D.: Multiple Objective Optimization with Vector Evaluated Genetic Algorithms. PhD thesis, Vanderbilt University (1984)
2. Schaffer, J.D.: Multiple Objective Optimization with Vector Evaluated Genetic Algorithms. In Erlbaum, L., ed.: Genetic Algorithms and their Applications: Proceedings of the First International Conference on Genetic Algorithms, Hillsdale, New Jersey (1985) 93–100
3. Smith, R.E., Forrest, S., Perelson, A.S.: Population Diversity in an Immune System Model: Implication for Genetic Search. In: Foundation of Genetic Algorithm 2. Morgan Kaufmann, San Mateo, CA (1993) 153–165
4. Kurpati, A., Azarm, S.: Immune Network Simulation with Multiobjective Genetic Algorithms for Multidisciplinary Design Optimization. Engineering Optimization **33** (2000) 245–260
5. Yoo, J., Hajela, P.: Immune Network Simulations in Multicriterion Design. Structural Optimization **18** (1999) 85–94
6. Coello Coello, C.A., Cruz Cortes, N.: An Approach to Solve Multiobjective Optimization Problems Based on an Artificial Immune System. In Timmis, J., Bentley, P.J., eds.: First International Conference on Artificial Immune Systems (ICARIS'2002), University of Kent, Canterbury, England (2002) 212–221 ISBN 1-902671-32-5.
7. De Castro, L., Timmis, J.: An Artificial Immune Network for Multimodal Function Optimization. In: Proceedings of the 2002 Congress on Evolutionary Computation, CEC'02. Volume 1. (2002) 699–704
8. Deb, K., Pratap, A., Agarwal, S., Meyarivan, T.: AFast and Elitist Multiobjective Genetic Algorithm: NSGA-II. IEEE Transactions on Evolutionary Computation **6** (2002) 182–197
9. Van Veldhuizen, D.A., Lamont, G.B.: On Measuring Multiobjective Evolutionary Algorithm Performance. In: 2000 Congress on Evolutionary Computation. Volume 1., Piscataway, New Jersey, IEEE Service Center (2000) 204–211
10. De Castro, L.N., Von Zuben, F.J.: Learning and Optimization Using the Clonal Selection Principle. IEEE Transactions on Evolutionary Computation, Special Issue on Artificial Immune Systems **6** (2002) 239–251
11. De Castro, L.N., Von Zuben, F.J.: Artificial Immune Systems: Part I Basic Theory and Applications. Technical Report RT DCA 01/99, Universidade Catolica de Santos, Coordenação de Pos-Graduação e Pesquisa (COPOP) (1999)
12. De Castro, L.N., Von Zuben, F.J.: Artificial Immune Systems: Part II A Survey of Applications. Technical Report RT DCA 02/00, Universidade Catolica de Santos, Coordenação de Pos-Graduação e Pesquisa (COPOP) (2000)
13. Tan, K. C. and, Y.Y.J., Goh, C.K., Lee, T.H.: Enhanced Distribtion and Exploration for Multiobjective Evolutionary Algorithms. In: Congress on Evolutionary Computation (CEC'2002). Volume 4. (2003) 1521–2528
14. Zitzler, E., Laumanns, M., Thiele, L.: SPEA2: Improving the Strength Pareto Evolutionary Algorithm. TIK Report 103, Computer Engineering and Networks Lab (TIK), Swiss Federal Institute of Technology (ETH) Zurich, Switzerland (2001)
15. Coello Coello, C.A., Toscano Pulido, G., Salazar Lechuga, M.: Handling Multiple Objectives with Particle Swarm Optimization. IEEE Transactions on Evolutionary Computation **8** (2004) 256–279
16. Lu, H., Yen, G.G.: Rank-Density-Based Multiobjective Genetic Algorithm and Benchmark Test Function Study. IEEE Transactions on Evolutionary Computation **7** (2003) 325–343

17. Zitzler, E., Thiele, L.: Multiobjective Evolutionary Algorithms: a Comparative Study and the Strength Pareto Approach. IEEE Transactions on Evolutionary Computation **3** (1999) 257–271
18. Fonseca, C.M., Fleming, P.J.: An Overview of Evolutionary Algorithms in Multi-objective Optimization. Evolutionary Computation **3** (1995) 1–16
19. Deb, K., Agrawal, S., Pratab, A., Meyarivan, T.: A Fast Elitist Non-Dominated Sorting Genetic Algorithm for Multi-Objective Optimization: NSGA-II. In Schoenauer, M., Deb, K., Rudolph, G., Yao, X., Lutton, E., Merelo, J.J., Schwefel, H.P., eds.: Proceedings of the Parallel Problem Solving from Nature VI Conference, Springer (2000) 849–858
20. Aguirre, A.H., Botello Rionda, S., Coello Coello, C.A., Lizarraga Lizarraga, G., Mezura Montes, E.: Handling Constraints Using Multiobjective Optimization Concepts. International Journal for Numerical Methods in Engineering **59** (2004) 1989–2017
21. Michalewicz, Z., Schoenauer, M.: Evolutionary Algorithms for Constrained Parameter Optimization Problems. Evolutionary Computation **4** (1996) 1–32
22. Coello Coello, C.A., Van Veldhuizen, D.A., Lamont, G.B.: Evolutionary Algorithms for Solving Multi-Objective Problems. Kluwer Academic Publishers, New York (2002) ISBN 0-3064-6762-3.
23. Schott, J.R.: Fault Tolerant Design Using Single and Multicriteria Genetic Algorithm Optimization. Master's thesis, Dept. Aeronautics and Astronautics, Massachussets Institue of Technology (1995)
24. Van Veldhuizen, D.A., Lamont, G.B.: Multiobjective Evolutionary Algorithm Research: a History and Analysis. Technical report tr-98-03, Graduate School of Engineering, Air Force Institute of Technology, Wright-Patterson AFB, OH (1998)
25. Bosman, P.A.N., Thierens, D.: The Balance between Proximity and Diversity in Multiobjective Evolutionary Algorithms. IEEE Transactions on Evolutionary Computation **7** (2003) 174–188
26. Van Veldhuizen, D.A.: Multiobjective Evolutionary Algorithms: Classifications, Analysis, and Innovations. Ph.d. dissetation, Graduate School of Engineering, Air Force Institute of Technology, Wright-Patterson AFB, OH (1999)
27. Knowles, J., Corne, D.: On Metrics for Comparing Non-Dominated Sets. In: Congress on Evolutionary Computation (CEC'2002). Volume 1., Piscataway, New Jersey, IEEE Service Center (2002) 711–716
28. Tanaka, M., Watanabe, H., Furukawa, Y., Tanino, T.: GA-Based Decision Support System for Multicriteria Optimization. In: Proceedings of the International Conference on Systems, Man, and Cybernetics. Volume 2., Piscataway, NJ, IEEE (1995) 1556–1561
29. De Jong, K.A.: An Analysis of Behavior of a Class of Genetic Adaptive Systems. PhD thesis, Dept. of Computer Science, University of Michigan, Ann Arbor, MI (1975)
30. Viennet, R., Fontiex, C., Marc, I.: New Multicriteria Optimization Method Based on the Use of a Diploid Genetic Algorithm: Example of an Industrial Problem. In Alliot, J.M., Lutton, E., Ronald, E., Schoenauer, M., Snyers, D., eds.: Proceedings of Artificial Evolution (European Conference, selected papers), Brest, France, Springer-Verlag (1995) 120–127
31. Zitzler, E., Deb, K., Thiele, L.: Comparison of Multiobjective Evolutionary Algorithms: Empirical Results. Evolutionary Computation **8** (2000) 173–195 MIT Press.
32. Deb, K.: Multi-Objective Genetic Algorithms: Problem Difficulties and Construction of Test Problems. Evolutionary Computation **7** (1999) 205–230

A Comparative Study of Real-Valued Negative Selection to Statistical Anomaly Detection Techniques

Thomas Stibor[1], Jonathan Timmis[2], and Claudia Eckert[1]

[1] Department of Computer Science,
Darmstadt University of Technology,
{stibor, eckert}@sec.informatik.tu-darmstadt.de
[2] Departments of Electronics and Computer Science,
University of York, Heslington, York
jt517@ohm.york.ac.uk

Abstract. The (randomized) real-valued negative selection algorithm is an anomaly detection approach, inspired by the negative selection immune system principle. The algorithm was proposed to overcome scaling problems inherent in the hamming shape-space negative selection algorithm. In this paper, we investigate termination behavior of the real-valued negative selection algorithm with variable-sized detectors on an artificial data set. We then undertake an analysis and comparison of the classification performance on the high-dimensional KDD data set of the real-valued negative selection, a real-valued positive selection and statistical anomaly detection techniques. Results reveal that in terms of detection rate, real-valued negative selection with variable-sized detectors is not competitive to statistical anomaly detection techniques on the KDD data set. In addition, we suggest that the termination guarantee of the real-valued negative selection with variable-sized detectors is very sensitive to several parameters.

1 Introduction

The field of Artificial Immune Systems (AIS) has seen the development of many algorithms. One of the major algorithms developed within AIS is the negative selection algorithm, first proposed by Forrest et al. [1] and then subsequently developed over the years [2,3,4,5]. This paper investigates the real-valued negative selection algorithm with variable-sized detectors [6] and its applicability to network intrusion traffic. The negative selection algorithm is oft cited for its potential use in intrusion detection problems due to its ability to generate a set of *detectors* from a single class of data (usually the *normal* network traffic), that is capable of identifying possible intrusions. However, there remains little work in the literature regarding the application of the negative selection algorithm with variable-sized detectors to network intrusion detection. This paper undertakes a comparative study between the negative selection with variable-sized detectors, another simple AIS algorithm, positive selection, and two well established

C. Jacob et al. (Eds.): ICARIS 2005, LNCS 3627, pp. 262–275, 2005.

statistical techniques. Our investigations reveal, that whilst appealing, negative selection with variable-sized detectors does not appear to perform as well as the more established techniques. The paper is organized as follows: Section 2 provides a simple overview of anomaly detection. Then, the immune negative selection principle and basic negative selection algorithm are briefly explained in section 3. Section 3.1 provides a review of the real-valued negative selection algorithm with variable-sized detectors. This is followed by a simple real-valued positive selection algorithm in section 3.2. Through the use of an artificial data set, in section 4 we explore the termination behavior of the real-valued negative selection algorithm. For comparative purposes, two novelty detection techniques are described in section 5. This is then followed by an analysis of the classification performance of the negative selection and is compared to the positive selection and to statistical novelty detection techniques in section 6.

2   Anomaly Detection

Anomaly detection, also referred to as novelty detection [7], outlier detection [7] or one-class learning [8,9], is a classification technique, which is used for classifying data where typically only a single class of data is available, or a second class of data is under-represented e.g. machine fault detection or medical diagnosis. In a probabilistic sense, novelty detection is equivalent to deciding whether an unknown test sample is produced by the underlying probability distribution that corresponds to the training set of normal examples. Such approaches are based on the assumption that *anomalous* data are not generated by the source of *normal* data. More formally, the task is to find a functional mapping $f : \mathbb{R}^N \rightarrow \{\mathcal{C}_0, \mathcal{C}_1\}$, using training data samples generated i.i.d.[1] according to an unknown probability distribution $P(\mathbf{x}, y)$

$$(\mathbf{x}_1, y_1), \ldots, (\mathbf{x}_n, y_n) \in \mathbb{R}^N \times Y, \qquad Y = \{\mathcal{C}_0, \mathcal{C}_1\}$$

such that f will correctly classify unseen examples $(\mathbf{x}, y)$. In the worst case, the training set contains *only* normal samples $(\mathbf{x}, y \in \mathcal{C}_0)$ and the challenge is to detect abnormal samples $(\mathbf{x}, y \in \mathcal{C}_1)$ with the function f which was trained[2] with only normal samples.

3   Negative Selection Principle

The negative selection principle is a process that takes place in the thymus gland, which helps to filter self reactive lymphocytes away from entering the lymphatic system. This principle inspired Forrest et al. [1] to propose a negative selection algorithm to detect data manipulation caused by computer viruses. The basic idea was to generate a number of detectors in the complementary space and then

---

[1] Independently drawn and identically distributed.
[2] The parameters are determined, based on the seen training samples.

to apply these detectors to classify new (unseen) data as self (no data manipulation) or non-self (data manipulation). The negative selection algorithm proposed by Forrest et al. is summarized in the following steps.

Given a shape-space U, self set S and non-self set N, where

$$U = S \cup N \quad and \quad S \cap N = \emptyset.$$

1. Define self as a set S of elements of length l in shape-space U.
2. Generate a set D of detectors, such that each fails to match any element in S.
3. Monitor S for changes by continually matching the detectors in D against S.

3.1   Real-Valued Negative Selection

The idea to generate detectors in the complementary space for continuous data, was proposed informally by Ebner et al. [10] and formally by Gonzalez et al. [4,5]. The real-valued negative selection algorithm, operates on a unitary hypercube $[0,1]^n$. A detector $d = (\mathbf{c}_d, r_{ns})$ has a center $\mathbf{c} \in [0,1]^n$ and a non-self recognition radius $r_{ns} \in \mathbb{R}$. Furthermore, every self element $s = (\mathbf{c}_s, r_s)$ has a center and a self radius r_s. The self-radius was introduced to allow other elements to be considered as self elements which lie close to the self-center. If an element lies within a detector (hypersphere), which in effect would be close to the self-center given a certain radius, then it is classified as non-self, otherwise as self. An element[3] $\mathbf{e}$ lies within a detector $d = (\mathbf{c}_d, r_{ns})$, if the Euclidean distance $dist(\mathbf{c}, \mathbf{e}) = \left(\sum_{i=1}^{n}(c_i - e_i)^2\right)^{1/2} < r_{ns}$. Ji and Dasgupta [6] proposed a real-valued negative selection algorithm with variable-sized detectors (termed *V-Detector*) — the algorithm is presented in the appendix and illustrated in figures 1(b), 1(c), 1(d). The algorithm randomly determines a center of a detector which must not lie within the hypersphere of a self-element. The radius is dynamically resized until the boundary of the region comes in contact with a self-element. The algorithm terminates if a predefined number of detectors are generated, or a pre-determined proportion of non-self space is covered. For all our experiments contained in this paper, we employed the algorithm proposed by Ji and Dasgupta [6].

3.2   Real-Valued Positive Selection

The real-valued positive selection algorithm was informally described by Ebner et al. [10] and formally by Stibor et al. [11]. The main difference to the negative selection is that *no* non-self detectors exists. Instead, each self element contains a self-detector which classifies unseen elements. An element which lies within the self-detector is classified as self, otherwise as non-self. This means that no detector generation phase is necessary, but the classification decision for each unseen element is computationally expensive, in contrast to the real-valued negative selection.

---

[3] n dimensional point.

4   Investigating the Real-Valued Negative Selection Algorithm with Variable-Sized Detectors

As explained above, the V-Detector algorithm randomly generates detectors with a variable-sized radius. In order to assess how well the algorithm generates a set of non-self detectors and terminates, we made use of a simple toy problem. We created a simple two-dimensional artificial data set with 9 self elements (see Fig. 1(a)). We ran the algorithm using the same parameters as [6] :

$$\text{Maximum Self Coverage } MSC = 99.99\,\%$$
$$\text{Maximum Number of Detectors } T_{max} = 1000$$

The results are visualized in figure 1. Figure 1(b) shows the generated detectors for the artificial data set for self-radius $r_s = 0.05$ and estimated coverage $c_0 = 99\,\%$. It can be noted that the algorithm generates variable-sized detectors which cover the non-self space with a limited number of overlapping detectors. Two *independent* algorithm runs for $r_s = 0.05$ and $c_0 = 80\,\%$ were also performed (see Fig. 1(c), 1(d)). It can be seen, that this random detector generation and coverage estimation method varies a great deal with equal parameter settings. To obtain a steady space coverage for each independent algorithm run, the parameter c_0 must be close to 100 %. Consequently, this increases the runtime complexity required to generate detectors. This is now analyzed in the following section.

4.1   Algorithm Termination

First, it can be seen (algorithm 1), that the termination condition in line 22 is not useful, because T *never* has a value higher than 1. Once increased to 1 (see line 21), T is set to 0 (see line 5) in the same outer repeat loop and therefore, the termination condition is line 22 is never satisfied.

Another algorithm termination is reached (see line 11), when the condition $t \geq 1/(1 - c_0)$ is satisfied. Let $\mathbf{x} \in \Delta$ denote, that $\mathbf{x}$ is covered by at least one detector. The variable t is only increased, when $\mathbf{x} \in \Delta$ (see line 9). When a random sample $\mathbf{x} \notin \Delta$ is chosen — falls within a self-element circle or an uncovered gap — then t is set 0 (see line 4). Therefore, the termination criteria is guaranteed, when a sample sequence $\mathbf{x}_1, \mathbf{x}_2, \ldots, \mathbf{x}_j \in \Delta$ of length j is found, where $j = t/\delta$. The term δ denotes the average number of detectors covering a sample $\mathbf{x}$. The justification behind δ is that a sample $\mathbf{x}$ can be covered by more than one detector, because the detectors can overlap and therefore the variable t can be increased multiple times. The probability of finding a sequence of length j, can be calculated with the geometric distribution and the approach $\mathbf{x}_{j+1} \notin \Delta$.

The probability to find in $j + 1$ random sampling trials j successes before the first failure is :

$$P(\mathbf{x}_{j+1} \notin \Delta) = p(1 - p)^j \tag{1}$$

Term 1 only depends on p and j. The higher the number of self elements or the larger the self-radius, the lesser the probability of finding a sample sequence

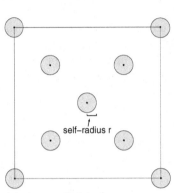

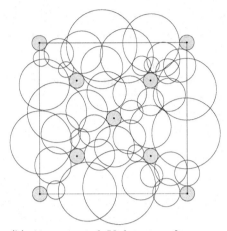

(a) An artificial data set containing 9 self-elements with self-
radius r_s pictured as the grey
circles with a black center $\mathbf{c}_s$. It
contains no V-detectors.

(b) 41 generated V-detectors for $r_s = 0.05$, $c_0 = 99\%$.

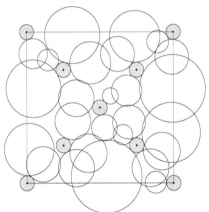

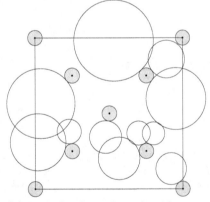

(c) First independent algorithm run
which generated 26 V-detectors for
$r_s = 0.05$, $c_0 = 80\%$.

(d) Second independent algorithm run
which generated 11 V-detectors for
$r_s = 0.05$, $c_0 = 80\%$.

Fig. 1. The real-valued negative selection algorithm with variable-sized detectors applied on an artificial data set for different estimated coverages

which guarantees the algorithm termination. Furthermore, the probability is
strongly biased by parameter c_0. A higher confidence of the estimated coverage c_0
decreases the probability of finding a termination sample sequence and therefore
increases the runtime complexity. In the work [6], the runtime complexity of
the V-Detector algorithm is estimated by $O(|D| \cdot |S|)$ *without* a probabilistic
approach. As the detectors are generated randomly, we suggest a probabilistic
runtime complexity estimation.

A final point to note is that the simple random generation and coverage estimation method employed, induces the steady space coverage problem. This is explored with a high-dimensional dataset and discussed in section 6.1.

5   Statistical Novelty Detection

Through the application of statistical methods, novelty can be quantified as a deviation from a probability distribution $p(\mathbf{x})$ which is generated from normal data. The quantity can be expressed by a threshold, where (unseen) data samples for which $p(\mathbf{x})$ falls below this threshold, are considered as abnormal samples. By applying such a threshold, all new data samples can be classified into two classes $\mathcal{C}_0$ or $\mathcal{C}_1$, where the training data are assumed to be drawn entirely from $\mathcal{C}_0$. To minimize the probability of misclassification, a new data sample $\mathbf{x}$ is assigned to the class with the larger posterior probability [12]. This classification decision is based on the Bayes theorem and can be written as :

$$\text{Decide} \quad \mathcal{C}_0 \quad if \quad p(\mathbf{x}|\mathcal{C}_0) > \frac{p(\mathbf{x}|\mathcal{C}_1)P(\mathcal{C}_1)}{P(\mathcal{C}_0)}; \quad \text{otherwise} \quad decide \quad \mathcal{C}_1$$

where $P(C_k)$ is the *prior* probability of a sample belonging to each of the classes C_k and $p(\mathbf{x}|C_k)$ is the class-conditional density. The class-conditional density $p(\mathbf{x}|\mathcal{C}_1)$ of the novel data represents the threshold and is unknown *a-priori*. Therefore, it can be modeled as a uniformly distributed density (see Fig. 2), which is constant over some large region of the input space [13]. The point of intersections divide the input space into two *decision regions* $\mathcal{R}_0$ and $\mathcal{R}_1$. An input sample falling in region $\mathcal{R}_0$ is assigned to class $\mathcal{C}_0$, otherwise it falls in region $\mathcal{R}_1$ and is assigned to class $\mathcal{C}_1$.

5.1   Parzen-Window Estimators

Parzen-Window is a nonparametric method for estimating density functions [14]. Given a set $\mathcal{A} = \{\mathbf{x}_1, \mathbf{x}_2, \ldots, \mathbf{x}_n\}$ of n i.i.d. samples drawn according to an unknown density function $p(\mathbf{x})$. The Parzen-Window method estimates $p(\mathbf{x})$ based on the n samples in $\mathcal{A}$ by

$$\hat{p}(\mathbf{x}) = \frac{1}{nh} \sum_{i=1}^{n} K\left(\frac{\mathbf{x} - \mathbf{x}_i}{h}\right)$$

where K is a kernel function which must satisfies the condition

$$\int_{-\infty}^{+\infty} K(x)dx = 1$$

and h the window width (also called smoothing parameter). For our experiments we choose the multivariate Gaussian kernel function

$$\hat{p}(\mathbf{x}) = \frac{1}{n(2\pi)^{d/2}\sigma^d} \sum_{i=1}^{n} \exp\left\{-\frac{||\mathbf{x} - \mathbf{x}_i||^2}{2\sigma^2}\right\}$$

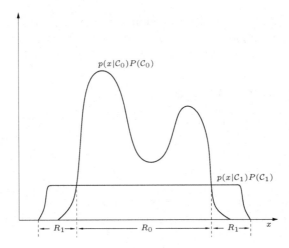

Fig. 2. Bayesian decision for determining whether an input sample belongs to class $\mathcal{C}_0$ (falling in region $\mathcal{R}_0$) or $\mathcal{C}_1$ (falling in region $\mathcal{R}_1$) modeled with class-conditional density functions

where $\mathbf{x}_i$ are training samples which characterize the normal behavior and d is the dimensionality of the data space. The Gaussian kernel function is completely specified by the variance parameter σ which control the degree of smoothness of the estimated density function. In our experiments (see section 6), we used the proposed variance parameter $\sigma = 0.01$ [15].

Through the combination of the Parzen-Window method and the Bayes classification method, it is possible to obtain a statistical classification technique. First, a density function $\hat{p}(\mathbf{x})$ is estimated based on the "normal" training samples and second, a uniformly distributed density function[4] $p_u(\mathbf{x})$ is *a-priori* modeled. An unseen sample which falls in region $\mathcal{R}_0$ is classified as normal, otherwise it is said to falls in the region $\mathcal{R}_1$ and is classified as an anomalous sample.

5.2   One-Class Support Vector Machine

In many applications it is sufficient to estimate the support of the probability distribution, as opposed to the full density. A one-class Support Vector Machine (termed one-class SVM) avoids estimating the full density. Instead, it estimates quantiles of the multivariate distribution, i.e. its support. The one-class SVM maps the input data into a higher-dimensional feature space $\mathcal{F}$ via a nonlinear mapping Φ and treats the origin as the only member of the second class. In addition, a fraction ν of "outliers" are allowed, which lie between the origin and the hyperplane (the hyperplane has maximum distance to the origin, see Fig. 3). In other words, the one-class SVM algorithm returns a function f that takes the value $+1$ in a region where the density "lives" and -1 elsewhere and therefore,

---

[4] The threshold.

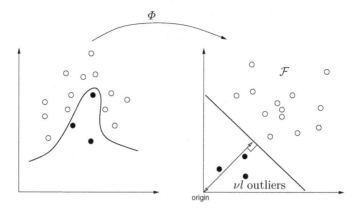

Fig. 3. Map the training data into a high-dimensional feature space $\mathcal{F}$ via Φ. Construct a separating hyperplane with maximum distance to the origin, with the constrains that νl outliers lie between the origin and the hyperplane.

for a new point $\mathbf{x}$, the value $f(\mathbf{x})$ is determined by evaluating which side of the hyperplane it falls on, in feature space.

More precisely, the optimal hyperplane is constructed, by solving the optimization problem

$$\min_{\alpha} \quad \frac{1}{2} \sum_{i,j=1}^{l} \alpha_i \alpha_j k(\mathbf{x}_i, \mathbf{x}_j)$$

$$\text{subject to} \quad 0 \le \alpha_i \le 1/(\nu l),\ i = 1, \dots, l$$

$$\sum_{i=1}^{l} \alpha_i = 1$$

where $\alpha_{1...l}$ are Lagrange multipliers, k the kernel function and $\mathbf{x}_{1...l}$ the training samples.

By solving this optimization problem, one obtains the decision function

$$f(\mathbf{x}) = \text{sgn}\left(\sum_{i=1}^{l} \alpha_i k(\mathbf{x}, \mathbf{x}_i) + \rho\right)$$

which will be positive for most examples $\mathbf{x}_i$ in the training set. The value of ρ can be recovered by exploiting the fact, that for any Lagrange multipliers α_i, the corresponding pattern $\mathbf{x}_i$ satisfies

$$\rho = (\mathbf{w} \cdot \Phi(\mathbf{x}_i)) = \sum_{j} \alpha_j k(\mathbf{x}_j, \mathbf{x}_i)$$

where $\mathbf{w}$ is the normal vector of a hyperplane.

For our experiments, we used the one-class SVM implementation LIBSVM 2.6 [16]. LIBSVM is a program, which provides several SVM algorithms for classification and regression, including the one-class SVM implementation proposed by Schölkopf et al. [8]. The default kernel (radial basis function) and the default values of the parameters for the one-class SVM are used.

6   Classification Results and Comparative Study

We wished to explore the effectiveness of all of these approaches on network intrusion detection problems. For our experiments we made use of the dataset from taken from KDD Cup 1999 [17]. This data set contains a wide variety of network intrusions and normal network traffic. The data set consists of connection-based network traffic data, where each record corresponds to one network connection. A network connection is a sequence of Internet packets sent during a period of time between two IP addresses. A complete record is described as a network connection vector which contains 38 continuous and 3 symbolic fields and an end-label (attack type or normal behavior).

Example 1.   0,icmp,ecr_i,SF,1032,0,0,0,0,0,0,0,0,0,0,0,0,0,0,0,
0,0,0,511,511,0.00,0.00,0.00,0.00,1.00,0.00,0.00,
255,243,0.95,0.01,0.95,0.00,0.00,0.00,0.00,0.00,smurf

Example 2.   0,tcp,http,SF,239,968,0,0,0,0,0,1,0,0,0,0,0,0,0,0,
0,0,3,3,0.00,0.00,0.00,0.00,1.00,0.00,0.00,3,239,
1.00,0.00,0.33,0.03,0.00,0.00,0.00,0.00,normal

Example 1 shows a connection vector which characterizes a Denial of Service (short DoS) attack. A DoS attack is an attack on a computer system, or network, that causes a loss of service to users by consuming the bandwidth of the victim network or overloading the computational resources of the victim system. As a concrete example 1 characterizes a smurf DoS attack which uses spoofed broadcast icmp messages to flood a target system. In contrast, example 2 shows a connection vector which characterizes a "normal" access to a HTTP server. The complete KDD dataset contains 3925650 abnormal (80, 14%) and 972780 normal (19, 86%) connection vectors and have a total size of ca. 700 mb. The abnormal samples are partitioned in four categories :

- DOS ($\approx 98, 92\%$) : denial-of-service, e.g. syn flood.
- R2L ($\approx 0, 0286\%$) : unauthorized access from a remote machine, e.g. guessing password.
- U2R ($\approx 0, 0013\%$) : unauthorized access to local superuser (root) privileges, e.g., various "buffer overflow" attacks.
- probing ($\approx 1, 05\%$) : surveillance and other probing, e.g., port scanning.

Due to the high runtime complexity of the Parzen-Window method and the real-valued positive selection, our experiments were performed on a reduced dataset. More precisely, we randomly created 20 subsets $S_1, \ldots, S_{20}$ from the complete KDD dataset. Each subset S_i contains randomly determined 1 % of normal and 1 % of anomalous data from the whole KDD dataset. There are 39256 anomalous and 9727 normal connection vectors in each subset. Furthermore, each discriminative symbolic string is mapped on to a natural number, i.e. icmp $\rightarrow$ 0, tcp $\rightarrow$ 1, udp $\rightarrow$ 2, and so on. The dataset is then normalized in the unitary hypercube $[0, 1]^{41}$ using the *min-max normalization*.

Each classification method is trained from subset S_i with normal samples *only*. The test run is performed on the whole subset S_i (normal and anomalous samples). After performing all 20 classification runs for each subset $S_1, \ldots, S_{20}$, the mean detection rate, mean false alarm rate and the standard deviations were recorded and are presented in table 1. The detection rate and false alarm rate is calculated as follows :

$$\text{detection rate} = \frac{\text{anomalous sample correctly classified}}{\text{total anomalous samples}} = \frac{TP}{TP+FN}$$

$$\text{false alarm rate} = \frac{\text{normal sample incorrectly classified}}{\text{total normal samples}} = \frac{FP}{FP+TN}$$

The abbreviations *TP,FP, TN,FN* are used in the ROC[5] [18] analysis to evaluate the performance of classification algorithms. Given a classifier and a sample, there are four different outcomes. If the sample is anomalous and it is classified as anomalous, it is counted as a *true positive* (TP); if it is classified as normal, it is counted as a *false negative* (FN). If the sample is normal and it is classified as normal, it is counted as a *true negative* (TN); if it is classified as anomalous, it is counted as a *false positive* (FP).

As the real-valued negative selection is the only method which has a random behavior[6] each run of the algorithm was repeated 20 times for each subset S_i.

The parameters for the real-valued negative selection were chosen as outlined in [6] ($MSC = 99.99\%$, $T_{max} = 1000$, $c_0 = 99\%$). Initial experiments with real-valued negative selection were performed with self-radius $r_s = 0.1$ and $r_s = 0.05$. For this radius, the algorithm produces very poor classification results. Therefore, several "empirical radius searching" runs were performed to find an effective self-radius. The radius lengths shown in table 1 resulted in the best classification performance. These radius lengths are also used for the positive selection algorithm.

6.1   Discussion

In table 1 one can see that real-valued positive selection (Self-Detector) method yields the highest detection rate and the lowest false alarm rate. A benefit of this method is that no training phase is required, and a nearly zero standard deviation of the detection rate for each threshold r_s is achieved. However, this method is computationally very expensive, due to the fact that the Euclidean distance is calculated from a sample to each self-element. The Parzen-Window method yields likewise a hight detection rate and a low false alarm rate. This

---

[5] Received Operating Characteristic.
[6] Generates detectors randomly.

Table 1. Classification Results for KDD dataset

Algorithm	Detection Rate		False Alarm Rate		# Detectors or # Support Vectors	
	Mean	SD	Mean	SD	Mean	SD
V-detector$^{r_s=0.000005}$	2.66	8.35	0.00	0.00	1.37	0.52
V-detector$^{r_s=0.00001}$	2.40	7.12	0.00	0.00	1.36	0.51
V-detector$^{r_s=0.00005}$	1.75	6.05	0.00	0.00	1.39	0.56
V-detector$^{r_s=0.0001}$	1.58	5.73	0.00	0.00	1.33	0.50
V-detector$^{r_s=0.05}$	1.21	4.59	0.00	0.00	1.48	0.59
V-detector$^{r_s=0.1}$	0.65	3.46	0.00	0.00	1.59	0.67
Self-Detector$^{r_s=0.000005}$	100	0.00	0.00	0.00	9727	0
Self-Detector$^{r_s=0.00001}$	100	0.00	0.00	0.00	9727	0
Self-Detector$^{r_s=0.00005}$	100	0.00	0.00	0.00	9727	0
Self-Detector$^{r_s=0.0001}$	100	0.00	0.00	0.00	9727	0
Self-Detector$^{r_s=0.05}$	100	0.00	0.00	0.00	9727	0
Self-Detector$^{r_s=0.1}$	99.99	0.02	0.00	0.00	9727	0
ocSVM$^{\nu=0.005}$	99.78	0.03	0.05	0.02	55.70	1.56
ocSVM$^{\nu=0.01}$	99.82	0.02	0.99	0.02	103.40	1.50
ocSVM$^{\nu=0.05}$	99.87	0.02	4.95	0.03	491.15	1.27
Parzen-Window$^{u=0.005}$	99.93	0.02	0.00	0.00	—	—
Parzen-Window$^{u=0.01}$	99.93	0.02	0.00	0.00	—	—
Parzen-Window$^{u=0.05}$	99.93	0.02	0.00	0.00	—	—

method also requires no training phase and has a very low standard deviation of the detection rate. However, this method is computationally expensive[7], because each training sample has to calculate the class conditionally probability for a test sample. The one-class SVM achieves similar high detection rates and low false alarm rates. Through the application of the default radial basis kernel, the test data is nearly optimally separable in high-dimensional feature space. This is shown by the fraction of outliers compared to the false alarm rate. For $\nu = 5\%$ outliers, the false alarm rate is nearly 5%. For $\nu = 0.5\%$ outliers, the false alarm rate is 0.5%. The main advantage of the one-class SVM, in comparison with the Parzen-Window method, is the low computational complexity to classify new elements. The one-class SVM considers only a subset of the training samples — the support vectors — to classify new elements. Results reveal, that the real-valued negative selection with variable-sized detectors is not competitive to the statistical techniques and to the Self-Detector method presented in this paper. It has a very low detection rate and a very high standard deviation — the standard deviation is far higher than the mean. Though the V-Detector parameter c_0 is 99 %, the estimated coverage method (see line 11) seems problematic in high-dimensional spaces. In the experiments performed, the algorithm terminates due to the estimated coverage with approximately 1.4 generated detectors.

---

[7] Exponential operation and several arithmetic operations.

7   Conclusion

In this paper we have briefly introduced the anomaly detection problem and have described two statistical anomaly detection approaches — the Parzen-Window and one-class SVM technique. It has been observed that immune system performs an anomaly detection, in part, through a process negative selection. This process eliminates self reactive lymphocytes and also ensures that all possible (including unseen) antigens are recognizable. This negative selection process motivated computer scientists to develop immune inspired algorithms which work in a similar way. On such algorithm, the real-valued negative selection algorithm, which employs variable-sized detectors, is such an anomaly detection approach. We have investigated the termination behavior of the real-valued negative selection algorithm with variable-sized detectors on an artificial data set. The investigations reveal that the algorithm termination behavior is sensitive to several parameters. A high confidence of the estimated detector coverage is necessary for obtaining a steady space coverage, but consequently increases the time complexity for the generation of detectors significantly. We then explored the performance of the algorithm on a high-dimensional data set for anomaly detection, and compared it to the real-valued positive selection and to two statistical anomaly detection techniques. The classification results revealed that the real-valued positive selection outperformed the other classification methods for this data set experiment. However, real-valued positive selection is limited due to the high complexity involved. The Parzen-Window method, likewise achieved a high classification performance, but has same complexity problems as the real-valued positive selection. The one-class SVM achieved a good classification performance and has an acceptable runtime complexity. The real-valued negative selection with variable-sized detectors has poor classification performance on the high-dimensional KDD data set.

It is difficult to conclude that the real-valued negative selection is in general not appropriate on high-dimensional data sets. However this work revealed several problems of the V-Detector algorithm which where not mentioned before. Nevertheless it may appear that the negative selection principle would seem to be a technique that is not appropriate for real-world anomaly detection problems [11,19].

References

1. Forrest S., Perelson A.S., Allen L., Cherukuri R.: Self-nonself discrimination in a computer. In: Proceedings of the 1994 IEEE Symposium on Research in Security and Privacy, IEEE Computer Society Press (1994)
2. D'haeseleer, P.: An immunological approach to change detection: Theoretical results. In: Proc. 9th IEEE Computer Security Foundations Workshop. (1996) 18–26

3. Hofmeyr S. A., Forrest S., D'haeseleer P.: An immunological approach to distributed network intrusion detection. In: First International Workshop on the Recent Advances in Intrusion Detection. (1998)
4. González, F., Dasgupta, D., Kozma, R.: Combining negative selection and classification techniques for anomaly detection. In: Congress on Evolutionary Computation, IEEE (2002) 705–710
5. González, F., Dasgupta, D., Niño, L.F.: A randomized real-valued negative selection algorithm. In Timmis, J., Bentley, P.J., Hart, E., eds.: Proceedings of the 2nd International Conference on Artificial Immune Systems (ICARIS). LNCS, Edinburgh, UK, Springer-Verlag (2003) 261–272
6. Ji, Z., Dasgupta, D.: Real-valued negative selection algorithm with variable-sized detectors. In: Genetic and Evolutionary Computation – GECCO-2004, Part I. Volume 3102 of LNCS., Seattle, WA, USA, Springer-Verlag (2004) 287–298
7. Marsland, S.: Novelty detection in learning systems. Neural Computing Surveys **3** (2003)
8. Schölkopf, B., Platt, J.C., Shawe-Taylor, S.T., Smola, A.J., Williamson, W.: Estimating the support of a high-dimensional distribution. Technical Report MSR-TR-99-87, Microsoft Research (MSR) (1999)
9. Müller, K.R., Mika, S., Rätsch, G., Tsuda, K., Schölkopf, B.: An introduction to kernel-based learning algorithms. Transactions on Neural Networks **12** (2001) 181–201
10. Ebner, M., Breunig, H.G., Albert, J.: On the use of negative selection in an artificial immune system. In: GECCO 2002: Proceedings of the Genetic and Evolutionary Computation Conference, New York, Morgan Kaufmann Publishers (2002) 957–964
11. Stibor, T., Mohr, P., Timmis, J., Eckert, C.: Is negative selection appropriate for anomaly detection ? In: Genetic and Evolutionary Computation – GECCO. (to appear) (2005)
12. Duda, R.., Hart, P.E., Stork, D.G.: Pattern Classification. Second edn. Wiley-Interscience (2001)
13. Bishop C.M.: Novelty detection and neural network validation. In: IEE Proceedings: Vision, Image and Signal Processing. Volume 141. (1994) 217–222
14. Silverman B.W.: Density Estimation for Statistics and Data Analysis. Chapman and Hall (1986)
15. Yeung, D.Y., Chow, C.: Parzen-window network intrusion detectors. In: Proc. of the Sixteenth International Conference on Pattern Recognition. (2002) 385–388
16. Chang, C.C., Lin, C.J.: LIBSVM: a Library for Support Vector Machines (http://www.csie.ntu.edu.tw/~cjlin/papers/libsvm.pdf). (2004)
17. Hettich, S. and Bay, S. D.: KDD Cup 1999 Data (1999) http://kdd.ics.uci.edu.
18. Fawcett, T.: ROC graphs: Notes and practical considerations for data mining researchers. Technical Report HPL-2003-4, Hewlett Packard Laboratories (2003)
19. Stibor, T., Timmis, J., Eckert, C.: On the appropriateness of negative selection defined over hamming shape-space as a network intrusion detection system. In: Proceedings of the 2005 IEEE Congress on Evolutionary Computation. (to appear), Edinburgh, UK, IEEE Press (2005)

Appendix

Algorithm 1: Generate V-Detector Set

---

    input : S = Set of self elements, T_{max} = max. number of V-Detectors,
              r_s = self radius, c_0 = estimated coverage, MSC = max. self
    coverage
    output: D = Set of generated V-Detectors

1 **begin**
2     $D \longleftarrow \emptyset$
3   **repeat**
4         $t \longleftarrow 0$
5         $T \longleftarrow 0$
6         $r \longleftarrow \infty$
7         $\mathbf{x} \longleftarrow$ random point from $[0,1]^n$
8   **foreach** $d \in D$ **do**
             // Euclid. distance between detector center $\mathbf{c}_d$ and $\mathbf{x}$
             // is lesser than Non-Self radius r_{ns} of detector d
9   **if** $dist(\mathbf{c}_d, \mathbf{x}) \leq r_{ns}$ **then**
                // point $\mathbf{x}$ is covered by a detector
10               $t \longleftarrow t + 1$
11   **if** $t \geq 1/(1 - c_0)$ **then**
12   **return** D
13   goto 5:
         // find the closest distance to a self element margin
14   **foreach** $s \in S$ **do**
15             $l \longleftarrow dist(\mathbf{c}_s, \mathbf{x})$
16   **if** $l - r_s \leq r$ **then**
17                $r \longleftarrow l - r_s$
18   **if** $r > r_s$ **then**
             // Add a new detector d to set D
19             $D \longleftarrow D \cup \{d = (\mathbf{x}, r)\}$
20   **else**
21             $T \longleftarrow T + 1$
22   **if** $T > 1/(1 - MSC)$ **then**
23   exit
24   **until** $|D| = T_{max}$
25 **end**

Immunity from Spam: An Analysis of an Artificial Immune System for Junk Email Detection

Terri Oda and Tony White

Carleton University, Ottawa ON, Canada
terri@zone12.com, arpwhite@scs.carleton.ca

Abstract. Despite attempts to legislate them out of existence, spam messages (junk email) continue to fill electronic mailboxes around the world. With spam senders adapting to each technical solution put on the market, adaptive solutions are being incorporated into new products. This paper undertakes an extended examination of the spam-detecting artificial immune system proposed in [1,2], focusing on comparison of scoring schemes, the effect of population size, and the libraries used to create the detectors.

1 Introduction

The first junk email was sent in 1978 [3]. Junk email messages were merely a curiousity in the early 1990's, but they soon became a nuisance, and then a serious problem to many people. Junk emails may account for 75-85% of email [4,5]. Despite attempts at legislation such as the CAN-SPAM act in the US [6], the problem does not seem to have lessened significantly, and may even be getting worse [7].

Artificial immune systems have been used for a diverse set of things, including spam detection [1,2] and email classification [8]. This paper focuses upon extending the work of [1,2]. The initial papers on a spam-detecting immune system showed positive results, but did not look at how the system performed over a longer period of time, or the effects of different alternatives such as variant libraries or varying population sizes. This paper compares results from different setups. In addition, this paper gives an algorithmic treatment of the spam immune system used, making it more clear what other parameters might be altered and which parts of the algorithm could be changed.

This system differs from AISEC [8] in several important ways, although they are both immunologically-inspired email classification tools. Firstly, it is specifically geared towards spam detection rather than a more general model of text classification. As such, it does not take into account known heuristics for email classification, and thus has a broader application field. The representation for AISEC is based upon vectors of words found in the subject and sender header fields of email, whereas the representation for this system can match upon any part of a given message. In part because of this representation, AISEC has the

C. Jacob et al. (Eds.): ICARIS 2005, LNCS 3627, pp. 276–289, 2005.

ability to do clonal mutations, something which is not seen in this system. The two systems, while performing similar functions, reach their classifications by very different means.

Section 2 gives a short overview of spam detection: what makes it an interesting problem, and how adaptive solutions can help. Section 3 describes the spam immune system as it was tested. The results of these tests are given in Section 4. Conclusions are discussed in Section 5, and some ideas for future work are outlined in Section 6.

2   Spam

While defining spam for the lawyers can be tricky, defining spam for the purpose of filtering is easy: Spam is what the recipient considers to be junk mail and does not wish to receive.

Spam is basically a two-class problem where the two classes are spam and non-spam (legitimate mail). Spam changes over time as new products become available or popular, but it also changes because the problem is co-evolutionary: spammers adapt to filters, and filters adapt to spam.

Although it does change, spam is not completely volatile: it tends to have many stable features and occasionally undergoes periods of rapid change [9]. This means that a semi-static solution will work for long periods, then break seemingly all at once, letting through a flood of messages. Obviously, this is not desirable. The hope with adaptive spam solutions is that they will be able to adapt to both slow and rapid changes.

Adaptive systems such as this one are also inherently diverse from one instance to the next. Although for the individual, diversity may not have immediate benefits (a given spam message might still go through an individual's filter), diversity in spam filters has a impact on the industry as a whole. If it is impossible for a spam sender to craft a message which will go through enough filters, then it will cost more to send messages than the spam senders can make in profit. This sort of economic disincentive may prove to be the only significant deterrent to spam, given the lack of success so far with legislation [7].

2.1   Spam Technologies

There are two broad classes of solutions to spam: those which are technological in nature, such as the many anti-spam products available, and those which are more social solutions, such as the legislations surrounding unsolicited email. Two of the technological solutions have lent ideas to the spam immune system, so these are described briefly here:

- **SpamAssassin.** SpamAssassin [10] is an excellent open source spam filter which uses a number of interesting heuristic techniques, including Bayesian style filtering, lookup in blacklists, and many others. Of particular interest to this paper are the text-based heuristics it uses, which are Perl regular expressions.

- **Bayesian-inspired spam filters.** The idea of using Bayes rule to sort spam was introduced in 1998 [11,12], but the idea became much more popular after a paper in 2002 [13] which boasted extremely high accuracies. Bayes rule is a result from probability theory that helps predict the classification of a given item based on features it has. ("Give me the probability that this message is spam, given that it contains the tokens 'Rolex' and 'replica'".)

3   The Spam Immune System

The human immune system distinguishes between self and non-self, so the spam immune system distinguishes between a self of legitimate email (non-spam) and a non-self of spam.

3.1   Detectors: Lymphocytes and Antibodies

The central part of the spam immune system is its detectors, which are regular expressions made by randomly recombining information from a set of libraries, as described in Section 3.2. These regular expressions match patterns in the entire message.

The digital lymphocyte consists of an antibody and two associated weights detailing what has been matched by that particular lymphocyte. Both of these weights are initialized to zero.

- *spam_matched*: the cumulative weighted number of spams matched
- *msg_matched*: the cumulative weighted number of messages matched

3.2   Libraries

The gene library contains partial patterns used to build the full patterns used in lymphocytes. (Algorithm 2 describes how this is done.) In order to create antibodies which match spam, a few different libraries were tested:

Dictionary of English Words. For the personal email of an English speaker, most messages are written in English. This is the case for the corpus used for testing and training. As such, the first library attempted was a list of American English words, taken from version 5-4 of the Debian package wamerican. This dictionary contains 96274 words.

Bayesian-Style Tokens. The Bayesian tokenizer divides a mail up into separate components, usually individual words. The SpamBayes [14] tokenizer was used to parse a training set of emails into Bayes tokens. Their implementation is based upon the work of Paul Graham [13], but includes many additions not found in his work [14]. This library contains 105248 tokens.

Heuristics. The library which gained the best results is a library of heuristics. Using full libraries of words wasted valuable knowledge that was available about spam and non-spam messages. For example, although both messages contain common words like "the" the presence or absence of such common words tells us little about the likelihood of the message being spam. By concentrating on words and phrases which are more likely to indicate a classification for the message, the system produces more "useful" detectors and can achieve results with a much smaller set of detectors.

Figure 1 gives some example heuristics. The syntax used is that of Perl regular expressions. The first of these looks for a pattern where the words "reply", "remove" and "subject" appear fairly close together (eg: "send a reply with remove in the subject"). The second is a simple string which represents the colour red in hexadecimal (this string might appear in HTML-formatted mail). The third contains the code for setting the background colour of an HTML document. Finally, the last matches strings such as "college diplomas" or "university diplomas" because these are periodically offered through spam messages.

```
reply.{1,15}remove.{1,15}subject
ff0000
\<BODY.*bgcolor="#?[^f]
\b(?:college|university)\s+diplomas
```

Fig. 1. Some heuristics from the Heuristic gene fragment library

The heuristic library is much smaller than its counterparts, with only 201 fragments. The heuristics used are drawn from SpamAssassin [10], information about the training results of Bayes classifiers [13] [15], as well as directly from examination of spam.

3.3   Assigning Scores to Messages: Is It Spam?

Given a set of weighted antibodies which have matched a given message, how do we make a determination as to whether that message is spam? First we combine all the individual antibody scores to assign a score to the message, and then we must set a threshold so that scores on one side of this threshold are spam, and those on the other are not.

In the first paper, scoring was done with a simple sum of the messages matched by each lymphocyte [1], as shown in Equation 1. Later work used a "weighted average" where this score was divided by the number of messages matched by all lymphocytes [2], as shown in Equation 2. Given the information stored by each lymphocyte, it is also possible to use a Bayes Score, as shown in Equation 3. In each of these, the sum or product is taken over all matching lymphocytes, so only the spam_matched and msg_matched values from those lymphocytes are used in the score. The results of testing these equations can be found in Section 4.2.

$$Straight\ sum = \sum_{matching\ lymphocytes} spam\_matched \tag{1}$$

$$Weighted\ average = \frac{\sum_{matching\ lymphocytes} spam\_matched}{\sum_{matching\ lymphocytes} msg\_matched} \tag{2}$$

$$Bayes\ score =$$

$$\frac{\prod_{matching\ lymphocytes} \frac{spam\_matched}{msg\_matched}}{\prod_{matching\ lymphocytes} \frac{spam\_matched}{msg\_matched} + \prod_{matching\ lymphocytes} 1 - \frac{spam\_matched}{msg\_matched}} \tag{3}$$

Ideally all spam would be on one side of the threshold and all non-spam on the other. Doing the threshold selection after initial training allows the user some control over the accuracy of the system. Some users may be willing to lose a few legitimate messages if it means they don't have to deal with all the spam, while others will prefer to sort through more spam rather than risk losing any legitimate mail. Although it has been suggested that a false positive should be weighted more heavily as an error than a false negative [13], there does not seem to be a consensus on an appropriate value for this weight. As a result, these tests have been done using a sum of the false positive and false negative scores to give a total error. The threshold was determined based on the score that gave a minimum total error over an average of all runs. For most tests, 20 runs were conducted. The results from this threshold determination are described in Section 4.2.

3.4   Lifecycle

The lifecycle of a digital lymphocyte starts when the lymphocyte is created and initialized (as described in Section 3.1). Once it has been created and initialized, it can be used to match messages. It is usually trained first on a set of pre-classified messages, then allowed to work with real, unclassified messages. The lymphocytes are culled periodically (on an interval set by the user, perhaps once a month or every two weeks), and new lymphocytes are generated. Algorithm 1 describes the overall functioning of the spam immune system.

The sub-algorithms describe the phases of the lifecycle in more detail: Algorithm 2 explains the generation of new lymphocytes, Algorithm 3 describes their initial training phase, Algorithm 4 explains the application of lymphocytes to messages, and Algorithm 5 details the process of culling and ageing of old lymphocytes.

4   Results

The system was tested against [16] because it is publicly available, contains sorted spam and non-spam which is relatively unaltered (messages are altered to preserve privacy and remove information added when they were donated). It

---

Algorithm 1. Spam Immune System

Require: *update_interval* ⇐ a time interval after which the system will age. {chosen by user} {e.g. 10 days from now}

repertoire ⇐ φ {Initialize repertoire (list) of lymphocytes to be empty}
update_time ⇐ *currenttime* + *update_interval* {time of next lymphocyte update}

Generate lymphocytes (See Algorithm 2)
Do initial training (See Algorithm 3)
while Immune System is running **do**
  if *message* is received **then**
    Apply lymphocytes (See Algorithm 4)
  end if
  if current time > *update_time* **then**
    Cull lymphocytes (See Algorithm 5)
    Generate lymphocytes to replace those lost by culling (See Algorithm 2)
    update_time ⇐ *currenttime* + *update_interval* {t}ime of next lymphocyte update
  end if
end while

Algorithm 2. Generation of lymphocytes

Require: *library* ⇐ a gene fragment library (cannot be empty)
Require: *repertoire* ⇐ the list of existing lymphocytes (may be empty)
Require: *p_appending* ⇐ the probability of appending to *antibody* {chosen by user}

while *repertoire* is smaller than the required size **do**
  lymphocyte ⇐ a new empty memory structure with space for an *antibody*, and the numbers *msg_matched* and *spam_matched*
  antibody ⇐ randomly chosen gene fragment from *library* {This starts the new antibody being created. This will be a regular expression made up of genes and wildcards.}

  lymphocyte.msg_matched ⇐ 0
  lymphocyte.spam_matched ⇐ 0
  repeat
    x ⇐ randomly chosen number between 0 and 1 {uniform distribution}
    while *x* < *p_appending* **do**
      newgene ⇐ new randomly chosen gene fragment from *library*
      antibody ⇐ concatenate *antibody*, an expression that matches 0 or more characters, and *newgene*
      x ⇐ new randomly chosen number between 0 and 1 {uniform distribution}
    end while
  until an *antibody* is created that does not not match any in the *repertoire*

  lymphocyte.antibody ⇐ *antibody*
  Add *lymphocyte* to *repertoire* of lymphocytes
end while

Algorithm 3. Training of lymphocytes

Require: *repertoire* ⇐ the list of lymphocytes (cannot be an empty list)
Require: *message* ⇐ a message which has been marked as spam or non-spam

  if the message is user-determined spam **then**
    spam_increment ⇐ 1
  else if the message is user-determined non-spam **then**
    spam_increment ⇐ 0
  else
    spam_increment ⇐ a number between 0 and 1 indicating how likely the message
    is to be spam {Chosen by user}
  end if

  for each *lymphocyte* in the *repertoire* **do**
    if *lymphocyte.antibody* matches the message **then**
      lymphocyte.msg_matched ⇐ *lymphocyte.msg_matched* + 1
      lymphocyte.spam_matched ⇐ *lymphocyte.spam_matched* + *spam_increment*
    end if
  end for

---

is no longer very recent (the bulk of the messages are from 2002), but it should be sufficiently recent for testing purposes.

The corpus was divided up by the information found in the Date: email header, as it was the only date information available. Messages whose date field were clearly inaccurate (such as messages where the year was listed as 2028) were discarded, and since all of the non-spam was sent during 2002, only the spam for that year was used. The messages were grouped by month.

4.1 Baseline Test

The baseline result used for comparison is a repertoire of 500 lymphocytes from the heuristic library, trained dynamically, retrained with a weight of 2 (meaning each retraining is equal to two trainings, once to reverse the original training and once as a new training), and culled if the *msg_matched* value falls below 1 and aged by 1 if the value is higher. Unless otherwise specified, these are the parameters used for each test.

This baseline was not chosen to be the best of the tests: as shown in Section 4.3, better classifications can be achieved by using larger populations. The benefit to using a non-optimal baseline is that there is more room to improve, so it is more evident if a given technique actually improves the results.

The average accuracy for the baseline test is 91.9% with 2.4% false positives. The standard deviation of this accuracy is 3.0%.

4.2 Scoring

As described in Section 3.3, three different weighting schemes have been used with the spam immune system. Each of the three systems produces a very different pattern of scores when applied to the messages. Figures 2, 3 and 4 show these scores for one instance of the baseline test. Only the first month (August) is graphed to avoid showing any effects related to culling and retraining.

Figure 2 shows the pattern of the straight sum scoring system. There is little clear division between the spam and the non-spam messages and there is a much wider range of scores. There is a large spike of spam and smaller spike of non-spam at the bottom end of the range – these represent messages for which few or

---

Algorithm 4. Application of antibodies with dynamically updated weights

---

Require: *repertoire* $\Leftarrow$ the list of antibodies (cannot be an empty list)
Require: *message* $\Leftarrow$ a message to be marked
Require: *threshold* $\Leftarrow$ a cutoff point valued between 0 and 1 inclusive; anything with a score great than or equal to this is spam {chosen by user}

Require: *increment* $\Leftarrow$ increment used to update lymphocytes
  Or...
Require: *confidence* $\Leftarrow$ a value between 0 and 1 inclusive, depending upon the user's confidence in the system. {chosen by user}

  $total\_spam\_matched \Leftarrow 0$ {initialize # of spams matched to 0}
  $total\_msg\_matched \Leftarrow 0$ {initialize # of messages matched to 0}
  $matching\_lymphocytes \Leftarrow \phi$ {Initialize empty list of matching lymphocytes}

  for each *lymphocyte* in the *repertoire* **do**
    if *lymphocyte.antibody* matches *message* **then**
      $total\_spam\_matched \Leftarrow total\_spam\_matched + lymphocyte.spam\_matched$
      $total\_msg\_matched \Leftarrow total\_msg\_matched + lymphocyte.msg\_matched$
      $lymphocyte.msg\_matched \Leftarrow lymphocyte.msg\_matched + 1$ {increment the # of messages matched by this antibody}
      add *lymphocyte* to *matching_lymphocytes*
    end if
  end for

  $score \Leftarrow \frac{total\_spam\_matched}{total\_msg\_matched}$ {Determine the score using a weighted sum}
  if $score < threshold$ **then**
    Message is spam
    for each *lymphocyte* in *matching_lymphocytes* **do**
      if *confidence* is set **then**
        $increment \Leftarrow confidence * score$
      else
        {$increment has been supplied by the user$}
      end if
      $lymphocyte.spam\_matched \Leftarrow lymphocyte.spam\_matched + increment$
    end for
  else
    Message is not spam
  end if

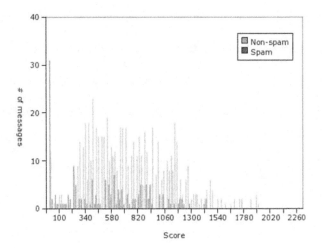

Fig. 2. Straight Sum Score Distribution

no lymphocytes matched. The average best threshold is at score 3808, with an average error rate of 20.11%. However, this error rate is almost identical to the rate of spam in the portion of the corpus being tested, so effectively the straight sum is not distinguishing any messages.

Figure 3 shows the bowl-shaped pattern of the Bayesian scoring system. There is mostly spam at the top of the score range, and mostly non-spam at the bottom of the range, with a spike in the middle of the distribution. (A weight of 0.5 is assigned to any message about which nothing is known.) The average best threshold is at 0.62 and the average best error rate is 7.08%.

Algorithm 5. Culling of antibodies: ageing and death

Require: *repertoire* ⇐ the list of antibodies (cannot be an empty list)
Require: *matched_threshold* ⇐ any lymphocyte with a *msg_matched* value below this threshold will be killed {chosen by user}
Require: *decrement* ⇐ amount by which to decrement ageing antibodies {chosen by user}

for each *lymphocyte* in the *repertoire* (list of all lymphocytes) **do**
    lymphocyte.spam_matched ⇐
    $\frac{lymphocyte.spam\_matched}{lymphocyte.msg\_matched}$ $* (lymphocyte.msg\_matched - decrement)$
    {the ratio between the two weights stays the same as it was before the ageing}
    lymphocyte.msg_matched ⇐ *lymphocyte.msg_matched − decrement*
    if *lymphocyte.msg_matched* < *threshold* **then**
        remove antibody from data store
    end if
end for

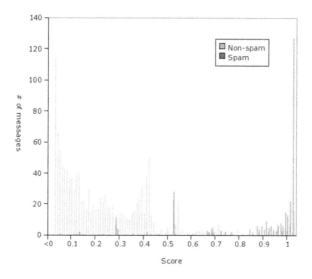

Fig. 3. Bayes Score Distribution

Table 1. Average threshold values for the three scoring systems

Scoring System	Threshold	Percent Error	Standard Deviation of Threshold
Straight Sum	3808	20.11	772.62
Bayes	0.62	7.08	0.12
Weighted Average	0.55	4.96	0.01

Figure 4 shows the pattern of the Weighted Average scoring system. The scores of the spam messages and the non-spam messages are somewhat distinct, falling in two bell-curves that partially overlap at the edges. As with the Straight Sum, there is a spike of messages at 0 because this is the score assigned to messages about which nothing is known. The average best threshold was 0.55, with an average best error rate of 4.96%.

Table 1 shows the thresholds as determined experimentally. Not only did the weighted average scores give a lower error rate on average, but the standard deviation of the best threshold was smaller, which makes it easier to assume that future tests at this threshold will yield similarly good results. As such, the weighted average is the scoring system used in the other tests.

4.3 Comparing Population Size

Using the heuristic library, lymphocytes were generated in batches of 1000, 900, 800, 700, 600, 500, 400, 300, 200, and 100. Each one was tested against all the messages of the testing set, using the parameters for the baseline test other than the number of lymphocytes in the repertoire. Figure 5 shows the percent error in

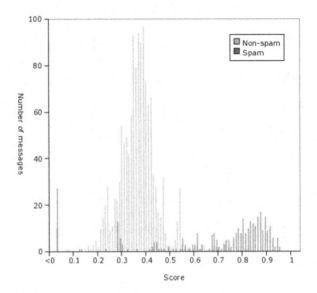

Fig. 4. Weighted Average Score Distribution

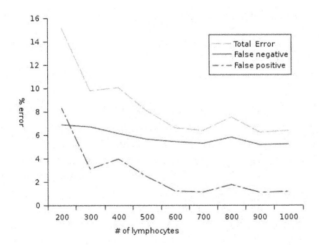

Fig. 5. Percent error versus population size

classification as a function of population size. All the values shown are averages for that population size.

"Useful" lymphocytes are those that have matched some messages and thus have scores larger than zero. These are shown in Figure 6. The graph was created by looking at the population of lymphocytes with any weight after the culling step of the lifecycle. Near the top of this graph, the lines for various popula-

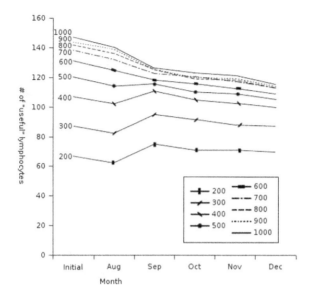

Fig. 6. The number of useful lymphocytes in each population

tion sizes converge, implying that we may have reached an optimal number of lymphocytes from this library for this corpus.

4.4 Libraries

The libraries were tested as with the baseline test, only with different libraries used. The results, in Table 2, show that the accuracy of the heuristic library is much higher. The numbers in brackets are the standard deviations of error for each of the libraries tested. Because the standard deviation of the error using the heuristic library is low, we can reasonably assume that the error will be consistent over a range of runs.

Table 2. Error for the three libraries

	False Positives	False Negatives	Total Error
Bayes	18.00 (11.13)	11.20 (2.69)	29.19 (8.94)
English	18.08 (9.84)	11.36 (3.16)	29.44 (8.18)
Heuristic	2.44 (2.10)	5.63 (1.13)	8.07 (3.02)

5   Conclusions

The spam immune system successfully adapts the artificial immune system model for use in spam detection. At 700 heuristic lymphocytes, the system averages 93.6% accuracy with 1.1% false positives. Thus, the spam immune system achieves accuracy comparable to that of commercial anti-spam solutions according to third-party reviewers of said products [17] [18]. Accuracy numbers cited by vendors are often higher than these numbers, but these third party reviews are probably closer to the accuracy that would be seen by typical users.

This system is even more compelling in that it uses only a single approach to achieve this accuracy. As shown in [17], many of the products they tested use multiple approaches, such as blacklisting combined with URL analysis. Presumably, if these approaches were added into a complete system including the spam immune system, it would be possible to achieve even higher accuracy. This demonstrates that not only is it possible to apply the artificial immune system model to spam detection, but it is also a viable alternate anti-spam solution.

The scoring system which produced the best results was the weighted average, originally proposed in [2]. While Bayes system achieved similar results, the larger variance between runs made it less attractive for a system which users would want to be relatively stable.

Three libraries were tested, but it was the heuristic library, originally proposed in [1] which emerged as the most accurate for classification. The Bayesian token and English word libraries performed significantly less well. Although the higher variance between runs implies that they could occasionally do as well as the heuristic library, most users will not be content with a system that "might" work – they want something which will work consistently for them on a given run.

6   Future Work

In order for research to continue, work should be done to produce a suitable corpus of messages that is more up-to-date and has a better distribution than the SpamAssassin corpus. In the past, mailing lists have been used as ways to gather spam and non-spam [12]. We have explored making modifications to the popular open source list management software Mailman [19], so that collection could be done with little additional work on the part of the list administrators, but this has not yet been explored on a live mailing list.

Ideally, the new corpus would be gathered over a period longer than the one-year span of the SpamAssassin corpus. If possible, it would be nice to have a higher ratio of spam, reflecting the greater ratio of spam found in the world currently. It would be nice to have a spam corpus which exhibits periods of volatility as described in [9], as well as messages known to be relatively stable.

Once a better corpus is prepared, other gene libraries should be explored:

Adaptive gene libraries. Currently, the system uses a library that is prepared in advance and does not change. However, as the system sees more spam, it could be gathering information that could be used to create new gene fragments. This could be done, for example, by looking at the Bayesian tokens found in messages.

Weighted gene libraries. When antibodies are generated, the entire library of gene fragments has an equal chance of being used, but it would be possible to weight the fragments so that those more likely to produce useful lymphocytes could be used more frequently. The "usefulness" of fragments could be based upon the weights assigned to lymphocytes that use them.

Other ideas include allowing mutations of lymphocytes, managing parameter settings adaptively (for example, using a genetic algorithm), varying the confidence values for training during application.

References

1. Oda, T., White, T.: Developing an immunity to spam. In: Genetic and Evolutionary Computation Conference (GECCO 2003), Proceedings, Part I. Volume 2723 of Lecture Notes in Computer Science., Chicago (2003) 231–242
2. Oda, T., White, T.: Increasing the accuracy of a spam-detecting artificial immune system. In: Proceedings of the Congress on Evolutionary Computation. Volume 1., Canberra, Australia (2003) 390–396
3. Templeton, B.: Reflections on the 25th anniversary of spam. (2003)
4. Postini Inc.: Postini - email stats (2005) accessed April 2005.
5. MessageLabs Ltd.: Monthly report: February 2005. Intelligence Newsletter (2005)
6. : Controlling the assault of non-solicited pornography and marketing (CAN-SPAM) act of 2003 (2003) S. 877 as it was passed by the US Senate.
7. Asaravala, A.: With this law, you can spam. Wired News (2004)
8. Secker, A., Freitas, A., Timmis, J.: AISEC: An Artificial Immune System for E-mail Classification. In: Proceedings of the Congress on Evolutionary Computation, Canberra. Australia, IEEE (2003) 131–139
9. Sullivan, T.: The myth of spam volatility. QAQD.com White Paper (2004) Presented at the 2004 MIT Spam Conference.
10. Apache Software Foundation: Spamassassin (2005) http://spamassassin.org.
11. Pantel, P., Lin, D.: Spamcop: A spam classification & organization program. In: Learning for Text Categorization: Papers from the 1998 Workshop, Madison, Wisconsin, AAAI Technical Report WS-98-05 (1998)
12. Sahami, M., Dumais, S., Heckerman, D., Horvitz, E.: A bayesian approach to filtering junk E-mail. In: Learning for Text Categorization: Papers from the 1998 Workshop, Madison, Wisconsin, AAAI Technical Report WS-98-05 (1998)
13. Graham, P.: A plan for spam. Hackers & Painters (2002)
14. : SpamBayes: Bayesian anti-spam classifier written in python (2004) Accessed October 13, 2004. http://spambayes.sourceforge.net/.
15. Graham, P.: Better bayesian filtering. In: 2003 Spam Conference. (2003)
16. : SpamAssassin public corpus (2003) http://spamassassin.org/publiccorpus/.
17. Anderson, R.: Filters take a bite out of spam. Network Computing (2004)
18. Metz, C.: Spam blockers. PC Magazine (2004)
19. Free Software Foundation: Mailman (2005) http://www.list.org.

Adaptive Radius Immune Algorithm for Data Clustering

George B. Bezerra[1], Tiago V. Barra[1], Leandro N. de Castro[2],
and Fernando J. Von Zuben[1]

[1] Laboratory of Bioinformatics and Bio-Inspired Computing (LBIC),
Department of Computer Engineering and Industrial Automation,
University of Campinas, Unicamp, CP: 6101, 13083-970, Campinas/SP, Brazil
{bezerra, tbarra, vonzuben}@dca.fee.unicamp.br
[2] Graduate Program on Informatics, Catholic University of Santos,
COPOP, R. Dr. Carvalho de Mendonça, 144, Vila Mathias, Santos/SP, Brazil
lnunes@unisantos.br

Abstract. Many algorithms perform data clustering by compressing the original data into a more compact and interpretable representation, which can be more easily inspected for the presence of clusters. This, however, can be a risky alternative, because the simplified representation may contain distortions mainly related to the density information present in the data, which can considerably act on the clustering results. In order to treat this deficiency, this paper proposes an Adaptive Radius Immune Algorithm (ARIA), which is capable of maximally preserving the density information after compression by implementing an antibody adaptive suppression radius that varies inversely with the local density in the space. ARIA is tested with both artificial and real world problems obtaining a better performance than the aiNet algorithm and showing that preserving the density information leads to refined clustering results.

1 Introduction

Many artificial immune clustering algorithms are based on data compression and information reduction procedures [2,6,9]. Inspired by immune principles and theories, the majority of these algorithms work by positioning a reduced number of prototypes (antibodies) on the most representative portions of the data set, producing an internal image that represents the antigens in a parsimonious manner. A partitioning or visualization technique can then be applied to the resulting arrangement, and the antibodies are thus separated into clusters.

The information reduction phase plays a key role in the clustering procedure. By positioning prototypes in the most important regions of the input space, it reduces the complexity of the problem: the redundancy within the data set tends to be eliminated and potential distortions due to noise are strongly alleviated; the data internal image assumes a more compact and interpretable form that is crucial for a reliable cluster analysis.

This practice, however, might be misleading in some situations. In problems where (*i*) clusters are placed considerably close to each other; (*ii*) densities vary from cluster to cluster; or (*iii*) their borders are fuzzy and overlap, the inherent distortion produced by the data compression can misrepresent key features of the data that are critically

C. Jacob et al. (Eds.): ICARIS 2005, LNCS 3627, pp. 290–303, 2005.

necessary for the proper identification of clusters (see [10] for real world examples). This problem arises because the antibody positioning usually does not take into account the density information within the data: there is no explicit compromise in maintaining the relative density distribution. As a result, relative distances between prototypes in the internal image do not correspond to relative distances between original data points. This circumstance can drastically affect the performance of the partitioning technique to be adopted.

This difficulty arises in information compression algorithms in general, and it is not a particular feature of immune algorithms. The Self-Organizing Maps (SOM) [7], a neural network clustering technique that also performs prototype positioning, suffers from the same problem. In [10] it was shown that the U-matrix, a commonly adopted distance-based criterion for separating the SOM prototypes into clusters, was not capable of solving a large class of problems because the relative distances among the trained neurons did not represented adequately the original data. In this same work, it was also demonstrated that by using the density information present in the data in combination with the U-matrix the SOM obtains a better performance for all cases.

In this paper we propose a new immune algorithm, named Adaptive Radius Immune Algorithm (ARIA), which uses mechanisms of clonal expansion and network suppression together with the density information present in the data in order to produce more accurate data representations. The algorithm is computationally fast and it is also very simple, in conception and implementation. ARIA makes use of an adaptive suppression radius that is inversely proportional to the local density for each antibody's neighborhood. In this way, for high density portions of data, antibodies are allowed to get closer to each other because of their small radii. For sparse regions, the radii tend to be large, so antibody distribution tends to be sparse too.

We apply the proposed algorithm to both synthetic and real world data and compare the results with those of the well-known aiNet algorithm [2]. aiNet was chosen for two main reasons: (*i*) it is one of the best known artificial immune clustering techniques of the AIS literature; and (*ii*) its efficiency in a large class of complex problems has already been attested [1,2]. Through these comparative analysis we intend to shown that the density information, if preserved after compression, leads to more accurate representations and, consequently, to better clustering results.

2   ARIA (Adaptive Radius Immune Algorithm)

ARIA is an iterative procedure that can be summarized into three main phases:

1. *Afinity maturation:* the antigens (data points) are presented to the antibodies, which suffer hypermutation in order to better fit the antigens (antigen-antibody interactions).
2. *Clonal expansion*: those antibodies that are more stimulated are selected to be cloned, and the network grows.
3. *Network suppression*: the interaction between the antibodies is quantified and if one antibody recognizes another, one of them is removed from the pool of cells (antibody-antibody interactions).

The pseudocode of ARIA is shown below in Algorithm 1. Table 1 presents the description of the parameters and symbols used in the pseudocode.

```
1 Initialize variables
2 For iteration 1 to gen do:
    2.1 For each antigen Ag do:
        2.1.1 Select the best matching antibody Ab;
        2.1.2 Mutate Ab with rate mi;
    end;
    2.2 Kill those antibodies that are not stimulated;
    2.3 Clone those antibodies that recognize antigens located
        at a distance larger than its radius R;
    2.4 Calculate the local density for each Ab;
    2.5 Calculate the suppression threshold (radius) of each Ab
        making R_Ab = r ×(den_max/den)^(1/dim);
    2.6 Suppress antibodies giving survival priority for those
        with smaller R;
    2.7 Make E = mean(R);
    2.8 If current generation is greater than gen/2:
        2.8.1 Reduce mi (mi = mi*decay);
    end;
end;
```

Algorithm 1. Pseudocode of ARIA

Table 1. Description of the symbols used in the pseudocode. Those symbols marked with an asterisk are user-tuned input parameters to the algorithm.

Symbol	Description
R	Radius of each antibody (suppression threshold).
$r*$	Radius multiplier. Determines the size of the smaller radius.
mi	Mutation rate.
$decay*$	Multiplier constant used to decrease the mutation rate.
E	Radius that defines the neighborhood for the density estimation.
$gen*$	Number of iterations.
dim	Dimension of the input data.

In Step 1 of the algorithm, the initial parameters are set and an initial population of antibodies is randomly generated. Only few antibodies need to be created because the network grows dynamically in order to appropriately represent the input data. Also, the initial radius R of the antibodies is set at random and so is the neighborhood radius E – coherent values for R and E will be automatically produced during the iterative procedure of adaptation. The mutation rate mi is initially set to 1.

The antigen-antibody interaction and affinity maturation phase takes place at Step 2.1. Antigens are randomly presented one at a time to the antibodies. For each presentation, the antibody with better affinity to the antigen (smaller Euclidean distance) is selected and mutated in the antigen's direction with a rate mi. Those antibodies incapable of recognizing antigens are eliminated from the population in Step 2.2.

The subsequent phase consists of clonal expansion (Step 2.3). Those antibodies that recognize antigens located at a distance larger than its suppression radius are cloned. A single antibody can recognize several antigens satisfying this condition, but only one clone per antibody is allowed to be generated. This constraint plays an important role: the network growth becomes smoother than it would be if the same antibody generated lots of clones in a single generation, thus making the self-organization process more stable. Besides, it prevents an overhead of antibodies, mainly in the initial generations, what makes the algorithm much faster. After a number of generations, however, as the prototypes are already well positioned, the number of clones tend to decrease or even to stop increasing, because few or no antigens will be uncovered by the antibodies. The mutation and cloning procedures are described in detail in Section 2.1.

In Step 2.4, the local density of each antibody's neighborhood is estimated. Its value is the number of data points within a hypersphere centered in the antibody and with radius E. The calculated densities are used to determine the radii R of the antibodies, using the formula presented in Step 2.5. Note that the radius of an antibody placed in a region with the highest density will have its value set exactly to r. The others will have a larger radius, as the density decreases. Note also that the radius is not really inversely proportional to the relative density. The density values are raised as a function of the inverse of the data dimension. This means that we want the hypervolume of the hypersphere to be inversely proportional to the density, and not directly the radius. In the two dimensional case, for example, if the area of the circle must be inversely proportional to the density, and the area is proportional to the square of the radius, so the radius must be inversely proportional to the square root of the density.

After the radii of all antibodies are defined, the network suppression phase takes place (Step 2.6). The suppression occurs as follows. If the distance between two antibodies is smaller than the radius of one of them (this means that they match), the one with larger radius is suppressed, i.e., it is removed from the pool of antibody cells. Note that survival priority is given to the antibodies presenting smaller radii (those in denser regions). The reason for this decision is simple: prototypes located at sparse regions are greedy. Their suppression radii tend to be larger than their neighborhood radius. This promotes an unstable behavior that is not desired.

In Step 2.7, the neighborhood radius E is updated to the mean of all suppression radii. Note that as the population of antibodies tend to vary in size and in radius, the neighborhood does not assume a fixed value, and it is particularly oscillatory in the initial generations. However, it quickly converges to a quasi constant value after a few generations.

In the next step, the mutation rate is also updated. It is kept the same for $gen/2$ generations and then starts to be geometrically decreased by a multiplier constant $decay$, as indicated in Step 2.8. The aim is to introduce a cooling process that forces the network convergence.

After convergence, the network topology has to be defined. To do that, a good alternative is to use the minimum spanning tree (MST), as was done in [1,6]. The MST is interesting because it imposes a parsimonious structure to the network. Cutting one of its edges always leads to subgraphs, and this strategy can be used to generate clusters. The criterion used for cutting the MST is discussed in Section 2.2.

2.1 Mutation and Cloning

The mutation mechanism is simple. Given an antibody vector **Ab** and an antigen vector **Ag**, the formula of the mutated antibody **Ab'** is:

$$\mathbf{Ab'} = \mathbf{Ab} + mi{\times}rand{\times}(\mathbf{Ag}{-}\mathbf{Ab}), \tag{1}$$

where *mi* is the mutation rate (initially set to 1) and *rand* is a random number uniformly generated between 0 and 1. Note that if *mi* and *rand* were set equal to 1, the new antibody would be exactly the same as **Ag**.

The cloning procedure uses the same equation. Each clone is nothing more than a mutated copy of its parental antibody. As many antigens can stimulate the cloning of a single antibody, we chose the first of the presented stimulating antigens to be the cloning target. An important observation here is that the cloning must occur for the parental antibody before it has been mutated. A copy of it is taken before Step 2.1 and this copy is then used in the cloning. The reason for this peculiarity is that if the antibody is mutated in the direction of the stimulating antigen, the distance between them may become very small. As a consequence, if the cloning is applied after this mutation, the resulting clone would be almost the same of its parent, and no diversity would be generated.

2.2 Partition Criterion

The separation of the data into clusters is performed indirectly by cutting the edges of the MST applied to the resultant network of antibodies. Each resulting subgraph corresponds to a cluster. To perform this task, a number of different criteria can be applied. The most direct and simplest approach is to remove the longest edges of the tree. However, it has been shown in [1] that this methodology completely neglects any information regarding density distribution, and fails to achieve good performance even in very simple problems.

A much more effective option is to adopt the elaborate criterion proposed by Zahn (1971) [11], which evaluates each edge based on the local density information (detailed information about this criterion can be found in [1]). An edge is cut if it is considerably longer than its immediate neighbors, rather than if it is long in relation to the whole tree. Using this information it is possible to detect clusters with arbitrary shape and size, what represents a great advantage over most common techniques. Zahn's criterion have been adopted in [1] with aiNet and in [6] with RABNET, both with successful results.

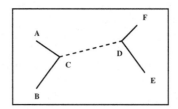

Fig. 1. Illustrative example of the criterion used for cutting the edges of the MST. When edge $\overline{CD}$ is being evaluated, the shortest of its immediate neighbors $\overline{AC}$, $\overline{BC}$, $\overline{DE}$ and $\overline{DF}$ is taken (in this case, $\overline{DF}$). For parameter $n = 2$, if $\overline{CD}$ is at least two times longer than $\overline{DF}$, $\overline{CD}$ must be removed from the tree. This is the case in this example, and the criterion yields two clusters: (A, B, C) and (D, E, F).

We have chosen to use here a simplified version of Zahn's criterion. An edge will be removed from the tree if it is at least n times longer than the shorter of its immediate neighbor edges. Fig. 1 illustrates how the criterion works.

This is clearly an intuitive measure, and follows the way human beings identify clusters in two or three dimensions [5]. The density information is represented by the length of the edges of the tree: high density clusters will have short edges connecting its points and low density clusters, large edges. As can be noted, the main idea remains the same as the original Zahn's proposal, but now we need only one parameter, n, rather than three, as described in [1]. An interesting value for n is about 2. It is worth reducing this value if no cluster can be found for a given data set even if no compression is performed.

3   Assessing Density Preservation

When information reduction is performed, the compact representation produced will always distort the original information contained in the data set. If the clusters' boundaries are not too evident, this misrepresentation can eliminate the possibility of a proper partitioning. In this section we illustrate this problem, and show that if the density information present in the data is maximally preserved, this difficulty is alleviated and the clustering performance can be enhanced.

3.1   When Relative Distances Are Distorted

The aim of this analysis is to investigate the effect of data compression on clustering when the only relevant piece of information for a correct cluster separation is the density distribution. The data set to be examined is shown in Fig. 2 – there are two clusters with 150 points each, but one of them is twice as dense as the other. The clusters were generated with a uniform distribution. Note in the figure that the difficulty of the problem is that the region between the two clusters is too narrow.

Fig. 2. Two classes with 150 points each and with different densities

As discussed in Section 2.2, the partition criterion should be capable of capturing the necessary information for a correct clustering. Nevertheless, it is not recommended to apply the criterion directly on the raw data. The reason is that at close look the uniform distribution is not perfect, i.e., the distance between data points is not constant and the noisy local variations can make the MST to be cut in several points – that is why the information reduction is needed.

We now compare the performance of ARIA and the aiNet algorithm to solve the problem. ARIA was run with parameters *gen* = 40, *decay* = 0.8 and *r* = 0.05. The compression rate obtained was 93.33%. Fig. 3a shows the final positioning of the prototypes after network convergence. Observe that the number of prototypes is approximately the same for each class. This is exactly what was expected, as the number of points for each class is also the same.

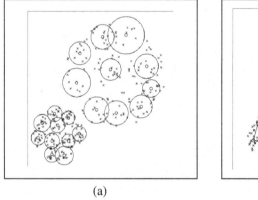 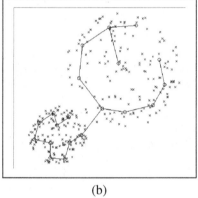

(a)   (b)

Fig. 3. ARIA results. (a) Prototype positioning after network convergence. (b) MST built on the prototypes. Circles correspond to the suppression radius of the antibodies.

Two points deserve comments here. Firstly, the reader should note that the degree of representation of each antibody tends to be uniform, that is, each antibody recognizes approximately the same number of antigens, albeit the individual recognition area (or hypervolume for an *n*-dimensional case) is different. Secondly, the relative distances are conserved after compression. This can be observed in the MST shown in Fig. 3b. The edge of the tree making the bridge between the two classes has more than two times the length of its left side neighbor. As a consequence, this edge is removed by the partition criterion and the clusters are correctly identified.

In order to make a fair comparison with aiNet, the parameters of the algorithm were setup in a manner that the compression rate was approximately the same. This was achieved by setting the suppression threshold (σ_s) – the aiNet parameter responsible for the resolution level – to 0.1. The final positioning of the antibodies is displayed in Fig. 4a. The overall compression rate obtained was 93%.

The difference between the two approaches becomes evident when analyzing Figs. 3 and 4. In the aiNet prototypes positioning, the relative density is neglected. Note in Fig. 4a that the distance between antibodies is practically the same, no matter which cluster they are representing. Also, the number of prototypes per cluster does not reflect the relative number of data points. As a consequence, all the edges of the MST have approximately the same length (see Fig. 4b) and it becomes impossible for the partition criterion to detect the existence of two classes under these circumstances.

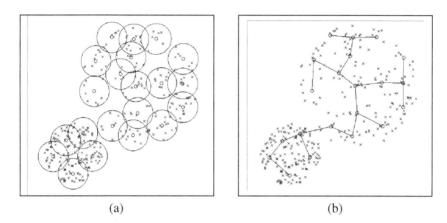

(a)   (b)

Fig. 4. aiNet results. (a) prototype positioning after network convergence. (b) MST built on the prototypes. Circles correspond to the suppression threshold of the antibodies.

3.2 Clusters with Fuzzy Boundaries

The next case study evaluates the influence of noise between the boundaries of two clusters, that is, when the frontier of the classes is not well defined. We propose a data set of two clusters generated by a normal distribution with a fixed variance – each class possesses exactly 200 points. The clusters are considerably far from each other; however, their boundaries are not well defined and overlap slightly. (Fig. 5.)

ARIA was run on this problem with parameters *gen* = 40, *decay* = 0.8 and *r* = 0.05. Fig. 6a demonstrates the state of the network after convergence and Fig. 6b shows the MST obtained. The compression rate achieved was 96%. Notice that, again, the edge connecting the classes is more than two times longer than each of its immediate neighbors, satisfying the condition for the partition criterion to detect both clusters.

For aiNet, the value used for σ_s was 0.11. Figs. 7a and 7b show the antibodies final position and the MST obtained, respectively. The compression rate was 96.25%.

Note in Fig. 7 that the aiNet prototypes hide the existence of an (almost) empty space between the clusters. This becomes clearer when analyzing the MST: all edges of the tree have similar length, even the one that is connecting the clusters. The problem is that aiNet antibodies cover a lot of unnecessary 'noise' points in the boundary of the clusters. As there are data points in the 'fuzzy' region separating the two classes, the antibodies are attracted to that region, no matter how sparse this region is in relation to other locations.

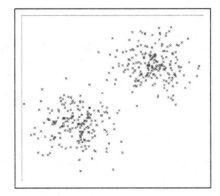

Fig. 5. Two classes with 200 points each, generated by a same normal distribution

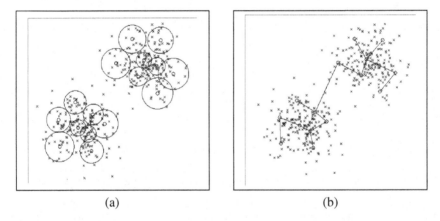

(a)   (b)

Fig. 6. ARIA results. (a) Prototype final position after network convergence. (b) MST built on the prototypes. Circles correspond to the suppression radius of the antibodies.

But what happens with ARIA? Why does it seem that the antibodies are not attracted to the sparse region, although there are antigens at that location? Actually, the antibodies do feel attracted to that region, indeed. Nevertheless, their radii tend to be large enough to enclose other antibodies with smaller radius, and these, in turn, will be pruned from the network. As smaller antibodies have survival priority over the larger ones, those prototypes located in the sparse regions are suppressed. To illustrate this situation, Fig. 8a shows the state of the network captured just before the suppression phase. Fig. 8b demonstrates what happens to the network after suppression. (The pictures were taken still at the beginning of the training process.)

As can be seen, ARIA misrepresents the sparse regions and concentrates its resources in representing the denser portions of the space. By doing that, the noise present in the data, if not in huge concentrations, is the first thing to be eliminated in the compact representation. The density preservation trait of the algorithm provides a higher noise tolerance than it would be expected for conventional algorithms.

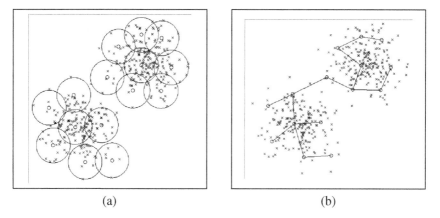

(a)   (b)

Fig. 7. aiNet results. (a) Prototype positioning after network convergence. (b) MST built on the prototypes. Circles correspond to the suppression threshold of the antibodies.

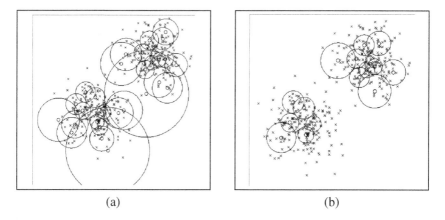

(a)   (b)

Fig. 8. Removal of greedy antibodies by the suppression phase. (a) Greedy antibodies with larger radius enclose a smaller amount of antibodies. (b) After suppression, the antibodies with larger radius are removed, because of the survival priority given to the ones with smaller radius.

4 Realistic Scenarios

In this section, we assess the performance of ARIA when applied to more complex problems and again we compare the results with aiNet. Two problems are analyzed here. The first one consists of a synthetic data set with five classes presenting fuzzy boundaries. The second one is a bioinformatics problem, consisting of two clusters of the yeast gene expression data.

4.1 Ellipses Problem

The ellipses data set consists of five classes with 300 points each. The disposition of the data points is shown in Fig. 9. Each class was generated with a different Gaussian distribution with varied principal components. The classes are located relatively close to each other, and their boundaries are not clearly defined and also overlap. All these properties make this problem an interesting challenge for data compression-based clustering algorithms. This data set is similar to that presented in [3], originally proposed for supervised data analysis.

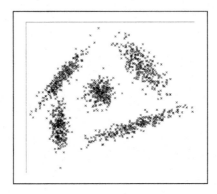

Fig. 9. Ellipses data set. Five classes with 300 points each generated with different normal distributions.

To solve this problem, ARIA parameters were set to *gen* = 40, *decay* = 0.8 and *r* = 0.025. The algorithm was executed 20 times, obtaining an average compression rate of 97.8%. For this level of resolution, aiNet was incapable of finding clusters. However, for a compression rate of 92.3% (and σ_s set to 0.03) the algorithm achieved a reasonable performance. Table 2 depicts the results obtained for both algorithms after 20 runs.

Table 2. Performance of ARIA and aiNet for the ellipses problem. The values show the average percentage of the number of cluters found after 20 runs for both algorithms.

nº of clusters	ARIA	aiNet
2	0 %	5 %
3	0 %	35 %
4	40 %	50 %
5	60 %	10 %

Table 2 indicates that ARIA was more efficient in identifying the clusters, achieving 60% of correct partitioning, against 10% of aiNet, while using 70% less antibodies on average. Fig. 10 compares an instance of the final prototype positioning of ARIA and aiNet after network convergence.

Notice in the figure that the boundaries of the clusters are misrepresented in the ARIA representation, while their core is maintained. This enhances the capability of the partition criterion in identifying clusters. Note also that the same does not happen to aiNet. As the boundaries of the clusters are also covered by antibodies, the classes come about to merge in some points and the MST cannot identify part of the cluster divisions.

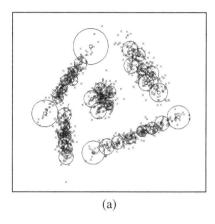 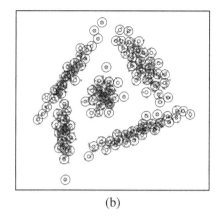

(a)   (b)

Fig. 10. (a) Example of the final representation of ARIA. (b) Example of the final representation of aiNet.

4.2 Yeast Expression Data

Gene expression data clustering is a classic bioinformatics problem [4]. Expression data are used to be extremely noisy and to present high dimensionalities, imposing a very difficult scenario for clustering algorithms. In this analysis we evaluate the performance of the algorithms when applied to the gene expression data of the budding yeast *Saccharomyces cerevisiae*. The data set consisting of 38 genes and 79 attributes has two clusters: B (11 functionally related genes involved in spindle pole body assembly and function) and C (with 27 proteasome genes). These clusters were previously labeled in [4]. They are part of a 2467 yeast genes and are considered a benchmark in the bioinformatics community.

In a first experiment, both algorithms were incapable of solving the problem. They found no clusters even for the least parsimonious representations, meaning that the partition criterion was not sensitive enough with $n = 2$. When reducing n to 1.5, however, the problem became somewhat easy for both techniques. They were capable of correctly separating the clusters for a variety of parameter combinations.

This scenario is drastically changed if some non-functionally related genes are introduced in the data set. Five yeast genes (of the 2467) presenting intermediary behavior relative to both clusters were used for this purpose (this is easy, given the gene ordering proposed in [4]). These genes can make the boundary between clusters B and C become fuzzy, thus increasing the difficulty of the problem.

Table 3. Performance of ARIA and aiNet for the yeast problem. The values show the average percentage of the number of clusters found after 20 runs for both algorithms.

n° of clusters	ARIA	aiNet
1	35 %	100 %
2	65 %	0 %

Running ARIA with parameters $gen = 40$, $decay = 0.8$ and $r = 0.5$, the problem can still be solved, with an average compression of 88.4%. For aiNet several parameter combinations were tested, but the algorithm has revealed to be incapable of finding the clusters. Table 3 summarizes the results obtained.

These results confirm the conclusion reached in Section 2.2. By assigning a large radius for antibodies belonging to sparse regions and consequently removing them from the network, ARIA is capable of reducing the undesired noise from the data, thus increasing the existent gap between the represented clusters.

5 Discussion and Future Work

This paper assesses the importance of the preservation of the density information for a clustering task when generating a compact representation of data. Conventional data compression algorithms tend to misrepresent the density information present in the original data, distorting the relative densities of the points intra- and inter-clusters. It is shown here that this deformation can drastically degrade the clustering results in several situations, and this is illustrated with the use of the aiNet algorithm.

In order to cope with this problem, we proposed the ARIA, which implements an adaptive antibody radius that is capable of capturing the relative density information, thus making it possible to preserve relative distances after compression. It is demonstrated that this adaptation capability provides the algorithm with a high noise tolerance and a superior performance considering artificial and real data sets.

ARIA has only one important user-tuned parameter, r, which determines the level of resolution of the internal image produced by the algorithm. Different problems might require distinct resolutions, and it is the user's responsibility to determine an appropriate value for this parameter. Although this might look as a deficiency of the algorithm, all other data compression techniques have an equivalent parameter, and the adequate value to be used in each problem also remains an open question.

As ARIA relies on the density information to construct its simplified representation, it is possible to make use of the data density distribution to automatically set an initial value to r. Although, this kind of information is hardly available, it is possible to estimate the density distribution of a data set using elaborate statistical techniques (like adaptive kernel methods [8]), which could serve as a suitable guess. Future work will thus concentrate in investigating statistical probability density estimation techniques and their applicability to the proposed intention. Success in this task implies turning ARIA into a completely automatic and user-independent technique. This would represent a remarkable advance regarding clustering techniques in general.

Acknowledgements

This work has been supported by grants from Fapesp, Capes, and CNPq.

References

1. Bezerra, G.B. & de Castro, L.N., "Bioinformatics Data Analysis Using an Artificial Immune Network", *Lecture Notes in Computer Sciences, Proc. of Second International Conference on Artificial Immune Systems, ICARIS 2003*, pp. 22-33, Edinburgh, UK, 2003.
2. de Castro, L. N. & Von Zuben, F. J., "aiNet: An artificial Immune Network for Data Analysis", In *Data Mining: A Heuristic Approach*, H. A. Abbass, R. A. Saker, and C. S. Newton (Eds.), Idea Group Publishing, USA, Chapter XII, pp. 231-259, 2001.
3. De Stefano, C., D'Elia, C. & Marcelly, A., "A Dynamic Approach to Learning Quantization", *Proc. Of the 17th International Conference on Pattern Recognition*, pp. 601- 604 Vol.4 2004.
4. Eisen, M.B., Spellman, P.T., Brow, P.O., & Botstein, D., "Cluster Analysis and Display of Genome-wide Expression Patterns", *Proc. Natl. Acad. Sci*, vol.95, pp. 14863-14868, USA, 1998.
5. Everitt, B., Landau, S. and Leese, M., *Cluster Analysis*, Fourth Edition, Oxford University Press, 2001.
6. Knidel, H., de Castro, L.N. & Von Zuben, F.J., Data Clustering with a Neuro-immune Network., International Conference on Natural Computation, China, 2005. (to be published)
7. Kohonen, T., *Self-Organizing Maps*, Springer Series in Information Sciences, Springer Verlag, 2001.
8. Silverman, B.W., *Density estimation for statistics and data analysis*, Champan and Hall, London, England, 1986.
9. Timmis, J. & Neal, M., "A resource Limited Artificial Immune System for Data Analysis", *Knowledge Based Systems*, 14(3-4):121-130, 2001.
10. Ultsch, A, "U*-Matrix: a Tool to Visualize Clusters in High Dimensional Data", in Technical Report No. 36, Department of Mathematics and Computer Science Philipps-University Marburg, 2003.
11. Zahn, C. T., "Graph-Theoretical Methods for Detecting and Describing Gestalt Clusters", *IEEE Trans. on Computers*, C-20(1), pp.68-86, 1971.

Quantum-Inspired Immune Clonal Algorithm

Yangyang Li and Licheng Jiao

Institute of Intelligent Information Processing, Xidian University, Xi'an 710071, China
lyy_791@yahoo.com.cn, lchjiao@mail.xidian.edu.cn

Abstract. This paper proposes a new immune clonal algorithm, called a quantum-inspired immune clonal algorithm (QICA), which is based on the concept and principles of quantum computing, such as a quantum bit and superposition of states. Like other evolutionary algorithms, QICA is also characterized by the representation of the individual, the evaluation function, and the population dynamics. QICA uses a quantum bit, defined as the smallest unit of information, for the probabilistic representation and a quantum bit individual as a string of quantum bits. In QICA, by quantum mutation operator, we can make full use of the information of the current best individual to perform the next search for speeding up the convergence. Information among the subpopulation is exchanged by adopting the quantum crossover operator for improvement of diversity of the population and avoiding prematurity. We execute the proposed algorithm to solve the benchmark problems with 30,100 and 2000 dimensions and very large numbers of local minima. The result shows that the proposed algorithm can close-to-optimal solution by the less computational cost.

1 Introduction

In the last few years we could perceive a great increase in interest in studying biologically inspired systems. Among these, we can emphasize artificial neural networks, evolutionary computation, DNA computation, and now artificial immune systems (AIS). The immune system is a complex of cells, molecules and organs which has proven to be capable of performing several tasks, like pattern recognition, learning, memory acquisition, generation of diversity, noise tolerance, generalization, distributed detection and optimization. Based on immunological principles, new computational techniques are being developed, aiming not only at a better understanding of the system, but also at solving engineering problems [1]-[5].

The clonal selection principle is the significant algorithm used by the immune system to describe the basic features of an immune response to an antigenic stimulus [4]. It establishes the idea that only those cells that recognize the antigens proliferate, thus being selected against those which do not. Immune clonal algorithm (ICA) [5] is principally a stochastic search and optimization method based on the clonal selection principle in AIS. Compared to traditional optimization methods, such as calculus-based and enumerative strategies, ICA are robust, global, and may be applied generally without recourse to domain-specific heuristics. In particular, ICA has the better ability of the local search. But with the scale of the problem increased, ICA did not solve effectively the complicated problem.

C. Jacob et al. (Eds.): ICARIS 2005, LNCS 3627, pp. 304–317, 2005.

We present a new algorithm, called a quantum-inspired immune clonal algorithm (QICA), which is based on merging quantum theory with immune clonal algorithm in AIS. There are three innovation points as follows based on previous ICA. Initially, individuals (antibodies) in a population are represented by quantum bits (qubits). The qubit individual has the advantage that it can represent a linear superposition of states (classical solutions) in search space probabilistically. As a result, the operation on a qubit chromosome is equivalent to that on several classical chromosomes simultaneously (namely the characteristic of quantum parallel). Secondly, for the novel representation, we put forward the quantum mutation operator which is used at the inner subpopulation to accelerate the convergence of ICA. Finally, information among the subpopulation is exchanged by adopting the quantum crossover operator for improvement of diversity of the population and avoiding prematurity. In this paper, the representation and immune genetic operation (namely quantum mutation and quantum crossover operators) are investigated to represent the antibodies effectively to explore the search space with the small number of antibodies (even with only one antibody for real-time application) and to exploit the global solution in the search space within a short span of time, respectively. To demonstrate its performance, experiments are carried out on Numerical Optimization and the convergence of the QICA is proved. The results show that QICA performs well—even with a small population—without premature convergence as compared to the other improved genetic algorithm.

The paper is organized as follows. Section 2 describes the theory of QICA. Section 3 contains the proof of convergence of QICA. Section 4 presents an application example with QICA and the improved genetic algorithm- OGA/Q [6] and BGA [7] for the numerical optimization problem, and summarizes the experimental results. Concluding remarks follow in Section 5.

2 Theory of QICA

Physics is the foundation of modern science and it gives a deeper understanding of nature. While digging into the evolution mechanism, people are also inspired by the idea of "simulating the matter". The two ideas learn from each other and produce many successful theories, such as the simulated annealing algorithm (SAA) who combines physics theory with an algorithm [8].

Quantum mechanics is one of the greatest achievements in the 20th century. Quantum information science is a result of merging physical science with information science. In the Quantum information theory, we must broaden our definition of information as merely a string of 0s and 1s and examine the consequence of the quantum nature of media for information, such as its uncertainty and entanglement of states [9]. It involves the study of Physics, Calculation, Communication, Mathematics etc; it also provides reliable physical base and new theory for the future development of information science.

Quantum computing is a research area that includes concepts like quantum mechanical computer (QC) and quantum algorithms. Although QC was shown to be more powerful than digital computers for solving various specialized problems, the QC hasn't walked out of laboratory for the difficulty of its physical realization up to now.

The researches on the combing of quantum mechanism with other classical methods focuses on two respects, one is designing more quantum algorithm in the classical computers [10]; the other is introducing the quantum idea into classical algorithms and modifying the conventional representation to get a better performance [11]. QICA is based on the latter consideration. Firstly we discuss the quantum chromosome.

2.1 Quantum Bit

The smallest unit of information stored in a two-state QC is called a quantum bit or qubit [9]. A qubit may be in the '1'state, signed as the state vector $|1\rangle$, in the '0' state, signed as the state vector $|0\rangle$, or in any superposition of the above two. This state of a qubit can be represent as: $|\varphi\rangle = \alpha|0\rangle + \beta|1\rangle$, where α and β are complex numbers that specify the probability amplitudes of the corresponding states, satisfying $|\alpha|^2 + |\beta|^2 = 1$. $|\alpha|^2$ gives the probability that the qubit will be found in the '0' state and $|\beta|^2$ gives the probability that the qubit will be found in the '1' state.. In other words, $|\varphi\rangle$ is a unit vector in two-dimensional complex vector space for which a particular basis has been fixed. One of the simplest physical examples of a qubit is the spin 1 2 of an electron. The spin-up and spin-down states of an electron can be taken as the states $|0\rangle$, $|1\rangle$ of a qubit. The state of a qubit can be changed by the operation with a quantum gate. A quantum gate is a reversible gate and can be represented as a unitary operator U acting on the qubit basis states satisfying $U^+U = UU^+$, where U^+ is the hermitian adjoint of U. There are several quantum gates, such as the NOT gate, controlled NOT gate, rotation gate, Hadamard gate, etc. [9]. If there is a system of n-qubits, the system can represent 2^n state at the same time, and therefore quantum computers were shown to be more powerful parallel than classical computers on various specialized problems. However, in the acting of observing a quantum state, it collapses to a single state. But if there is no quantum algorithm that solves practical problems, quantum computer hardware may be useless [12]. It could be considered as a computer without operating system [13]. In this paper, QICA can imitate parallel computation in a digital computer.

2.2 The Coding of Quantum Chromosome

In AIS, we encode the solution as different representations the same as that in evolutionary computation. The classical representation can be broadly classified as binary, numeric, and symbolic. QICA use a novel representation, for the probabilistic representation that is based on the concept of qubits, and a qubit antibody as a string of qubits. One qubit is defined with a pair of complex numbers (α , β), where $|\alpha|^2 + |\beta|^2 = 1$. $|\alpha|^2$ gives the probability that the qubit will be found in the '0' state and $|\beta|^2$ gives the probability that the qubit will be found in the '1' state. A qubit may be in the '1' state, in the '0' state, or in a linear superposition of the two. An m-qubit antibody as a string of qubits is defined as:

$$\begin{pmatrix} \alpha_1 & \alpha_2 & \cdots & \alpha_m \\ \beta_1 & \beta_2 & \cdots & \beta_m \end{pmatrix}, \tag{1}$$

where $|\alpha_i|^2 + |\beta_i|^2 = 1 (i = 1, 2, ..., m)$. This presentation has the advantage of representing any superposition of states. For example, if there is a three-qubit system with three pairs of complex numbers such as:

$$\begin{pmatrix} \dfrac{1}{\sqrt{2}} & 1 & \dfrac{1}{2} \\ \dfrac{1}{\sqrt{2}} & 0 & \dfrac{\sqrt{3}}{2} \end{pmatrix}, \tag{2}$$

the states of the system can be represent as:

$$\frac{1}{2\sqrt{2}}|000\rangle + \frac{\sqrt{3}}{2\sqrt{2}}|001\rangle + \frac{1}{2\sqrt{2}}|100\rangle + \frac{\sqrt{3}}{2\sqrt{2}}|101\rangle. \tag{3}$$

The above result means that the probabilities to represent the states $|000\rangle, |001\rangle, |100\rangle$ and $|101\rangle$ are $\dfrac{1}{8}, \dfrac{3}{8}, \dfrac{1}{8}$ and $\dfrac{3}{8}$, respectively. By consequence, the three-qubit system of (2) contains the information of eight states.

Owing to its probability representation, QICA has a better characteristic of diversity than classical version, since it can represent linear superposition of states probabilistically. In the above example, one qubit chromosome is enough to represent four states, but in the classical representation, at least four chromosomes (called on also classical chromosome) (000), (001), (100), and (101) are need.

2.3 Immune Clonal Algorithm

Clonal Selection Theory is put forward by Burnet in 1958 [14]. Its main ideas lie in that the antigen can selectively react to the antibodies, which are native production and spread on the cell surface in the form of peptides. When exposed to antigen, the antigen stimulates an immune cell with appropriate receptors to proliferate (divide) and mature into terminal plasma cells. The process of cell division generates a clone, i.e., a set of cells that are the progenies of the single cell, in addition to proliferating into plasma cells; the immune cells can differentiate into long-lived memory cells. Memory cells circulate through the blood, lymph and tissues, and when exposed to a second antigenic stimulus commence to differentiate into large immune cells (lymphocyte) capable of producing high affinity antibody pre-selected for the specific antigen that had stimulated the primary response. Based on the clonal selection theory, Immune Clonal algorithm (ICA) is proposed [5]. The used ICA in this paper is an antibody random map induced by the avidity including: clone operation, immune genetic operation and clonal selection operation. The state transfer of antibody population is denoted as follows:

$$C : A(k) \xrightarrow{clone \quad operation} A'(k) \xrightarrow{immune \quad genetic \quad operation} A''(k) \xrightarrow{selection \quad operation} A(k+1).$$

Here $A(k)$ is antibody population based on classical chromosome at k-th genera-tion. Antibody, antigen, avidity between antibody and antigen are similar to the defi-nitions of the possible solution, the objective function (and restrictive condition), the fitness between solution and the objective function in the artificial immune system (AIS), respectively. According to the avidity function, a point $a_i(k)$ which represents antibody i in antibody population $A(k)$, in the solution space will be divided into c_i same points $a_i'(k) \in A'(k)$, by using clone operation. A new antibody population $A(k+1)$ is attained after performing the immune genetic operation which can include mutation and crossover operator and the clonal selection operation. In this paper, the avidity function is defined as the objective function $f(*)$. It can be found out that ICA obtains good local searching ability at a cost of adding the scale of the population (namely clone operation). As a result, we adopt quantum bit representation which has powerful parallel in order to speed up the convergence of ICA. We present the pro-posed algorithm in the following.

2.4 The Quantum-Inspired Immune Clonal Algorithm

In Fig 1, we describe its critical steps in detail. We adopt quantum chromosome as the representation of antibody, where $Q(t)$, $P(t)$, $f(*)$ and $B(t)$ mean the antibody popula-tion based on quantum chromosome at the t-th generation , the antibody population based on classical chromosome, the objective function, and the best solutions at the t-th generation, respectively.

Algorithm1: The quantum-inspired immune clonal algorithm

Step1. Initial the quantum population $Q(t) = \{q_1, q_2, \cdots q_n\}, t = 0$.

Step2. Produce $P(t)$ by observing $Q(t)$.

Step3. Evaluate the avidity of $P(t)$ and store the best solutions among $P(t)$ into $B(t)$.

Step4. Judge the termination condition, if it is satisfied, then output the best solu-tion, and else continue.

Step5. Generate the next generation population $Q(t+1)$ from $Q(t)$ by the clonal operator Θ, the immune genetic operator and the clonal selection operator.

Step6. go to step2.

Fig. 1. The quantum-inspired immune clonal algorithm

The major elements of QICA are presented as follows.

The quantum population :

At the t-th generation it has a quantum population $Q(t) = \{q'_1, q'_2, \cdots q'_n\}$, where n is the size of population, and m is the length of the chromosome q'_j which is defined as:

$$q'_j = \left\{ \begin{matrix} \alpha'_1 & \alpha'_2 & \cdots & \alpha'_m \\ \beta'_1 & \beta'_2 & \cdots & \beta'_m \end{matrix} \right\}, j = 1, 2, \ldots, n \quad . \quad \text{In } step1 \text{ all } \alpha'_i \text{ and } \beta'_i \text{ of } q'_j \ ($$

$i = 1, 2, \ldots, m; t = 0$) are randomly generated between 0 and 1.

Observing operator:

In *Step2*, we observe $Q(t)$ and produce binary stings $P(t) = \{x_1^t, x_2^t, ..., x_n^t\}$, where each x_j^t (j=1,...,n) is a binary string of length m which derives from $|\alpha_i^t|^2$ or $|\beta_i^t|^2$ (i=1,..,m). The process is: generate a random number $p \in [0,1]$. If it is larger than $|\alpha_i^t|^2$, the corresponding bit in $P(t)$ takes '1', else takes '0'.

Clonal operator:

The clonal operator Θ is defined as:

$$\Theta(Q(t)) = [\Theta(q_1) \quad \Theta(q_2) \quad \cdots \quad \Theta(q_n)]^T, \tag{4}$$

where $\Theta(q_i) = I_i \times q_i, i = 1, 2 \cdots n$, and I_i is C_i dimension row vectors. Generally, C_i is given by:

$$C_i = Int\left(N_c * \frac{f(q_i)}{\sum_{j=1}^{n} f(q_j)} \right) \quad i = 1, 2 \cdots n \tag{5}$$

N_c is a given value relating to the clone scale, which can be adjusted self-adaptively by the avidity. *Int(x)* rounds the elements of x to the least integer bigger than or equal to x. After clone, the population becomes:

$$Q'(t) = \{Q(t), q'_{1,} \cdots q'_n\}, \tag{6}$$

where:

$$q'_i(t) = \{q_{i1}(t), q_{i2}(t), \cdots, q_{iC_i-1}(t)\}, q_{ij}(t) = q_i(t) \; j = 1, 2, \cdots, C_i - 1. \tag{7}$$

Immune gene operator:

We adopt quantum mutation and quantum crossover operation as the immune genetic operator. Quantum mutation is used firstly at the inner subpopulation, and information among the subpopulation is exchanged by adopting the quantum crossover operator.

Quantum mutation

In the following, we give a simple mutation method to evolve the chromosome. It deduces a probability distribution in terms of the current best antibody. It is also much simpler, whose process is: define a guide quantum chromosome from the current best antibody which is stored in $B(t)$ and spread the mutated quantum bit antibody subpopulation with this guide chromosome being the center. It can be written as:

$$Q_{guide}(t) = \alpha \times P_{currentbest}(t) + (1-a) \times (1 - P_{currentbest}(t)), \tag{8}$$

$$q_i"(t) = Q_{guide}(t) + b \times normrnd(0,1), \quad (i = 1, 2, ..., n), \tag{9}$$

Where $P_{currentbest}(t)$, Q_{guide} and $normrnd(0,1)$ are the current best antibody based on classical chromosome, the guide quantum chromosome at the t-th generation and the normal distribution with mean 0 and standard deviation 1, respectively. $q_i''(t)$ is the mutated quantum bit subpopulation; a is the guide factor of Q_{guide} ; b is the spread variance. For easy to comprehend, an example is given. Obviously, we only need to let $q'' = (0\ 0\ 1\ 1\ 0)$ to get $P = (1\ 1\ 0\ 0\ 1)$ with probability 1, i.e., $q'' = \overline{P}$. If P is the optimum, the probability of getting the optimum becomes larger with a becoming smaller. When $a=0, Q_{guide} = \overline{P}$, one will get P with probability 1 after observing Q_{guide} . Often we let $a \in [0.1, 0.5]$, $b \in [0.05, 0.15]$.

Quantum crossover

The common crossover operator is limit to between two individuals. By using quantum theory (namely interference characteristic), the quantum crossover– All Interference Crossover [15] is used in this paper. All the antibodies of population are involved in the crossover operation, so the algorithm has better diversity of the population. Let the population size is 5, and the chromosome length is 8 described as the following Table 1 in detail:

Interference Crossover occurs as follows: take the 1st element of chromosome 1, take the 2nd element of chromosome 2, take 3rd element of chromosome 3, take the 4th element of chromosome 4, etc.

Table 1.

No.	Chromosome (before)							
1	A(1)	E(2)	D(3)	C(4)	B(5)	A(6)	E(7)	D(8)
2	B(1)	A(2)	E(3)	D(4)	C(5)	B(6)	A(7)	E(8)
3	C(1)	B(2)	A(3)	E(4)	D(5)	C(6)	B(7)	A(8)
4	D(1)	C(2)	B(3)	A(4)	E(5)	D(6)	C(7)	B(8)
5	E(1)	D(2)	C(3)	B(4)	A(5)	E(6)	D(7)	C(8)

Table 2.

No.	Generated Chromosome (after)							
1	A(1)	A(2)	A(3)	A(4)	A(5)	A(6)	A(7)	A(8)
2	B(1)	B(2)	B(3)	B(4)	B(5)	B(6)	B(7)	B(8)
3	C(1)	C(2)	C(3)	C(4)	C(5)	C(6)	C(7)	C(8)
4	D(1)	D(2)	D(3)	D(4)	D(5)	D(6)	D(7)	D(8)
5	E(1)	E(2)	E(3)	E(4)	E(5)	E(6)	E(7)	E(8)

As a summary, the quantum mutation can guide the quantum chromosome in the subpopulation to evolve to a better antibody with a larger probability. By using the evolutionary theory, the crossover operator is adopted [16] and the quantum crossover can bring more diverse antibodies among subpopulation and avoids prematurity.

After quantum crossover operation, the new population is shown as the following Table 2:

Clonal Selection Operator:
The operation as follows, if we will search minimal value of object function:

For $\forall i = 1, 2, \cdots n$,   if   there   is   crossed   antibody b
$f(b) = \min\{f(p"_{ij}) \mid j = 2, 3, \cdots C_i - 1\}$, namely: $f(p"_i) > f(b),\ i = 1, 2, \cdots C_{i-1}$.

Then b replaces the antibody individual $p"_i$ in the aboriginal population. And quantum chromosome representation of the antibody b is noted as the next quantum chromosome in $Q(t+1)$. The antibody population is updated, and the information exchanging among the antibody population is realized.

The termination condition:
It is defined as:

$$\left| f^* - f^{best} \right| < \varepsilon, \tag{10}$$

where f^* is the optimum value of object function in theory, f^{best} is best value of object function among the current generation and ε is the acceptable error. The termination condition in this paper is synthesis of formula (10) and the maximum number of generation.

3   Convergence of the Algorithm

Definition 3.1. Let $X(t) = (x_1(t), x_2(t), \cdots, x_n(t))$ in S^n be the population at time t and for $X(t)$, defined:

$$M = \{\bar{X} \mid f(\bar{X}) = \max\{f(X_i(t)), i \leq n\}\}, \tag{11}$$

$$M^* = \{\bar{X} \mid f(\bar{X}) = \max\{f(X), X \in S^n\}\}. \tag{12}$$

M is called the satisfied set of population X_t and M^* is defined as the global satisfied set of state S^n.

Definition 3.2. Supposes arbitrary initial distribution, the following equation satisfies:

$$\lim_{t \to \infty} P\{M \subseteq M^*\} = 1 \cdot \tag{13}$$

Then we call the algorithm is convergent.

Theorem 3.1. The population series of QICA $\{Q_t, t \geq 0\}$ is finite homogeneous Markov chain.

Proof: Like the evolutionary algorithms, the state transfer of QICA are processed on the finite space, therefore, population is finite, since

$$Q(t+1) = T(Q(t)) = T_s \circ T_g \circ \Theta(Q(t)). \tag{14}$$

T_s, T_g and Θ indicate the clonal selection operator, the immune genetic operator and the clone operator respectively. Note that T_s, T_g and Θ have no relation with t, so $Q(t+1)$ only relates with $Q(t)$ [16]. Namely, $\{Q_t, t \geq 0\}$ is finite homogeneous Markov chain.

Theorem 3.2. The M of Markov chain of QICA is monotone increasing, namely, $\forall t \geq 0, f(Q_{t+1}) \geq f(Q_t)$.

Proof: Apparently, the individual of QICA does not degenerate for our adopting holding best strategy in the algorithm.

Theorem 3.3. The quantum-inspired immune clonal algorithm is convergent.

Proof: For Theorem 3.1 and Theorem 3.2, the QICA is convergent with the probability 1.

4 Experiments

We execute the QICA to solve the following test functions:

$$f_1(x) = \sum_{i=1}^{m} x_i^2$$

$$f_2(x) = \sum_{i=1}^{m} |x_i| + \prod_{i=1}^{m} |x_i|$$

$$f_3(x) = \sum_{i=1}^{m} \left(\sum_{j=1}^{i} x_j \right)^2$$

$$f_4(x) = \sum_{i=1}^{m} i x_i^4 + random[0,1)$$

$$f_5(x) = \frac{1}{m} \sum_{i=1}^{m} (x_i^4 - 16 x_i^2 + 5 x_i)$$

$$f_6(x) = mA + \sum_{i=1}^{m} (x_i^2 - A\cos(2\pi x_i)),$$ where A is a given constant, in this paper

$A=10$.

$$f_7(x) = -\sum_{i=1}^{m} x_i \sin\left(\sqrt{|x_i|}\right)$$

$$f_8(x) = \sum_{i=1}^{m} \frac{x_i^2}{4000} - \prod_{i=1}^{m} \cos(\frac{x_i}{\sqrt{i}}) + 1$$

$$f_9(x) = -20\exp\left(-0.2\sqrt{\frac{1}{m}\sum_{i}^{m} x_i^2}\right) - \exp\left(\frac{1}{m}\sum_{i=1}^{m} \cos(2\pi x_i)\right) + 20 + \exp(1)$$

Table 3 lists the basic characteristics of these test functions.

Table 3. The basic characteristics of these test functions

The functions	Feasible solution space	The global optimum	Number of the **local** optimum
f_1	$[-100,100]^m$	0	NA
f_2	$[-10,10]^m$	0	NA
f_3	$[-100,100]^m$	0	NA
f_4	$[-1.28,1.28]^m$	0	NA
f_5	$[-5,5]^m$	-78.33236	2^m
f_6	$[-5.12,5.12]^m$	0	NA
f_7	$[-500,500]^m$	-12569.5	NA
f_8	$[-600,600]^m$	0	NA
f_9	$[-30,30]^m$	0	NA

In our study, we execute QICA to solve these test functions with the dimensions given in Table 4. The above test functions were examined by the OGA/Q in [6] and the OGA/Q outperforms the other algorithms. As a result, the existing results reported in [6] can be used for a direct comparison in Table 4.

The experiment results of QICA to optimize the function above are shown in Table 4, where F, m, E, and M(δ) are corresponding to the function above, the dimensions of the function, the mean number of function evaluations, the mean best solution (the standard deviation of best function value). ICA did not search the optimum of the above functions and we did not take it in this paper. For QICA, p_c=0.3, p_m=0.88. And because a quantum chromosome can represent several the classical chromosomes at the same time, the size of initial individual population is 5 and the clonal sizes N_c=10 in this article, where ε=10^{-3} and the maximum generation is 10^3.

We performed 50 independent runs for QICA on each test function and recorded: 1) the mean number of function evaluations, 2) the mean best solution (i.e., the mean of the function values found in the 50 runs), and 3) the standard deviation of best function value. We see that the mean function values are equal or close to the optimal ones, and the standard deviations of the function values are relatively small; hence it has a very stable quality of solution. And owing to the termination condition adopted in QICA, the precision of some outcome is poorer than that of OGA/Q, but the mean number of function evaluations of QICA is very small; hence it has a lower computational cost. The results show that QICA performs well even with a small population and QICA found the better solutions within the less the computational number compared to OGA/Q.

Table 4. The comparing results of QICA and OGA/Q for the function f_1-f_9

F	m	E		M(δ)	
		QICA	OGA/Q	**QICA**	OGA/Q
f_1	30	**1,238**	112,559	**8.646×10^{-4}** **(7.403×10^{-5})**	0 (0)
f_2	30	**1,304**	112,612	**1.926×10^{-10}** **(2.815×10^{-10})**	0 (0)
f_3	30	**1,236**	112,576	**3.581×10^{-10}** **(3.597×10^{-10})**	0 (0)
f_4	30	**1,244**	112,652	**5.6467×10^{-4}** **(1.7403×10^{-4})**	6.301×10^{-3} (4.069×10^{-4})
f_5	100	**1,752**	245,930	**-78.33145** **(2.339×10^{-4})**	-78.3000296 (6.288×10^{-3})
f_6	30	**1,395**	224,710	**5.481×10^{-10}** **(2.191×10^{-10})**	0 (0)
f_7	30	**2,083**	302,166	**-12569.4866** **(4.035×10^{-5})**	-12569.4537 (6.447×10^{-4})
f_8	30	**1,424**	134,000	**3.723×10^{-14}** **(3.716×10^{-14})**	0 (0)
f_9	30	**1,293**	112,421	**1.521×10^{-14}** **(2.323×10^{-14})**	4.440×10^{-16} (3.989×10^{-16})

The experiment results of QICA to optimize the function above whose dimensions are increased are shown in Table 5 and Table 6, where m, n and E mean the dimensions of the function, initial the population size of individual and the mean number of function evaluations, respectively. The BGA was executed to solve the test functions f_6–f_9, and the results were reported in [7]. We will use these existing results for a direct comparison in Table 5 and Table 6. '↗' denote that the BGA did not carry through the experiment in literature 7. The number of runs was 10; the clonal sizes $N_c=20$; ε is 10^{-5} and the other parameters for QICA are the same as the above.

Table 5. The comparing results of QICA and BGA for the function f_6 and f_7

		f_6					f_7	
m	n	E		m	n	E	
		QICA	BGA				QICA	BGA
100	20	4123	25040	100	20	12472	92000
200	20	6181	52948	200	20	15991	248000
400	20	13217	112634	400	20	24890	699803
1000	20	22410	337570	1000	20	41450	╱
2000	20	31269	╱	2000	20	65563	╱

Table 6. The comparing results of QICA and BGA for the function f_8 and f_9

		f_8					f_9	
m	n	E		m	n	E	
		QICA	BGA				QICA	BGA
100	20	6713	361722	100	20	5100	53860
200	20	7930	748300	200	20	8578	107800
400	20	15719	1630000	400	20	12971	220820
1000	20	26012	╱	1000	20	29940	548306
2000	20	41199	╱	2000	20	41748	╱

We can find that the mean number of function evaluations of BGA is rapidly increased with the dimensions expanded from the above two tables and the relation between those of QICA is approximate to linear from Fig.2. The results for QICA are very much more precise than[1] BGA but the computational cost of QICA is obviously less than that of BGA. And QICA can find the high quality solutions when the dimensions of these functions are 1000 or 2000. Hence the ability of QICA to optimize the high-dimension function outperforms BGA obviously.

---

[1] The acceptable error to the function 6-9 in BGA is 0.1, 10^{-4}, 10^{-3} and 10^{-3} respectively.

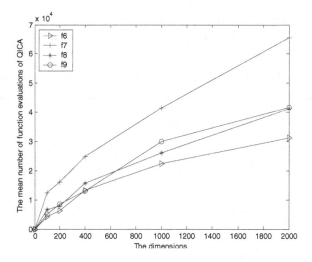

Fig. 2. The relation curve between the mean number of function evaluations and the dimensions of f_6 - f_9 for QICA

5   Conclusions

This paper proposed a novel QICA, inspired by the concept of quantum computing. Our objective was to apply the quantum theory to enhance the immune clonal algorithm, so that it could be more robust and statistically sound. In particular, a quantum bit antibody was defined as a string of quantum bits for the probabilistic representation. Due to the novel representation, we put forward the quantum mutation operator which is used at the inner subpopulation to accelerate the convergence of ICA. Information among the subpopulation is exchanged by adopting the quantum crossover operator for improvement of diversity of the population and avoiding prematurity. As a result, the proposed QICA has automatic balance ability between exploration and exploitation. We executed QICA to solve benchmark problems. The dimensions of these problems are 30, 100 or 2000 and some of them have numerous local minima. The results show that QICA can find optimal or close-to-optimal solutions. The application of QICA to application example such as the combinatorial optimization problems deserves our further research.

References

1. De Castro, L. N., Timmis, J.: Artificial Immune Systems: A New Computational Intelligence Approach. London, U.K.: Springer-Verlag (1996)
2. Dasgupta, D.: Artificial Immune Systems and Their Applications. Berlin, Germany: Springer-Verlag (1999)
3. Hofmeyr, S. A., Forrest, S.: Immunity by design: An artificial immune system. in Proc. Genetic and Evolutionary Computation Conf., July (1999) 1289–1296

4. De Castro, L. N., Von Zuben, F. J.: Artificial Immune Systems: Part I—Basic Theory and Applications. FEEC/Univ. Campinas, Campinas, Brazil. [Online]. Available: http://www.dca.fee.unicamp. br/~lnunes/immune.html (1999)

5. De Castro, L. N., Von Zuben, F. J.: Artificial Immune Systems: Part II—A Survey of Applications. FEEC/Univ. Campinas, Campinas, Brazil. [Online]. Available: http://www.dca.fee.unicamp.br/~lnunes/immune.html (2000)

6. Leung Y.W., Wang Y.P.: An Orthogonal Genetic Algorithm with Quantization for Global Numerical Optimization. IEEE Transactions on Evolutionary Computation, 5(1) (2001) 41-53

7. Heinz M., Dirk S.V.: Predictive Models for the Breeder Genetic Algorithm. Evolutionary Computation, 1(1) (1993) 25-49

8. Davis, T.E., Principe, J.C.: A simulated annealing like convergence theory for the simple genetic algorithm, in Proc.4th Conf.Gentic Algorithms, R.K.Belew and L.B.Booker, Eds., San Mateo,CA, (1991)

9. Hey, T.: Quantum computing: An introduction,in Computing & Control Engineering Journal. Piscataway, NJ: IEEE Press, Vol. 10, No. 3, June (1999) 105–112

10. Grover, L.K.: A framework for fast quantum mechanical algorithms, in Proceeding of the 30th Annual ACM Symposium on Theory of Computing ACM Press, New York (1998) 53-62

11. Altaisky, M.V.: Quantum neutral network, arXiv: quant-ph/0107012 v2 5 Jul (2001)

12. Yao, A.: Quantum circuit complexity. Proceedings of the 34th IEEE symposium on Foundations of computer science, (1993) 352-361

13. Aharonov, D., Kitaev, A., Nisan, N.: Quantum circuits with mixed states, LANL e-print quant-ph/ 9806029 (1998)

14. Burnet, F. M.: Clonal Selection and After .In Theoretical Immunology, Bell, G. I., Perelson, A. S., pimbley Jr, g. H.(eds.) Marcel Dekker Inc., (1978) 63-85

15. Narayanna, A., Moore, M.: Quantum-inspired genetic algorithms. In Proceedings of IEEE International Conference on Evolutional Evolution, (1996) 61-66

16. Liu, R.C., Du, H.F., Jiao, L.C.: Immunity Poly-Clonal Strategies. Journal of Computer Research and Development, Vol. 41, No. 4, (2004) 571-576

A Markov Chain Model of the B-Cell Algorithm

Edward Clark[1], Andrew Hone[2], and Jon Timmis[3]

[1] Computing Laboratory, University of Kent, Canterbury CT2 7NF, UK
ebc3@kent.ac.uk
[2] Institute of Mathematics, Statistics & Actuarial Science, University of Kent
anwh@kent.ac.uk
[3] Departments of Electronics and Computer Science, University of York,
Heslington, York. YO10 5DD
jt517@ohm.york.ac.uk

Abstract. An exact Markov chain model of the B-cell algorithm (BCA) is constructed via a novel possible transit method. The model is used to formulate a proof that the BCA is convergent absolute under a very broad set of conditions. Results from a simple numerical example are presented, we use this to demonstrate how the model can be applied to increase understanding of the performance of the BCA in optimizing function landscapes as well as giving insight into the optimal parameter settings for the BCA.

1 Introduction

Whilst there have been successes in the development of AIS (Artificial Immune Systems) [13] to date, there has been limited work on more theoretical aspects. For example, in terms of convergence proofs only one paper [7] presents a complete proof of convergence for a specific multi-objective clonal selection algorithm using Markov chains. As pointed out by Hone and Kelsey [4] a useful avenue to explore would be into the dynamics of immune algorithms based on nonlinear dynamical systems inspired by biological models [5], and stochastic differential equations [15]. Given the use of clonal selection based algorithms within AIS, the community could benefit a great deal from further theoretical investigations, such as the exploration of the mutation operator, which could provide information for optimizing mutation rates for specific functions.

There are many clonal selection based algorithms in the literature, most of which have focused on developing optimisation approaches, such as the work by De Castro and Von Zuben on CLONALG [12], the work by Nicosia et al. [14] and the work by Kelsey et al [1,2]. From a computational perspective, the clonal selection idea leads to algorithms that evolve (through a cloning, mutation and selection phase) candidate solutions to a given problem.

Taking the challenge from [4] we have developed an exact[1] stochastic model of the B-cell algorithm (BCA) [1,2], based on a single member population using elitism. In

---

[1] Exact: meaning the parts of the algorithm that were modeled were modeled exactly with no simplifying assumptions or approximations.

C. Jacob et al. (Eds.): ICARIS 2005, LNCS 3627, pp. 318–330, 2005.

the case where the BCA has a clonal pool size of one, it can also be considered complete[2]. In line with [7] we adopted the use of a Markov chain. We have chosen to develop the theoretical basis for the BCA due to the simple nature of the algorithm. The simplicity comes from that fact that within the BCA, although a population of B-cells (candidate solutions) are evolved, they do not interact with each other i.e. each member of the population is unaware of the existence of any other member. Therefore, multiple member populations can be treated as independent; hence the results of the single member model can be re-applied using basic probability theory to populations of multiple members. This allows us to simplify the mathematical model of the BCA. It should be noted, that we have developed the underlying theory of the BCA independent of implementing the algorithm. This methodology removes the chance of accidentally back fitting the predictions of the theory to the algorithm.

In some algorithms, simple GAs (Genetic Algorithms) for example, having large population or clonal pool sizes causes coupling which produces a positive effect on the search mechanism. However, based on thought experiments, we expect that coupling in the clonal pool can only have zero or negative effects on the BCA (in terms of performance vs. number of function evaluations). Thus we propose that the BCA, and consequently the model, should be restricted to a clonal pool of one, to remove the negative coupling effects.

Currently, the only way to model elitist immune algorithms has been through the maintenance of a separate elitist set of current best solutions as in [7]. However, we present a model that does not require the maintenance of such a separate set. We show that the BCA can be represented by a Markov chain via a novel construction of a "possible transit matrix". In order for us to present our proofs, it is necessary to define two new terms to articulate some issues more clearly. Therefore, we define the following:

Search space global optima (SSGO): A point in the search space is considered to be a global optimum if there is no other point with higher affinity (points with equal affinity are equally valid global optima). All functions have at least one SSGO as long as the search space is not the empty set.

Convergent Absolute: An algorithm can be said to be convergent absolute if and only if it can be shown to converge on the search space global optima with probability 1 from all points in the search space, for all functions, in any number of dimensions.

We would also like to point out that it is important to make a distinction between the true objective function space and the search space grid that is used to represent the objective function. The BCA, and consequently the theory, is only aware of the search space. We cannot therefore say anything about the position of an optimum in the function space without additional knowledge. For example, consider a function with a global optimum at some large value of x, but the search space being used is limited moderate values. The algorithm will converge on the SSGO with probability 1, which is the true optimum from the perspective of the BCA. The problem of defining an appropriate search space, grid size and refinement, although important, is a separate

---

[2] Complete: meaning all parts of the algorithm were taken into account and represented in the modelling process.

problem to that of determining the convergence properties of the algorithm. This paper is concerned only with the properties of convergence of the BCA on SSGO.

The major contributions of this paper are: introduction of a novel method for the construction of transition matrices for elitist algorithms; proof that the BCA is convergent absolute and an example of the numerical application of the novel method.

The remaining sections of the paper are structured as follows: section 2 provides a brief overview of the BCA algorithm, and relevant background material on Markov chains. This is then followed in section 3 with the presentation of a mathematical model of the BCA. Here we present a model of the mutation function employed within the BCA, and demonstrate how it is possible to construct a transition matrix of the algorithm and present the theory to demonstrate that the BCA is convergent absolute. This is then followed by a demonstration of the numerical application of the model. We then conclude with comments regarding the application of our theory and future work.

2 Background Material

As mentioned above, the B-cell algorithm (BCA) is based purely on clonal selection and mutation mechanisms, without any interaction between the different members of the cell populations. For algorithms such as the BCA, if the state of the cell population at time t is specified, then the subsequent state at time $t+1$ is a random variable. Moreover, the changing behavior of the population with the time t (which varies in discrete steps $t \rightarrow t+1$) is naturally described in terms of a Markov chain (see [5, 6] for the relevant background material).

2.1 The B-Cell Algorithm

In this section, we present a brief overview of the B-cell algorithm (BCA) before we progress to the mathematical model and proofs in the following sections. The reader is directed to [1] for a full description of the algorithm. However, the BCA is outlined in pseudo-code here:

Step 1: Create an initial random population P of individuals.

Step 2: For each $\underline{v} \in P$, evaluate $g(\underline{v})$ and create a clone population C.

Step 3: Select a random member of $\underline{v}' \in C$ and apply the contiguous region hypermutation operator.

Step 4: Evaluate $g(\underline{v}')$; if $g(\underline{v}') > g(\underline{v})$ then replace $\underline{v}$ by clone $\underline{v}'$.
(The BCA in [1] is minimizing, but could just as easily be maximizing. We refer to it as minimizing/maximizing where appropriate for a given example and optimizing in general.)

Step 5: Repeat steps 2-4 until stopping criterion is met.

An important feature of the BCA is its use of a unique mutation operator, known as *contiguous somatic hypermutation* (also known as the *contiguous region hypermutation operator CRHO).* Evidence of an analogous biological mechanism in the immunological literature is sparse [3], however, the authors do argue that mutation occurs in *clusters* of regions within cells: this is broadly analogous to contiguous regions. The representation employed in the actual implementation of the BCA in [1] takes an *N*-dimensional vector of 64-bit strings, which represents bit-encoded double precision numbers. These vectors are considered to be the B-cells within the system. Each B-cell within the population is evaluated by the objective function, *g(x)*. More formally, the B-cells are defined as a vector $v \in P$ of bit strings of length $L = 64$ where P is the population of vectors (B-cells). However, it should be noted, that from a theoretical point of view, and the work concerned in this paper, *L* does not have to be restricted to 64 bits and can be generalized to any integer.

Empirical work presented in [1,2,4] indicates that an efficient population size for many functions is low, in contrast with genetic algorithms; a typical size would be #P $\in$ *[3 .. 5]*. For the purposes of our work, in order to simply the complexity of the mathematical model of the BCA, we consider a population size of 1. This is because population members do not interact, thus allowing us to calculate independent probabilities for each B-cell.

After evaluation by the objective function, a B-cell v is cloned to produce a *clonal pool, C*. It should be noted that there exists a clonal pool *C* for each B-cell within the population and also that all the adaptation (mutation) takes place within *C*. The size of *C* is typically the same size as the population *P* (but this does not have to be the case). In order to maintain diversity within the search, one clone is selected at random and each element in the vector is randomized. Each B-cell $v' \in C$ is then subjected to a novel contiguous somatic hypermutation mechanism (described below). The BCA typically uses a distance function as its stopping criterion: when it is within a certain prescribed distance from the optimum, the authors consider the algorithm to have converged. However, this is more of a stopping criterion than a statement that the algorithm has converged on the SSGO.

The unusual feature of the BCA is the form of the mutation operator. This operates by subjecting bits contained within a *contiguous* region of v' to mutation with probability *r* such that $0 \le r \le 1$. As shown in figure 1, the CRHO selects a random site (or *hotspot*) within v', along with a hotspot length of *L* (which is determined randomly and may be up to the full length of the vector); the vector is then subjected to mutation from the hotspot onwards for the length of the contiguous region. It is important to note that the mutation does not wrap around the vector.

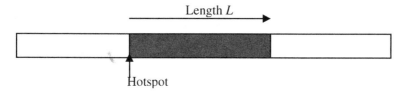

Fig. 1. Hypermutation operator within the BCA

2.2 Markov Chains

An important property of the B-cell algorithm from a modeling perspective is that it has a non-interacting population. A model for a population of one is completely general, as they can be scaled to a population of any size by using rules for independent probabilities. This greatly simplifies the modeling process.

For a maximization problem, we can represent the state of our system by a random variable X_t, which changes with the time t, and then the objective will be to maximize a given objective function $g(x)$. The state X_t corresponds to the value of the bit string corresponding to a cell. The aim of the algorithm is to find the state value x that maximizes the function $g(x)$, by making many iterations in time. At each time t, a clone is taken from the cell, hypermutation is applied to the clone, and if it happens that $g(C_t) > g(X_t)$ then the next state value is $X_{t+1} = C_t$, otherwise the original cell is kept and $X_{t+1} = X_t$; see [1] for more details. At each stage there is a probability for transition to a new state (bit string) value for X_{t+1}, and the BCA is purely elitist in the sense that only mutations that result in improvement are kept (so that the value of $g(x)$ is non-decreasing with t). To describe the evolution of a cell in the BCA in terms of a Markov chain, we label the possible states by an index j running from 0 to $N-1$, where $N = 2^L$ is the number of possible states (i.e. the number of possible strings of length L). Then we choose the value of the bit string at time t to be given by the probability distribution $\mathbf{v}_t = (v_{t,1}, v_{t,2}, ..., v_{t,N})$, with the jth component of the row vector $\mathbf{v}_t$ being just

$$v_{t,j} := P(X_t = j),\tag{1}$$

that is the probability of being in state j at time t. Furthermore, the probability of transition between state j and another state k is independent of the time t, and so can be represented by the $N \times N$ transition matrix $\mathbf{P} := (P_{jk})$ with entries

$$P_{jk} = P(X_{t+1} = k \mid X_t = j)\tag{2}$$

To work out the probability distribution at time $t+1$, the standard rules of conditional probability imply that

$$v_{t+1,k} = \sum_{j=1}^{N} v_{tj} P_{jk},\tag{3}$$

Therefore, rewriting the equation (3) in matrix notation we have

$$\mathbf{v}_{t+1} = \mathbf{v}_t \mathbf{P}\tag{4}$$

which describes the time evolution of the row vector $\mathbf{v}_t$. The row vector $\mathbf{v}_t$ is the probability distribution of the state X_t at time t. Note that $\mathbf{P}$ is a stochastic matrix: all of its entries lie between 0 and 1, and the row sums satisfy

$$\sum_{k=1}^{N} P_{jk} = 1 \tag{5}$$

i.e. from state j, the cell must make a transition somewhere (including null transitions) with probability 1.

Because the transition matrix $\mathbf{P}$ is time-independent, equation (4) means that the probability distribution vector $\mathbf{v}_t$ at time t can be written immediately in terms of the initial distribution, as

$$\mathbf{v}_t = \mathbf{v}_0 \mathbf{P}^t . \tag{6}$$

It is evident from the form of (6) that if we wish to understand the long-term behavior of the algorithm, we need to understand what happens to the powers of the transition matrix $\mathbf{P}^t$ as $t \to \infty$. In fact, for the BCA it is further possible to prove that where there is a unique optimum state, it is reached with probability one in the limit $t \to \infty$; in the terminology of Markov chains [6], a unique optimum is an absorbing state. Similarly, if there are several optima (i.e. different values of x for which $g(x)$ takes the same optimal value) then it turns out that the overall probability of lying in at least one of these optima also tends to one as $t \to \infty$.

For our detailed analysis of the Markov chain model of the BCA in section 3 we will rely on some standard properties and results concerning Markov chains. It is helpful to introduce the notation

$$P_{jk}(n) = P(X_{t+n} = k \mid X_t = j) \tag{7}$$

for the entries of the matrix $\mathbf{P}^n$ (the nth powers of the transition matrix). A state j can be said to be persistent if the sum

$$\sum_{n=0}^{\infty} P_{jj}(n) = \infty . \tag{8}$$

Otherwise if the sum converges, so that

$$\sum_{n=0}^{\infty} P_{jj}(n) < \infty , \tag{9}$$

then the state j is transient. By the Decomposition Theorem (see [6] p.123) any Markov chain can be decomposed into the set of transient states together with some irreducible closed sets of persistent states. In Section 3 we show that for the BCA, all of the non-optimal states are transient, while all the optima are persistent. Furthermore, the optima turn out to be *absorbing* states of the chain, in the sense that once an optimum is reached it is never left (due to the elitist nature of the BCA). Since the BCA corresponds to a Markov chain with a finite number of states, we can calculate the transition matrix $\mathbf{P}$ explicitly for a given objective function.

3 Mathematical Model of the BCA

We shall outline some key features of the BCA and how they effect the modeling process and then give the full stochastic model and demonstrate that the model takes the form of an absorbing Markov chain irrespective of the function to be optimized.

3.1 The Contiguous Region Hypermutation Operator

As an initial modeling step the stochastic nature of the contiguous region hypermutation operator was examined. In the case where the clonal pool C has only one member, it is possible to obtain formulae to calculate the probabilities of all possible mutation masks. These were deduced by counting all possible ways each mutation mask could occur, for an exhaustive set of mutation masks.

$$f_T = \frac{1}{L^2}\left[\sum_{n=1}^{a}\sum_{m=b}^{L-1}(1-r)^{m+1-n-k}\,r^k + \sum_{n=1}^{a}n(1-r)^{L+1-n-k}\,r^k\right]. \tag{10}$$

The above formula includes the following notation:

f_T the probability of transition from zero to some number T

L the length of binary string

a the bit position of the first "on" bit starting from the most significant bit

b the bit position of the last "on" bit starting from the most significant bit

k the total number of bits that must be flipped to mutate from 0 to T

r the probability of a bit being mutated given it is in the contiguous region

$$\{L,a,b,k,T\}\in \mathbb{Z}^+ \; ; \; 0\le T\le 2^L-1 \, ; \, a\le b\le L \; ; \; \{f_T,r\}\in \mathbb{R} \; ; \; 0\le r\le 1$$

Equation (10) can generate the probabilities of all non-zero mutation masks. To be exhaustive the zero mutation mask is also needed

$$f_0 = \frac{1}{L^2}\left[\sum_{n=1}^{L}\sum_{m=n}^{L-1}(1-r)^{m+1-n} + \sum_{n=1}^{L}n(1-r)^{L+1-n}\right]. \tag{11}$$

With this formulation only the probability of the mutation mask occurring is generated, so the formula is general (for a clonal pool of one). The results can be applied to binary, Gray code or any other binary system. The probability of a mutation mask is given as a polynomial in r. After formulation of equations (10) and (11) the CRHO was implemented to compare theory (figure 2) with experiment (figure 3).

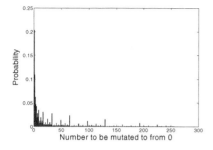

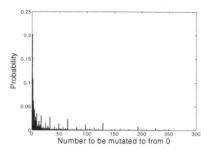

Fig. 2. Theoretically determined probabilities of generating mutation masks from the CRHO: String Length L=8, Probability of mutation $r = 0.5$.

Fig. 3. Probabilities determined experimentally by averaging one million results from the implemented CRHO: String Length L=8, Probability of mutation $r = 0.5$.

3.2 The Transition Matrix

Due to the elitist nature of the BCA, existing methods of obtaining the transition matrix cannot be successfully applied. Hence a new approach to obtaining the transition matrix has been pioneered. We will determine two matrices, the sample matrix and possible transit matrix and combine them to form the transition matrix.

The Sample Matrix

Since the probabilities of all the mutation masks are now known it is possible to construct the sample matrix. The sample matrix contains the probabilities that the algorithm will "sample" a given point within search space. Sampling a point is equivalent to generating a new potential solution via the CRHO and it being selected to be evaluated by the objective function. The sample matrix is entirely dependent on the search space and representation, but is independent of the function space.

To construct the sample matrix from equations (10) and (11) the binary representation being used must be employed as an interpreter between real search space values of states and the mutation mask required to transit between the states. This is done by converting the initial and final states into binary strings and using the exclusive or operator to determine the mutation mask. From the mutation mask, equation (10) or (11) can be utilized to give the algebraic sampling probability, dependant on the mutation rate r (or a numeric answer if r is known).

There are 2^L possible functions that can be defined by equations (10) and (11). As no two end states (of any initial state) are the same and each row has 2^L elements, it is clear that mutation masks only occur exactly once per row on all rows. Once one line of the sample matrix has been calculated it is possible to unpack the rest of the matrix using just the exclusive or operator and copying the relevant entry from the completed row.

The Possible Transit Matrix

The possible transit matrix is dependant on the search space and the function space but is independent of the representation. For a given initial state affinity, consider the affinity all the possible end states. If the affinity of the end state is greater than the affinity of the initial state then the matrix element representing that transition is assigned the value 1. If the affinity is *equal* or less than that of the initial state then the matrix element is assigned the value 0.

By means of an element-to-element multiplication of the possible transit matrix and sample matrix it is possible to produce a transition matrix that is correct except for the values of diagonal elements. During the element-to-element multiplication, some of the values in the sample matrix will have been multiplied by 0, in order that the rows will no longer sum to 1. In the BCA, a rejected move results in a null move; therefore the probabilities that were multiplied by 0 must be added to the diagonal element of the appropriate row. Thus the transition matrix is produced.

3.3 Proof of Convergence

In order to prove that the BCA is convergent absolute, we shall show that the BCA model will always take the form of an absorbing Markov chain with a non-zero one step transition probability from all points in the space to a global optima. In the terminology of Markov chains, all non-optimal states of the BCA are transient. Moreover, all the optima are absorbing states.

Proposition 1: All non-optimal states are transient provided $0 < r < 1$

Proof: Under the condition $0 < r < 1$, the sample matrix contains only non-zero elements. By inspection of equation (10) it is clear that $f_T > 0$ if $(1 - r) > 0$ and $r > 0$. Thus, we impose the condition $1 > r > 0$, this condition also makes $f_0 > 0$ as can be seen in equation (11). (The formulae (10), (11) would need to be modified in the case when the clonal pool C has more than one member but the condition for $f_T > 0$ is the same.) Hence it is possible to reach the absorbing state in one step from any initial state. This is irrespective of the function due to the fact that by definition of the possible transit matrix, transition from a non-optimal state to an optimum is allowed with probability 1. Hence, for a non-optimal state j the probability of remaining in that state for one time step is $p = P_{jj} < 1$. Once a state has been left for a state of higher affinity, it can never return to a previously occupied state, due to the possible transit matrix forbidding transitions to states of lower affinity, hence $P_{jj}(n) = p^n$; it follows that

$$\sum_{n=0}^{\infty} P_{jj}(n) = \sum_{n=0}^{\infty} p^n = \frac{1}{(1-p)} < \infty , \tag{12}$$

and hence state j is transient.

The general theory of Markov chains is particularly effective in the case of irreducible chains. The chain corresponding to the BCA is reducible, however: by the Decomposition Theorem [6] it can be partitioned into the set of transient non-optimal states together with the (disjoint) closed sets of absorbing states corresponding to the optima. Adopting the terminology of [7], we can say that the non-optimal states of the BCA are *inessential*, in the sense that for all such non-optimal states j there exists another state k such that j can make a transition to k but not vice-versa: it is sufficient to choose any state k with a larger value of the objective function. Then if there are M optima we can partition the transition matrix $\mathbf{P}$ as follows

$$\mathbf{P} = \begin{pmatrix} \mathbf{1} & 0 \\ \mathbf{R} & \mathbf{Q} \end{pmatrix} \tag{13}$$

where $\mathbf{1}$ denotes the $M \times M$ identity matrix, $\mathbf{Q}$ corresponds to the transitions between the inessential states and $\mathbf{R}$ corresponds to transitions from inessential to optimal states. It follows from standard properties of stochastic matrices (see e.g. [8]) that the powers $\mathbf{Q}^t \to 0$ as $t \to \infty$. Using this partitioning, we arrive at the following:

Proposition 2: All optima are absorbing states

Proof: By definition, the possible transit matrix prohibits transition from a global optimum to any other state, even another global optima. Therefore once the algorithm enters a global optimum it satisfies the condition for persistence (equation 8). Clearly for an optimum state j we have $p = P_{jj} = 1$ (i.e. once an optimum is reached then one remains there with probability one), so the corresponding sum (12) diverges and the optima are all persistent states; since they do not communicate with any other state, they are also absorbing.

Theorem: The BCA is convergent absolute provided $0 < r < 1$, where r is the probability of mutation for bits contained within the contiguous region.

Proof: We have the state vector calculated from powers of the transition matrix according to

$$\mathbf{v}_t = \mathbf{v}_0 \mathbf{P}^t . \tag{14}$$

Now

$$\mathbf{P}^t = \begin{pmatrix} \mathbf{1} & 0 \\ \mathbf{R}_t & \mathbf{Q}^t \end{pmatrix} \tag{15}$$

for some matrix $\mathbf{R}_t$ constructed from sums of powers of $\mathbf{Q}$ acting on $\mathbf{R}$. Also, it follows from standard properties of stochastic matrices (see e.g. [8]) that the powers $\mathbf{Q}^t \to 0$ as $t \to \infty$. So in the limit $t \to \infty$, the powers of $\mathbf{P}$ take the form

$$\mathbf{P}^\infty = \begin{pmatrix} \mathbf{1} & 0 \\ \mathbf{R}_\infty & 0 \end{pmatrix} \tag{16}$$

Acting with this matrix on the initial state vector $\mathbf{v}_0$ we see that the probability of being in any of the non-optimal transient states tends to zero as $t \rightarrow \infty$, and hence the probability of ending up in an optimum tends to one, as required.

4 Demonstration of Numerical Application of the Model

Other complete and exact Markov chain models, for example in the GA literature [9] provide good analytical follow up work [10] but numerical application of the model [11] is constrained by the complexity of the model to unrealistically small variables, e.g. string length 2. The BCA produces a model simple enough to do numerical work with realistic values of the models variables, string length ~ 16.

Potentially, the BCA model can be utilized to gain insight into all facets of the BCA, the most obvious of these is the effect of the mutation rate on the convergence rate of the algorithm. We have probed this application of the model on a simple one-dimensional quadratic function space. In this example, all values are accurate within the limits of double precision. Figure 4, presents a coarse sweep of the range of mutation rates, and produced two features of particular interest.

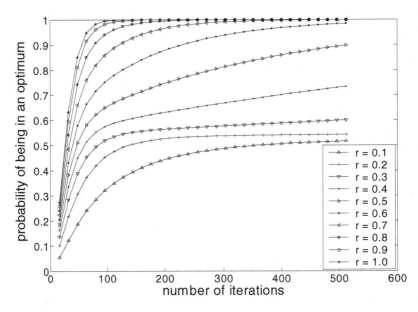

Fig. 4. Examination of the effect of mutation rate, r, on the B cell algorithm convergence rates for a one-dimensional quadratic. String length L = 8.

First, a mutation rate of 1 is shown to be the optimal mutation rate for the problem, this is interesting because $r = 1$ lies outside the conditions for the BCA to be convergent absolute. Hence $r = 1$ can produce persistent non-optimal states in the BCA as some of the one step transition probabilities to the SSGO are zero. However, the function space in this example is simple enough for all states to have a non-zero multi-step probability of reaching the SSGO allowing the BCA to converge on the SSGO with probability 1.

Second, the line for $r = 0.1$ looks flat considering that the BCA has been shown to be convergent absolute given $0 < r < 1$. This raised the question when dose the probability of being in the optimum become 1? Further investigation showed that at 2^{20} iterations the probability of being in the optimum had risen to ~ 0.85, at 2^{40} iterations the probability had risen to 1 (to within the limits of double precision). This result was obtained by squaring the transition matrix at each step; hence only 40 matrix multiplications were required. This example demonstrates the power of the model to look at the extreme long-term behavior of the model numerically as well as analytically.

5   Conclusions

Within the area of Artificial Immune Systems (AIS) there has been limited theoretical work. In this paper we model an immune inspired algorithm, the B-cell algorithm (BCA) as a Markov Chain. Our model is exact and can be considered complete in the case where the clonal pool size is one.

We have introduced a possible transit matrix that provides a novel method for the modelling of elitist algorithms.   In addition, we have shown that the BCA is convergent absolute provided $0 < r < 1$ where r is the probability of mutation for bits contained in the contiguous region. The conditions for this proof are also met by elitist random search, and hence it is also convergent absolute.

In terms of future work, we intend to attempt to derive the optimal mutation rate algebraically from the model, for any given function.   From a wider perspective, we intend to apply our technique to a variety of immune inspired algorithms such as CLONALG.

References

1. Kelsey, J and Timmis, J. Immune Inspired Somatic Contiguous Hypermutation for Function Optimisation. Springer Lecture Notes in Computer Science **2723**. pages 207-218. CantuPaz et al (Eds) Proc. of Genetic and Evolutionary Computation Conference (GECCO) 2003.
2. Kelsey, J, Timmis, J and Hone, A. Chasing Chaos. In R. Sarker, R. Reynolds, H. Abbass, T. Kay-Chen, R. McKay, D Essam, and T. Gedeon, editors, *Proceedings of the Congress on Evolutionary Computation*, pages 413-419, Canberra. Australia, December 2003. IEEE.
3. Rosin-Arbesfeld, R., Townsley, F. and Bienz, M. The APC tumour suppressor has a nuclear export function. *Letters to Nature* **406**: pages 1009-1012, 2000.
4. Hone, A., Kelsey, J.: Optima, extrema and artificial immune systems. In: LNCS 3239, Springer (2004) 80–90.
5. J D Farmer, N H Packard, and A S Perelson. The Immune System, Adaptation, and Machine Learning. Physica D **22**: 187–204, 1986.

6. Grimmett, G.R. & Stirzaker, D.R.: *Probability and Random Processes*. Oxford: Oxford University Press (1982).
7. Villalobos-Arias, M., Coello Coello, C.A. & Hernández-Lerma, O.: Convergence Analysis of a Multiobjective Artificial Immune System Algorithm, in *Proceedings of ICARIS 2004*, G.Nicosia, V.Cutello, P.J.Bentley & J.Timmis (Eds.), Springer Lecture Notes in Computer Science **3239** Springer-Verlag (2004) 226-235.
8. Seneta, E.: *Non-Negative Matrices and Markov Chains*. New York: Springer-Verlag (1981).
9. Nix, A.E., & Vose, M.D.: Modeling genetic algorithms with Markov chains. *Annals of Mathematics and Artificial Intelligence* **5**, 79-88, 1992.
10. Vose, M.D.: Modeling Simple Genetic Algorithms. *Evolutionary Computation* **3**, Number 4, 1996.
11. Kenneth A. De Jong, William M. Spears, and Diana F. Gordon. Using Markov Chains to Analyze GAFOs, In *Proceedings of FOGA94*, Estes Park, CO, pages 115-137. Morgan Kaufmann., 1994.
12. de Castro, L., Von Zuben, F.J.: Learning and optimization using the clonal selection principle. *IEEE Transactions on Evolutionary Computation*, Special Issue on Artificial Immune Systems **6**. 239–251, 2002.
13. de Castro, L., Timmis, J.: *Artificial Immune Systems: A New Computational Intelligence Approach*. Springer-Verlag 2002.
14. Cutello, V., Nicosia, G., Parvone, M.: Exploring the capability of immune algorithms: A characterisation of hypermutation operators. In: Springer LNCS **3239**, 263–276, 2004.
15. Brzezniak, Z., Zastawniak, T.: *Basic Stochastic Processes*. Springer, 1999.

Fuzzy Continuous Petri Net-Based Approach for Modeling Helper T Cell Differentiation⋆

Inho Park, Dokyun Na, Kwang H. Lee, and Doheon Lee

Department of BioSystems, KAIST,
373-1, Guseong-dong, Yuseong-gu, Daejeon, Republic of Korea
dhlee@biosoft.kaist.ac.kr

Abstract. Helper T(Th) cells regulate immune response by producing various kinds of cytokines in response to antigen stimulation. The regulatory functions of Th cells are promoted by their differentiation into two distinct subsets, Th1 and Th2 cells. Th1 cells are involved in inducing cellular immune response by activating cytotoxic T cells. Th2 cells trigger B cells to produce antibodies, protective proteins used by the immune system to identify and neutralize foreign substances. Because cellular and humoral immune responses have quite different roles in protecting the host from foreign substances, Th cell differentiation is a crucial event in the immune response. The destiny of a naive Th cell is mainly controlled by cytokines such as IL-4, IL-12, and IFN-γ. To understand the mechanism of Th cell differentiation, many mathematical models have been proposed. One of the most difficult problems in mathematical modeling is to find appropriate kinetic parameters needed to complete a model. However, it is relatively easy to get qualitative or linguistic knowledge of a model dynamics. To incorporate such knowledge into a model, we propose a novel approach, fuzzy continuous Petri nets extending traditional continuous Petri net by adding new types of places and transitions called fuzzy places and fuzzy transitions. This extension makes it possible to perform fuzzy inference with fuzzy places and fuzzy transitions acting as kinetic parameters and fuzzy inference systems between input and output places, respectively.

1 Introduction

Two types of helper T(Th) cells, called Th1 and Th2, have been defined based on the profile of cytokines they produce and are differentiated from common Th cell precursors(Th0). These two subsets of Th cells have quite different roles in the immune response. Th1 cells induce cellular immune response by activating cytotoxic T cells, which defend a host against infectious intracellular microorganisms such as viruses and some types of bacteria by killing infected cells. Th2

⋆ This work was supported by National Research Laboratory Grant (2005-01450) from the Ministry of Science and Technology. We would like to thank CHUNG Moon Soul Center for BioInformation and BioElectronics and the IBM-SUR program for providing research and computing facilities.

C. Jacob et al. (Eds.): ICARIS 2005, LNCS 3627, pp. 331–338, 2005.

cells lead to humoral immune response by activating B cells to produce antibodies, protective proteins used by the immune system to identify and neutralize foreign substances. The humoral immune response helps a host remove extracellular pathogens. Thus, Th1/Th2 cell differentiation from a naive Th cell is an important event in the immune response. Although there are many different factors affecting Th cell differentiation, it is mainly controlled by cytokines such as IL-4, IL-12, and IFN-γ [1]. To understand the mechanism of Th cell differentiation with cytokine network, many mathematical models have been developed[2,3,4]. One of the most difficult problems in mathematical modeling is to find appropriate kinetic parameters needed to complete a model. However, it is relatively easy to get linguistic, incomplete or qualitative knowledge of a model dynamics. For example, we can easily find sentences like 'FN-γ and IL-12 promote Th1 differentiation' and 'L-4 helps Th2 differentiation' using literature search. Linguistic knowledge can be very useful in modeling the immune system, but previous approaches do not use it. Here we present a novel approach based on Petri nets and fuzzy inference systems for incorporating qualitative knowledge when constructing a immune system model.

2   Method

2.1   Petri Nets

A Petri net is a graphical and mathematical modeling tool successfully used in a number of fields for concurrent, asynchronous, and parallel system modeling. Recently, Petri nets have been widely applied to represent biological pathways or processes. Following is the definition of basic Petri nets[5,6].

Definition 1. *A Petri net is a 5-tuple* $R = < P, T, F, W, M_0 >$ *where* $P = \{p_1, p_2, \cdots, p_n\}$ *is a finite set of places,* $T = \{t_1, t_2, \cdots, t_n\}$ *is a finite set of transitions. The set of places and transitions are disjoint,* $P \cap T = \emptyset$. *F* $\subseteq$ $(P \times T) \cup (T \times P)$ *is a set of arcs.* $W : F \to \{1, 2, 3, \cdots\}$ *is a weight function. And* $M_0 : P \to \{0, 1, 2, 3, \cdots\}$ *is the initial marking.*

The behavior of a Petri net is described in terms of changes of tokens in places according to the firing of transitions. If every input place of a transition has more tokens than the weight of the arc between the transition and the place, the transition is enabled. Of enabled transitions, only one transition can fire. After a transition is fired, as many tokens as the weights of the arc are removed from the input place and as many tokens are added to output places.

Because of its discrete nature, basic Petri net is not suitable for immune system modeling so that we used a continuous Petri net, an extension of basic Petri net, instead. The differences between the basic Petri net and the continuous Petri net are following: In the continuous Petri net, places can have real value marking and transitions fire continuously with some velocity. The velocity of a transition firing is affected by the marking of places. Shown below is the definition of continuous Petri nets[7].

Definition 2. *A continuous Petri net is a 6-tuple* $R = < P, T, V, F, W, M_0 >$ *where* P, T, F, W, M_0 *are identical to those of the basic Petri net.* $V : T \rightarrow V(p_1, p_2, p_3, \cdots) \in R^+$ *is the firing speed function.*

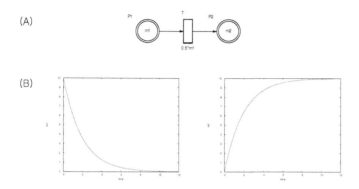

Fig. 1. Continuous Petri net. In the graphical representation of the Petri net (A), a circle represents a place and a rectangle represents a transition. Two graph (B) show the changes of tokens of places with respect to time.

In our immune system model, places represent immune cells or external entities (e.g. antigen or virus) and transitions represent interactions (e.g. B cell activation by antigen).

2.2   Fuzzy Inference System

Fuzzy inference systems are reasoning systems based on fuzzy set theory, fuzzy if-then rules and fuzzy reasoning. The strength of fuzzy inference systems lies in their capability of handling uncertain linguistic concepts. They are composed of several parts; fuzzification interface, fuzzy rule base, fuzzy inference and defuzzification interface[8].

Fuzzy if-then rules are generally expressed in the form *'If x is A, then y is · B'* where A and B are linguistic values defined by fuzzy sets on the universe of discourse $x \in X$ and $y \in Y$, respectively. For example,

If pressure is high, then volume is small.

where *pressure* and *volume* are fuzzy variables, *high* and *small* are linguistic values. By applying inference operation upon fuzzy rules, fuzzy inference systems can deduce consequences. Followings are the steps of fuzzy inference.

1. Compare the input variables with the membership functions on the premise part to obtain the membership values of each linguistic label. (This step is often called *fuzzification.*)
2. Combine the membership values on the premise part to get the firing strength of each rule.

3. Generate the qualified consequence of each rule depending on the firing strength.
4. Aggregate the qualified consequents to produce a crisp output. (This step is called *defuzzification.*)

There are many inference methods; Mamdani, Larsen, Tsukamoto and TSK.

2.3 Fuzzy Continuous Petri Nets

In mathematical modeling and simulation, we usually need appropriate kinetic parameters of a system. However, it is difficult to find parameter values of a system. Therefore, various methods are used to estimate unknown parameters. On the other hand, it is relatively easy to get linguistic or qualitative knowledge. To make use of linguistic and qualitative knowledge in the estimation of kinetic parameters, we employed fuzzy inference systems.

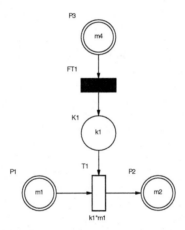

Fig. 2. A fuzzy continuous Petri net. In the figure, a black transition represents a fuzzy transition and a single circle represents a fuzzy place. Fuzzy transition FT1 inferences k_1 value from fuzzy if-then rules given the value of input place P_3. And k_1 is used in the firing speed function of a continuous transition, T1.

To include a functionality of fuzzy inference, we add new types of transitions and places so-called, fuzzy transitions and fuzzy places. The role of fuzzy transitions is to inference parameter from fuzzy if-then rules between input and output places. And only fuzzy places can be a output place of a fuzzy transition. Fuzzy places act as kinetic parameters of reactions represented by continuous transition. Fig. 2 shows a simple example of a fuzzy continuous Petri net.

3   Model

Dendritic cells are stimulated by recognizing antigens. Stimulated dendritic cells act as APC, antigen presenting cell, by presenting processed antigen fragments

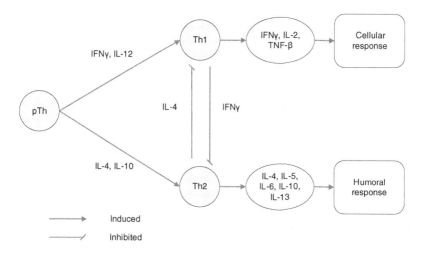

Fig. 3. The schematic diagram of a cytokine network

using MHC-II molecules and produce signals required for the proliferation and differentiation of naive Th cells. A naive Th cell differentiates into Th1 or Th2 cell upon interaction with MHC-peptide complex presented on the membrane of APC. The dynamics of interaction between naive Th cell and APC is affected by many factors such as the density of MHC-peptide complex and the strength of interaction[9]. APC produces cytokines such as IL-10 and IL-12 which affect naive Th cells differentiation.

Fig. 3 shows a schematic diagram of cytokine network of Th cell differentiation. IFN-γ and IL-12 induce Th1 differentiation. On the other hand, IL-4 and IL-10 promote Th2 differentiation. Activated Th1 produces such cytokines as IFN-γ, IL-2 and TNF-β which induce cellular immune response whereas activated Th2 produces such cytokines as IL-4, IL6 and IL-10, which induce humoral immune response. Besides, IL-4 and IFN-γ inhibit Th1 and Th2 differentiation, respectively.

In our fuzzy continuous Petri nets approach, we integrated signals affecting behaviors of immune cells by fuzzy inference, which simplifies rate equations. All the variables appearing in the reaction equations in continuous transitions are directly related to the reaction.

Fig. 4 shows important reactions in the Th cell differentiation with cytokines. Listed below are examples of rules in fuzzy transitions depicted in Fig. 4.

Example 1. Th1 differentiation: FT2 in Fig. 4(b)

- The concentration of IL-12 is higher than $0.5ng/ml$ and that of IL-4 is lower than $10ng/ml$, the differentiation rate is about $4day^{-1}$.
- The concentration of IL-4 is higher than $10ng/ml$, the differentiation rate is about $2day^{-1}$.
- The concentration of IL-4 is higher than $100ng/ml$, the differentiation rate is nearly 0.

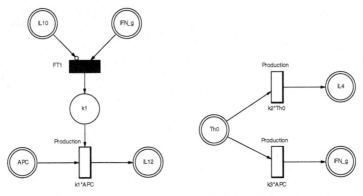

(a) APC cytokines production   (b) Th0 cytokines production

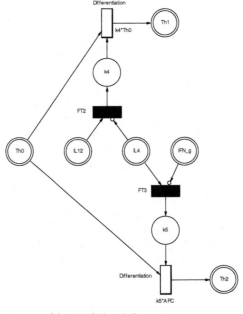

(c) Th1/Th2 differentiation

Fig. 4. Important reactions of Th cell differentiation

Example 2. Th2 differentiation: FT3 in Fig. 4(b)

- The concentration of IL-4 is higher than $100ng/ml$, the differentiation rate is about $6day^{-1}$.
- The concentration of IL-4 is lower than $10ng/ml$, the differentiation rate is about $1.2day^{-1}$.

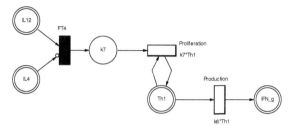

(a) Th1 proliferation and cytokine production

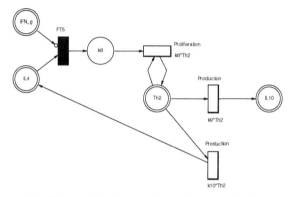

(b) Th2 proliferation and cytokine production

Fig. 5. Important reactions of Th cell differentiation

- The concentration of IL-4 is lower than $10ng/ml$ of IL-4 and that of IFN-γ is higher than than $10ng/ml$ of , the differentiation rate is nearly 0.

Even though we just have partial knowledge about a system being modelled, we can easily include the knowledge in the model. On top of that, newly discovered knowledge can be easily incorporated into the fuzzy rule based system[8].

4 Discussion

In conclusion, we propose a new approach to the immune system modeling, a fuzzy continuous Petri net. The advantage of the modeling method is that we can make use of qualitative or linguistic knowledge that are relatively easier to obtain than kinetic parameters. We show that fuzzy inference systems successfully used in expert systems in various domains can be also used in the immune system modeling. To make it more useful, we need to develop more robust methods for constructing fuzzy rules from immunological knowledge. Moreover, we have to develop analysis techniques such as reachability and boundedness for traditional Petri nets.

The challenge of recent research is how to integrate molecular transcriptional network and cellular communication via cytokines in the immune response[10]. Hierarchical Petri nets approach could be a good candidate formalism for integration of knowledge from different levels.

References

1. Stephanie L. Constant and Kim Bottomly, INDUCTION OF TH1 AND TH2 CD4+ T CELL RESPONSES: The Alternative Approaches., Annu. Rev. Immunol. 1997. 15:297-322
2. Andrew Yates, Claudia Bergmann, J. Leo Van Hemmen, JarStark, and Robin Callard, Cytokine-modulated Regulation of Helper T Cell Populations, J. theor. Biol., 206:539–560, 2000.
3. Claudia Bergmann and J. Leo Van Hemmen, Th1 or Th2: How an Approate T Helper Response can be Made, Bulletin of Mathematical Biology, 63:405–430, 2001.
4. Michael A. Fishman and Alan S. Perelson, Th1/Th2 Differentiation and Cross-regulation, Bulletin of Mathematical Biology, 61:403–436, 1999.
5. J. L. Peterson., Petri net theory and the modeling of systems. Prentice Hall, englewood Cliff, NJ, 1981
6. T. Murata., Petri nets: Properties, analysis and applications, Proc. IEEE Vol. 77, No. 4, April 1989
7. H. Alla, R. David., A modeling and analysis tool for discrete event systems: continuous Petri net. Performance Evaluation, Vol. 33, No. 3, August 1999
8. Kwang H. Lee, First Course on Fuzzy Theory and Applications, Springer, 2005
9. Anja Langenkamp, Mara Messi, Antonio Lanzavecchia and Federica Sallusto, Kinetics of dendritic cell activation: impact on priming of Th1, Th2 and nonpolarized T cells, Nat. Immunol. Vol. 1, No. 4, October 2000
10. Andrew Yates, Robin Callard, Jaroslav Stark., Combining cytokine signalling with T-bet and GATA-3 regulation in Th1 and Th2 differentiation: a model for cellular decision-making., Jour. Theor. Biol., 231 (2004) 181-196

A Peer-to-Peer Blacklisting Strategy Inspired by Leukocyte-Endothelium Interaction

Bruce C. Trapnell, Jr.

TopGun Software, Inc. and the University of Maryland,
15104 Peartree Drive, Bowie, MD, 20721
trapnell@topgunsoftware.com

Abstract. This paper describes a multi-agent strategy for blacklisting malicious nodes in a peer-to-peer network that is inspired by the innate immune system, including the recruitment of leukocytes to the site of an infection in the human body. Agents are based on macrophages, T-cells, and tumor necrosis factor, and exist on network nodes that have properties drawn from vascular endothelial tissue. Here I show that this strategy succeeds in blacklisting malicious nodes from the network using non-specific recruitment. This strategy is sensitive to parameters that affect the recruitment of leukocyte agents to malicious nodes. The strategy can eliminate even a large, uniform distribution of malicious nodes in the network.

1 Introduction

A Peer-to-Peer (P2P) network is "a class of systems and applications that employ distributed resources to perform a critical function in a decentralized manner" [9]. P2P systems are typically composed of clients, or *peers*, in ad-hoc networks or on the Internet, and these clients communicate through one or more protocols to perform a task in a decentralized way. A peer-to-peer (P2P) network's function depends on the reliable and accurate routing and processing of its protocols' messages. However, it is entirely possible that a computer or a set of computers within the network can severely disrupt the operation of the network by sending incorrect messages, or by altering or dropping correct messages. These 'malicious' clients are, in effect, an *infection* of the P2P network. However, it is possible to simply 'amputate' these nodes from the rest of the network, usually without severely degrading its performance. [8]

Malicious nodes are dangerous because they can masquerade as benign nodes while quietly disrupting the network. The problem of separating the benign nodes from the malicious is non-trivial, and solutions can be expensive in terms of protocol overhead. One technique, described in [8], relies on the comparison of timestamped messages in logs maintained by network nodes to prohibit the sending of illegal messages. The system also assumes a (possibly offline) Certificate Authority (CA) to enforce node identities that cannot be forged.

This task of separating the benign from the malicious is not unlike the charge of the human immune system. It must discriminate between the body's own cells (self) and harmful foreign bodies (non-self). However, even if we knew instantly and easily

C. Jacob et al. (Eds.): ICARIS 2005, LNCS 3627, pp. 339–352, 2005.
© Springer-Verlag Berlin Heidelberg 2005

which nodes were malicious and which were benign, we would still need a strategy for somehow removing the malicious nodes or marginalizing their negative impact. Moreover, since we must assume that malicious nodes can behave arbitrarily, we would prefer their removal. Without knowing the exact nature of their dysfunction, it would be difficult to marginalize it.

Fortunately, removing the nodes is fairly straightforward: all benign neighbors of malicious nodes need to be instructed not to listen to those malicious nodes anymore. Viewing the P2P network as a graph, this amounts to deleting edges that connect good nodes to bad. Jelasity, *et al.*, describe one such strategy for gossip-based protocols. This approach, called *blacklisting*, is aptly named: each benign node maintains its own list of other nodes, and refuses to communicate with nodes on its blacklist [8]. Once all benign nodes connected to a malicious node have blacklisted that node, it can no longer communicate with the network.

This task of deleting specific edges is fairly similar to a task assigned to the natural immune system: 'destroy the foreign body, which looks like XYZ.' Eliminating an infection typically involves the targeting and destruction of a large number of bacteria, viruses, or other foreign particles within the body. That work is *specific* because some of the effector mechanisms responsible for destroying antigen, such as phagocytosis and opsonization, require the biochemical identification of small features of the antigen [1]. These antigen features will not appear on any self body, and all antigen will have them. They are, in effect, targeting markers for the adaptive immune system.

When a network is infected with a large number of malicious nodes, there is obviously a lot of work to do, and that work is specific, but the immune-inspired response will not be targeting a single node. It will target a set of nodes, for each of which there is a fairly small amount of work to do. For example, say that a network of 10,000 nodes has an infection of 500 nodes. Each of those nodes is connected to an average of 10 other (benign) nodes. Thus, about 5,000 edges must be deleted. That is a lot of work, but we are also looking for edges connected to 500 different nodes, each with its own identity, and thus its own specificity. It is shown below that features of the innate immune system are useful in tackling this problem.

The blacklisting problem begs an agent-based approach inspired by mechanisms found in the human immune system. Such an approach is natural to Artificial Immune System (AIS), and some agent-based, immune-inspired systems have been developed [15, 9]. Sathyanath and Sahin described AISIMAM, a general agent model inspired by the human immune system, and drew useful analogies between basic agent behavior and the cells of the immune system. AISIMAM focuses primarily on the sensory information processing and communication between agents and their role in self/non-self discrimination [15]. Many of these systems use agents modeled after B-Cells, antibodies, and the other components of the adaptive immune system [13, 12, 7]. They generate a diverse set of receptors by a variety of methods, and often feature clonal expansion of agents specific to the task they are meant to solve. The components of the innate immune system are often ignored because they do not feature the specificity and memory capabilities of the adaptive immune system.

Recently, a biologically inspired, agent-based approach to P2P protocol design and analysis has been taken. Anthill, described in [2], is a P2P design and analysis framework inspired by ant colonies. The usefulness of ant algorithms has been well established, and some principles of their operation are known [6]. In particular, *stigmergy*, which is the communication between agents via modifications to their external environment, has been shown to be effective in a variety of applications. In the case of ant agents, pheromones deposited on nodes or edges a network graph inform the ant's movement through the network, effectively communicating shortest paths, etc [4].

This paper describes a multi-agent blacklisting strategy inspired by the leukocyte recruitment mechanism used by the natural immune system. The strategy uses agents to blacklist malicious nodes in a P2P network. These agents are modeled after the cells involved in the inflammation that follows an infection. It uses macrophage-like detector agents to locate malicious nodes, and T-Cell-like agents to blacklist the nodes. The agents use a form of stigmergy to migrate to the site of a detection. The strategy presented here uses a very similar mechanism for stigmergy to the one found in AntNet [4]. This immune inspired strategy is highly effective in blacklisting malicious nodes. The innate immune system is often ignored in favor of the adaptive, but it has many useful features that can be applied to real-world applications.

2   The Innate Immune System

The innate immune system is the body's first line of defense [1]. It consists of a collection of a number of different mechanisms that prevent the entry of antigen into the body's tissues, and the non-specific destruction of antigen that manages entry. The cells of the innate immune system have the ability to recognize broad categories of antigenic features. For example, the presence of *lipopolysaccharides* (LPS) indicates an infection by gram-negative bacteria, as LPS is present in their cell wall. *Macrophages* are responsible for the identification of LPS and other microbial features. When a macrophage detects the presence of LPS, it secretes a cytokine called *Tumor Necrosis Factor* (TNF), which then initiates the process of local inflammation, the recruitment of other leukocytes to the site of infection, and the activation of those leukocytes to combat the antigen.

Inflammation is the key inspiration to the blacklisting strategy presented in this paper. When vascular endothelial cells encounter TNF, they are *activated*, which means they express higher levels of proteins, called *selectins*, embedded in their cell walls. Leukocytes 'roll' along the endothelium, forming and dissolving low affinity bonds between the endothelial selectins and their reciprocal ligands, which are embedded in the cell walls of the leukocytes. While 'rolling', they become activated themselves, and can now form higher affinity bonds between their *integrins*, which are features of the leukocyte cell wall, and ligands on the endothelial cells. Thus, the leukocytes are recruited and can now pass into the surrounding tissue.

TNF induces inflammation, which is responsible for getting other leukocytes into the tissue around the infection. TNF is secreted by a macrophage that was activated as the result of a limited-specificity detection event. Thus, the macrophage, which does not know much about the specific nature of the antigen, initiates a chain of events that recruits other cells, some of which might know exactly what the antigen is, and specifically how to kill it.

3   The Leukocyte-Endothelial Blacklisting Strategy (LEBS)

This section presents an immune-inspired strategy for removing malicious nodes from a P2P network. The leukocyte-endothelial blacklisting strategy (LEBS) uses agents modeled after macrophages, TNF, and T-Cells. The network nodes are its endothelium, and they express a 'selectin' that informs the migration of macrophages and T-Cells. When a macrophage 'detects' a malicious node, it emits TNF, which raises the expression of selectin in any node it moves across. Other macrophages and T-Cells prefer to move onto nodes that have higher selectin expression levels, and thus into the area of 'inflammation'.

LEBS uses a multi-agent system (MAS) that employs a kind of stigmergy. The interaction between leukocytes and endothelial cells, which is stimulated by TNF and results in recruitment to infection sites. A macrophage, upon detecting an edge from a benign node to a malicious one, secretes TNF. This TNF diffuses into the surrounding nodes, inducing a local gradient of selectin expression in the nodes around the site of detection. Other agents move onto these nodes and interact with the selectin expression gradient differently according to their type. LEBS does not approach the problem of actually *detecting* which nodes are bad, as that problem is distinct from blacklisting, and at least one solution has been demonstrated [8]. Instead, the strategy aims to distribute blacklisting information to benign nodes to at least partially remove the malicious nodes from the P2P network.

Let N be the graph representation of a P2P network with some arbitrary topology. N is assumed to be connected and undirected. The vertices of N are the clients in the network, and the edges of N are the communication lines between clients. Each node thus has a *neighborhood*, which is the set of nodes connected to it [3]. Each node is also assumed to be marked either malicious or benign. Each node has a unique label or 'identity'. Nodes also each have a real-valued *selectin expression level* that ranges from 0 to 1, and is initially 0 for all nodes. This selectin expression level decays at a fixed rate, to a minimum of 0.0, across all nodes in the network. All nodes have a blacklist, which is initially empty. A benign node will not send or receive any communications from any node on its blacklist.

3.1   Overall Agent Execution

The strategy uses three types of agents, modeled after macrophages, T-Cells, and TNF. *Macrophage* agents are responsible for detecting malicious nodes, while *T-Cell* agents blacklist the malicious nodes detected by macrophages. *TNF* agents induce the recruitment of the other two agent types to the area around a malicious node after it has been detected. All agents 'live' on nodes of the network, and may move from one node to one of that node's neighbors via the edge connecting them. Agents may not exist on or move onto malicious nodes. Agents can also determine which of a node's neighbors are benign and which are malicious. All agents follow the same basic program, which is outlined below. The agent program controls both movement and execution. Each agent moves to a new node or stays on the same node it is currently occupying. That agent then *executes*, performing a function determined by its type.

```
run()
    currNode = nextNode(neighborsOf(currNode));
    execute();
```

Where `currNode` is the node that the agent being run is currently occupying. The function `neighborsOf()` takes a node as its argument, and returns a set of nodes, which is the union of the neighborhood of the argument and `currNode`. This effectively allows agents to stay on the same node, so they are not forced to move through the network.

Each agent has a *selectin adhesion function* ϕ that assigns a node a weight based on that node's selectin expression level. The function `nextNode()` uses the function ϕ to assign weights to the nodes in the set returned by `neighborsOf()`. `nextNode()` then selects the next node in a weight-proportionate manner, similar to how individuals are selected fitness-proportionately in a basic genetic algorithm [11]. More specifically, `nextNode()` determines the node occupied by the agent using ϕ–weight-proportionate roulette wheel selection. The motivation for using ϕ-weight-proportionate selection is to allow each agent type to respond differently to the selectin expression gradient. As we describe below, each agent type has its own ϕ-function and its own `execute()` function.

3.2 Macrophage Agents

A macrophage agent is responsible for moving from node to node, surveying the neighbors of its host node for maliciousness. If it detects a malicious node, it becomes *activated*, which means it presents the identity of this node for other agents to see and secretes t TNF agents, which will initially occupy the same node. T-Cells sharing the same node will see the presented node identity, become activated themselves, and seek out the edges connecting malicious nodes to benign. Upon activation, a macrophage starts a counter, called its *activation counter*. This counter has a positive (integral) initial value and is decremented on each subsequent call to `execute()`. The initial value of this counter is a parameter of the system called the *activation duration*. When the counter drops below zero, the macrophage returns to its unactivated state. The macrophage agent's `execute()` function is outlined below:

```
execute()
    if(!activated)
        foreach node in neighborsOf(currNode)
            if(node.malicious == true)
                secreteTNF(t); //creates t TNF agents
                target = node;  //present this node
                counter = activationDuration;
                activated = true;
    if(counter < 0)   //activation counter
        activated = false;
    counter = counter - 1;
```

The macrophage agent's selectin adhesion function ϕ is a simple polynomial function of the `currNode`'s selectin expression level:

$$\phi_M(s) = s - s^3. \tag{1}$$

In this equation, s is the selectin expression level of the argument node. This function was chosen somewhat arbitrarily. Since this function has a maximum over the interval $[0,1]$ at $\sqrt{3}$, macrophages should have the highest probability of moving on to nodes which express a selectin level of around $\sqrt{3}$. This encourages macrophages to avoid the very center of the selectin expression gradient. Instead of migrating straight to the site of detection, a macrophage should 'surround' the malicious node by moving around the center of the gradient area, resulting in new detection events from other neighbors of that malicious node, provoking further inflammation.

3.3 T-Cell Agents

T-Cell agents function in much the same way as macrophages, but their purpose is different. If a T-Cell shares a node with an activated macrophage, that T-Cell becomes activated. It then seeks out nodes with connections to the malicious node that the macrophage was presenting when the T-Cell encountered it. This malicious node is now called the T-Cell's *target*. A T-Cell's selectin adhesion function behaves differently depending on whether it is activated or not. An unactivated T-Cell seeks out the node with the highest selectin expression level, while an activated T-Cell tries to seek out nodes with a moderate level of selectin expression. The T-Cell agent's selectin adhesion function is listed below:

$$\phi_T(s) = \begin{array}{ll} activated, & s - s^3 \\ unactivated, & s^2 \end{array}. \tag{2}$$

When an activated T-Cell occupies a node, it checks that node's neighborhood for the malicious node that it is currently targeting. If the neighborhood contains the target node, the T-Cell adds the malicious node to the benign (current) node's blacklist. The T-Cell then returns to its unactivated state. Below is the `execute()` function for T-Cells:

```
execute()
    if(activated)
        if(counter > 0)
            if(neighborsOf(currNode).contains(target))
                currNode.blackList(target);
                activated = false;
        else
            activated = false;
        counter = counter - 1;
    else
        if(currNode has activated macrophage macro)
            target = macro.target;
            counter = activationDuration;
```

3.4 TNF Agents

TNF agents are secreted by a macrophage agent when it detects a malicious node. They are otherwise absent from the network. Moreover, they have a finite lifetime, determined by a decrementing counter similar to the counters that track the activation duration in T-Cells and macrophages. When the macrophage 'secretes' the TNF agents, it initializes this lifetime counter to a positive integer less than 100. The TNF agent's selectin adhesion function is the constant function $\phi_{TNF} = c$, which means that the probability of a particular node being selected from a set of k nodes is 1/k, since the ratio of that node's weight is c divided by the total weight of all the nodes, which is ck. This means they effectively ignore the selectin expression gradient. However, the TNF agents' purpose is to induce the gradient. They achieve this by adding the remaining value of their lifetime counter (divided by 100 for scaling to the range [0,1]) to the selectin expression level for their current nodes. Here is their comparatively simple execute():

```
execute()
    if(counter > 0)
        currNode.selectinExpr = currNode.selectinExpr +
            (counter/100.0);
        if(currNode.selectinExpr > 1.0)
            currNode.selectinExpr = 1.0;
        counter = counter - 1;
    else
        die() //delete this TNF agent from the network
```

3.5 Agent Interactions

LEBS aims to allocate agents to perform blacklisting through a combination of stigmergy and direct agent interaction. The selectin expression level is the medium for the stigmergy. Direct agent interaction occurs when T-Cell agents detect an activated macrophage on the same node and become activated themselves. On activation, T-Cell agents begin to target the malicious node presented by the activated macrophage. They remain activated until they find a node connected to their target node or until their activation counter runs out. Figure 1 illustrates an example of the LEBS agents detecting and subsequently blacklisting a malicious node. The figure shows the detection of a malicious node and the subsequent recruitment of agents to the site of the detection. Each TNF agent has a lifetime counter which is decremented at the end of the TNF agent's turn. TNF agents add the remaining value (divided by 100, for scaling to the range [0,1]) of their lifetime counter to the selectin expression level of their current node each turn. At the start of each turn, the selectin expression level of each node is reduced by 0.01. Thus, the selectin expression level is elevated around sites of node decection, and then decays over time, resulting in a transient local gradient that forms the basis of T-Cell and Macrophage agent recruitment.

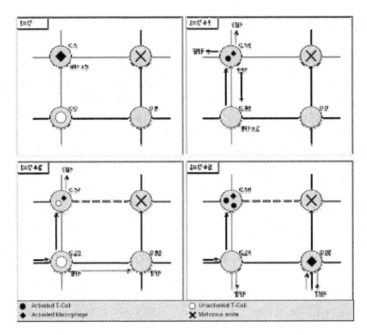

Fig. 1. Recruitment of agents to site of malicious node detection. Each frame is taken at the end of a cycle, beginning at top left at the time of detection t^*. The selectin expression level is shown at the top right of each node. From top left, (t^*) a macrophage detects a malicious node, and secretes five TNF agents which raise the selectin level at their node, ($t^* + 1$) a nearby T-Cell is recruited to the site of detection, ($t^* + 2$) the newly activated T-Cell blacklists a malicious edge (*dotted edge*), ($t^* + 3$) other agents are recruited to the area around the malicious node.

4 Experimental Methods

This section summarizes the methods used to evaluate the effectiveness of LEBS. Only a brief examination of the strategy is described. Specifically, the performance impact of variations in agent population, TNF lifetime, and the number of TNF agents secreted per detection are explored. A common network is used for all tests.

LEBS was tested using the PeerSim framework [14], a P2P simulator designed for scalability. A cycle-driven protocol was used to provide hosting services for agents in the simulator. Each node has an instance of this protocol, which allows it to host agents as they move through the network.

The same network was used in all tests, though the placement of malicious nodes was random in each test. Although it is not a realistic model of a real P2P network, a toroidal grid topology[1] was used for these initial simulations for simplicity. The network was composed of 10,000 nodes. For all experiments, 500 of these nodes were labeled as malicious before the run of the simulation, and they were uniformly distributed throughout the network. The network size and number of malicious node

---

[1] All nodes are arranged in a square grid, each node having exactly 4 neighbors. The nodes on an edge are connecting to the corresponding nodes on the opposite edge of the grid.

were chosen to match the work of Jelasity, *et al.* in [8]. All nodes had degree 4. The simulations each ran for 1,000 *cycles*. A cycle in this experiment is defined as one call to run() for each agent in the network. Recall that run() allows each agent to move to a new node and then execute once.

All benign nodes were capable of hosting an unlimited number of agents of any type. T-Cell agents and macrophage agents were uniformly distributed throughout the network at the beginning of each simulation. At no time was any agent placed on, or allowed to move on to, a malicious node. At the end of each cycle, the fraction of malicious edges that had been marked blacklisted was recorded. That is, for each malicious node, the number of its 4 neighbors that had that malicious node in their blacklist was recorded, and the resulting sum divided by the total number of edges to malicious nodes in the network.

A common control set of values for T-Cell and macrophage populations, number of malicious nodes, maximum activation durations, TNF lifetime, and TNF per detection was determined. This control was used as a performance benchmark for all other tests of LEBS. The control macrophage and T-Cell populations were both 500. As mentioned above, 500 malicious nodes of the 10,000 total were marked malicious. The TNF agent lifetime after secretion by a macrophage was 10 cycles. The T-Cell maximum activation duration was 10 cycles, and the macrophage activation duration was 50 cycles. On each macrophage activation, 5 TNF agents were secreted and placed at the node hosting the newly activated macrophage. The selectin expression level decay rate for each node was 0.01 per cycle, and the level was decayed at the start of each cycle.

Each of these parameters was varied over a reasonable range. Since this is a brief, primarily qualitative evaluation of LEBS, only a handful of values were tested. For each value, 30 tests were run. The data presented are cycle averages of the fraction of blacklisted edges over all 30 trials.

5   Results

The data from the evaluation of LEBS are presented here. For each experiment, the cycle averages of the fraction of blacklisted edges are plotted against the time in

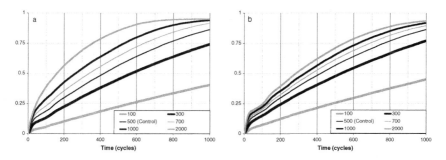

Fig. 2. Selected population values for (a) macrophage and (b) T-Cell agents. Each curve shows a distinct value for the number of agents in the network. Selected values range from 100 to 2000 macrophage or T-Cell agents.

cycles. The fraction of the malicious edges that have been blacklisted is reported as a number between 0 and 1.0, with 1.0 being 100% of all malicious edges blacklisted. Each plot shows several values of the variable for the experiment. In all experiments, the common control is used as a reference for determining relative performance.

When more macrophage or T-Cell agents were present on the network, LEBS performed better. The performance data for selected population values are shown in Figure 2 above. Six different values for initial populations for macrophages (Fig. 2a) and T-Cells (Fig. 2b) were examined. More macrophages or more T-Cells clearly results in faster blacklisting. Figure 3, below, shows how LEBS responds to changes in the parameters that affect how well it can recruit other agents to the site of malicious node detection. LEBS is very sensitive to changes in both the number of TNF agents secreted per detection (Fig. 3a), and the TNF lifetime (Fig. 3b).

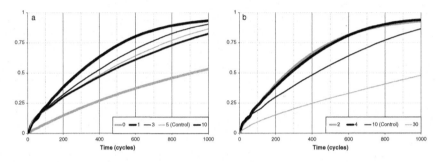

Fig. 3. Selected values for (a) the number of TNF agents secreted per detection and (b) the lifetime of TNF agents in cycles.

All experiments featured a nondecreasing sequence of values for the fraction of blacklisted edges. This is unsurprising, since the network was static and no additional malicious nodes were introduced to the network after the start of each run. Because the data is nondecreasing, the time (in cycles) to reach a particular blacklisting milestone, such as a 50% blacklisting of malicious edges, is a useful performance metric. The values for the time to blacklist 50% of malicious edges (BL50) and the terminal blacklisting fraction (time = 1000 cycles) are presented in tables 1-4 below. A BL50 value of 'X' means that for the value tested, LEBS failed to blacklist 50% of the malicious edges by the end of the simulation. All values were checked for statistical significance with a Student's t-test. The t-test results against the common control are listed in the tables. A result of greater than 2.0 confirmed with a 95% probability that the difference between the tested value and the control was statistically significant. T-test results marked with an asterix (*) indicate that the value tested cannot be confidently said to be significantly different from the control.

The above data represents only a short look at the performance of LEBS. For the values used in the common control, LEBS is very successful at blacklisting the malicious nodes. 86.4% of all edges to malicious nodes were blacklisted within 1000 cycles. Moreover, 50% of the malicious edges were blacklisted within 422 cycles in the common control. Unsurprisingly, LEBS is more successful at blacklisting malicious

Table 1. Macrophage population values

Macrophage Population	BL50(cycle)	BL50 t-test	Terminal Blacklisting (%)	TBL t-test
100	X	X	40.5	23.992
300	573	201.35	74.2	5.8064
500 (Control)	422	0	86.4	0
700	339	116.09	91.6	2.8778
1000	264	233.23	94.1	4.4029
2000	160	411.29	95.1	411.29

Table 2. T-Cell population values

T-Cell Population	BL50(cycle)	BL50 t-test	Terminal Blacklisting (%)	TBL t-test
100	X	X	45.0	19.777
300	534	101.37	77.1	4.4765
500 (Control)	422	0	86.4	0
700	373	50.878	89.5	1.7636*
1000	335	93.792	91.8	3.1196
2000	286	143.38	93.5	4.0357

Table 3. Values for TNF secreted by macrophage per detection of malicious node

TNF Detection	BL50(cycle)	BL50 t-test	Terminal Blacklisting (%)	TBL t-test
0	910	515.71	53.2	16.424
1	287	201.75	93.3	3.9842
3	371	71.824	90.4	2.2350
5 (Control)	422	0	86.4	0
10	443	29.32	82.4	29.324

Table 4. TNF lifetime in cycles

TNF Lifetime (cycles)	BL50(cycle)	BL50 t-test	Terminal Blacklisting (%)	TBL t-test
2	265	236.67	92.8	3.3460
4	281	212.05	94.0	4.0740
10 (Control)	422	0	86.4	0
30	X	885.85	48.0	17.553

nodes with more T-Cell (Table 2) and Macrophage (Table 1) agents at its disposal, given a constant number of malicious nodes. LEBS is also very sensitive to the parameters that directly influence the generation of the selectin expression gradient around the site of malicious node detection. The number of TNF agents secreted per detection and their lifetime in cycles has a dramatic influence over the ability of LEBS to blacklist malicious nodes.

Table 3 illustrates LEBS' sensitivity to the number of TNF agents secreted per detection. When only 1 or 3 TNF agents were secreted, performance was somewhat better than the global control value of 5. A 100% increase in TNF per detection of the control value resulted in a marginally higher BL50. This suggests that the number of TNF agents secreted per detection has a diminishing marginal impact on performance.

It is worth noting that the performance of LEBS without any selectin expression gradient at all was measured. Table 3 shows the BL50 cycle and terminal blacklisting fraction for a TNF per detection value of zero. This means that no TNF agents ever entered the network, and so never induced a selectin expression gradient. As a result, all movement of macrophages and T-Cells through the network was totally random. That is, given any set of nodes to move to in the next cycle, a T-Cell or macrophage will choose from them with equal probability. Thus, it was relatively unlikely that T-Cells would move onto a node with an activated macrophage. As one might expect, the performance of LEBS in this case was poor: a BL50 cycle of 910.

LEBS also appears to be sensitive to the lifetime in cycles of a TNF agent. Table 4 shows that a short lifetime resulted in better performance for the small number of values tested. The topology of the network was chosen to promote the effectiveness of the selectin expression gradients in getting agents to the site of detection of a malicious node. The selectin adhesion functions were chosen to promote a good covering of the gradient by activated agents. One can imagine that if this gradient is too large, or isn't "steep" enough, the agents will be directed away from the target malicious node. In other words, if the gradient covers too much of the local area around the malicious node, the T-Cells will never find the neighbors of that node, and so it will not be blacklisted.

LEBS performed admirably in may cases. For example, when only one TNF agent per detection was secreted, 93.3% of all edges to malicious nodes were blacklisted using the same population levels as the global control. In addition, LEBS achieved BL50 at cycle 287 with one TNF per detection.

6 Discussion

This paper described LEBS, a strategy for blacklisting malicious nodes from a P2P network inspired by the leukocyte recruitment mechanism of the human immune system. A type of stigmergy was used to direct agents to the neighbors of malicious nodes. This communication was modeled on the interaction between leukocytes and endothelial cells via selectins and their reciprocal ligands. In LEBS, macrophage agents secrete TNF agents, which induce a selectin-like gradient on node of the network. T-Cell and macrophage agents then prefer to move on these nodes. LEBS was effective in blacklisting a high percentage of malicious nodes in the network. It was shown to be sensitive to several parameters, including the population sizes of T-Cell and macrophage agents. LEBS was also shown to be sensitive to the parameters that influence the selectin expression gradient. This is somewhat unsurprising, because the selectin expression gradient is part of the 'inflammation' that is the basis for LEBS' operation.

The data presented here is not enough to make strong statements about the correlation between the performance of LEBS and parameters such as agent populations, TNF lifetime, and TNF secretion rate. Moreover, the performance data here relied on a network topology that promoted, or at least did not significantly hinder, the effectiveness of a selectin expression gradient in recruiting agents to the site of detection. Unfortunately, as noted earlier, P2P networks are very often *not* a toroidal grid. For LEBS to be deemed useful in blacklisting malicious nodes from real P2P networks, it must be tested on more realistic P2P network topologies. The network used in the study was also static. In a real P2P network, clients join and leave constantly, resulting in a dynamic network. LEBS must be tested on a dynamic network as well.

In this study, the values tested for the population sizes, the TNF lifetime, and the TNF per detection were chosen somewhat arbitrarily. A more thorough investigation of LEBS' response to variations in these parameters is needed. More importantly, the selectin adhesion functions were not varied at all in this study. Given how sensitive LEBS seems with respect to changes in parameters responsible for inducing the selectin expression gradient, the selectin adhesion functions are likely to have an equally dramatic impact on performance.

The malicious node distribution over the network in this study was uniform. It is possible that LEBS would perform much better if the malicious nodes were concentrated in one local region of the network. One can imagine that a macrophage, having detected a malicious node, might recruit other macrophages to the nodes around the site of detection. Once there, they might detect other malicious nodes, causes more inflammation, etc. until most of the agents in the network were concentrated on attacking this group of malicious nodes. However, a full blacklisting of a cluster of malicious nodes might also result in isolating some non-malicious nodes. Moreover, if the blacklisting of a cluster of nodes partitioned the network, some agents would also be isolated. Care must be taken to ensure that LEBS remains effective in the presence of a non-uniform distribution of malicious nodes in the P2P network. This should be a focus of future work on LEBS.

Acknowledgements

The author would like to thank James Reggia for editing, review, and general support. Scott Weems reviewed the data from the simulation study and provided guidance with the statistical investigation of the data. Gian Paolo Jesi suggested a useful approach on implementing the simulation study using the Peersim framework. This work was supported in part by NSF Award IIS-0325098.

References

1. A. Abbas, A. Lichtman, J. Pober, *Cellular and Molecular Immunology*, 4th edition, Philadelphia: W.B. Saunders Company, 2000
2. O. Babaoglu, H. Meling and A. Montresor, "Anthill: A framework for the development of agent-based peerto-peer systems," Proceedings of the 22nd International Conference on Distributed Computing Systems(ICDCS), Vienna, Austria, 2002, pp. 15-22.
3. Balakrishnan, R. and Ranganathan, K. "Vertex Cuts and Edge Cuts." §3.1 in *A Textbook of Graph Theory.* New York: Springer-Verlag, p. 3, 1999.
4. G. Di Caro and M. Dorigo. AntNet: Distributed Stigmergetic Control for Communications Networks. Journal of Artificial Intelligence Research, 9:317–365, 1998.
5. P. Dasgupta, "Incentive Driven Node Discovery in a Peer-to-Peer Network Using Mobile Intelligent Agents," Proceedings of the 7th International Conference on Artificial Intelligence, Las Vegas, June 2003, pp. 750-756.
6. M. Dorigo, V. Maniezzo, and A. Colorni. "The Ant System: Optimization by a Colony of Cooperating Agents." IEEE Transactions on Systems, Man, and Cybernetics-Part B, 26(1):29– 41, 1996.
7. C. Jacob, J. Litorco, L. Lee, "Immunity Through Swarms: Agent-Based Simulations of the Human Immune System", Proceedings of ICARIS 2004: 3rd International Conference on Artificial Immune Systems, Catania, Sicily, Italy, 2004.
8. M. Jelasity, A. Montresor, and O. Babaoglu. "Detection and removal of malicious peers in gossip-based protocols." In 2nd Bertinoro Workshop on Future Directions in Distributed Computing: Survivability: Obstacles and Solutions (FuDiCo II: S.O.S.), Bertinoro, Italy, June 2004. invitation only workshop, proceedings online at http://www.cs.utexas.edu/users/lorenzo/sos/
9. Henry Y. K. Lau, Vicky W. K. Wong, "Immunologic Control Framework for Automated Material Handling". Proceedings of ICARIS 2003: 57-68
10. D. Milojicic, V. Kalogeraki, R. Lukose, K. Nagaraja, J. Pruyne, B. Richard, S. Rollins and Z. Xu, "Peer-to-peer computing", HP Technical Report, 2002 HPL-2002-57
11. M. Mitchell, *An Introduction to Genetic Algorithms*, Cambridge, MIT Press, 2001, 166
12. H. Nishiyama, F. Mizoguchi, "Design of Security System Based on Immune System", Proceedings of the 10th IEEE International Workshop on Enabling Technolgies: Infrastructure for Collaborative Enterprises, Massachusetts, 2001, 138-143
13. Y. Pang, Y. Yan, H. Yafei, Z. Yiping, Z. Shiyong, "Securing Ad Hoc Networks through mobile agent", Proceedings of the 3rd International Conference on Information Security, Shainghai, China, 2004, 125-129
14. M. Jelasity, A. Montresor, G. P. Jesi, *Peersim Peer-to-Peer Simulator*, http://peersim.sourceforge.net, January 7th 2005.
15. S. Sathyanath, F. Sahin., "AISIMAM – An Artificial Immune System Based Intelligent Multi Agent Model and its Application to a Mine Detection Problem", Proceedings of ICARIS 2002: 1st International Conference on Artificial Immune Systems, University of Kent, 2002.

Self-regulating Method for Model Library Based Artificial Immune Systems

Zejun Wu[1,2] and Yiwen Liang[1]

[1] School of Computer / State Key Lab of Software Engineering, Wuhan University,
430079 Wuhan, Hubei, China
wu_zejun@hotmail.com, ywliang@whu.edu.cn
[2] School of Information Science, Zhongnan University of Economics and Law,
430060 Wuhan, Hubei, China

Abstract. In most of the existing artificial immune systems, instabilities mainly stem from the empirical pre-definition of a scenario-specific model. In this paper we introduce a self-regulating algorithm into an integrated platform of artificial immune systems based on Model Library. The algorithm can dynamically configure multi-AIS-models according to the "pressure" produced during the course of training and testing, so that the system can automatically adapt to detect various objects. In addition, a novel hybrid evaluation method is proposed to improve the self-adaptability of the system. Experimental results demonstrate that the self-regulating algorithm can achieve better performance as compared with traditional artificial immune systems in terms of false positive and false negative rates.

1 Introduction

A family of techniques originated from the community of immunology, known as artificial immune systems (AIS), has been emerging as a new branch of Artificial Intelligence (AI) and gained increasing popularity in the past decade. By investigating the mechanism of human immune system (HIS), researchers in the computational fields have successfully introduced AIS to solve a wide range of anomaly detection problems, such as cancer diagnose, virus detection, mortgage deceit and fault diagnose [1][2].

The immunological principles employed by AIS models, such as the immune network theory, the mechanisms of negative selection, the clonal selection principles and the danger theory, are by far treated separately although there are underlying correlations amongst them. Most state-of-the-art anomaly detection systems are designed for detecting a particular kind of objects using pre-tuned AIS models, resulting in numerous variations of the general AIS models. In other words, the choice of an AIS model, including its expression, matching, training, evaluation, and various controlling parameters, is in general pre-determined by experts based on their experience on hypothesized problem space. The model is then iteratively adjusted until satisfactory outcome has been achieved in training and testing. If there is no or few improvements during this process, one need resort to other models.

C. Jacob et al. (Eds.): ICARIS 2005, LNCS 3627, pp. 353–365, 2005.
© Springer-Verlag Berlin Heidelberg 2005

Hence, there are two issues to be addressed in conventional approaches: model predefinition and model evaluation. For the first one, due to limited experience of each individual expert, it is nontrivial to define a robust model for detecting all possible objects. Taking network security for an instance, a model predefined to cope with worm viruses could be prone to flood packet attack. For the second problem, we argue that single model evaluation alone is inadequate for evaluating anomaly cases varying in such a dynamic way, as features used in one kind of detectors could be quite limited. Following the previous example, in order to detect an attack involving both worm viruses and flood packets, it is necessary to use two kinds of detectors with the expressions of regular language as well as finite-state automata.

In this paper, we propose an Integrated Platform of Artificial Immune Systems (IPAisys) based on the detector population mode to tackle the aforementioned problems. In this platform, a group of model prototypes are integrated in a unified framework, wherein the model structure can be automatically regularized by using the output of training and testing as so-called "pressure". A self-regulating algorithm is developed with the use of Model Library to achieve optimal multi-AIS-models through dynamic configuration. Therefore, as compared with the traditional single model evaluation process shown in Figure 1, our platform is more flexible and intelligent in that it is capable of choosing an optimal combination of different models to cooperatively evaluate each unknown case.

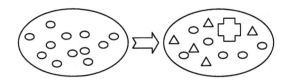

Fig. 1. Evaluation from single model to multi-AIS-models

The remainder of this paper is organized as follows. In Section 2, some related work is reviewed with a brief introduction of AIS model and IPAisys. After that, the self-regulating algorithm based IPAisys is discussed in detail in Section 3. We analyze three control experiments in Section 4, followed by concluding remarks and future work in Section 5.

2   Related Work

2.1   Detector Population Based AIS Model

S. Forrest *et al.* proposed in [3][4] an AIS model based on binary string expression, r-contiguous matching and negative selection algorithm (NSA). They defined "Self" as the normal behavior patterns of a network monitoring system. Some random patterns are produced as immature detectors and tested by "Self". An immature detector will be abandoned in case that it is matched with one pattern of "Self".

J. Kim [5] pointed out that NSA could cause severe scaling problem in face of tremendous network traffic data. Apart from that, r-contiguous matching, as a continuous matching method, is inappropriate for network traffic data with discrete features. She thereby proposed an AIS model based on a semantic expression of detectors, i.e. multi-dimensional features, and the IF-THEN matching rule, and replaced NSA by the clonal selection algorithm (CSA), alleviating the scaling problem to certain extent.

To further enlarge the problem space of anomaly detection, F. González [6] developed the rules-based NSA, in which several real-value based expressions were detailed, including hyper-rectangle, fuzzy rules and hyper-sphere and corresponding detector generation algorithms.

It can be seen from the approaches above that detector population based AIS models are mainly assembled by expression method, matching function, detector training algorithm, evaluation system and neutralization way. A typical AIS model works as follows. Immature detectors are randomly generated with the 0-1 strings expression and then transferred to a training host, where they evolve into mature ones based on a training algorithm. At the same time, the matching function will calculate the fitness values. These matured detectors will then be combined to evaluate an unknown object, which will be annihilated by predefined neutralization way if a danger is assumed. According to this process, the structure of detector population based AIS models can be summarized in Figure 2 to reflect the common characteristics among diverse AIS models as described in [7][8][9][10].

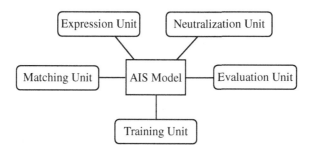

Fig. 2. Structure of AIS model based on detector population mode

As discussed in our previous work [11], the five units in Figure 2, i.e. expression unit (Ex), matching unit (Ma), training unit (Tr), evaluation unit (Ev) and neutralization unit (Ne), can define an AIS model based on detector population mode. In this paper, as only one genetic algorithm is predefined (see Section 3 and 4), Tr unit can be fixed. In the consideration that most AIS experts are mainly concerned with detection rather than elimination of anomaly, we also ignore Ne unit for simplicity. As such, we shall mainly focus on the effects of Ex, Ma and Ev units in this paper and represent an AIS model by a triple of units as:

$$AisModel \equiv (Ex, Ma, Ev)$$

2.2 Integrated Platform of AIS (IPAisys)

In general, IPAisys consists of two main modules: data pre-processing module and model evolution module, each with its own components. All components are integrated into a unified framework as illustrated in Figure 3.

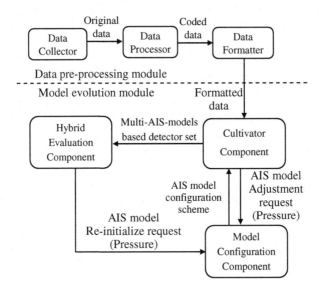

Fig. 3. Architecture of the integrated platform of AIS

In the data pre-processing module, antigen data are collected by the data collector and transferred to the data processor, wherein the original data are coded for compression and concatenation. Following the data processor is the data formatter, which translates coded data into XML format to provide a data-independent interface to the model evolution module so that the AIS model can be uniformly configured regardless of the format of original data. After that, the XML format data are delivered to the cultivator component of the model evolution module.

In the model evolution module, the model configuration component is responsible for providing an optimal configuration of multi-AIS-models to the cultivator component. With formatted data and the optimal configuration scheme, the cultivator component trains multi-AIS-models based detector set for hybrid evaluation component using genetic algorithm, and meanwhile return fitness values as "pressure" to the model configuration component. After receiving the matured detector set from the cultivator component, the hybrid evaluation component further improves it by testing and sends re-initialization request to the model configuration component if the testing results are unsatisfactory.

Controlling the development of multi-AIS-models, the model configuration component and cultivator component are the core constituent elements of IPAisys and have been explained in detail in our previous work [11]. In this paper, a self-regulating algorithm together with a hybrid evaluation method is proposed to further enhance the self-adaptability of IPAisys.

3   Self-regulating and Hybrid Evaluation

The self-regulating algorithm aims to dynamically configure multi-AIS-models based on Model Library and its lifecycle. According to multi-AIS-models chosen, the hybrid evaluation method detects an anomaly based on the cooperative decision of different detector subsets.

3.1   Model Library and Its Lifecycle

Model Library is built on both unit information and parameter information. The unit library, consisting of Ex, Ma, Ev, Tr and Ne, should be established first, followed by the predefinition of corresponding parameters. As we have excluded Tr and Ne units from the unit library, the configurability of an AIS model rests on units Ex, Ma and Ev. Taking Ex unit for example, Binary String (BS), Digital Sequence (DS), and Hyper-rectangle (HR) are optional expression items, as shown in Figure 4.

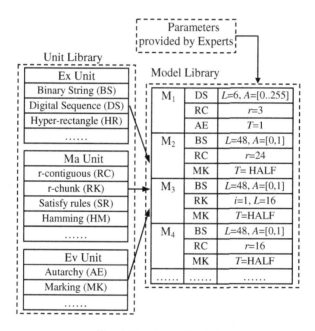

Fig. 4. Structure of Model

Model Library is then constructed as follows. One optional item is randomly chosen from each unit list in the unit library to create an abstract model Ma_i. Several abstract models compose an abstract model set $Ma=\{Ma_1, Ma_2 \ldots Ma_n\}$, which is then empirically initialized with parameters as $M=\{M_1, M_2 \ldots M_n\}$. For M_1, the length of the digital sequence expression is six ($L=6$), and each number in the digital sequence can take from 0 to 255 ($A=[0\ldots255]$), and the r value of r-contiguous matching function is three ($r=3$). $T=1$ indicates autarchy evaluation way, i.e. an anomaly is detected if any detector suggests so, and T=HALF implies marking evaluation way, that is, an anomaly is detected if more than half detectors suggest so. Note that the configuration of an AIS model should also be constrained by the Ex-Ma relationship to prevent invalid AIS models from being assembled. Table 1 lists several typical relationships between Ex and Ma. For instance, "BS+RC" can be expressed as a dependence relationship between BS (Ex Unit) and RC (Ma Unit) while "HR−RC" as a restriction relationship between HR (Ex Unit) and RC (Ma Unit).

Table 1. Ex-Ma relationships of dependency and restriction

Unit name	Unit name	Type of relationship	Relationship list
Ex	Ma	Dependence (+)	BS+RC; DS+RC; BS+RK; DS+RK; HR+SR
Ex	Ma	Restriction (−)	BS−SR; DS−SR; HR−RC; HR−RK;

As unpredictable parameters make it infeasible to manifest all possible models in Model Library, the lifecycle of Model Library need to be designed in demand of limited resources. In Model Library, the total number of models is fixed, and the life value of each model M_i, $Life_i$, will increase or decrease according to the feedback of the self-regulating algorithm (see Section 3.2). When $Life_i$ drops below a threshold, M_i will be replaced by a new model.

3.2 Self-regulating Algorithm

IPAisys can automatically choose models from Model Library and combine them into multi-AIS-models using some regulating methods.

In [11], we attempted to regulate multi-AIS-models by iteratively transforming a detector set D={D_1, D_2 ... D_k} according to a transition matrix, P_{matrix}, defined as

$$P_{matrix} = \begin{pmatrix} p_{11} & p_{12} & \cdots & p_{1k} \\ p_{21} & p_{22} & \cdots & p_{2k} \\ \cdots & \cdots & \cdots & \cdots \\ p_{k1} & p_{k2} & \cdots & p_{kk} \end{pmatrix},$$

where $\sum_{j=1}^{k} p_{ij} = 1 \ (i = 1...k)$.

The transition probability P_{ij} ($i = 1...k, j = 1...k$) is the chance for detectors D_i to change into detectors D_j. Therefore, the number of detectors D_j should be proportional to $\sum_{i=1}^{k} p_{ij}$ after one round of regulation. We set P_{ii}=1.0 (i=1...k) and P_{ij}=0 ($i \neq j$) for initialization to equally weight each model without other prior knowledge.

The change of P_{matrix} is decided by the fitness values of D={D_1, D_2 ... D_k} obtained during training. After N generations of evolution, the average fitness of D_i (i=1...k), denoted by F_{Di}, is calculated as "pressure" and P_{matrix} changes according to the following rules:

(1) $P_{ij}' = P_{ij}$ iff $F_{Di} \geq F_{Dj}$ $(i \neq j)$;

(2) $P_{ij}' = P_{ij} + p_{change}$ iff $F_{Di} < F_{Dj}$ $(i \neq j)$;

(3) $P_{ii}' = 1 - \sum_{j=1}^{k} P_{ij}'$ $(i \neq j$ and $i = 1...k)$;

where P_{change} is a predefined offset constant to P_{ij}.

Figure 5 shows a regulation example of multi-AIS-models, $M = \{M_1, M_2, M_3\}$, where each M_i $(i=1, 2, 3)$ contains 100 detectors at the very beginning. With the transformation of P_{matrix}, the number of detectors of M_1, M_2 and M_3 changes to 120, 100, 80 after the first round and to 140, 100, 60 after the second round.

$$P_{matrix} = \begin{pmatrix} 1.0 & 0 & 0 \\ 0 & 1.0 & 0 \\ 0 & 0 & 1.0 \end{pmatrix} \boxed{\text{1st change}} \Rightarrow P_{matrix}' = \begin{pmatrix} 1.0 & 0 & 0 \\ 0.1 & 0.9 & 0 \\ 0.1 & 0.1 & 0.8 \end{pmatrix} \boxed{\text{2nd change}} \Rightarrow P_{matrix}'' = \begin{pmatrix} 1.0 & 0 & 0 \\ 0.2 & 0.8 & 0 \\ 0.2 & 0.2 & 0.6 \end{pmatrix} \cdots$$

Fig. 5. P_{matrix} changes from initialization to other states

The P_{matrix} method is based on intuition that the more useful a detector the larger proportion it should grow into. However, experimental results show that this method usually leads to the impoverishment of diversity. When multi-AIS-models $M=\{M_1, M_2 ... M_n\}$ is iteratively regulated according to the transition matrix, the number of detectors of M_i $(i=1...n, i \neq k)$ will gradually reduce to zero and the detectors in the detector set D are dominated by those from M_k.

To keep the diversity of detectors for the purpose of cooperative evaluation, we propose a self-regulating algorithm in this paper to dynamically configure multi-AIS-models without changing the density of each model. The main procedures are diagrammatized in Figure 6 and described below.

(1) A primitive multi-AIS-models is initialized by choosing a model set $M=\{M_1, M_2 ... M_n\}$ from Model Library according to Ex-Ma relationship;

(2) In the cultivator component, genetic algorithm is performed for each M_i $(i=1...n)$;

(3) Detector set $D=\{D_1, D_2 ... D_n\}$ is produced after one generation of genetic algorithm ($D_i=\{d_1, d_2...d_{wi}\}$, $i=1...k$, is the detector subset from model M_i, and w_i is the detector number of D_i);

(4) The average fitness value of all detectors in D_i, F_{Di}, is compared with a threshold μ; if $F_{Di} < \mu$, the parameters of Ma unit in M_i is regulated for the next generation and the value of $Life_i$ decreases, and vice versa; Given $D_i=\{d_1, d_2 ... d_{wi}\}$, function $d\_match\_self()$ computes the degree of mismatch between d_j $(j=1...w_i)$ and self training set, and function $match\_nonself()$ computes the degree of match between d_j $(j=1...w_i)$ and nonself training set. F_{Di} is then obtained by:

$$F_{Di} = \frac{1}{w_i} \sum_{j=1}^{w_i} (d\_match\_self(d_j)/x_1 + match\_nonself(d_j)/x_2)$$

where x_1 and x_2 are weighting parameters.

(5) The total regulation times of Ma unit parameters in M_i, $Retry_i$, is compared with a threshold ; if $Retry_i >$, the Ma unit of M_i is replaced by another one in the next generation and the value of $Life_i$ decreases, and vice versa;

(6) Genetic algorithm is run for N generations to obtain a mature detector set $Dm=\{Dm_1, Dm_2 ... Dm_n\}$;

(7) In the hybrid evaluation component, the False Positive rate (FP) and False Negative rate (FN) of Dm are compared against thresholds and ; if $FP <$ or $FN <$, re-initialization request is sent to the model configuration component and a new model set will be chosen; N is reset to zero;

(8) Excellent detector set $De=\{De_1, De_2 ... De_n\}$ is output with an evaluation function for real applications.

We now apply the proposed regulating algorithm to the data described in Figure 4. In Step 4, based on the comparison between F_{Di} and the threshold μ, M_i is regulated according to Model Library, where M_2 and M_4 are similar models except for r in Ma unit. M_2 can thus be substituted by M_4 as one regulation operation in this step. In Step 5, M_2 and M_3 are similar models expect for Ma unit, i.e. M_2 has r-contiguous matching while M_3 has r-chunk matching. M_2 can be replaced by M_3 as one regulation operation in this step. In Step 7, according to comparison between values (*FP* and *FN*) and thresholds (and), current multi-AIS-models, M, is replaced by another model set, M', which is re-initialized from Model Library.

It can be seen from Figure 6 that the self-regulation of multi-AIS-models consists of three types of regulation operations: parameter-regulation, unit-regulation and model-set-regulation.

3.3 Hybrid Evaluation Method

The hybrid evaluation component is responsible for testing $D = \{D_1, D_2...D_k\}$ in terms of *FP* and *FN* to decide whether multi-AIS-models need to be re-initialized. The testing function, $f_{testing}(x)$, also referred to as evaluation function, can be defined in two forms below, representing two evaluation rules:

(1) $f_{testing}(x) = g_{D_1}(x) \otimes g_{D_2}(x) \otimes ......g_{D_k}(x)$;

(2) $f_{testing}(x) = \sum_{i=1}^{k} g_{D_i}(x)$;

where $g_{Di}(x)$ $(i=1...k)$ is an evaluation function of detector subset D_i, depending on Ev unit selected in the model configuration component. $g_{Di}(x) = 1$ (positive response) means that D_i detects x as anomaly, and vice versa. In Function (1), x is detected as anomaly as long as any detector subset D_i $(i \in [1...k])$ gives positive response; and detected as normality only if all D_i $(i=1...k)$ are negative. On the other hand, x is detected as anomaly in Function (2) if $f_{tesing}(x) > \eta$ $(0 \le \eta \le k)$, and vice versa, i.e. the decision is made by cooperative marking of each D_i. In our case, η is set to $k/2$ based on the major voting rule. We can see that Function (1) accords with an Autarchy evaluation way and Function (2) stands for a Marking evaluation way.

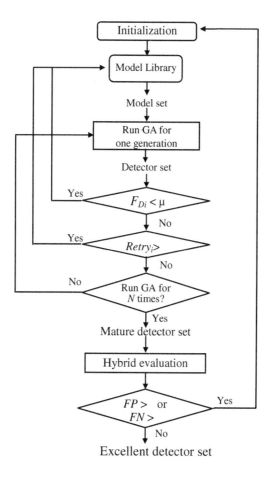

Fig. 6. Self-regulating algorithm flow chat

A problem arises that the first testing function lacks cooperation among different models while the second one ignores the relative importance of each D_i ($i=1...k$). We thus propose a Hybrid evaluation function to emphasize detectors with good fitness values.

$$(3) \quad f_{tesing}(x) = \sum_{i=1}^{k} \frac{F_{Di}}{\sum_{j=1}^{k} F_{Dj}} g_{D_i}(x)$$

where F_{Di} is an average fitness value of detector subset D_i and $g_{Di}(x)$ ($i=1...k$) is the evaluation function of detector subset D_i.

In Function (3), Self-training-set, T_s, and Nonself-training-set, T_n are used as argument x to train two adaptive thresholds,   and , so that $f_{tesing}(x_s) <$ and $f_{testing}(x_n) >$. (x_s is any element of T_s and x_n is element unit of T_n).

For an testing or unknown object x_u:

- If $f_{tesing}(x_u) < $, x_u is a normal activity;
- If $f_{tesing}(x_u) > $, x_u is assumed as an anomaly activity;
- If $ < f_{tesing}(x_u) < $, x_u is regarded as ambiguous (manual arbitration required).

After testing, excellent detector set De (see Section 3.2), is produced. Functions (1) (2) and (3), as evaluation functions, can be assembled to De for real applications.

4   Experiment Analysis

Two data sets R_1 and R_2 are used in our experiments. R_1 is a version of the 1999 DARPA intrusion detection evaluation data set maintained by MIT Lincoln Lab [12]. The statistics of the original data, including the number of bytes per second, the number of packets per second and the number of ICMP packets per second, are obtained by the data pre-processing module in IPAisys. As there are two weeks of data at hand, we use the data of the first week (attack free) for training and the second week (attacks included) for testing. R_2 is 20-minute network traffic data obtained by capturing TCP packet headers passed both within intra-LAN and between intra-LAN and external networks [13], where internal data are considered as normal behavior while external data as anomaly. The source IP addresses and ports together with destination IP addresses and ports are parsed by the data pre-processing module. For R_2, the first 15-minute data are used for training and the rest for testing.

Four isolated AIS models, M_1, M_2, M_3 and M_4, are initialized in Model Library and described in Figure 4, three of which are chosen each time to build multi-AIS-models. The population size of multi-AIS-models is set to 300, with 100 for each AIS model. The number of generations in genetic algorithm is set to 100, i.e. $N=100$. The reproduction, crossover and mutation rate are 0.7, 0.25 and 0.05, respectively. μ is set to 50, and   to 5.   and   are both equal to 0.3. x_1 and x_2 are assigned with value 1 and 0.1, respectively. Table 2, 3 and 4 compare the means and standard deviations of detection performances of several different models over 10 trials in terms of *FP* and *FN*. $Life_i$ is not included in current experiments.

Table 2. A control experiment of *FP* and *FN* comparison between single model and multi-AIS-models ("Hybrid" in the parenthesis means Hybrid testing function is used while evaluating; when single model is used, *k* is set to 1 in Hybrid testing function; self-regulating algorithm is used while configuring multi-AIS-models)

	M_1 (Hybrid)	M_2 (Hybrid)	M_3 (Hybrid)	Multi-AIS-models Self-regulation (Hybrid)
FP(%) R_1	5.78 (2.31)	2.57 (1.45)	2.35 (1.53)	1.12 (0.93)
FN(%) R_1	33.67 (6.11)	42.53 (6.02)	47.12 (8.56)	12.65 (4.12)
FP(%) R_2	3.69 (1.71)	2.44 (1.22)	2.21 (1.06)	0.77 (0.32)
FN(%) R_2	24.39 (5.76)	28.12 (8.25)	33.65 (7.82)	3.51 (1.79)

From Table 2, *FP* and *FN* of multi-AIS-models are obviously lower than those of any single model when using the same Hybrid testing function, demonstrating the effectiveness of the proposed approach.

Table 3. A control experiment of *FP* and *FN* comparison between P_{matrix} method and self-regulating method while using multi-AIS-models (using Autarchy testing function, Marking testing function and Hybrid testing function, respectively)

	P_{matrix} (Autarchy)	P_{matrix} (Marking)	P_{matrix} (Hybrid)	Self-regulation (Autarchy)	Self-regulation (Marking)	Self-regulation (Hybrid)
FP(%) R_1	1.35 (0.74)	1.73 (0.89)	1.31 (0.87)	1.19 (0.68)	1.55 (1.35)	1.12 (0.93)
FN(%) R_1	13.21 (4.42)	7.33 (2.64)	13.15 (3.65)	6.21 (1.28)	7.16 (2.27)	12.65 (4.12)
FP(%) R_2	1.69 (0.74)	1.36 (1.12)	0.93 (0.41)	1.23 (1.31)	1.15 (1.28)	0.77 (0.32)
FN(%) R_2	23.81 (5.78)	17.94 (6.65)	15.63 (4.22)	15.35 (6.11)	11.82 (4.79)	3.51 (1.79)

From Table 3, our self-regulating method is superior to the P_{matrix} method with lower *FP* and *FN*, under either evaluation function. An interesting finding is that Autarchy testing function is more efficient for R_1 while for R_2 Marking testing function is more suitable. In addition, Hybrid evaluation function achieves higher detection rates than both Autarchy and Marking methods.

Table 4. A control experiment of best *FP* and *FN* comparison between different multi-AIS-models (using Hybrid testing function; four multi-AIS-models are fixed)

	$M_1 M_2 M_4$ (Hybrid)	$M_1 M_3 M_4$ (Hybrid)	$M_2 M_3 M_4$ (Hybrid)	$M_1 M_2 M_3$ (Hybrid)
Best FP(%) R_1	1.16 (0.71)	1.12 (0.93)	1. 09 (0.97)	1.01 (0.64)
Best FN(%) R_1	12.72 (3.27)	12.43 (2.74)	12.27 (2.39)	12.21 (1.82)
Best FP(%) R_2	1.13 (0.85)	0.65 (0.52)	0.57 (0.41)	0.39 (0.55)
Best FN(%) R_2	3.92 (1.21)	3.16 (1.22)	2.69 (1.83)	1.51 (1.34)

In Table 4, we compare three different multi-AIS-models. It can be seen that multi-AIS-models $\{M_1 M_3 M_4\}$ has similar *FP* and *FN* values with $\{M_2 M_3 M_4\}$, while their best *FP* and *FN* are both lower than those of $\{M_1 M_2 M_4\}$ and both higher than other of $\{M_1 M_2 M_3\}$. However, the difference is not so evident when using R_1 as training and testing set. Comparing $\{M_1 M_3 M_4\}$ and $\{M_1 M_2 M_3\}$, different values of parameter *r* in M_2 and M_4 bring out a result that $\{M_1 M_2 M_3\}$ is more efficient than $\{M_1 M_3 M_4\}$, especially for R_2.

The following conclusions can be safely reached from the experimental results:

(1) The "pressure", such as F_{Di}, $Retry_i$, *FP* and *FN*, produced by self-regulating algorithm effectively invokes the dynamic configuration to achieve better self-adaptability and detection performance;

(2) Self-regulating method improves the detection performance with lower *FP* and *FN* as compared with P_{matrix} method;

(3) R-chunk matching function performs better for R_2; value of parameter *r* can be regulated to gain better performance for R_2; and the proposed Hybrid evaluation

function achieves higher detection rates than both Autarchy and Marking methods;

(4) Although multi-AIS-models outperform each single model, it is computationally more expensive, especially when $FP >$ or $FN >$ in testing. According to our statistics, multi-AIS-models are re-initialized for 5 to 6 times out of 10 in the experiments.

5 Conclusion

In this paper, we propose a novel self-regulating algorithm to improve the adaptability of AIS by optimally integrating and configuring various detector population based AIS models in a unified framework. In addition, Model Library is introduced to this algorithm to provide optional items to set up multi-AIS-models. In particular, self-regulating algorithm based IPAisys is superior to the traditional application-specific model in the following aspects:

(1) It preserves the diversity of various detectors, offering a possibility of cooperative evaluation;
(2) It is able to find the optimal multi-AIS-models by self-learning;
(3) It provides a platform for convenient comparison among different combinations of models, so that the one most suitable for certain problem can be selected;
(4) Artificial interference is partially replaced by automatic selecting process through Model Library.

In the future work, the self-regulating algorithm could be further improved. Currently, units of models are automatically regulated by the "pressure", but parameters of units have been pre-defined by experts. It is desirable to automate the regulation of parameters based on some regular changing rules. For model library, the influence of lifecycle on detection results will be further studied in our next paper. In addition, offline data are now used for both training and testing, resulting in a system unable to detect new anomaly. To design training and testing schemes based on real-time data will benefit from the perspective of practical use.

Acknowledgement

This work is supported with Key Research Grant No. 90204011 from National Natural Science Foundation of China.

References

1. D. Dasgupta and J. Zhou, Reviewing the development of AIS in last five years, in the proceedings of the 2003 IEEE Congress on Evolutionary Computation, vol.3, pp.123-130, 2003.
2. Zejun Wu, Hongbin Dong, Yiwen Liang, R. I. McKay, A Chromosome-based Evaluation Model for Computer Defense Immune Systems, in the proceedings of the 2003 IEEE Congress on Evolutionary Computation, vol.3, pp.1363-1369, 2003.

3. S. Forrest, A. Perelson, L. Allen, and R. Cherukuri, Self-nonself discrimination in a computer, in the proceedings of IEEE Symposium on Research in Security and Privacy, pp. 202-212, 1994.
4. J. Balthrop, S. Forrest, and M. R. Glickman, Revisting LISYS: Parameters and normal behavior, in the proceedings of the 2002 IEEE Congress on Evolutionary Computation, pp.1045-1050, 2002.
5. J. Kim, Integrating Artificial Immune Algorithms for Intrusion Detection, Ph.d thesis, University College London, 2002.
6. F. Gonzalez, A Study of Artificial Immune Systems Applied to Anomaly Detection, Ph.d thesis, The University of Memphis, 2003.
7. S. Hofmeyr and S. Forrest, Architecture for an artificial immune system, Evolutionary Computation, vol. 8, no. 4, pp. 443-473, 2000.
8. L. de Castro and J. Timmis, Artificial Immune Systems: A New Computational Intelligence Approach, Springer press, 2002.
9. F. Gonzalez and D. Dasgupta, Anomaly detection using real-valued negative selection. Journal of Genetic Programming and Evolvable Machines, 4:383–403, 2003.
10. U. Aickelin, J. Greensmith, and J. Twycross, Immune System Approaches to Intrusion Detection – A Review, in the proceedings of the Third International Conference on Artificial Immune Systems (ICARIS'2004), pp.316–329, 2004.
11. Zejun Wu, Yiwen Liang, Integrated Platform of Artificial Immune System for Anomaly Detection, WSEAS Transactions on Information Science and Applications, vol. 2 (2), pp.144-149, 2005.
12. 1999 Darpa intrusion detection evaluation, MIT Lincoln Labs, 1999.
13. Qiong Yu, Zejun Wu, Yiwen Liang, Feature Interval Matching Based Negative Selection Algorithm for Anomaly Detection, in the proceedings of 2005 International Symposium on Intelligence Computation and its Application, pp. 445-449, 2005.

Polymorphism and Danger Susceptibility of System Call DASTONs

Anjum Iqbal and Mohd Aizaini Maarof

Group on Artificial Immune Systems N Security (GAINS),
Faculty of Computer Science and Information Systems (FSKSM),
Universiti Teknologi Malaysia, 81310 UTM Skudai, Johor, Malaysia
anjum@siswa.utm.my, maarofma@fsksm.utm.my

Abstract. We have proposed a metaphor "DAnger Susceptible daTa codON" (DASTON) in data subject to processing by Danger Theory (DT) based Artificial Immune System (DAIS). The DASTONs are data chunks or data point sets that actively take part to produce "danger"; here we abstract "danger" as required outcome. To have closer look to the metaphor, this paper furthers biological abstractions for DASTON. Susceptibility of DASTON is important parameter for generating dangerous outcome. In biology, susceptibility of a host to pathogenic activities (potentially dangerous activities) is related to polymorphism. Interestingly, results of experiments conducted for system call DASTONs are in close accordance to biological theory of polymorphism and susceptibility. This shows that computational data (system calls in this case) exhibit biological properties when processed with DT point of view.

1 Introduction

We proposed a novel metaphor [1], DAnger Susceptible daTa codON (DASTON), after having inspired from Uwe Aicklein's proposals [2][3] and others work [3][4][5] referring Danger Theory [6][7][8][9][10] to resolve issues pertaining to self-nonself (SNS) view point in Artificial Immune Systems (AIS). The idea of presence of DASTONs, in data processed by Danger Theory based AIS (DAIS), confers a new look towards data. The DASTONs are data chunks or various combinations of data points (data point sets) that actively participate in process for delivering required outcome. This metaphor derives its strength from important biological phenomena and substances, for example, susceptibility, host-pathogen interactions, danger signaling, codons, etc. [11][12][13][14][15][16][17][18][19].

Proposing biologically inspired metaphors for computational research involves ability to precisely map abstractions in two fields [20]. We have tried [1] to come up with analogies that help us extend our understandings and contribute more for AIS research. This paper extends the understanding of DASTON with concrete abstractions and clear experimental results.

Susceptibility might be considered a vital biological property for inferring potential danger [6][7][8][9][10] to host body and genetic polymorphism (see section 3 for details) might provide direct measure for susceptibility. Our DASTON is also highly

C. Jacob et al. (Eds.): ICARIS 2005, LNCS 3627, pp. 366–374, 2005.
© Springer-Verlag Berlin Heidelberg 2005

concerned about susceptibility. The basic research question we address in this effort is; is there any link between polymorphism and susceptibility of DASTON while studying in biological context? The answer to this question might enable us to have deeper look into metaphor and device more computational abstractions closer to biological associates.

Though, the study might be carried out for variety of data and applications, current scope is limited to system call sequences, normal and intrusion trace, available from the University of New Mexico (UNM) [21]. This data might have potential to elaborate the metaphor. Interestingly, experimental results show good compliance with theory in biology, opening new avenues for our research.

Following section 2 describes biological procedure of danger signal production by infection susceptible cell, when attacked by pathogen. Section 3 elaborates link between susceptibility and polymorphism in biology. Section 4 gives brief overview of DASTON, reader may refer [1] for details. Section 5 establishes link between polymorphism and susceptibility of DASTON in given biological context. This section portrays mythology and results of the study. Finally, section 6 concludes the effort elaborating its significance in AIS research.

2 Host Susceptibility to Pathogens: A Potential Danger

According to Polly Matzinger [6][7][8][9][10], the substances made or modified by cells under distress or suffering from abnormal death serve as danger signals for immune system. Here we introduce the term "potential danger" and link it to the infectious disease susceptibility of host. A pathogen may contribute in producing poisonous products (danger signal), leading to infectious disease, during an interplay with susceptible host. The pathogen may not interplay with unsusceptible host, hence not producing danger signal. This infers that host susceptibility might be considered as

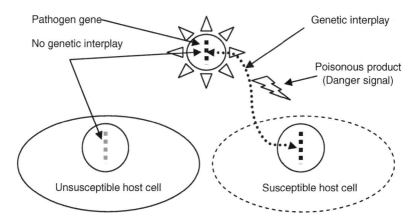

Fig. 1. The susceptible host genes are interacting with pathogen genes to produce poisonous products that cause danger signal for immune system. While, unsusceptible host genes might not interplay with pathogen. The susceptibility of host is "potential danger".

potential danger producing factor (see figure 1). The details of infectious disease susceptibility may be better understood by reviewing related biological references [11][12][13][14][15][16][17][18][19].

The susceptibility of a host is conferred by the susceptible genetic regions. These are the high interest regions to our research. We want to closely see these regions to understand their behavior (principle) and then mapping that behavior to our case study in computation. Following paragraphs might help us understand the biological behavior of susceptible genetic regions that we will be successfully mapping to DAS-TONs in system calls data.

3 Polymorphism and Susceptibility

The word polymorphism is combination of "poly" means many and "morph" form or shape. In biology it is "the occurrence together in the same population of more than one allele (alternative form of a genetic locus) or genetic marker at the same locus with the least frequent allele or marker occurring more frequently than can be accounted for by mutation alone. Different eye colors or hair shapes result from genetic polymorphism, see figure 2.

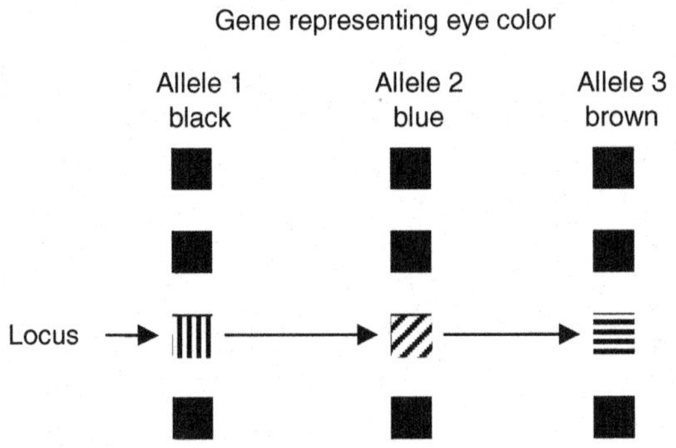

Fig. 2. A gene may have different forms (alleles) to result various phenotypes. Same gene is having alleles to result different eye colors, is an example of polymorphism.

The polymorphism may arise from single genetic unit (nucleotide) to multiple units. Currently, we are not concerned about the detailed mechanisms of biological polymorphism. We are only interested in learning that polymorphism gives rise to susceptibility. The importance of single nucleotide polymorphism (SNP) project in revealing susceptibility is worth mentioning (http://snp.cshl.org/). The polymorphism of tumor necrosis factor (TNF) gene is related to susceptibility of hepatitis B virus infection [22]. The major histocompatibility complex (MHC) includes the highly polymorphic human leukocyte antigen (HLA) genes that confer susceptibility to various infections including malaria, tuberculosis, HIV infections, and hepatitis B [23][25]. Polymorphism of a gene related to interleukin imparts susceptibility to hepatitis C [24] and other infections [26]. This suggests that polymorphism might be linked to potential danger susceptibility.

4   What Is DASTON?

Based on the biological concept, briefly described in section 2, we have proposed the presence of DASTONs (DAnger Susceptible daTa codON) in data [1]. These are the data chunks or combination of data points, DATONs (DATa codONs), present in data heap that actively participate in data processing to retrieve specific information from that data when subjected to triggering data or process (figure. 3). It is like presence of genetic segments in host that are susceptible to pathogenic interactions resulting in the production of toxic substances signaling danger (see fig-ure 1). The type and size of DATONs may depend upon the nature of application, data type, and depth of details required from the data. Real examples might be that; a) only potential fields in a data-base might interact with query fields to result required information, and b) only poten-tial system calls in a process might interact with exploit scripts to compromise the at-tacked system. One may exploit his own creative analogy to implement this biologically inspired idea. The success of analogy depends on the degree of creativity and clarity in understanding the biological concept upon which it is based [20].

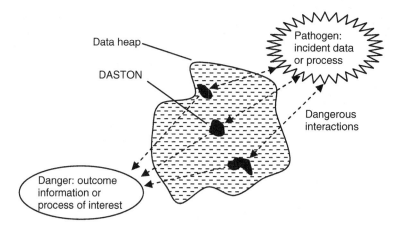

Fig. 3. DASTON present in data heap interact with incident data (named as pathogenic data) to produce required information or process (analogous to danger in danger theory)

5   Polymorphism and Susceptibility of System Call DASTONs

As discussed in section 3, biological polymorphism is "the occurrence together in the same population of more than one allele or genetic marker at the same locus". It is also learned that biological polymorphism might provide the susceptibility measure of host body for infectious diseases [22][23][24][25][26]. We have applied the concept for establishing link between polymorphism and susceptibility of DASTON.

To enhance the worth of DASTON, we have conducted interesting experiments. Though, the metaphor might be mapped to various computational applications and data types but we stick to our constrained application - intrusion detection – and the dataset - system call sequences. These have potential to clearly illustrate the metaphor in given biological context (see Table 1).

Table 1. The abstractions corresponding to system call DASTONs

Abstractions	
Biology	Computation
Danger	Intrusion
Pathogen	Exploit script
Nucleotide	A system call
Hosts' genetic sequence	Sequence of system calls for a process/task
Triplet of nucleotides (Codon)	Set of system calls (DATON)
Susceptible Codon/segment	Danger Susceptible DATON (DASTON)

5.1 Methodology

We have conducted comparative analysis of normal and intrusion trace benchmark data, system call sequences, available from the University of New Maxico [21]. The system call pairs (DATONs), as shown in flow diagram of figure 5, are of three types; a) present in both normal and intrusion trace data, b) present in normal data only, and c) present in intrusion trace data only. The DATONS present only in intrusion trace system call sequences might be designated as the most susceptible system call pairs that are DASTONs.

DASTON associated system call	Other system calls in sequence

Fig. 4. Format of DASTONs associated system call pair used to get polymorphic measure of DASTONs

The "polymorphic measure" of a DASTON (system call pair present in intrusion trace sequence only) is defined as the number of distinct pairs each essentially containing one of two members from DASTON associated system calls (the system calls constituting DASTONs) , see figure 4.

In these experiments we have used the data of "synthetic sendmail" exploits (we have performed experiments with other exploits also but for simplicity presenting these results only). The normal sequences have been tested against sequences obtained from three intrusion traces (sunsendmailcp intrusion, decode intrusion, and forwarding loops). Results of experiments are in agreement with our hypothesis of "polymorphic susceptibility", as shown in plots of figures 6 and 7.

5.2 Results

The plots of figures 6 and 7 present results with Decode Intrusion and Forwarding Loops respectively. In first experiment with Decode Intrusion there are 32 system calls associated with DASTONs, and only 3 of these have lesser polymorphic measure (number of distinct system calls combining with a DASTON associated system

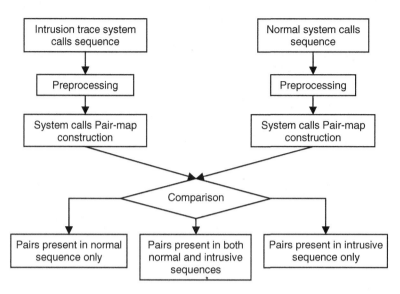

Fig. 5. Flow of the process for identifying system call DASTONs from normal and intrusion trace sequences

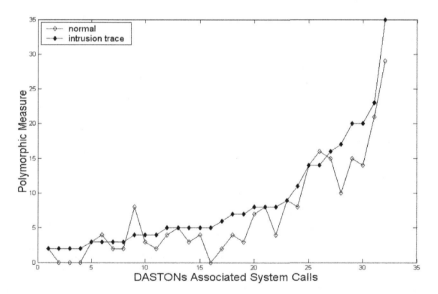

Fig. 6. Experimental results for polymorphic measure with normal and decode intrusion trace sequences

call to form distinct pairs) in intrusion trace data (filled diamond markers) than their companions in normal data (unfilled diamond marks). In second experiment with Forwarding Loops the number of DASTONs associated system calls is 35 out which only one has lesser polymorphism. This clearly demonstrates that polymorphism would be a useful parameter to estimate Danger Susceptibility of DASTONs, like their biological buddies. It also suggests that frequency based analysis alone, of system calls sequences, should not be sufficient for describing their anomalous behavior, though it has shown success [27].

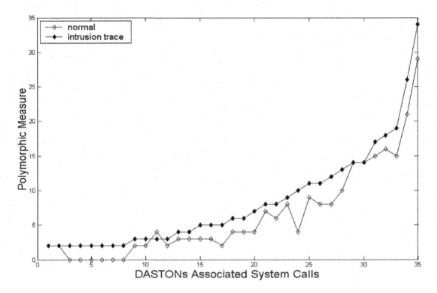

Fig. 7. Experimental results for polymorphic measure with normal and forwarding loops intrusion trace sequences

6 Conclusions

In biology, susceptibility of host cell to infectious pathogen (a case of danger producing activity) might be determined through genetic polymorphism. The same hypothesis we have applied to our proposed metaphor, DASTON, which shows compliance with the biological theory. It is a beautiful illustration of biological properties possessed by a bio-inspired computational metaphor. The data used for this illustration is system calls data that has significance in intrusion detection applications. The DASTON associated system calls have higher polymorphic values (means they combine with greater number of distinct system calls to produce distinct system call pairs) in intrusion trace sequences than those in normal sequences. Only negligible numbers of deviations appear in results. This suggests that DASTON has potential to be explored more for furthering biological abstractions in Danger Theory based AIS (DAIS) research. The idea confers a novel look towards data that DAIS processes. The established link between polymorphism and danger susceptibility recommends that frequency based analysis alone should not be sufficient for detecting anomalous behavior of system call sequences. Considering polymorphic behavior of system calls we might be able to device good anomaly detectors. Though we have successfully applied the concept to computations but immuno-informaticians and immunologists might help to verify and further explore the immunological basis of the idea. It needs their straightforward confirmation that danger susceptibility of host for infectious pathogens is related to polymorphism of genetic segments. Their confirmation might improve the status of DASTON and bring it closer to immuno-genetics. This will open new avenues for DAIS researchers and will help devising novel computational metaphors closer to immunology theory. Remember, all this works with the creativity of the best designed machine, the human.

Acknowledgment

The authors are grateful to Ministry of Science Technology and Environment (MOSTE) Malaysia for supporting this pioneering AIS research in Malaysia. We are thankful to AIS research community for their encouraging cooperation.

References

1. Anjum Iqbal and Mohd. Aizaini Maarof (2004), Towards Danger Theory based Artificial APC Model: Novel Metaphor for Danger Susceptible Data Codons, In Proc. of International Conference on Artificial Immune Systems (ICARIS 2004).
2. Uwe Aickelin, and Steve Cayzer (2002), The Danger Theory and Its Application to Artificial Immune Systems, In Proceedings of the International Conference on Artificial Immune Systems (ICARIS, 2002), Edinburgh, UK.
3. U. Aicklein, P. Bentley, S. Cayser, J. Kim, and J. McLeod (2003), Danger Theory: The Link between AIS and IDS, In Proceedings of the International Conference on Artificial Immune Systems (ICARIS, 2003), Edinburgh, UK.
4. Emma Hart and Peter Ross (2003), Improving SOSDM: Inspirations from the Danger Theory, In Proceedings of International Conference on Artificial Immune Systems (ICARIS 2003), Springer LNCS 2787, pp. 194–203.
5. Andrew Secker, Alex A. Freitas, and Jon Timmis (2003), A Danger Theory Inspired Approach to Web Mining, In Proceedings of International Conference on Artificial Immune Systems (ICARIS 2003), Springer LNCS 2787, pp. 156–167.
6. Polly Matzinger (2002), The Danger Model: A Renewed Sense of Self, Science, Vol. 296, pp. 301-305.
7. P. Matzinger (2001), The Danger Model In Its Historical Context, Scand. J. Immunol, Vol. 54, pp. 4-9.
8. Stefania Gallucci, Martijn Lolkema, and Polly Matzinger (1999), Natural Adjuvants: Endogenous Activators of Dendritic Cells, Nature Medicine, Vol. 5, No. 11, pp. 1249-1255
9. Polly Matzinger, The Real Function of The Immune System, Last accessed on 06-04-04, URL:http://cmmg.biosci.wayne.edu/asg/polly.html
10. Polly Matzinger (1998), An Innate sense of danger, Seminars in Immunology, Vol. 10, pp. 399-415.
11. Michael A. Lutz, Francine Gervais, Alan Bernstein, Arthur L. Hattel, and Pamela H. Correll (2002), STK Receptor Tyrosine Kinase Regulates Susceptibility to Infection with Listeria Monocytogenes, Infection and Immunity, Vol. 70, No. 1, p. 416–418.
12. S Roy, A V S Hill, K Knox, D Griffithsand, D Crook (2002), Association of Common Genetic Variant with Susceptibility to Invasive Pneumococcal Disease, BMJ Volume 324, page 1369.

13. Wilfred Goldmann (2003), The Significance of Genetic Control in TSEs, Microbiology-Today, Vol. 30/Nov. 03, pp. 170-171
14. Jennie Blackwell (2002), Genetics and Genomics in Infectious Disease, CIMR Research Report, Last accessed on 06-04-04, URL:http://www.cimr.cam.ac.uk/resreports/report2002/pdf/blackwell_low.pdf
15. Paul M. Coussens, Brian Tooker, William Nobis, and Matthew J. Coussens (2001), Genetics and Genomics of Susceptibility to Mycobacterial Infections in Cattle, On-line publication on the 2001 IAAFSC web site.
16. Adrian VS Hill (1999), Genetics and Genomics of Infectious Disease Susceptibility, British Medical Bulletin, Vol. 55, No. 2, pp. 401-413.
17. Sean V. Tavtigian1, et al (2001), A Candidate Prostate Cancer Susceptibility Gene at Chromosome 17p, Nature Genetics, Volume 27, pp. 172-180.
18. Jean-Laurent Casanova (2001), Mendelian Susceptibility to Mycobacterial Infection in Man, Swiss Med Weekly, Vol. 131, pp. 445–454.
19. P. Denny, E. Hopes, N. Gingles, K. W. Broman, W. McPheat, J. Morten, J. Alexander, P. W. Andrew, and S. D.M. Brown (2003), A major Locus Conferring Susceptibility to Infection by Streptococcus Pneumoniae in Mice, Mammalian Genome, Springer, Volume 14, pp. 448–453.
20. S. Forrest, J. Balthrop, M. Glickman and D. Ackley (2002). "Computation in the Wild." In the Internet as a Large-Complex System, edited by K. Park and W. Willins: Oxford University Press. July 18, 2002.
21. Intrusion Detection Data Sets, URL:http://www.cs.unm.edu/~immsec/systemcalls.htm, Last cited on 01-05-2005.
22. Yue-Su Zhou, Fu-Sheng Wang, Ming-Xu Liu, Lei Jin, Wei-Guo Hong (2005), Relationship between susceptibility of hepatitis B virus and gene polymorphism of tumor necrosis factor-α, World Chin J Digestol, Vol. 13, No. 2, pp. 207-210.
23. Dominic Kwiatkowski (2000), Susceptibility to infection, BMJ, Vol. 321, pp. 1061-1065.
24. Susanne Knapp and Branwen J. W. Hennig (2003), Interleukin-10 promoter polymorphisms and the outcome of hepatitis C virus infection, Immunogenetics, Vol. 55, pp. 362–369.
25. Adrian VS Hill (1999), Genetics and genomics of infectious disease susceptibility, British Medical Bulletin, Vol. 55, No. 2, pp. 401-413.
26. Amir H. Sabouri, and Mineki Saito (2004), Polymorphism in the Interleukin-10 Promoter Affects Both Provirus Load and the Risk of Human T Lymphotropic Virus Type I–Associated Myelopathy/Tropical Spastic Paraparesis, Journal of Infectious Diseases, Vol. 190, pp. 1279-1285.
27. D-K. Kang, D. Fuller, and V. Honavar, "Learning Classifiers for Misuse and Anomaly Detection Using a Bag of System Calls Representation," Technical Report ISU-CS-TR 05-06, Computer Science Department, Iowa State University, Ames, IA, USA, Mar 3, 2005.

General Suppression Control Framework: Application in Self-balancing Robots

Albert Ko, H.Y.K. Lau, and T.L. Lau

Intelligent Systems Laboratory, The University of Hong Kong,
Pokfulam Road, Hong Kong SAR
aux1496@hkusua.hku.hk

Abstract. The General Suppression Control Framework (GSCF) is a framework inspired by the suppression hypothesis of the immune discrimination theory. The framework consists of five distinct components, the Affinity Evaluator, Cell Differentiator, Cell Reactor, Suppression Modulator, and the Local Environment. These reactive components, each responsible for a specific function, can generate long-term and short-term influences to other components by the use of humoral and cellular signals.

This paper focuses in the design of a control system that aims to balance and navigate a self-balancing robot though obstacles based on the five components in GSCF. The control system demonstrates how simple combination of suppression mechanism can filter and fuses two unstable measurements together to obtain reliable measurement to maintain the balance of a dynamically unstable system. The control system is implemented in a two-wheeled self-balancing robot for its inherited instability can best demonstrate the systems responsiveness to dynamic changes.

Keywords: Artificial Immune Systems, Distributed Control, Self-balancing Robots, Service Robots.

1 Introduction

Artificial Immune Systems (AIS) [10] has been studied widely in the fields of Artificial Intelligence and Computer Science due to its deep inspiration to the engineering sciences. The essences of human immune system properties are imitated to perform complicated tasks, for example, learning strategies, adaptive control, memory managements and self-organization. These special properties of the immune system have adapted in solving various engineering problems. Lau & Wong [15] developed a control framework to operate a group of autonomous agents with the ability to evolve and learn in a dynamic environment. Segel & Cohen [18] examined how biological ideas can help to solve engineering problems, and inversely how the artificial system can inspire new conjectures to unrecognized methods by which the immune system is organized. de Castro & Timmis [5] presented the application of AIS in computer network security, machine learning, and pattern recognition. Tarakanov et al. [23]

C. Jacob et al. (Eds.): ICARIS 2005, LNCS 3627, pp 375–388, 2005.

introduced Immunocomputing as a new computing approach based on the fundamental concept of formal protein (FP).

This research is a continuation of [13] and employs the same General Suppression Control Framework (GSCF) [12] to design a control system for a self-balancing autonomous robot to perform search operations over difficult terrain [7]. The development of GSCF was initially motivated by the need for a distributed control system that can scale, evolve, and reconfigure in response to the dynamic environment. Features such as cell proliferation allow the system memory and communication range to scale in response to external stimulant, and cell evolution enables the system to adapt and to generate new knowledge. The ability to proliferate and evolve dynamically, distinct the system from other biologically inspired systems which can only learn with a fixed network, or can only generate solution with a fixed number of agents.

Preceding works at Intelligent Systems Laboratory employed GSCF to design a highly scalable distributed system for controlling a *homogeneous* modular robot to reach a common goal under multi-constraints. The modular robot was configured in the form of a hyper redundant manipulator similar to those used in space [11]. The modular robot illustrated the scalable homogeneous systems, designed based on GSCF, can effectively general constructive behaviors to direct the modular robot to reach a common goal. The system also developed a minimal communication strategy to communicate goal status to all modules using only signal proliferation. The work described in this paper, in contrast to the previous, will employ GSCF to design a *heterogeneous* control system for an autonomous self-balancing robot with multiple sensors and actuators. The self-balancing robot has input signals from gyroscope, accelerometer, shaft encoders, sonar transducers, and thermal array sensor. The objective is to test the control framework's ability to continuously fuse suppressive and stimulative signals from different sources to produce useful control parameters. The system treats these sensors as groups of heterogeneous cells that exist in the *Local Environment*. Suppressor cells with specific sensitivity towards different sensors are responsible for monitoring and reporting sensors data. These data are then filtered or combined to suppress or to stimulate motors to drive forward and backward to navigate the robot. The contributions of this work are in two folds; one, to better understand how heterogeneous control systems may be designed using GSCF, and two, to further demonstrate AIS theories can be employed to solve practical engineering problems.

This paper proceeds as follows. **Section 2** provides an overview of the immune system and the major concepts associated to GSCF. **Section 3** gives a general overview of current development of self-balancing robots and their advantages over conventional three-wheeled and four-wheeled robots. Basic mechatronic design of the robot will also be presented. **Section 4** introduces the suppression hypothesis in the discrimination theory and explains the five components in GSCF. The design of a GSCF based heterogeneous control system is also presented. **Section 5** concludes the work in this research and discusses future works to be taken.

2   The Immune Systems

Bio-inspired systems [21] has been helping to solve engineering problems in many disciplines, to name but a few, genetic algorithms [3] creates diversified answers for complex problem, artificial neural networks enable systems to learn effectively [9], and swarm behavior [17] inspired highly scaleable multi-agent systems [24]. Human Immune System [22] in its own stand is an extremely effective system that can identify abnormal activities, solve the problem using existing knowledge, and generate new solutions for unseen events; in short it is a network of players who cooperate to get things done [19]. Strictly speaking Human Immune Systems [2] consists of two major parts, the Innate Immune System and the Acquired Immune System. This section provides a brief overview of the basic components associated with the analogy exploited in GSCF.

Innate Immune System [16] consists of elements that are always present and available at very short notice to foil challenges from "foreign" invaders. These elements include skin, mucous membranes, and the cough reflex, which act as barriers to environmental invaders. Internal components such as fever, interferons, macrophages, and substances released by leukocytes also contribute to terminating the effect of invaders directly or to enhance the effectiveness of host reactions to them.

Acquired Immune System is a supplement to the innate system and presents only in vertebrates. The major recognition and reaction functions of the immune response are performed by T-lymphocytes (T-cells) and B-lymphocytes (B-cells) which exhibit specificity towards antigen. B-cells synthesize and secrete into the bloodstream antibodies with specificity against the antigen, the process is termed Humoral Immunity. The T-cells do not make antibodies but seek out the invader to kill, they also help B-cells to make antibodies and activate macrophages to eat foreign matters. Acquired immunity facilitated by T-cells is called Cellular Immunity.

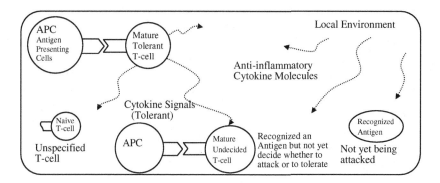

Fig. 1. Cell Suppression Mechanism of the immune system

Despite the many details in immunology theory, there are four unique functions that contribute to the operation of the entire system. These functions are:

Clonal Selection - This theory holds that each B-cell makes antibodies that fit only one specific type of antigen, called its "cognate" antigen. When the specific B-cell binds to its cognate, the B-cell proliferates to clone many copies of itself which recognize that same antigen. The newly cloned cells will become plasma B-cells and continue to produce and export huge quantities of antibodies and will continue to clone more

B-cells. This simple action is recognized as one of the major concepts in immunology for its simplicity and high effectiveness.

Immunological Memory - After B and T cells have been activated and proliferated to build up clones and destroy the foreign invaders, most of them will die off but some of them will live to pass on their knowledge of the antigen. These leftover B and T cells become immunological memory of the system and therefore are called Memory Cells. These cells are much easier to activate than "inexperience" cells and can spring into action quickly to protect the body.

Antibody Diversity - This is a modular design process which mix and matches segments of B-cell genes to create Modular diversity and Junctional diversity. The result of this mix and match strategy is a small number of gene segments can create incredible antibody diversity.

Discrimination - The most unique function of the immune system, perhaps the most important one too is to discriminate Non-Self Cells from Self Cells. Self Cells are the good cells that exist and work inside our body. Non-Self Cells are external elements that does harm to the system (antigen). The distinction and the recognition of foreign antigen is done by B-Cells and T-Cells, which allows the system to identify harmful bodies to response (to kill) and leave the good bodies (self-cells) untouched.

3 Self-balancing Robots

The inherent instability of inverted pendulum systems has always been an excellent test bed for control theory experimentations. In recent years, control theories derived from such systems has been implement to a class of mobile robots by research institutes, commercial companies, and independent hobbyists to develop robots for different applications. This type of two-wheel robots based on the design of an inverted pendulum are usually called self-balancing robots. The Swiss Federal Institute of Technology has developed a mobile inverted pendulum called JOE [8] to test a control system made up of two decoupled state space controllers. The Robotic Mobile Platform (RMP) based on Segway Company's human transporter is being used for a variety of robotic research including outdoor path planning [14] for its high mobility on uneven terrain. Independent researcher Blackwell [4] uses off-the-shelves components to build a balancing scooter similar to the commercial vehicle Segway. Anderson [1] uses a commercial IMU (Inertia Measurement Unit) to construct a miniature self-balancing robot that can go up and down steep slopes with high stability. Most self-balancing robots uses gyroscope and accelerometer to determine the robots' level of tilt in respect to ground, BaliBot [20] on the other hand uses a pair of infra-red range finders to obtain information that helps the robot to stay balance.

Conventional mobile robots with three and four wheels offer reliability and stability in most daily operations due to their well developed mechatronics and control system. Yet, two-wheeled self-balancing robots carries practical advantages in many ways, for example, self-balancing robots has genuine zero round-about radius, small foot-print, high tolerant to impulsive force, and greater stability over slopes. Conventional robots with four wheels of equal size maximize platform stability by locating the Center of

Gravity (CG) between front and rear wheels as shown in Figure 2a. This design works well on level ground, but when going up hill (Figure 2b) the robot's line of CG begins to shift towards the rear wheels; as the gradient increases the front wheels start to lose traction and the robot will tip backward when the line of CG is beyond the rear support. The same situation occurs when going down hill (Figure 2c). Three-wheeled robots (Figure 2d) often have two larger differential driving wheels at the back (or front) and one smaller wheel in front for support. This type of robots can usually go up a steeper slope (assuming the larger driving wheels are at the back) than down because when going down hill the rear driving wheels will lose traction even before the robot tips (Figure 2f).

Two-wheeled self-balancing robots (Figure 2g) are inherently unstable; therefore they must have a balancing mechanism to keep their CG vertically above their wheels to prevent the robot from falling. To keep the robot standing straight, the balancing mechanism drives the wheels forward when the CG is accelerating forward, and backward when it is accelerating backward. Therefore by making the robot lean forward (offsetting CG forward); the balancing mechanism will automatically drives the wheels forward with an appropriate torque (speed) to cancel out the acceleration. This mechanism enables self-balancing robots to drive up and down slopes (Figure 2h-g) with a straight body, hence preventing the robot from tipping over.

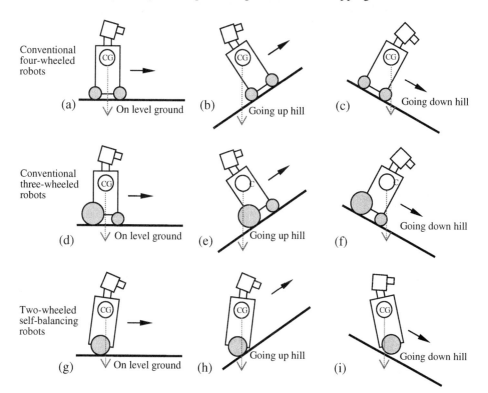

Fig. 2. Conventional robots with three and four wheels easily lose traction and tip over when going up and down slopes (a-f). Self-balancing robots maintain good traction by shifting its CG above its wheels at all time.

Fig. 3. The self-balancing robot equipped with optical encoder, sonar transducers, thermal array sensors, gyroscope, and accelerometer

Though the primary focus of this paper is on control system design, understanding the mechatronic design of the robot may help to appreciate the simplicity of the control system in contrast to the complexity of the mechanical system under control. Figure 3 shows the general appearance of the self-balancing robot. To balance a two-wheeled robot, four terms must be known in order to model the motion and position of the robot; they are platform position, platform velocity (horizontal), angular rate, and tilt-angle. In our design, the platform velocity and position are estimated using a pair of optical encoders (HEDS-5500) from Hewlett Packard. The encoders have a resolution of 512 counts per revolution, platform displacement (position) can be estimated by knowing the number of counts and wheel diameter; integrating number of counts in respect to time gives the platform velocity. A gyro (ADXRS150EB) from Analog Device and an accelerometer (Memsic 2125) from Memsic are used to estimate the angular rate and the tile angle. Angular rate can be obtained directly from the gyro, where tilt angle can be obtained by integrating the angular rate in respect to time. However, readings from gyro tend to drift over time; hence an accelerometer is needed to correct the drift and to give a reference of the absolute vertical angle. Though accelerometer can produce accurate angle readings in respect to gravitational acceleration, it is also very sensitive to acceleration caused by other forces, such as driving force from the motor, therefore an intelligent filtering mechanism that can combine the two outputs to produce a reliable tilt angle is a fundamental requirement for self-balancing robots. The following section will describe how a control system can be built to balance a robot on two wheels and how simple suppression mechanism can generate reliable control parameter from unstable sources. Due to the complexity and ample details of the mechanical system, the following sections will focus on high level system design and ignore the lower level control details to maintain a keen focus on the topic.

4   Control System

The control system designed for the self-balancing robot is based on the *General Suppression Control Framework (GSCF)* (see Figure 4) developed in our previous research [13]. The design of GSCF was based around the analogy of the immuno-suppression hypothesis [6] in the discrimination theory. When a T-cell receptor binds to a peptide with high affinity presented by an APC (Antigen Presenting Cells), the T-cell recognized the antigen become mature and it has to decide whether to attack the antigen aggressively or to tolerate it in peace. An important decision factor is the local environment within which the T-cell resides. The present of inflammatory cytokine molecules such as interferon-gamma (INF-γ) in the environment tend to elicit aggressive behaviors of T-cells, whereas the anti-inflammatory cytokines like IL-4 and IL-10 tend to suppress such behavior by blocking the signaling of aggression. In brief, a T-cell matured after recognizing an antigen does not start killing unless the environment also contains encouraging factors for doing so.

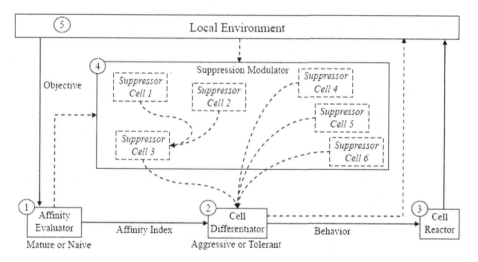

Fig. 4. The General Suppression Framework. Dashed lines represent humoral signal transmissions, where solid lines represent cellular signals. The suppression modulator can host any number of suppressor cells.

The control framework consists of five major components. The most notable difference between the natural mechanism shown in Figure 1 and the framework shown in Figure 4 is that the T-cell's functions are divided into three separate components, the *Affinity Evaluator, Cell Differentiator* and the *Cell Reactor*. Delegating the three unique functions into separate components enables the system to be organized in a modular manner and when programming for an application, the result and effect of each component can be analyzed easier.

The first step in designing a GSCF based control system is to identify the system objective and assign basic suppressor cell functions. In this experiment a self-balancing robot equipped with a heat array sensor is used and the system objective is to track abnormal present of heat in the laboratory. The robot is also equipped with two sonar transducers to prevent it from bumping into obstacles, one gyro and one accelerometer to keep the robot balance on two wheels, and one pair of encoder to monitor the wheel position and speed.

4.1 GSCF Components

The functions of the five components and the assignment of suppressor cell duties are explained below.

(1) *Affinity Evaluator* – evaluates information in the *Local Environment* against the system objective and output an affinity index to *(4) Suppression Modulator* and to *(2) Cell Differentiator* when the heat array sensor senses an abnormal heat. The affinity index is highest when the heat object is close to the robot.

(2) *Cell Differentiator* – evaluates affinity index from the *(1) Affinity Evaluator* to confirm if there is an abnormal heating body nearby and to decide whether the robot should trace the heat source based on suppression indexes from the *(4) Suppression Modulator*. The decided behavior is sent to *(3) Cell Reactor* using cellular signaling. The component can also send humoral signals directly to influence the *(5) Local Environment*.

(3) *Cell Reactor* – reacts to the cellular signal from the *(2) Cell Differentiator* and execute corresponding behaviors which take effect in the *(5) Local Environment*. This component is responsible for converting logical and computational results into mechanical actions.

(4) *Suppression Modulator* – is a collection of *Suppressor Cells*. The function specific *Suppressor Cells* continuously react to external stimulants to adjust their sensitivity, and perform proliferation. The overall function of *Suppression Modulator* is comparable to the cytokine signaling mechanism which uses INF-γ, IL-4, IL-10, etc. to perform intercellular communication and to cause the environment to inflame, so to elicit or suppress aggressive behaviors in the T-cells. There can be 0, 1, 2, 3, ..., n number of *Suppressor Cells* and their response to stimulation may influence other *Suppressor Cells* inside the Modulator and may evolve over time.

(5) *Local Environment* – is where interactions between different components take place. The importance of this component within the framework is to act as an interface that links to the *Global Environment* which contains other *Local Environments* with different sets of *Suppression Modulators*. In addition, it provides a theoretical space to integrate the physical objects and the abstract system in an analyzable form.

4.2 Suppressor Cells

The fundamental idea of GSCF is to let *Affinity Evaluator* to decide whether there is a problem to solve (an objective to meet), and then consult the *Cell Differentiator* to decide whether the system has the resources to solve the problem under imposed constraints. These constraints may be predefined system constraints or maybe newly developed due to changes in the environment. GSCF define these constraints and system variables as suppressor cells (SC), these cells may evolve to adapt to new changes and may proliferate to increase their sensitivity to specific stimulants. This section discusses how suppressor cells are designed and how individual suppressive action can be combined to produce useful result.

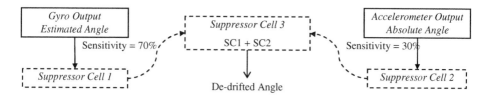

Fig. 5. The three suppressor cells responsible for determining the robots tilt angle. SC1 and SC2 monitor gyro and accelerometer data and adjust their sensitivity in response to changes in the environment. SC3 fuses the data for *Cell Differentiator* to evaluate.

To balance a robot on its two wheels the system must know which way the robot is tilting and how fast is the tilt angle changing, this require readings from the gyro and the accelerometer. Since gyro can produce better integrated angular reading at higher frequency and accelerometer can produce accurate angular reading when the robot is stable (slow motion), these two measurements can be fused to obtain a more accurate reading by assigning suppressor cells to monitor their status. The cell corresponding to a sensor is said to have high sensitivity to the sensor and its sensitivity may varies in response to changes in the environment.

SC1 is assigned to have high sensitivity to gyro outputs; the relative angle from the vertical axis is calculated by angular rate times Δt (sample rate in millisecond). The calculated angle is subject to gyro drift and is therefore only reliable in short term. The reliability is directly proportional to the system's stability; sensitivity is initially set to 70%, SC1 automatically adjust the sensitivity before outputting to SC3.

The accelerometer assigned to SC2 measures the deviated angle between the robot and the vertical axis. This instrument is more reliable in long term because it measures absolute angle in respect to earth's gravitational force and its reading does not drift over time. The reliability of this instrument is inversely proportional to the system's stability; sensitivity is automatically adjusted by SC2 in response to environment changes, which is initially set to 30%.

While SC1 and SC2 continuously adjust their sensitivities in response to the system's stability (angular rate of change), SC3 is sensitive to the output of SC1 and SC2. SC3 combines the estimated angle from SC1 and the absolute angle from SC2 to produce a de-drifted angle reading that is biased to gyro reading when the system is

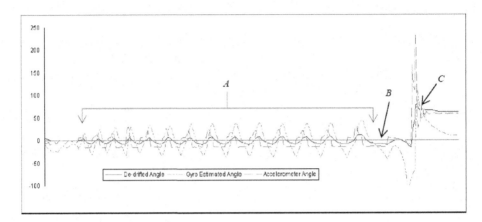

Fig. 6. (A) on the graph shows the robot oscillates back and forth near to its vertical position, then an external impulse force applied to it (B) caused it to fall flat on its face (C)

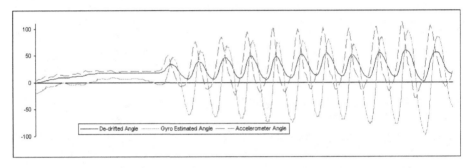

Fig. 7. The physical robot corresponding to this graph was tilted 30 degree towards its front and oscillates back and forth near this angle in the positive region (0-90 degree) only. However, the gyro and the accelerometer were both reporting realistic angles in the positive region as well as the negative region.

unstable and to accelerometer when the system is relatively stable. Figures 6 and 7 show the result of this simple suppression mechanism.

The y-axis of the graph in Figure 6 ranges from -100 to 250 degree, but the actual deviation is only possible from -90 degree (fall flat in front) to +90 degree (fall flat on the back) with 0 degree being absolutely straight. The readings beyond ±90 are either due to gyro drift or due to dynamic acceleration that influenced the accelerometer reading. This graph shows the accelerometer reading obtained when the robot oscillates back and forth at low speed is more reliable than the gyro estimated reading, therefore the solid line (de-drifted angle) tends to agree more with the accelerometer. However after the robot being pushed and fall at high speed (C), the accelerometer is no longer reliable, hence the sensitivity of SC2 drops and SC1 increases, causes the output from SC3 (solid line) to agree more with the gyro estimated angle at that instance.

The graph in Figure 7 further demonstrates how this simple suppression mechanism filters unstable readings from two sources to produce one reliable reading. This time the robot is tilted 30 degree towards its front and oscillates back and forth near this angle. Notice even the robot was only oscillating in the positive region (0-90 degree), the gyro estimated angle and the accelerometer angle still fluctuate severely into the negative region. By continuously adjusting the sensitivity of SC1 and SC2, a reliable reading that resembles the actual physical motion of the robot was produced.

There are three other cells inside the *Suppression Modulator*, SC4 and SC5 are sensitive to the sonar transducers' readings, their suppression index increases when obstacles are near. SC6 is sensitive to readings from the thermal array sensor; suppression index is highest when a heating object is found. The functions of these six SCs are summarized in Table 1.

Table 1. Summary of suppressor cells in the *Suppression Modulator*

	Sensitive Element	Suppressor Cell Duties	Output to Cell Differentiator
SC1	Gyroscope	Sensitive highest when system is unstable	Output to SC3
SC2	Accelerometer	Sensitivity highest when system is stable	Output to SC3
SC3	Summation Cell (SC1 and SC2)	Combines signals from SC1 and SC2 to provide a reliable suppression signal to Cell Differentiator. Suppression index highest when robot is not balanced.	De-drifted Angle
SC4	Left Sonar	Suppression index highest when obstacle is close	Suppression Signal 1-10
SC5	Right Sonar	Suppression index highest when obstacle is close	Suppression Signal 1-10
SC6	Thermal Array Sensor (TAS)	Suppression index highest when heat is found	Suppression Signal 1-10

4.3 Cell Differentiator

The functioning of *Cell Differentiator* is similar to the cell differentiation mechanism, in which cells develop aggressive or tolerant behavior in response to the type of cytokines present in the immune system. Like *Suppression Modulator*, *Cell Differentiator* is the heart of GSCF; it is responsible for integrating complex information from different sources into simple instructions and converts intricate problems into quantitative outputs. The decision flow of the *Cell Differentiator* can be summarized using a simple flow chart as shown in Figure 8.

The suppression indexes from the suppressor cells has priority over all others, it is being evaluated first to see if the robot is balance (SC1, SC2, and SC3) and if any obstacles present in front of the robot (SC4 and SC5). If the suppression index is high, the robot will perform no work except to keep the robot balance, and if the suppression index is low the system will check the affinity index to see whether a heating body is found. If a heating body is found, the system will perform aggressive behavior, alarm the command centre and remain still to monitor the heat source. If there is no heating body found within sensory range, the robot will continue to patrol around. Note that the

Cell Differentiator is only responsible to produce high level behavioral instructions such as "sound the alarm", "keep balance", "search for heat", etc. Low level commands for mechanical controllers are translated by the *Cell Reactor*. Since mechanical control schemes varies greatly between different operation platforms, GSCF delegates this work to *Cell Reactor*, so the high level design of other components can remain platform independent.

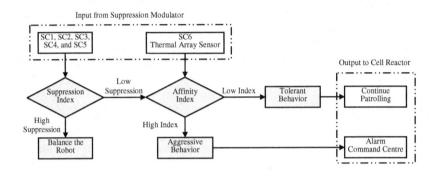

Fig. 8. Decision scheme in Cell Differentiator

5   Conclusion and Future Work

Artificial Immune System is a large and complex system that covers some biological mechanisms that are already being employed to solve engineering problems, and many more that are not yet exploited. This research demonstrated how simple suppression mechanism can help the robot to stay balance while searching through an obstructed environment. The exploitation of integration and proliferation of distributed signals (cell affinity, cell aggressiveness, and cell maturity) to suppress counter-productive behavior in a dynamic environment distinct AIS from other biologically inspired systems.

This paper is not intended to discuss hardware implementation details in the *Cell Reactor* but to show how GSCF based control system is designed at a higher level. The design of this heterogeneous control system for self-balancing robot is an attempt to further investigate flexibility of GSCF to different application requirements. Our previous research used GSCF to design a control system for a homogeneous MSR (Modular Self-Reconfigurable) robot to reach a light source under the constraints of torque limit and joint angle. The new system designed for the autonomous self-balancing robot employs the same system structure and added many features that were not explored in the previous one.

Firstly, the new system is a heterogeneous system with six independent suppressor cells that has adjustable sensitivity level towards different sensors, where previous homogeneous system has only one suppressor cell.

Secondly, the previous homogeneous system has six modules and one sensor, whereas the new heterogeneous system has one module but six sensors. This poses radical challenges to the design of *Suppression Modulator* and *Cell Differentiator*.

Thirdly, the simple suppression mechanism between SC1, SC2 and SC3 shows that SCs inside of the suppression modulator may communicate with neighboring cells as well as to the external environment. The proliferation of suppression signals provided a simple way to adjust cell sensitivity, hence increased system adaptability. This mechanism was not exploited in the homogeneous system.

In general, both the homogeneous and heterogeneous control systems built on the idea of GSCF served well in their respective application. Though the current applications are relatively simple, their under laying principles are applicable to many other engineering problems. Our future work will continue to apply GSCF to solve engineering problems at different level, in particular to problems that require high level learning. To do so, it is necessary to develop more sophisticate suppressor cells to study the dynamics of a diverse group of suppressor cells, and to explore more on the evolution aspect of the framework. The storage, retrieval and selection of distributed immune memories generated during the learning process would probably bring new ideas to distributed data manipulation for behavior based systems.

References

[1] D.P. Anderson. (20th April, 2005) nbot, a two wheel balancing robot [Online], Available from: http://geology.heroy.smu.edu/~dpa-www/robo/nbot/. [26.04.2005]

[2] E. Benjamini, G. Sunshine, and S. Leskowitz. Immunology: A Short Course. Wiley-Liss, New York, 1996.

[3] P.J. Bentley. Evolution Design by Computers. Morgan Kaufmann, Bath, U.K., 1999.

[4] T. Blackwell. (26th April, 2005) Building a Balancing Scooter [Online], Available from: http://www.tlb.org/scooter.html. [26.04.2005]

[5] L.N. de Castro, and J. Timmis. Artificial Immune Systems: A New Computational Intelligence Approach. Springer-Verlag, New York, 2002.

[6] D. Dasgupta. Artificial Immune Systems and Their Applications. Springer-Verlag, Germany, 1999.

[7] I. Erkmen, and A. Erkmen. Snake Robots to the Rescue. *IEEE Robotics & Automation Magazine*, vol. 2, pp. 1513-1518. 2002.

[8] F. Grasser, A. D'Arrigo, S. Colombi, and A. C. Rufer. JOE: A Mobile, Inverted Pendulum. IEEE Transactions on Industrial Electronics, vol. 49, No. 1, pp. 107-114. 2002.

[9] M. H. Hassoun. *Fundamentals of Artificial Neural Networks*. MIT Press. Massachusetts, 1995.

[10] Y. Ishida. *Immunity-Based Systems - A Design Perspective*. Springer-Verlag, Germany, 2004.

[11] S. Kimura, M. Takahashi, and T. Okuyama. A Fault-Tolerant Control Algorithm Having a Decentralized Autonomous Architecture for Space Hyper-Redundant Manipulators. IEEE Transaction on Systems Man, and Cybernetics-Part A: Systems and Humans, vol. 28, No.4 pp. 521-528. 1998.

[12] A. W. Y. Ko, T. L. Lau, and, Y. K. H. Lau. An Immuno Control Framework for Decentralized Mechatronic Control, to appear in *International Journal of Unconventional Computing - 2005 Special Issue,* 2005.

[13] A. W. Y. Ko, T. L. Lau, and Y. K. H. Lau. An immuno control framework for decentralised mechatronic control, *Proc. 3rd International Conference on Artificial Immune Systems (ICARIS 2004)*, Catania, Italy, September, pp. 91 – 105. 2004.

[14] M. B. Kobilarov, and G. Sukhatme. Near Time-optimal Constrained Trajectory Planning on Outdoor Terrain. To appear in *Proc. IEEE International Conference on Robotics and Automation (ICRA2005), Barcelona,* Spain, April 18-22, 2005.

[15] Y. K. H. Lau, and W. K. V. Wong. Immunologic responses manipulation of AIS agents handling, *Proc. 3rd International Conference on Artificial Immune Systems (ICARIS 2004)*, Catania, Italy, 13 – 16 September. pp. 65-79. 2004.

[16] J. H. L. Playfair, B. M. Chain. Immunology at a Glance. Blackwell Science, Bodmin, Cornwall, 2001.

[17] T.S. Ray. Overview of Tierra at ATR, in "Technical Information, no. 15, Technologies for Software Evolutionary Systems", ATR-HIP. 2001. <http://www.isd.atr.co.jp/~ray/pubs/overview/Overview.doc>

[18] L. A. Segel, and I. R. Cohen. Design Principles for the Immune System and Other Distributed Autonomous Systems. Oxford University Press, Oxford, 2001.

[19] J. Sharon. Basic Immunology. Williams & Wilkins, Pennsylvania, USA, 1998.

[20] B. Sherman and M. Sherman. (18th April, 2005) BaliBot, An Inverted Pendulum Robot [Online], Available from: http://home.earthlink.net/%7Ebotronics/index/balibot.html. [26.04.2005]

[21] M. Sipper. Machine Nature: the Coming Age of Bio-inspired Computing. McGraw-Hill, New York, 2002.

[22] L. Sompayrac. How the Immune System Works. Blackwell Science, Massachusetts, USA, 1999.

[23] A. O. Tarakanov, V.A. Skormin, and S.P. Sokolova. Immunocomputing: Principles and Applications. Springer-Verlag, New York, 2003.

[24] M. J. Wooldridge. An Introduction to multiagent systems. John Wiley & Sons, West Sussex, England, 2002.

Application of an Artificial Immune System in a Compositional Timbre Design Technique

Marcelo Caetano[1,2], Jônatas Manzolli[2], and Fernando J. Von Zuben[1]

[1] Laboratory of Bioinformatics and Bio-inspired Computing (LBiC)
[2] Interdisciplinary Nucleus for Sound Studies (NICS),
University of Campinas (Unicamp), PO Box 6101 - 13083-970, Brazil
{caetano, vonzuben}@dca.fee.unicamp.br;
jonatas@nics.unicamp.br

Abstract. Computer generated sounds for music applications have many facets, of which timbre design is of groundbreaking significance. Timbre is a remarkable and rather complex phenomenon that has puzzled researchers for a long time. Actually, the nature of musical signals is not fully understood yet. In this paper, we present a sound synthesis method using an artificial immune network for data clustering, denoted aiNet. Sounds produced by the method are referred to as immunological sounds. Basically, antibody-sounds are generated to recognize a fixed and predefined set of antigen-sounds, thus producing timbral variants with the desired characteristics. The aiNet algorithm provides maintenance of diversity and an adaptive number of resultant antibody-sounds (memory cells), so that the intended aesthetical result is properly achieved by avoiding the formal definition of the timbral attributes. The initial set of antibody-sounds may be randomly generated vectors, sinusoidal waves with random frequency, or a set of loaded waveforms. To evaluate the obtained results we propose an affinity measure based on the average spectral distance from the memory cells to the antigen-sounds. With the validation of the affinity criterion, the experimental procedure is outlined, and the results are depicted and analyzed.

1 Introduction

Computer music is an ever-growing field partly because it allows the composer such great flexibility in sound manipulation when searching for the desired result. Once the search space and the goals are defined, a technique for achieving the final product is required. Many different approaches have been proposed to meet the requirements of the process, i.e. creating interesting music, with results that vary from the unexpected to the undesired, depending upon a vast number of factors and on the methodology itself. Traditional sound synthesis techniques present limitations especially due to the fact that they do not take into consideration the subjective and/or the dynamic nature of music, by using processes that are either too simple or not specifically designed to handle musical sounds [14].

In this work, we are focusing primarily on the production of complex sounds for musical applications taking timbre design as paradigm. Complex sounds pertain to a

C. Jacob et al. (Eds.): ICARIS 2005, LNCS 3627, pp. 389–403, 2005.
© Springer-Verlag Berlin Heidelberg 2005

distinctive class of sounds that present certain characteristics. Such sounds usually have dynamic spectra, i.e. each partial has a unique temporal evolution. They are slightly inharmonic and the partials possess a certain stochastic, low-amplitude, high-frequency deviation in time. The partials have onset asynchrony, i.e. higher partials attack later than the lower ones. Our ears are highly selective and often reject sounds that are too mathematically perfect [4].

Music composition has been studied for a long time using many kinds of computational techniques, including statistic and stochastic methods [22][34], chaos theory [19], and other non-linear methods [21]. Many researchers have recently suggested the creation of Artificial Intelligence (AI) based systems for music composition [1][4][16][32]. Applications of AI in music composition involve artificial neural networks [6], cellular automata [3][23], and evolutionary computation (EC) [13][16][20][24][32]. Refer to the work of Santos et al. [29] for a detailed review of the application of EC in music systems.

As a preliminary step toward the current proposal, Caetano et al. [4] suggested the use of EC to pursue stationary/fixed target sounds that are considered the user's desired timbral outcome. The reported results can be interpreted as a sort of spectral blend between the initial and target sounds. An objective and a subjective criterion were adopted to evaluate the results. The approach of creating new timbres by the algorithmic evolution of a population of candidate solutions, having targets as references, presents a vast range of possibilities. It should be noted that, despite the fact that the process of algorithmic evolution searches for an optimum guided by the fitness function, this optimum cannot be properly specified from the musical point of view. So, the denoted targets should not be considered ideal solutions, but solely indicative modes.

Here, we present a timbre design method that allows the composer to express a certain degree of subjectivity by simply adjusting the input parameters according to prerequisites. The user is enabled to find candidate solutions that meet certain musical requirements by using a set of waveforms as examples of the desired timbre. Instead of describing the sounds using numerical parameters or any other linguistic tool, we used a set of sounds to characterize timbre. Smalley [31] declared that the information contained in the frequency spectrum cannot be separated from the time domain, because "*spectrum is perceived through time and time is perceived as spectral motion*". Thus, by specifying the target waveforms (antigen-sounds), the user is also specifying the spectral contents and the timbral characteristics of the tones. Grey [14] discusses the advantages of time domain representation. We aim at sound design by means of the specification of the spectral contents. In practical terms, the induced immune response will provide results (antibody-sounds) highly correlated with the target waveforms, albeit preserving local diversity.

The main objective of this paper is to verify the music potential of an immune inspired clustering technique in the specific task of timbre design by simulating the process under different conditions, and posteriorly showing that the results are consistent with the expected outcome. Artificial immune systems (AIS) for data clustering are generally based on the immune network theory of Jerne [18], thus producing a self-organizing process with diversity maintenance and a dynamic control of the network size [10].

Concerning the application of immune-inspired approaches in the aesthetical domain, we may emphasize two initiatives. AISArt [17] is an interactive image generation tool. The user conducts the system according to the aesthetic appreciation of areas of the images, which is also an original approach in the context of interactive evolutionary systems [1]. Chao and Forrest [5] also describe an interactive search algorithm inspired by the immune system, devoted to synthesizing biomorphs [9]. They report that this algorithm is capable of consensus solutions, given that distinct selection criteria may be associated with modules that compose the biomorph. To the best of our knowledge, there has been no previous application of AIS in timbre design.

The next section describes theories of timbre and how they are related to the development of sound synthesis techniques. Then, the fundamentals of AIS are briefly reviewed and the proposed approach is presented. The experiments performed are described and the outcomes, followed by analysis, are presented. Finally, concluding remarks and perspectives for further research are considered.

2 Timbre Design

2.1 Musical Timbre

Timbre is defined by the ASA (American Standard Association) as "that attribute of the auditory sense in terms of which the listener can judge that two sounds similarly presented which have the same intensity and pitch are dissimilar" [28]. Therefore, musical timbre is the characteristic tone quality of a particular class of sounds. As a diverse phenomenon, timbre is more difficult to characterize than either loudness or pitch. No one-dimensional scale – such as the loud/soft of intensity or the high/low of pitch – has been postulated for timbre, because there exists no simple pair of opposites between which a scale can be made.

Because timbre has so many facets, computer techniques for multidimensional scaling have constituted the first major progress in quantitative description of timbre [14], since the pioneering work of Hermann von Helmholtz [33] in the nineteenth century. From then on, researchers have determined a more accurate model of natural (complex) sounds. Digital recording has enabled the contemporary researcher to show that the waveform (and hence the spectrum) can change drastically during the course of a tone. Risset [27] observed that complex sounds have dynamic spectra and the evolution in time of the sound's spectrum plays an important part in the perception of timbre. Timbre variations are perceived, for example, as clusters of sounds played by a particular musical instrument, or said by a particular person, even though these sounds might be very distinct among themselves, depending upon its pitch, intensity or duration. In fact, the concept of timbre has always been related to sounds of musical instruments or voice, and it is in this scope that the majority of research on timbre has been developed [14][15][27]. These works identified innumerable factors that form what is called timbre perception.

2.2 Theories of Timbre

2.2.1 Classical Theory of Timbre

Herman von Helmholtz [33] laid the foundations for modern studies of timbre. He characterized tones as consisting of a sum of sinusoidal waves enclosed in an amplitude envelope made up of three parts: the attack, the steady-state, and the decay as shown in Figure 1.

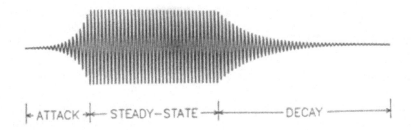

Fig. 1. A simplified Helmholtz model: the three principal segments of a tone

Helmholtz concluded that sounds which evoke a sensation of pitch have periodic waveforms (refer to Figure 2 (b) for an example) and further described the shape of these waveforms as fixed and unchanging with time. He also established that the nature of the waveform has great effect on the perceived timbre of a sound. To determine which characteristics of a waveform correlate best with timbre, he made use of the work of Fourier and concluded that the spectral description of a sound has the most straightforward correlation with its timbre. As a consequence, almost every synthesis technique proposed is concerned with the production of a signal with a specific spectral content, rather than a particular waveform.

The spectral envelope of a sound is one of the most important determinants of timbre [12], because it outlines the profile of energy distribution in a frequency spectrum.

2.2.2 Modern Studies of Timbre

Since then, researchers have determined a more accurate model of natural sound. Digital recording has enabled researchers to show that the waveform, and hence the spectrum, can change drastically during the course of a tone. Such changes can be visualized by a plot of the evolution of the partials in time, herein denoted dynamic spectrum and depicted in Figure 2 (c).

The Fourier transform enables researchers to obtain the spectrum of a sound from its waveform. Risset [27] obtained the spectral evolution of the partials of trumpet tones, being able to determine the time behavior of each component in the sound. He found that each partial of the tone has a different amplitude envelope.

This clearly contrasts with the basic Helmholtz model in which the envelopes of all the partials have the same shape. Grey [15] wondered whether such fine-grained, intricate evolution of the partials could be approximated and still retain the tone's characteristic timbre. He found out that of the three forms of simplification attempted with the tones, the most successful was a *line-segment approximation* to time-varying amplitude and frequency functions for the partials.

Although this method does decrease dramatically the amount of data required to reconstruct the tones, it still takes a large number of oscillations to satisfactorily accomplish the desired result. In computer music, synthesis algorithms that directly recreate the partials of a tone generally use data stored as line segments. It is important to be aware that this methodology is usually effective only within a small range of frequencies. For instance, a tone based on the data but raised an octave from the original will most often not evoke the same sensation of timbre.

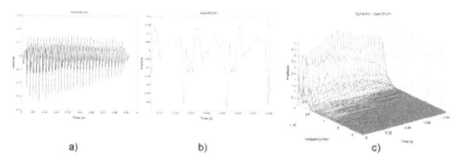

a)   b)   c)

Fig. 2. Example of a waveform and dynamic spectrum of a natural (complex) sound (tenor trumpet). Part (a) shows the waveform and (b) a detail of the periodicity, characteristic of the harmonic spectra of musical instruments. Part (c) emphasizes the evolution of the partials in time (dynamic spectrum).

When presented with a group of spectral components, a listener may or may not fuse them into the percept of a single sound. One of the determining factors is the onset asynchrony of the spectrum that refers to the difference in entrance times among the components [15] (see Figure 2(c)). The fluctuations in frequency of the various partials are usually necessary for the partials to fuse into the percept of a single tone [7].

3   The Artificial Immune Musical System

The immune system is a complex of cells, molecules and organs with the primary role of limiting damage to the host organism by pathogens, which elicit an immune response and thus are called antigens. One type of response is the secretion of antibody molecules by B cells. Antibodies are receptor molecules bound on the surface of a B cell with the primary role of recognizing and binding, through a complementary match, with an antigen. Antigens can be recognized by several different antibodies. The antibody can alter its shape to achieve a better match (complementarity) with a given antigen. The strength and specificity of the antigen-antibody interaction is measured by the affinity (complementarity level) of their match [11].

3.1 Artificial Immune Network (aiNet)

AISs are adaptive procedures inspired by the biological immune system for solving several different problems [10]. Dasgupta [8] defines them as *"a composition of intelligent methodologies, inspired by the natural immune system for the resolution of real world problems"*.

The aiNet is an artificial immune network whose main role is to perform data clustering by following some ideas from the immune network theory [18], the clonal selection [2], and affinity maturation principles [25]. The resulting self-organizing system is an antibody network that recognizes antigens (input data set) with certain (and adjustable) generality.

The clonal selection principle proposes a description of the way the immune system copes with the pathogens to mount an adaptive immune response. The affinity maturation principle is used to explain how the immune system becomes increasingly better at its task of recognizing and eliminating these pathogens (antigenic substances). The immune network theory hypothesizes the activities of the immune cells, the emergence of memory and the discrimination between reactive and tolerant regions in the shape-space [26] [30].

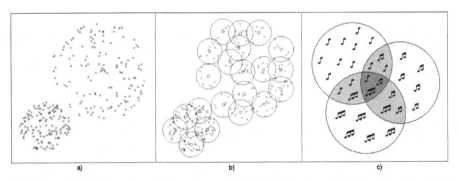

Fig. 3. Depiction of the feature extraction capability of aiNet. Part (a) shows the original data, part (b) shows the resultant memory cells representing the original data, and part (c) illustates the common timbral features of three classes of sounds.

The aiNet clusters will serve as *internal images* (*mirrors*) responsible for mapping existing clusters in the data set (Figure 3 (a)) into network clusters (Figure 3 (b)). The resultant memory cells represent common features present in the data set that were extracted by aiNet. Let us picture a set of sounds as antigens and its internal (mirror) image as variants. Inspired by Risset's sound variants idea [27], it is possible to imagine, for example, variants as a type of immune-inspired transformation applied to the sound population. Smalley's time and spectrum integration [31] also induces a timbre adaptation in time or, using a more suitable terminology for the context, a dynamic process in which an immunological timbre is generated. In this sense, the waveforms can be regarded as the repertoire to which the system is exposed, and the associated timbre may be linked to the specific response it elicits. It is of critical importance to notice that when an antibody-sound is representing more than one antigen-sound, it is placed in such a spot in soundspace that allows it to present features that are common to all the sounds it is representing. Figure 3 (c) depicts the intersection of characteristics shared by three different sounds.

3.1.1 Representation

The input parameters of the present implementation are shown in Table 1. Each individual is codified as a vector composed of L samples of a given waveform at a sampling frequency of FS samples per second. The individuals are, thus, represented in time domain, as vectors in $\mathbb{R}^L$. The affinity is given by the multidimensional Euclidean distance between antigen-sounds and antibody-sounds and is shown in equation (1). This is the time-domain evaluation of distance.

Table 1. Input parameters that can be controlled by the user

L	Number of samples per individual
FS	Sampling rate
G	Number of antigens
ts	Suppression threshold
$number$	Initial number of antibodies
n	Number of best-matching cells selected
gen	Number of generations
CM	Clone number multiplier
qi	Percentile amount of clones to be re-selected
sc	Minimum distance between antibodies and antigens

$$d(ag,ab) = \sqrt{\sum_{n=1}^{L}(ag_n - ab_n)^2} \tag{1}$$

3.1.2 Methodology of Analysis

A measure of spectral distance was developed to verify whether approaching the target sounds in time domain also corresponds to approximating the desired timbral attributes in virtue of this spectral distance measure. It measures the distance from the antigen-sound's dynamic spectrum to the dynamic spectrum of each antibody-sound it represents, as shown in equation (2), which utilizes the same notation of Figure 4. Figure 4 depicts a schematic representation of a dynamic spectrum matrix. The parameters are explained in Table 2.

$$\alpha_g^{kh} = \sqrt{\frac{1}{FT}\sum_i^F\sum_j^T \left(\left|a_g^k(i,j)\right| - \left|a_g^h(i,j)\right|\right)^2} \tag{2}$$

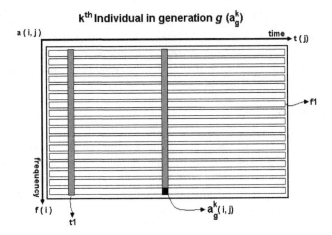

Fig. 4. Depiction of a dynamic spectrum matrix representation. X-axis represents time domain by the index j. Y-axis represents frequency domain by the index i. Each white row is a frequency (partial) temporal evolution (e.g. f1). The gray columns are instantaneous spectra in determined moments (e.g. t1). The intersection of row and column gives the amplitude of a given partial (frequency) at a given moment, represented by a(i,j) (black square).

Table 2. Parameters of Equations (2) and (3)

k	k^{th} antigen
h	h^{th} antibody
g	Generation
F	Dimension of frequency vector
T	Dimension of time vector
D	Number of antibodies representing antigens

Then, the minimum distance for each antigen and the respective antibody-sound set representing it are extracted from α_g^{kh}, obtaining a subset $\tilde{\alpha}_g^{k1}$, where $k_1 \leq k$ because one antibody-sound may be representing more than one antigen-sound (data compression). In the latter case, the distances are averaged for each antigen-sound. Finally, this vector of values is averaged for each generation, as shown in equation (3).

$$\overline{A}_g = \sum_{k1}^{D} \tilde{\alpha}_g^{k1} \tag{3}$$

This way, an average spectral distance from the potential solutions to the target spectrum is obtained at each generation. Two different experiments were performed to validate the method. They will be explained in what follows.

Experiment 1:

The spectral distance can be used to test whether the suppression threshold (*ts*) would produce the expected result. The suppression threshold (*ts*) controls the specificity level of the antibodies, the clustering accuracy and network plasticity. Refer to de Castro & Von Zuben [11] for sensitivity analysis of the parameters. One can conclude that decreasing *ts*, the antibody-sounds are expected to become more specific, decreasing the average distance from the antigen-sounds they represent while increasing in number. As a consequence, the resultant waveforms approach the target sounds as close as the user wishes.

Experiment 2:

In this experiment we wish to verify the potential of the method to generate high quality variants, regardless of the type of initialisation of the antibody network, i.e. regardless of the initial spectral content. We used three types of initialisation: white noise (a vector randomly generated), pure tones (sinusoidal waves with random frequencies from 180 Hz to 16 kHz) and complex sounds (loaded waveforms of another musical instrument). The spectra used in the experiments can be seen in Figure 5. They represent the dynamic spectra of the original antibody-sounds, that is, the spectral content which will be moulded into the target spectra by means of temporal immunological manipulation.

The dynamic spectra of four antigen-sounds are shown in Figure 6. They represent the target spectra, the ultimate goal of the method. We expect to obtain immunological internal images, which would represent timbral variants.

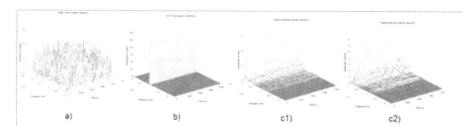

Fig. 5. Dynamic spectrum of the original antibody-sounds used in experiment 2. Part (a) shows white noise; Part (b) a pure tone and parts (c1) and (c2) show examples of the dynamic spectrum of a harmonica representing a natural (complex) sound.

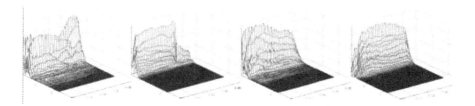

Fig. 6. Example of dynamic spectra of the tones used as antigens

4   Results

The parameters used in all experiments were as follows in Table 3. Refer to Table 1 for the definition of all input parameters. These values of *L* and *FS* represent a wave-format sound segment of approximately 0.1s. In experiment 1, the value of *ts* varies as shown in Table 4.

Table 3. Parameters utilized in both experiments (1) and (2)

L	*FS*	*G*	*number*	*n*	*gen*	*CM*	*qi*	*sc*
4096	44100	10	5	1	50	7	70%	0.1

4.1   Experiment 1

In this experiment we wished to confirm the data compression capability of the method. This characteristic allows the user to choose how close to the target sounds one wishes the results to be. The smaller the number of memory cells (resultant antibody-sounds), the farther they are from the antigen-sounds they represent for they represent more than one antigen-sound. The results shown in Table 4 confirm this assertion both in time and in spectrum domain. Due to the relatedness of the spectral contents and the associated timbre, it can be inferred that the same holds true for the corresponding timbral space. That is, this representation contains characteristics that are common to all the sounds it is representing (Figure 3).

Table 4. Result of Experiment 1

ts	D	Distance	
		Temporal	**Spectral**
0.5	4	3.16	41.89
0.3	6	1.44	35.46
0.1	9	0.49	21.66
0.05	10	0.27	20.05

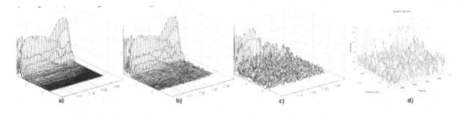

Fig. 7. Depiction of the different results obtained by adjusting the parameters and randomly perturbing the antigen-sounds

Figure 7 (a) shows an antigen-sound's dynamic spectrum and its memory cell representation when *ts* is 0.05 (b) and 0.5 (c). Part (d) shows the result of randomly perturbing the antigen-sounds, i.e. adding a gaussian-noise (white-noise) vector (with variance 0.1) to it. Clearly the result is very different between Figures 7 (c) and (d). Psychoacoustically, the resultant sound in Figure 7 (c) is a timbral merger of the corresponding antigen-sounds. In Figure 7 (d) it is a noisy version of Figure 7 (a). It is interesting to notice that the spectral result was achieved through waveform (temporal) manipulation.

4.2 Experiment 2

This experiment was set to prove the independence of the method from the type of initialization of the original antibody-sounds. All the parameters remained the same in experiment 2, except for *ts* that was set to 0.05. The results of the second experiment are depicted in Figure 8, which shows only four resultant antibody-sounds to illustrate the results. It is important to stress that 10 memory cells (resultant antibody-sounds) were obtained in all instances of this experiment. Compare the results with the antigen-sounds shown in Figure 6. In terms of spectral contents and dynamics, these antibody-sounds bear a striking resemblance to the antibody-sounds' dynamic spectra, representing a variant

4.2.1 Generational Distance Analysis
This second result intends to show the rapid dynamics of the convergence process, independently from the initialisation, both in time and spectrum domain. It can also be

Fig. 8. Memory cells resulting from the initialization of the algorithm with white noise (top), pure tones (middle) and complex sounds (bottom)

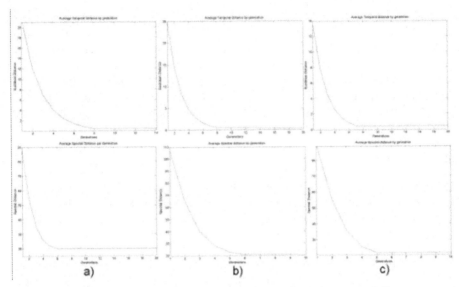

Fig. 9. Detail of the generational distance evolution. Top shows the temporal distance measure and bottom shows the spectral metric evolution. Column (a) shows the distances for the white-noise case; column (b) for the pure-tone case; and column (c) for the complex-sound case. Only the transient part of the curve is shown, i.e. the first generations.

inferred that the same holds true for the timbral domain. Figure 9 shows the adaptation of both the temporal and spectral affinity between antibody-sounds and the antigen-sounds they represent. Only the first generations are shown for the sake of clarity and to emphasize the rapid convergence in both cases. Notice that in all instances convergence was achieved before the tenth generation. It means that, no matter the starting point in soundspace, the result can always be expected to be approximately the same (for the same input parameters). This is an extremely important characteristic of the method.

5 Analysis

Both experiments base the method as a robust, yet flexible, timbre design technique. In experiment 1 we showed that the user can achieve a result that is as close as one wishes to the preset antigen population, depending on only one input parameter, the suppression threshold (ts).

It should be noted that, in experiment 2, both distances decreased exponentially with the generations and stabilized fairly quickly. The measure of spectral distance developed confirms the temporal behaviour observed. Here we should stress the important fact that this is hardly the first proposal for a measure of timbral distance. Many other techniques are available, including multidimensional scaling [15] and subjective analyses [4], among others.

In experiment 2 the results show that the method does not depend on the initialisation of the original antibody-sounds. Also, the dynamic spectra obtained represent timbral variants of the antigen-sounds.

The experiments show that aiNet is capable of producing sounds that have the desired spectral content with flexibility and robustness. The method makes possible to avoid the burden of trying to describe the desired result in terms of timbral attributes or to exhaustively search the entire soundspace for the desired result interactively, such as is the case for Interactive Genetic Algorithms [1].

6   Conclusions

A novel method of timbre design was presented, which utilizes aiNet, an immune-inspired clustering technique, in the task of obtaining sounds. These sounds possess a set of desired timbral characteristics that are inherent to musical sounds and that cannot be precisely described due to the intrinsic multidimensional nature of timbre and the subjective characteristics involved. There is no consensus on how many or what these dimensions are, let alone their subjective relation to the spectral contents of the tone. A spectral measure of distance was developed to confirm the results. It is a mathematical measure that can be linked to the subjective, aesthetic percept of timbre.

We showed that the method is robust in original spectral content to be transformed, as well as it is adjustable according to the input parameters. We also demonstrated that random variation alone is not enough to produce the same results, generating only noisy results. The characteristics of maintenance of diversity and the adjustable size of population provided by aiNet are essential in the results.

Many extensions can be envisaged and tested. It can be used to compose soundscapes, as a timbre design tool or in live electroacoustic music where an immunological timbre is generated, which evolves in real time along with other music materials. Future trends might include using the technique in AI-based musical systems and adapting the method for dynamic environments, i.e. using time-varying antigen-sounds.

Acknowledgements

The authors wish to thank FAPESP (process no. 03/11122-8) and CNPq (process no. 300910/96-7 and 308765/2003-6) for their financial support.

References

[1]   Biles, J. A. "GenJam: A Genetic Algorithm for Generating Jazz Solos", Proceedings of the 1994 International Computer Music Conference, (ICMC'94), pp. 131-137, 1994.

[2]   Burnet, F.M. The Clonal Selection Theory of Acquired Immunity, Cambridge University Press, 1959.

[3] Burraston, D., Edmonds, EA, Livingstone, D. and Miranda, E. "Cellular Automata in MIDI based Computer Music" Proceedings of the InternationalComputer Music Conference, pp. 71-78, 2004.

[4] Caetano, M., Manzolli, J., Von Zuben, F. J. Interactive Control of Evolution Applied to Sound Synthesis. Proceedings of the 18th International Florida Artificial Intelligence Research Society (FLAIRS), Clearwater, EUA, 2005.

[5] Chao, D., Forrest, S. "Generating biomorphs with an aesthetic immune system". Proceedings of the eighth international conference on Artificial life, pp 89 – 92, MIT Press, 2002.

[6] Chen, C. J. and Miikkulainen, R., "Creating Melodies with Evolving Recurrent Neural Networks", Proceedings of the International Joint Conference on Neural Networks (IJCNN-01), 2241-2246, 2001.

[7] Chowning, J. "Computer Synthesis of the Singing Voice" In Joan Sundberg (ed.), Sound Generation in Winds, Strings, and Computers. Stockholm: Royal Swedish Academy of Music, 1980.

[8] Dasgupta, D. Artificial Immune Systems and their Applications, Springer-Verlag. (ed.), 1999.

[9] Dawkins, R., The Blind Watchmaker, Penguin Books, 1986.

[10] de Castro, L. N. & Timmis, J. I. Artificial Immune Systems: A New Computational Intelligence Approach, Springer-Verlag, London, 2002.

[11] de Castro, L.N and Von Zuben, F. aiNET: An Artificial Immune Network for Data Analysis, in Data Mining: A Heuristic Approach. Abbas, H, Sarker, R and Newton, C (Eds). Idea Group Publishing, 2001.

[12] Dodge, C. and Jerse, T. A. Computer Music, synthesis, composition and performance. Schirmer Books, ISBN 0-02-873100-X, 1985.

[13] Fornari, J.E. Evolutionary Syhnthesis of Sound Segments. Ph.D. Thesis, Dept. of Semiconductors, Instruments and Photonic, University of Campinas, 2001. *in Portuguese*.

[14] Grey, J. M. An Exploration of Musical Timbre, Doctoral dissertation, Stanford Univ, 1975.

[15] Grey, J. M., and Moorer, J. A., "Perceptual Evaluations of Synthesized Musical Instrument Tones". Journ. Ac. Soc. Am., 62, 2, pp 454-462, 1977.

[16] Horowits, D. "Generating Rhythms with Genetic Algorithms". Proceedings of the 1994 International Computer Music Conference (ICMC'94), pp. 142-143, 1994.

[17] http://aisart.hybridsociety.net/. Accessed in March 2005.

[18] Jerne, N. K. "Towards a Network Theory of the Immune System", Ann. Immunol. (Inst. Pasteur), pp. 373-389, 1974.

[19] Johnson, K. Controlled chaos and other sound synthesis techniques, BSc thesis, University of New Hampshire Durham, New Hampshire, 2000.

[20] Manzolli, J, A. Maia Jr., J.E. Fornari & F. Damiani, "The Evolutionary Sound Synthesis Method". Proceedings of the ninth ACM international conference on Multimedia, September 30-October 05, Ottawa, Canada, 2001.

[21] Manzolli, J. "FracWav sound synthesis". Proceedings of the International Workshop on Models and Representations of Musicals Signals, Capri, 1992.

[22] Manzolli, J., Maia, A. "Interactive composition using Markov chain and boundary functions". Proceedings of the 15th Brazilian Computer Society Conference, II Brazilian Symposium on Computer Music, 1995.

[23] Miranda, E. R. On the Music of Emergent Behavior: What Can Evolutionary Computation Bring to the Musician?, Leonardo, vol. 36, no. 1, pp. 55-58, 2003.

[24] Moroni, A., Manzolli, J., Von Zuben, F. & Gudwin, R. Vox Populi: An Interactive Evolutionary System for Algorithmic Music Composition, San Fracisco, USA: Leonardo Music Journal –MIT Press, Vol. 10, 2000.

[25] Nossal, G.J.V. The Molecular and Cellular Basis of Affinity Maturation in the Antibody Response, Cell, 68, pp. 1-2, 1993.

[26] Perelson, A.S. & Oster, G.F. Theoretical Studies of Clonal Selection: Minimal Antibody Repertoire Size and Reliability of Self-Nonself Discrimination. J. Theoret. Biol., vol. 81, pp. 645-670, 1979.

[27] Risset, J. C. Computer Study of Trumpet Tones. Murray Hill, N.J.: Bell Telephone Laboratories, 1966.

[28] Risset, J. C., Wessel, D. L. Exploration of timbre by analysis and synthesis. In D. Deutsch (ed.) *The Psychology of Music* (pp. 26-58). New York: Academic, 1982.

[29] Santos, A., Arcay, B., Dorado, J., Romero, J. & Rodríguez, J.: "Evolutionary Computation Systems for Musical Composition". International Conference Acoustic and Music: Theory and Applications (AMTA 2000). vol 1. pp 97-102. ISBN:960-8052-23-8. 2000.

[30] Segel, L. & Perelson, A.S. "Computations in Shape Space: A New Approach to Immune Network Theory", in: ed. A.S. Perelson, Theoretical Immunology, vol. 2, pp. 321-343, 1988.

[31] Smalley, D. Spectro-morphology and Structuring Processes. In the Language of Electroacoustic Music, ed. Emmerson, pg. 61-93, 1990.

[32] Thywissen, K., GeNotator: An Environment for Investigating the Application of Genetic Algorithms in Computer Assisted Composition, Univ. of York M. Sc. Thesis, 1993.

[33] von Helmholtz, H. On the Sensations of Tone. London, Longman, 1885.

[34] Xenakis, I. Formalized Music. Bloomington: Indiana University Press, 1971.

Immunising Automated Teller Machines

Modupe Ayara[1], Jon Timmis[2], Rogério de Lemos[1], and Simon Forrest[3]

[1] Computing Laboratory, University of Kent. Canterbury, UK
{moa2, r.delemos}@kent.ac.uk
[2] Departments of Electronics and Computer Science, University of York. York, UK
jt517@ohm.york.ac.uk
[3] NCR Financial Solutions Group, Discovery Centre. Dundee, UK
simon.forrest@scotland.ncr.com

Abstract. This paper presents an immune-inspired adaptable error detection (AED) framework for Automated Teller Machines (ATMs). This framework two levels, one level is local to a single ATM, while the other is a network-wide adaptable error detection. It employs ideas from vaccination, and adaptability analogies of the immune system. For discriminating between normal and erroneous states, an immune inspired one-class supervised algorithm was employed, which supports continual learning and adaptation. The effectiveness of the local AED was confirmed by its ability of detecting potential failures on an average 3 hours before the actual occurrence. This is an encouraging result in terms of availability, since measures can be devised for reducing the downtime of ATMs.

1 Introduction

Automated Teller Machines (ATMs) are embedded systems for financial-related services. Work presented in this paper is concerned with how to improve the availability of these systems through adaptable error detection. The proposed technique aims to reduce system downtime by detecting states that are precursors of system failure. This is achieved by employing immune inspired continuous learning for updating the set of error detectors in a system. The technique relies on the existence of sequences of states that represent the operational status of an ATM, from which the adaptable error detection is able to identify those sequences that might contain fatal states.

This paper details the investigations undertaken to develop an immune-inspired adaptable error detection (AED) technique for ATMs. Underlying the immune-inspired adaptable error detection is a framework that is based on the architecture of a network of ATMs, which consists of individual ATMs that are networked to a central management system. The network supports a two-way communication mechanism between the central management system and connected ATMs. Likewise, the proposed framework for adaptable error detection consists of two levels of error detection. One level of the framework is local to a single ATM, while the other is a network-wide adaptable error detection. The latter is for exchanging information on new and common error behaviours amongst

C. Jacob et al. (Eds.): ICARIS 2005, LNCS 3627, pp. 404–417, 2005.

individual ATMs. In this architecture, each ATM hosts a local AED, while the network-wide AED is implemented within the central management system. By exploiting the communication mechanism between the central management system and individual ATMs, exchange of information amongst the local AED is made possible through the network-wide AED.

The implementation undertaken in this work was limited to the local adaptable error detection (AED). An ATM is made up of several modules, but a single module - the cash dispenser - was employed for the implementation. The basis for the local adaptable error detection technique was an artificial immune system originally developed for email classification [10], and it was evaluated by using relevant criteria that include: (1) classification performance of the algorithm in discriminating fatal from non-fatal sequences, and (2) the measurement of availability. From the outcome of the evaluation, it was demonstrated that the proposed AED technique could detect an incipient system failure. Based on these results, it is concluded that the framework, and subsequent prototype, is an effective first step towards adaptable error detection.

The rest of the paper is structured as follows. The next section error detection is motivated in the context of dependable systems. Section 3 reports on related work in the area of artificial immune systems (AIS) applied to fault tolerance. In section 4, we describe the proposed framework for adaptable error detection in context of a single ATM, and a network of ATMs. Section 5 presents an AIS algorithm for adaptable error detection, and the results of some experiments performed are discussed in the following section. The final section of the paper presents some concluding remarks concerning the application of AIS techniques to error detection in systems that are continuously subjected to change.

2   Artificial Immune Systems for Fault Tolerance

Fault tolerance aims to avoid service failures despite the presence of faults, and is carried out via error detection and recovery. Error detection is responsible for identifying the presence of an error in a system. Recovery transforms a system state that contains one or more errors and (possibly) faults into a state without detected errors and without faults that can be activated again. Error detection is the trigger for fault tolerance, therefore a fault tolerant system is reliant on an effective error detection capability.

Error detection techniques usually exploit known error profiles for detecting error states and behaviours. Such techniques are the monitoring of system's behaviour with respect to a given set of rules that include (1) adherence to given control-flow paths, (2) execution time limits, (3) data integrity checks, (4) comparison among redundant components and (5) algorithm-based plausibility checks of data [9]. However, these approaches restrict the detection of errors to those that are known at design-time.

The analogy between fault tolerance and the immune system was first expressed by [1]. In that paper, four attributes of the immune system that support the idea are: (1) the immune system functions continuously and autonomously, independent of cognition; (2) its elements (lymph nodes, other lymphoid organs, and lymphocytes) are distributed throughout the body to serve all of its organs; (3) it has its own communication links - the network of lymphatic vessels and (4) its elements (organs and vessels) are themselves redundant and in some cases diverse. Properties such as *diversity, redundancy, self-organisation, anomaly detection, learning,* and *memory* are all important from a fault tolerance perspective.

Research into hardware fault tolerance can be described under fault diagnosis and error detection. Work on fault diagnosis has focused on applying immune network concepts for defining relationships between data from sensors such as [8]. More pertinent to this research is the investigations of AIS to error detection, which can be found in [2,3,4]. By taking ideas from, [1] and [12], Bradley and Tyrell have examined the application of AIS to error detection in hardware [5]. The name *immunotronics* was coined for immune-based hardware fault tolerance. They proposed a mapping from the immune system to hardware fault tolerance which later led to the development of models for a hardware immune system using the attributes specified by [1].

3   Framework for Adaptable Error Detection

The framework for adaptable error detection (AED) being proposed, employs ideas from vaccination, and adaptability analogies of the immune system. *Vaccination* or *immunisation* is a process of priming the immune system against the occurrence of a disease by introducing attenuated antigens of the disease [7]. This process allows the immune system to generate antibodies for the introduced antigens, with the effect that subsequent invasions by similar antigens induce secondary immune responses. Therefore, this process endows the immune system with knowledge about antigens which it had not previously encountered and enables it to adapt to novel antigens during the primary immune response. This confers on the immune system the ability to detect novel patterns and react accordingly thereby supplementing existing knowledge about antigens.

In the proposed framework, the immunisation metaphor corresponds to the traditional error detection approach of deploying a set of error detectors, which are representative of known error signatures. However, the problem of traditional techniques is the inability to detect unexpected erroneous behaviors. What is required is a system that can continually learn about these unknown behaviors and adapt a set of detectors capable of identifying them in the future. This requirement motivated us to adopt ideas from the continuous learning nature of the immune system.

The framework consists of two phases, namely *design-time immunisation* and *run-time adaptation* that are comparable with the immune metaphors of immunisation, and continual learning, respectively. The design-time immunisation caters for the distribution of generic error detectors amongst systems from an off-line process of detector generation. To be more precise, assume there is a family of embedded systems with similar functions and behaviours whereby each system is characterised by its own unique features. The idea is to extract

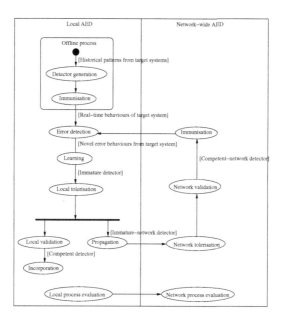

Fig. 1. Activity diagram of the framework for adaptable error detection

generic error detectors corresponding to error signatures common to these systems. Therefore, these generic error detectors serve as the minimum set of detectors across all the systems compared to populations of detectors that are unique to individual systems. In contrast, the run-time adaptation phase confers on each system a more specialised set of detectors and is responsible for augmenting the detectors that are more generic (through the use of an evolutionary process). The specialised error detectors are generated from error sequences observed during run-time operations of the system. Furthermore, the framework divides the learning mechanisms into two levels of (1) learning within a system and (2) learning amongst systems. The two levels are represented as local AED and network-wide AED systems as illustrated in figure 1.

4 Prototype for Local Adaptable Error Detection in ATMs

In this section we outline a prototype system that has been realised as part of the research. We initially outline the architecture of the solution over an ATM network, then discuss issues relating to the data and immune inspired techniques employed.

4.1 Artificial Immune Systems for Adaptable Error Detection

Assuming a network of ATMs, as depicted by figure 2, we can place the framework outlined in the previous section within context. Our framework for AED exploits the network infrastructure to support local and network-wide learning, which is integrated with the ATM architecture as shown by figure 2. In this figure, we see ATMs labelled *SST 1*, *SST 2*, *SST 3*, and *SST 4* connected to a *Central Manager*, which is able to receive and send information to connected ATMs.

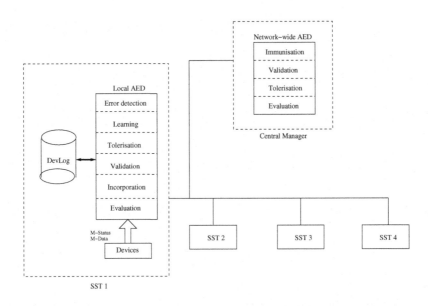

Fig. 2. System Architecture for adaptable error detection in ATMs

A local AED system is implemented within an ATM, while the network-wide AED is hosted by the Central Manager to support the central information exchange amongst local AEDs. Figure 2 shows a detailed view of the major activities associated with a single local AED for *SST 1*, and the network-wide AED. Altogether, the connection of each ATM to a central system that contains the network-wide AED enables learning amongst ATMs.

Data. The data source we were provided with were ATM log files. These files record histories of error events. Each log file records error events related to different modules in an ATM, for example, an error in the magnetic card reader (MCRW) module. Furthermore, each error state of a module in an ATM is presented under the *M-Status* field, while the *Start Time* field presents the time when the error state was recorded. Throughout our work, we investigated alternatives on how to use the data, ranging from time stamps, M-Status, M-Data and combinations thereof. After careful investigation, we concluded that whilst combining a number of data (such as M-Status and time) may be beneficial, we adopted the line of taking the simplest approach first. To that end, we made use of M-Status values only. These are discrete values that represent the state of operation of an ATM, and through preliminary investigations we found that this was sufficient to identify potential failure in the machine. For the purposes of out work, this value is represented by 10.

Data Representation. For the purposes of our investigations, fixed length sequences were employed due to the absence of information on markers that tag the beginning of sequences of states. Hence, fatal sequences are fixed length sequences that are terminated by fatal states, while non-fatal sequences do not terminate with fatal states. Figure 3 shows examples of fatal and non-fatal sequences.

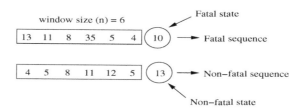

Fig. 3. Illustration of fatal and non-fatal sequences

For our implementation of the prototype, a fatal state is assumed as a M-Status value of 10, therefore the fatal sequence illustrated by figure 3 terminates with a state value of 10. Non-fatal sequences do not terminate with a 10, but any other value in the allowable range of machine state values.

Affinity Measure. In order for a detector within local AED to identify if a sequence of data is a precursor to failure, some form of affinity measure between the two is required. Given that a sequence is being used, any affinity metric should take into account the number of states (a history) to make the prediction. To this end, the most obvious choice is to adopt some form of *window* on the incoming sequence which allows it to be matched against a detector. If sufficient states within the sequence are matched against a *fatal sequence detector* then a classification can be made whether the sequence is a precursor to a fatal state.

An Artificial Immune System for E-mail Classification (AISEC) Algorithm. In order to develop our solution, we have taken as a basis, the artificial immune system for e-mail classification (AISEC) [10]. AISEC was developed for a two-class problem, to discriminate between interesting and uninteresting e-mails. However, it has properties such as continual learning and adaptation which are required for our application to ATMs. Other techniques were investigated, such as rule induction, and we concluded that this algorithm had the simplicity and properties that are required.

4.2 AISEC for Adaptable Error Detection

We now present the AISEC algorithm as adapted for use within the local AED. The algorithm cannot be applied directly to adaptable error detection, since the algorithm was designed for e-mail classification. In line with the view of [6], the algorithm had to be redesigned according to the new application area. In particular, we needed to pay attention to the choice of suitable data and their transformation for implementing the local AED, affinity measure, evolutionary mechanism and parameters.

Representation. B-cells in the AISEC algorithm for adaptable error detection (AED) are simply detectors of sequences, which identify sequences that terminate at fatal states. B-cells are generated from ATM log files during the off-line detector generation phase. Prior to the detector generation process, the ATM log files are initially pre-processed. Data obtained from the output of the pre-processing are divided into the training, testing and validation partitions. The training partition provides training data for the detector generation process. Parameters of the AISEC algorithm are then optimised with the validation partition, while the AISEC is tested with the testing data partition. By training, validating and testing the AISEC algorithm with separate data sets, an accurate or unbiased measure of the classification performance could be reported from experiments [11].

The error detectors generated are used to immunise the local AED for the classification of potential failure sequences:

- *Off-line generation*: Error detectors are fixed length sequences, hence an appropriate window size must be selected to initiate the detector generation process. For the training data, *M-Status* sequences terminated by fatal states are generated from the states of the cash dispenser;
- *Online generation*: During the testing phase of the AISEC algorithm, fixed-length sequences of run-time ATM states are generated using the same format as the off-line detector generation process. The same window size applied during the generation of B-cells is adopted. Similarly, the window size provides the marker for the beginning and ending of non-fatal sequences, while it signifies the beginning of fatal sequences at run-time. Sequences are generated using a non-overlapping sliding window of selected window size. The reason for adopting non-overlapping sliding window originates from empirical studies. It was observed that the AISEC algorithm could not discriminate between fatal and non-fatal sequences when sequences are generated through an overlapping mode. This is because a fatal sequence and a preceding non-fatal sequence have last (n-1) states in common, where n is the length of each sequence.

Affinity Measures. The affinity measure employed for the AISEC algorithm adapts the r-contiguous bits matching rule for the problem, which defines the affinity between two data items, when they have a number of contiguous bits in common. Consequently, affinity between a sequence of run-time ATM states (antigen), and an error detector (B-cell) is computed by identifying the number of contiguous states that are common to them. An illustration is shown in figure 4, whereby the value of r is the minimum number of contiguous states required to define affinity.

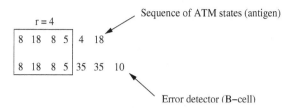

Fig. 4. R-contiguous bits matching rule

In our prototype, affinity is calculated from the r-contiguous states common to an antigen and a B-cell. The affinity measure also takes into account the proximity of the common contiguous states present in the B-cells in relation to the fatal state. For example, in figure 4, the B-cell has two states *35, 35* between contiguous states *8 18 8 5* and fatal state of 10. The antigen has two states *4, 18* after the contiguous states *8 18 8 5*. These states that lie in between the contiguous states and the fatal state provide another factor for the affinity. Affinity is calculated as a value between 0 and 1, and it is computed using equation 1 based on the following notations:

affinity - variable to store affinity between *antigen* and *B-cell*;
r-contiguousbits - contiguous bits common to *antigen* and *B-cell*;
windowSize - window size for generating sequences;
abs(x) - absolute value of *x*;
antigenInterval - number of states between r-contiguous bits and fatal state in *antigen*;
b-cellInterval - number of states between r-contiguous bits and fatal state in *B-cell*;

$$affinity = \frac{r\text{-}contiguousbits}{windowSize + abs(antigenInterval - b\text{-}cellInterval)} \qquad (1)$$

Algorithm. Within the prototype, the basic AISEC algorithm was implemented in addition to *generalisation* and *specialisation* of B-cells as mutation mechanisms. Generalisation substitutes a valid state in a B-cell with a don't care (*), while specialisation substitutes a state with another valid state in the gene library. The gene library constrains the algorithm to mutating with only valid states.

In addition to this, new B-cells can be introduced into the detector set through the incorporation of undetected fatal sequences. Unlike cloning and mutation, which are characterised by a guided random process, the incorporation of fatal sequences allows the learning of specific failure sequences. That is, if there is a recurrence of these sequences, they will be detected.

Experimental Setup. Two data sets were applied during the empirical experiments for the case study and to identify them, they are tagged *ATM-data-set-A* and *ATM-data-set-B*, respectively. In order to provide sufficient data test the local AED, we collated several log files from geographically located ATMs into *ATM-data-set-A*. Whilst the framework is based on the notion that only local information will be used to immunise the ATM, we have made the reasonable assumption that geographically located ATMs provide us with a common enough data set to allow for experimentation. Other experiments undertaken during our research indicate that this is not the case for non-geographically located ATMs. Our second data set *ATM-data-set-B* was used to test for availability, and is made up of records from a single ATM, and therefore is a subset of *ATM-data-set-A*. For testing availability we had to restrict tests to a single ATM, in order to have a clear indication on how much availability can be improved. Each data set was divided into three separate parts. $\frac{2}{3}^{rd}$ of each data set was for training, while the remaining $\frac{1}{3}^{rd}$ of each data set was divided into halves for validation and testing. In total, there were 4588 records for *ATM-data-set-A*, and 543 records for *ATM-data-set-B*. All experiments were repeated for 30 independent runs, and the average taken. AISEC has a number of parameters, for more detail on these see [10]. We undertook an extensive analysis of the parameter space, and the parameters used in our experiments were determined empirically and are detailed in the table caption.

5   Results

Experiments were carried out using four variants of the AISEC algorithm to understand the role of the off-line and online processes, as well as the different evolutionary mechanisms by recording classification performance.

The variants of the local AED include:

- *Static AED*: This is the AISEC algorithm, without off-line evolutionary process during training of naive B-cells, without online feedback on classification, and without online evolutionary process;
- *Static AED with evolution*: This is the AISEC algorithm, which includes the off-line evolution of naive B-cells, but without online feedback on classification, and without online evolutionary process;
- *Online AED with evolution*: This is the full ASIEC algorithm, which includes online feedback on classification, online evolutionary process through cloning and mutation, and off-line evolutionary process during training of naive B-cells;
- *Online AED with incorporation of fatal sequences*: This is the full AISEC algorithm but instead of the evolutionary process by cloning and mutation, new B-cells are recruited into the naive pool by incorporating undetected fatal sequences.

5.1   Classification Performance

Results from the experiments based on these variants of the local AED, are presented in table 1. Column (a) represents results from executing the *static*

Table 1. Comparison of classification performance of the AISEC algorithm using testing data from *ATM-data-set-A*. Parameters include: window size = 6, classification threshold = 0.98, affinity threshold = 0.95, memory seed = 65, clone constant = 7, mutation constant = 1.0, stimulation count (naive) = 25, stimulation count (memory) = 15, train data = 68 detectors, test data = 38 (24 fatal sequences and 14 non-fatal sequences).

| | *Static AED* | *Static AED with evolution* | *Online AED with evolution* | *Online AED with incorporation of fatal sequences* |
	(a)	*(b)*	*(c)*	*(d)*
Classification accuracy	94.74% (0.00)	92.19% (2.89)	92.81% (2.49)	93.68% (1.48)
True positive	91.67% (0.00)	87.64% (4.58)	88.61% (3.94)	90.00% (2.35)
True negative	100.00% (0.00)	100.00% (0.00)	100.00% (0.00)	100.00% (0.00)
False positive	0.00% (0.00)	0.00% (0.00)	0.00% (0.00)	0.00% (0.00)
False negative	8.33% (0.00)	12.36% (4.58)	11.39% (3.94)	10.00% (2.35)
Naive detectors	3.00 (0.00)	0.83 (0.65)	55.13 (8.52)	2.97 (0.85)
Memory detectors	65.00 (0.00)	65.00 (0.00)	65.00 (0.00)	65.20 (0.41)

AED, column (b) shows results from *static AED with evolution*, column (c) is for *online AED with evolution*, and column (d) provides the outcomes from *online AED with incorporation of fatal sequences*.

As can be seen from table 1, in terms of classification accuracy (i.e., how well it predicts a fatal sequence) the local AED is consistently high. What is very encouraging is the low rate of false positives (i.e. how many times the AED system said there was a potential failure, when there was not). This figure should be as low as possible, as a high false positive rate would generate a high false alarm rate. However, what should be noted is that there is very little difference between the performance of all four variants. This is attributed to the relatively small amount of data that was available. Data employed in these experiments come from real ATMs in operation, and retrieval of this data (at present) is difficult. This restriction has not enabled the immune mechanism within the AED with evolution sufficient experience and time to improve.

In summary, the following deductions can be made from the results on this data set, clearly further analysis is required with other data sets to see if these observations hold, however this was not possible due to the difficulty in collecting data from ATMs:

- Continuous incorporation of undetected fatal sequences into the local AED achieves comparable classification performance with the evolutionary mechanism of cloning and mutation;

- Population of naive B-cells increases exponentially with respect to time, using cloning and mutation. In contrast there is a linear increase of naive B-cells with the incorporation of fatal sequences. Given this observation, it is deduced that the incorporation of fatal sequences employs minimal B-cells to achieve classification accuracy comparable to using cloning and mutation;
- Population of memory B-cells is stable over time, although it is expected to show minor variations over an extended period;
- The classification accuracy of the local AED starts off from a high value of 100% based on sufficient training data, but it degrades over time due to the presence of ineffective B-cells resulting from incorrect learning. After a period of reinforcing effective B-cells and removing ineffective ones, the classification accuracy stabilises to indicate that the local AED has reached an equilibrium;
- The local AED was able to detect fatal sequences successfully. For example, the local AED stabilised around a classification accuracy of roughly 90.00% using *ATM-data-set-A*;
- The local AED produces specialised detectors that are useful for further analysis of precursors to system failure.

5.2   Availability

The other criterion for evaluating the local AED is the impact on availability of ATMs. This criterion exploits the time interval between detection of fatal sequences and the occurrence of fatal states. An increase in the detection time interval might translate to an increase in mean time to failure (MTTF). Also, based on the inference that the time interval serves as the time for the early detection and successful avoidance of a failure event, the early detection of a fatal sequence might increase availability through allowing for preventative maintenance, or reducing the mean time to repair (MTTR).

Experiments on availability were carried out using data associated with a single ATM *ATM-data-set-B*, and the average results over 30 runs are presented in table 2. The mean detection time intervals were calculated from the timestamps associated with each state in the ATM data.

As can be seen from the results in table 2, whilst the predictive accuracy is relatively low, the local AED was able to detect problems up to 3 hours in advance. As it can be observed, there is a trade off between the accuracy and the availability. The accuracy is lower in this set of experiments (compared to those presented in table 1), due to not only the small amount of data that was used (only 543 records were available), but the fact that because of the data, different parameters of the algorithm had to be employed, in particular the classification threshold. This allowed for more general matching to take place (i.e. less discrimination) to overcome the deficiency in the data, but at the sacrifice of accuracy. Other experiments were undertaken with a variety of parameters, and alternative data sets. For a different data set we are able to detect up to one day in advance, but with an increase in the classification threshold.

Table 2. Comparison of classification performance of the local AED using testing data from *ATM-data-set-B*. Parameters include: window size = 6, classification threshold = 0.5, affinity threshold = 0.95, memory seed = 5, clone constant = 7, mutation constant = 1.0, stimulation count (naive) = 25, stimulation count (memory) = 15, , train data = 7 detectors, test data = 9 (5 fatal sequences and 4 non-fatal sequences).

| | *Static AED no evolution* | *Static AED with evolution* | *Online AED with evolution* | *Online AED with fatal sequences* |
	(a)	*(b)*	*(c)*	*(d)*
Classification accuracy	55.56% (0.00)	55.19% (11.48)	52.96% (12.61)	58.15% (7.54)
Mean detection time interval	0:3:15:15 (0:0:0:0)	0:2:36:12 (0:1:19:26)	0:2:16:40 (0:1:31:0)	0:2:29:41 (0:1:23:59)

5.3   Discussion of Results

From these results, we can conclude that the local AED, as implemented in our protoype, detects fatal sequences prior to the occurrences of failures. This, of course, depends on adequate training data and appropriate parameters. Consequently, these experiments have proven the feasibility of adaptable error detection based on the framework. These results translate to the enhancement of availability in ATMs by anticipating potential failures. The assumption is that the a priori knowledge of impending failures initiates mechanisms for circumventing their occurrences. As a result, the mean time to failure (MTTF) of target system is increased. It can be also assumed that the mean time to repair (MTTR) could be reduced since the fault in the system is now known. We also note that one has to be careful drawing general conclusions from these results, as we have only presented results from two data sets. Ideally, more testing would be done with other data sets as and when it becomes available.

6   Conclusions

We have proposed a framework for potentially improving the availability of ATMs in which a key component is a local adaptable error detection (AED) that was implemented by adapting the artificial immune system for email classification (AISEC) algorithm. The effectiveness of the local AED was established using data that correspond to the error incidences in the cash-handler module of an ATM. Results from the empirical studies has confirmed the efficacy of the local AED at forecasting system failures. A summary of the findings are presented below:

– *Detection of failure occurrences*: The classification performance was derived from the classification accuracy of the AISEC algorithm (employed in the local AED), which is simply the number of failure occurrences detected out of the total number of failure occurrences reported in the system. From the outcome, classification accuracies of approximately 90% was recorded for one of the data sets;

- *Enhancement of availability*: The local AED was assessed with regards to its ability to detect potential failures in the system before their occurrences. Through the early detection of failures, it is assumed that necessary repair actions could be undertaken to prevent system downtime. In other words, the mean time to failure of the system can be increased, and mean time to repair can be reduced. Based on this criterion, the time intervals between the detection and occurrences of failures were monitored. From the estimated mean of these time intervals based on a particular data set, it was demonstrated that the local AED detected failure occurrences on an average of 3 hours before failures. Given another data set, it was observed that the failures were detected with an average of one day prior to the incident. These mean time intervals are absolute values, but their significance for carrying out repairs to circumvent failures are dependent on domain expert's opinion.

Acknowledgments. This research was fully funded by NCR Financial Solutions Group, and the authors would like to thank the company for their continued support of this research.

References

1. A. Avizienis. Towards systematic design of fault-tolerant systems. *IEEE Computer*, 30(4):51–58, April 1997.
2. D. W. Bradley and A. M. Tyrell. Immunotrics: Hardware fault tolerance inspired by the immune system. In *Proceedings of Third International Conference on Evolvable Systems (ICES 2000)*, volume 1801, pages 11–20, April 2000.
3. D. W. Bradley and A. M. Tyrell. The architecture for the hardware immune system. In Didier Keymeulen, Adrian Stoica, Jason Lohn, and Ricardo S. Zebulum, editors, *Proceedings of The Third NASA-DoD workshop on Evolvable Hardware*, pages 193–200, Long Beach, California, July 2001. IEEE Computer Society.
4. D. W. Bradley and A. M. Tyrell. A hardware immune system for benchmark state machine error detection. In *Proceedings of Congress on Evolutionary Computation. Part of the World Congress on Computational Intelligence.*, pages 813–818, Honolulu, HI. USA, 2002.
5. D. W. Bradley and A.M. Tyrell. Hardware fault tolerance: An immunological solution. pages 107–112. IEEE, 2000.
6. A. A. Freitas and J. Timmis. Revisiting the foundations of artificial immune systems: A problem-oriented perspective. In P. J. Bentley J. Timmis and E. Hart, editors, *Proceedings of the 2nd International Conference on ARtificial Immune Systems (ICARIS)*, pages 229–241, Edinburgh, UK, September 2003. Springer.
7. B. Hérve. A brief history of the prevention of infectious diseases by immunisations. *Comparative Immunology, Microbiology, and Infectious Diseases*, 26(5):293–308, 2003.
8. Y. Ishida. Active diagnosis by self-organization: An approach by the immune network metaphor. In *Proceedings of the International Joint Conference on Artificial Intelligence (IJCAI'97)*, pages 1084–1089, Nagoya, 1997.

9. C. Scherrer and A. Steininger. Dealing with dormant faults in an embedded fault-tolerant computer systems. *IEEE Transactions on Reliability*, 52(4):512–522, December 2003.

10. A. Secker, A. Frietas, and J. Timmis. Aisec: An artificial immune system for e-mail classification. In R. Sarker, R. Reynolds, H. Abbass, T. Kay-Chen, R. McKay, D Essam, and T. Gedeon, editors, *Proceedings of the Congress on Evolutionary Computation*, pages 131–139–167, Canberra, Australia, December 2003b. IEEE.

11. S. M. Weiss and K. A. Casimir. *Computer Systems that Learn: Classification and Prediction Methods from Statistics, Neural nets, Machine learning, and Expert systems*. Morgan Kaufmann Publishers, Inc., 1991.

12. S. Xanthakis, S. Karapoulios, R. Pajot, and A. Rozz. Immune sytem and fault tolerant computing. *Lecture Notes in Computer Science*, 1063:181–197, 1996.

Fault Detection Algorithm for Telephone Systems Based on the Danger Theory

José Carlos L. Pinto[1] and Fernando J. Von Zuben[2]

[1] Telecommunications Research and Development Center,
CPqD, Rod. Campinas – Mogi-Mirim Km 118,5, Campinas/SP, Brazil
`jcarlos@cpqd.com.br`
[2] Department of Computer Engineering and Industrial Automation,
State University of Campinas, Unicamp, CP: 6101, 13083-970, Campinas/SP, Brazil
`vonzuben@dca.fee.unicamp.br`

Abstract. This work is aimed at presenting a fault detection algorithm composed of multiple interconnected modules, and operating according to the paradigm supported by the danger theory in immunology. This algorithm attempts to achieve significant features that a fault detection system is supposed to have when monitoring a telephone profile system. These features would basically be adaptability due to the strong variation that operational conditions may exhibit over time, and the decrease in the number of false positives, which can be generated when any abnormal behavior is erroneously classified as being a fault. Simulated scenarios have been conceived to validate the proposal, and the obtained results are then analyzed.

1 Introduction

According to the danger theory in immunology, the guiding principle is the presence or absence of second signals determining responsiveness or tolerance [9]. The fault detection model to be proposed here will follow this driving force to synthesize a fault detection system capable of providing an adaptive coverage for a highly changeable environment as well as memorizing reactions in the face of the required adaptations.

Alternative approaches based on process history [13], and even algorithms based on artificial immune systems that adopt the self–non-self view, have problems with the rates of false positives (FP), to be drastically reduced here with the presence of second signals. When the self–non-self view is applied to static scenarios for fault detection, high levels of performance may be achieved [7], but it is not the case here.

These features become greatly relevant in telephone networks, due to the existence of events that may express distinct behavior along time and that should be satisfactorily attended such as, for instance, the peaks and valleys of call attempts, which can be unpredicted in the normal functioning of the network. Another issue to be pondered is the erroneous classification of a given anomaly as a fault. What a detection system can basically perceive is the deviation of situations that are said to be normal. The further step of classifying such deviation from normality as a fault generally requires a steady human intervention.

C. Jacob et al. (Eds.): ICARIS 2005, LNCS 3627, pp. 418–431, 2005.

We intend to perform this classification automatically and adaptively [11]. Additionally, a voting process is implemented to provide robustness to the fault detection activity, with multiple immune-inspired systems operating in parallel.

The paper is organized as follows. Section 2 describes the essentials of telephone systems and fault detection requirements. Sections 3 outlines the most relevant concepts associated with the danger theory paradigm, and related work is briefly reviewed in Section 4. The proposed fault detection system is fully described in Section 5, and Section 6 presents and analyzes the obtained results. Finally, further steps of the research and concluding remarks are pointed out.

2 Telephone Systems and Fault Detection Requirements

In a broad sense, it is currently possible to consider telephone systems as based on circuit networks, packet networks or hybrid networks [6][8]. Packet networks utilize protocols such as RTP (Real-Time Transport Protocol) and RTCP (Real-Time Transport Control Protocol), which make voice communication possible and try to support the quality of telephone service in real time. The need for some protocol to establish the communication among users is also to be observed, such as the SIP (Session Initiation Protocol), for example. In relation to circuit networks, although there is no need for a voice transmission protocol – as it is usual for package networks –, the use of a protocol that gives way to complete the telephone call is necessary. These traditional networks (circuit telephone networks) have a coupled signaling network. This signaling network is a package network which utilizes specific protocols such as the SS7 protocol (Signaling System Number 7), which is used either for the completion of calls or for offering services that are not oriented to connection.

The protocols used to complete a telephone call make use of ordinary information, such as the originating address, the destination address, the time of the call attempt, information on specific features (associated with functionality and type of service), etc., which are quite relevant to control such information among users. In order for the telephone service quality to be maintained, it is possible to have a management system that analyzes these parameters by indicating the occurrence of faults generated by undesired network situations or conducts. An example of undesired conduct is the occurrence of an excessive number of unsuccessful calls within a given time period. This kind of fault can be verified by the simple counting of unsuccessful calls.

An aspect to be considered in relation to telephone communication is that the traffic intensity as well as the characteristics (parameters) of the call attempts vary at distinct rates over time. Examples of changes that can occur within the parameters of call attempts concerning a network over time include the appearance of calls whose duration is approximately zero, or whose status is of a generic non-completed call. Within a given time period, this occurrence should be considered a normal event. Meanwhile, within another time period, this occurrence may take place due to a fault in the destination or be caused by any other type of fault. Under these circumstances, a simple event counting is not able to indicate precisely the difference between a normal condition and a real fault occurred in the network. The algorithm to be proposed in what follows relies on an elaborate immune-inspired learning device to make this discernment. This process aims at following up the evolution of the conduct of call attempts regardless of the speed of this evolution, and it also attempts to avoid human intervention for the acquisition of these fault diagnoses.

The obtained results, i.e. the indication of faults occurred in the telephone system, aim to supplement the information which has been obtained by the generated alarms, which use the simple counting of events. This information complementation acts for: (*i*) the indication of the continuity of faults which have already been alarmed; (*ii*) the indication of faults or the propensity to faults which have not been alarmed yet; (*iii*) the association of call attempts with a specific alarm (so that one is able to know the calls that have really originated an alarm); and (*iv*) the association of call attempts (related to an alarm) with a given region of parameters to facilitate the search for the cause of the generated fault.

3   The Human Immune System and the Danger Theory

The immune system can be described as a complex of cells, molecules and organs capable of protecting the entire body against harmful actions. This system is composed of several layers: skin and mucus, physiological conditions, innate immune system, and adaptive immune system. The adaptive system has manifold characteristics that inspire the formulation of algorithms which lead to the solution of ordinary problems. Among these characteristics, it is possible to mention the capacity to react against structures which have never come forth before, capacity to express adaptive behavior, and also the capacity to memorize antigenic structures.

The simplified performance of the adaptive immune system can be observed from the moment when T cells (T helper lymphocytes) are triggered by Antigen Presenting Cells (APCs). Through their receptors, the T lymphocytes (helpers) recognize a new peptide-MHC (Major Histocompatibility Complex) combination in the surface of an Antigen Presenting Cell (APC). Next, these T lymphocytes (helpers) secrete chemical substances that activate other types of lymphocytes (B lymphocytes). Through their receptors, the B lymphocytes are able to recognize antigens, which have been previously presented by the APC, in a free manner in the body. When activated, the B lymphocytes secrete antibodies that adhere to the identified antigens, for signaling and neutralizing purposes. Another type of lymphocyte is the T killer, which is capable of fighting abnormal cells, virus-infected cells, and certain types of antigens.

The interpretation on how the initial reaction of the immune system takes place (from the APC) admits distinct views. According to a more classic approach, the immune system is triggered by external stimuli (non-self). At this point, the immune system needs to recognize which molecules belong to it (self) and which molecules do not (non-self). Nevertheless, this view presents some points that cannot be answered, including: why doesn't the immune system defend us against the air we breathe or against the food we eat? By means of an alternative approach, which throws a more comprehensive explanation for this last issues, Matzinger [9] presents the Danger Theory, according to which another dichotomy is stressed: "dangerous / inoffensive" [4]. The Danger model is based on the principle that the immune system is controlled by internal signals (danger signals), and not external ones. Such signals are emitted by cells as they suffer any injury.

According to the Danger Theory, whenever a cell displays a danger signal, a danger zone is created around it. The APCs in this area are activated and send off co-stimulation signals that can be received by the T cells. In their environment, the APCs capture the antigens randomly (for professional APCs, i.e., dendritic cells) or non-randomly (for B cells) and present them to the T cells. The B cells may act as APCs by co-stimulating experienced T cells (memory cells – which have already passed through some previous activation).

According to the theory at issue, lymphocyte behavior can be analyzed based on the combination of two signals. The former (signal 1) would be the one obtained by the immune cell as it recognizes an antigen. The latter (signal 2) would be the previously mentioned co-stimulation signal, which acts as a confirmation for signal 1.

In a condensed form, the danger theory paradigm can be expressed in the form of the laws of lymphotics [9]:

- A lymphocyte requires two signals to be activated. An inactive lymphocyte dies whenever it receives a signal 1 without a signal 2 and it is activated whenever it receives both signals. A signal 2 received without a signal 1 is ignored.
- T cells can only receive a signal 2 from APCs, and B cells from active T cells or memory cells. There is one exception to this rule. During the initial phase of the negative selection, the lymphocytes are not able to receive signal 2, no matter which source it comes from.
- Active T or B cells ignore signal 2. They execute their functions as they receive a signal 1, regardless of the presence of a signal 2. After a certain period of time, these cells either die or return to the inactive status (memory cells).

This approach is intended to justify issues that remained unanswered, for instance, the absence of attack, on part of the immune system, against certain structures which are external to the body (e.g.: food, silicon prostheses, bone fragments, among others). Some mechanisms are added with this purpose. Thus, by searching the analogy with the mechanisms that have been inherited and proposed by the Danger Theory, the AIS can achieve new solutions and improve solutions that were previously encountered by other immune approaches.

4 Related Work

Several pieces of work related to fault detection by using AIS have been developed in the last few years. The most common approach, however, is based on the self–non-self view, which presents some shortcomings when the system under supervision must provide an adaptive coverage for a highly changeable environment.

Nonetheless, recent work utilizing the DT has been developed. In their work, Aickelin et al. [1] proposed the use of DT for intrusion detection. They model a system in which the correlation among the multiple signals provides a groundwork method for the immune response. This work attempts to identify alerts of the apoptotic type (corresponding to legitimate system actions and to the requirements of an attack) and alerts of the necrotic type (corresponding to the real damage generated by successful attacks). Actions taken by the intrusion detection system are based on the equilibrium between these two alert types.

Sarafijanovic and Boudec [10] presented an elaborate framework to detect misbehavior in mobile ad-hoc network with a DT perspective. In a simplified manner, this proposal is based upon the utilization of a virtual thymus in which the antigens that possess authorization to take part in it (antigens that are not related to danger signals) generate detectors for the system through a constant negative selection process. These detectors, when co-stimulated by danger signals, identify the misbehavior in the network.

The main distinction of these previous approaches to the present proposal is stressed in what follows. As far as the death and the deactivation of detectors (lymphocytes) are concerned, the present proposal tries to explicitly emphasize the laws of lymphotics. Another relevant aspect is the existence of a voting process, so that multiple fault detection systems should be implemented and have to operate in parallel. This is akin with a strong tendency in machine learning [12]. This approach provides an analysis which is less prone to false diagnoses and offers an enhanced adaptability of the detector population in relation to the constant change of the system. It also uses a maturation procedure concerning the detector population, which is based on the affinity of each detector with the population of antigens (Global Affinity). This is accomplished by considering the need to maintain the diversity in the detector population and the variable speed that the detector population is supposed to have in its evolution as it attempts to follow the variation speed in the profile of the antigen population. In addition, an analysis is performed regarding the concentration of active detectors in the observation space. Its objective is to detect the causes of the faults by checking the regions with high concentration levels.

5   The Fault Detection Algorithm

The algorithm that is proposed here is aimed at detecting faults in telephone systems. At first, four variables assuming major significance for a system with such profile were chosen: Origin, destination, duration, and feature. In this essay, these variables mean, respectively, the origin of a call, the destination of a call, the duration of a call, and a given feature or specific quality of this call.

Each call of the telephone system is represented in the fault detection system by an antigen, which must be compared with the detector population of this system. Both antigens and detectors are modeled as heterogeneous strings, i.e., composed of linear attributes (origin, destination and duration) and nominal attribute (feature). The attributes origin and destination were considered as being linear ones, although they could have been deemed as nominal attributes.

Then it was defined a function that indicates the affinity among detectors and antigens. This function indicates whether an antigen is inside or outside a region that surrounds the detector, which is defined as the affinity region. The function is based on affinity intervals as the comparison of linear attributes takes place, and the equality of such attributes, when nominal attribute are been compared.

It should be noticed that a fault detection algorithm that is based on anomaly verification in a telephone system may find such anomalies without actually detecting the faults. If every anomaly is considered to be a fault, there will be an increase in the number of false positives (FP). This happens as the detection of an anomaly may merely stand for the detection of a call outside the patterns which are said to be more common for that telephone system at that moment, and this call is perhaps not a fault. At this point there is a relevant aspect to consider in regard to the application of the Danger Theory. If it is possible to define an adequate danger signal (signal 2), the number of FPs can be decreased, for the danger signal will confirm whether the occurrence of an anomaly actually refers to a fault. In case an anomaly occurs without the danger signal, it will not be considered as being a fault.

The following is a definition of the signals used here according to the basis provided by the danger theory:

- Signal 1: perception of the presence of the antigen (by means of detectors).
- Signal 2: co-stimulation. In this case, the non-completed call rate will be used ($NC > Th_{NC}$, where NC = non-completed call attempt rate, and Th_{NC} is the threshold for the non-completed call attempt rate).

Therefore, once the presence of an antigen is noticed by means of a detector, a **signal 1** will be triggered. This happens when an antigen is inside the recognition region of the detector, as mentioned before.

The signal 2, as well as in the biological case, must alarm a danger situation. In telephony, several situations can be alarmed, for instance, congestion situations, not-completed calls, hardware failure, etc. In the present case, the non-completed call rate was chosen because it is a measurement that can be obtained directly from the call data, and also because it is directly related to the stimulated situation of the ongoing simulation.

5.1 Detector Activation and Fault Detection

Whenever a signal 2 is triggered, the antigens in a danger zone must be identified. This zone refers to a region covered by signal 2, where signal 2 takes effect. Therefore, a region expressing a causal relationship with signal 2 must be defined. The region to be adopted will be a temporal region, i.e., once the indication of a signal 2 is at hand, the region to be analyzed will be the last time interval t_d, thus verifying the detectors that caused the triggering of a signal 1 inside this time interval. Probably, the antigens that matched these detectors contributed to the triggering of signal 2.

Inside this space (danger zone), the detectors that received signal 1 as well as signal 2 are activated and they indicate faults in the respective call attempts (antigens) with which they matched.

During the system adaptation in order to work with a new detector profile (due to the changes in the call profiles), the co-stimulation signal turn out to be essential to avoid confirming as faulty the abnormal calls that will compose the new call profiles of the system (which will become the normal call behavior). Moreover, the co-stimulation signal also prevents the generation of FP in response to diffuse occurrence of abnormal calls that do not cause system faults.

An active detector does not need signal 2 to indicate a fault. It is sufficient to match it with an antigen.

5.2 Death of Detectors

According to the dictation of the danger theory, a detector must be eliminated if it receives a signal 1 without the occurrence of a signal 2. From the algorithm standpoint, this elimination is quite significant, since these detectors are potential False Positive generators.

As changes in the profile of call attempts occur, especially in changes at high rates, although the detector renewal routine searches for adapting itself to such changes, there may be the matching between detectors and antigens that are not effectively related to danger signals. So, if at a near time there is the triggering of a signal 2 linked to some other event, so that the danger zone is broad enough to comprise the first mentioned detector (the one that has already received signal 1 without signal 2, though it does not have any link to any danger signal), a co-stimulation for this detector will be generated. Then, an FP will occur. A well adjusted danger zone is necessary to avoid such occurrences.

5.3 Detector Deactivation

After a period of time T_{deact} has elapsed, an active detector becomes inactive. This point of the danger theory is observed according to the system's adaptive character. An antigen, which indicates a profile of a call attempt related to a fault in a given period of the analysis, can be an ordinary call attempt after a certain period of time has elapsed. These detectors, which have passed through the active status, become memory detectors, making it possible to provide an effective secondary response.

5.4 Voting

As a means to increase the reliability of the algorithm diagnosis, a voting routine is utilized. Parallel processes are used to analyze, in an independent manner, the same call attempts. A call attempt is effectively considered as a fault if a given percentage of the processes that take part in the analysis regards that call as being a fault within a voting process. Although a process of constant adaptation is used, the processes used in the analysis are not deterministic. Therefore, the use of some processes to make the same analysis in parallel increases the robustness of the algorithm.

5.5 Detector Population Renewal

The algorithm tries to explore the adaptability feature through the constant formation of a population of mature detectors inspired by the clonal selection algorithm [3] [5].

As a means to obtain a good performance, the algorithm manages the generation of detectors by assuring that this population is sufficient to cover the observation space. In this context, the number of detectors is now adaptive, according to the complexity of the environment to be covered.

Essentially, the purpose is to generate detectors with enhanced adaptation over time. Therefore, the affinity of each detector with the set of the latest antigens is measured (Global Affinity). After that, this measure is normalized, acting as a mutation parameter, and the detectors are cloned. Following the negative selection principle, the higher the affinity of the detector with the antigens (notice that the great majority of the antigens correspond to normal behavior), the higher the mutation rate suffered by their clones, because you need detectors capable of identifying abnormal behavior. Next, the affinity of the detectors with the antigen population is observed. Only the detectors that do not match with either the antigen in population or with other detectors are maintained (Figure 1(a)). The issue of not matching other detectors is intended to increase the efficiency of the detector population.

Hence, it is possible to observe important remarks concerning the constant renewal of the detector population, such as: the search for maturation and for the diversity in its population, based on the total number of detectors, and the adaptation of the size of this population to the observation space.

This renewal procedure is considerably significant as it offers a global maturation of the detector population by following the speed of changes that the profile of call attempts of the system under observation suffers over time.

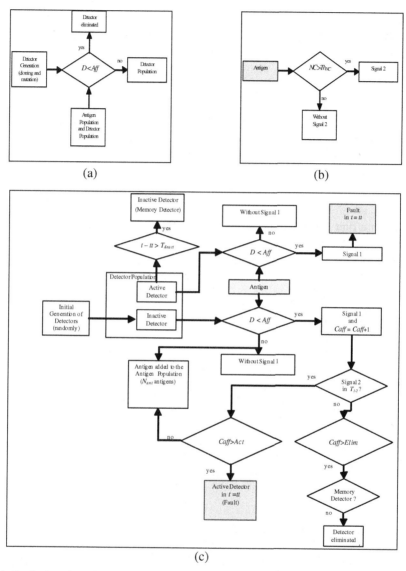

Fig. 1. Fault detection algorithm based on the danger theory paradigm: (a) generation of new detectors over time; (b) alarm generation (signal 2); (c) algorithm overview showing the detector activation procedure and fault detection in each call attempt

5.6 Algorithm Synthesis

In a simplified manner, for each voting process, the algorithm can be viewed according to the following steps:

1. *Random initial generation of detectors;*
2. *If signal 1 is received without signal 2, the detector (or detectors) is eliminated (negative selection);*

3. *If necessary, new detectors are generated to cover the defense space (utilizing cloning and hypermutation similar to what have been done with CLONALG [5]);*
4. *If signals 1 and 2 are received, the detector (or detectors) is activated;*
5. *After a period of time T_{deact}, an active detector becomes inactive;*
6. *An active detector detects danger with the presence of signal 1 (without requiring signal 2);*
7. *A signal 2 received without a signal 1 is ignored.*

The algorithm is depicted in further details in the flows of Figure 1. The following variables should be considered to understanding the whole steps in the flowcharts of Figure 1:

D	:	distance between two elements (detectors and antigens)
Aff	:	affinity threshold (affinity area around the detector).
C_{aff}	:	affinity counter (checks the number of times that signal 1 is triggered)
Act	:	threshold for detector activation
$Elim$	:	threshold for detector elimination
N_{an}	:	maximum quantity of antigens at the antigen population.
T_{1-2}	:	period of time after the occurrence of signal 1 so that, through the occurrence of signal 2, the detector is activated.
tt	:	triggering time of signal 2 or fault detection
T_{deact}	:	time threshold for the deactivation of the active detector
t	:	call attempt time
NC	:	non-completed call attempt rate
Th_{NC}	:	threshold for non-completed call attempt rate

It is worth noticing that after the initial generation of detectors (Figure 1(c)) this population is constantly renewed as indicated in Figure 1(a). The flow in Figure 1(c) aims at showing what occurs when an antigen appears in the system (generation of a call attempt), as well as what occurs when the activity time of a detector expires. Figure 1(b) shows how the signal 2 is generated. Some arrows were removed from the figure to make it clearer.

6 Algorithm Implementation: Results

The objective of algorithm implementation was to validate the proposition and to analyze the emergence of their main features. The most relevant aspects to be monitored are FP rates and the issues involving detector adaptability over time. The following intervals were defined for the call attributes:

- Origin: 0 – 11 (indices of the telephone network nodes)
- Destination: 0 – 11 (indices of the telephone network nodes)
- Duration: 0 – 359 (in seconds)
- Feature: 0 – 3 (admits four distinct types of calls)

Relevant parameters of the algorithm have been defined as follows:

- threshold for detector activation (*Act*): 3 call attempts
- threshold for detector elimination (*Elim*): 3 call attempts
- maximum quantity of antigens at the antigen population (N_{ant}): 50 antigens
- period of time after the occurrence of signal 1 so that, through the occurrence of signal 2, the detector is activated (T_{1-2}): 20 call attempts (the average time of 20 call attempts)
- time threshold for the deactivation of the active detector (T_{deact}): 60 call attempts (the average time of 60 call attempts)
- threshold for non-completed call attempt rate (Th_{NC}): 3 call attempts
- threshold for voting: 25% (the amount of votes must exceed this threshold for a call attempt be considered a fault)

In total, 500 calls were generated. The variables *origin*, *destination* and *feature* related to these calls followed a uniform random distribution, whereas the variable *duration* followed, within the interval of calls from 1 to 70, an asymmetric distribution skewed to the right with an average of 70 seconds and, within the interval of calls from 71 to 500, a symmetric distribution centered in 180 seconds (the middle point of the interval 0-359). The motivation for a skewed distribution regarding the variable duration was to verify the adaptation of detectors at the end of the process. In real systems the distribution adopted here may indeed not occur. However, the most significant for analysis is the behavior change. This phenomenon can really occur and therefore this is what the simulation aims to verify.

In the entirety of the generated calls, a fault event was inserted after call number 400. Every call generated in the origins from 1 to 6, using feature 2, would not be completed (would have duration equal to 0). Except for this, in the generation of calls from 1 to 500, other non-completed calls may occur, though this should be understood as a normal system behavior (e.g., a non-completed call due to absence of response from the destination user). The calls are randomly generated and some of them can show this profile. They occur in a dispersed way, with duration equal to zero and possibly with origin, destination and feature different from those chosen for generating the faults. Therefore, diagnosis systems running in parallel (see section 5.4) diagnosed the tested calls by means of voting.

For the purpose of demonstrating the adaptation of detectors along the process, the profiles of Figure 2 illustrate the emergence of an expected behavior: they refer to the distribution of antigens and detectors according to the parameter *duration*, in the performed experiment. By observing the variable *duration*, it was possible to notice the detectors settlement in the space that is complementary to the generated calls.

In Figure 3, it is possible to observe the best case that was found among 50 executions. This figure presents the non-completed calls among the 500 generated call attempts, the alarms generated due to an overflow of non-completed calls (signal 2), the activation of detectors and fault detection (signal 1 + signal 2), and the fault detection after detector activation (signal 1 received with active detector). Table 1 shows the test results. As additional information, call attempt number 291 (Figure 3), though an anomaly (it is not a fault), could not be detected as a fault in none of the 50 executions due to the lack of signal 2. This is another desired behavior.

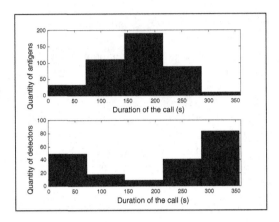

Fig. 2. Distribution of antigens and detectors according to the parameter *duration*. Population of cells in the interval from 71 to 500 calls and detector population at the end of the 500 calls.

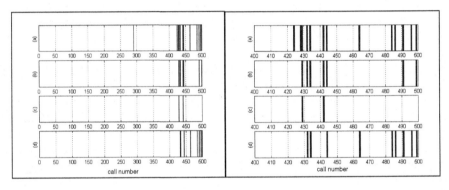

Fig. 3. Sequence of calls from 0 to 500 and from 400 to 500: (a) non-completed call attempts; (b) alarms (signal 2); (c) detector activation and fault signal generation (signal 1 + signal 2); (d) fault signal generation (signal 1 with active detector)

As an additional result, the behavior of the activated detectors was observed for fault detection purposes. Thus, a plot is presented in Figure 4 (a), indicating the coverage level generated by those detectors. Each process that takes part of the voting to look for faults activates a set of detectors. Each of these detectors has an acting region where it is possible to recognize the antigens (recognition region). The graph presented is formed by the sum of areas covered by these detectors. The observation area is in the origin-destination plan, assuming that the call duration equals zero and the feature equals 2 (fault situation). In this graph, the stars correspond to the faults. The elevation of the surface corresponds to the coverage level, i.e., the more elevated the surface, the higher the incidence of active detectors in the region of the origin-destination plan. The behavior of the algorithm corresponds to the expectations, i.e., the region that the active detectors attempt to cover is the one which holds the largest fault concentration. The regions which should not be covered (as they do not have faults) have a low coverage rate due to being able of generating False Negatives.

Table 1. Results obtained from the test with the proposed algorithm. The results consider the possible detection faults (faults after the first alarm – signal 2).

Average percentage of detected faults considering the 50 fault detection systems operating in parallel and that will take part in the voting phase (notice that the performance depicted in Figure 3 corresponds to the fault detection system with the best performance)	91.0 %
Percentage of faults undetectable by the alarm (signal 2), but detected in average by the 50 fault detection systems operating in parallel	100 %
Percentage of False Positives	0%

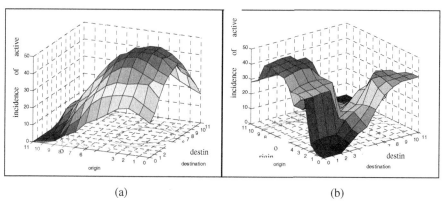

(a)   (b)

Fig. 4. (a) Average behavior of fault detection algorithm in the test with a fault region; (b) average behavior of the fault detection algorithm in the test with two fault regions. The stars correspond to the faults. The more elevated the surface, the higher the incidence of active detectors in the region.

In order to verify the possibility of having a separation between the groups of call attempts whose failures have been originated by different reasons, another test was performed, where two separate fault regions were generated in the space of parameters of the call attempts. A graph, similar to the previously mentioned, was drafted. It shows the differences in regions by the formation of two peaks (Figure 4 (b)). The regions that presented the highest incidence of call attempts, the sufficient amount to trigger the signal 1 of a detector, and which were settled within a danger zone, were covered by the peaks and can be identified in Figure 4 (b).

It is important to notice that there are regions in the figure which, although having a concentration of call attempts with duration equal to zero, were not covered by the algorithm. This occurred owing to the fact that these call attempts are dispersed, temporally separated from each other. Thus, these call attempts, with similar characteristics, did not occur at a time sufficiently close to each other so that, when summed up, they trigger a signal 1. Hence, they are viewed by the algorithm as a normal behavior. This is an important point as it shows the ability of the algorithm to make the distinction between call attempts with similar characteristics but distinct diagnoses. Therefore, Figures 4 (a) and (b) show clearly that it is possible to search for the cause of the faults as well as to indicate the reliability of fault diagnoses by observing the coverage level that is indicated by the graph and associated with a given call attempt.

7 Future Research

The following steps can be quoted as a follow-up of this study: the identification of processes that could automatically set the most relevant thresholds of the algorithm. A fuzzy approach, based on the degeneracy concept [2], could be used for affinity description as well. By using this approach, the diversity or the number of detectors could be reduced and even so the coverage of the antigenic space could remain at the same level. The detector activation could be seen as the result of an analysis involving the combination of the obtained signal 1 intensity, i.e. the affinity level with each antigenic structure, and a related signal 2 level. In relation to the generated surfaces, which identify the coverage level by the active detectors (Figures 4 (a) and (b)), the generated failure diagnosis can have a reliability level associated with each encountered fault.

In the proposed experiments, the dimension of the telephone network, the number of calls, and the number of variable capable of characterizing the whole scenario are reduced, not corresponding to what effectively characterizes a real application. As the main purpose here has been to validate the proposal and to verify its ability to express adaptability and proper operation in terms of avoiding false positives, then the experiments suffice to fulfill the objectives. More realistic experiments will be part of the further steps of the research, as well as efforts toward sensitivity analysis of parameters such as danger zone length and threshold of votes used for detection.

8 Concluding Remarks

This paper proposed and implemented a fault detection algorithm based on concepts that support the danger theory paradigm. The most prominent aspects of the algorithm are the adaptability and the low index of false positives (FP). The distribution of one of these characteristics observed by the algorithm underwent some changes at a certain moment of the execution. As the detector population is constantly updated by the use of a clonal selection procedure, high levels of matching and diversity maintenance are made possible, at reasonable computational cost [5].

By using the danger theory paradigm, where a co-stimulation is necessary to confirm the danger implied by the presence of a detected antigen, anomalies external to the reach of signal 2 were not, as expected, considered as faults. A meaningful result was the percentage of algorithm coverage in the detection of faults concerning the regions that were not covered by the alarm (signal 2). This coverage is quite significant, as it indicates the possibility of the continuity of a fault or the tendency to recover it. As this fault is presented in a dispersed form, it does not allow the observed system to alarm. Thus, the use of the algorithm in this context provides an important complement for fault detection. The number of FPs was meaningless. The percentage of detected faults was also highly significant, although it was not possible to detect all faults, in average.

The algorithm can be used for diagnosis generation, identifying regions (clusters) of high concentration of active detectors, which makes it possible to specify the characteristics that result in faults, i.e. configuration of the set of parameters that originates a fault.

Acknowledgements

This work has been supported by grants from CNPq and Fapesp.

References

[1] Aickelin, U., Bentley, P., Cayzer, S., Kim, J. & McLeod, J. (2003) Danger Theory: The Link between AIS and IDS?, 2nd International Conference on AIS (ICARIS 2003), pp. 147-155.

[2] Atamas, S.P. (2005) Les affinities electives, Dossier Pour La Science, 46.

[3] Ayara, M., Timmis, J., De Lemos, R., de Castro, L.N. & Duncan, R. (2002) Negative Selection: How to Generate Detectors, 1st International Conference on AIS (ICARIS 2002), pp 89-98.

[4] Bersini, H. (2002) Self-Assertion versus Self-Recognition: A Tribute to Francisco Varela, 1st International Conference on AIS (ICARIS 2002), pp 107-112.

[5] de Castro, L.N. & Von Zuben, F.J. (2002) Learning and Optimization Using the Clonal Selection Principle. IEEE Transactions on Evolutionary Computation, vol. 6, no. 3, pp. 239-251.

[6] Faynberg, I., Lawrence, G., Lu, H.-L. (2000) Converged networks and services: Internetworking IP and the PSTN. New York: John Wiley & Sons.

[7] González, F.A. & Dasgupta, D. (2002) An Immunogenetic Technique to Detect Anomalies in Network Traffic, Proceedings of the Genetic and Evolutionary Computation Conference (GECCO), pp. 1081-1088.

[8] Hersent, O., Petit, J.P. (1999) IP Telephony: Packet-Based Multimedia Communications Systems, Addison-Wesley.

[9] Matzinger, P. (1994) Tolerance Danger and the Extended Family, Annual Review of Immunology, vol. 12, pp. 991-1045.

[10] Sarafijanovic, S. & Boudec, J. (2004) An Artificial Immune System for Misbehavior Detection in Mobile Ad-Hoc Networks with Virtual Thymus, Clustering, Danger Signal, and Memory Detectors, 3rd International Conference on AIS (ICARIS 2004), pp. 316-329.

[11] Secker, A., Freitas, A.A. & Timmis, J. (2003) A Danger Theory Inspired Approach to Web Mining, 2nd International Conference on AIS, pp 156-167.

[12] Schapire, R.E., Freund, Y., Bartlett, P., Lee, W.S. (1998) Boosting the margin: A new explanation for the effectiveness of voting methods. The Annals of Statistics, vol. 26, no. 5, pp. 1651-1686.

[13] Venkatasubramanian, V., Rengaswamy, R., Yin, K. & Kavuri, S.N. (2003) A review of process fault detection and diagnosis: part I – Quantitative model-based methods, Computer and Chemical Engineering, vol. 27, pp. 293-311.

Design and Simulation of a Biological Immune Controller Based on Improved Varela Immune Network Model

Fu Dongmei, Zheng Deling, and Chen Ying

Department of automation, college of information engineering,
university science technology beijing,100083
FDM2003@163.com

Abtract. Biological immune system is a control system that has strong robusticity and self-adaptability in complex disturbance and indeterminacy environments. The B cell and the antibody in biological immune dynamic process are described in the basic Varela immune network model(BVINM), But the antigen doesn't exist in this model. An improved Varela immune network model(IVINM) has been presented by appending the antigen in the BVINM in this article. Based on the improved Varela immune network model, An immune controller model is designed and its structure is proposed in the paper. Finally the paper puts forward a simulation example, and analyses the characteristic of the immune controller.

Keywords: Artificial immune, Varela immune network model(VINM), Immune controller, Simulation.

1 Introduction

The Biological immune system is a control system that has strong robusticity and self-adaptability in complex disturbance and indeterminacy environments[1]. It is the research object which the computer and the intelligent domain always pay attention to. Computation immunology already has formed which was a special branch[2]. Research scope of the computation immunology is from biological immune process simulation to immune mechanism, immune algorithm, immune model and practical application. International artificial immune system academic conference was convened every year, since the first international artificial immune system academic conference was held in the Kent University of England in 2002. Obviously, the scientists hoped to introduce the biological immune rule and the mechanism to the actual project domain effectively, in order to provide kinds of brand new effective technologies and the methods for the science and the project domain.

Design of the controller aims to enhance the quality of the control system and obtain requested control goal. It is the key for guaranteeing the quality and the characteristic of the control system once the model of the object is determinate. Therefore the design and the analysis of controller is a focal point which the whole control domain pays attention to. There are two method for design traditional controller: One is the classical control theory design method, including linear method such as the method of the root-locus, the method of frequency domain, PID

C. Jacob et al. (Eds.): ICARIS 2005, LNCS 3627, pp. 432–441, 2005.
© Springer-Verlag Berlin Heidelberg 2005

adjustment and non-linear method such as phase plane, description function; Another is the modern control theory design method, including the state feedback controller, the auto-adapted adjustment controller, change the structure controller, based on H^∞ and so on. The design and realization of controller mentioned above already had a series of relative more complete and strict theory methods, but still some defaults left, For example, the object is often limited strictly to be linear, or having been known at least. When the object is disturbed by the factors which cannot be surveyed or cannot be estimated, the control capability will fall off greatly.

There are two sorts of artificial immune models[2,3], one is the immune model based on the immune system theory (mainly clones choice theory nowadays), and another is the immune network model based on the immune network theory. As far as the immune network model was concerned. two immune network models are covered, one is continual and another is discrete. If we introduce the artificial immune model to the controller model for the continuous process control system, it is advisable means to adopt the simplified continuous immune network model. This is because: Firstly, all the continuous immune network models at present are the ordinary differential equation of time, which conforms to the real continuous control system. Secondly the discrete immune network model is not the common discrete model based on time in the control system, but it means that the immune cells or molecules are separated ones. The discrete immune network model describes the quantity changing of the immune factors or molecules. The basic Varela immune network model (BVINM) belongs to the continuous immune network model. Based on the Varela immune network model, this article proposed an improved Varela immune network model. Through simplifying the IVNM, a new immune controller that has the learning and memorizing characteristic was structured. Finally, the simulation application result of the immune controller was shown in this paper

2 Basic Varela Immune Network Model[4,5]

The model that proposed by Varela and his confreres is called the second generation network model. The model contains three important concepts: structure, dynamics and metadynamics. The structure indicate the relation pattern of the each part immune network. Usually the structure is expressed by the matrix. Dynamics indicate the dynamic change of the density and affinity of immune factor. The metadynamics indicate that the network composition may change. This change denotes that new elements will appear in the network and old ones disappear at any moment.

The fundamental assumption of the BVINM is:

1) The BVINM only considered the B cell and the antibody produced by it. The identical kind of the cell and the antibody are called the clone or the unique feature. The antibody only can be produced by the mature B cell.
2) The effects of the different kinds of the clone are expressed by the matrix M. The optional value of the matrix is 0 or 1.
3) The new B cells are produced and the old ones disappeared unceasingly. The probability of the mature and the reproduction of the B cell depends on the clone in the immune network.

The BVINM includes the two equations as follows:

$$\begin{cases} \dot{T}_i = -k_1\sigma_i T_i - k_2 T_i + k_3 M(\sigma_i)B_i \\ \dot{B}_i = -k_4 B_i + k_5 P(\sigma_i)B_i + k_6 \end{cases} \tag{1}$$

In the formula, T_i expresses the quantity of the ith kind of the antibody. B_i expresses the quantity of the ith kind of the B cell. The parameter k_1 indicates the mortality of the antibody which is caused by the antibodies interaction. k_2 expresses the natural mortality of the antibody. k_3 indicates the reproduction rate of the antibody which is caused by the mature B cell. k_4 expresses the mortality of the B cell. k_5 expresses the reproduction rate of the B cell which is caused by the B cell itself. k_6 expresses the new reproduction rate of the B cell which is caused by the marrow. $M(\sigma_i)$ is the mature function of the B_i cell. $P(\sigma_i)$ is the reproduction function of which the B_i cells reproduce the T_i antibodys. The mature function and the reproduction function have the "bell" function which is shown in Figure 1.

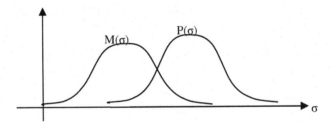

Fig.1. $M(\sigma_i)$ is the mature function of the B_i cell. $P(\sigma_i)$ is the reproduction function of which the B_i cells reproduce the T_i antibodys. The mature function $M(\sigma)$ and the reproduction function $P(\sigma)$ have the "bell" function.

σ_i expresses the network sensitivity of the ith kind of clone:

$$\sigma_i = \sum_{j=1}^{n} m_{i,j}T_j \tag{2}$$

$m_{i,j}$ denotes the Boolean value of the affinity between ith and jth clone in the formula. The Boolean value is 1 when the affinity exists, and the value is 0 when the affinity disappears. n is the type of B_i cell and T_i antibody, i=1,2,... ... n.

The "bell" function implies the basic fact of the biological immune process: Insufficient or the superfluous sensitivity can suppress the B cells' reproduction and capability of which B cells produce T antibody[2].

The formula (1) and (2) denote the dynamic process of the interaction between the B cell and the antibody in the biological immune process to some extent. If the formula (1) and (2) are be used for designing the immune controller in the control system, they have some insufficiencies:

1) BVINM haven't reflected the infection that antigen act on immune network, which is adverse for the VINM transform to the controller model, for the system error is often considered as the antigen when design the immune control system. One of the final control effects is to eliminate or reduce the error of control system as far as possible.

2) Formula (1) describes that the B_i cell can only promote the T_i antibody. In the fact, B cell can excrete many kinds of immune antibodies. The reproduction of the B_i cell mainly depends on the B cell itself and the marrow. Moreover the reproduction of the B_i cell radically is elicited by the antigen which have intruded organism. (To be concise, the other factors are not considered).

3 Improved Varela Immune Network Model

After the antigen invaded organism, the organism had two different kinds of responses. One is the self-duplication of antigen. Another is the elimination of the antigen caused by the phagocyte and the killing cell. That can be described with the under dynamic equation[6]:

$$\dot{Ag}_i = q'Ag - H(T_i)Ag_i \tag{3}$$

Among them, q' denote the reproduction rate of the antigen when the immune process doesn't exist, $H(T_i)$ is the function of which antigen is eliminated by antibody. $H(T_i)$ can be shown as follows[6]:

$$H(T_i) = h + K_e T_i \tag{4}$$

h denote the rate of the non-special killing. K_e denote the approximate rate of antigen's being specially eliminated. Take (4) into (3):

$$\dot{Ag}_i = qAg_i - K_e T_i Ag_i \tag{5}$$

in the formula (5), q expresses the rate of the antigen reproduction. K_e expresses the rate of antigen's being eliminated. We suppose that the elimination rate of the antigen mainly depends on the probability of the antibody meeting and uniting with the antigen, while the probability is determined by the quantity of the antibody and the antigen. The product of the antibody quantity and the antigen quantity is use for expressing the probability of the antibody and the antigen meeting each other [7,8], that is $T_i Ag_i$. Considering (1) and (5), we can obtain the IVINM as follows:

$$\begin{cases} \dot{Ag}_i = qAg_i - K_e T_i Ag_i \\ \dot{T}_i = -k_1 \sigma_i T_i - k_2 T_i + k_3 M(\sigma_i)B_i \\ \dot{B}_i = -k_4 B_i + k_5 P(\sigma_i)B_i + k_6 + K_{Ag}Ag_i \end{cases} \tag{6}$$

Ag , q and K_e in the formula (6) is the same as in the formula (5). And $M(\sigma_i)$, $P(\sigma_i)$, σ_i in the formula (6) is the same as in the formula (1) and (2). K_{Ag} denotes the B cell reproduction rate which is caused by the antigen.

4 Design and Analysis of Immune Controller

We need a SISO controller for SISO system., and then the formula (6) can be shown as follows:

$$\begin{cases} \dot{A}g = qAg - K_eTAg \\ \dot{T} = -k_1\sigma T - k_2T + k_3M(\sigma)B \\ \dot{B} = -k_4B + k_5P(\sigma)B + k_6 + K_{Ag}Ag \end{cases} \qquad (7)$$

When we use the IVINM (7) for constructing new immune controller, we must clarify which are similar or heuristic between this IVINM and the control system, we also must clarify which are different that needs to be improved. The similarity is shown as follows: the first is that the IVINM (7) describe the immune process between the B cell and the antibody after the antigen invaded organism. That is similar to the relation of the error variable and the control variable in control system, when the error e(t) replace the antigen Ag and the control u(t) replace the B cell. The second is the IVINM (7) describes the dynamic process between the B cell and the antibody. The B cell is the important cell in recognizing and memorizing antigen as well as in secreting antibody. It is already proved that the plasma-cell created by the B cell was one of the important reasons why the immune system has the memory characteristic in the medicine.

Dissimilarity is shown as follows:

(1) The changing rate of the antigen intruded organism is composed of the antigen self-duplication and the rate of antigen being killed by the antibody in the IVINM (7). The error of the control system cannot be divided into two parts like that, for the error of the control system is unable to self-duplicate. Moreover the control error relates widely to the object model, the external disturbance, the control input as well as the controller model and so on. Therefore only the rate of antigen being killed is considered in this paper.

(2) The quantity of the antigen, the antibody and the B cell each is certainly bigger than zero in biological immune system. But the error and control quantity may be positive or negative in the control system. So it is necessary that the IVINM (7) should be improved and simplified for making the formula of the immune controller.

We abandon the antigen self-duplication item in formula (7) basing on the condition (1). Considering the condition (2), the function of the mature $M(\sigma)$ as follows is taken:

$$M(\sigma) = K_m(e^{p_1|\sigma|} - e^{p_2|\sigma|}) \bullet sign(\sigma) \qquad (8)$$

K_m is a constant and $K_m > 0$ in the formula (8). p_2 and p_1 are the constants and $p_2 < p_1 < 0$. sign(σ) is the mark function. The formula (8) is appropriate for the error that may be positive or negative in the control system. The formula (8) has the curve which is shown in figure 2, it's upper part of the curve is similar to the "bell" shape in figure 1. The reproduction function $P(\sigma)$ also adopts formula (8).

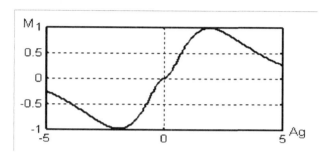

Fig. 2. The $M(\sigma)$ and $P(\sigma)$ curve of actual control system. They were both expressed by formula (8).

We combine the first item with the second one in the formula (7). e(t) replace Ag , u(t) replace B. We can obtain the control model based on the IVINM as follows:

$$\begin{cases} \dot{e}(t) = -K_e T(t)e(t) \\ \dot{T}(t) = -k_T T(t) + k_3 M(\sigma)u(t) \\ \dot{u}(t) = -k_4 u(t) + k_5 P(\sigma)u(t) + k_6 + K_{Ag}e(t) \end{cases} \qquad (9)$$

$k_T = k_1\sigma + k_2$. It is too complex that the formula (9) is used for the controller. Therefore the formula (9) will be further simplified: 1) because k_T is too small, we suppose $k_T = 0$; 2) we neglect the self-duplication item in the equation (9); 3) we suppose the independent variable of $M(\sigma)$ is u(t) ,that is $M(u)$. We suppose the independent variable of $P(\sigma)$ is $\dot{u}(t)$, that is $P(\dot{u})$. 4) Get one order derivative of the third formula in formulary (9), and omit the complex non-linear item, and take the first formula into the third formula, and then we obtain the formula (10) as follows:

$$\begin{cases} \dot{T}(t) = k_3 M(e(t))u(t) \\ \ddot{u}(t) = -(k_4 - k_5 P(e(t)))\dot{u}(t) - kT(t)e(t) \end{cases} \qquad (10)$$

$k = K_{Ag}K_e$, the formula (10) is an immune controller model based on the IVINM in this paper. This immune controller model is called an improved Varela immune network controller (IVINC).The structure of the IVINC is shown in figure 3.

The IVINC shown in figure 3 is a non-linear controller. It has the characteristics as follows:

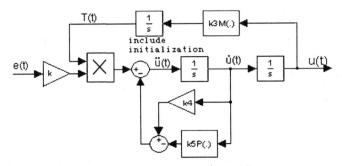

Fig. 3. A biological immune controller based on improved varela immune network , e(t) is an error of the control system, and it is an equivalence of the Ag antibody in the biological immune system.u(t) is the output of the immune controller, it is an equivalence of the B cell concentration in the biological immune system. The waves of $M(\cdot)$ function and $P(\cdot)$ function are shown in fig.2.

1) If k_4 and $k_5 P(\dot{u})$ are chosen reasonably, the inner feedback in the IVINC brings the positive feedback when $\dot{u}(t)$ belongs to the appropriate spectrum. When the inner feedback is the positive feedback, $\dot{u}(t)$ will increase fast, and the larger $\dot{u}(t)$ will cause the negative feedback. That accord with the biological immune feedback mechanism (the Ding immortal article).

2) When the choosing of parameter is reasonable, it can be ensured that if the error e(t)<>0 then T (t)<>0 at the same time, so the larger T (t) is good for the controller to response more sensitively to the small error e(t). When the control system repeatedly respond to the series of same input signal, the second reaction speed of the system will be accelerated due to increasing the antibody density. That accords with the memory mechanism of the biological immune response.

3) When u(t) is too large, $k_3 M(u)u(t)$ approximate to zero due to $M(u)$. That is quite effective to control the excessively increasing of T(t). If k_T takes a very small value in the formula (9), that is advantageous to the system stability, but that also will sacrifice the memory characteristic of the immune response to some extent.

5 Simulation Result

The structure of the control system which includes the IVINC is shown in fig. 4.

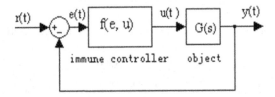

Fig. 4. Artificial immunie control system structure. f(e,u) is an immune controller shown in fig.3, while G(s) is an object controlled by the immune controller.

The anti-lag ability, memory characteristic and parameter choice of the IVINC are studied with simulation in this paper.

5.1 Long-Lag and Big-Inertia Object Control

The object with long-lag and big-inertia is hard to be controlled in practice. We suppose the object model is:

$$G_0(s) = \frac{e^{-\varepsilon s}}{50s + 1} \tag{11}$$

The inertia constant is 50 in this model. If $\tau > 3$, it is very difficult that the object realizes the stable control with the PID.

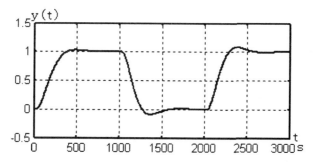

Fig. 5. long-lag and big-inertia object control curve. $y(t)$ is an output of the system when the square-wave signal $r(t) = 1$. We take $\tau = 30$, P0=0.1, k=0.1, k_3 =5, k_4 =1.5 k_5 =0, K_m = 5, $p_1 = -0.1$, $p_2 = -0.10001$.

From the simulation curve in figure 5, it is learned that the second response is obviously quicker than the first response, and the third response is little quicker than the second, subsequently the responses is nearly constant. This characteristic is extremely similar to the mechanism of the immune response. Moreover, from the simulation result, it is learned that the IVINC ensure the control system to track the constant input with the error approximating to zero.

5.2 Long-Log and Big-Oscillation Object Control

The object with long-lag and big-oscillation is hard to be controlled in practice. We suppose the object model is:

$$G_0(s) = \frac{e^{-\varepsilon s}}{25s^2 + s + 1} \tag{12}$$

The inertia time-constant is 5, ξ=0.1, If $\tau > 2.5$, it is very difficultly that the object realizes the stable control with the PID. Though the formula (12) greatly differs from the formula (11), the satisfying control effect can be obtained if only the parameters of the IVINC change little.

The square-wave signal whose value equals 1 is chosen as the control signal in the paper. We take $\tau=30$, P0=0.1, k=0.2, k_3 =5, k_3 =5, k_4 =1.5, k_5 =0, K_m =5 , $p_1 = -0.1$, $p_2 = -0.10001$. The simulation result is shown in figure 6.

The same conclusion can be gotten when comparing the figure 6 to the figure 5:

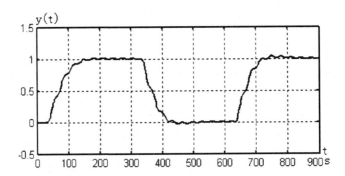

Fig. 6. long-log and big-oscillation object control curve. $y(t)$ is an output of the system when the step function $r(t) = 1$. The square-wave signal whose value equals 1 is chosen as the control signal in the paper. We take $\tau=30$, P0=0.1, k=0.2, k_3 =5, k_3 =5, k_4 =1.5, k_5 =0, K_m =5, $p_1 = -0.1$, $p_2 = -0.10001$. The simulation result is shown in figure 6.

the second response is obviously quicker than the first response, and the third response is little quicker than the second, subsequently the responses is nearly constant, the IVINC ensure the control system to track the constant input with the error approximating to zero. Otherwise, it is learned from the selection of parameter that the IVINC has the well auto-adapted ability.

5.3   The Parameter Characteristic of The IVINC

When the parameters of the object change, the parameters of the IVINC should be adjusted to achieve the control goal. The rule of the parameters being selected is very important for the control system design and analysis. We have discovered the following several rules through the simulation research:

1) When the object pure-lag is increased(e.g. $\tau=4$, 10, 20... 60) , the good control effect still could be obtained without the parameters of the IVINC changing , while the characteristic of the dynamic response dropped slightly.
2) The value of the B cell mortality rate k_4 greatly affects system. The system stability is improved by increasing k_4 suitably, but it is possible to cause overmuch immune and to make the system to be unable to track the control signal, vice versa.

3) The proportional factor k has the same effect on the immune control system as on the linear system.
4) The stability of the artificial immune system is also influenced by the parameter of nonlinear function $M(\sigma)$ and $P(\sigma)$. K_m is often not very large as well as p_1 and p_2 . When p1 is close to p2 and p1 is less than p2, the performances of the immune control system are preferable usually.
5) The non-zero initial value P0 is influential to the system stability, the response rate and so on, generally that is complex.

6 Conclusions

(1) The paper proposes the IVINM based on the BVINM. An artificial immune controller is obtained based on the IVINM, which is called the IVINC.
(2) The paper gives the structure of the IVINC and approximately described the characteristics of the IVINC.
(3) For two classical control objects that is usually hard to be controlled, the simulation research which adopts the IVINC obtained the good control result.
(4) Several control variables of the IVINC are researched with the simulation method.

Although the IVINC has beening studied in this paper, still some problems left to be resolved. For example, why the IVINC have such egregious ability in overcoming the pure-lag? Can we further decrease the controller's parameter number which is too much for practice? How to prove the stability of the control system which includes the IVINC in theory? But no matter how, the IVINC which is proposed in this paper already displayed the well immune characteristic to some extent. Perhaps it is worth to be further researched.

References

1. D.Dasgupta, Z.Ji, F.González. Artificial Immune System (AIS) Research in the Last Five Years. Published in the proceedings of the Congress on Evolutionary Computation Conference (CEC) Canberra, Australia December 8-12 2003.
2. L.Tong. Computer Immunology. Publish House of Electronics Industry. Beijing. 2004
3. Lydyard P M. & Whelan A. and M.W.Panger. Instant Notes in Immunology[M]. Science Publish House. BeiJing. 2001
4. Varela F J, Stewart J. Dynamics of a class of immune networks.I)Global behavior. J. Theory. Biology. ,1990,144: 93~101
5. Bersini,H.and Varela,F.J. The immune recruitment mechanism: Reinforcement, Recruitment and Their Applications. Computing with Biological Metaphors, Vol 1. 1994
6. AnShen.X, & ChanYing. D. Nonlinear Models in Immunity [M]. ShangHai Scientific and Technological Educationg Publish House. 1998
7. Gutnikov.S &Melnikov.Y. A Simple Non-linear Model of Immune Response[J]. Chaos. Solitons and fractals 16(2003): 125-132
8. DongMei. Fu & DeLing. Zheng. Design for Biological Immune Controllers and Simulation on Its Control Features [J]. Journal of University of Science and Technology BeiJing. 2004,26(4):442-445

Applying the Clonal Selection Principle to Find Flexible Job-Shop Schedules

Z.X. Ong, J.C. Tay, and C.K. Kwoh

Evolutionary and Complex Systems Lab,
Nanyang Technological University
asjctay@ntu.edu.sg

Abstract. We apply the Clonal Selection principle of the human immune system to solve the Flexible Job-Shop Problem with recirculation. Various practical design issues are addressed in the implemented algorithm, ClonaFLEX; first, an efficient antibody representation which creates only feasible solutions and a bootstrapping antibody initialization method to reduce the search time required. Second, the assignment of suitable mutation rates for antibodies based on their affinity. To this end, a simple yet effective visual method of determining the optimal mutation value is proposed. And third, to prevent premature convergence, a novel way of using elite pools to incubate antibodies is presented. Performance results of ClonaFLEX are obtained against benchmark FJSP instances by Kacem and Brandimarte. On average, ClonaFLEX outperforms a cultural evolutionary algorithm (EA) in 7 out of 12 problem sets, equivalent results for 4 and poorer in 1.

Keywords: Immune Algorithm, Clonal Selection, Flexible Job-Shop Scheduling Problem, Optimization.

1 Introduction

The Flexible Job-Shop Scheduling problem (FJSP) is a NP-hard problem [7] that has attracted much research [8][9][10][11][12] due to its practical application in modeling the constraints frequently found in modern manufacturing and production facilities. The FJSP specifies a series of jobs to be processed by a list of machines. The constituent operations of the jobs are to be processed on predetermined machines with different processing times. An operation can be executed on a machine chosen from a set of available alternatives. The task is twofold; to allocate operations to machines and to order the allocated operations on each machine so as to give the shortest makespan, or the minimum time to complete all jobs. Due to the combinatorial number of possible schedules, general methods to find the global minimum will not return results in a reasonable amount of time.

In recent years, the development of evolutionary algorithms based on immunological metaphors has introduced a new paradigm for solving such combinatorial problems. In particular, immune algorithms, such as CLONALG, designed based on the Clonal Selection principle of adaptive immunity have shown considerable success in

C. Jacob et al. (Eds.): ICARIS 2005, LNCS 3627, pp. 442–455, 2005.
© Springer-Verlag Berlin Heidelberg 2005

solving a variety of multi-modal and combinatorial problems [4][6]. However, a successful application of this principle requires careful design to avoid problem-specific representational inefficiencies, premature convergence due to undirected mutation and insufficient diversity. In this sense, clonal selection-based algorithms are like genetic algorithms (GAs) which require proper designs of chromosomal representations and recombination operators [11][12] to allow an effective parallel and sampled search, intelligently locating basins in the solution space where optimal results can be reached. The objective of this paper is therefore to share our experiences for an effective application of the Clonal Selection principle, through the design of an algorithm called ClonaFLEX that effectively approximates the global optimal solution for the FJSP.

This paper is organized as follows: Section 2 begins with a description of the vertebrate immune system and explains how Clonal Selection can in principle, be used to solve combinatorial search problems. Section 3 gives the FJSP problem formulation. Section 4 describes the design parameters for the ClonaFLEX algorithm; namely, antibody representation, initialization, affinity computation and mutation. Section 5 describes practical considerations for maintaining antibody diversity and the derivation of mutation rates. Section 6 presents the performance results of benchmark tests while Section 7 summarizes and gives concluding assessments.

2   The Vertebrate Immune System

The vertebrate immune system comprises the innate and adaptive defense mechanisms which provide the host body with a means of protection against infectious agents. Its basic elements consist of lymphocytes belonging to two main types: B-cells and T-cells. Both B-cells and T-cells perform the task of combating and eliminating pathogens (foreign invading cells) in different but complementary ways. As our approach in this paper is inspired mainly from the function of B-cells, the mechanism of T-cells will not be discussed. Interested readers can refer to material in [1].

B-cells carry on their surface, receptor molecules or antibodies (AB) which are capable of recognizing harmful antigens and binding with them. After the antigen has been bound by the antibodies, it will subsequently be recognized and ingested by phagocytes. B-cells are mono-specific in nature, each producing a single type of antibody which can recognize and bind to only a certain antigenic protein. This results in the need for a large repertoire of antibodies in order to afford the effective recognition of a diverse range of antigens, known and unknown. The Clonal Selection principle is an adaptive immune mechanism to overcome this problem.

2.1   The Principle of Clonal Selection

This theory (also known as the Clonal Expansion principle) [2] explains the response of lymphocytes (in this case, the B-cells) in the face of an antigenic stimuli. It is illustrated in Figure 1.

When the antibodies on a B-cell recognize an antigen with a certain affinity (degree of match), the B-cell will be stimulated to proliferate (divide) and eventually mature into terminal (non-dividing) antibody secreting cells, called plasma cells [5]. Proliferation of the B-cells is a mitotic process whereby the cells divide themselves, creating a set of clones identical to the parent cell. The proliferation rate is directly proportional to the affinity level, meaning that B-cells with higher affinity levels will be more readily selected for cloning and cloned in larger numbers compared to others. More specifically, during asexual reproduction, the B-cell clones experience somatic hyper-mutation; a random structural change. More often than not, a large proportion of the cloned population becomes dysfunctional or develops into harmful anti-self cells after the mutation. These anti-self cells are programmed for cell death by the immune system through a process called apoptosis. However, occasionally an effective change enables the offspring cell to bind better with the antigen, hence affinity is improved. In the event that a mutated cloned cell with higher affinity is found, it in turn will be activated to undergo proliferation.

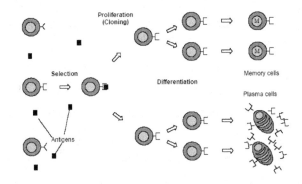

Fig. 1. Illustration of the Clonal Selection principle (taken from [3])

The mutation on the cloned cells occurs at a rate which is inversely proportional to the antigen-affinity. Clones of higher affinity cells are subjected to less mutation compared to those from cells which exhibit lower affinity. This process of constant selection and mutation of only the B-cells with antibodies which can better recognize specific antigens is known as affinity maturation. Though the repertoire of antibodies in the immune system is limited; through affinity maturation, it is capable of evolving antibodies to successfully recognize and bind with known and unknown antigens, leading to their eventual elimination.

The immune system also possesses memory properties as a portion of the B-cells will differentiate into memory cells, which do not produce antibodies but instead remembers the antigenic pattern in anticipation of future re-infections. These memory cells circulate within the host body. In response to a second antigenic stimulus, they differentiate into plasma cells to produce antibodies which have high affinity.

3 Problem Definition

The FJSP can be defined as follows:

- There are n jobs, indexed by i, and these jobs are independent of each other.
- Each job, J_i has l_i operations, and a set of precedence constraints P_i.
- Each job, J_i is a set of operations $O_{i,j}$ for $j = 1, ..., l_i$.
- There are m machines, indexed by k.
- For each operation $O_{i,j}$, there is a set of machines capable of performing it. The set is denoted by $M_{i,j}$, $M_{i,j} \subseteq \{1, ..., m\}$. A matrix is used to denote $M_{i,j}$.
- The processing time of an operation $O_{i,j}$ on machine k is predefined and denoted by $t_{i,j,k}$. A matrix is used to denote $t_{i,j,k}$.
- Each operation cannot be interrupted during its performance.
- Each machine can perform at most one operation at any time.
- The objective is to find a schedule with the shortest makespan, where the makespan of a schedule is the time required for all jobs to be processed in the job shop according to the schedule.

4 Applying Clonal Selection to Find Flexible Job-Shop Schedules

In this paper, an immune algorithm called ClonaFLEX, designed using the Clonal Selection principle, is proposed to solve the FJSP. Similar to CLONALG [4], it contains the features of the Clonal Selection Algorithm, but with several customizations to handle the FJSP objective. In ClonaFLEX, possible job schedules to solve the FJSP are modeled as antibodies. An affinity value is assigned to each antibody depending on its fitness. The shorter the makespan of a schedule, the fitter an antibody is. The algorithm identifies good antibodies, by means of their affinity values, and conducts an intelligent search in the search space around them to find better solutions. This process is repeatedly carried out and the information gained from each generation is used as feedback to conserve and propagate good features. As more than one good antibody can be identified each time, ClonaFLEX allows for a parallel search, substantially decreasing the time needed to solve the problem. In spite of this apparent simplicity, the application of clonal selection to effectively find good schedules has not been trivial. This is due to the practical effect of premature convergence due to insufficient antibody diversity. In this section, we present the main practical design considerations for the successful application of the Clonal Selection principle; in particular, to solve the FJSP.

4.1 Antibody Representation

The first consideration is the choice of representation for an antibody. We take inspiration from research in applying GAs to solve the FJSP [9][11]. In GAs, the solutions are represented as chromosomes. In [11], Ho and Tay proposed a chromosome representation (and associated recombination operators) for generating only feasible FJSP schedules. Detailed results in Wibowo and Tay [12] showed that less computational time is required as a result of avoiding a repair mechanism. With regards to the FJSP, the chromosomes of GAs are the same as antibodies of ClonaFLEX. Therefore, the representation of GA chromosomes can be readily adapted to that of ClonaFLEX's antibodies. In this work, Ho and Tay's encoding scheme is used.

Table 1. Example of a 2x3 FJSP (taken from [11])

		M_1	M_2	M_3
	O_{11}	4	5	XXX
J_1	O_{12}	9	2	2
	O_{13}	XXX	6	3
J_2	O_{21}	6	5	XXX
	O_{22}	3	3	5

Basically, the representation comprise of two parts:

- Operation Order String: This part of the chromosome follows Ramiro *et al.* [13]. The string encodes the order of the operations to be processed by specifying the job number which the operation belongs to. The order of operations for each job remains unchanged to avoid creating infeasible solutions during mutation. Consider the 2x3 FJSP in Table 1 where Job 1 (J_1) has 3 operations (O_{11}, O_{12}, O_{13}) and Job 2 (J_2) has 2 operations (O_{21}, O_{22}). One possible schedule could be (O_{21} O_{11} O_{22} O_{12} O_{13}). We obtain the resulting string by replacing each operation by the corresponding job index; giving the result (2 1 2 1 1). This encoding prevents the creation of infeasible schedules.
- Machine Order String: This part represents the assignments of machines to operations. Here, an array of binary numbers is used to indicate specifically which machine each of the operations has been allocated to. Fig. 2 shows one possible encoding under this scheme. A value of 1 indicates that a machine is selected.

O_{11}		O_{12}			O_{13}		O_{21}		O_{22}		
M_1	M_2	M_1	M_2	M_3	M_2	M_3	M_1	M_2	M_1	M_2	M_3
0	1	0	0	1	1	0	0	1	0	1	0

Fig. 2. Scheme for representing the machine assignment of the operations

4.2 Antibody Initialization

Before the antibody can be used, its operation order and machine order strings (as discussed in the previous section) need to be initialized. Instead of using a randomized mutation approach, a bootstrapping method is employed. This is described as follows.

In the creation of an antibody, a random schedule of the job operations is generated and encoded as the operation order string. The bootstrapping mechanism is applied to the machine order. For each operation, instead of randomly choosing a machine to be assigned, the machine offering the shortest processing time is chosen. The purpose of the proposed bootstrapping initialization method is to ensure that the machine order of the antibody is optimized by selecting the best machine for each operation. In this way, less mutation needs to be performed on the machine order before the best combination is found. As the processing time of each operation is initially a minimum, this helps to reduce the initial makespan value of the antibodies. By fixing the initialization of the machine order, it may seem that the diversity of a given group of generated antibodies will be compromised. However, it should be noted that the machine order string is only half of the antibody representation. The random generation of the other half, which is the operation order, provides a diversifying effect that offsets the localization effect of the machine order initialization.

4.3 Makespan Computation

Each antibody represents a possible job schedule that may satisfy a given FJSP. Its makespan value can be computed by interpreting both the operation and machine order. We use the Makespan Computation Algorithm [11] shown in Figure 3.

```
1.  for (i := 1 to m) do
2.      j := operation_order(i)
3.      k := operation_index(j)
4.      l := get_machine_index(j,k)
5.      p := get_processing_time(j,k,l)
6.      L := set of operations processed on machine l
7.      middleList := false
8.      for (i := 1 to size_of(L)-1) do
9.          if (p <= time between L(i) & L(i+1)) then
10.             insert operation k between L(i) & L(i+1)
11.             middleList := true
12.             break
13.         endif
14.     endfor
15.     if (!middleList) then
16.         insert operation k at the end of L
17.     endif
18. endfor
19.     max := maximum finishing time of a machine in a set of machine M
20. return max
```

Fig. 3. The Makespan Computation Algorithm [11]

In the algorithm, m is the length of *operation order*, operation_order(i) returns the index of the job at position i in *operation order*, operation_index(j) returns the index of the operation of job j, get_machine_index(j,k) returns the index of the machine performing $O_{j,k}$, get_procdessing_time(j,k,l) returns processing time of $O_{j,k}$ on machine l and M is the set of machines in the scheduling problem.

The algorithm works by detecting a left-most time gap between two operations processed on the same machine. If this gap is big enough to accommodate a new operation, the new operation will be inserted into the slot. Thus, the algorithm attempts to find the shortest possible makespan value for a schedule by packing all the operations processes as closely as possible.

4.4 Mutation of Antibodies

The main purpose of the mutation process is to produce variants of the existing antibodies which can offer better makespan values. Since an antibody is represented by two parts; the operation order and machine order, two separate mutation operators are devised to act on each of these parts of the antibody. These operators will be named as the *operation order mutation operator* and the *machine order mutation operator* respectively.

In *operation order mutation*, only the operation order of an antibody is mutated. Two random operations will be selected and swapped in position with each other (see Figure 4). The number of operation swaps depends on the mutation rate – the higher the mutation rate, the more operations to be swapped.

2	1	2	1	1

Operation order before mutation (swapping)

1	1	2	1	*2*

Operation order after mutation (swapping)

Fig. 4. Example of a mutation on the operation order string

In *machine order mutation*, random operations are chosen to have their assigned machine bits changed. This means that they will now be processed by a machine different from the originally assigned one (see Figure 5). With a higher mutation rate, more operations experience a change in their assigned machine.

O_{11}		O_{12}			O_{13}	
M_1	M_2	M_1	M_2	M_3	M_2	M_3
0	1	0	0	1	1	0

Machine order before mutation

O_{11}		O_{12}			O_{13}	
M_1	M_2	M_1	M_2	M_3	M_2	M_3
0	1	*1*	0	*0*	0	1

Machine order after mutation

Fig. 5. Example of a mutation on the machine order string

In adhering to the Clonal Selection principle, the rate of the mutations is set to be inversely proportional to the antibody's fitness. If an antibody is weak, a larger amount of mutation is likely to cause an improvement in fitness. However, if the antibody is already fit, a similar mutation is more likely to cause deterioration in fitness which is an adverse effect. In this case, a small mutation is favored.

4.5 Design of the ClonaFLEX Algorithm

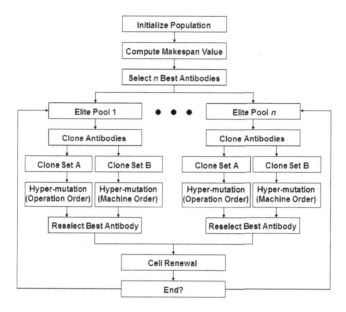

Fig. 6. Flow diagram of the ClonaFLEX algorithm

Figure 6 shows the design of the proposed algorithm. The individual steps are described as follows:

1. Create an initial pool of m antibodies (candidate solutions).
2. Compute the makespan value of each antibody using the Makespan Computation Algorithm (see Figure 3).
3. Select n best (fittest) individuals from the m original antibodies, where $n < m$, based on their makespan values. These antibodies will be referred to as the *elites*.
4. Place each of the n selected elites in n separate and distinct pools. They will be referred to as the elite pools. (Note: there is no special arrangement for the subsequent placement of elites in the elite pools. After the initial selection of the first batch of elites, each will simply be given a pool to populate. The subsequent elites chose from each pool after cloning and mutation will then replace only its predecessor in their respective pools. There is no crossover of antibodies between pools).
5. Clone the elites in each elite pool with a rate proportional to its fitness. The fitter the antibody (the lower the makespan), the more clones it will have.
6. Subject the clones in each pool through a hyper-mutation process. Half of the clones will undergo *operation order mutation* while the other half will undergo *machine order mutation*. The mutation rate for both cases is inversely proportional to the fitness of the parent antibody.

7. Determine the fittest individual in each elite pool from amongst its mutated clones to become the elite for the next generation. All other clones are discarded.

8. Replace each elite in the worst *l* elite pools with a new antibody (cell renewal) once every *k* generations to introduce diversity and prevent the search from being trapped in local optima.

9. Determine if the number of generations to evolve is reached. If it has, terminate and return the best antibody; if it has not, return to Step 4.

5   Analysis

The ClonaFLEX algorithm was designed based on the Clonal Selection principle, involving certain elements of evolutionary computation. In ClonaFLEX, there is no crossover process. Instead, the algorithm relies solely on a dynamic mutation rate as the only means to drive the evolution of its population of antibodies (solutions).

After the identification of a good antibody, ClonaFLEX massively clones it and mutates the newly generated clones. Due to the large number of mutated clones, there is effectively a wide coverage of the solution space around the original antibody. This is much akin to doing a greedy search, but is intelligently guided by the relative strength of the conserved features denoted by the fitness of each antibody. Depending on these fitness values, different mutation rates allow for a variation of search radius.

The cloning and mutation approach provides an effective method for the global search of good solution basins. However, there are also other factors that contribute to the efficacy of the ClonaFLEX algorithm.

5.1   Maintaining Population Diversity

In the ClonaFLEX implementation, the *n* chosen elites are placed in distinct pools. This feature is to ensure a more effective parallel search.

Due to the Clonal Selection principle, intense competition can arise among antibodies and the weaker ones will never have the chance to be expressed. During selection, the fitter antibodies will always be considered over the weaker ones. After a certain number of generations of evolution, these fit antibodies start to dominate the pool with their fitness, resulting in the selection of the same few individuals to move into the next generation each time. This problem is made worse by the cloning process where fit antibodies are cloned more in number, resulting in even greater competition. The population space then rapidly converges and loses diversity. The system soon finds itself with antibodies all cloned from the same parent cell. If the population space converges too early during a search, the result found might only be a local optimum instead of the global one.

By placing the elites in independent pools, it enables each individual to develop at their own pace without having to face disturbance or competition from the others. As there is no communication or crossing over between the pools, the antibodies in each pool become distinctively different from the rest in the other pools, thus preventing premature population convergence.

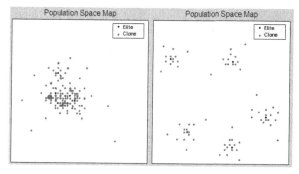

Fig. 7. Effect of Elite Pools. The left graph shows the population space when one antibody pool is used. The right graph shows that when five separate antibody pools are used.

Figure 7 shows the antibodies being mapped out using Sammon's Mapping [15]. Sammon's Mapping is a non-metric multidimensional scaling technique [14] that attempts to map the elements of a multivariate data set onto a lower dimensional plane while retaining the original spatial distances that existed among them. Here, the multivariate antibodies are mapped onto a two dimensional plane with the principal direction of change represented by the two axes. The left graph shows the mapping when only one pool is used to house all the antibodies. The elites and their clones are all clustered together indicating population space convergence. The right graph shows the mapping using five different pools. It can be seen that five distinct and separate clusters, each headed by an elite, has been formed as they are more able to maintain a relative distance from one another.

The search now becomes more effective since each pool covers candidates in a different area of the solution space. If a pool was to get stuck in a local optimum, the other pools remain unaffected and can continue their search unaffected.

5.2 Determining the Optimal Mutation Rate by Visual Experimentation

One important factor in the design of ClonaFLEX is the mutation rate for the cloned antibodies. According to the Clonal Selection principle, it is to be inversely proportional to its antigen-affinity. In our application, the antigen affinity (or fitness) is measured by an integral quantity which is the makespan of a given FJSP schedule. The mutation rate is then in principle determined by the inverse of the antigen affinity; that is, the higher the affinity, the lower the mutation rate, vice versa. However, one cannot decide the 'goodness' of an affinity value without a measure of relative distance to the optimal for a given problem instance. In other words, it cannot be decided if an affinity value is considered high (or low) without knowing how far it is from the optimal (which differs for each instance)? One possibility is instead to equate the mutation rate to be proportional to the relative change in affinity from one generation to another. However, since the fitness landscape need not be monotonic and unimodal, such an approach will inevitably cause premature convergence to local optimums. The approach we use to solve this problem is to experimentally partition the makespan domain for a problem instance into separate zones and then assign mutation rates to each zone. Therefore in ClonaFLEX, the mutation rate is assigned as follows:

1. Divide the possible makespan range into zones (e.g. makespan values of 1 – 20 will be zone 1 and makespan values of 21 – 40 will be zone 2).
2. Assign mutation rates to each of the makespan zones such that the lower zones (indicating lower makespan) have lower mutation rates.
3. Determine the makespan zone which an antibody belongs to by using its makespan value.
4. Mutate the antibody using that zone's assigned mutation rate.

There is an optimum value for the mutation rate of each of the zones. If these parameters are not properly set, the mutation process will not yield fruitful results. Optimization of the mutation rates is a difficult process; which we determine by using a visualization approach. We illustrate this approach with an example. The graphs in Figure 8 are plots of an antibody's makespan against time for different runs. The first plot shows the initial algorithm run against an 8 x 8 FJSP instance from Kacem [9], where the best makespan found is seen to decrease steadily as the number of rounds increases. However, a slight adjustment of the mutation rate for the topmost zone can induce the makespan to reduce at a much faster rate, as shown by the steeper gradient in the second plot (marked with a green circle). This process is repeated for the individual zones until a near-optimal mutation rate is obtained which can be inferred from the steepness of makespan decent. Due to this rapid drop in makespan value, the algorithm wastes less time in each zone, having more time to search for better antibodies in the lower zones, as shown in the third plot.

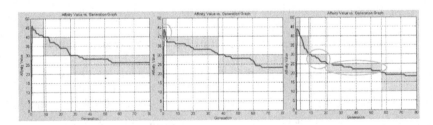

Fig. 8. Mutation rate analysis graphs. From left to right: the first plot gives the result of the initial run, the second shows the result after the mutation rate of the topmost makespan zone has been adjusted and the third gives the results after all the zones have been optimized.

As the direct application of the Clonal Selection principle leads to premature population convergence, this visualization approach identifies specific makespan zones to evaluate the effectiveness of the assigned mutation rate. Each zone can then be targeted individually for improvement by changing the mutation rate till it gives the best drop rate.

6   Empirical Results

The ClonaFLEX algorithm was applied to 12 sets of benchmark FJSP instances. These included problem sets from both T-FJSP and P-FJSP to illustrate the ability of the algorithm to handle both cases without any change to the implementation. The algorithm was set to run for 200 generations each time with an initial antibody population of 100 of which only 10 elites would be chosen. Each problem set was repeated 30 times and the results were collected. Table 2 shows the tabulated result of ClonaFLEX versus the first four sets of problems taken from Kacem *et al* [10] as well as those from GENACE [11]; a cultural EA. The next eight sets of problems were taken from Brandimarte *et al* [8] and the results are tabulated in Table 3.

Table 2. Results of problem sets from Kacem *et al* [10]

Problem Set	Kacem *et al.*	GENACE	ClonaFLEX	
			Best Result	Average Result
T-FJSP 4 x 5	16	11	11	11.0
T-FJSP 10 x 7	15	12	**11**	11.0
T-FJSP 10 x 10	7	7	7	7.5
T-FJSP 15 x 10	23	12	12	13.33

Table 3. Results of problem sets from Brandimarte *et al* [8]

Problem Set	Brandimarte *et al.*	GENACE	ClonaFLEX	
			Best Result	Average Result
P-FJSP 10 x 6 (1)	42	41	**39**	39.54
P-FJSP 10 x 6 (2)	32	29	**27**	28.3
P-FJSP 10 x 15	86	68	*70*	73.0
P-FJSP 15 x 4	186	176	**173**	174.67
P-FJSP 15 x 8	81	67	**65**	66.67
P-FJSP 20 x 5	157	148	**145**	148.13
P-FJSP 20 x 10 (1)	523	523	523	523.0
P-FJSP 20 x 10 (2)	369	328	**311**	325.07

The above results clearly indicate that the ClonaFLEX algorithm is able to obtain better upper bounds than the GENACE algorithm for 7 out of the 12 problems sets (in bold), equivalent results for 4 other instances while poorer in 1 (in italic). *T*-tests conducted at a 10% significance level also confirmed the hypothesis that the ClonaFLEX algorithm is able to perform on average, better than the GENACE algorithm for 6 of the 12 test cases, with another 5 cases showing that they are of equal performance. There is only 1 case whereby the performance of ClonaFLEX is inferior to GENACE.

7   Conclusion

In this paper, the Clonal Selection principle of the immune system was examined and a new algorithm based on it - ClonaFLEX, was designed to solve the NP-hard FJSP. Several practical considerations were presented. First, to encode the FJSP schedule in

ClonaFLEX, an antibody representation [11] that produced feasible schedules (hence without the need for a repair mechanism) was adopted. The mutation process in ClonaFLEX involved the use of two specific operators, the *operation order mutation operator* and the *machine order mutation operator*, which operate on each of the two parts of the antibody string. Second, due to the differing relationship between antigen affinity and mutation rates for every problem instance, we experimentally preallocated makespan zones and used a visual method to decide the optimal mutation rates for assignment to each zone. A bootstrapping antibody initialization technique was also presented to aid in optimizing the antibodies when they are first created during the start of the algorithm. Third, the straightforward implementation of clonal selection resulted in premature convergence of the population space. To overcome this problem, elite pools are used to incubate antibodies of various strains where they can evolve in an uncontested environment. Without communication between the pools, these antibodies are able to retain their strain distinctiveness and stay structurally different from one another, thus allowing a more effective parallel search.

The ClonaFLEX algorithm was tested against 12 benchmark FJSP instances taken from Kacem *et al* [10] and Brandimarte *et al* [8]. The results gathered were compared to those obtained by GENACE, a cultural EA [11]. From the experimental results, ClonaFLEX obtained better makespans for 7 problem sets, equivalent results for 4 other instances while a poorer result for 1.

The main aim of this paper lies in presenting the practical design considerations for solving the FJSP through an application of Clonal Selection theory. Though a manual approach of mutation rate determination was required due to the practical limitation of a straightforward use of the principle, the results nonetheless prove the efficacy of these immune algorithms in solving such NP-hard problems.

References

1. Weissman I., Cooper M.., "How the Immune System Develops", *Scientific American*, pp. 64-71, 1993.
2. Burnet F., *The Clonal Selection Theory of Acquired Immunity*. Cambridge, U.K.: Cambridge Press, 1959.
3. de Castro L., Von Zuben F., "Artificial Immune System: Part 1 - Basic Theory and Applications", Technical Report, State University of Campinas, Campinas, 1999.
4. de Castro L., Von Zuben F., " Learning and Optimization Using the Clonal Selection Principle", *IEEE Transactions on Evolutionary Computation, Special Issue on Artificial Immune Systems*, vol. 6(3), pp. 239-251, 2001.
5. de Castro L, Timmis J., *Artificial Immune System: A New Computational Intelligence Approach*. London, U.K.,: Springer-Verlag, 2002.
6. Doyen A., Engin O., Ozkan C., "A New Artificial Immune System Approach to Solve Permutation Flow Shop Scheduling Problems", *Turkish Symposium on Artificial Immune Systems and Neural Networks TAINN'03*, 2003.
7. Garey M., Johnson D., Sethi R., "The Complexity of Flow Shop and Job-shop Schedules", *Mathematics of Operations Research*, vol. 1(2), pp. 117-129, 1976.
8. Brandimarte P., "Routing and Scheduling in a Flexible Job-Shop by Tabu Search", *Annals of Operations Research*, vol. 2, pp. 158-183, 1993.

9. Kacem I., Hammadi S. and Borne P., "Approach by Localization and Multiobjective Evolutionary Optimization for Flexible Job-shop Scheduling Problems", *IEEE Transactions on Systems, Man and Cybernetics*, vol. 32(1), pp. 1-13, 2002.
10. Kacem I., Hammadi S. and Borne P., "Pareto-optimality Approach for Flexible Job-Shop Scheduling Problems: Hybridization of Evolutionary Algorithms and Fuzzy Logic", *Mathematics and Computer in Simulation*, vol. 60, pp. 245-276, 2002.
11. Tay J. C. and Ho N. B., "GENACE: An Efficient Cultural Algorithm for Solving the Flexible Job-Shop Problem", *Proceedings of the IEEE Congress of Evolutionary Computation*, pp. 1759-1766, 2004.
12. Tay J. C. and Wibowo D., "An Effective Chromosome Representation for Evolving Flexible Job Shop Schedules", *Proceedings of AAAI Genetic and Evolutionary Computation*, vol. 2, pp. 210-221, 2004.
13. Ramino V., Camino R., Vela J.P., Alberto G., "A knowledge-based evolutionary strategy for scheduling problems with bottleneck", *European Journal of Operations Research*, vol. 145(1), pp.57-71, 2003.
14. Kadluczka M., Nelson P., Tirpak T., "N-to-2-Space Mapping for Visualization of Search Algorithm Performance", *16th IEEE International Conference on Tools with Artificial Intelligence*, pp.508-513, 2004.
15. Sammon J. W. Jr, "A Nonlinear Mapping for Data Structure Analysis", *IEEE Transactions on Computers*, vol. C-18(5), pp. 401-409, 1969.

The Medical Applications of
Attribute Weighted Artificial Immune System (AWAIS):
Diagnosis of Heart and Diabetes Diseases

Seral Şahan[1], Kemal Polat[1], Halife Kodaz[2], and Salih Güneş[1]

[1] Selcuk University, Eng.-Arch. Fac. Electrical & Electronics Eng.
42031-Konya/Turkey
{seral, sgunes, kpolat}@selcuk.edu.tr
[2] Selcuk University, Eng.-Arch. Fac. Computer Eng.
42031-Konya/Turkey
hkodaz@selcuk.edu.tr

Abstract. In our previous work, we had been proposed a new artificial immune system named as Attribute Weighted Artificial Immune System (AWAIS) to eliminate the negative effects of taking into account of all attributes in calculating Euclidean distance in shape-space representation which is used in many network-based Artificial Immune Systems (AISs). This system depends on the weighting attributes with respect to their importance degrees in class discrimination. These weights are then used in calculation of Euclidean distances. The performance analyses were conducted in the previous study by using machine learning benchmark datasets. In this study, the performance of AWAIS was investigated for real world problems. The used datasets were medical datasets consisting of Statlog Heart Disease and Pima Indian Diabetes datasets taken from University of California at Irvine (UCI) Machine Learning Repository. Classification accuracies for these datasets were obtained through using 10-fold cross validation method. AWAIS reached 82.59% classification accuracy for Statlog Heart Disease while it obtained a classification accuracy of 75.87% for Pima Indians Diabetes. These results are comparable with other classifiers and give promising performance to AWAIS for that kind of problems.

1 Introduction

A new artificial intelligence area named as Artificial Immune Systems (AISs) is going forward gradually. There are many AIS algorithms in which recognition and learning mechanisms of immune system were modeled. As a representation method of immune system cells, shape-space approach is used in many of the AIS classification algorithms. Shape-space model, which was proposed by Perelson and Oster in 1979 [1], is used as a representation mechanism modeling the interactions between two cells in the immune system.

In the systems that use a distance criterion as a similarity metric, some shape-space related problems may exist in case of irrelevant attributes [2], [3]. One attribute value

C. Jacob et al. (Eds.): ICARIS 2005, LNCS 3627, pp. 456–468, 2005.
© Springer-Verlag Berlin Heidelberg 2005

in shape space can cause two data in the same class to be distant from each other and therefore to be recognized and classified by different system units. If that attribute is irrelevant for class discrimination process, the algorithm may result in erroneous classes.

In our previous study [4], it was aimed to reach higher classification accuracy by assigning weights to important attributes in classification. This was done with some modifications to affinity measures of AISs and then a system named AWAIS (Attribute Weighted Artificial Immune System) has come into existence. In that paper, we had conducted the performance analyses of AWAIS for chainlink and two-spirals datasets which are commonly used machine learning benchmarks and for wine dataset representing a real-world problem. For all of those problems, the performance of AWAIS was very satisfactory and promising. In this paper we carried applications of AWAIS for real-world situations further and used AWAIS as a classifier in medical domain to diagnose diseases. The problems dealt in this study are Heart Disease and Diabetes Diagnosing problems via classification. Used datasets were taken from UCI Machine Learning Repository carrying the names Statlog Heart Disease and Pima Indians Diabetes respectively [5]. A form of k-fold cross validation which is a very commonly used method was used to evaluate classification accuracies more reliably in the experimental studies. The obtained classification accuracies were 82.59% and 75.87% for Heart Disease and Diabetes respectively.

This paper is organized as follows. In the second section of this paper, the background information is given including natural and artificial immune systems, shape-space representation and curse of dimensionality problem. The third section is reserved for introduction of AWAIS. The used datasets and k-cross validation are all given in fourth section of the paper under the title of method. Results and discussions about these results were given in section five which is then followed by the conclusion in section six.

2 Background

2.1 Natural and Artificial Immune Systems and Shape-Space Representation

The natural immune system is a distributed novel-pattern detection system with several functional components positioned in strategic locations throughout the body [6]. Immune system regulates the defense mechanism of body by means of innate and adaptive immune responses. Between these, adaptive immune response is much more important for us because it contains metaphors like recognition, memory acquisition, diversity, self-regulation...etc. The main architects of adaptive immune response are Lymphocytes, which divide into two classes as T and B Lymphocytes (cells), each having its own function. Especially B cells have a great importance because of their secreted antibodies (Abs) that takes very critical roles in adaptive immune response. For detailed information about immune system refer to [7].

AISs emerged in the 1990s as a new computational research area. AISs link several emerging computational fields inspired by biological behavior such as Artificial Neural Networks and Artificial Life [8].

Among the studies conducted in the field of AIS, *B* cell modeling is the most encountered representation type. Different representation methods have been proposed in that modeling. Among these, shape-space representation is the most commonly used one [1].

The shape-space model (*S*) aims at quantitatively describing the interactions among antigens (*Ag*s), the foreign elements that enter the body like microbe,...etc., and antibodies (*Ag-Ab*). The set of features that characterize a molecule is called its *generalized shape*. The *Ag-Ab* representation (binary or real-valued) determines a distance measure to be used to calculate the degree of interaction between these molecules. Mathematically, the generalized shape of a molecule (*m*), either an antibody or an antigen, can be represented by a set of coordinates $m = <m_1, m_2,...m_L>$, which can be regarded as a point in an *L*-dimensional real-valued shape-space ($m \in S^L$)[6]. In this work, we used real strings to represent the molecules. Antigens and antibodies were considered of same length *L*. The length and cell representation depends upon the problem.

2.2 Problems with Euclidean Distance as an Affinity Measure

The shape-space representation gives a good model of interactions in immune system but because the affinities between Abs to Ags are calculated based on a distance criterion, some problems exist like other distance-based approaches. The distances between instances are calculated based on all attributes of the instances and so distance can be dominated by irrelevant attributes [2]. To illustrate this, let us think the two points of a same class shown in Fig. 1. Again we will assume second attribute is not so important for class determination. The first and the third attributes of these two points are the same but the difference in second attribute value results the two data point to be apart from each other. If we take second attribute into account in a same degree with other two attributes, a possible wrong decision about the class of points can be done. This is also a problem because each attribute value is squared while determining Euclidean distance as stated in [9].

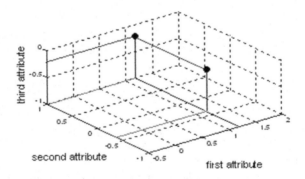

Fig. 1. Two points in same class illustrating curse of dimensionality problem

This difficulty, which arises when many irrelevant attributes present can be solved by using attribute weights. Using weighted attributes is a common way to get rid of the problem like this as done in ML algorithms like in [10], [11] and etc.

3 AWAIS (Attribute Weighted Artificial Immune System)

As mentioned before, most of network-based AIS algorithms use shape-space representation and the problem stated above related with irrelevant attributes inevitably appeared in turn affects the system performance. The AWAIS algorithm proposed for minimizing the effect of this problem is a supervised Artificial Immune System based on attribute-weighted distance criterion. The supervision in the algorithm shows itself while determining the weights of attributes and during the process of developing memory cells in the training by taking the class of the input data into account. AWAIS is a two-stage classification system in which attribute weights of each class are formed in one level and a training procedure with these weights takes place at the other.

3.1 Attribute Weighting

In most real valued shape-space representations, the distance between two points is calculated by the Euclidean distance criteria (Eq. (1)):

$$D = \sqrt{\sum_{i=1}^{L} (ab_i - ag_i)^2} \, . \tag{1}$$

Where **ab** and **ag** are the two points in the shape-space represented by a vector respectively and L is the length of these vectors. According to this formula, all of the attributes have same effect in determining distance. However, there are such data sets that some attributes of them have no effect on the class of data while some other attributes are more important in determining class. So, if it is assigned higher weights to the attributes that are more important in determining one class and if these weights are used in calculation of distance, it can be prevented to make a misclassification of the two distant data according to the Euclidean norm in the same class [2]. Starting from this point, the used attribute weighting depends on the following base: if one attribute doesn't changing very much among the data of one class, this attribute is one of the characteristic attributes of related class and it must have a higher weight than others [12].

The applied attribute weighting procedure in the AWAIS is as follows:

```
(1) Normalization of each attribute in data set between
    0-1.
(2) Determine  the  antigens  of  each  class→ Ag_class_j
    (j:1,....n, n: number of class)
(3) For each class do:
    For Ag_class_(LxNc) to be a matrix that involves the
    antigens of that class;
    (L: attribute num., Nc: ag num. of that class);
```

(3.1) For i^{th} attribute do: $(i:1,.....L)$
Evaluate standard deviation of ith attribute
with Eq. (2):

$$std\_dev_i = \sqrt{\frac{1}{Nc}\sum_{k=1}^{Nc}\left(Ag_{k,i} - mean\left(Ag_i\right)\right)^2}. \qquad (2)$$

Here $Ag_{k,i}$ is the ith attribute of kth Ag in j^{th}
class; $mean(Ag_i)$ is the mean of ith attribute
of all Ags in j^{th} class.
Calculate the weights as follows:

$$w_{j,i}=1/std\_dev_i , \quad (i=1,...L; \; j=1,...n) \qquad (3)$$

(3.2) normalize the weights of jth class.

The calculated w_{nxL} matrix is a normalized weight matrix involving the weights of each attribute for each class and this matrix is used in distance calculations of the training algorithm of AWAIS.

Here, in the attribute weighting procedure, a means of normalization of attributes for each class by standard deviation is performed. By doing so, each class has its own set of attribute weights.

3.2 AWAIS Training Algorithm

The training procedure of the algorithm conducts the following steps:

(1) For each Ag_i do : ($i: 1,...N$)
    (1.1) Determine the class of Ag_i. Call memory Abs of
    that class and calculate the
    distances between Ag_i and these memory Abs with
    Eq. (4):

$$D = \sqrt{\sum_{k=1}^{L} w_{j,k}\left(Ab_{j,k} - Ag_{i,k}\right)^2}. \qquad (4)$$

    Here $Ab_{i,k}$ and $Ag_{i,k}$ are the kth attribute of Ab_j
    and Ag_i respectively; $w_{j,k}$ is the weight of kth
    attribute that belongs to the class of Ab_j.
    (1.2) If the minimum distance among the calculated
    distances above is less than a threshold value
    named as suppression value (supp) then return
    to step 1.
    (1.3) Form a memory Ab for Ag_i:
        At each iteration do:
        (1.3.1) Make a random Ab population with
        Ab=[Ab_mem ; Ab_rand] and   calculate the
        distances of these Abs to Ag_i.

> (1.3.2)   Select *m* nearest *Abs* to *Ag_i*; clon
> and mutate these *Abs*   (*Ab_mutate*).
> (1.3.3)   Keep the *m* nearest *Abs* in the
> *Ab_mutate* population to *Ag_i* as *Ab_mem* tem-
> porary memory population.
> (1.3.4)   Define the nearest *Ab* to *Ag_i* as
> *Ab_cand*, candidate memory *Ab* for *Ag_i* and
> stop iterative process if the distance of
> *Ab_cand* to *Ag_i* is less that a threshold
> value named as stopping criterion (*sc*).
> (1.3.5) Concatenate *Ab_cand* as a new memory
> *Ab* to memory matrix of the class of *Ag_i*.
> (1.4) Stop training.

The mutation mechanism in the algorithm which is used in many AIS algorithms and named as *hypermutation* is performed proportional to distance between two cells (Eq. (5)):

$$Ab_{j,k}{}'=Ab_{j,k}\pm D_{j,I}*(Ab_{j,k})$$ (5)

Here $Ab_{j,k}{}'$ is the new value and $Ab_{j,k}$ is the old value of kth attribute of jth Ab. $D_{j,i}$ stands for the distance between Ag_i and Ab_j.

The used affinity measure is no more a pure Euclidean Distance and the attribute weights are used in distance criteria. The classes of memory *Abs* in the AWAIS after training are known with the aid of a labeling vector that contains the information about which memory *Abs* belong to which class.

After memory Antibodies is formed by this training procedure, test samples are presented to these Antibodies and the classes of these samples are determined by using k-nearest neighbor method.

4   Method

4.1 Statlog Heart Disease and Pima Indians Diabets Datasets

The Statlog Heart disease dataset was taken from UCI Machine Learning Respiratory [5]. 270 samples belong to patients with heart problem while the remaining 150 samples are of healthy persons. The samples taken from patients and healthy persons include 13 attributes which are: 1. age, 2. sex, 3. chest pain type (4 values), 4. resting blood pressure, 5. serum cholestoral in mg/dl, 6. fasting blood sugar > 120 mg/dl, 7. resting electrocardiographic results (values 0,1,2), 8. maximum heart rate achieved, 9. exercise induced angina, 10. oldpeak = ST depression induced by exercise relative to rest, 11. the slope of the peak exercise ST segment, 12. number of major vessels (0-3) colored by flourosopy, 13. thal: 3 = normal; 6 = fixed defect; 7 = reversable defect This dataset has 13 attributes and 2 classes. The class information is included in the dataset as 1 and 2 regarding absence and presence of disease respectively.

The other used data set for Diabetes problem was also taken from the same database and it is named as Pima Indians Diabetes [5]. This dataset contains 768 samples taken from healthy and unhealthy persons. 500 of these samples belong to persons with no diabetes problem while the remaining 286 sample are of persons with diabetes. The class information contained in this data set is given by 0 for healthy persons and by 1 for diabetic patients. The number of attributes in samples is 8. These attributes are: 1. Number of times pregnant, 2. Plasma glucose concentration a 2 hours in an oral glucose tolerance test, 3. Diastolic blood pressure (mm Hg), 4. Triceps skin fold thickness (mm), 5. 2-Hours serum insulin (mu U/ml), 6. Body mass index (weight in kg/(height in m)^2), 7. Diabetes pedigree function, 8. Age (years).

4.2 K-Fold Cross Validation

In this study, the classification accuracies for the datasets were measured according to the Eq. (6):

$$accuracy(T) = \frac{\sum_{i=1}^{|T|} assess(t_i)}{|T|}, t_i \in T$$

$$assess(t) = \begin{cases} 1, & if \ classify(t) = t.c \\ 0, & otherwise \end{cases}$$

$$(6)$$

where T is the set of data items to be classified (the test set), $t \in T$, $t.c$ is the class of the item t, and classify(t) returns the classification of t by AIRS.

For test results to be more valuable, k-fold cross validation is used among the researchers. It minimizes the bias associated with the random sampling of the training [13]. In this method, whole data is randomly divided to k mutually exclusive and approximately equal size subsets. The classification algorithm trained and tested k times. In each case, one of the folds is taken as test data and the remaining folds are added to form training data. Thus k different test results exist for each training-test configuration. The average of these results gives the test accuracy of the algorithm [13]. We used this method as 10-fold cross validation in our applications.

5 Results and Discussion

5.1 Results for Statlog Heart Disease

Whereas AWAIS has a number of parameters that affect the classification performance of the algorithm, the key parameter to adjust in AWAIS algorithm is *supp* parameter since it determines the number of memory Abs so the classification accuracy. The other parameters in the system were found to have little effect on classification accuracy, they would rather affect the classification time of the algorithm. The number of best memory cells selected in each iteration, which is given by m, was selected as 25. An Ab population that consists of 100 members was used. This population consists of 25 best Abs from previous iteration and 75 randomly generated Abs. The percentage of memory Abs was chosen experimentally and from these experimentations it was found that if there were less number of memory Abs, the algorithm had tended to be more like a random search algorithm while if the percentage of memory Abs were chosen to be high, the population had dominated with memory Abs and the algorithm had converged to the best individual. But this had no serious effect on classification accuracy, it only affected the classification time of the algorithm.

The value of supp parameter is selected in the [0,1] range. If this value is selected too high, the number of Abs will be too low and in contrary if this value is too low, there will be more memory Abs. The number of memory Abs highly affects the classification performance. Besides of supp parameter the k value for k-nn also affects the classification accuracy. Because the number of memory Abs is different for each supp value, the k value was changed for each supp value to obtain highest classification accuracy.

The classification accuracy with respect to the supp parameter is plotted in Fig. 2 (a) with respect to the supp parameter. The number of memory Abs and variation of k-value for which the highest accuracy was obtained with respect to the supp value are shown in Fig. 2 (b).

The dashed line in Fig. 2 (b) shows the memory Ab number for each supp value and the straight line represents the k-values at which highest classification accuracies were obtained for each supp value. As stated above, the number of Abs grows with decreasing supp while this growing results in higher classification accuracy to a degree. The maximum classification accuracy was obtained for 0.08 value of supp parameter as 82.59%. For this value of supp parameter, the number of memory Abs was about 160. Also, as can be seen from the Fig. 2 (b), k value increases with decreasing supp value as proportional to the number of memory Abs.

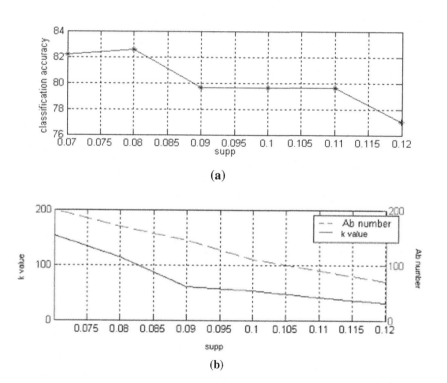

Fig. 2. (a) obtained classification accuracies with respect to the supp parameter, (b) k value and Ab number versus supp parameter (for Statlog Heart Disease)

Table 1. Classification accuracies obtained by AWAIS and other classifiers for the Statlog Heart Disease dataset

Author	Method	Accuracy (%)
WEKA, RA	Naive-Bayes	83.60
Our Study (2005)	**AWAIS**	**82.59**
Newton Cheung (2001)	Naive Bayes	81.48
Newton Cheung (2001)	BNND	81.11
Newton Cheung (2001)	C4.5	81.11
Newton Cheung (2001)	BNNF	80.96
Robert Detrano	Logistic regression	77.00
WEKA, RA	K*	76.70
WEKA, RA	IB1c	74.00
WEKA, RA	1R	71.40
WEKA, RA	T2	68.10
ToolDiag, RA	MLP+BP	65.60
WEKA, RA	FOIL	64.00
ToolDiag, RA	RBF	60.00
WEKA, RA	InductH	58.50

The classification accuracy obtained by AWAIS is shown in Table.1 with accuracies obtained for the same problem with other classifiers in Literature [14]. 10-fold cross validation was used in all of the classifiers in the table. The table shows that, AWAIS is the second best performed classifier after the study of WEKA group with respect to the classification accuracy. This promising result gives the way for AWAIS to be used in real-world problems as other classifiers. Whereas AWAIS couldn't reach the highest accuracy for the problem, the obtained accuracy is good for an AIS algorithm that uses a distance criterion as an affinity measure. When we look at the table, the highest accuracy was obtained by Naïve-Bayes classifier and Bayes classifiers are known to be optimal classifiers for some kind of problems. It is promising to see that an AIS algorithm performs comparable with a good classifier and if appropriate algorithm formulation for the problem at hand is constructed, even an over-performed AIS algorithm can be found.

5.2 Results for Pima Indians Diabetes

As for the Statlog Dataset, supp parameter was adjusted to obtain highest classification accuracy. Fig. 3 (a) shows the classification accuracy with respect to the supp parameter. The number of memory Abs and k value for corresponding supp parameter values are presented in Fig. 3 (b).

The maximum classification accuracy was obtained for 0.06 value of supp parameter as 75.87%. For this value of supp parameter, the number of memory Abs was about 230.

The dashed line in Fig. 3 (b) shows the memory Ab number for each supp value and the straight line represents the k-values at which highest classification accuracies were obtained for each supp value. Again, k value increases with decreasing supp value as proportional to the number of memory Abs.

The classification accuracy obtained by AWAIS for Pima Indians Diabetes dataset is shown in Table.2 with accuracies obtained for the same problem with other classifiers in Literature [14]. Indeed, Pima Indians Diabetes is a popular medical classification dataset among Machine Learning researchers. So many studies have been conducted related with this classification problem. Whereas high classification accuracies were reached, the accuracies couldn't go above 80% with cross validation scheme. This is also a reason why researchers are dealing with this problem. Because of the vast amount of classifiers were used for this dataset, only some of them are reported in the Table 2 and this is enough to have an opinion how is the performance of AWAIS is.

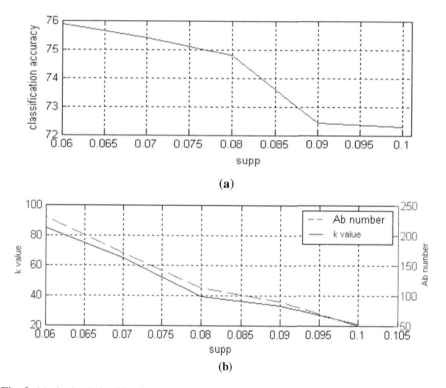

Fig. 3. (a) obtained classification accuracies with respect to the supp parameter, (b) k value and Ab number versus supp parameter (for Pima Indians Diabetes dataset)

According to the table, AWAIS is comparable with other classifiers. Whereas the classification accuracy obtained by AWAIS is also less than those of some classifiers, it was satisfactory to see AWAIS as an average classifier for this dataset if we remember that this dataset is hard to classify. Also, as can be seen from the table, an other AIS, AIRS, was applied by Watkins for this problem and a classification accuracy of 74.10% was obtained [16]. It is good to see that AWAIS has been overperformed to another AIS algorithm for this problem. Also, as it can be seen from the

Table 2. Classification accuracies obtained by AWAIS and some other classifiers for the Pima Indians Diabetes datasets

Method	Accuracy (%)	Reference
Logdisc	77.70	Statlog
IncNet	77.60	Norbert Jankowski
DIPOL92	77.60	Statlog
Linear Discr. Anal.	77.50	Statlog
SMART	76.80	Statlog
GTODT (5xCV)	76.80	Bernet and Blue
kNN,k=23,Manh,raw,W (3xCV)	76.7±4.0	WD-GM,feat. Weigh.
kNN,k=1:25,Manh,raw	76.6±3.4	WD-GM
ASI	76.60	Ster & Dobnikar
Fisher discr. Analysis	76.50	Ster & Dobnikar
MLP+BP	76.40	Ster & Dobnikar
AWAIS (10xCV)	**75.87**	**Our study**
MLP+BP	75.8±6.2	Zarndt
LVQ	75.80	Ster & Dobnikar
LFC	75.80	Ster & Dobnikar
RBF	75.70	Statlog
NNEE (2004) [15]	75.57	Y.Jiang &Z.-H.Zhou
NB	75.5-73.8	Ster & Dobnikar
kNN, k=22, Manh	75.50	Karol Grudzinski
MML	75.5±6.3	Zarndt
SNB	75.40	Ster & Dobnikar
BP	75.20	Statlog
SSV DT	75.0±3.6	WD-GM
kNN, k=18,Euclid,raw	74.8±4.8	WD-GM
ILAS	74.80	Jaurne et. al
CART DT	74.7±5.4	Zarndt
CART DT	74.50	Statlog
DB-CART	74.40	Shang & Breiman
ASR	74.30	Ster & Dobnikar
AIRS (13xCV) [16]	74.10	Watkins
SSV DT	73.7±4.7	WD-GM
C 4.5 DT	73.00	Statlog
CART	72.80	Ster & Dobnikar
C 4.5 DT	72.7±6.6	Zarndt
Kohonen	72.70	Statlog
Bayes	72.2±6.9	Zarndt
C 4.5 (5xCV)	72.00	Bernet and Blue

table, another algorithm with distance criterion, k-nn algorithm, was used for this problem with manhattan distance. The obtained results for this algorithm are better than AWAIS for k=23 with 3xCV and for k=1:25. The classification accuracy is better but in this case the classification time of AWAIS is probably less than k-nn because the used system units in k-nn algorithm are the raw training data whereas for AWAIS the memory Abs are used for classification which are far less than training data. Besides of this, for k-nn, the used distance criterion is Manhattan instead of Euclidean. If we conduct the comparison of AWAIS with k-nn algorithm in the same context, we must take the classification result of k-nn with Euclidean distance which was found to be 74.8% according to the table. Than it is straightforward to say that the use of Manhattan distance can improve the performance of algorithm which is also stated in [9].

6 Conclusions

Shape-space representation, especially used in many network-based AIS algorithms is a means of representing immune system units as system units and this representation scheme also defines the interactions of the system units with the environment by means of distance criteria. A problem caused by irrelevant attributes based on distance criteria appeared in the distance-based classification systems affects the classification performance in negative manner especially for nonlinear data sets. A system named as AWAIS had been proposed for minimizing these negative effects by weighting attributes and using these weighted attributes in calculation of distances. In this paper the real-world performance of this system was analyzed through two medical classification problems. These are heart and diabetes diseases classification problems and the used datasets for these problems were taken from UCI machine learning repository carrying names Stotlog Heart Disease and Pima Indians Diabetes respectively. These datasets were taken especially for their hardness in classification. In performance evaluation of our system for regarding problems, 10 fold cross validation scheme was used.

AWAIS has performed very well for used datasets by reaching 82.59% and 75.87% classification accuracy for Statlog Heart Disease and Pima Indians Diabetes respectively. These results are not the highest ones among other classifiers applied to corresponding datasets so far but the place of AWAIS among them is satisfactorily high. Besides, as stated above, the used datasets are among the medical classification datasets that are hard to classify. Furthermore, another AIS, AIRS, had been applied for Pima Diabetes dataset and the classification accuracy of AWAIS is higher than it's.

Without a doubt, the weighting procedure that was adapted in AWAIS is not the only way for weighting. This weighting procedure assumes that the attribute values in one class doesn't change so much. However, there can be lots of practical problems that don't obey this assumption and for these problems AWAIS may not do so much. Also, weighting each attribute independently seems to be ineffective for datasets that have highly correlated attributes. There are lots of methods to determine the relevancy of attributes in literature and they can be used for determining attributes weights. The use of these methods may add to the performance of AWAIS more than our method. But the key point in AWAIS is to eliminate the negative effects of taking into account all attributes in calculation of distances due to the possible disadvantages of this scheme. It has not strictly stated that the AWAIS can be used with only its weighting procedure. Also, instead of Euclidean distance, Manhattan distance can be used as affinity measure and this opens the way for further studies in this context.

Acknowledgements

This work is supported by the Coordinatorship of Selçuk University's Scientific Research Projects Grant.

References

1. Perelson, A.S. and Oster, G. F., Theoretical Studies of Clonal Selection: Minimal Antibody Repertoire Size and Reliabilty of Self-Nonself Discrimination, Journal of Theoretical Biology, Vol. 81(1979) 645-670
2. Mitchell, T.M., Machine Learning, The McGraw-Hill Companies Press (1997) 234-236
3. Hart, E., Immunology as a Metaphor for Computational Information Processing: Fact or Fiction?, Doctor of Philosophy, Artificial Intelligence Applications Institute, Division of Informatics, University of Edinburgh (2002) 28-34
4. Şahan, S., Kodaz, H., Güneş, S., Polat, K., A New Classifier Based on Attribute Weighted Artificial Immune System, Lecture Notes in Computer Science, Vol. 3280. Springer-Verlag, Berlin Heidelberg (2004) 11-20
5. Blake, C.L., and Merz, C.J., UJI Reporsitory of Machine Learning Databases, (1996) http://www.ics.uci.edu./~mlearn/MLReporsitory.html
6. De Castro, L.N. and Von Zuben, F. J, Artificial Immune Systems: Part I-Basic Theory and Applications, Technical Report, TR-DCA 01/99 (1999) 3-14
7. Abbas, A.K., Lichtman, A.H., Pober, J.S.,Cellular and Molecular Immunology, 4th ed., W.B. Saunders Company (Ed.), 2000
8. De Castro, L.N and Timmis, J., Artificial Immune Systems: A New Computational Intelligence Approach, Springer-Verlag Press (2002)
9. Freitas, A. and Timmis., J., Revisiting the Foundations of Artificial Immune Systems: A Problem Oriented Perspective, Timmis, J., Bentley, P., and Hart, E. (editors), Proceedings of the 2nd International Conference on Artificial Immune Systems, volume 2787 of Lecture Notes in Computer Science, Springer, (2003) 229-241
10. Emam, K. E., Benlarbi, S., Goel., N., and Rai, S. N., Comparing case-based reasoning classifiers for predicting high risk software components, The Journal of Systems and Software, Vol. 55. Elsevier, (2001) 301-320
11. Liao, T.W., Zhang, Z., and Mount, C.R., Similarity measures for retrieval in case-based reasoning systems, Applied Artificial Intelligence, Vol. 12. (1998) 267-288
12. Cherkassky, V. and Mulier, F., Learning From Data, John Wiley & Sons, Inc. (Ed.), 1998
13. Delen, D., Walker, G., Kadam, A., Predicting breast cancer survivability: a comparison of three data mining methods, Artificial Intelligence in Medicine, in Pres (Sep. 2004)
14. http://www.phys.uni.torun.pl/kmk/projects/datasets.html#Sheart (last modified 2002)
15. Jiang, Y. and Zhou, Z.-H., Editing training data for kNN classifiers with Neural Network ensemble, Lecture Notes in Computer Science, Vol. 3173. Springer-Verlag, Berlin Heidelberg (2004) 356–361
16. Watkins, A., AIRS: A Resource Limited Artificial Immune Classifier, Master Thesis, Mississippi State University 2001

Designing Ensembles of Fuzzy Classification Systems: An Immune-Inspired Approach

Pablo D. Castro, Guilherme P. Coelho,
Marcelo F. Caetano, and Fernando J. Von Zuben

Laboratory of Bioinformatics and Bioinspired Computing - LBiC,
Department of Computer Engineering and Industrial Automation - DCA,
School of Electrical and Computer Engineering - FEEC,
University of Campinas - UNICAMP,
PO Box 6101, 13083-852 Campinas, Brazil
{pablo, gcoelho, caetano, vonzuben}@dca.fee.unicamp.br

Abstract. In this work we propose an immune-based approach for designing of fuzzy systems. From numerical data and with membership function previously defined, the immune algorithm evolves a population of fuzzy classification rules based on the clonal selection, hypermutation and immune network principles. Once AIS are able to find multiple good solutions of the problem, accurate and diverse fuzzy systems are built in a single run. Hence, we construct an ensemble of these classifier in order to achieve better results. An ensemble of classifiers consists of a set of individual classifiers whose outputs are combined when classifying novel patterns. The good performance of an ensemble is strongly dependent of individual accuracy and diversity of its components. We evaluate the proposed methodology through computational experiments on some datasets. The results demonstrate that the performance of the obtained fuzzy systems in isolation is very good. However when we combine these systems, a significant improvement is obtained in the correct classification rate, outperforming the single best classifier.

1 Introduction

Fuzzy Systems are fundamental methodologies to represent and process linguistic information, with mechanisms to deal with uncertainty and imprecision. With such remarkable attributes, fuzzy systems have been widely and successfully applied to control, classification and modeling problems [1] [2].

One of the most important tasks in the development of fuzzy systems is the design of its knowledge base. An expressive effort has been devised lately to develop or adapt methodologies that are capable of automatically extracting the knowledge base from numerical data. Particularly in the framework of soft computing, significant methodologies have been proposed with the objective of building fuzzy systems by means of genetic algorithms (GAs).

Genetic Algorithms have demonstrated to be a powerful tool to perform tasks such as [3]: generation of fuzzy rule base, optimization of fuzzy rule bases,

C. Jacob et al. (Eds.): ICARIS 2005, LNCS 3627, pp. 469–482, 2005.

generation of membership functions, and tuning of membership functions. All theses tasks can be considered as optimization or search processes. Fuzzy system generated or adapted by genetic algorithms are called Genetic Fuzzy Systems [4]. The combination of Fuzzy Systems with Genetic Algorithms have great acceptance in the scientific community, once these algorithms are robust and can search efficiently large solution spaces [5]. However, a basic GA together with a significant portion of its variants are not effective in dealing with multimodal optimization [6]. And a simultaneous search for multiple high-quality solutions are strongly desired in certain applications of fuzzy systems. Interpretability issues may require qualitatively distinct proposals with a quantitatively similar behavior [7].

A relatively novel computational paradigm, namely Artificial Immune System (AIS), was originated from attempts to model and apply immunological principles to problem solving in a wide range of areas such as optimization, data analysis, computer security and robotics [8] [9]. One advantage of AIS over other search strategies is that it is able to maintain population diversity and to find many good solutions simultaneously, if they exist.

In this work, we investigate the use of an artificial immune system, namely Copt-aiNet [10], to generate at the same time a pool of diverse and high-performance fuzzy classification systems designed to produce complementary aspects of the solution. In addition, we also implement an ensemble of the generated fuzzy classification systems, in order to obtain a more accurate fuzzy classifier. According to Hansen and Salamon [11], reliable classifier systems can be built by combining multiple classifiers into a single one.

A key point for the good performance of an ensemble of classification systems is that the classifiers should present good results when applied in isolation and they should be diverse between themselves [12].

In order to evaluate the proposed approach, it will be applied to one artificial and two real classification datasets. The computational simulations indicate that our AIS is able to generate accurate and diverse fuzzy classification systems. Besides, the proposals of ensembles of these fuzzy classifiers may further improve the performance when compared with a single model.

This paper is organized as follows. Section 2 shows the fuzzy classification rule format and the fuzzy reasoning method employed. Section 3 describes the Copt-aiNet algorithm. Section 4 presents the application of Copt-aiNet for fuzzy rule base generation. An overview on ensemble and how to implement an ensemble of fuzzy system for classification problems is presented in section 5. Experimental results are presented and discussed in section 6. Finally, section 7 draws some concluding remarks.

2   Fuzzy Classification Rule Format and Fuzzy Reasoning Method

This section describes the fuzzy rule format and fuzzy reasoning method employed in this work.

We use fuzzy rules for pattern classification problems of the following type:

$$R_k: \text{IF } X_1 \text{ is } A_1 \text{ and } \ldots \text{ and } X_n \text{ is } A_n, \text{ THEN } Class_j$$

where R_k is the rule identifier , $X_1, \ldots, X_n$ are attributes of the input pattern, A_i is the linguistic term defined by a fuzzy set used to represent the attribute X_i, and $Class_j$ represents the class.

In a Fuzzy Classification System, the reasoning method is based on fuzzy logic. It derives conclusions from a set of fuzzy rules and a pattern. This work uses the Winner Fuzzy Rule Reasoning Method [13] to classify a new pattern as described below.

Let $e_p = \{a_{p_1}, a_{p_2}, \ldots, a_{p_n}\}$ be the pattern to be classified, $a_{p_1}, \ldots, a_{p_n}$ the values of the corresponding attributes $X_1, \ldots, X_n$ and $R = \{R_1, R_2, \ldots, R_S\}$ the fuzzy rule set. The Winner Rule Fuzzy Reasoning Method is performed by the following steps:

Step 1: Calculate the compatibility degree, $Compat(R_k, e_p)$, between the pattern e_p and each rule R_k, $k=1\ldots S$, applying a T-norm [1] [2] to the membership degree of the pattern attribute values, a_{p_i}, in the corresponding fuzzy sets that appear in the antecedent part of the rule, A_i, $i=1\ldots n$.

$$\text{Compat}(R_k, e_p) = T\left(\mu_{A_1}(a_{p_1}), \ldots, \mu_{A_n}(a_{p_n})\right) \quad (1)$$

Step 2: Find the rule with higher compatibility degree with the given pattern,

$$\text{Max}\{\text{Compat}(R_k, e_p)\} \quad , k=1\ldots S \quad (2)$$

Step 3: The pattern e_p will be classified in the class $Class_j$, such that $Class_j$ is the class of the rule R_k that possess the highest compatibility degree with the pattern.

If two or more rules present the same compatibility degree with the pattern but different consequent, then the first rule that appears will be fired. Although this fuzzy reasoning method seems too simple, it presents a satisfactory level of accuracy and its simplicity give us the advantage of understanding how it derives the conclusions.

3   The Copt-aiNet Algorithm

This section presents the origins of Copt-aiNet (Artificial Immune Network for Combinatorial Optimization) algorithm and the immune inspirations utilized to develop it.

The Copt-aiNet has been derived from other immune-inspired algorithms. Firstly, an immune algorithm named aiNet (Artificial Immune Network) was proposed by de Castro and Von Zuben in [14] to perform data analysis and clustering tasks. In a subsequent work, de Castro and Timmis developed a version of aiNet for multimodal optimization problems, called opt-aiNet (Artificial

Immune Network for Optimization) [15]. The Copt-aiNet was further proposed by Gomes et al. in [10] as an extension of opt-aiNet for combinatorial optimization tasks. The authors demonstrated empirically the suitability of the cited algorithms for optimization problems and presented results where they outperform other approaches.

The Copt-aiNet is based mainly on two immune principles, namely clonal selection [16] and immune network [17]. The clonal selection theory states that when an antigen invades the organism, some antibodies that recognize this antigen start proliferating. The higher the affinity between an antibody and an antigen, the more offsprings, called clones, will be generated. During proliferation, the clones suffer mutation with rates proportional to their affinity with antigens: the higher the affinity, the smaller the mutation rate, and vice-versa. The other important theory is the so-called immune network theory, which proposes that antibodies are not only capable of recognizing antigens, but they are also capable of recognizing each other. When an antibody is recognized by another one, it is suppressed. These two theories are fundamental to the maintenance of diversity in the population and to the search for multiple good solutions.

The Copt-aiNet algorithm may be explained by the following steps:

Step 1 - Generation of the initial population: the initial population is constructed randomly. Each antibody represents a feasible solution to the problem. Initially the population contains 20 individuals and it is allowed to grow and shrink dynamically.

Step 2 - Population evaluation: the fitness value of each antibody is calculated using the objective function.

Step 3 - Clonal Selection: each antibody gives origin to a number of clones, denoted by C. This number is proportional to the antibody fitness value.

Step 4 - Hypermutation: the clones generated in the previous step suffer a mutation process. The mutation rate of each clone is inversely proportional to its fitness: clone with higher fitness will be submitted to lower mutation rates and vice-versa.

Step 5 - Suppression: the antibodies interact with each other in a network form by determining their similarity. If two or more antibodies are similar within a similarity threshold, the antibody with lower fitness value is eliminated from the population. This process avoids redundancy and therefore tends to preserves population diversity.

Step 6 - If none of the k best solutions is improved along a predefined number of iterations, all the antibodies in the population suffer a maturation process. During the maturation process, the antibodies suffer a series of guided mutations in order to better match the antigens. This process is implemented by a local search heuristic. In Copt-aiNet, a Tabu search heuristic [20] is employed as a local search procedure.

Step 7 - If the stopping condition was not met, return to Step 2.

4   The Copt-aiNet Algorithm for Fuzzy Systems Designing

This section describes the application of the Copt-aiNet algorithm to fuzzy rule bases generation, once the automatic building of fuzzy rules is usually interpreted as search and combinatorial optimization processes [22].

The first attempts to develop fuzzy systems using an AIS was proposed by Alves et al. in [21] and promising results were obtained. However, their algorithm is based only on the clonal selection and hypermutation principles while the Copt-aiNet also utilizes the immune network theory, a powerful mechanism to maintain diversity and to obtain multiple optimum solutions.

Starting from a dataset representing samples or examples of the problem and with membership functions previously defined, the proposed method applies the Copt-aiNet to find suitable fuzzy rule bases that correctly classify these examples. Next, we detail the fuzzy membership function generation, the rule bases coding scheme, the fitness function, and the hypermutation and suppression operators adopted in the present work.

− Definition of Membership Functions

In this work the linguistic terms associated with each input attribute are represented by triangular membership functions uniformly distributed in the universe of discourse. In Figure 1 there is an example of this kind of fuzzy partition, where the variable is represented by 3 linguistic terms (fuzzy sets).

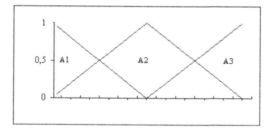

Fig. 1. Example of fuzzy partition

We adopted triangular membership functions for the sake of simplicity though other shapes could have been defined.

− Coding of Fuzzy Rule Base

Each antibody encodes a entire fuzzy rule base while the antigen represents the training patterns. The rules are coded by integer numbers that represent the index of fuzzy sets that appear in the antecedent and consequent part of the rule. The number 0 is associated to the *"don't care"* condition.

For instance, suppose a classification problem where the patterns are described by four attributes - X_1, X_2, X_3 and X_4 - and one class - C_j. The attributes are associated with the domains $D_1 = \{A_{1_1}, A_{1_2}, A_{1_3}\}$, $D_2 = \{A_{2_1}, A_{2_2},$

$A_{2_3}\}$, $D_3 = \{A_{3_1}, A_{3_2}, A_{3_3}\}$ and $D_4 = \{A_{4_1}, A_{4_2}, A_{4_3}\}$, respectively and the classes are $C = \{Class_1, Class_2, Class_3\}$.

Figure 2 presents an antibody coded with k rules and each one is represented by 4 genes, where the first three genes indicate the index of the fuzzy sets of the attributes X_1, X_2, X_3 and X_4 and the fourth gene represents the class.

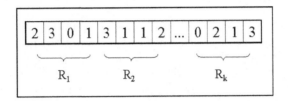

Fig. 2. Example of antibody

The fuzzy rule base coded in the antibody of the Figure 2 is as follow:

R_1: IF X_1 is A_{1_2} and X_2 is A_{2_3} and X_3 is *"don't care"*, THEN $Class_1$
R_2: IF X_1 is A_{1_3} and X_2 is A_{2_1} and X_3 is A_{3_1}, THEN $Class_2$
$\vdots$
R_k: IF X_1 is *"don't care"* and X_2 is A_{2_2} and X_3 is A_{3_1}, THEN $Class_3$

The use of *"don't care"* condition provides better generalization capacity of correctly classifying new patterns. Besides, the introduction of *"don't care"* has also an important effect on rule comprehensibility, once these rules have fewer attributes on the antecedent part. Short rules can be more easily understood by human beings than long rules with many attributes [18].

– Initial Population
The initial population is randomly generated. It is formed by random numbers that can assume values from 0 to q_i, where q_i is the number of fuzzy sets to represent the attribute a_i.

– Fitness Function
The fitness function is defined based on performance of the fuzzy rule base, calculated by the number of training patterns correctly classified, using the fuzzy reasoning method presented in section 2. The fitness function is expressed by:

$$\text{Fit}(Ab_i) = NPC(Ab_i) \tag{3}$$

where *NPC(Ab$_i$)* is the Number of Patterns Correctly Classified by the fuzzy rule base coded in the antibody Ab_i.

– Cloning
All antibodies of current population suffer a cloning process. The number of clones per antibody is proportional to its fitness value (affinity with antigen).

Higher fitness corresponds to a higher number of clones. The function used to implement this procedure is presented in equation (4).

$$C(Ab_i) = \begin{cases} Min\_C & \text{if Fit}(Ab_i) \leq (\text{Max\_Fit} * 0.3) \\ Max\_C & \text{if Fit}(Ab_i) \geq (\text{Max\_Fit} * 0.7) \\ Fit(Ab_i)/\beta & \text{otherwise} \end{cases} \qquad (4)$$

where Min_C and Max_C are the minimum and maximum number of clones, respectively. $Fit(Ab_i)$ is the fitness value of antibody Ab_i, Max_Fit is the highest fitness value found in the current iteration and β is a parameter that can vary during the process. The values 0.3 and 0.7 were obtained empirically by preliminary experiments.

– **Hypermutation**

The clone mutation rate is inversely proportional to its affinity with antigen. The mutation rate is given by:

$$Mut\_Rate(Ab_i) = Max\_Mut\_Rate * \frac{(Fit(Ab_i) - Max\_Fit)}{(Min\_Fit - Max\_Fit)} \qquad (5)$$

where,
$Mut\_Rate(Ab_i)$ is the mutation rate for clone i;
Max_Mut_Rate is the highest value that mutation rate can assume;
$Fit(Ab_i)$ is the fitness of clone i;
Max_Fit is the highest fitness value found in the current iteration;
Min_Fit is the lowest fitness value found in the current iteration.

– **Suppression**

In this phase, similar antibodies are eliminated in order to avoid redundancy and thus maintain diversity. This stage is very important to generate different candidates to compose the ensemble in the future.

The degree of similarity between the antibodies is measured based on their individual outputs. If two or more classifiers classify correctly the same patters and also misclassify the same patterns, the degree of similarity is maximum. Antibodies with a degree of similarity above a certain threshold are eliminated from population, being kept only the one with higher fitness.

– **Stopping Condition**

In computer simulations of this work, we used the maximum number of generations as stopping condition.

5   Ensemble of Fuzzy Classification Systems

Ensemble [11] [19] is a learning paradigm where alternative proposals, called components of the ensemble, combine their individual outputs to derive a solution to a given problem. The reasons for combining multiple components are

compelling, because different components may implicitly represent different useful aspects of the intended solution. Figure 3 depicts a general ensemble framework. Suppose it is operating as an ensemble of classifiers. Each component of
the ensemble is a classifier (e.g., neural network, decision tree, rule-based classifier) independently proposed and they can operate in isolation. For each input x,
the output y_i, $i=1...M$, generated by the M components is combined to produce
the ensemble output, y.

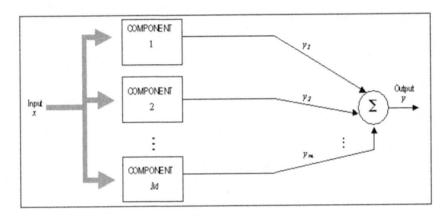

Fig. 3. Scheme of an ensemble

The good performance of an ensemble relies on the quality and diversity
of its components. The quality of an available component is related to its performance when applied in isolation and the components are considered diverse
when they diverge on the individual output, proposing distinct classes for the
same input values. Of course, two high-performance classifiers must provide the
same outcome to the great majority of the input patterns. So the divergence
will be expressed solely as a function of the patterns incorrectly classified. To
be useful as components of an ensemble the two classifiers should disagree when
they take wrong decisions [23].

In this work we investigate the ensemble of fuzzy classification systems, in
order to obtain a more accurate and robust classifier. Ensemble of fuzzy system
have been explored for regression and classification problems and very good
results are reported in the literature [24] [25].

The construction of an ensemble involves 3 stages: generation of components,
selection of components and combination of components. Firstly, the dataset
must be divided into 4 subsets: training, validation, selection and test.

The generation of components is performed by means of the Copt-aiNet
algorithm, once this immune algorithm is able to produce diverse and high-
quality solutions, as presented in the previous sections. In this stage the training
dataset is adopted.

As soon as the components are created, we have to select the most useful to compose the ensemble. A reason for not adding all generated classifiers in the ensemble is that some ensemble candidates may degrade the performance of the whole ensemble [26]. The selection process adopted here consists of sorting the candidates to compose the ensemble according to the performance of each one when considered in isolation and taking the validation dataset. The candidate with the best performance is considered as the first component of the ensemble. The next candidate (the one with the second best performance) is then added to the ensemble. If the performance of the ensemble w.r.t. the selection dataset is improved, then the ensemble has now two components. Otherwise, the newly-inserted candidate is extracted from the ensemble. The same procedure should be performed considering the remaining candidates, one after the other.

After selecting the components of the ensemble, the next step is to define how to combine the individual outputs into just one. We use the majority voting method so that a pattern is classified in the class C_j if C_j is the individual output of the majority of components. The ensemble performance is measured w.r.t. the test dataset.

6   Experimental Results

In order to evaluate the performance of the proposed immune-inspired algorithm for generation of fuzzy rule bases, the algorithm was applied to one artificial dataset, available on http://www.lbic.fee.unicamp.br/homepage/downloads/ar tificial.txt, and to two well-known classification problems from UCI Repository of Machine Learning Databases [27].

Table 1 summarizes the knowledge domain characteristics giving the total number of instances, the number of attributes, and the number of classes per dataset. The Bupa and Iris datasets are well-known and frequently used in machine learning tasks. The Artificial dataset was created to perform preliminary experiments. Figure 4 gives a graphical representation of this dataset.

Table 1. Datasets Characteristics

Dataset	# Instances	# Attributes	# Classes
Artificial	3000	2	3
Bupa	345	6	2
Iris	150	4	3

Each dataset was partitioned according to section 5 as follows: 60% for training, 10% for validation, 10% for selection and 20% for test. This partitioning was performed randomly in each run of the algorithm. For each dataset, we applied the algorithm 10 times so that you have 10 distinct partitions at each execution.

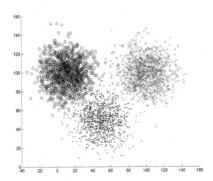

Fig. 4. Artificial Dataset

Firstly, we demonstrate the ability of Copt-aiNet for designing fuzzy classification systems with high performance. For all experiments, the maximum number of generations was 1000.

Table 2 presents an average of the results over 10 executions for test data using the best classifier obtained. The 4th column of Table 2 is the average number of rules per rule base. Note that the rule bases are composed of a few number of fuzzy rules.

Table 2. Results using a single fuzzy classifier

Dataset	Classif.(%)	Std. Dev.	# Rules
Artificial	97.1	1.87	5
Bupa	68.6	1.24	10
Iris	93.5	0.96	6

From Table 2 we can see that the immune algorithm is able to generate fuzzy systems with a satisfactory level of accuracy. For Bupa and Iris datasets, the results obtained are better or very close to results from other fuzzy classification systems reported in the literature. A fuzzy system generated by an AIS in [21] achieved 57.4% of accuracy in Bupa dataset. A genetic fuzzy system was applied to Iris dataset classifying correctly 96.4% of test patterns in [28].

As expected, the Copt-aiNet found not only one but many good fuzzy classification systems in a single run. The individual performance of each fuzzy classifier for Iris dataset in the best run is shown in Table 3.

The fuzzy rule base of the best classifier of Table 3 is presented below. The terms sl, sw, pl and pw represent the attributes sepal length, sepal width, petal length and petal width, respectively. Each one is represented by 3 fuzzy sets of triangular shape: low, medium, and high.

Table 3. Results using a single fuzzy classifier

Fuzzy Classifier	Classif.(%)	Std. Dev.	# Rules
1	93.0	0.96	6
2	92.4	0.94	6
3	92.4	0.96	8
4	91.1	0.94	5
5	90.7	0.92	4
6	93.5	0.96	6

R_1: IF sl is low AND sw is high AND pl is high AND pw is low THEN Iris-Setosa

R_2: IF sl is high AND sw is medium AND pl is medium AND pw is low THEN Iris-Setosa

R_3: IF sl is *"don't care"* AND sw is low AND pl is *"don't care"* AND pw is medium THEN Iris-Versicolor

R_4: IF sl is low AND sw is *"don't care"* AND pl is high AND pw is high THEN Iris-Virginica

R_5: IF sl is high AND sw is low AND pl is medium AND pw is low THEN Iris-Setosa

R_6: IF sl is high AND sw is *"don't care"* AND pl is medium AND pw is high THEN Iris-Setosa

With multiple high-performance fuzzy classifiers we can combine the individual output of these classifiers as explained in section 5, aiming to achieve an improvement in performance. The performance of the obtained ensembles can be seen in Table 4. The average number of ensemble components is presented in the fourth column.

From Table 4, we can see that the ensemble of fuzzy classifier systems improved the classification accuracy, outperforming the single best classifier. Albeit

Table 4. Results using ensemble

Dataset	Classif.(%)	Std. Dev.	# Components
Artificial	98.8	0.90	3
Bupa	74.4	0.78	11
Iris	97.2	1.02	7

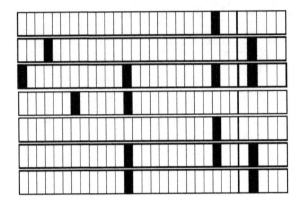

Fig. 5. Individual errors for the Iris test dataset

there are some extra computational requirements underlying ensemble construction, they are justified in the sense of the good performance achieved.

To provide a better visualization of the decisions taken, individual errors made by each classifier on each example of the Iris test dataset are presented in Figure 5. White squares represent patterns correctly classified while black squares mark errors. The patterns are disposed along the horizontal axis and the classifiers vertically.

Figure 5 reinforces that the combination of classifiers leads to more robust results, since the decision is always taken by the majority of them. Although there are scattered errors, the final performance of the combined classifiers tends to filter out a portion of them. This picture also shows that the obtained classifiers have similar difficulties to classify correctly the patterns 13, 23, and 27.

7   Concluding Remarks

This work proposed an immune-based learning method for obtaining fuzzy classification systems. From numerical data and with membership functions defined previously, the algorithm evolves a population of fuzzy rule bases using the clonal selection, hypermutation and immune network principles. The multimodal characteristic of the presented algorithm allows many high-performance and diverse solutions to be achieved. Therefore a combination of individual outputs of the generated fuzzy systems is performed, giving rise to ensembles with improved classification rates.

Experiments on three datasets have demonstrated that the immune algorithm presented here is able to generate accurate fuzzy systems and that ensembles of fuzzy classifiers have outperformed the single best classifier.

The experimental results can be further improved in several aspects. For example, other formats for the membership functions may be considered, together with a different fuzzy reasoning method and other mechanisms for ensemble construction. We also intend to apply the proposed methodology to datasets with higher dimensionality, in order to verify the scalability of the algorithm.

Acknowledgments. This work has been supported by grants from Fapesp, Capes, and CNPq.

References

1. G. Klir and B. Yuan, "Fuzzy Sets and Fuzzy Logic - Theory and Applications", Prentice-Hall, 1995.
2. W. Pedrycz and F. Gomide, "An Introduction to Fuzzy Sets: Analysis and Design", MIT Press, 1998.
3. O. Cordón, F. Herrera, F. Gomide, F. Hoffmann and L. Magdalena, "Ten years of genetic-fuzzy systems: a current framework and new trends", *Proceedings of Joint 9th IFSA World Congress and 20th NAFIPS International Conference*, pp. 1241-1246, Vancouver, Canada, 2001.
4. O. Cordón, F. Herrera, F. Hoffmann and L. Magdalena, "Genetic Fuzzy Systems. Evolutionary tuning and learning of fuzzy knowledge bases", vol. 19 of Advances in Fuzzy Systems: Applications and Theory, World Scientific, 2001.
5. Y. Yuan and H. Zhuang, "A genetic algorithm for generating fuzzy classification rules", *Fuzzy Sets and Systems*, vol. 84, no. 4, pp. 1-19, 1996.
6. D. E. Goldberg and J. J. Richardson, "Genetic algorithms with sharing for multimodal function optimization", Proceedings of the 2nd International Conference on Genetic Algorithms, pp. 41-49, Cambridge, 1987.
7. P. Bonissone, N. Eklund and K. Goebel, "Using an Ensemble of Classifiers to Audit a Production Classifier", Proceedings of the 6th International Workshop on Multiple Classifier Systems, Monterey, CA, June 13 -1, 2005.
8. D. Dasgupta (ed.), "Artificial Immune Systems and Their Applications", Springer-Verlag, 1999.
9. L. N. de Castro and J. Timmis, "An Introduction to Artificial Immune Systems: A New Computational Intelligence Paradigm", Springer-Verlag, 2002.
10. L. C. T. Gomes, J. S. de Sousa, G. B. Bezerra, L. N. de Castro and F. J. Von Zuben, "Copt-aiNet and the Gene Ordering Problem", In: Second Brazilian Workshop on Bioinformatics, Macaé, Brazil, 2003.
11. L. K. Hansen and P. Salamon, "Neural network ensembles", IEEE Transactions on Pattern Analysis and Machine Intelligence, vol. 12, pp. 993-1001, 1990.
12. D. Opitz and J. Shavlik, "Generating accurate and diverse members of a neural network ensemble", In D. Touretsky, M. Mozer, and M. Hasselmo (Eds.), Advances in Neural Information Processing Systems, vol. 8, pp. 535-541, MIT Press, 1996.
13. O. Cordón, M. J. del Jesus and F. Herrera, "A proposal on reasoning methods in fuzzy rule-based classification systems", *International Journal of Approximate Reasoning*, vol. 20, pp. 21-45, 2001.
14. L. N. de Castro and F. J. Von Zuben, "aiNet: An Artificial Immune Network for Data Analysis", in Data Mining: A Heuristic Approach, H. A. Abbass, R. A. Sarker, and C. S. Newton (eds.), Idea Group Publishing, USA, Chapter XII, pp. 231-259, 2001.
15. L. N. de Castro and J. I. Timmis, "An Artificial Immune Network for Multimodal Function Optimization", Proceedings of IEEE Congress of Evolutionary Computation, vol. 1, pp. 699-674, Hawaii, 2002.

482   P.D. Castro et al.

16. G. L. Ada and G. J. V. Nossal, "The Clonal Selection Theory", Scientific American, vol. 257, no. 2, pp. 50-57, 1987.
17. N. K. Jerne, "Towards a Network Theory of the Immune System", Ann. Immunol. (Inst. Pasteur) 125C, pp. 373-389, 1974.
18. Alex A. Freitas, "Data Mining and Knowledge Discovery with Evolutionary Algorithms", Springer-Verlag New York, Secaucus, NJ, USA, 2002.
19. A. Krogh and J. Vedelsby, "Neural Network Ensembles, Cross Validation, and Active Learning", in G. Tesauro, D. Touretzky, and T. Leen (Eds.), Advances in Neural Information Processing System, vol. 7, pp. 231-238, MIT Press, 1994.
20. F. Glover and M. Laguna, "Tabu Search", Kluwer Academic Publishers, 1998.
21. R. T. Alves, M. R. B. Delgado, H. S. Lopes and A. Freitas, "Induction of Fuzzy Classification Rules with an Artificial Immune System",Proceedings of Brazilian Symposium on Neural Networks, Brazil, 2004.
22. H. A. Camargo, M. G. Pires and P. A. D. Castro. "Genetic Design of Fuzzy Knowledge Bases - a study of different approaches", Proceedings of 23rd IEEE International Conference of NAFIPS, vol. 2, pp. 954-959, Canada, 2004.
23. M.P. Perrone and L.N. Cooper, "When networks disagree: Ensemble method for neural networks", In R.J. Mammone (ed.), Neural Networks for Speech and Image processing. Chapman-Hall, 1993.
24. C. A. M. Lima, A. L. V. Coelho and F. J. Von Zuben, "Fuzzy Systems Design via Ensembles of ANFIS", Proceedings of the IEEE International Conference on Fuzzy Systems (FUZZ-IEEE2002), vol. 1, pp. 506-511, Hawaii, 2002.
25. H. Ishibuchi and T. Yamamoto, "Evolutionary Multi-objective Optimization for Generating an Ensemble of Fuzzy Rule-Based Classifiers", Proc. of the Genetic and Evolutionary Computation Conference, pp. 1077-1088, USA, 2003.
26. Z. H. Zhou, J. Wu and W. Tang, "Ensembling Neural Networks: Many Could Be Better Than All", Artificial Intelligence, vol. 137, no. 1-2, pp. 239-263, 2002.
27. C. L. Blake and C. J. Merz. UCI Repository of machine learning databases [http://www.ics.uci.edu/m̃learn/MLRepository.html], Irvine, CA: University of California, Department of Information and Computer Science", 1998.
28. Hisao Ishibuchi and Takashi Yamamoto, "Fuzzy rule selection by multi-objective genetic local search algorithms and rule evaluation measures in data mining", *Fuzzy Sets and Systems*, vol. 141, pp. 59-88, 2004.

Application Areas of AIS: The Past, The Present and The Future

Emma Hart[1] and Jonathan Timmis[2]

[1] School of Computing, Napier University
e.hart@napier.ac.uk
[2] Departments of Electronics and Computer Science, University of York
jt@york.ac.uk

Abstract. After a decade of research into the area of Artificial Immune Systems, it is worthwhile to take a step back and reflect on the contributions that the paradigm has brought to the application areas to which it has been applied. Undeniably, there have been a lot of successful stories — however, if the field is to advance in the future and really carve out its own distinctive niche, then it is necessary to be able to illustrate that there are clear benefits to be obtained by applying this paradigm rather than others. This paper attempts to take stock of the application areas that have been tackled in the past, and ask the difficult question "was it worth it ?". We then attempt to suggest a set of problem features that we believe will allow the true potential of the immunological system to be exploited in computational systems, and define a unique niche for AIS.

1 Introduction

The AIS community has been vibrant and active for a number of years now, producing a prolific amount of research ranging from modelling the natural immune system, solving artificial or bench-mark problems, to tackling real-world applications, using an equally diverse set of immune-inspired algorithms. Whilst it is natural, and indeed healthy, for a somewhat scattergun approach to be taken in the early days of developing any new paradigm, in the sense that high-level, often naive metaphors are selected and applied to problem areas that have often been tackled with other paradigms, there comes a point at which research effort needs to have a more coherent focus in order to more clearly define the field, and allow it to go forward and be fully exploited. We argue that this point has now been reached in the AIS world — with a solid foundation of published work to build on, the time has come to try and define the role that AIS can play and the type of applications that will really allow its potential to be realised.

Without a doubt there have been a lot of successful applications of AIS, and these should not be ignored. However, at this point, there are still no exemplars that really stand out as instances of successfully applying an AIS to a hard, real-world problems, or of AIS being used in industry. This is in contrast for example to the field of Evolutionary Algorithms, where at the most recent flagship conference in the field, GECCO 2004 [5], there were 38 papers describing the applications of EAs

C. Jacob et al. (Eds.): ICARIS 2005, LNCS 3627, pp. 483–497, 2005.

to real-world problems, and the EVONET repository [3] is able to list 39 examples of *Evolution at Work*, i.e practical applications of EAs. On the one hand, this is somewhat of an unfair comparison, given the relative time-periods that the two fields have been active, however it illustrates the importance of focussing research effort in the next few years in order to provide hard evidence of a distinctive niche for AIS.

For any new paradigm to prove itself is always a difficult task — there is a lot of good competition from existing tried and tested algorithms. There has perhaps been a natural tendency for AIS to be compared to other biologically inspired paradigms such as Evolutionary Algorithms, Neural-networks, and to other more traditional classification or clustering algorithms. Scientifically, it is essential that such comparisons to be made; however, we argue that it is not sufficient for AIS simply to outperform other algorithms on any given set of problem instances to be declared useful. For a start, test instances (particularly benchmarks) are not necessarily difficult, and any number of other problem instances can be generated on which performance will be unknown. Secondly, in the light of the no-free lunch theorem [47], we cannot expect any one algorithm to outperform all others given all possible problem instances. We argue that for a paradigm to be truly successful, it should contain features that *are not present* in other paradigms and thus make it distinctive. In this position paper, we hope to extract some general features of problems that we believe will allow AIS to really bring some benefit, and thus distinguish it from other techniques. We suggest that the way forward for AIS is in part a focussed attempt to carefully select application areas based on mapping problem features to mechanisms exhibited by the IS, taking the problem-oriented perspective outlined by example in [38,22,10], and discussed further in section 4.2. However, we emphasise that application development needs to be under-pinned with a continuing line of research into the theoretical basis of AIS and with the overriding need for extraction of novel and accurate metaphors from immunology.

2   Survey of Existing Application Areas

In order to place the following discussions in context, we first present a general review of application areas to which AIS has currently been applied. The following brief summary is based in part on a bibliography produced by De Castro [14], used in a tutorial at ICARIS 2004 [15] on Engineering Application of AIS. The information contained in this tutorial has been expanded to include references from ICARIS 2004 [4] and is available from [1]. A useful summary of application areas can also be found in [16] though as this was produced in 2000 it is slightly outdated. Whilst we stress that it does not represent all publications in the AIS domain, we believe it is reflective of the general picture. Note that this section does not describe in detail the application areas that AIS has been applied to. The reader is referred to the above publications for further information — the section is intended to provide an overview of the field as a whole and provide a basis for the following discussion.

Figure 1 therefore shows a summary of 97 papers which have been classified into 12 headings. Note that the categories are chosen simply to reflect the natural grouping of papers and in some cases are rather broad, and in others very narrow. For example, computer security and virus detection could be classified as examples of anomaly detection, and the majority of the bio-informatics papers are essentially performing classification or clustering. However, where more than one paper has been written on a particular application area, these papers have been grouped together. Also, in several cases there are multiple papers published over a period of time by the same authors on the same application; in this case, only one paper per author is included in the list, as the intention is to reflect the diversity of applications and give some indication of the effort being directed towards a particular application area.

In brief, papers falling under the heading *Anomaly Detection* include a diverse range of topic areas, ranging for example from detection of temperature fluctuations in refrigeration units [41] to aircraft fault detection [13]. As previously mentioned, computer security and virus detection applications could also be classified under this heading; these sub-headings speak for themselves as to the type of application covered. Some specific features of anomaly detection applications are discussed in more detail in section 3.1.

A very large number of papers fall under the general heading of *Learning*. Learning can generally be understood to be the process of acquiring knowledge from experience and being able to re-apply that knowledge to previously unseen problem instances — this generic title applies to a variety of sub-topics such as pattern recognition, concept-learning, and supervised and unsupervised versions of clustering data and classifying data. Papers relating to *clustering and classification* have been separated out from the general learning topic as a sub-topic where they relate specifically to clustering or classifying a particular data-set and have been compared to conventional classification techniques, and have been benchmarked used the standard accepted quality tests in data-mining such as classification accuracy. Almost all clustering applications which have gone beyond the conceptual stage focus on benchmark sets of data such as those available from the UCI repository which are static in nature, although there are few attempts to apply immune-based algorithms to dynamic data, e.g [26,33].

As previously mentioned, papers relating to *bio-informatics* have also been separated a distinct topic, as these form a natural group; however, it is important to realise that this topic essentially is just another set of applications of clustering algorithms — again the data being clustered is static in nature.

Combinatoric Optimisation covers a number of real-world application areas such as travelling salesman problems, scheduling (including inventory and job-shop scheduling), and routing problems. Typically, the publications report results on benchmark problem instances rather than real-world problem instances.

Robotic applications tend to be based on controlling simulated robots around small, artificial environments, generally addressing the problem of behaviour arbitration and autonomous navigation, although work by [28] attempts to lay a foundation for using an AIS to provide the basis of an architecture for a robot to acquire

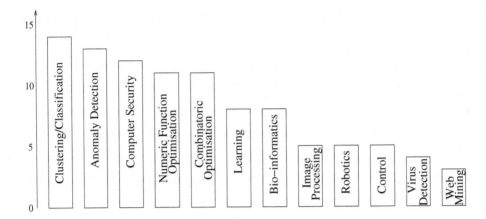

Fig. 1. Summary of Application Areas of AIS

new, more complex skills throughout its lifetime. *Adaptive control systems* form a related category of papers, for example pertaining to controlling a robotic arm [32]. The small topics of *Image Processing* and *Web-Mining* are self-evident.

2.1   Summary of Application Areas

Having presented the above categorisations of application areas, it seems that application areas that have been addressed by AIS techniques can be broadly summarised as (1) Learning (2) Anomaly Detection and (3) Optimisation. Thus, *learning* includes clustering, classification and pattern recognition, robotic and control applications; *Anomaly Detection* includes fault detection and computer and network security applications, and *Optimisation* includes real-world problems which essentially boil down to combinatoric and also numeric function optimisation. To some extent, the fact that applications of AIS have fallen into the above categories is somewhat an accident of history. Early immune-based algorithms, proposed in the main by computer scientists with little if any immunological background, seized on what appeared to be be the obvious functions of the immune system as a defensive system, able to perform pattern recognition and learn over time. Hence, although very early work in the area was performed from an interdisciplinary slant, e.g. [9], there has been a tendency to *reason by metaphor* [38], and apply simplistic models such as clonal selection, immune-networks and negative-selection in isolation to problems which appear at first glance to be amenable to such techniques. Furthermore, again perhaps by accident, many of the AIS practitioners arrive in the field by way of working in other biologically inspired fields such as Evolutionary Computing, and thus there is a tendency to apply AIS algorithms to the same problems as have been tackled in other domains (e.g. optimisation), which often results in un-natural problem representations, and rather contrived mechanisms for mapping a problem to an AIS algorithm.

3   "Was It Worth It " - A Look at the Added Value of the AIS

It is now pertinent to re-evaluate the application of immune algorithms to the above application areas, and question whether there is really any added value in applying AIS to the three areas listed above. Again we re-iterate that there is no doubt that AIS has been successful in these areas; however, we question as to whether they AIS brings any benefits that could not have been gained from applying a different sort of algorithm. Recall the seminal list of features of an AIS, originally due to Dasgupta in [12] and so often quoted in AIS publications. This defines the features of an immune system that are relevant from a computational perspective as: recognition, feature extraction, diversity, learning, memory, distributed detection, self-regulation, thresholds, co-stimulation, dynamic protection and probabilistic detection. Although later in we question as to whether the features on this list really distinguish an AIS from many other paradigms, it is useful to bear in mind during the following analysis of the three application areas.

3.1   Anomaly Detection

Anomaly detection has been an area of application that has found favor with the AIS practitioner. Such techniques are required to decide whether an unknown test sample is produced by the underlying probability distribution that corresponds to the training set of normal examples. Typically, only a single class is available on which to train the system. The goal of these immune inspired system was to take examples from one class (usually what was considered to be normal operational data) and generate a set of detectors that was capable of identifying when the *normal* or *known* system had changed, thus indicating a possible intrusion.

The early pioneering work of Forrest et al [21] led to a great deal of research and proposal of immune inspired anomaly detection systems [20]. Results reported in these works, did hint at the possibility that the immune approach was useful to some degree as both known and novel intrusions could be detected. This was extended by work of [31], who combined the clonal selection algorithm with a negative selection algorithm to help reduce the false positive rates. The interest of this immune approach was in part, due to the fact that it appeared possible to train a system with only a single class of examples and the intuitive link between the role of the natural immune system as the "great protector" and the development of intrusion detection systems. Notable work in [8] proposed the *r-chunk* matching rule which was to replace the computational expensive *r-contiguous bits* matching rule that had *dogged* the approaches to date. The *r-chunk* rule made it computationally more efficient to generate a set of detectors of the non-self space (in hamming shape space) and later computationally more efficient methods were developed in real-valued shape space [25,29], again based on only a single class of examples. This potentially made the use of the immune approach more attractive, as the main issue that had been raised to date was one of scalability with respect to the size of the *normal* data.

Recent work in [19], proposed a formal framework for the negative selection approach, and when one examines this work, it is possible to see hints that the *r-chunk* may well suffer certain scaling problems. Indeed, this has now been confirmed by [39,40] who present an in-depth theoretical analysis of the negative selection algorithm over real and hamming shape spaces. The investigations reveal that defined over the hamming shape-space, the approach is not well suited for real-world anomaly detection problems. Problems arise with the generated detector set which under-fits exponentially for small values of r (where r is the size of the chunk. They suggest that in order avoid this under-fitting behavior, the matching threshold value r must lie near l (the length of the string). However, they point out that this has a consequence. This is that the detector generation process is once again infeasible, since all proposed detector generating algorithms have a runtime complexity which is exponential in r. In addition to their theoretical arguments, they undertook a simple study of comparison between the negative selection approaches on a one-class support vector machine (SVM) [34]. When comparing the work of [29], (the real-valued negative selection algorithm with variable-sized detectors) results revealed, that the classification performance of the method not only crucially depended on the size of the variable region, but results from the one-class SVM provides as good, if not better results. In addition, they noted that in order to tune the parameters of the system by [29] it was necessary to have the second class, as the probability distribution of this class impacted a great deal on the overall performance of the system.

So, from a "value added" perspective, at present it is not clear from the literature that the immune approach offers anything. It is necessary to use two classes of data to train and tune the system, a high false positive rate seems to blight systems and the computational complexity of generating detectors seems prohibitive in large dimensional data sets. In order to overcome some of these shortfalls, work proposed in [6] and later expanded on in [7] proposes the adoption of the *danger theory* approach. The authors claim that it should be possible to move away from the need to define what is *normal* for a system, and dynamically identify *normal* through the adoption of danger signals and context dependent responses, however these ideas have yet to be proven in practice. Therefore, despite that the fact that at first glance, anomaly detection does appear to map to many of the features in the list given at the start of this section; i.e the problems are often distributed in nature, require feature extraction, recognition, memory and continuous learning, immunology has not yet provided all the answers.

3.2   Optimisation

A number of publications relate to to function optimisation problems, often declaring some success when compared against other state-of-the-art algorithms. The majority of these publications are based on the application of the clonal selection principle, resulting in a number of algorithms such as Clonalg algorithm [17], opt-AINET [18] and the B-Cell algorithm [42]. Thus, for example, [11] applies Clonalg with a variety of modified hyper-mutation operators to solving static 'trap functions" — complex but toy problems often used in evolutionary algorithm trap investigations, and [42] compare versions of opt-AINET and the B-Cell algorithm to a variety of optimisation functions of various dimensions found in the literature.

All of these algorithms essentially evolve solutions to problems via repeated application of a cloning, mutation and selection cycle to a population of candidate solutions (B Cells). A single antigen represents some function to be optimised, and good solutions are allowed to remain in the population, mimicking the memory cell mechanisms believed to exists in the natural immune system. The authors of optAINET state that it is characterised by the following features; it performs exploitation and exploration of the search space, it can determine the locations of multiple optima, it maintains many optimal solutions, and has defined stopping criteria. The main differences between this and Clonalg or the B-Cell algorithm lie in whether or not they maintain a static or adaptive population size, whether or not they include elitist mechanisms and in type of mutation operators they use. Anyone familiar with the EA literature will recognise all of these features as equally applicable to an EA, and even the differences between the immune algorithms are recognisable as differences between the various flavours of EA. We further conjecture that the only two features of Dasgupta's list that recommended immune-algorithms as a mechanism for performing function optimisation are that the algorithms require a diversity mechanism and a memory mechanism — however, these features are common components of many other algorithms. Therefore, we conjecture that there is no added value in applying an immune algorithm to static function optimisation problems. Admittedly, the B-Cell algorithm described has been found to use significantly fewer evaluations than a hybrid GA on some problems [42], however, we hypothesise that static function optimisation will not prove to be the Holy Grail of immune algorithms. Similar arguments apply to the use of AIS in Combinatorial Optimisation Problems. Thus, although AIS algorithms have provided superior results on benchmark job-shop scheduling problems when compared to other state-of-the art optimisation algorithms such as GRASP, these are again static problems, in which there is no obvious benefit to be gained from applying an AIS.

Perhaps a more obvious optimisation area is that of *dynamic* function optimisation. In these problems, the goal is to find and track a continuously moving target — this at least fits better with the view of the immune system as a dynamic, and continuously adapting system. Gaspar and Collard [23] used a network-based AIS to perform dynamic function optimisation. Walker *et al* [45] have applied a version of Clonalg to a number of dynamic optimisation problems which they compare to an evolutionary strategy and find that generally an evolutionary strategy can optimise more quickly than the clonal selection algorithm. Recently, Kelsey *et al* [30] have adapted the B-Cell algorithm to perform dynamic optimisation, and found that the fast adaptable nature of the algorithm enabled the tracking of multiple moving optima. Although there is little other work in this area, we also hypothesise that continuing research effort will reveal little of value; the immune system is not a natural model for extracting metaphors to perform optimisation.

There is perhaps a caveat to the above statements. We are aware of work by Clark *et al* who have produced a theoretical analysis of the B-Cell algorithm discussed above. We believe this paper is in review for ICARIS 2005. This work provides a complete and exact model of the B-cell algorithm with a proof of convergence. In addition, from their model, it would appear that it is possible to locate the optimum mutation rate for a given function. In addition, work by [44] provides a complete proof for their multi-objective immune inspired algorithm. Thus, as there have been no convincing theoretical analyses that enable performance prediction in the EA world, there is perhaps value in applying a properly understood algorithm to a problem, regardless of the nature of the problem.

3.3   Clustering and Classification

Immune-based algorithms which perform clustering make up a large number of the application areas shown in figure 1. These range from supervised algorithms such as AIRS [46] and Carter, to aiNET [18] and algorithms based on idiotypic network models such as those of Neal and Timmis [33]. However, as already stated, the application areas to which these models are to clustering or classifying *static* data sets, where comparable or improved performance is achieved on many datasets, when compared to traditional algorithms. Classification/clustering require *feature extraction, recognition* and *learning* — key features of the AIS — however, we conjecture that these are also key features of any machine-learning algorithms, and that there are no unique features of the *problem domain* that indicate an AIS based algorithm can offer anything over and above the more traditional machine learning algorithms. One potential distinguishing feature of the IS which *has* been exploited in classification is its *distributed* nature, which is used to advantage by Watkins [46] in a parallel version of AIRS.

A more promising application area for AIS may lie in the area of *dynamic* clustering or classification. Advances in technology now make it incredibly straightforward for huge amounts of data to be collected and stored cheaply and easily, and hence many companies and researchers now routinely collect data on a daily or even hourly basis. By tracking patterns and trends in the data, companies may be able to gain a competitive advantage. There are some existing learning algorithms which can cluster dynamic data — however, in an era of ever increasing computational processing power coupled with continually decreasing costs, it is pertinent to question why dynamic algorithms need even to be considered for time-varying problems. It is trivial for example to re-apply established "static" algorithms at each time-instant in a dynamic problem to the data in-hand; however, this type of approach totally disregards any information captured in either the current information or in previous time-series, therefore may miss vital clues. Therefore, we propose that AIS algorithms by definition, incorporate some form of memory, and can therefore outperform other state-of-the-art learning systems which are purely reactive. Most learning systems have very limited memory and hence no mechanism to balance the need to keep a record of currently under-used knowledge acquired in the past against the need to store newly-acquired knowledge that is valuable in the current climate.

Note that there is some existing, although limited, work in this area. Neals algorithm [33] is meta-stable in that it can in theory be continuously applied to a data-set. The work of Hart [26] models a self-organising system which is able to dynamically cluster moving data, whilst maintaining some memory of the past, but has only been tested with artificial data-sets. Work by Secker et al [35] developed a dynamic supervised learning algorithm for the filter of emails, and work by Kim and Bentley [31] a dynamic classification algorithm for use in intrusion detection.

4   A New Approach to AIS

The above discussion has shed a rather gloomy light on future of AIS in solving real-world applications. Perhaps this is a suitable point to take a step backwards and first re-evaluate our approach to designing AIS algorithms, as well as attempting to define what kind of applications they may be suitable for. With this in mind, we take brief look at both sides of the coin and take first an algorithm-oriented and then a problem-oriented view of the situation.

4.1   A Conceptual Framework for Algorithm Development

Work by Stepney el. al [38] proposes a conceptual framework that allows for the development of more biologically grounded AIS, through the adoption of an interdisciplinary approach. Metaphors employed have typically been simple, but somewhat effective. However, as proposed in [38], through greater interaction between computer scientists, engineers, biologists and mathematicians, better insights into the workings of the immune system, and the applicability (or otherwise) of the AIS paradigm will be gained. These interactions should be rooted in a sound methodology in order to fully exploit the synergy. The basic outline of the approach proposed by Stepney et al. is to first *probe* the biological system in question. When one probes such a system, one has to bear in mind what it is you want to extract or observe. For example, you may be interested in initiation of danger signals, so one would undertake experimentation to observe that. This process is then followed by the development of suitable mathematical models. Properties of the system can then be modelled at a mathematical level, which allows for possible insights into the biological model that are not possible with "wet lab" experiments. From this, it is then possible to construct a computation model, based on the mathematical model. The creation of the computational model allows for the execution of the model, to observe and gain insight into the workings of the model. This model can then more easily be abstracted into an algorithm, or set of algorithms for deployment in an application area. Clearly, this is an iterative process, that allows for a great deal of interaction between all stages. Arising from this may be various *computational frameworks* that are suitable for instantiation into applications.

Stepney *et al* then go onto propose that once such frameworks are developed, it is possible to ask suitably posed *meta-questions* about the framework, that may give attention to interesting properties. The questions are concerned with openness (e.g. how much continual growth or development is required within the system), diversity (e.g how many agents are required), interaction (e.g. level of communication between agents), structure (e.g are the different levels required between agents) and scale (e.g how many agents are required). These are known as the ODISS questions. The potential benefit of adopting this approach is clear not only do all disciplines benefit from such work, but the immune algorithms developed at the end of the process will, all being well, be more grounded in the immunology than the simple *observe, implement* approach so dominant in the AIS literature today.

4.2   A Problem Oriented Perspective

Freitas and Timmis [22] outline the need to consider carefully the application domain when developing AIS. They review the role AIS have played in the development of a number of machine learning tasks, including that of classification. However, Freitas and Timmis point out that there is a lack of appreciation for possible inductive bias within algorithms and positional bias within the choice of representation and affinity measures. Indeed, this observation is reinforced by the work of Hart and Ross [27] with the development of their simple immune network simulator with various affinity metrics. They make the argument that seemingly generic AIS algorithms, are maybe not so generic after all, and each has to be tailored to specific application areas. This may be facilitated by the development of more theoretical aspects of AIS, which will help us to understand how, when and where to apply various AIS techniques.

It should be noted that there have been some previous attempts at providing *design principles* for immune systems, such as work by Segal et al. [36], Bersini and Varela [10] and Somayaji *et al* [37] (which was specifically focussed on design of computer immune systems). However, work by Segal, whilst extremely interesting, focussed primarily on network signalling, and did not provide a comprehensive set of general design principles, or provide any test application areas for those principles. Work by Bersini, focussed on the immune network and *self assertion* ideas of the immune system to create his design principles and whilst being more concrete, are still quite high level. We assert that these potentially useful principles need to be tested in various application areas, and refined to allow for the creation of not only a generic set of AIS design principles that are useful to the community, but also specific ones for specific application areas. With this, may come a better understanding of how to apply AIS, and not fall into the traps highlighted by Freitas and Timmis.

5   Suggestions as to the Way Forward

We have outlined what we believe to be the problems with the current applications to which AIS has been applied, from the perspective that although reasonably successful on a narrow range of problems, they do not add sufficient value over and above that which is offered by other paradigms to make them anything other than another tool in the engineers application tool-box. Although from some points of view, any tool is a worthwhile addition, we believe there is still a wealth of unexploited potential in the AIS domain. Adopting the methodology and problem oriented perspectives outlined above rather than the scatter gun approaches taken to date will surely help us tap into this potential. However, there are some crucial missing ingredients in our current perspectives in AIS that limit our current progress. Here we suggest three of the areas that we feel will play some part in defining the future of AIS — note that there will of course be several others.

The Innate Immune System. The natural immune system is known to comprise of two sub-systems, working in tandem with each other; the *innate* immune system, and the *adaptive* immune system. Almost without exception, the AIS community has chosen to model the adaptive immune system. This may partially reflect the historical interest in the adaptive immune system in the immunological community, which over a period of years, dismissed the innate system as the minor partner in the functioning of the immune system. Recently however there has been a resurgence of interest in the innate immune system in immunological circles — witness for example the work described in [24], and the influence it may have on the adaptive system. Directing some attention therefore towards understanding and modelling the innate system maybe prove fruitful in producing better immune-models. For example, we may choose to focus on a certain aspect such as signalling mechanisms within the innate immune system and apply the conceptual framework model to abstract useful mechanisms based on this.

Strikingly, one of the key problems identified in section 3 with optimisation and clustering applications is that immune algorithms are applied to *static* systems without any justification. Yet, the inspiration behind the algorithms applied to such systems is the *adaptive* immune system, where we model clonal selection and learning on relatively fast time-scales. Perhaps such applications areas should be re-evaluated in the light of what we can learn from modelling the *innate* immune system. Many creatures, e.g. the nematode worm have *only* an innate immune system and yet function perfectly well — perhaps in many cases we have been too ambitious by trying to model the complete immune system and could achieve equally impressive results by abstracting mechanisms from a more simplistic yet still incredible system.

The immune system does not operate in isolation. Living organisms show a remarkable ability to maintain homeostasis, that is, achieve a steady-state of internal body function in a varying environment. This is precisely what we wish to achieve in many practical anomaly detection systems, for example in maintaining a secure computing environment. In nature, this is made possible via the —em interaction of both a number of systems, for including the immune system, neural system and endocrine system, and via multiple components within each of these systems. Any one of these systems cannot and does not operate in isolation — this suggests that perhaps the true potential of modelling immune systems might only be achieved via combining them with other sub-systems. This is clearly an exciting new area of research to which attention should be paid. There has been some exploratory work in this area — [43] — yet much remains unknown. Furthermore, the fact that the immune system does not act in isolation gives us yet another important pointer; the immune system must be *embodied*. This fact has been acknowledged in robotic research for a long time, where it is well known that "there can be no intelligence without embodiment", however it is largely ignored in AIS research.

Life-long learning. Although many application papers allude to this aspect of the immune system in their introductory text, few systems have really attempted to capture this feature of the IS, and those that have exhibit only a weak version of this. For instance, some optimisation and clustering algorithms have been applied in dynamic environments. However, there has been no published work on problems which *naturally* require a system to *improve its own performance* over the course of a life-time, as a result of its own experience. As this feature of the IS clearly distinguishes it from most other biologically inspired paradigms such as EAs or neural-nets which produce a fixed solution (or solutions) to a problem and then terminate, choice of application areas should focus on those problems which naturally require continuous learning.

6   Conclusions: Features of AIS Applications

We summarise by proposing a list of features that draw together some of the preceding discussion and that we believe point to the way forward for AIS. Some of these features are currently absent in any of the AIS literature. Others, such as life-long learning, have been modelled in a limited sense. We emphasise that it is by the *combination* of these principles that a distinctive niche is carved for AIS.

1. They will exhibit *homeostasis*
2. They will benefit from interactions between *innate* and *adaptive* immune models
3. They will consists of *multiple, interacting, communicating components*
4. Components can be easily and naturally *distributed*
5. They will be required to perform *life-long learning*

An exciting example which represents a step forward in this direction is work currently in progress at the University of Kent, which proposes a technique that aims to prevent system down-time by detecting states that are precursors of system failure in Automated Teller Machines (ATM). This is achieved through the development of an immune inspired continuous learning approach for updating the set of error detectors in a system. Unlike the typical anomaly detection techniques discussed in section 3.1, this technique relies on the existence of sequences of states that represent the operational status of an ATM when errors are occurring (so not when the ATM is operating within normal bounds). The adaptable error detection process is able to identify those sequences that might contain fatal states and identify potential sequences that might lead to system failure. The system is embodied, distributed, has multiple components and its purpose is to maintain homeostasis in a distributed ATM network, therefore must exhibit life-long learning, and therefore exactly encapsulates the principles just outlined.

Acknowledgements. Many of the ideas in this paper have evolved from useful and stimulating discussions at the ICARIS conferences with many people in the field, and in particular at meetings of the UK based ARTIST network [2].

References

1. http://www.dcs.napier.ac.uk/~emmah/research_interests/AIS.html.
2. Artist - uk based network, funded by esprc.
3. http://evonet.lri.fr.

4. *Artificial Immune Systems: Proceedings of ICARIS 2004*. Springer, 2004.
5. *Proceedings of Genetic and Evolutionary Computation Conference*. Springer, 2004.
6. Uwe Aickelin and Steve Cayzer. The danger theory and its application to artificial immune systems. In Jonathan Timmis and Peter J. Bentley, editors, *Proceedings of the 1st International Conference on Artificial Immune Systems ICARIS*, pages 141–148, University of Kent at Canterbury, September 2002. University of Kent at Canterbury Printing Unit.
7. U Aicklen, P Bentley, S Cayzer, J Kim, and J McLeod. Danger Theory: The Link Between AIS and IDS? In *LNCS 2787*, pages 147–155. Springer, 2003.
8. J. Balthrop, F. Esponda, S. Forrest, and M. Glickman. Coverage and generalization in an artificial immune system. In *GECCO 2002: Proc. of the Genetic and Evolutionary Computation Conf.*, page 310, 2002.
9. H. Bersini. Immune network and adaptive control. In *Proceedings of 1st Conference on Artificial Life*, pages 217–226. MITpress, 1991.
10. H Bersini and F Varela. *The Immune Learning Mechansims: Recruitment, Reinforcement and their Applications*. Chapman Hall, 1994.
11. V. Cutello, G. Nicosia, and M. Pavone. Exploring the capability of immune algorithms: A characterization of hypermutation operators. In *Artificial Immune Systems: Proceedings of ICARIS 2004*, pages 263–273. Springer, 2004.
12. D. Dasgupta, editor. *Artifificial Immune Systems and their Applications*. Springer, 1999.
13. D. Dasgupta, K. KrishnaKumar, D. Wong, and M. Berry. Negative selection algorithm for aircraft fault detection. In *Artificial Immune Systems: Proceedings of ICARIS 2004*, pages 1–14. Springer, 2004.
14. L. De Castro. Artificial immune systems bibliography. `http://www.dca.fee.unicamp.br/ lnunes/AIS.html`.
15. L. De Castro. Engineering applications of artificial immune systems. Tutorial at ICARIS 2004, available from `http://artificial-immune-systems.org/ICARIS2004/icaris2004.htm`, 2004.
16. L. De Castro and F. Von Zuben. Artifical immune systems: Part ii - a survery of applications. Technical Report DCA-RT 02/00, Department of Computer Engineering and Industrial Automation, State University of Campinas, Brazil, 2000.
17. L. De Castro and F.J. Von Zuben. The clonal selection algorithm with engineering applications. In *GECCO 2002 - Workshop Proceedings*, pages 37–37, 2000.
18. L.N. De Castro and F.J. Von Zuben. Ainet: An artificial immune network for data analysis. In H.A. Abbass, R.A. Sarker, and C.S. Newton, editors, *Data Mining: A Heuristic Approach*. Idea Group Publishing, USA, 2001.
19. F. Esponda, S. Forrest, and P. Helman. A formal framework for positive and negative detection schemes. *IEEE Transactions on Systems, Man and Cybernetics Part B*, 34:357–373, 2004.
20. S Forrest, S Hofmeyr, and A Somayaji. Computer Immunology. *Communications of the ACM*, 40(10):88–96, 1997.
21. S Forrest, A Perelson, L Allen, and R Cherukuri. Self-Nonself Discrimination in a Computer. In *Proc. of the IEEE Symposium on Research in Security and Privacy*, pages 202–212, 1994.
22. A Freitas and J Timmis. Revisiting the Foundations of Artificial Immune Systems: A Problem Oriented Perspective. In *LNCS 2787*, pages 229–241. Springer, 2003.
23. A. Gaspar and P. Collard. From gas to artificial immune systems: Improving adaptation in time-dependent optimization. In *Proceedings of the Congress on Evolutionary Computation*, pages 1859–186. IEEE Press, 1999.

24. R. Germain. An innately interesting decade of research in immunology. *Nature Medicine*, 10(12):1307–1320, 2004.
25. F. Gonzalez, D. Dasgupta, and L.F. Nino. A randomized real-valued negative selection algorithm. In *Proceedings of the 2nd International Conference on Artificial Immune Systems (ICARIS). Lecture Notes in Computer Science*, page 261272, 2003.
26. E. Hart and P. Ross. Exploiting the analogy betweeen the immune system and sparse distributed memories. *Genetic Programming and Evolvable Machines*, 4:333–358, 2003.
27. E Hart and P Ross. Studies on the implications of shape-space models for idiotypic networks. In *LNCS 3239*, pages 413–427. Springer, 2004.
28. E. Hart, A. Webb, P. Ross, and A. Lawson. A role for immunology in next generation robot controllers. In *Artificial Immune Systems: Proceedings of ICARIS 2003*, pages 46–57. Springer, 2003.
29. Z. Ji and D Dasgupta. Real-valued negative selection algorithm with variable-sized detectors. In *Genetic and Evolutionary Computation GECCO-2004, Part I. Volume 3102 of Lecture Notes in Computer Science*, page 287298, 2004.
30. J Kelsey, J Timmis, and A Hone. Chasing chaos. In *Congress on Evolutionary Computation*, pages 89–98, Canberra, Australia., December 2003. IEEE.
31. J Kim and P Bentley. Immune Memory in the Dynamic Clonal Selection Algorithm. In J Timmis and P Bentley, editors, *Proceedings of the First International Conference on Artificial Immune Systems ICARIS*, pages 59–67, 2002.
32. A. Ko, H.Y.K. Lau, and T.L. Lau. An immuno control framework for cedcentralized mechatronic control. In *Artificial Immune Systems: Proceedings of ICARIS 2004*, pages 46–57. Springer, 2004.
33. M. Neal. Meta-stable memory in an artificial immune network. In *Artificial Immune Systems: Proceedings of ICARIS 2003*, pages 168–181. Springer, 2003.
34. B Scholkopf, J. Platt, A ShaweTaylor, A. Smola, and A Williamson. Estimating the support of a high-dimensional distribution. Technical Report MSR-TR-99-87, 1999.
35. A. Secker, A. Freitas, and J. Timmis. AISEC: An Artificial Immune System for E-mail Classification. In *Proceedings of the Congress on Evolutionary Computation*, pages 131–139. IEEE, December 2003.
36. L Segal and I Cohen, editors. *Design Principles for the Immune System and Other Distributed Systems*. Oxford University Press, 2001.
37. A Somayaji, S Hofmeyr, and S. Forrest. *Design Principles for the Immune System and Other Distributed System*, chapter Principles of a Computer Immune System. 2001, Oxford University Press.
38. S Stepney, R Smith, J Timmis, and A Tyrrell. Towards a Conceptual Framework for Artificial Immune Systems. In *LNCS 3239*, pages 53–64. Springer, 2004.
39. T. Stibor, K. Bayarou, and C. Eckert. An investigation of R-chunk detector generation on higher alphabets. In *LNCS 3102*, pages 26–30, 2004.
40. T. Stibor, P. Mohr, J. Timmis, and C. Eckert. Is negative selection algorithm suitable for anomaly detection? In *Proceedings of GECCO 2005. LNCS*, 2005.
41. D. Taylor and D. Corne. An investigation into negative selection algorithm for fault detction in refrigeration systems. In *Artificial Immune Systems: Proceedings of ICARIS 2003*, pages 34–45. Springer, 2003.
42. J. Timmis, C.Edmonds, and J. Kelsey. Assessing the performance of two immune inspired algorithms and a hybrid genetic algorithm for optmisation. In *Proceedings of Genetic and Evolutionary Computation Conference, GECCO 2004*, pages 308–317. Springer, 2004.
43. J. Timmis and M. Neal. Once more unto the breach: Towards artificial homeostasis. *Recent Developments in Biologically Inspired Computing*, pages 340–365, 2005.

44. M Villalobos-Arias, C A Coello Coello, and O Hernandez-Lerma. Convergence analysis of a multiobjective artificial immune system algorithm. In *Lecture Noted in Computer Science 3239*, pages 226 – 235, 2004.

45. J. Walker and S. Garrett. Dyanmic function optimisation: Comparing the performance of clonalg and evolution strategies. In *Artificial Immune Systems: Proceedings of ICARIS 2003*, pages 273–285. Springer, 2003.

46. A. Watkins and J.. Timmis. Exploiting the parallelism inherent in airs, and artificial immune classifier. In *Artificial Immune Systems: Proceedings of ICARIS 2004*, pages 427–438. Springer, 2004.

47. D. Wolpert and W. Macready. No free lunch theorems for optimisation. *IEEE Transactions on Evolutionary Computing*, 1997.

Author Index

Lecture Notes in Computer Science

For information about Vols. 1–3519

please contact your bookseller or Springer

Vol. 3569: F. Bacchus, T. Walsh (Eds.), Theory and Applications of Satisfiability Testing. XII, 492 pages. 2005.

Vol. 3568: W.-K. Leow, M.S. Lew, T.-S. Chua, W.-Y. Ma, L. Chaisorn, E.M. Bakker (Eds.), Image and Video Retrieval. XVII, 672 pages. 2005.

Vol. 3567: M. Jackson, D. Nelson, S. Stirk (Eds.), Database: Enterprise, Skills and Innovation. XII, 185 pages. 2005.

Vol. 3566: J.-P. Banâtre, P. Fradet, J.-L. Giavitto, O. Michel (Eds.), Unconventional Programming Paradigms. XI, 367 pages. 2005.

Vol. 3565: G.E. Christensen, M. Sonka (Eds.), Information Processing in Medical Imaging. XXI, 777 pages. 2005.

Vol. 3564: N. Eisinger, J. Małuszyński (Eds.), Reasoning Web. IX, 319 pages. 2005.

Vol. 3562: J. Mira, J.R. Álvarez (Eds.), Artificial Intelligence and Knowledge Engineering Applications: A Bioinspired Approach, Part II. XXIV, 636 pages. 2005.

Vol. 3561: J. Mira, J.R. Álvarez (Eds.), Mechanisms, Symbols, and Models Underlying Cognition, Part I. XXIV, 532 pages. 2005.

Vol. 3560: V.K. Prasanna, S. Iyengar, P.G. Spirakis, M. Welsh (Eds.), Distributed Computing in Sensor Systems. XV, 423 pages. 2005.

Vol. 3559: P. Auer, R. Meir (Eds.), Learning Theory. XI, 692 pages. 2005. (Subseries LNAI).

Vol. 3558: V. Torra, Y. Narukawa, S. Miyamoto (Eds.), Modeling Decisions for Artificial Intelligence. XII, 470 pages. 2005. (Subseries LNAI).

Vol. 3557: H. Gilbert, H. Handschuh (Eds.), Fast Software Encryption. XI, 443 pages. 2005.

Vol. 3556: H. Baumeister, M. Marchesi, M. Holcombe (Eds.), Extreme Programming and Agile Processes in Software Engineering. XIV, 332 pages. 2005.

Vol. 3555: T. Vardanega, A.J. Wellings (Eds.), Reliable Software Technology – Ada-Europe 2005. XV, 273 pages. 2005.

Vol. 3554: A. Dey, B. Kokinov, D. Leake, R. Turner (Eds.), Modeling and Using Context. XIV, 572 pages. 2005. (Subseries LNAI).

Vol. 3553: T.D. Hämäläinen, A.D. Pimentel, J. Takala, S. Vassiliadis (Eds.), Embedded Computer Systems: Architectures, Modeling, and Simulation. XV, 476 pages. 2005.

Vol. 3552: H. de Meer, N. Bhatti (Eds.), Quality of Service – IWQoS 2005. XVIII, 400 pages. 2005.

Vol. 3551: T. Härder, W. Lehner (Eds.), Data Management in a Connected World. XIX, 371 pages. 2005.

Vol. 3548: K. Julisch, C. Kruegel (Eds.), Intrusion and Malware Detection and Vulnerability Assessment. X, 241 pages. 2005.

Vol. 3547: F. Bomarius, S. Komi-Sirviö (Eds.), Product Focused Software Process Improvement. XIII, 588 pages. 2005.

Vol. 3546: T. Kanade, A. Jain, N.K. Ratha (Eds.), Audio- and Video-Based Biometric Person Authentication. XX, 1134 pages. 2005.

Vol. 3544: T. Higashino (Ed.), Principles of Distributed Systems. XII, 460 pages. 2005.

Vol. 3543: L. Kutvonen, N. Alonistioti (Eds.), Distributed Applications and Interoperable Systems. XI, 235 pages. 2005.

Vol. 3542: H.H. Hoos, D.G. Mitchell (Eds.), Theory and Applications of Satisfiability Testing. XIII, 393 pages. 2005.

Vol. 3541: N.C. Oza, R. Polikar, J. Kittler, F. Roli (Eds.), Multiple Classifier Systems. XII, 430 pages. 2005.

Vol. 3540: H. Kalviainen, J. Parkkinen, A. Kaarna (Eds.), Image Analysis. XXII, 1270 pages. 2005.

Vol. 3539: K. Morik, J.-F. Boulicaut, A. Siebes (Eds.), Local Pattern Detection. XI, 233 pages. 2005. (Subseries LNAI).

Vol. 3538: L. Ardissono, P. Brna, A. Mitrovic (Eds.), User Modeling 2005. XVI, 533 pages. 2005. (Subseries LNAI).

Vol. 3537: A. Apostolico, M. Crochemore, K. Park (Eds.), Combinatorial Pattern Matching. XI, 444 pages. 2005.

Vol. 3536: G. Ciardo, P. Darondeau (Eds.), Applications and Theory of Petri Nets 2005. XI, 470 pages. 2005.

Vol. 3535: M. Steffen, G. Zavattaro (Eds.), Formal Methods for Open Object-Based Distributed Systems. X, 323 pages. 2005.

Vol. 3534: S. Spaccapietra, E. Zimányi (Eds.), Journal on Data Semantics III. XI, 213 pages. 2005.

Vol. 3533: M. Ali, F. Esposito (Eds.), Innovations in Applied Artificial Intelligence. XX, 858 pages. 2005. (Subseries LNAI).

Vol. 3532: A. Gómez-Pérez, J. Euzenat (Eds.), The Semantic Web: Research and Applications. XV, 728 pages. 2005.

Vol. 3531: J. Ioannidis, A. Keromytis, M. Yung (Eds.), Applied Cryptography and Network Security. XI, 530 pages. 2005.

Vol. 3530: A. Prinz, R. Reed, J. Reed (Eds.), SDL 2005: Model Driven. XI, 361 pages. 2005.

Vol. 3528: P.S. Szczepaniak, J. Kacprzyk, A. Niewiadomski (Eds.), Advances in Web Intelligence. XVII, 513 pages. 2005. (Subseries LNAI).

Vol. 3527: R. Morrison, F. Oquendo (Eds.), Software Architecture. XII, 263 pages. 2005.

Vol. 3526: S. B. Cooper, B. Löwe, L. Torenvliet (Eds.), New Computational Paradigms. XVII, 574 pages. 2005.

Vol. 3525: A.E. Abdallah, C.B. Jones, J.W. Sanders (Eds.), Communicating Sequential Processes. XIV, 321 pages. 2005.

Vol. 3524: R. Barták, M. Milano (Eds.), Integration of AI and OR Techniques in Constraint Programming for Combinatorial Optimization Problems. XI, 320 pages. 2005.

Vol. 3523: J.S. Marques, N. Pérez de la Blanca, P. Pina (Eds.), Pattern Recognition and Image Analysis, Part II. XXVI, 733 pages. 2005.

Vol. 3522: J.S. Marques, N. Pérez de la Blanca, P. Pina (Eds.), Pattern Recognition and Image Analysis, Part I. XXVI, 703 pages. 2005.

Vol. 3521: N. Megiddo, Y. Xu, B. Zhu (Eds.), Algorithmic Applications in Management. XIII, 484 pages. 2005.

Vol. 3520: O. Pastor, J. Falcão e Cunha (Eds.), Advanced Information Systems Engineering. XVI, 584 pages. 2005.